The Colonial American Stage, 1665–1774

The Colonial American Stage, 1665–1774: A Documentary Calendar

Odai Johnson and William J. Burling
Cartography by James Coombs

Madison • Teaneck
Fairleigh Dickinson University Press
London: Associated University Presses

© 2001 by Rosemont Publishing and Printing Corp.

All rights reserved. Authorization to photocopy items for internal or personal use, or personal use of specific clients, is granted by the copyright owner, provided that a base fee of $10.00, plus eight cents per page, per copy is paid directly to the Copyright Clearance Center, 222 Rosewood Drive, Danvers, Massachusetts 01923. [0–8386–3903–8/01 $10.00 + 8¢ pp, pc.]

Associated University Presses
440 Forsgate Drive
Cranbury, NJ 08512

Associated University Presses
16 Barter Street
London, WC1A 2AH, England

Associated University Presses
P.O. Box 338, Port Credit
Mississauga, Ontario
Canada L5G 4L8

The paper used in this publication meets the requirements of the American National Standard for Permanence of Paper for Printed Library Materials Z39.48–1984.

Library of Congress Cataloging–in–Publication Data

Burling, William J.
   The colonial American stage, 1665-1774: a documentary calendar / Odai Johnson and William J. Burling; cartography by James Coombs
     p. cm.
   Includes bibliographical references and index.
   ISBN 0–8386–3903–8 (alk. paper)
   1. Theatre--United States--History--17th century. 2. Theater--United States--18th century. I. Burling, William J. II. Coombs, James A. III. Title.

PN 2237.J64 2001
792'.0973'09032--dc21   2001023284

PRINTED IN THE UNITED STATES OF AMERICA

*For Amie and Deb, as always.
For Bonnie.*

Contents

Preface / 9
Acknowledgments / 13
Maps / 15–17
   Map 1 The Range of Theatrical Venues in Colonial America / 15
   Map 2 Theatrical Venues in Colonial West Indies / 16
   Map 3 Theatrical Venues in Colonial Maryland and Virginia / 17

Introduction / 21
   Companies / 21
   Scenery, "Habits," and Music / 36
   Theatrical Venues / 44
   Repertory / 62
   Negotiating Authority / 70
   Company Finances / 80
   Audiences / 87
   Works Frequently Cited / 91

The Calendar / 92
Bibliography / 479
Indexes / 489
   Person Index / 489
   Place and Subject Index / 499
   Title and Author Index / 505

Preface

This work is designed to offer a working calendar of colonial American theatrical activity from the beginning of the colonial period to the closing of the theatres at the outbreak of the Revolutionary War in October of 1774. The intention is to record every known performance by a professional or amateur company or solo performer and all related information. Thus this project (1) seeks to gather into a single record all the existing material relating to the theatres, productions, and personnel of companies and individuals performing in the American colonies; (2) reexamines all previously published primary evidence and claims; and (3) offers extensive new information from sources unknown or unavailable to previous researchers.

The geographic range of this study is the British American colonies, from Halifax, Nova Scotia, to Savannah, in the Georgia colony on the continent (see Map 1), and the British West Indies. During the seventeenth and eighteenth centuries, the status of the West Indies, and in particular, Jamaica, differed very little from that of the American colonies. The latter was an English outpost, ceded to England in 1670, with transplanted English culture, including a public theatre. By the middle of the eighteenth century Jamaica had a Master of the Revels and an active pool of actors. Theatrical activity was also present on Barbados, the Bahamas, Montserrat, Cuba, and the Dutch West Indies, all extensions of a Caribbean touring circuit (see Map 2). Of these colonial outposts, Jamaica was by far the most important, being not only the southernmost terminus of a touring circuit, but also the port to which colonial companies repaired to resupply when their northern markets were saturated, or to retreat to in times of conflict, as during the Seven Years' War (i.e., French and Indian War) and again immediately prior to the Revolution. Unfortunately, very little information is known concerning theatrical activity in the West Indies, though we have uncovered hitherto unknown significant data for 1770–72.

This type of reference work has been long overdue for two major reasons. The first is that the study of colonial theatre is dominated by local histories. Although several substantial earlier studies of the colonial stage are available (chiefly Hugh F. Rankin's *The Theatre in Colonial America*), most of the major works are focused on individual cities: Charles Durang, and later, Thomas Pollock have written on the Philadelphia stage; Joseph Ireland, T. Allston Brown, and George Odell have all worked successively on the history of the New York stage; while similarly treated are the Charleston stage, and the early theatres in Providence, Albany, Annapolis, Halifax, and Jamaica. While these studies necessarily offer some limited expanded coverage, primarily they focus on localized theatrical activity. An impressive group of recent studies, particularly the *Cambridge History of American Theatre* (1998), *Cambridge Guide to American Theatre* (1993, 1996), and *Theatre in the United States: A Documentary History* (Volume 1, 1750–1915; 1996), provide excellent overviews, analyses, and select, useful documents, but they are by their nature general and therefore are not expressly dedicated to presenting the comprehensive data respecting colonial theatre necessary for detailed scholarly research.[1] Thus, until now, no single work has gathered up all of the individual productions and isolated histories into a single calendar and source book.

One hazard that has resulted from the production of isolated histories is that the local histories do not overlap and are contextually incomplete. Gaps often occur between the highly detailed annals of one city and that of the next. As we have found, the history of the Philadelphia stage does not necessarily begin where the history of the New York stages leaves off. Also the current histories do not sufficiently account for the activity in less populous, nearby sites, though these venues functioned for the companies in important ways. Sometimes they were layover sites, like the small Maryland towns of Chester, Upper Marlborough, or Piscataway, where the company could play for ten days or a fortnight and move on (see Map 3). Some were local circuit sites like the run between Williamsburg, Fredericksburg, Alexandria, and Norfolk, Virginia. Occasionally—and usually in the summer—the

---

[1] Indeed, as the essays and calendar entries which follow will demonstrate, we offer substantial new evidence not known to the authors of those works, and we interpret in quite different ways some of the data which they present.

company branched out from major centers into pilot sites, where the market or moral climate of a community like Newport (1761) or Providence (1762), Rhode Island, Albany, New York (1769), or Baltimore (1772) could be tested without the financial commitment of a full season. Our work has thus attempted to collate, update, and, when needed, correct the separate histories and, more importantly, to account for the gaps that occur in between them.

A colonial calendar has also allowed us to chart the itineraries of the companies and to reconstruct annual and long term patterns in their movements. This data has allowed us to predict the probable locations of companies when records become scarce or ambiguous. Once touring companies began to work on a semi-permanent schedule, they settled into a circuit that made their whereabouts in any given month—if not orbitally predictable—at least probable. This is particularly true in the case of annual events like the June Fair at Fredericksburg or the Autumnal Provincial Court and October Races at Annapolis.

The second reason for such a study grows out of the need to clear up the many inconsistencies that have crept into the record over successive retellings. From William Dunlap (1797) to T. Allston Brown (1903) to Arthur Hobson Quinn (1943), the early scholarship of the colonial American stage has relied heavily on often anecdotal evidence. The assumptions of one historian became the facts of another, and in the case of colonial theatre this practice has become all too frequent. Some are lapses, as, for example, when Arthur Hornblow (1:118) tells us that after the New York season closed on 26 April 1762, David Douglass and his company adjourned to the West Indies. As pointed out by other scholars, we know now, rather, they went to Virginia and Rhode Island instead. And, for another example, scholars have long thought that the company performing in Halifax, Nova Scotia, in 1768 was the American Company; we show that this was the Mills Company, having worked its way northward from North Carolina, and that while in Nova Scotia they traded upon the "American Company" name.

Others involve the misdating of crucial primary evidence that has often been codified by subsequent historians. One example is the case of the letter of introduction carried by David Douglass in 1761, written by the governor of Virginia. This letter Douglass carried to Rhode Island and offered to the Newport Town Council for clearance to perform when he and his company arrived sometime in late July 1761. Seilhamer, however, incorrectly citing *Gaine's Mercury*, dates it November

9, 1761. In fact, the *Boston Gazette* (21 September 1761) extracts a 10 September letter from Newport quoting the Douglass letter, clearly indicating it had been in print prior to that date. In this matter our research corroborates George Willard, who, working from material that perhaps no longer exists, states that the letter appears in the *Newport Mercury* (11 August 1761) and reprints it. Hornblow also errs, and has the company in Newport performing on 10 June 1761, though their letter of introduction is dated from Virginia on 11 June 1761. Scores of similar problems exist in regard to repertoire, company, and casting, and even dates of playbills in the Harvard Theatre Collection. Nor are these errors the sole domain of last century's scholars. We hope, of course, that we have not, ourselves, introduced any patently misleading new errors or ghosts, though we can hardly expect that our *Calendar* is without blemishes.

Conceived as a source book, *The Colonial American Stage, 1665–1774: A Documentary Calendar* therefore includes extensive pertinent information relating to theatrical matters: complete play and cast lists (where available), actor and civic benefits, building contracts, pricing schedules, advertisements relating to personnel, dates, seasons, premieres of plays, authors, companies, sources, occasional reviews, and juridical acts that impacted the theatre. Our intention is to provide a foundation for future, more complete calendars, as our successors fill in the gaps and correct the misconceptions of our own era.

A NOTE ON THE TEXTS

The inconsistencies and vagaries of printing practices during the colonial period are well known to all of us who work in the field. Therefore, in texts quoted directly from contemporary sources, we have transcribed the material as it appears in the original documents. In our head notes and commentaries we have tried to modernize whenever possible, but proper names are difficult to reconcile due to the many variants.

Acknowledgments

The most pleasant task for us is to acknowledge the contributions made to a project of this scope, necessarily resting as it does upon the extensive groundwork provided by numerous scholars and the assistance of many additional persons. While we are the grateful heirs to all of the scholarship cited in this *Documentary Calendar*, we must especially note the pioneering work of Glen Hughes, George C. D. Odell, Thomas Clark Pollock, Hugh Rankin, Eola Willis, Arthur Hobson Quinn, and George O. Seilhamer. We are likewise indebted to all of our contemporaries who have provided research assistance, information, and other kinds of advice and support. Therefore we present our grateful thanks to the following individuals, groups, and libraries (in no particular order): Ms. Francie Wolfe, Interlibrary Loan Guru, Southwest Missouri State University; Ms. Alecia Parker, Historical Annapolis Foundation; Ms. Annette Fern, Harvard Theatre Collection; Professor Barry Witham; Professor Mary Julia Curtis; Mr. A. C. Elias; Professor Etta Madden; Professor James Tierney; Professor James May; Mr. James Green, Library Company of Philadelphia; Professor Gay Gibson Cima; Mr. Nelson D. Lankford, Virginia Historical Society; Professor Dorothy Holland; Ms. Melissa Miller, Harry Ransom Humanities Research Center; Professor Errol Hill; the National Library of Jamaica; Mr. Wade Dorsey, South Carolina Department of Archives and History; Ms. Gwyn Pace, Dalhousie University; Mr. Philip Hartling, Nova Scotia Archives and Records Management; Mr. Harry McKown, North Carolina Collections; Mr. Charles Bush of Williamsburg; Mr. Tom Goyens, Ms. Lisa Fischer, Ms. Gail Greve, and Mr. George H. Yetter, Colonial Williamsburg Foundation.

A special note of recognition and appreciation is extended to the team which created the University Music Editions CD-ROM, *The Performing Arts in Colonial American Newspapers, 1690-1783*: Ms. Mary Jane Corry, Ms. Kate Van Winkle Keller, and Mr. Robert M. Keller. The timely 1997 appearance of this research tool greatly facilitated the cross-checking of many entries and allowed us to explore newspapers in a way hitherto unimaginable.

We must also gratefully acknowledge the support and patience of the AUP staff for "holding the press" at the last minute so that we could include some important information concerning the West Indies that was discovered even as the book was in last-minute stages of publication preparation.

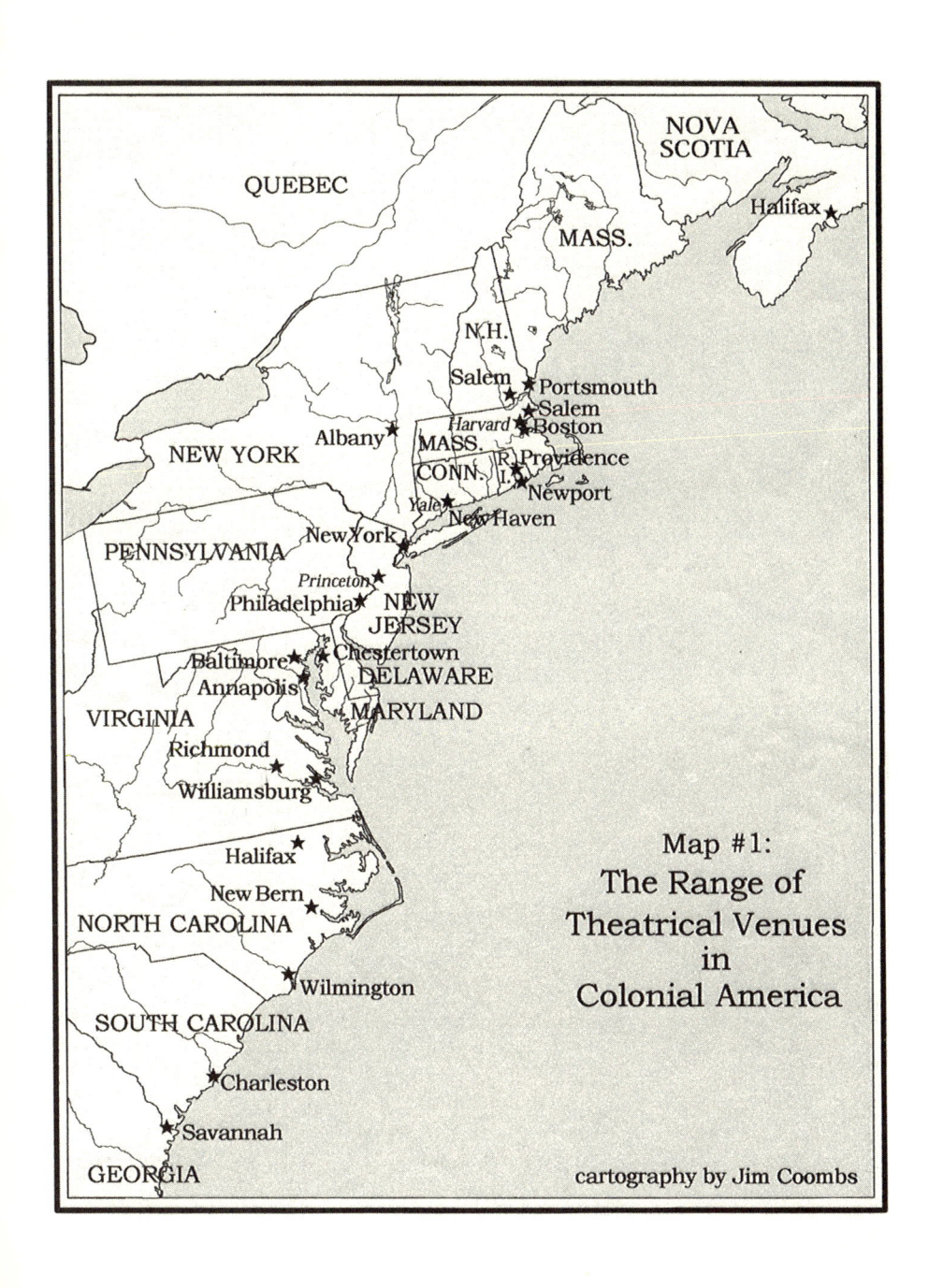

Map #1: The Range of Theatrical Venues in Colonial America

cartography by Jim Coombs

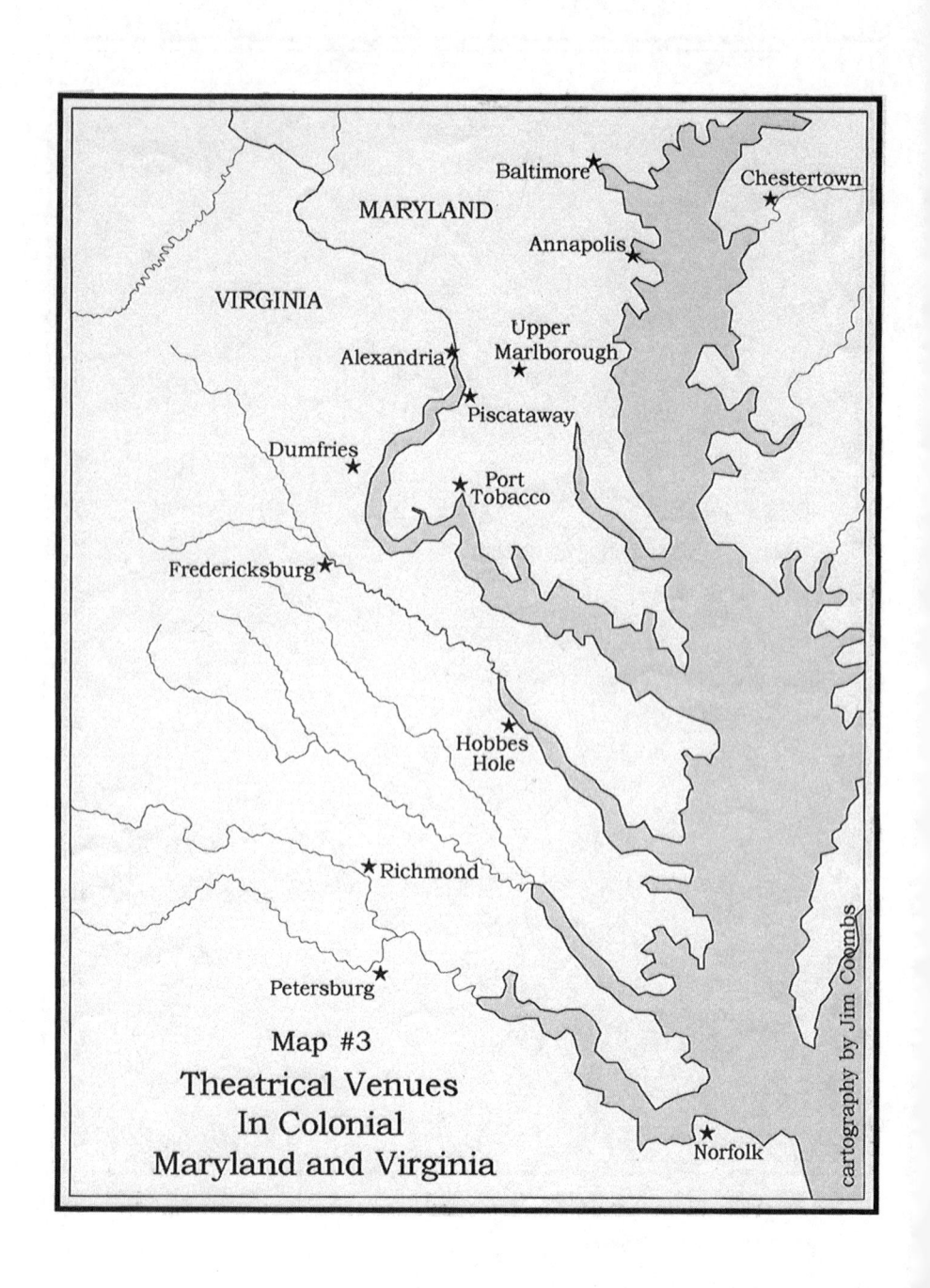

Map #3
**Theatrical Venues
In Colonial
Maryland and Virginia**

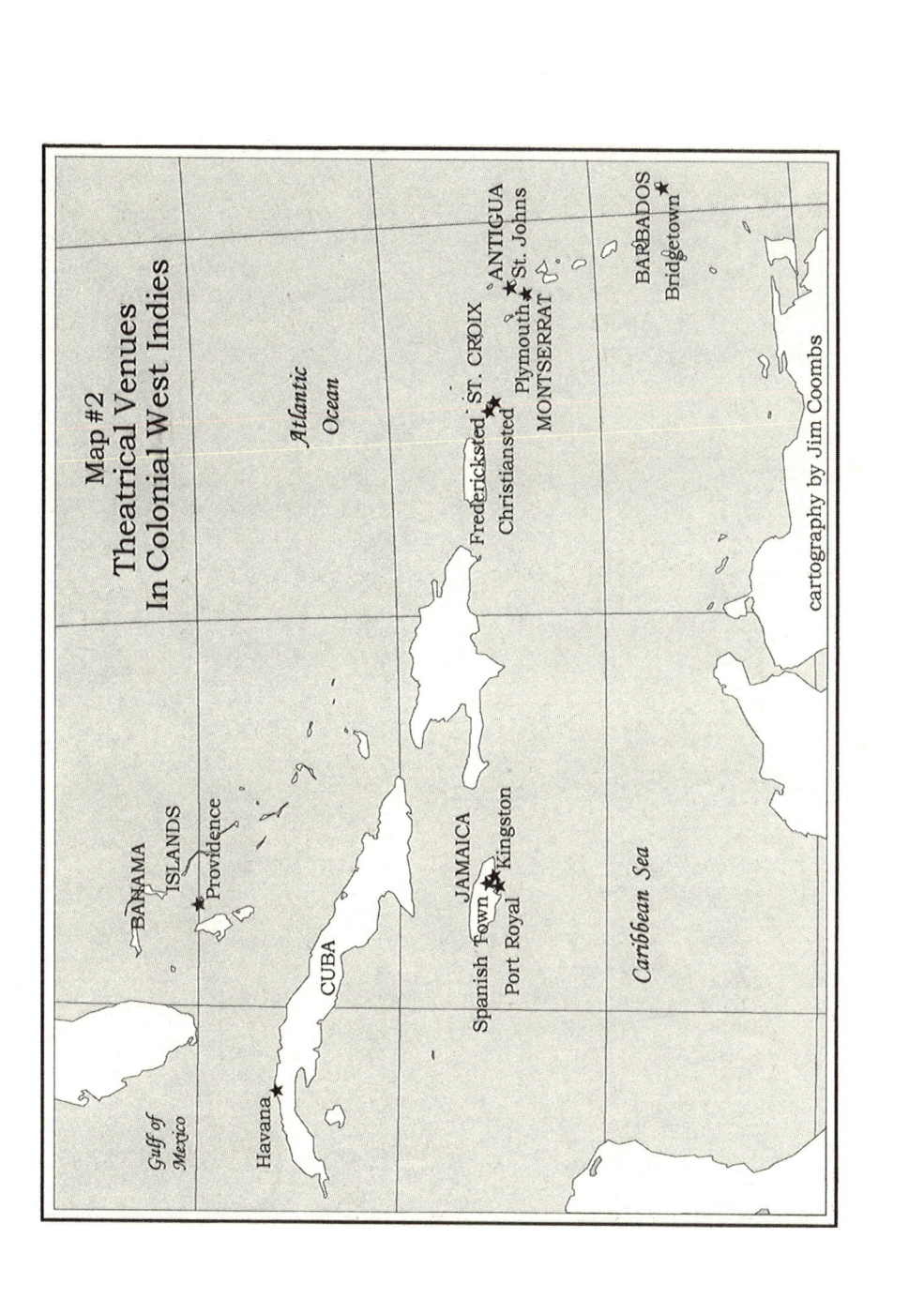

Map #2
Theatrical Venues
In Colonial West Indies

cartography by Jim Coombs

The Colonial American Stage, 1665–1774

Introduction

The following essays seek to provide useful overviews of the complex and extensive information to be found in the *Calendar*. As with any exercise in synthesis, our remarks represent an interpretation of the data as it struck us, though we have attempted to provide a balanced assessment. This essay comprises seven sections: companies; scenery, "habits," and music; theatrical venues; repertory; negotiating authority; company finances; and audiences. We must point out, however, that the following introductory analysis is based on a woefully incomplete record. This inadequacy is particularly apparent in the years up to the mid-eighteenth century, where scattered entries offer very little upon which to base conclusions of even the most speculative nature. The data in the *Calendar* itself, of course, can foster other interpretations, and we eagerly invite such analyses.

Companies

A wide range of companies performed in the colonies, most temporarily assembled and few fully professional, even by provincial touring standards. The temptation—and certainly the historic tradition—has been to make divisions based upon vocational intent: (1) amateur companies who acted for their own diversion and not as a primary profession; (2) mixed companies made up of leading professional actors filled out with amateurs; and (3) full professional companies who subsisted primarily by performance. This tradition—inaugurated in American theatre studies by William Dunlap and followed by every subsequent writer—offers a clear privilege of the "professional" and ample opportunity to dismiss the pioneering work that contributed so much to the development and maintenance of the professional company. This propensity has led to the exclusion of many companies from the histories of the period. Dunlap's infatuation with the Hallam Company, for example, is so pervasive that he takes little notice of its predecessors, in particular the Murray-Kean Company, even when confronted with rather extensive evidence, such as the notice of the Annapolis theatre and the early *Maryland Gazette* play bills, concerning which he quotes and concludes, "The claim for Annapolis of having erected the first theatre ...appears very unaccountable" (22). This bias likewise appears in otherwise solid contemporary scholarship, such as Weldon Durnam's *American Theatre Companies, 1749-1887* (1986), which offers no entries for the lesser Bayly, Holt, Levingston, Morgan, Mills, and Heady companies, or even the more important Verling Virginia Company.

Another fallacy of the traditional divisions is to dismiss the amateur troupes on an implied aesthetic ground, as if the quality of their work was necessarily inferior to that of the professional. As we know little about actual productions and next to nothing about the abilities of the actors—amateur or professional—such a division seems particularly short-sighted. We have only two references to a little-known company of strollers working North Carolina in 1768, but the closing remarks of a reference letter from the governor of that colony, William Tyron, praises one of the actors, Henry Giffard, as the best player on the American stage. That we know so little about this company has more to do with where they were performing than the quality of their performance.

We therefore propose the following simplified definitions: eschewing aesthetic distinctions, any company performing for money—touring or local—is **professional**; any company playing solely for charity or their own diversion is **amateur**. In addition, the principal professional companies maintained large repertories and mounted sustained seasons, though some troupes performing for money did so on a very limited basis. We have added to this simple dichotomy a category for **unidentified companies**, about which we do not have enough information to make a determination. And lastly, we have offered a heading of **solo acts**, such as the many one-person touring versions of Stevens's *Lecture on Heads*. A chronological summary listing of colonial American companies would thus appear as follows.

Professional
Levingston/Stagg Company (1716–1720s?, Williamsburg)
Thomas Heady and Company (1732–34?, New York)
Henry Holt/Charles Shepherd Company (1735–36, Charleston; 1739 New York)

John Moody and the Jamaican Company (1745–?)
Murray/Kean Company (August 1749–December 1752)
Robert Upton Company (December 1751–March 1752)
Lewis Hallam's Company (1752–55)
David Douglass's Company (later the American Company, 1756–74)
Tomlinson's Company (1765–1766, New York)
William Verling's Virginia Company (later the New American Company, 1767–69?)
Mr. Bayly's Company (1767–68)
Mr. Mills's Company (1768?–69?)
Leeward Islands Company, St. Croix (1770–72)
West-End Company, St. Croix (1770)
Antigua Company (1772)
Mr. Morgan's Company (1772–73)

Unidentified or problematic companies
Richard Hunter (c. 1700)
Antony Aston (c. 1703)
Unknown (Philadelphia 1723)
Unknown (West Indies 1729?–?)
Unknown (Lancaster, Pennsylvania / New York c. 1740)
Unknown (Richmond, Virginia, 1774)
Unknown (New York, 1774)

Amateur Companies
Students
Soldiers
Gentlemen

Solo Acts
Mr. Stokes (1749)
Mr. Garner (1766–67)
Mr. Joan (1769–70)
Mr. M. A. Warwel (1769–70)
"A gentleman lately arrived from London" (1772)
Mr. Martin Foy (1772)
Mr. Morgan (1772)
Mr. Hoar (1773)

Though we see more amateur activity early in the colonial period, the development from amateur to professional was far from evolutionary. Examples of small companies of amateurs which assembled for single productions or brief seasons span the entire era, beginning with the 1665 first record of William Darby, Cornelius Watkinson, and Philip Howard (who staged

The Bear and the Cub), to British soldiers seeking to ease their boredom, to the students of Mr. Oliver Dale, who performed *Cato* in Charleston only a short while before the Revolution. Indeed, often in the calendar amateur and professional companies played concurrently, though we found no occasion when they played competitively in the same city. As will also be noticed, few of even the professional companies had any longevity. It is a testimony to the resourcefulness of David Douglass that he alone, of all the professional players, succeeded in maintaining a company in the colonies longer than a few seasons.[1]

We have also included a heading for unidentified companies whose presences, but little else of their activity, personnel, or longevity are known, for example, the company playing in Barbados in the 1730s of which we have only a few names. This may have been the same company which played in Jamaica in 1733, and may perhaps have still been touring the West Indies well into the 1740s. They were allegedly from England, and, given the status of the unpatented theatres after the Licensing Act of 1737, the islands may have provided a profitable alternative market for a touring company. We also find curious and maddeningly limited references to early New York companies, such as the 12 February 1741 production of *The Beaux' Stratagem* in which the character Aimwell was "perform'd by a Person who never appear'd on any Stage before," suggesting that the other members of the production company all had enjoyed some stage experience. But of these companies, we do not have enough information from which to determine their status. No doubt many more companies existed than those listed above, but unfortunately they have left no record of their activities.

Amateur Companies

Most of the amateur companies were assembled for a single production; occasionally they produced two or three plays, but never anything like a season. They were also local to the city in which they performed and did not tour. Most importantly, amateurs are amateurs because there is a marked social

---

[1] Douglass's Company, which originated under Lewis Hallam's direction in 1752 and is also sometimes called the "Old American Company" in its later years, continuously operated from 1752 until 1806, a remarkable achievement.

disdain for playing for profit. To recall the stigma attached to acting we need only review the innumerable playbills which advertise an unnamed "gentleman" acting a role for his own diversion (such as the 7 April 1760 production by the Douglass Company at The New Theatre in Annapolis which advertised *Romeo and Juliet*, "Romeo—by a young gentleman for his diversion"). The names never appear in print to avoid even typographic association with this class of vagrants. This stigma is articulated best in a letter from the *New York Gazette & Weekly Post-Boy* of 26 June 1769 which announces the postponement of an amateur production of *The Orphan* because it was let out that the company was selling tickets:

> ... the 'young gentlemen' were informed by some of their friends, that there were a parcel of counterfeited tickets then selling about the town ... (... if he asserts so, he is mistaken; for there were only 52 genuine tickets struck off, which were given to the "Exhibitor's" particular friends) they immediately on this information, resolved to postpone the performance till some other opportunity, their intention being only amusement, (as may be seen by the tenor of their tickets) they thought it below their rank and characters to perform for the sake of a little paltry gain ....

The most frequent assembly of amateurs were students who performed at the early colonial colleges. Entries occur for such "young scholars" from 1690 on through to the closing of the theatres in 1774 (see entries for 1690, 1702, 1736, 1757, 1758, 1759, 1767, and rival productions in 1774). These productions were hosted by colleges throughout the colonies, as in Cambridge, Philadelphia, Williamsburg, and Charleston, etc., including Harvard and Yale Colleges in colonies that were otherwise hostile theatre marketplaces.

Amateur productions often acquired a certain legitimacy (or tolerance) that was not always conferred upon their more professional counterparts. When the students at the college in Philadelphia in the winter of 1756–57 arranged for four performances of *The Masque of Alfred the Great*, the prologue for this performance was published in the *Pennsylvania Gazette* of 20 January 1757, while a lengthy review praising the piece appeared in the *New Hampshire Gazette* of 18 March 1757. Two years later, when David Douglass arrived in Philadelphia with his company, the Commonwealth of Pennsylvania passed a law forbidding plays, with the severe penalty of £500 for violation.

Likewise, student productions were also often the first and only venues for theatrical performances in New England. New

Haven (Connecticut colony) and the township of Pamfret saw student productions in 1755, 1756, 1762, 1771, 1772, and 1773; professional companies would not break in until well after the Revolution.[2] At Cambridge, Massachusetts Bay Colony, Harvard as well, hosted early student productions: in 1690 Benjamin Colman's *Gustavus Vasa* was presented; in June 1758 students performed *The Roman Father* (William Whitehead, 1750), followed by *Cato* in July[3] and again in 1759; and on at least one occasion (20 November 1765), a Harvard collegiate production (unidentified) was cast entirely with faculty.

In other colonies, student productions also flourished. In 1702, the students at William and Mary College, Virginia colony, presented *A Pastoral Colloquy* (Anonymous).[4] In Williamsburg a company advertised as "Young Gentlemen of the College" (these we assume to be students at William and Mary) mounted a production of *Cato* in September 1736. This occasion was a busy theatrical week in colonial Williamsburg. Apart from the student production, a second company of amateurs known as "the gentlemen and ladies of this country" presented on the following Monday, Wednesday, and Friday, *The Busy-Body*, *The Recruiting Officer*, and *The Beaux' Stratagem*, respectively (*The Virginia Gazette*, 3–10 September 1736). Not to be outdone, the students at the college the following week offered a second production, this time Addison's *The Drummer, or the Haunted House*.

Student productions continued right through the colonial period. The last records we have are from 1774. Two amateur performances took place in Charleston following (inspired by?) the departure of the American Company: on 29 June 1774 pupils of James Thomson, late tutor of New Jersey College, performed *Cato*; six weeks later pupils of Oliver Dale presented the same play.

Another form of amateur company was the assembly of gentlemen in theatre-free communities who gathered and

---

[2] See Bloom, *A History of the Theatre in New Haven Connecticut before 1860*.

[3] Odell 1:108; following the diary of Dr. Nathaniel Ames. Cf. *Records of the Massachusetts Colonial Society*, 48:295.

[4] Davis (1284) claims that there were two colloquies. See Quin (1:5), following Lyon G. Tyler, *Williamsburg, The Old Colonial Capital*, 224–31.

performed for their own amusement. Though not annual events, and often only on ceremonial occasions, performances by these companies of gentlemen were certainly frequent enough before professional companies appeared with any regularity to be recorded in newspapers and letters abroad. Many communities enjoyed some kind of amateur theatrical of this nature (see entries for 1729, 1730, 1736, 1746, 1748, 1760, etc.). Of these, a representative example was the company assembled under the direction of Dr. Henry Potter, who, with other members of the Williamsburg community—painters and apothecaries—produced a short season during the General Court in August 1736. Their efforts were quite successful as "they have already got about one hundred and fifty pounds subscriptions, to encourage their entertaining the country with the like diversions at future public meetings of our general court and assembly" (*American Weekly Mercury*, 19–26 August 1736). Potter, it seems, had a long-standing affair with the theatre, as he had written and composed an opera, *The Decoy*, "printed and performed in London in 1733," so he most certainly was connected to the London theatre scene.[5] The productions of Potter's company also sparked a rival company of students from the college (William and Mary) who began to offer their own program of plays. This kind of activity goes a long way to evidence the support on the part of the community for the theatre, prior to the arrival of professional players.

Finally, companies of British soldiers also occasionally offered private theatricals, such as those stationed in Albany in 1757 and 1760, the company at Fort Cumberland in 1758, the troop of English soldiers in Boston who mounted plays for their own diversion in 1769, and the "Gentlemen of the Army and Navy" in Halifax, Nova Scotia, in 1773. Of these early soldier-thespians, unfortunately, we have the least information, but it was a tradition that continued right through the Revolutionary War, and indeed, offered the only theatrical activity (albeit partisan) during the occupation.

PROFESSIONAL COMPANIES

Although the Hallams initially had quarrels with the companies that preceded them (e.g., the Murray-Kean Company) and sought to distance themselves publicly from

---

[5] See Davis, *Intellectual Life in the Colonial South*, 1269.

such "pretenders," they nonetheless found markets more favorable in communities like Williamsburg that had already created their own theatre. Thus they may have seemed all the more professional following, as they did, on the heels of less experienced companies.

The professional players were characterized by several features that set them apart from the amateur companies which had little to do with the quality of their work, and chief among these distinctions was that their primary occupation was playing for profit. Though in times of financial crisis members may have supplemented their income by teaching dance, music, or fencing, teaching was a stopgap and their primary livelihood remained the theatre. Some performers were itinerant and some were local; most were from London, Jamaica, or the provincial touring circuit. The more successful companies were composed of players who had prior London or provincial touring experience; they were trained, not just in acting, but in the life of a touring player. The less successful were new to the vagaries of touring life, and attrition was constant. The professional companies tended to be better connected to the London and Jamaican theatrical resources, so they had advantages for recruitment and resupply. An example: though both were composed of professional provincial players, the Hallam Company largely replaced the Murray-Kean Company because it was better trained, better equipped, better organized, and certainly better financed.

If amateurs were local and temporary, being a professional was by no means synonymous with permanence or a guarantee of success. Apart from David Douglass and the American Company, none of the many attempts to organize and sustain companies and establish permanent theatres had any longevity in the colonies. For example, during fall 1767 the Douglass Company is the only one on record performing. By the following spring there are four companies: Douglass's, Verling's in Virginia, Mr. Mill's Company touring North Carolina, and Mr. Bayly's playing in Charleston. By the fall of 1769 three of these four troupes had apparently failed, and the American Company was in the greatest disarray and financial straits of its ten-plus-years' existence.

The primary obstacles were the poverty of the market and the exigencies of touring. As few colonial cities had near the numbers to support a professional theatre, companies like Bayly's quickly exhausted their markets, and those who were forced to travel endured the vagaries of travel: year in, year out, living in temporary lodging, soliciting permission, raising subscriptions, building or converting theatres, offering short seasons, and always moving on. Attrition was inevitable, recruitment never ending. A brief scroll down the roster of the companies playing in 1768–69 reveals the fluid exchange of personnel between the American Company playing between Philadelphia and New York and William Verling's Virginia Company playing in Virginia and Maryland. Dropping from the record entirely is Bayly's Company in 1768.

On occasion a company could be placed in one location then disappear entirely from sight only to reappear in a totally different location far from the original region. Such was the case with Mr. Mills's Company in 1768. The first records place the company probably in Wilmington, North Carolina, next in Providence, Rhode Island colony, and then, after a curious gap in the record, in Halifax, Nova Scotia, trading upon the name of the American Company, while those performers were in Philadelphia. Likewise, after spring 1769 Verling's Company moves to St. Croix to become (or join) the Leeward Islands Company during 1770–72.

Yet "local" companies fared no better. Bayly's struggles in Charleston, as Henry Holt's in Charleston, documented in the 1735–36 season, go a long way to remind us of the difficulty of establishing professional theatre in cities of ten or twelve thousand people. Holt supplemented his production schedule with a dancing academy and occasional balls yet still abandoned the project after three years and moved to New York. Bayly first opened his company in New York and moved down to Charleston in hopes of better prospects. Both failed. It was not until the early 1770s that the theatrical circuit was sufficiently established to support the professional player with any security. Ironically, the Continental Congress discouraged theatre at exactly the moment it was finally on secure footing.

We need also to mention that the Caribbean area often hosted one or more companies. While records are scarce for earlier decades, during the early 1770s the *Royal Danish American Gazette* in St. Croix records ample evidence of ongoing theatrical activities. Two companies actually contened with each other in 1770, the Leeward Islands Company and the West-End Company, on St. Croix, while a third company (not personnel yet identified) operated on Antigua at least during 1772. The evidence suggest, however, far more companies and more frequent performances throughout the area than have yet been established.

Unidentified Companies

Unfortunately many companies left little or no record of their activities. To the above list we must add a few oblique and wispy references to the many unidentified companies that have escaped attention or have survived with such scant records as to cast doubt on their very existence as companies. Though the evidence is not strong, nonetheless, taken in composite, it offers a far more complex picture of the colonial theatrical scene than the occasional touring company.

Richard Hunter and Antony Aston, for example, both very early strollers in the colonies, may have organized other actors to mount their productions. Sometime between 1699 and 1702 Hunter applied to the governor of New York, John Nanfan, for permission to act plays in the city. Odell (1:5) quotes the petitioner as having "been at great charge and expense in providing persons and necessary's in order to the acting of Play's in the City." We do not know if permission was ever granted and the "company" ever realized. Aston as well claims to have acted in the colonies, and we can assume he was not alone. When he traveled to New York he met up with a fencing master, Jack Charlton, formerly of London, who may have abetted Aston in his theatrical venture in that city and elsewhere, but again, not enough evidence survives to even surmise.

In Philadelphia in 1723 professional actors arrived in Philadelphia, "led by a player who had strowled hither to act as a Comedian ... [and] chose for their Stage a place just without the verge of the City ... [then] printed bills ... [and began] to act accordingly" (Pollock 4–5). The governor, Sir William Keith, apparently supported the performers, much to the displeasure of James Logan, mayor of Philadelphia, as evidenced by his remarks in a letter:

> How grievous this proves to the sober people of the place, thou wilt easily judge, but it happens at p'sent to be more particularly so on me, having, unfortunately, been chosen Mayor of Philad [sic] for this year, there is an expectation that I should exert that authority to suppress their

acting. But as ... ye Gov. himself resorts thither, I can by no means think it adviseable to embroil myself with the governor to no purpose.[6]

Nothing else is known of this troupe.

A company of some nature, of which we have only a few names, played in Barbados as early as 1728. This may have been the same company which appeared in Jamaica in 1733, or in Montserrat, British West Indies, where by December 1734 a playhouse had been built. This company may perhaps have still been touring the West Indies well into the 1740s when John Moody arrived. The players were allegedly from England, and, given the status of the unpatented London theatres after the Licensing Act of 1737, the islands may have provided a profitable alternative market for a touring company.

Finally, quite late in the colonial period, we find a broadside of 4 June 1774 attacking the theatre on moral grounds. The broadside is labeled as having been "stuck up at Richmond ...close to the playbill for that day." We have no other record of the identity of this Virginia company; indeed, the only other troupe of record that spring was the American Company of David Douglass, who had finished their season in Charleston on 19 May 1774 and had broken up for the summer. The whereabouts of most of their principals are accounted for, in England, New York, Philadelphia and Charleston. If this is a legitimate company in Virginia, and if they are printing and posting playbills, then this is the only one in operation in the colonies in June of 1774. The possibility exists that the company in Richmond was under the management of the intrepid William Verling, whose company played in Virginia as late as 1769, and who appeared briefly again in Virginia after the Revolution; if so, this is the only clue to the company's activities and whereabouts.

FREE AGENCY, ATTRITION, AND RECRUITMENT

Outside of obtaining permission to play, perhaps the largest single problem the colonial American companies faced was the difficulty of maintaining a stable company. It was a rare season, for even the most solid colonial company, when the manager began and ended with the same personnel. Like the strollers in the British provincial circuit, the major colonial

---

[6] Quoted in Pollock (5); corroborating evidence comes from the *Pennsylvania Archives*: "Comedians in town before 9th 2mo" (2d Series, 7, 70–72).

companies were organized around a nuclear core of familial relations: extended families such as the Hallams, and the Hallam-Douglasses, or husband-wife teams, such as Owen and Mary Morris, Mr. and Mrs. Malone, Mr. and Mrs. Tomlinson, Mr. and Mrs. Adcock, or John Henry and his marriages to successive Storer sisters. Beyond the familiar core, however, the peripheries of the colonial companies could be very unstable, losing their numbers to free agency in a highly opportunistic business.

From the very inception of the first professional company—when the Hallam project was little more than a well planned idea—attrition to free agency and recruitment problems characterized their struggles. According to Lewis Hallam, when Robert Upton arrived in New York in December 1751, ostensibly as an advance agent, he immediately abandoned the Hallam Company and took up with a "set of pretenders." When Upton later assembled his own small company, he in turn picked up at least five players who had themselves all abandoned the Murray-Kean Company: Mr. and Mrs. Leigh, Miss Osborne, her mother "Widow" Osborne, and John Tremaine. In three months' time the Upton Company became defunct, and at least one of the actors returned to the Murray-Kean Company, who had since moved on to Virginia.

This free agency was a hallmark of the early companies. Almost upon arrival in the colonies, two of Hallam's actors, Wynnel and Herbert, abandoned the Hallam Company for the Murray-Kean Company. At the end of Hallam's second season in the colonies, he lost his musicians, Mr. Charles Love and William Hulett, both of whom remained in New York to open music schools. That same year Charles Woodham, an actor with the Murray-Kean Company in 1753, quit for the Jamaican Company. At the end of the Douglass Company's first engagement in Philadelphia, they lost as many as six actors who chose to remain in that city, numbers a company of twelve to fifteen could ill afford. Later, William Verling joined the Douglass Company sometime in 1765, but by spring 1766 he left to perform as a solo, and by late 1767 operated a rival company composed of at least six other former members of the Douglass Company. One of these new members was the most well-traveled of colonial actors, Henrietta "Widow" Osborne, who played successively with the Murray-Kean, Robert Upton, John Moody, David Douglass, and William Verling companies, for various disgruntled engagements during her career in the colonies, and later performed stints in Jamaica with John Moody and in London.

All this attrition and free agency necessitated almost continual recruitment, and with the less connected companies, recruitment must have been a local affair. We have included in the calendar notes many occasions of "gentlemen" making first appearances on the stage. Some of these occasions were for diversion only (e.g., 22 February 1769), but others were essentially try-outs. This may very well have been the principle recruitment strategy for companies with no London or Jamaican contacts.

For the more intra-national companies—the Hallam and the Douglass companies—recruitment meant a long and costly summer trip back to major theatre centers. On the average these recruitment trips occurred every two-and-a-half to three years. David Douglass, or an emissary like John Henry, would return to London for actors, musicians, new scripts, and scenery. The promise of the colonial circuit was not always enticing, and recruitment was uneven. At the close of the 1764 season in Charleston, Douglass returned to London, and this particular trip was the company's best recruitment catch, yielding six new actors including the young Nancy Hallam, and Miss Wainwright and Stephen Woolls, both excellent singers, and both tutored by the important London composer Dr. Thomas Arne. In 1767 the Henrys and the Storers from the theatre in Jamaica all joined the Douglass Company. Likewise, when the Parkers joined the Verling Company in 1768 they too are billed as "from the theatre in Jamaica." In the summer of 1771 Douglass sent John Henry back to London for recruitment purposes and to purchase scenery. New scenes and new plays arrived, but, unfortunately no actors. Again, in the summer 1774 Lewis Hallam Jr. returned to London and netted quite a crop of recruits, but their untimely arrival coincided with the closing of the theatres (see 15 December 1774).

These London recruits were in addition to the local talent mentioned above. Companies on occasion allowed an infatuated amateur to try out: "The part of Othello to be attempted by a Gentleman, assisted by other Gentlemen, in the Characters of the Duke and Senate of Venice" (10 April 1768). Occasionally these novices would be invited into the company: Richard Goodman, a young law student, tried out on the last day of the 1769 season in Philadelphia and remained with the company until it broke up for the summer of 1774. Women were also allowed to audition. One Mary Richardson appeared incognito on 12 December 1769 and joined the company shortly thereafter, performing with them until she married and retired from the stage in 1773.

Companies also supplemented their numbers with local actors who joined the troupe when in town but did not travel with them. For example, the Douglass Company advertised a host of new names in Philadelphia in 1759, none of whom traveled on with the company to Annapolis. Upon their arrival in Annapolis, the company employed an entirely new crop of recruits, including the veteran Walter Murray, to play roles vacated by those actors who remained in the previous city. Later, in New York, the company hired the able John Tremaine from the defunct Murray-Kean and Robert Upton companies, but he did not continue with the company beyond its New York season. And, as a final example, in 1768 Miss Cheer (by then Lady Rosehill) rejoined the Douglass Company in Philadelphia for a limited and lucrative engagement (ten pounds per week and a benefit), which evidences the star system at work on a local level.

Causes of Attrition

Apart from low and uncertain wages, perhaps the most trying aspect of life in an itinerant company was the vagaries of the touring life which could keep a player on the road for years at a stretch and offer only temporary residencies. From what evidence we have of the 1751 New York season, for example, the Murray-Kean Company struggled all spring with small audiences, disappointing and postponed benefits, and even bad weather that seriously impacted attendance. These factors must have taken their toll, as the small company lost at least six members after their New York season. Even the manager quit: on 29 April 1751 Thomas Kean announced his retirement to take up writing. When Robert Upton arrived later that year and tried his hand at the New York audience, he met with even greater disappointment; he cut his losses and returned to England. At the conclusion of the Hallams's first season in Williamsburg during 1752–53, though successful by colonial standards, many of the players nonetheless left Williamsburg with debts, and Hallam forfeited his deed to the playhouse to cover the costs.

Life as a touring actor in colonial America was not easy. Henrietta Osborne, in her prologue for 19 January 1768, complains of being "doom'd perpetually to roam," though a more telling piece of evidence comes in the form of a recommendation letter of 11 June 1768 from the Governor of North Carolina, William Tryon, to the Bishop of London on behalf of an actor in the Mills Company who wished to leave off playing:

I was solicited a few days ago by Mr. Giffard a young man who is engaged with a company of comedians now in this province to recommend him to your Lordship for ordination orders .... He assured me it was no sudden caprice that induced him to make this application but the result of very mature deliberation, that he was most wearied of the vague life of his present profession .... He takes this letter by way of Providence being under obligation of contract to attend the company there. If your Lordship grants Mr. Giffard his petition you will take off the best player on the American stage.[7]

Some left the company to take up "honest" work (John Tremaine became a cabinet maker, Charles Love opened a music school); some left to marry (Miss Cheer left the stage to become Lady Rosehill—a temporary promotion); some were killed in transportation accidents (Mrs. Henry and Mrs. Morris were both casualties in separate nautical tragedies), while others like Adam Allyn and Mrs. Douglass died of natural causes. Occasionally the loss of patronage could cause severe hardship, evidencing the fragility of the company's ties to the community. In the summer and fall of 1769 David Douglass's American Company suffered two such disappointments: the collapse of their subscription plan in Charleston and the death of a patron in Philadelphia which prompted Douglass to solicit public permission for a short season.

In the twenty-five year history of the professional company in colonial America, it was a rare city that accommodated the actors for longer than six months. This meant a life of perpetual motion, soliciting permission, perhaps securing it, converting a space into a theatre, performing a short season, and then moving on to the next city, year in and year out.

Solo Acts

Still to consider is the presence of numerous one-person shows touring the colonies from quite early in the century. These were performers with some experience on the established London or provincial stage, traveling without a company. Their ranks included Mr. C. H., the "characterizer" of whom the Boston papers claimed to be "the first of that profession"; Mr. Stokes, a professional "who for several years acted on the stages in Dublin, Edinburgh and Goodman's Fields" (see 1 December 1749) and who offered "several dramatick entertainments" in Charleston in 1749; Mr. Joseph

---

[7] For further details and the complete text of the letter, see the *Calendar* entry for 11 June 1768.

Garner, Mr. Hoar, Mr. Foy, Mr. Morgan, Mr. Joan, Mr. Warwell, and Mr. Allyn, all of whom toured solo acts throughout the colonies. Company actors also worked solo during down times. John Henry, Patrick Malone, David Douglass, William Verling, and Lewis Hallam Jr., to mention a few, all performed solo acts (singing, lectures, rope-dancing etc) to see them through the lean summer months.

The nature of the performances varied. There were lectures of various sorts, excerpts of plays, and songs from the ballad operas, as well as spectacle exhibitions of rope dancing and other variety acts. Patrick Malone offered an evening of rope dancing; the Storers and Miss Hallam sang; Mr. Joan offered one-man versions of musicals, such as *The Beggar's Opera* in which he impersonated all the roles. But by far the choicest vehicle for solo performers was Stevens's *Lecture on Heads*, enormously popular from the fall of 1769. David Douglass performed it, as did Mr. Wall, Mr. Henry, Mr. Martin Foy, Mr. Joseph Garner, Mr. Hallam, William Verling, and several unidentified gentlemen "lately arrived from London."

To appreciate fully the contributions of these solo acts we need also to consider the nature of their venues. David Douglass performed in Boston, a town he was never able to crack with his full company. Mr. Joan also ventured into this theatrically hostile region, playing in Salem, Massachusetts colony, Portsmouth, New Hampshire colony, and Providence, Rhode Island colony. Also of interest is the brief sojourn of Mr. Stokes in 1749, who had earlier performed at Goodman's Fields in London. His appearance in the colonies suggests a possible Hallam Company connection: i.e., he may have reconnoitered the theatrical landscape for Hallam in ways that Upton was presumably hired to do in 1751.

Scenery, "Habits," and Music

Details from the first contract of Levingston's Company in Williamsburg in 1716 make clear that even quite early in the record, a major part of the attraction of a colonial theatrical performance was its spectacle: the sets, scenery, music, costumes, etc. Information concerning these topics is limited, but what does exist allows for some useful observations on the practices of colonial theatre operations.[8]

---

[8] For developments during the post-revolutionary era, see Duerr, "Charles Ciceri and the Background of American Stage Design."

SCENERY

The records from Williamsburg suggest much about early practices in that city. When Charles and Mary Stagg were indentured to Levingston, they were contracted to provide "scenery and music out of England," as well as actors (see 11 July 1716). Indeed, scenery, costumes, and related materials were essential for success. In the same city—Williamsburg—in 1736 when Dr. Henry Potter assembled an amateur company to refit the old theatre that Levingston had used, he had a painter with him, Abraham Nichols. This same Nichols may have gone on to garner a career as a painter of scenes, as Rosenfeld (249) lists a Nichols who had provided sets for English provincial companies some years later. Again, when the Murray-Kean Company traveled to Williamsburg in the summer of 1751, they operated on short capital and were driven to advertise for additional funds to supply "proper scenes and dresses" (see 24 October 1751). Lewis Hallam, on the other hand, had come supplied with a stock of necessities and used them to his advantage, on stage and off. When appealing to the initial New York authorities for permission to play in 1753, Hallam claimed he was out "a vast expense to Procure Scenes, Clothes, People &c." That scenery was an essential component of the theatrical experience is articulated quite vividly by a writer in the *New York Mercury* of 7 December 1767 who praised "The Pomp and Parade of the Theatre, the Decoration of the Scenes, the Novelty and Splendour of the Dress, the Sprightly and animated Music." By the close of the colonial period one reviewer in Charleston would sum up the entire "spectacle text" of actor, costume, set, music, lights, and playhouse:

> Indeed all the performers did great justice to their characters.... The house is elegantly finished, and supposed, for the size, to be the most commodious on the continent. The scenes, which are new and well designed, the dresses, the music, and what had a very pleasing effect, the disposition of the lights, all contributed to the satisfaction of the audience, who expressed the highest approbation of their entertainment. (*South Carolina Gazette,* 13 December 1773)

There is no doubt of the fact that the scenery, costumes, and music contributed significantly to the professionalism that became the hallmark of the colonial theatre.

When sets got old, or sustained the wear of travel, new scenery proved harder to come by in the colonies than new actors, so the performers stretched the life of their scenery.

Though the Hallams brought scenery in 1753, not until 1759 do we have the first evidence that the company (by then the Douglass troupe) refurbished their scenes: in Philadelphia, William Williams, a painter, who also earned the distinction of introducing Benjamin West to oil painting, provided the company with new painted drops when they opened their season at the new Theatre at Society Hill in June 1759. Costing the company over £100 at a time when funds were scarce, they are described in an advertisement for a production of *Theodosius*. The "decorations are intirely new and proper," offering the audience "a grand view of the Temple; the transparent altar-piece, shewing the vision of Constantine the Great, before his battle against the Christians; the bloody cross in the air; inscribed about in golden character, In Hoc Signo Vinces" (*Pennsylvania Gazette*, 9 August 1759).

In addition to Williams, the American Company employed other local painters through the years. While we know virtually nothing about his work, Jacob Snyder was discovered by Douglass in Providence sometime in 1762 (Seilhamer 284) and may have been employed even earlier by the Hallams (Duerr 983–84). In 1769 Douglass found another local painter for the special occasion of a Gentleman assaying the part of Othello, "assisted by other Gentlemen, in the Characters of the Duke and Senate of Venice." For this debut a new set of scenes was painted "at great expense," but unfortunately the artist was not recorded (see 10 April 1769). In the 1770s one Thomas Burrows apparently designed sets for productions in New York (Duerr 984), but, again, no information exists by which to reconstruct his style or accomplishments.

Though local painters could be found, the standard practice was to purchase scenery in England. For example, evidence suggests that during summer 1764 Douglass was in London procuring "new scenes, machinery, and abundance of other playhouse decorations" (*New York Post-Boy*, 5 July 1764). In London Douglass contracted with Nicholas Doll of Covent Garden, and when he returned to the colonies in the fall of 1765, he brought with him actors, singers, and scenes painted by Doll. Again, in the summer of 1771 Douglass contracted for more sets, advertising on 6 June 1771 that he "expects a new set of scenes painted by Mr. Doll in a few weeks" (*Maryland Gazette*, 13 June 1771). This activity was part of the dressing of his new theatre in Annapolis that was under construction. The theatre and the season did indeed open on the ninth of September, but the new scenes did not arrive until a short while later, and a Mr. Richards ultimately produced the scenes, not Doll. Despite the tardiness of the sets, one reviewer wrote "several of the scenes reflect great credit on the ability of the painter" (quoted in Rankin, 162).[9] These were probably the same scenes that impressed viewers in Annapolis the following season. Of these one reviewer remarked, "When the curtain drew up, the new scenes painted by Mr. Richards [of London], presented themselves to us, and exhibited a view of a superb apartment, at the end of a fine colonnade of pillars of the Ionic order, which, by a happy disposition of the lights, had a most pleasing effect" (see 1 September 1772).

Two years later, the scenes may still have appeared new enough to serve, at least new to the Charleston audiences. When Douglass opened his Church St. Theatre in Charleston on 22 December 1773, Kelly's *Word to the Wise* was an unusually spectacular production. Beyond the exceptional talents of Hallam praised by a reviewer, special notice was given to "The scenes, which are new and well designed, the dresses, the music, and what had a very pleasing effect, a disposition of the lights, all contributed to the satisfaction of the audience, who expressed the highest approbation of their entertainment" (*South Carolina Gazette*, 13 Dec-30 May 1774).

Smaller companies as well felt the need to use scenery. When Mr. Morgan expanded his solo act into a small company in Portsmouth, New Hampshire in 1772, he promised "elegant scenes and machinery and every other decoration after the manner of the entertainments at Sadler's Wells" (see 19 June 1772). Even among solo acts, design figures prominently. In the summer of 1773 Thomas Wall performed a new solo piece modeled on Stevens's *Lecture on Heads*, for which he advertised "the paintings &c are entirely new, and never before exhibited in America." He carried this show to Annapolis at the conclusion of the summer when he rejoined the company and again advertised the paintings as "entirely new," qualifying them only slightly: "never before exhibited in Annapolis" (*Maryland Gazette*, 7 October 1773).

Spectacle also played a large part in many traditional plays. The funeral procession that had crept into competing productions of *Romeo and Juliet* in London was employed as bait in advertisements even in transitional venues, such as in Upper Marlborough for 1 July 1760. Other processions were

---

[9] A scene painting from this new crop may be that which forms the backdrop of Peele's well-known painting of Nancy Hallam as Imogen emerging from a forest cave, as performed in *Cymbeline* on 7 October 1771.

later added, such as "a Procession of Roman Youths and Virgins, with an Ovation" in the 6 October 1767 Philadelphia production of *The Roman Father*. In the 1770s, when companies were sustaining longer seasons, more elaborate spectacle was introduced. The 19 January 1770 *Tempest* production (also in Philadelphia) is an example:

> The Tempest is to be acted to-morrow, written by Shakespeare, and altered by Dryden ... The scenery, machinery, and decorations for this representation, we are informed, have been prepared at a very great expense, and from the general impatience among all ranks of people for its performance, it is imagined there will be a crowded audience. (*Pennsylvania Journal*, 18 January 1770)

It was indeed an event, being performed four nights straight, a highly unusual run for Philadelphia or any other city. During the same season "Machinery for the Grand Masque of Neptune" was advertised for the *Neptune and Amphitrite* afterpiece, and later that spring, the extravagant masque of *Comus* debuted in March.

Just as their trans-Atlantic colleagues were becoming ever more committed to spectacle, so, too, the colonial performers continued to raise the bar, especially in the 1770s. The machinery of the New York revival of *The Tempest* on 5 May 1773 was reported in the *New York Mercury* of 10 May 1773 as "elegant," and this particular production garnered universal praise, as they toted scenes and machines from city to city. Of the 2 February 1774 production of *The Tempest* in Charleston, the press remarks as follows: "The characters were in general, well supported; but the deceptions, machinery, and decorations, surpassed everybody's expectations" (*Rivington's New York Gazette*, 24 February 1774). Another flashy show was premiered in Philadelphia on 3 March 1773. Garrick and Arne's *Cymon* concluded with "a Procession of the Different Orders of Chivalry; and the Shepherds of Arcadia. With a set of transparent Scenes" (*Pennsylvania Chronicle*, 22 February–1 March 1773). This same production was enticingly advertised to New York audiences the following May, as reported in the *New York Mercury* (31 May 1773):

> The scenery, decorations, dresses and machinery of the opera of Cymon, to be performed this evening, are allowed by the most critical judges of theatrical splendor, to be more magnificent than cou'd be expected at so early a period, on the American stage. During its run at Philadelphia, several gentlemen from London, attended the representation, and made comparisons much to the honour of our infant Western theatre.

This puff, written by Douglass, no doubt, reveals more about the company's interests than about critical reception. As far as can be determined, the "run at Philadelphia" consisted of only one performance, though gaps do exist in the calendar.

One final example of staging merits inclusion. For the martial epic *The Conquest of Canada* (Philadelphia, 22 February 1773), Douglass pressed real soldiers into the conflict, the stage becoming so crowded with artillery, boats, soldiers, and other authentic military properties that Douglass dispensed with the afterpiece, a program change almost unheard of in colonial playbills. Rankin (174) calls this production "the most spectacular production in the twenty-one year existence of the American Company." But the grandeur of this version of *The Conquest of Canada* was not, and could not be, repeated.

The productions surveyed here make clear the possibilities and the limits of staging during the colonial period. Of greatest significance remains the fact that staging was a crucial parameter of colonial production, and that when resources allowed, the companies would stretch their resources to the limits to achieve the strongest impact.

"HABITS" AND MUSIC

Scenery and machinery were not the only elements of colonial production. Habits, or costumes, and music were also de rigueur. Very little information survives concerning costuming, but a great deal of the music of the era has survived and has received scholarly attention.[10] We refer here not simply to the obvious matter of musical plays. Rather, the presentation of music was an integral part of the theatrical "whole show," as it was in London, and any evening's program virtually always featured not only a main play and an afterpiece, but also assorted miscellaneous musical numbers. Nevertheless, as we suggest elsewhere in our discussions of repertory and company personnel, music becomes increasingly important after the mid-1760s, when David Douglass recruits a talented group of singers for the American Company.

Although too few costume notices exist to form definitive conclusions, they are occasionally noted in reviews. The critic

---

[10] The standard study of the era is Sonneck, *Early Opera in America*.

"Y. Z.," in a lengthy review of a performance of *Cymbeline* in Annapolis in 1770, remarked that "The dresses are remarkably elegant" (*Maryland Gazette*, 6 September 1770). This detail indicates that audiences were, indeed, aware of costuming. We are not surprised to learn, therefore, that the Douglass Company, at least on one occasion, imported new costumes from London: "We hear that The Rival Queens or Alexander the Great will shortly be presented, and that the play will be entirely new dressed; a set of most superb habits having been just imported from London" (*Rivington's New York Gazette*, 24 February 1774). Unfortunately, these are the sole items available regarding this important, but elusive, subject.

As a large part of the repertoire was English comic opera, singers and musicians were essential to any company. To this end the major companies were routinely staffed with many actors who were also competent vocalists and musicians and were occasionally capable of assembling a small band. Actor-musicians like Charles Stagg (violin), Charles Love (harpsichord), William Hulett (harpsichord and violin), John Singleton (composer), as well as vocalists Miss Wainwright, Margaret Cheer, Miss Hallam, Thomas Wall, and Stephen Woolls were all sufficient instrumentalists and vocalists to fill out the scoring requirements of such well-known ballad operas as *Love in the Village* and *The Beggar's Opera*. Beyond the traveling company talents, a common practice was to hire local professional musicians such as Williamsburg's Cuthbert Ogle (d. 1755) and later Peter Pelham, or Charleston's Peter Valton, to accompany the productions.[11] Though orchestras are not routinely mentioned, a small core group of musicians was certainly present for many, perhaps all, performances, and occasionally additional instruments would be required for the more spectacular operas, such as *The Masque of Comus*, advertised with the special notice that "The orchestra [is] to be conducted by Mr. Hallam" (*Pennsylvania Journal*, 9 March 1770). Even the smaller companies employed musicians, as attested by George Washington's observation of the Moody Company, playing in Barbados in 1751, that the "Music [was] adapted and regularly conducted" (Ford 6–7), and the Virginia Company, when performing *The Beggar's Opera*, made a point of advertising that "the musick of the opera [is] to be conducted by Mr. Pelham, and others" (*Virginia Gazette*, 3 June 1768).

---

[11] For a more detailed account of the inter-relations of players and musicians, see Davis, 3:1265–72.

Additional songs and musical interludes were also regularly added to the program to showcase the talent of a favorite performer. This was particularly true for benefit nights, when the playbill would be padded with announced songs. Perhaps an extension of this practice, followed by many of the actors of the Douglass Company, was the staging of segments of separate musical shows, a forerunner of the modern cabaret. Usually presented at a minor venue on off nights, though sometimes staged in the afternoon of the same date of a regular evening performance, these concerts were often for the benefit of the local community in some form, or for the relief of a distressed performer. This was the case with a musical concert of 14 January 1768, when several members of the Douglass Company performed at Mr. Burns's Long Room for the benefit of "the poor debtors in gaol." These out-reach programs were, no doubt, very endearing to the community, but also they kept the players in the public eye. Such performances were just as frequently packaged as concerts for the players' benefits. Miss Cheer, Mr. Furell, Mr. Barry, and Mrs. Morris all mounted benefit concerts in Charleston during spring 1764, and the practice was repeated many times throughout the colonies during the colonial period.

Occasionally the number of musicians was expanded. For example, the Masonic lodges offered their talents to Mason-sponsored productions with appropriate songs between the acts, such as the performance in Charleston in January 1755 (*South Carolina Gazette*, 9 January 1755; Cohen 94). Likewise the military sometimes participated. At the benefit performance for Miss Hallam and Miss Storer at the John Street Theatre in New York on 5 July 1773, a concluding song consisted of "by particular desire, The Soldier Tired of War's Alarms, by Miss Hallam, accompanied by the band of his Majesty's 23rd Regiment" (*New York Mercury*, 5 July 1773).

All of these examples, and many more that could be marshaled, evidence the significance of music to theatrical programs. Music was more than simply popular; it was a cultural institution and expectation, and theatre companies provided one of the most important and effective outlets for the consumption of musical entertainment.

Theatrical Venues

American colonial companies performed in virtually any type of space that could be adapted for the purposes of acting.[12] As few cities had theatres, and almost no towns or villages, the companies made do with inns, "great rooms," "long rooms," assembly rooms, ballrooms, hospitals, schools, warehouses, and, no doubt, other types of facilities. Of those locations which actually could boast of a bonafide theatre, we know almost nothing of the exact plans. Nevertheless this survey attempts to gather such information as has survived concerning physical structures built as or converted into theatres, the vast majority of which appertains to Annapolis, Charleston, New York, Philadelphia, and Williamsburg, though fragmentary but suggestive evidence has survived regarding theatres in Baltimore, Halifax (North Carolina), and Providence. All told, approximately thirty-five verified theatres were built during the colonial era, with virtually all of them being constructed between 1732 and 1772. Still, caution should be exercised when attempting to arrive at a precise census of facilities, as some performances, such as those in Norfolk, Virginia, in 1772, are advertised as being "at the theatre," though no evidence has turned up to verify this venue, and a similar mystery concerns Richmond, where evidence from 1774 suggests that perhaps a theatre existed in that city, too. To these must be added the fact that George Washington provides the suggestion of a playhouse in Fredericksburg (Ford 9), and some evidence suggests a theatre in Petersburg (Scott and Wyatt 148), so the following survey must be understood as tentative. In addition to the prominent venues, a wide range of minor facilities was employed, concerning which we have supplied a survey.

Annapolis (3 Theatres)

As one of the most important of the colonial capitals, Annapolis enjoyed frequent theatrical activity, especially during the fall racing season. Up to the time of the Revolution at least three theatres were erected in the city, all in a twenty-year period between 1752 and 1771.

---

[12] For other useful surveys of early American venues, see Young, *Famous American Playhouses, 1716-1899*, and Henderson, "Scenography, Stagecraft, and Architecture in the American Theatre: Beginnings to 1870."

The first notice of theatricals in Annapolis, almost certainly amateur, appears in very early 1748, but the performances, in all likelihood, were presented in a ballroom. The first bonafide theatre in Annapolis, appropriately referred to as the "New Theatre," opened by at least 22 June 1752 and was built by the Murray-Kean Company (*Maryland Gazette*, 18 June 1752). The structure is known to have contained seating in the pit and boxes, and at least one gallery. Few other details have survived, but a notice in the *Maryland Gazette* (7 December 1752) relates that "The house is intirely lined throughout, fit for the reception of ladies and gentlemen; and they have also raised a porch at the door, that will keep out the inclemency of the weather." This theatre was seldom used after 1752, and its ultimate fate is unknown.

A second theatrical structure was erected in early 1760. The *Maryland Gazette* of 7 February 1760 reports that "By permission of his Excellency the Governor, a Theatre is erecting in this city, which will be opened soon by a Company of Comedians, who are now at Chester-Town." The company in question was the Douglass troupe, which duly opened the facility to a "polite and numerous audience" on 3 March 1760. The next information concerning this facility appears in the *Maryland Gazette* of 16 February 1769, which describes an unusual means of access to a new set of boxes: "Upper Boxes are now preparing, the passage to which, must be from the Stage; 'tis therefore hoped, such ladies and gentlemen as choose to fix on their seats, will come before the Play, as it is not possible they can be admitted after the curtain is drawn up." This theatre was used from time to time for about a decade.

Apparently the 1760 structure eventually became obsolete, as yet a third theatre was announced for construction in Annapolis in 1770. A lengthy proposal, well worth quoting in full, was published in the *Maryland Gazette* of 4 October, as follows:

> The encouragement that the ladies and gentlemen of Maryland have always given to theatrical representations, and the approbation that has attended the performances of the American [i.e., Douglass] Company, though under every disadvantage from the situation, size, and aukward construction of the House, induce Mr. Douglass to imagine, that if a commodious theatre was erected in a convenient part of the city of Annapolis, a decent company, and he flatters himself his friends are not too partial when they pronounce the present to be such, might, for about six weeks every year, including the Autumnal Provincial Court and Races, be resorted to by sufficient audiences, to stimulate them to a grateful exertion of their

faculties for the entertainment of the publick, whose favours this season they acknowledge to have been infinitely superior to their expectations. But as the expenses of building a Theatre would be more than the company could possibly pay out of the receipts of one season, after deducting the incidental nightly charge, and allowing the performers a moderate support; Mr. Douglass, urged by a number of his friends, begs leave to solicit the assistance of the publick to a scheme, which will enable him effectually to carry the design into execution, and at the same time will not be disadvantageous to the ladies and gentlemen, whose publick spirit, and taste for the rational entertainments of the stage, may lead them to patronise the undertaking. It is proposed, then, to deliver to any lady or gentleman, subscribing five pounds or upwards, the value of their respective sums in tickets; one half of which will be admitted the first season, and the remainder the season following; the money to be deposited with William Paca and Samuel Chase, Esqrs; of the city of Annapolis, and the land conveyed to them in trust to the subscribers, until the House is built, and this proposal be fully complied with on the part of the company.

The subscription and construction efforts were well along by early the next year. A letter of 18 January 1771 by William Eddis, a surveyor, provides the details regarding the American Company's ongoing efforts to open the new venue:

My pleasure and my surprise were therefore excited in proportion, on finding performers in this country equal, at least, to those who sustain the best of the first characters in your more celebrated provincial theatres. Our governor ... patronizes the American Company; and as their present place of exhibition is in a small scale, and inconveniently situated, a subscription, by his example, has been rapidly completed to erect a new theatre, on a commodious, if not an elegant plan. The manager is to deliver tickets for two seasons, to the amount of the respective subscriptions, and it is imagined, that the money received at the doors, from non-subscribers, will enable him to conduct the business without difficulty; and when the limited number of performances is completed, the entire property is to be vested in him. This will be a valuable addition to our catalogue of amusements. The building is already in a state of forwardness, and the day of opening is anxiously awaited. (Quoted in Rankin, 158)

Eddis's account is not quite accurate regarding the progress of construction, however, despite his apparent familiarity with the details of the project. The *Maryland Gazette* of 13 June 1771 offers much information on the actual state of affairs, for work was, in fact, delayed, for several months:

Mr. Douglass begs leave to acquaint the gentlemen, who have subscribed to the new Theatre in Annapolis, that all the materials for the building are now purchased, and workmen engaged to complete it by the First of September: He assures them, that nothing will be wanting on his part, nor on the parts of the gentlemen who have undertaken to superintend the work, to render it as commodious and elegant as any theatre in America. He has sent to London to engage some performers, and expects them, and a new set of scenes, painted by Mr. Doll, in a few weeks. In short, the publick, whose favours he most gratefully acknowledges, will, he flatters himself, be convinced, by the efforts he makes to entertain them, that he has a proper sense of their goodness, and an unremitting desire to make every return in his power, for the obligations he is under to them. He would esteem it as a very great favour, if the gentlemen who have neglected to pay their subscription money, will be good enough to send it as soon as possible, as the sum collected, is by no means sufficient to answer the necessary demands that will very soon be made. Annapolis, June 6, 1771.

Despite Douglass's insistent claims, however, not until three months later, on 9 September 1771, did the new "West Street Theatre" open with performances of *The Roman Father* and *The Mayor of Garratt*. The theatre is described in the *Maryland Gazette* of 12 September 1771 as "thought to be as elegant and commodious, for its size, as any theatre in America." This venue was the jewel of Annapolis and was actively used until 15 October 1773. The players did not return in 1774, and the Revolution soon followed, ending professional theatricals in Annapolis until after the war.

Caribbean (9 theatres)

We know nothing beyond the facts that theatres did exist in the Caribbean during the colonial period in at least nine places. Verified playhouses are mentioned in the newspapers as existing at Antigua; Havana (Cuba); Spanish Town, Port Royal, and Kingston (Jamaica); Christiansted and Fredericksted on St. Croix (Danish West Indies); Plymouth (Montserrat); and Bridgetown (Barbados). Hopefully future theatre historians will be able to provide documentation of these facilities, and, no doubt, other venues will be discovered.

Charleston (5 theatres)

Charleston seems to have enjoyed plays early in the eighteenth century, perhaps by 1712 (see headnote for that season), and certainly at the Court Room in 1734 and 1735.

Not until 12 February 1736, however, is the first dedicated theatre structure authenticated, the first of four to be erected by 1774. This was the Queen Street theatre, owned by Charles Shepherd and managed by Henry Holt, an early but apparently unsuccessful colonial theatrical entrepreneur, who was forced to sell the building barely four months later. A notice in the *South Carolina Gazette* of 1–8 May 1736 offers some of the sales details but, more importantly, also provides suggestive information concerning the size of the facility:

> To be sold to the best bidder on Wednesday next the 12th instant at the Theatre in Queen street, one half (or the whole) of the said Theatre with the ground thereunto belonging, containing front in Church-street 57 feet, depth 119 feet, with all the scenes, cloathing, &c. N.B. The conditions of sale to be seen at the theatre upon the day of sale.

The lot dimensions of the Queen Street Theatre suggest a building size comparable to the smaller London theatres, such as the Little Theatre in the Haymarket, which is known to have been 48 feet by 136 feet, and to have held at least 650 in its early configurations.[13] From newspaper notices we know that the Charleston theatre contained seating in the usual arrangement of pit, box, and gallery. The sale of the theatre prompted a poem in the *South Carolina Gazette* of 22–29 May 1736, part of which ran as follows:

> ON THE SALE OF THE THEATRE.
>
> How cruel Fortune, and how fickle too,
> To crop the method made for making you.
> Changes, tho' common, yet when great they prove,
> Make men distrust the care of mighty Jove
> Half made in thought, (tho' not in fact) we find
> You bought and sold, but left poor H--- behind.

Holt may have lost the title to the building, but he continued to present plays and balls at that venue from November 1736 until May 1737, when he disappears from the record in Charleston (though reappears in New York three years later). The theatre lasted only fifteen years, when, as Rankin (72) explains, the great hurricane of 15 September 1752 levelled

---

[13] See Burling, *Summer Theatre*, chapter 3.

"over 500 buildings . . . one of which was probably the old Queen Street Theatre."

A second theatre, the location of which is unknown, opened by 7 October 1754. This facility, presumably constructed by the Hallam Company, also had a pit, boxes, and a gallery. The company played on into early 1755, but the theatre was thereafter abandoned, and several years went by without theatricals in the city.

Two more theatres followed. A third theatre, also built in Queen Street and called by that name, was constructed and opened by the Douglass Company in December 1763. The *South Carolina Gazette* of 5 November 1763 provides the following pertinent details: "A theatre is already contracted for 75 feet by 35, to be erected near where that of Messrs. Holliday and Comp. formerly stood and intended to be opened the 5th of December next." This theatre, too, followed the usual seating plan of pit, box, and gallery, but within a very few years was deemed unsuitable by Douglass, no doubt due to its rather small interior. We find clear information that John Henry, a leading member of the Douglass Company, was sent by Douglass to Charleston in summer 1769 to attempt to raise subscription funds for the erection of yet a fourth theatre. He arrived at an inopportune time, however, and was unsuccessful, as the following lengthy but informative letter from John Henry to the citizens of Charleston, published in the *South Carolina & American General Gazette* of 24–31 July 1769, makes clear:

> To the Publick. The repeated encouragement, countenance, and protection the American theatre has met with here from an audience of one of the most respectable on the continent is deeply known and has deeply imprinted the sentiment of gratitude in the breasts of the American Company of comedians; in consequence of which Mr. Douglas, the manager of that company, has sent me here from New York to build an elegant theatre fit for the accommodation of so numerous and polite an assembly as formerly honored this stage with their patronage. On these principles, with a strict charge to the elegance of the decorations on which neither pains or cost were to have been spared, I set out for this metropolis, but on my arrival was very much disappointed to find the colony involved in the present disagreeable, though glorious struggle. I thought my duty to enquire of our former patrons their opinion with regard to erecting a theatre at this juncture, but found that, until those unhappy differences were subsided, it would be disagreeable to the majority of the inhabitants. Under these circumstances it would be doing the highest injustice to the worthy and respectable public, as well as to our own private principles of

> gratitude for the innumerable favours received here, to have the most distant thought of what never was meant but as a grateful proof of our constant endeavours to entertain, in the most elegant manner, so generous and judicious an audience; therefore without the least hesitation, in compliance with the general desire, I declined it until a more favourable opportunity. The ladies and gentlemen of this town have always been as particularly conspicuous in their taste for every kind of rational amusement as for their encouragement of the polite arts in general, among which the theatre has always claimed, and as constantly received, their generous protection; and I am fully convinced, did not matters of the utmost importance merit their highest attention at this critical juncture, it would not fail of that patronage it has hitherto been honoured with. I shall beg leave to observe, before I conclude, that from the most sincere gratitude and to endeavour at meriting the favour so generously bestowed on the theatre, the manager has been at a most considerable expence in every decoration belonging to it to render it compleat for the purpose, amounting to some thousand pounds; and it is hoped, as soon as every political affair which concerns the welfare of this valuable colony is settled to general satisfaction, that under such generous and respectable patrons, like every other of the polite arts, the British may not exceed, if equal, the American stage. I have the honour to be, with the utmost respect and deference, the publick's most devoted and very humble servant. July 31, 1769. John Henry.

Not until four years later was a new theatre constructed.

Serious efforts toward building a new theatre resumed in 1773. A news letter from Charleston, dated 5 July 1773, and published in the *Maryland Journal* of 20–28 August 1773 reports that "A large subscription has been solicited and is raising, for building an elegant Theatre in this town, in which Mr. Douglass's American Company will perform during the winter." The subscription effort, however, ran into difficulties. "Benevolus" reports in the *South Carolina Gazette* of 9 August 1773 that Douglass had been circulating printed petitions which present "an exertion of the abilities of a Company of Comedians, under his direction, the ensuing winter, to the favour and patronage of the ladies and gentlemen of South-Carolina." Douglass's "exertion" apparently was successful, as the *South Carolina Gazette* of 17 August 1773 contains a letter from Douglass to the citizens of the city in which he remarks that

> the subscription is in great forwardness, and a considerable part of the money already collected, and deposited in the proper hands for carrying the design into execution; the receipts for which are lodged at Mr. Wells's, on the Bay, for the inspection of the

subscribers.—Materials are collecting, builders engaged, and every possible step taken to compleat the undertaking, early in November.

The press reports that by early September construction is rapidly progressing, and on 22 December 1773 the Church Street Theatre finally opened. *Rivington's New York Gazette* of 24 February 1774 reports that "The House is elegantly finished, and supposed, for the size, to be the most commodious on the continent. The scenes, which are new and well designed, the dresses, the music, and what had a very pleasing effect, the disposition of the lights, all contributed to the satisfaction of the audience, who expressed the highest approbation of their entertainment," so Douglass apparently made good on his promises to create a first-rate venue in Charleston. In this facility the Douglass Company presented the final professional performances in the colonies prior to the outbreak of the Revolution.

Yet one final venue in Charleston deserves a word, the Bacchus Theatre on the Bay, for although the likes of the American Company never performed there, the venue saw significant activity during 1768 by Mr. Bayly's Company, who had migrated there from New York. Newspaper advertisements specify that pit, box, and gallery seating was available, but, alas, no exact account is provided of either the building or the location of the theatre.

NEW YORK (5 THEATRES)

The first playhouse in New York opened by 6 December 1732, though plays are thought to have been performed as early as 1700 in that city. The "New Theatre" has not left any clues as to its dimensions, but it was apparently located on the east side of Broadway, just above Beaver Street, according to a manuscript map from 1735 (reproduced in Odell, oppos. 1.12). An advertisement from *Zenger's Journal* (repeated 2 and 9 February 1741) also names the "New Theatre" and corroborates the location on Broadway (though the slim possibility exists that this 1741 theatre was a second facility[14]).

The "New Theatre" was either not available or no longer extant by 1750, when a company that year presented plays in "a convenient Room for their Purpose, in one of the Buildings lately belonging to the Hon. Rip Van Dam, esq; deceased, in

---

[14] Cf. Henderson, *The City and the Theatre* and head note for 1732 in the *Calendar*.

Nassau St; where they intend to perform as long as the season lasts" (*Weekly Post-Boy*, 6 March 1750). This facility, which lasted not even three years, came to be known as "the Theatre in Nassau Street" and is initially advertised on its opening of 5 March 1750 as having only pit and gallery seating. A notice ten months later in the *Post-Boy* of 21 January 1750/51 provides some additional details concerning the capacity of this structure and indicates that alterations had been undertaken. In answering reports concerning a benefit performance, James Parker, publisher of the *New York Gazette & Weekly Post-Boy* and the printer of the tickets, claims he produced 161 pit tickets, 10 for the boxes, and 121 for the gallery, for a total of 292. This capacity, if correct, would have meant the theatre was about one-half the size of the smallest contemporary London venue, the Haymarket (as noted above). We must note at this juncture that the Hallam Company, in a lengthy letter in the *New York Mercury* of 2 July 1753, remarked that they had sent Robert Upton to New York in 1751 to arrange for the construction of a theatre, but that he had deserted their cause and had joined the local players, i.e., the Murray-Kean Company. When the Hallams finally arrived in New York in 1753, they did erect a new theatre on the location of the former Murray-Kean building, as they had done in Williamsburg, symbolically and literally upon the ground of their great rivals.

This new structure, which opened on 17 September 1753 and is termed by historians as the "Second Nassau Street Theatre," was built on the site of the previous structure, as verified by a notice in the *Post-Boy* for 17 September: "The Company of Comedians who arrived here the past Summer, having obtained Permission from the Proper Authority, to Act, have built a very fine, large and commodious Theatre in the place where the old One stood ...." This theatre also had a short life.

In 1758 the Douglass Company erected the fourth theatre in New York, the venue referred to as "Cruger's Wharf Theatre." The *New York Mercury* of 11 December 1758 publishes a letter by David Douglass, wherein he pleads for permission to perform. The letter relates the following pertinent item, establishing the construction of the new theatre: "The expenses of our coming here, our living since our arrival, with the charge of building, etc. (which let me observe, we had engaged for before we had any reason to apprehend a denial) amount to a sum that would swallow up the profits of a great many nights acting, had we permission." No details have survived about its capacity, but seating was arranged in the traditional pit, box, and gallery format. The waterside location, however, which Odell terms "curious" (1:75) was apparently an impediment to success, and this structure, too, was soon abandoned.

The Douglass Company built yet another theatre in New York, termed the "Chapel Street [i.e., Beekman Street] Theatre," which duly opened on 18 November 1761. For this theatre an actual box office report of sorts has survived, being an account published in the *New York Mercury* for 1 February 1762 of a benefit performance on 25 January. The theatre that evening held 352 people, with 116 in the boxes, 146 in the pit, and 90 in the gallery, producing just over £133. The building was apparently ninety by forty feet,[15] costing some £650 to erect.[16] Fortune was not kind to the Chapel Street Theatre, for during a performance on 5 May 1766 (see entry for that date), a riot ensued, and the theatre was badly burned (Odell 1:94).

In 1767 Douglass built his third theatre, one which would enjoy a longer life than its many predecessors and which was the fifth and last colonial theatre in New York. The "John Street Theatre" was erected during late 1767 and opened on 7 December of that year. The structure was quite large, being compared by Dunlap to George Colman's London Haymarket Theatre, though Dunlap does not specify which of the many versions of that London theatre he meant, or even which Colman (father or son). Dunlap (51–52) reports two rows of boxes, a pit, and gallery, and that the house apparently could generate $800 at capacity, suggesting seating in the 600–800 person range. For this theatre, alone, of all colonial venues, an image has survived. Depicting the house interior of the theatre but revealing few details—not even the boxes are visible—this print from the late eighteenth century (no earlier than 1791) is reproduced in Odell (opp. 1:114). The John Street Theatre, which was used only sparingly by the Douglass Company (and not at all during 1769–73), survived until 1798.

---

[15] The dimensions are stated in an advertisement in the *New York Gazette* of 2 April 1764.

[16] See Douglass's letter in the *New York Mercury* of 28 December 1761.

Philadelphia (3 theatres)

Despite being one of the most important stops on the colonial circuit, Philadelphia never had a theatre which could compare with those of its sister theatrical cities. Not one of the three playhouses of the era ever rose above the level of mediocrity, and the theatre of most importance, the Southwark Theatre, had a reputation for ugliness.

The earliest evidence of actors in Philadelphia comes from 1723, and the following year produces the first notice of a theatrical structure, called the "New Booth" on Society Hill (*American Weekly Mercury*, 7 May 1724). The New Booth, however, was apparently used for variety entertainments, such as rope dancing, though the possibility exists that drolls or pantomimes may have been presented. Not until 1749 is there solid confirmation of the first theatre used for dramatic purposes, Plumsted's, which was a converted warehouse situated on Water Street, between Pine and Lombard (Pollock 6, 74). This facility was later termed "The New Theatre in Water Street" when the Hallam troupe used it during their first visit in 1753–54.

The first genuinely theatrical facility, "The Theatre on Society Hill," was erected by David Douglass for his company in 1759. Located outside the city limits at the corner of Vernon and Cedar Streets and costing £300 for the building and £100 for scenery (Pollock 14), the theatre opened on 25 June 1759. The theatre featured box, pit, and gallery seating and was used by Douglass for only one season.

In 1766 when the company returned to Philadelphia, Douglass built yet another structure, called "The Theatre in Southwark." Being ninety-five by fifty feet, this facility, strictly utilitarian and lacking aesthetic merit, met the minimal needs of the company and no more (Pollock 19). When compared with the many elegant and comfortable structures which Douglass erected elsewhere, this apparently ill-contrived, dingy, and incommodious venue stands out as a very odd project (Rankin 211, n. 7). Whatever its demerits, and there were many, the facility endured for a half century and is the last and only theatre the company used whenever they appeared in Philadelphia up to the time of the Revolution.

WILLIAMSBURG (3 THEATRES)

Relatively speaking, Williamsburg is unique in that information concerning theatrical facilities is fairly extensive. Being a colonial capital, the city was frequented by numerous visitors who recorded their observations; further, municipal authorities maintained detailed public records, many of which have survived, including deeds and other documents of relevance to theatre historians. From these sources we can verify that theatres were built in 1716 and 1751.

The first theatre in colonial America was constructed in Williamsburg in 1716. William Levingston, a merchant, entered into an agreement at Yorktown dated 11 July 1716 with Charles and Mary Stagg, " 'actors,' to build a theatre in Williamsburg and to provide actors, scenery and music out of England, 'for the enacting of comedies and tragedies in said city'" (quoted in Odell 1: 9; cf. Rankin 12–13). In 1718 the theatre was measured as being eighty-six feet six inches by thirty feet two inches on a brick foundation.[17] The company evidently was not successful, and by 1723 the record shows that the mortgage on the theatre was foreclosed (Hornblow 1:36). The structure remained intact, however, at least until the early 1730s, when performances were presented there sporadically.

The first theatre apparently was pulled down at some point between 1737 and 1751, as news of a new theatre appears. A notice in the *Virginia Gazette* of 29 August 1751 offers the following information:

> By permission of his Honour the President, whereas the Company of Comedians that are in New-York intend performing in this city; but there being no room suitable for a play-house, 'tis proposed that a theatre shall be built by way of subscription: Each subscriber, advancing a pistole, to be entitled to a box ticket, for the first night's diversions. Those gentlemen and ladies who are kind enough to favour this undertaking, are desired to send their subscription money to Mr. Finnie's, at the Raleigh, where tickets may be had. N.B. The house to be completed by October court.

Opening for performances by the Murray-Kean Company by at least 21 October 1751, this second Williamsburg theatre, located on Eastern (later Waller) Street had an active history.

---

[17] See Stephenson, "The First Theatre."

Apparently, however, the expenses for the facility exceeded estimates. A notice in the *Virginia Gazette* of 24 October 1751 offers the following information:

> The Company of Comedians having been at a greater expence than they at first expected in erecting a theatre in the city of Williamsburg, and having an immediate occasion for the money expended in that particular, in order to procure proper scenes and dresses, humbly hope that those gentlemen who are lovers of theatrical performances, will be kind enough to assist them, by way of subscription, for the payment of the house and lots, each subscriber to have a property therein, in proportion to the sum subscribed. As the money is immediately wanted, we hope the gentlemen will be kind enough to pay it as they subscribe, into the hands of Messrs. Mitchelson and Hyndman, who have obliged us so far as to receive the same, and to whom deeds will be delivered, on the subscription being compleated, for the purpose above mentioned. Which shall be gratefully acknowledged, by their most obliged humble servants, [signed] Charles Somerset Woodham, Walter Murray, Thomas Kean.

The company departed from Williamsburg by early 1752 but returned in April before again moving on to Annapolis. The Williamsburg audience was most fortunate, however, to enjoy a second professional company that same year, as the Hallam Company, the first fully professional theatrical troupe in the colonies, arrived from London in June, choosing to begin operations in Williamsburg.

The Hallams purchased the new 1751 structure for £150 10s. (Rankin 52) but ascertained that it did not meet their standards or needs. We find in the *Virginia Gazette* of 21 August 1752 a rather sarcastic notice which informs the public that the company "have obtain'd his honour the Governor's permission, and have, with great expence, entirely altered the play-house at Williamsburg to a regular theatre, fit for the reception of ladies and gentlemen, and the execution of their own performances." Apparently the Murray-Kean Company was not aware that they had built and had been performing in a non-regular theatre.[18] This altered structure, in which the Hallams began performances on 15 September 1752 and sometimes incorrectly identified as the "third" Williamsburg Theatre, had a pit, boxes, and a gallery, though its seating capacity is unknown. When Hallam left in 1752 he offered the

---

[18] See Rankin's useful analysis of this Williamsburg theatre and related features, such as seating, stage, and lighting (52–54).

theatre as collateral for debts which were never repaid, and he thus lost title (Rankin 58–59).

The Douglass troupe built a new theatre in 1760, located east of the Capitol, which they enjoyed in 1762–63, as did the Verling Company in 1768.[19] After 1768, information on the structures becomes difficult to untangle. Notices from 7 September 1769 in the *Virginia Gazette* show that a building was converted into a school house. Was this the second theatre? Then in May 1770 the players returned and once again used the "Old Theatre." Is this the 1760 facility? During the early 1770s apparently the seating was rearranged, as a playbill for 1 May 1771 (in the Colonial Williamsburg Foundation collection) states that only box and pit tickets are being sold. This altered facility is therefore presumably the same one which was the location of the final performances in colonial Williamsburg during late spring 1772. The last verified program occurred on 28 April 1772, though newspaper notices suggest the strong likelihood that performances at this "Old Theatre" continued into May.

OTHER LOCATIONS (5 THEATRES)

Especially after 1758, touring companies required something more than a large room for performances. The size of the casts, the complexity of the plays, especially musicals, and the space needed for scenery, dressing areas, and musicians simply could not be accommodated except in actual theatres. Thus a number of locations built theatres, even though the performers appeared only at irregular intervals: Baltimore, Halifax (North Carolina), Newport (Rhode Island), Norfolk (Virginia), and Petersburg (Virginia).

Being far less important during the eighteenth century than its nearby neighbor Annapolis, Baltimore did not attract theatrical attention until very late in the colonial period. Anecdotal information suggests that companies almost certainly performed there from time to time in earlier years, but the first hard data consists of a playbill dated 10 July 1772 (see the entry for that date), with the performance by the American Company having taken place at what is termed the

---

[19] Recent excavations of the site by the Colonial Williamsburg Foundation team have verified the location and dating of this structure. No scholarship about this theatre has yet appeared in print, but Odai Johnson observed and participated in the dig.

"New Theatre," but which is described more prosaically in a handwritten note on the playbill as "an Old Stable belonging to Mr. Little." Douglass's company apparently entertained the town satisfactorily, as reported in a letter in the *Maryland Gazette* of 20 August 1772:

> I have spent my time here most agreeably ... from an entertainment I received here as agreeable as it was unexpected; I mean the Theatre. The American Company have performed here the greater part of the summer, and notwithstanding the disadvantages of an inconvenient playhouse, and hot nights, have been universally well received and encouraged.

In 1773 the American Company very likely returned to Baltimore. A historian of the city records that "In the year 1773 a large warehouse, which stood at the corner of Baltimore and Frederick Streets, was occasionally converted into a theatre, on the boards of which the company of Messrs. Douglass and Hallam performed plays from time to time for the edification of the colonists."[20] The fact that the venue is specifically referred to as a warehouse, as opposed to the stable employed in 1772, strongly suggests that the 1773 dating is correct. After the Revolution Baltimore is known to have had a theatrical venue, the "New Theatre," being in 1782 the home of Wall's (later Ryan's) Maryland Company, a well documented troupe. Though nothing is known of its arrangements other than the traditional box, pit, and gallery seating, this theatre may have been the same as the one used in 1773 by the American Company.

Though almost nothing is known of the next playhouse, on a survey map of Halifax, North Carolina, from June 1769, a theatre appears. Rankin (211, n. 7) estimates the size at about sixty by thirty feet. While evidence is frustratingly short in supply, in all likelihood it was built for performances by a company headed by a Mr. Mills and his troupe, known to have been active in the area in 1768–69 (Henderson 25–26; cf. headnotes for 1768 and 1769).

Little is also known about the third provincial venue. In the early days of its existence the Douglass Company regularly sought out new audiences, and one of the areas of first exploration was Newport, Rhode Island. Predictably, the company experienced considerable resistance at first from the

---

[20] Scharf (*Chronicles of Baltimore*, 112–13) makes this claim but offers no documentation for his assertion.

local religious zealots, but sufficient numbers of vacationing southern planters desired theatricals. Therefore the company prepared a temporary theatre, a license was eventually issued, and a short two-month season was initiated on 2 September 1761. Of this "theatre," we know virtually nothing. The following year when the company returned they performed at the King's Arms Tavern.

The provincial theatres in Petersburg, Virginia, and Halifax, Nova Scotia, are known only by the most minimal information. In 1782 Petersburg documents refer to a structure known as "the old playhouse,"[21] and a local history of the city offers the following tantalizing assertion:

> Evidences of theatrical activity and interests appeared soon after the middle of the eighteenth century. The Methodist revival of 1773 was held in the Old Street Theatre. These and other scraps of information on the subject are more intriguing than enlightening, but it is certain that 'the old play house' on Old Street, as it was listed in the real estate assessment of 1784, was an interesting place. It was visited by the company of Kean and Murray and probably by Lewis Hallam's company also. (Scott and Wyatt 148)

Until and unless specific evidence comes to light, the origins and history of the Petersburg Old Theatre will remain a mystery, but concerning the theatre in Halifax we know even less, that being only the fact of its existence as mentioned in advertisements in the *Nova Scotia Gazette* for 1768, though Y. S. Bains (36) postulates that the theatre is actually a converted assembly room in the Pontiac Inn. Nevertheless, *Gazette* notices in 1773–74 refer to the space as "The Theatre."

We see, then, that numerous facilities were erected or converted for theatrical performances during the colonial era. The resourcefulness and flexibility of those companies had to have been limitless, as they faced new challenges wherever they traveled. In sum, the records demonstrate the great desire, on the part of both performers and audiences, to present and sustain the theatrical experience under the most trying of conditions.

---

[21] See Wyatt, "Three Petersburg Theatres" (83–110); cf. Davis 3.1193, 1679n94.

Minor Venues

Apart from the building or converting of buildings into formal theatres, a large variety of other theatrical venues provided temporary or introductory spaces for itinerant companies and solo performers. The many Long Rooms, Great Rooms, Court Rooms, Assembly Halls, and Concert Halls were all likely locations in which a newly arrived performer or company would make their presence known, offer samples of their wares to the town, and frankly sample the local audience potential, as well. For example "the gentleman who lately arrived from London" invited the patronage of New York for his introductory exhibition of the *Lecture on Heads* at Mr. Hull's Assembly Room. In many towns below the threshold of supporting a subscription to build a proper playhouse, these Long Rooms may have offered the only theatrical space available. Dumfries, Virginia, did not boast a theatre, but Washington saw performances there at the Assembly Room. In smaller towns these minor venues might also have functioned as sites of audience development. Mr. Morgan who performed solo in the Long Rooms of Portsmouth, New Hampshire, in the early 1770s found his audience so encouraging that he "enlarged his plan," assembled a company, and converted the Academy House into a theatre for variety entertainments, á la Sadlers' Wells in London (*New Hampshire Gazette*, 19 June 1772). This undertaking involved substantially reconfiguring the space, as we learn from his advertisement that "Complaints having been made that the first gallery was very incommodious, Mr. Morgan takes this opportunity of informing the town, that he has alter'd it as much for the better as the house will allow, in order to do which he has been oblig'd to take away the upper gallery intirely" (*New Hampshire Gazette*, 23 October 1772). Such endeavors as Morgan's established the idea of theatre upon which a community subscription base was founded that would ultimately produce the playhouse itself.

Sometimes communities never developed into a sustainable audience. For example, Mr. Lyon's Long Room in Savannah appears briefly in 1768, after which we hear no more. More often than not, they did not compete with the playhouses, but functioned as adjacent venues, outside the regular theatre season. They offered incidental entertainment of music, entre'act material. Even when they did not necessarily function as precursors to theatres, nonetheless these Long Room venues kept the performer in a public sphere, as when

David Douglass advertised his *Lecture on Heads* at Mr. Burns's Assembly Room, in New York throughout the summer of 1767, with singing by Woolls. Though the company itself traveled to Philadelphia for the fall season, Douglass was keeping himself visible in the city, and after the Philadelphia engagement, the entire company repaired to New York for a lengthy season that began in December and carried them into June of the following year. These kinds of summer appearances in non-theatrical venues, therefore, may have functioned to maintain a presence in the city without full company support. In essence, they were publicity investments for upcoming engagements. The Douglass Company had not been in New York for many years prior to the summer of 1767. Indeed as the rest of the company was, at the time, in Rhode Island, Douglass may very well have been feeling out the market with these summer shows without the necessity (or the expense) of moving the full company, and he had good reason to be leery. When Douglass first ventured into New York in 1758 his company was denied permission to perform, and only after several months' residence with little or no income was he finally able to negotiate with local authorities to gain permission to play. Thus this 1767 summer sojourn was a low-profit, high profile reconnaissance mission to a historically unfriendly city.

Douglass later employed the same strategy of one-man performances to feel out the markets in Boston in August 1769 at the "Bunch of Grapes in King-Street," and in Portsmouth New Hampshire, announcing a series of "lectures" at Mr. Stavers's Long Room in September of that year.

Occasionally these non-theatrical venues may have been chosen for their political profile. For example, when the Douglass Company played New York on 30 December 1767, they performed a benefit for the debtors at the New City Hall building. They reprised this benefit "for the poor debtor in gaol" two weeks later, this time at Mr. Burns's Long Room. That they are not performing civic benefits at the theatre at John St. is itself telling. This may be a case of fulfilling the obligation of a relief performance, without donating the proceeds of a full house, the Long Room being a smaller capacity than John St. The company's round of benefits later in the spring, of course, took place at the theatre, where the possibility of higher proceeds was certainly expected. This pattern of offering petit-benefits at alternative venues continued. In June of 1769 several members of the Douglass company, again in New York, assembled a benefit performance for a fellow actress, Mrs. Harmon, at Mr. Burns's Long Room. A few weeks later, after the departure of the main body of the company, many members remained in New York performing at Mr. Burns's Long Room and also at the Vaux-Hall Garden.

Also to be considered are the venues employed by the dedicated solo performers who made brief but aggressive inroads throughout the colonies. For example, in New England, Warwell, Mr. Morgan, and more importantly Mr. Jones, who advertised himself as a "person who has read and sung in most of the great towns in America," performed one-man renditions of popular plays and operas in the Long Rooms and small venues across New Hampshire and Massachusetts. These early assays into New England and other locations assisted and perhaps even allowed the later companies to establish more permanent theatre plants. Also of interest are the little-known activities of a Mr. Bayly, who in May 1767 set up shop at The Orange Tree, Golden Hill, in New York, while the American Company was in Philadelphia, eventually moving on to the Bacchus Theatre on the Bay, Charleston, in April 1768, when Douglass's troupe returned to New York. Bayly's hitherto unknown productions at these minor venues make clear that audience demand was high even when the major companies were out of town.

Repertory

The various colonial companies drew almost entirely upon plays well known to playgoers in London, Dublin, Edinburgh, and throughout the British empire generally. Being, in a very real sense, the most distant provincial circuit, the preferences of the audiences of the colonies moved in some relation to the tastes of the imperial cosmopolitan trends, but important differences can be noted, as the colonists did not have available to them anything like the timely variety and flow of new plays present in London and other cities. The most popular plays in colonial America consisted of a small sub-set of plays which also appealed to London and other audiences, but often with intense distortions.

The evening's bill of fare consisted principally of a full-length "mainpiece" followed by an afterpiece, which was always a farce, a pantomime, or a short musical play, and sometimes several of these in combination. Also included were various entr'acte entertainments, such as vocal or instrumental pieces, dancing, comic routines, and orations. These latter entertainments we have not recorded due to their non-dramatic content, but they do constitute an interesting dimension of audience tastes. An important caveat, however, must be added in regard to the following analysis. While, as Samuel Johnson so correctly stated, "the Drama's Laws the Drama's Patrons give, / For we that live to please, must please to live," we cannot be sure, due to the fact that we lack records for the vast majority of probable evenings of performance in colonial America,[22] whether we are seeing what audiences "wanted," as a clear sign of audience tastes, or whether the data reflect only what the acting troupes could present, given their resources. Almost surely both factors are at play. Nevertheless, the known data offer some intriguing results.

MAINPIECES

Among mainpieces, the most frequently represented plays consist almost equally of comedy and serious drama, a ratio quite similar to David Garrick's era at Drury Lane Theatre[23] (the London standard we have selected). In London the ratio of comedy to tragedy, as made clear in statistical analyses prepared by George Winchester Stone for the period 1747-76, was about six to four. From the meager existing data, the provincial colonial companies, though lacking the enormous variety of the London patent houses, nevertheless apparently presented a similar balance of plays. Eight of the thirteen most frequently performed mainpiece plays in the colonies also were seen frequently at Drury Lane, including the top two shows of the era, *The Beaux' Stratagem* and *Romeo and Juliet*. *Richard III, The Orphan,* and *The Fair Penitent*, among tragedies, and among comedies, *The Beggar's Opera* and *The Provoked*

---

[22] To add to the difficulties, we have the unusual category of known performances identified by earlier scholars who failed to record the complete details. For example, Rankin apparently found "evidence" of two performances of *Venice Preserved* in Albany (no dates), one of *Jane Shore* in Perth Amboy in 1759 (but which is probably a shaky inference from a remark by Dunlap [22]), and of 37 performances of *The Padlock* (where we have identified only 26), all without any corroborating sources materials (see Armstrong, *passim*). This type of unfortunate loss of evidence makes all the more evident the need for a collective calendar such as the present project attempts.

[23] These details appear in Stone, *The London Stage, 1660-1800*, clxii-clxiv. Unfortunately the assumptions we apply here must be only approximate, as Stone employs a system of classification which varies from our statistical categories and ranks plays by major theatre. Still, the general trends and proportions are representative for our purposes.

Husband were often seen by audiences on both sides of the Atlantic. Of great interest here, however, irrespective of the relative balance of comedy and tragedy, are the plays seen often in the colonies but not nearly as frequently in London.

Among comedies, the most obvious difference is in the colonial preference for the plays of George Farquhar, which constitute literally a trend in themselves. Though continually popular in London as well, Farquhar's plays were presented on the colonial stage in far greater proportions, appearing early and often in the records. While *The Beaux' Stratagem* and *The Recruiting Officer*, both first recorded in 1732, stand among the earliest known plays in the colonies, the considerable popularity of the latter is a feature of interest which is difficult to interpret. *The Constant Couple*, though not appearing until 1750, was, nevertheless, among the "second wave" of plays introduced in the colonies and enjoyed a more successful stage life in the colonies than in London.

What follows is a summary table according to available data of the most popular plays staged in colonial America. Readers must understand that a vast amount of performance information is not available, so the following ranking is conjectural. For comparative purposes we have also included the relative popularity of these plays in London during the mid-eighteenth century.

TABLE 1: MAINPIECES

Name of Play	1st Colonial Season	# of Known Performances	London Ranking
Romeo and Juliet	1730	35	1
The Beaux' Stratagem	1732	34	6
Richard III	1750	33	5
The Beggar's Opera	1733	32	2
The Provoked Husband	1752	30	9
George Barnwell; or, The London Merchant	1736	29	—
Cato	1732	28	—

The Recruiting Officer	1752	28	—
The Orphan	1735	27	13
The Fair Penitent	1750	25	17
Hamlet	by 1752	24	4
The Gamester	1754	24	—
Douglas	1759	22	—

Also of interest are plays popular in London which did not receive equal representation in the colonies, especially during the era for which we have fairly complete records. For example, *The Suspicious Husband*, first among all comedies at Drury Lane, is far down the list in the colonies (introduced in 1754), with only fifteen known performances. Shakespeare's *Much Ado about Nothing*, highly ranked in London, is unknown in the colonies, though most of the other popular London comedies eventually appeared, including (with year of first colonial performance) *Cymbeline* (1767), *The Conscious Lovers* (1753), *The Clandestine Marriage* (1767), *The Tempest* (1770),[24] *The Jealous Wife* (1764), and *The West Indian* (1771), all with ten or more performances.

Among serious plays, colonial patterns also show important distinctions. While sharing with London audiences an abiding interest in *Romeo and Juliet* (1730), *Richard III* (1750, as adapted by Colley Cibber),[25] *The Orphan* (1735), and *The Fair Penitent* (1750), colonial audiences viewed a much higher proportion of performances of other serious plays which were not nearly as popular in London during 1747–1776, though each for different reasons. *George Barnwell; or, The London Merchant* (1736) is a clear case in point. Though the play was wildly popular in London during the 1730s and 40s, after 1747 it had become the sort of play which appeared only a few times per season. In the northern colonies Lillo's play appeared regularly for many years and seems to have appealed to the

---

[24] Stone includes this play among "comedies," but it more properly should be classified a musical, as the version presented in the colonies was the Dryden/Davenant adaptation, which contains extensive music.

[25] For a discussion of the importance of this play, see the introduction to it in Burling and Viator, *The Plays of Colley Cibber*.

moral imperatives of the struggling colonists, in its staunch advocacy of Christian temperance and a stringent work ethic, as did *The Gamester* (1754, Edward Moore and Garrick's version). The political sentiments of *Cato* (1732) also resonated strongly with the colonists, despite the well-known fact that even in London both Whigs and Tories claimed it for their own. The last of the most popular serious plays, *Douglas* (1759) is perhaps the most interesting. To be sure, the play was well received upon its first appearance in London and did enter the continuing repertory. In the colonies, however, the play's impact and success were immediate and lasting, a cultural phenomenon well worth studying in detail.[26] Thus the serious plays which the colonists viewed, as with the comedies, differed in important ways from the tastes of Londoners, but would not have been seen as anything outside general cultural norms.

Always of interest is the situation regarding the plays of Shakespeare. We have noted the performances of some plays, but as a group, additional observations can be made. Of the thirteen plays presented for a total of 181 known performances, all but three are the same plays which were popular in London, and we now include both the Drury Lane and Covent Garden repertories as our basis of comparison. Plays popular in London but not so favored in the colonies include *Henry IV (Part 1)*, *King John*, and *Julius Caesar*, and two of the most well received London plays were never performed in the colonies—*Much Ado About Nothing* and *Henry VIII*. In general, however, the colonial audiences saw few surprises as compared to what Londoners could expect on the patent theatre stages.

TABLE 2: PERFORMANCES OF PLAYS BY SHAKESPEARE

Title	Date First Performed	# of Performances
Romeo and Juliet	1730	35

---

[26] The popularity of this play in the southern colonies may have been due to the increasingly large numbers of Irish and Scotch immigrants in that region; thus the anti-English theme would have appealed to their nationalistic fervor. This possibility and many other excellent insights and suggestions were offered to us by the anonymous Reader who reviewed our manuscript for publication.

Richard III (Cibber version)	1750	33
Hamlet	by 1752	24
Othello	1751	13
Cymbeline	1767	13
The Tempest (Davenant version)	1770	13
Macbeth (Dryden/Davenant version)	1759	12
The Merchant of Venice	1752	11
King Lear [Tate version]	1754	10
Henry IV, Part 1	1761	9
King John	1768	5
Julius Caesar	1770	2
The Merry Wives of Windsor	1770	1

AFTERPIECES

In terms of afterpieces, the colonial stage was in many respects a virtual mirror of London preferences. As seen in the accompanying table, five of the six most popular afterpieces at Drury Lane also were regularly performed in the colonies. The one notable difference is that pantomimes were not performed nearly as often in the colonies as in London, no doubt due to the fact that elaborate and expensive machinery was required for such productions. As such, only *Harlequin Collector* received regular performance in the colonies.

By far the most frequently staged creator of farces in this era was David Garrick, whose plays constitute the first three positions in the rankings. *Lethe* (1751), *The Lying Valet* (1750), and *Miss in Her Teens* (1751) all appear within a year of one another in the colonies and become important staples of the various companies. Garrick's *Catherine and Petruchio* (1766) also shows up regularly in programs, as do his *The Guardian*

(1768) and *The Irish Widow* (1773), confirming his appeal on both sides of the Atlantic.

The rest of the shows consist of two types, farce and musical romance. Robert Dodsley's *The King and the Miller of Mansfield* (1752), whose many performances are yet to be explained, and James Townley's *High Life below Stairs* (1767), both farces, were often performed in the colonies, with the popularity of the latter being quite intense in the years immediately before the congressional ban on play performance in 1774. The factor tying the rest of the afterpieces together is that they were all musicals of one sort or another. Charles Coffey's *The Devil to Pay* (1736), Henry Carey's *Damon and Phillida* (1751),[27] Isaac Bickerstaffe's *The Padlock* (1769), and Carey's *The Honest Yorkshireman* (1752) all catered to the increasing interest in musicals after the 1728 London appearance of *The Beggar's Opera* in London.

TABLE 3: AFTERPIECES

Name of Play	First Season	# of Known Performances	London Ranking
Lethe	1751	42	2
The Lying Valet	1750	41	—
Miss in Her Teens	1751	38	6
Damon and Phillida	1751	35	—
The Devil to Pay	1736	34	4
Catherine and Petruchio	1766	27	—
The Padlock	1769	26	3
High Life Below Stairs	1767	26	5

[27] Long thought to be the work of Colley Cibber because this play is a two-act version of Cibber's *Love in a Riddle* (Drury Lane, 1729), evidence now suggests this is the work of Carey. See Burling, "New Light on the Colley Cibber Canon: *The Bulls and Bears* and *Damon and Phillida.*"

The King and the Miller of Mansfield	1752	25	—
The Honest Yorkshireman	1752	24	—
Harlequin Collector	1753	24	—

Indeed, the trend is very clear in the data that the short musical was the most popular afterpiece genre on the colonial stage. Additional musical plays not listed among the most popular, but still performed quite regularly, include Henry Fielding's *The Mock Doctor* (1750) and *The Virgin Unmasked* (1751), Kane O'Hare's *Midas* (1769), John Hippisley's *Flora* (1735), and additional Bickerstaffe favorites, such as *Thomas and Sally* (1766), *Love in a Village* (1766), and *the Maid of the Mill* (1769). Musical afterpieces mounted but without documented larger numbers of performances include Coffey's *The Beau in the Suds* (1750), Carey's *The Contrivances* (1767), and Moses Mendez's *The Chaplet* (1767). As these dates make clear, in the colonies musicals became more important in the mid-1760s, due to the fact that David Douglass recruited several excellent singers at that time.

In sum, colonial audiences enjoyed a selection very closely aligned with the theatres of London. As for the time delay, to be sure many of the plays were not seen abroad until several years after their London premieres, such as the seven-year lapse between the 1747 London premiere of Benjamin Hoadly's wildly popular *The Suspicious Husband* and its 1754 arrival in the colonies, but even this factor was eventually greatly diminished. From the late 1760s onward, only a few months might elapse between a play's appearance in London and its colonial premiere. For example, only six months after its London premiere (3 October 1768), Bickerstaffe's *The Padlock* was mounted in New York (29 May 1769); William O'Brien's *Cross Purposes* received its initial London staging on 5 December 1772 and was seen along with *Hamlet* on 28 May 1773; and Oliver Goldsmith's *She Stoops to Conquer* appeared first in London on 15 March 1773 and was staged in New York on 2 August of the same year.

Nevertheless, despite the best efforts of the colonial troupes, the challenge of the Atlantic Ocean was formidable, and, in fact, only a tiny fraction of new London plays, regardless of their popularity, appeared anytime soon in the colonies. The colonial companies were often desperate for new material, even being forced to advertise in the hopes of locating a copy of a play that they might borrow in order to work up a new show, as revealed in the *New York Gazette & Weekly Post-Boy* of 6 May 1751: "If any gentleman or lady, has the farce call'd The Intriguing Chambermaid, and will lend it a while to the players, it will be thankfully acknowledged."

We must never forget, however, that new plays, despite their great appeal, never constituted a great percentage of total performances in London during the Age of Garrick. Revivals were the standard fare, and the continuing popularity of plays such as *The Beggar's Opera, Romeo and Juliet,* and *Richard III* reflected audience expectations and tastes in a very real sense, just as syndicated reruns of popular television series do in our own time.

Negotiating Authority

From the first record of the performance of *The Bear and the Cub* in Virginia in 1665, evidence of very early colonial theatre in America largely survives through records of its opposition. Indeed, almost all of the evidence for the presence of theatrical activity in the colonies for the first fifty years comes to us in the form of prohibitions. The opposition itself later played a crucial role in the shaping of the theatrical marketplace, yet, lest the detractors of the theatre be overemphasized, it should be recalled that in the first example of litigation against the theatre, the actors of the 1665 play, *The Bear and the Cub*, were acquitted, and the accuser was forced to pay court costs. It should also be noted that almost without exception the opposition against the theatre was localized in the northern colonies (Pennsylvania, New York, and particularly in New England), while the Carolinas and Maryland offered no resistance to the theatre beyond an early prohibition of 1712 in Charleston against playing on Sundays, and some initial resistance to the introduction of the Hallam Company in 1752 in Virginia.

The absence of prohibitions, however, did not constitute blanket permission. Securing the permission of the authorities proved a continual negotiation for the colonial companies, and in every colony and island permission from the governor had to be secured prior to any public performance. The headers of playbills and newspaper notices are routinely marked in their boldest print "by permission." To this end, the governor of each colony had to be solicited, and when such solicitations did not prove successful, theatre managers courted wealthy and influential patrons, lobbied openly in newspapers, and even donated complimentary tickets to procure support, as was the case with the Rhode Island colonial House of Representatives in 1761.

To ease the negotiations in a new colony, the managers of the companies carried with them letters of character attesting to their integrity as citizens and players. Yet they were still often required to post bails of assurances against debts and good behavior. And when all else failed, managers pleaded hardship and begged for a minimal season to cover travel expenses out of the colony. All of this was a timely process. While thus awaiting permission, some of the more entrepreneurial players advertised other services, sych as dancing lessons and musical instruction (see further discussion under "Company Finances"). The time between engagements may also have been spent in refurbishing a theatre, as was certainly the case with the Hallam Company in their inaugural summer in Williamsburg, 1752. Sometimes permission was never granted, as was the case of Mr. Mills, whose North Carolina company tried—unsuccessfully—to secure a summer season in Rhode Island in 1768.

Once permission was secured, it was never permanent. As the moral landscape of the colonies varied from city to city and governor to governor, permission had to be renegotiated and re-secured many times each year, and often even in the same city. Likewise, permission for one company did not guarantee permission for the next, as Lewis Hallam discovered when he entered New York on the heels of the Upton Company in 1753. Also, when a company returned to a colony in which they had previously played, permission had to be re-secured. This ambivalence toward the theatre was particularly pointed in early New York, with successive governors banning plays, permitting plays, and even writing plays. In 1699 or 1700 the governor of New York, John Nanfan, granted permission for one Richard Hunter to perform plays in the city.[28] Nanfan's successor, however, sided with the Quakers and in 1709 forbad play acting altogether in New York. Yet another New York governor, Robert Hunter, was the author of *Androboros, A Bi[o]graphical Farce in Three Acts*, published in New York in 1714. This pattern of gubernatorial ambivalence continued right through the 1760s, providing the touring companies with

---

[28] The license is extant but no records exist of any performances. See "Notes and Queries," 118.

runs of remarkable seasons followed by periods of denied permission. Thus any victory the theatre gained over its opponents was seldom conclusive and never permanent.

Nor did the permission of the governor guarantee the permission of local authorities. City mayors were occasionally at odds with the governor of the colony, thus creating factional rifts which complicated negotiations. This was clearly the case in Philadelphia in 1723 when the city pressured the mayor to suppress performances that the governor himself attended. An unknown company (Tomlinson's?) was also apparently caught up in similar factional disturbances during the Stamp Act riots in New York in 1766, when a mob destroyed a theatre associated with the then ex-governor. In Newport in September 1761, permission had to be bought, as Douglass apparently offered the full membership of the House of Representatives complimentary tickets in exchange for defeating the proposed bill to deny the players permission. The following summer when Douglass returned to Rhode Island, the opposition was better organized and the players were denied their license and forced into a subterfuge of performing "concerts," between the parts of which plays were offered gratis. Even in a theatre-friendly community like Charleston, a local and very factious disturbance gave the Douglass company a great disappointment in 1769, and no subscription money could be found. That same fall when a notable patron in Philadelphia died, David Douglass was forced to publicly plead for permission to open a short season in that city, "to save [the company] from Destruction" (see 5 October 1769).

One of the lengthier negotiations with the colonial authorities occurred in New York in the summer of 1753 when Lewis Hallam first introduced his company of comedians from London. They arrived in the city sometime in June after the Upton Company had beat a hasty retreat. By 2 July the Hallams had met with sufficient repulsions to publish a lengthy account of their trials in the *New York Mercury*. Negotiations must have continued throughout the summer, as Hallam lobbied for the support of prominent citizens. The season did not open that year until 17 September, nearly three months after their arrival. The following year they met with more resistance in Philadelphia. Negotiations in this city culminated with a contract that promised the company's reputable behavior and required the posting of bail before a short season of twenty-four plays was allowed. The season was later extended, but this was far from a lasting victory, for when the company returned to Philadelphia in 1759, they encountered similar resistance. Likewise when the company—now the Douglass Company—returned to New York in the fall of 1758, they applied for permission and were met with "absolute denial" (see 6 November 1758). After pleading for nearly seven weeks, the company was finally granted permission to perform a brief season of thirteen nights.

Beyond obtaining permission, the companies often encountered opposition of other natures, chiefly moral, legal, and economic. Though the distinctions were often blurred—for example, moral opposition was easily translated into legislation, or economic objections were often simply moral protests in disguise—nonetheless the adversaries of drama were a continual obstacle to the colonial companies even after they had secured the proper license to play.

Moral Opposition

Moral opposition is characterized by a climate that made the production of plays largely unwelcome and that often involved statutory prohibitions. Boston provides a lasting example. Boston did not legally prohibit plays until 1750, but there was zero tolerance for the institution well before the need arose to enact legislation. Indeed, if Boston newspapers are any index of public sensibilities, great lengths were covered to remind their readers of the moral hazards of theatre and the wages of attending playhouses. Compounding whatever anti-theatrical rhetoric ran from the pulpits, the press was very active in exerting a subtler, indirect coercion that created a hostile ideological environment for the theatre. It is a curiosity of New England that throughout the bulk of the eighteenth century, as theatres and theatre-going were becoming established throughout the lower colonies and attempting in-roads further north, Boston papers reprinted little of their victories, their seasons, charities, or significance, while studiously reprinting every tragic accident that befell players, playhouses, and theatre-goers, in the colonies and in Europe, however old. Indeed Boston press coverage vis-à-vis drama was little more than a catalogue of playhouse catastrophes, each more devastating than the last. The Boston press piled one natural disaster upon another in hyperbolic doses like Hollywood blockbusters: fires, earthquakes, hurricanes, volcanoes. Here is an early example from the *Boston News Letter*, 18–25 February 1706. The news was hardly current:

> Bristol, August 4 [1703]. On Thursday last our players acted near this city: a comedy called *the Metamorphoses*, in which there's a song in

praise of the devil, page 14, the first four lines are thus, 'Hail powers beneath! whose influence imparts / the knowledge of infernal arts, / By whose unerring gifts we move / to alter the decrees above.' Near the end of the play the seats gave a great crack, and afterwards fell, so that the auditors were all rumbled together, and frighten'd as if there had been conjuration. The candles fell among the wood, and were like to have set all on fire. The crowd of the people stopt up the doors and made the passage very slow; some lost their swords, others their hats and wigs, and women their head-dresses and scarves; several persons were bruis'd but not killed; and the upper part of the gallery falling, several women tumbled down upon their heads, and were expos'd in the throng to great indecencies. The players run out at the back-door, and there was a report that something more than ordinary appear'd, but that is false, the devil was too sensible of his own interest to disturb those who invok'd him, and paid him such adoration. However several who were there look upon it as a judgement, and resolve never to go thither any more; but the players are so hardened, that they intend to act it again this evening.

No account was published as to what disasters ensued the next evening, nor needed there be: the moral imperatives were clear enough. Again, from the *Boston Gazette*, 1 December 1741:

Clonmell, Sept. 23. On Monday last was acted here the *Recruiting Officer* with the *Devil in the Wine Cellar*. As the actors began to play the devil (the farce) the lofts of the house not only fell down, but also the stage and front seats, with 200 persons that sat thereon, several of whom had their arms and legs broke, and others were so much bruised that their lives are despair'd of.

The good citizens of New England, with their belief in the emblematic nature of the world, no doubt took these examples to heart.

But to the opponents of the stage, play-going was equally condemnable. Theatres were of themselves the sites of God's wrath, a judgement that made little distinction between player and auditor. In 1719 the *Boston News Letter* reports an earthquake in Venice: "the shock was most felt at the Opera and playhouse, where the performers and actors let fall the curtains, and the company ran out" (17–24 August 1719). In 1757 Bostonians read of the playhouse in Havre-de-Grace, Paris, that was destroyed by a "most violent hurricane" during a performance of *Samson*: "Upwards of 100 persons were buried in the ruins, which being set on fire by the candles and lamps, the whole was consumed" (*Boston News Letter*, 14 July 1757). There is nothing incidental or off-hand about the details that these reports include. The production itself—*Samson*—indicts the Parisian audience as Philistines, gathered to watch the spectacle, and the destruction of the theatre is unequivocally equated with the destruction of the temple of the heathens. If the providential nature of the event was not convincing enough to dissuade the hardened playgoer, the account closed with a summary of the target-specific calamity: "happily, the flames were not communicated to any other building."

Perhaps the most remarkable story of God's judgement visited upon theatres came from the distant past. When the city of Pompeii was under excavation in the late 1740s, the story of the discovery was carried in several colonial papers, but only Boston papers leaped from news coverage to moral parable. It was the discovery of the theatre of Pompeii that attracted the attention of the Boston press, "that theatre which according to historians, was buried by an earthquake in the reign of the emperor Titus" (*Boston News Letter*, 26 May 1748).

In the moral climate of New England, theatres were the sites of destruction where the wrath of God was visited upon the over-indulgent. That a fire broke out in the theatre in Petersburg, Russia, during a performance of *Tartuffe* (*Boston Evening Post*, 31 July 1749), or an actor in a production of *Dr. Faustus* fell from one of the flying machines "by which accident his skull was fractur'd [and he] died in a miserable manner" (*Boston Gazette*, 29 November 1736) makes for remedial local reading: given an environment of anti-theatrical rhetoric, accounts of theatre disasters were evidence of the judgment of God.

In the absence of recent catastrophes, those of the past could be recycled to serve as vivid and lasting reminders of the dangers of play-going. That these stories were received as considerably more parable than news is illustrated by the following event that was reported in the Boston papers *thirty-seven years* after its occurrence:

> The following tragical event happened in the county of Cambridgeshire, not many years since. Some strollers having brought down a puppet-show, it was exhibited in a large thatched barn, at Barnwell, a little village near Cambridge on the 8th of September, 1727. Just as the shew was about to begin an idle fellow attempted to thrust himself in without paying, which the people of the shew prevented; and a quarrel ensued; after some altercation, the fellow went away, and the door being made fast, all was quiet; but this execrable villain, to revenge the supposed incivility he had received by the shewmen, went to a heap of hay and straw which stood close to the barn, and secretly set it on fire .... (*Boston Evening Post*, 29 October 1764)

The fire burned the closed thatch barn and numerous spectators died in the conflagration. Quite noticeably, most of these accounts–revisited for the edification of modern readers–are not carried in other colonial newspapers. That the editors *cum* writers of these accidents were on the watch for such moral testimonials and such coverage created a frigid moral atmosphere and assured prospective managers that players and playhouse would meet with a chilly reception.

Outside of New England, the moral opposition to the theatre was most pronounced during the late 1730s and early 1740s when British evangelist George Whitefield toured the colonies, initiating the religious hysteria known as the Great Awakening. Whitefield's campaign against luxury extended of course to play-going but also included balls, dancing, gaming, and even card playing. The popularity of both preacher and platform that so vehemently discouraged dramatic productions may help to account for the paucity of theatrical activity during this decade. He was, however, not without his detractors who saw little harm in innocent amusements.

The Quakers of Philadelphia presented a perennial challenge. In Philadelphia we encounter the only known examples of play texts expunged to suit the tastes of the community. This was no doubt a practice that occurred more frequently than has been recorded, but it was publicly advertised in Philadelphia, 10 May 1770, with Congreve's *Love for Love*: "no line in this play, offensive to delicacy, will appear in the representation."

Legal Opposition

In the Quaker colony, moral opposition easily translated to legal opposition. Statutes were enacted by local legislative bodies only to be repealed in England. In 1700 the Assembly of Pennsylvania passed a law prohibiting "stage plays, masks, revels." In 1705 it was repealed in Parliament. The following session, the prohibition against playing was repassed in Pennsylvania assembly. In 1709 it was again repealed in Parliament. In 1711, the Quaker Assembly in Pennsylvania passed their prohibition for the third time which in 1713 was a third time repealed in Westminster. This adversarial climate found an early expression again in 1723 when a troupe of players arrived in Philadelphia and the mayor of that city found himself at odds with the governor of the colony:

> How grievous this proves to the sober people of the place, thou wilt easily judge, but it happens at p'sent to be more particularly so on me, having,

unfortunately, been chosen Mayor of Philad [sic] for this year, there is an expectation that I should exert that authority to suppress their acting. But as . . . ye Gov. himself resorts thither, I can by no means think it adviseable to embroil myself with the governor to no purpose. (See entry for 1723.)

The subject of drama was indeed inflammatory.

Yet even in Boston, in spite of the strong moral climate to the contrary, occasional clandestine performances slipped in, necessitating formal legislation. After an amateur performance in 1750, when the "eagerness of the public to witness [a] performance occasioned a serious disturbance at the door" (Willard 4), Boston drafted and formally enacted a prohibition against plays and play-going.

Yet in spite of the legislative efforts to ban the theatre (and some hefty fines for their violation), bans against the theatre were not always effective. In Boston from 1759 on, there were almost annual clandestine theatricals that upset the zero tolerance community. Indeed the 1750 ordinance had to be publicly republished in 1759, implying some illicit performances. Clandestine performances continued, occurring in 1760, 1763, 1765, and 1767 with heated debates, followed by an attempt to repeal the act to prevent stage plays, but the repeal was unsuccessful. Again in the spring 1769 opposition arose when some military personnel undertook to organize a company and perform a series of plays. It was on this occasion that one of the supporters of this venture reminded the Boston public of the unconstitutionality of the theatrical prohibition:

> ... there is an Act of Parliament licensing theatrical performances throughout the King's dominions, which I take upon me to say (and no one can contradict) intirely supersedes the Act of this province, the Assembly are restricted to the making laws not contrary to the laws of England, and if so, certainly the act of this province abovementioned can be of no force. (*Boston Evening Post*, 20 March 1769)

Well reasoned as this argument was, nonetheless the performances were suspended, and the act to suppress theatricals was not formally repealed until 1793.

Newport, Rhode Island, enacted a ban on theatrical presentations in the attempt to prevent the Douglass Company from building a subscription theatre in the summer of 1761, though the company performed in spite of the bill. Providence followed suit in 1762, while Portsmouth, New Hampshire, refused the actors admittance altogether in the same year (1762).

Economic Opposition

Beyond the moral and legal opponents to the theatre, the more frugal minded also objected to the extravagance of the playhouse. For example, economic objections may also have contributed to the New York theatre riot of 5 May 1766. Ironically, when the theatres were finally closed prior to the Revolution, the reasons are economic, not moral. The Continental Congress in October of 1774 discouraged the theatre as part of a sweeping field of expensive diversions that dissipated income. Earlier the same year citizens in South Carolina had also objected that "large sums are weekly laid out for amusements," though this may be a moral argument in masquerade. Economic objection was perhaps a new approach for the old enemies; having failed in their appeal on moral grounds, they resorted to economic objections. This was also certainly the case in Rhode Island in 1761, where the zealous anti-theatrical camp used the economic argument against the theatre. Claims of financial extravagance were levied against the Douglass Company in New York in 1761, as well, which necessitated the manager to publish a defense of his income and expenditures. Moral objections masquerading as financial objections continued sporadically throughout the 1760s and 1770s, and critics even called upon evidence from England to support their case (see entry for 27 August 1767; cf., entry for Richmond, Virginia, 4 June 1774).

Charity Benefits

To appease the opposition and to curry favor companies routinely presented benefits where the proceeds of the evening were donated to civic charities: for the relief of the poor, a charity school, the hospital, etc. This strategy offered an opportunity for the companies publicly to extend their gratitude to their supporters and to purchase credit among the detractors of the theatre. Some begrudgers, however, saw through the charity as a shallow stunt to buy legitimacy. One objector (in Boston, naturally) in 1761 published a lengthy letter in which he accused the players of stealing the goose and giving the giblets in alms in Newport, Rhode Island. The benefit, he complains, was

> artfully contriv'd to accomplish the design [i.e., of establishing a theatre], in opposition to the avow'd sentiments of the town, and 'tis needless to mention the indefatigable measures pursued, to draw persons of every rank into the game. (*Boston Gazette*, 21 September 1761)

Such resistance, however, was not widespread, and communities generally welcomed and appreciated the community services of the theatre companies. These charities generally fell at the end of the local season, typically the last performance or two. In Philadelphia at the conclusion of the 1759 engagement, the proceeds of the last performance went to the Pennsylvania Hospital. In Newport in 1761, where opposition was high, two benefits were offered at which substantial sums were raised. Other recipients included the charity schools in New York, Philadelphia, and Annapolis; "the debtors" of New York and Philadelphia; and a hospital to be erected in New York.

SUBTERFUGES

When negotiations broke down, and the strategies failed to placate the authorities, Douglass was not above evasive maneuvers to support his company. One such maneuver took place during fall 1758 when Douglass returned to New York and found the environment hostile. Having been denied permission to play, Douglass advertised the opening of a supposed "Histrionic Academy," and when that subterfuge was challenged, he went public with his intentions in an open letter in which he claimed hardship (see further discussion under "Company Finances"). The campaign solicited enough support—or sympathy—to earn him and his company a short season. These toe-holds proved foundational when the company returned to New York two years later.

Douglass employed other devices to evade prohibitions, such as the presentation of concerts, with performances of plays offered gratis. This device—the well-known "concert" formula, which was developed in London by illegal entrepreneurs to evade the Licensing Act—proved successful in Providence, Rhode Island, in the summer of 1762, only because he had popular support if not legal license. Here he advertised concerts of music, noting that "between the several parts of the concert will be given (gratis) the tragedy of *Cato*" (*Boston Post Boy*, 16 August 1762). There was also the presentation of *Othello* thinly arranged for public instruction, transmogrified into and retitled as *Moral Dialogues, in Five Parts, Depicting the evil effects of jealousy and other bad passions, and proving that happiness can only spring from the pursuit of virtue. Mr. Douglass will present a noble and magnanimous Moor called Othello, who loves a young lady named Desdemona, and after he has married her, harbours (as in too many cases) the dreadful passion of jealousy* . . . . Such devices, however, were rare, and by no means the normal modus operandi.

This brief survey should make clear the sharply contrasting moral positions regarding the performance of plays that were present in the colonies from their very origins and which inevitably shaped the evolving cultural milieu of the young nation. Nevertheless one should not infer that negotiating authority substantially interfered with the work-a-day business of playing except in limited geographical regions.

Company Finances

The economic stability and success of colonial theatrical companies, as well as their internal financial policies, are difficult to assess. Almost no company records are extant, and the few details which have survived, many of which are anecdotal, allow for few inferences regarding investors, shares, profits, salaries, and related expenses. As for other dimensions of company finances, such as nightly ticket pricing and subscription strategies, the record is far more complete. The tentative, overall conclusion is that audience demand was often very high, but that the scale of expenses involved with touring on such a large scale required creative supplementary strategies for raising funds. Further, we need to bear in mind that the companies experienced considerable time without engagements, sometimes lasting for months, a fact that mitigates against anything like a regular weekly income. The financial lot of a colonial actor was indeed quite tenuous.

Hallam Company Arrangements

The only company for which we have information concerning internal financial arrangements is the Hallam Company, which arrived in the colonies from London in 1752. The information has come down to us via Dunlap, who recorded the reminiscences of Lewis Hallam Jr. This type of third-party "telephone" transmission does not instill much confidence, but the details are worth relating because no other source exists. The company, we are told, was financed by William Hallam, who received four out of the eighteen shares into which the company profits were to be divided. The other fourteen shares were allocated as follows: Lewis Hallam received a share as an actor and an additional share for his efforts as manager, and his three children collectively owned one share, while the twelve adult members of the troupe split the remaining eleven shares (Rankin 48). The chances are very good, indeed, whatever the exact breakdown, that the company divided up the net proceeds on the basis of shares. This type of financial arrangement was commonplace among provincial companies in England and even by major London theatre companies during summers.[29] By 1754, however, William Hallam journeyed to Philadelphia to sell his shares to his brother, Lewis, thus ending his affiliation with the company.

FINANCIAL RECORDS

Almost no bonafide financial records for the colonial period are extant, a fact hardly surprising considering that accountability was not an issue for the essentially self-contained itinerant troupes which performed in colonial America, as opposed to permanently fixed companies with outside investors, as in London. As the earliest manuscript contracts and other records are not known until the 1780s,[30] what information we have has come from newspapers.

While the paucity of information heightens the importance of the few accounts which have survived, the reports must be treated with great caution. For example, the *Boston Gazette* of 21 September 1761 prints a letter which refers to a benefit on 7 September 1761 at the theatre in Newport, Rhode Island colony, which claims that the company raised "a thousand pounds" at a benefit for the poor, and that the community "can throw away three or four thousand pounds a week at a playhouse," which resulted in a total of some "£30,000 ... in the short space of eight or ten weeks." These figures would at first imply that the company was grossing £500–600 per night, six nights a week, for the two months of the season in Newport, but a seemingly contradictory figure of £50 for the house's potential is reported in *Parker's Gazette* (1 October 1761) for a benefit performance on 7 September 1761. The solution to this puzzling problem points to one of the challenges facing scholars who investigate the colonial period, namely, that variant currencies and values existed (a point to which we shall return). In the case of Newport, the Rhode Island colony was operating on "old tenor" values, which were greater than "new" values by a factor of twenty and which were not brought into

---

[29] See Burling, *Summer Theatre in London,* chapters 1–3.

[30] See Haims, "First American Theatre Contracts."

line with neighboring colonies until 1763.[31] Therefore, the benefit figures do square within rough limits and allow us to extrapolate that the company made about £1,500 during the full term of the Newport engagement, or, in other words, about £150 a week, or £50 a night (assuming three performances a week). That the company was popular and well received is confirmed by a letter in the *Boston Gazette* (21 September 1761) which reports a crowded house for the 2 September opening of the Newport season. This £50 figure is also supported by the probability that the theatre held about half the audience of the Chapel Street Theatre in New York, which produced about £130 when completely full (see analysis below).

Also from 1761 a general set of figures appears in the *New York Mercury* (28 December 1761). Douglass, responding to charges that the company was reaping excessive profits, published figures which may well describe their financial conditions in that city in 1761 and shed some light on how we might reconstruct figures for other seasons. The theatre, we are told, could produce £180 at the maximum, but that the average take was £120, or ⅔ capacity, thus generating £1,920 for the sixteen nights of the two-month season. Expenses for constructing the theatre came to £650, for costumes and scenery £400, and for operating expenses £250. Therefore the company saw a profit of £620, or an average of just under £39 per evening. These figures thus provide the only ostensibly precise amounts for any extended performance sequence during the entire colonial period.

The most complete, and presumably reliable, financial information for a single evening of the era appears in the *New York Mercury* of 1 February 1762. This well-known set of figures represents the evening's receipts for a charity benefit for the poor at the Chapel Street Theatre in New York, when the Douglass Company performed *Othello* and *The Lying Valet* on 25 January 1762 (see entry for that date for more complete data). This is, of course, the same theatre described by the figures discussed above for December 1761. We learn that the benefit produced gross receipts of £133 6d. and net receipts of £114 10s. These figures resulted from an audience of 352 people, which we know constituted about three-fourths of the presumed capacity of 470. While the gross receipts are of

---

[31] On the monetary conversion rate in Rhode Island, see McCusker, *Handbook*, 136.

interest, however, the house charges represent the most important information, revealing a precise breakdown of the fixed, minimal costs of running the company, less salaries (which, of course, are not included, being a benefit performance) on a nightly basis. We learn that the charges for this benefit evening were £18 10s. 6d., a figure somewhat greater than the £15 average implied by Douglass in the 28 December 1761 letter but still well within reasonable limits. Advertising and lighting, at more than £5 each, take up the bulk of the expenses, but salaries for musicians, dressers, and door keepers are also significant. Collectively these figures make clear the extensive and complex nature of the company's operations, and the fact that numerous auxiliary personnel were employed. This company was a fully professional operation in every sense of the term.

Pricing Information

Ticket prices remained remarkably consistent over the forty years (i.e., 1735–74) for which we have information, with prices representing often extreme fluctuations in local currency values and denominations throughout the colonies.

Charleston, South Carolina colony, seems to have operated in an economic context quite separate from the rest of the colonies for the entire eighteenth century. John J. McCusker highlights this unique situation by remarking that "South Carolina's paper money had attained a security and stability rare in the colonies" (220). The earliest known pricing information of any kind comes from Charleston in 1735, when tickets are advertised as 40 shillings at the Court Room (not a true theatre). A year later when the Queen Street Theatre opened in 1736, the prices were 30s. for boxes, 20s. for the pit, and 15s. for gallery seats. These figures seem shockingly high, but, in fact, merely reflect the local currency values, as the Charleston economy simply operated on a 200–500 percent difference from the rest of the colonies. While prices vary to a small degree during 1736–37, they correspond quite well with ticket fees for 1774, the last year of theatre before the Revolution in that city, when viewers paid 35s. for the pit and box and 25s. for the gallery. The rest of the continent appears to have been relatively consistent, though differences in currencies occasionally complicate comparisons. In Williamsburg in 1751, the earliest date for pricing in that city, we find 7s. 6d. for boxes, 5s. 9d. for the pit, and 3s. 9d. for the gallery, figures which remain fixed through 1770, the last year for which we have data, though in 1751 the Spanish pistole was also advertised in ticket pricing. In Maryland the situation was slightly more complex, as that colony operated under a dual currency for many of the years covered by the *Calendar*. Prices for all goods and services actually declined through the years beginning in the early 1750s.[32] Thus in Annapolis in 1752 tickets cost 10s. for boxes, 7s. 6d. for the pit, and 5s. for the gallery but by 1772 they were 7s. 5d. for pit and box and 5s. for the gallery.

New York experienced only slight inflation during the eighteenth century. In New York in 1741 prices were 5s. for the boxes and 2s. 6d. for the pit, while by 1753, with the appearance of the Hallam Company, the first truly professional company in the city, prices were raised to 8s for boxes, 6s. for the pit, and 3s. for the galleries, figures which were basically the same in 1773. The 1753 prices, when compared to contemporary London rates of 5s., 3s., 1s. 6d., are actually nearly identical in adjusted value, as the New York to London exchange rate ran at about 160–170 percent.[33] Hallam and Douglass, it would seem, were very aware of currency values.

Pennsylvania was similar to South Carolina, not in the elevated currency values, but in the "commercial and financial importance" of the local economy, especially in Philadelphia (McCusker 181). When theatrical productions began in earnest in 1754, tickets were 6s. for boxes, 4s. for the pit, and 2s. 6d. for the gallery, a scale which increased somewhat to 7s. 6d. for boxes, 5s. for the pit, and 3s. for the gallery by 1772. We see here the best example of a genuine increase in real prices, as the basic exchange rate was virtually unchanged during the eighteen-year period.[34] We deduce, therefore, that Philadelphia was a wealthy city that could well afford slightly higher prices than other venues.

Very little pricing information exists for theatres outside the major theatrical venues, and such data as we have is complicated by the fact of often being in variant currencies. A production of *The Beggar's Opera* in Providence, Bahamas in 1746 required the hefty price of one dollar during the "old tenor" days, as compared to a half-dollar charged at various concerts and recitations in the late 1760s (e.g., David Douglass's *Lecture on Heads*, 8 September 1769). In

---

[32] On the vagaries of the Maryland system, see McCusker, *Handbook*, 192–95.

[33] See McCusker, *Handbook*, 164–65.

[34] See McCusker, *Handbook*, 185–86.

Portsmouth, New Hampshire colony, in June 1772, the pricing actually was advertised in two different currencies: subscribers were asked to pay eight dollars for two tickets per night for twelve nights, while single tickets were available for one, two, or three pistereens. And the American Company, while touring in Virginia in May 1771, charged 6s. for tickets in Fredericksburg (see 28 May 1771), which is known from the only extant playbill for a major company for a venue outside the major cities. This last item is especially noteworthy, as it makes clear that the company was able to command prices equivalent to those for performances in more populous regions.

SUBSCRIPTION STRATEGIES

The precarious nature of audience support in the colonies often demanded some minimal level of financial guarantee for the various troupes, for both erecting theatres and mounting productions, and the strategy most commonly used was to raise subscriptions. This practice appeared literally with the first known company in Charleston in 1735 and was still present in the 1770s. Of interest, however, is the fact that for nearly twenty years, between 1752 and 1770, the practice disappeared from the record.

The earliest subscription notices, from Charleston, Williamsburg, and Providence, Bahamas, appeared during the period 1735–1751. The terms are not specified for the early Charleston subscription, but Henry Holt, the manager, was clearly anxious to garner support for his fledgling enterprise (see May 1735). The information for Williamsburg in 1736 is a bit more specific, with a figure of 20s being asked per season ticket. A local company in Providence, Bahamas, built a playhouse and mounted a season in 1746–47 using the subscription method, and in 1751 the Murray-Kean company, again in Williamsburg, incurred "a greater expence than they at first expected in erecting a theatre" (see 24 October 1751) and thus sought to raise funds "in order to procure proper scenes and dresses." This subscription request seems to be the last of record until 1769, when John Henry of the Douglass Company met with humiliating failure in Charleston in attempting to raise subscriptions.

The last few years before the Revolution saw a return to subscription requests, but the two examples from major cities were both building fund campaigns. In Annapolis in October 1770 Douglass sought community assistance to the tune of £600 for the structure because the company was in town only about six weeks a year and thus could not support the costs of a new building due to such a limited engagement period. By January 1771 the money had been raised (see 18 January 1771). Likewise in Charleston a new theatre was needed for the American Company in 1773, as notices pertaining to the subscription drive appeared in the *South Carolina Gazette* during July and August of that year, with the theatre opening on 22 December 1773. Outside of the main circuit, a new company headed by one Mr. Morgan advertised on 19 June 1772 for subscription support in Portsmouth, New Hampshire colony, on the following terms: "Subscribers to pay eight dollars, and to have two tickets each, for twelve nights, one for the front seats, and one for the second seats." His subscription efforts were successful, and the company duly opened by at least October of that year, though they disappear from the record after the early months of 1773.

SUPPLEMENTAL INCOME STRATEGIES

The fact that many of the performers of the colonial era engaged in remunerative activities outside of their theatrical duties makes clear that additional income was always needed and welcomed. Predictably, the range of these efforts corresponds to the talents of the individuals, and the record is replete with examples for many years during the period 1735–1774.

One of the most common income supplements for performers with vocal talent was to sing at special concerts. As numerous incidences of this sort of activity are known, a few examples will serve to demonstrate the fact. During summer (13 June, 3 July, etc.) and fall (28 September, 5 October, etc.) 1769, Woolls, Miss Hallam, Miss Wainright, Miss Maria Storer, and other members of the American Company, all of them vocalists, presented musical concerts at Mr. Burns's Tavern (also known as The Long Room) and at Vauxhall Gardens in New York. This activity was repeated by additional company members at various New York locations during subsequent summers through 1774.

For those unable to sing, the unique eighteenth-century monologue entertainment by George Alexander Stevens known as the *Lecture on Heads* afforded an opportunity for extra income. The *Lecture* seems to have been a consistently popular one-man entertainment which could be readily mounted by a sufficiently talented individual in virtually any location. None other than the manager himself, David Douglass, offered such "lectures" on a regular basis during

1766–69 in various locations throughout the colonies. Lewis Hallam Jr. did likewise during 1768–69, and fellow company member John Henry in 1769 also offered the *Lecture*, as did Thomas Wall in 1773 in Annapolis. After the seasonal disbanding of the American Company for the summer in 1774, Allen and Goodman worked their way northward to Philadelphia by presenting a similar program.

Dancing schools also appeared. For example, Henry Holt supplemented his original company with balls and dance lessons in Charleston in 1735–36. Later William Hulett, who performed with the Hallam Company, opened dancing schools at different times in Hartford and New York. Likewise, Sarah Hallam, after her retirement, opened a dancing school in Williamsburg.

And as a final instance of scrambling, the versatile Thomas Wall, already mentioned as a singer and a lecturer, exploited another dimension of his musical talents. In several locations, including Annapolis, Charleston, New York, and Philadelphia, Wall offered guitar or mandolin lessons during the years 1768–1773, and, in the true spirit of the Enlightenment, even presented lectures on electricity.

The examples just noted all concern the activities of "regular" members of the various companies, but do not pertain to the non-touring local performers, often hired by a company to perform only while the company resided in a particular city. These people, of course, had alternative occupations which supported them on a regular basis, as their engagements with the companies were always quite limited.

AUDIENCES

Colonial American audiences, in their socioeconomic make-up, were not unlike English provincial audiences, i.e., gentry mixed with working class.[35] Yet unlike their English counterparts, colonial American audiences were a tame lot. While London during this period was enjoying the heyday of theatre riots—with hardly a full season going by without some manner of disturbance prompting the redecoration of the house—in the colonies there were few disturbances and only one recorded riot. Companies went out of their way to appease

---

[35] For analyses of eighteenth-century London audiences, see Scouten and Hume, "'Restoration Comedy' and its Audiences, 1660–1776," and Pedicord, *The Theatrical Public in the Time of Garrick*.

their clientele, and we do not find reported in the press the sort of mischief that "Thady" Fitzpatrick planned against David Garrick in London, or Thomas Kelly against Thomas Sheridan at the Smock Alley Theatre in Dublin. Rather, in the colonies, the theatre hosted a more agreeable population.

From the time of the arrival of the first professional company, the theatre offered a veneer of culture on a landscape that was but marginally civilized. The liminal nature of the early theatre is well characterized by the diversity of the audience at the Hallams' first theatre in Williamsburg. Charles Durang relates Lewis Hallam Jr.'s recollection of the opening night in Williamsburg in 1752:

> All roads leading to Williamsburg [were] crowded with old vehicles of every imaginable construction, driven by the negroes, and filled with ladies in their gayest attire—their young gallants attending them on horseback, and all directing their way to the theatre. [36]

The anticipation of a professional theatre company from London must have been intense to generate such crowds. To capitalize on the greatest possible size of audience, the seasonal calendars in Annapolis, Williamsburg, Fredericksburg, and Petersburg paralleled the Court and racing sessions, guaranteeing a higher number of gentry than the town normally boasted. This strategy had the additional benefit of proliferating the cultural tastes of the gentry into the general population, thus establishing an accepting, and acceptable, climate for theatrical companies.

Because no single population center could sustain a permanent company until well after the Revolutionary War, for the colonial players touring was essential. Yet the diversity of the colonies offered challenges to the companies that their counterparts in more culturally homogenous English provincial circuits never encountered. The cultural terrain of the colonies offered a diverse reception. The southern colonies were genteel and tolerant; New York was predominantly Dutch, frugal and, working class; Philadelphia was Quaker and resistant to theatre; while New England was Puritanical and openly hostile. In terms of performance, this meant that plays that were anticipated and applauded in Annapolis had to be sanitized in Philadelphia; likewise the cosmopolitan and genteel audience

---

[36] See Charles Durang, "The Philadelphia Stage from 1749 to 1821," which ran as a serial in the *Philadelphia Sunday Dispatch* in May 1854.

of Charleston received plays that were the targets of eggs thrown by spectators in New York, as described in our entry for 3 May 1762. About a year later, on 6 June 1763, the following notice appeared in the *New York Mercury*:

> This day are published, and sold by Rivington and Brown ... Description of a quack doctor, and a company of stroling players .... An humorous survey of the audience at the play, the behaviour of persons in the boxes, pit, gallery, of the ladies of pleasure, and of the fine gentlemen on the stage.

This bookseller's advertisement would seem to suggest that the New York audience could also be the object of someone's displeasure.

Indeed the trouble with boisterous audiences tended to be associated more with working-class markets such as New York, rather than with the Southern colonies. No notice of any audience disturbances during a performance comes from the Carolinas or Maryland, while all the recorded disturbances are localized to the northern colonies, in particular New York, where incidences of egg-throwing and rowdyism inspired David Douglass to public reprimands. Quite late in the record, 1773, the Douglass Company was plagued by undesirables in the gallery and responded by shutting up the gallery:

> A Pistole Reward, WILL be given to whoever can discover the Person who was so very rude to throw Eggs from the Gallery, upon the Stage last Monday, by which the Cloaths of some Ladies and Gentlemen in the Boxes were spoiled, and the Performance in some Measure interrupted. (*New York Mercury*, 3 May 1773).

By and large, however, audiences seemed to be more civil than their English counterparts; indeed, many accounts acknowledge the players being "warmly countenanced and supported by the publick" (see 19 May 1774).

The single recorded instance of riot took place on 12 May 1766 in New York. An extensive newspaper account, most unusual for the period, records many—though not all—of the salient facts:

> Our Grand Theatre in Chapel-Street on Monday night last had a grand Rout. When the Audience were fixed, (agreeable to the Assurance of performing the Play of the Twin-Rivals) about the Middle of the first Scene a more grand Rout instantly took Place both Out and In the House, for by the usual English Signal of one Candle, and an Huzza on both Sides, the Rivals began in earnest, and those were best off who got out first, either by jumping out of Windows, or making their Way through the Doors, as the Lights

> were extinguished, and both Inside and Outside soon torn to Pieces and burnt by Persons unknown about Ten and Eleven a Clock at Night, to the Satisfaction of Many at this distressed Time, and to the great Grievance of those less inclined for the Publick Good. Thus ended the Comedy, in which a Boy unhappily had his Skull fractured, his Recovery doubtful; others lost their Caps, Hats, Wigs, Cardinals and Cloaks Tails of Smocks torn off (thro' a Mistake) in the Hurry; and a certain He (who was to act the Part of Mrs.Mandrake) being caught in the She-Dress, was soon turn'd topsey-turvey, and whipped for a considerable Distance. (*New York Gazette*, 12 May 1766)

The motivation for this "rout," caused by "Persons unknown," is difficult to determine, but apparently it represented an illogical connection between the theatre company's activities and local economic woes. The article adds the curious phrase, "to the great Grievance of those less inclined for the Publick Good," which, by way of typical eighteenth-century ironic understatement, suggests, though does not specify, a social cause for the riot. Another account of the same incident in the *Maryland Gazette* of 22 May 1766 adds further details in recording that the theatre had

> given offence to many of the inhabitants of this city, who thought it highly improper that such entertainments should be exhibited at this time of public distress, when great numbers of poor people can scarce find means of subsistence, whereby many persons might be tempted to neglect their business, and squander that money, which is necessary to the payment of their debts, and support of their families.

The cause of the riot, therefore, originated in a more profound issue, namely economic distress afflicting the community. That the theatre was the focus of the mob's animosity, however, reveals the deep resentment of many New Yorkers toward theatrical performances, as suggested above in our discussion of "Negotiating Authority." The results of this May riot were considerable: "The multitude immediately demolished the house, and carried the pieces to the common, where they consumed them in a bonfire" (*Maryland Gazette*, 22 May 1766). The identity of the company performing that evening is not known, but it was not the Douglass troupe, who were in Charleston at the time and had not been in New York since 1762. When Douglass returned to New York in 1767, he erected a new theatre in John St. Perhaps the political pressures of an increasingly hostile and abusive British military presence during the Stamp Act Riots added to the foment. In any event, this single riot is the only known instance of such violent activity.

The few records extant thus suggest that audiences were generally docile and predictable. The possibility for dissension certainly existed, but, for the most part, the professional theatre companies faced few problems with audiences once permission to perform was granted.

❋❋❋

Works Frequently Cited

BD	*A Biographical Dictionary of Actors, Actresses, Musicians, Dancers, Managers, and Other Stage Personnel in London, 1660–1800.*
Curtis	"The Early Charleston Stage: 1703–1798."
Odell	*Annals of the New York Stage.*
Pollock	*The Philadelphia Theatre in the Eighteenth Century.*
Quinn	*A History of the American Drama. From the Beginning to the Civil War.*
Rankin	*The Theatre in Colonial America.*
Seilhamer	*History of the American Theatre.*
Willis	*The Charleston Stage in the XVIII Century.*

The Colonial American Stage, 1665–1774: A Documentary Calendar

Note: First known performances of plays are marked in **bold print** and highlighted with an asterisk (*).

1665

The first continental colonial performance on record occurred in Pungoteague, Accomac County, Eastern Virginia in the summer of 1665, when William Darby, Cornelius Watkinson, and Philip Howard performed Darby's *The Bear and the Cub*. This event may also have occasioned the first example of anit-theatrical hostility. On the complaint of Edward Martin, the three actors were arraigned on 16 November 1665 and ordered to appear in court with costumes and script on 18 December. The justices found nothing offensive in the performance. In the following court session of 17 January 1666, the players were found not guilty of any indiscretion, and Martin was saddled with the court costs. It has been traditionally related to have been performed in Cowles [i.e., Cole's] Tavern. The court records however do not stipulate the site of the original production, only that it was reproduced in Cole's Tavern—as it was known at the time—functioning as a temporary court. Susie Ames ("*The Bear and the Cub*") has argued that Cowles, or Cole's, Tavern was more properly Fowke's Tavern in 1665, as it was still in the possession of Thomas and Amy Fowkes and not sold to John Cole until sometime after 1672. Whitelaw (*Virginia's Eastern Shore*, 1: 712–13) notes that the defendants and Edward Martin were all neighboring property owners, so perhaps something more than a distaste of theatre was at stake in the litigation.

***

27 August 1665   Cowle's Tavern, Pungoteague, Virginia colony
The Bear and the Cub* (William Darby).
Performers: William Darby; Philip Howard; Cornelius Watkinson.
[Source: *Accomac County Records*, vol. 1663–66, f. 102; cf., Wise, *Ye Kingdome of Accawmacke*, 325–26.]

16 November 1665   Cowle's Tavern, Pungoteague, Virginia colony
Court action.
[A court examination of the affair led to the following decision:

> Whereas Corelius Watkinson, Phillip Howard, and William Darby were this Day arrested by Mr. John Fawsett his Majesties's Attorney for Accomack County for acting a play by them called the Bare and the Cubb on the 27th of August last past, Upon examination of the same The Court have thought fitt to suspend the Cause till the next Court, and doe order the said Cornelius Watkinson, Phillip Howard and William Darby appear the next Court in those habilments that they then acted in, and gave a draught of such verses or other Speeches and passages, which were then acted by them, and that the Sheriff detaine Cornelius Watkinson and Phillip Howard in his Custody untill they put in Security to perform this order. Its ordered that the Sheriff arrest the Body of William Darby for his appearance the next Court to answer at his Majestie's Suit for being artour [author] of a play commonly called The Beare and The Cubb.

Source: *Accomac County Records*, vol. 1663–66, f. 102.]

18 December 1665   Cowle's Tavern, Pungoteague, Virginia colony
Court action.
[The following additional legal details pertain to *The Bear and the Cub*:

> It is ordered that the Sheriff Sumons Edward Martin to the next Court to show cause why hee should not pay the Charges which accrue upon the Informacon given by him against Cornelius Watkinson, Phillip Howard and William Darby.

Source: *Accomac County Records*, vol. 1663–66, f. 102.]

1666

This year saw the juridical resolution of *The Bear and the Cub* trial when the court found no fault with the actors and charged the informant Edward Martin with the court costs.

16 January 1665/6   Virginia colony
Court action.
   [The legal action concluded as follows:

>   Whereas Edward Martin was this Day examined Concerning his informacon given to Mr. Fawsett his Majestie's Attorney for Accomac County about a play called the Bare and the Cubb, whereby several persons were brought to Court and Charges thereon arise but the Court finding the said persons not guilty of same suspended the payment of Court charges, and for as much as it appeareth upon the Oath of the said Mr. Fawsett that upon the said Edward Martin's informacon the charge and trouble of that suit did accrew, Its therefor ordered that the said Edward Martin pay all the charges in the suit.

Source: *Accomac County Records*, vol. 1663–66, f. 102.]

1682

Hill (*Jamaican Stage*, 19) remarks on the adverse implications of the English Puritan cultural policies: "When in 1655 Jamaica became an English colony, public theatricals were officially banned by the imperial government." After the restoration of Charles II in 1660, however, the ban on theatricals was lifted throughout the empire. The effects were not realized in Jamaica until 1682, however, when the first mention appears of a public theatre, though the location is not known, presumably in either Spanish Town or Port Royal. Wright (*Revels in Jamaica*, 6) quotes Wood, *Laws of Jamaica* [1716] on the revival of theatricals: "The manner of living there for Gallantry, Good Housekeeping and Recreations (as Horse-Races, Bowls, Dancing, Musick, Plays at a Publick Theatre, etc.) sufficiently demonstrate the flourishing condition of the island." From "Francis Hanson's Account of the Island and Government of Jamaica, which was wrote in or about the year 1682." Cf. Hill, *Jamaican Stage*, 20.

On 7 December 1682 the following proposal (*Charter to William Penn*, 114) was ratified by colony of Pennsylvania:

The Colonial American Stage 95

Whosoever shall introduce into this Province, or frequent such rude and riotous sports and practices as prizes, stage-plays, masques, revels, bull-baitings, cock-fightings, with such like, being convicted thereof, shall be reputed and fined as Breakers of the peace, and suffer at least ten days' imprisonment at hard labour in the house of correction, or forfeit twenty shillings.

1686

Increase Mather, in the preface to his *Testimony Against Several Profane and Superstitious Customs* remarks, "There is much discourse now of beginning stage plays in New England."

1690

Rankin (5) follows Hornblow (1:30) in suggesting that in this year in Cambridge, Massachusetts Bay Colony, students at Harvard College presented Benjamin Colman's *Gustavus Vasa*, the first play written by an American and acted in America. Quinn (1:5) questions this assertion.

1692

This year the ban on theatre in Pennsylvania was repealed in England.

1699

The colony of Pennsylvania re-ratified the Charter of William Penn this year with much the same language in regard to theatrical prohibitions:

> Whosoever shall introduce into this province and territories any rude or riotous sports, as prizes, stage-plays, masks, revels, bull baitings, cock-fighting, bonfires ... or shall practice the same and be lawfully convicted thereof ... for every such offense such persons will be reputed as breakers of the peace and shall forfeit and pay twenty shillings, and suffer ten day's imprisonment at hard labor in the House of Correction. (*The Statutes at Large of Pennsylvania*, 2:4–5)

1700

Sometime between 1699 and 1702 one Richard Hunter applied to the governor of New York, John Nanfan, for permission to act plays in the city. Odell (1:5) quotes the petitioner as having "been at great charge and expense in providing persons and necessary's in order to the acting of Play's in the City." No record has survived of the outcome of the petition or of any subsequent performances. It may not be coincidental that in Philadelphia this same year the Assembly of Pennsylvania passed a law prohibiting "stage-plays, masks, revels." The juridical preparations against plays in Philadelphia may suggest an awareness of theatrical activity in New York.

※※※

c. 1700　　　　　　　New York
Request for permission to perform.
　[Richard Hunter applied to the governor of New York, John Nanfan, for permission to act plays in the city. While there is no record of any performances, Henderson (13) claims that Hunter did receive permission. Source: Odell (1:5–6), citing the *American Magazine* 9 (April 1865), 118.]

1700　　　　　　　　Philadelphia
Law passed.
　[The Assembly of Pennsylvania passed a law prohibiting "stage-plays, masks, revels." Source: *Act of the Assembly*, 1; *Statutes at Large of Pennsylvania*, 2:4, as cited in Pollock 4, 73.]

1702

A student production (or recital) was performed during the late spring of this year. Davis (1284) writes that two pastoral colloquies were presented, "the first at least being in English verse and the second in Latin or English. Governor Nicholson enclosed copies of these works, perhaps written by the professors, in a letter of July 22, 1702 to the Archbishop of Canterbury."

1702　　　　　　William and Mary's College, Virginia colony
A Pastoral Colloquy (Anonymous).

Students of William and Mary.
[A student production was presented during this year. Source: Quinn (1:5), following Tyler, *Williamsburg*, 224–31; Davis, *Intellectual Life*, 1284.]

1703

Anthony Aston, a one time actor at Drury Lane Theatre, London turned adventurer, claims in the preface to his *The Fool's Opera* to have acted in Charleston, South Carolina, and unspecified locations in "New York, East and West Jersey, Maryland, [and] Virginia (on both sides of the Chesapeek)," during the winter of 1703–4.

1705

The 1700 Pennsylvania prohibition against plays was repealed in England (cf. Pollock 4).

1706

The prohibition against "stage-plays, masks, revels" was repassed in Pennsylvania (*Acts of the Assembly*, 80–81, as cited in Pollock 4, 73).

1709

The 1706 Pennsylvania prohibition was repealed in England: "An Act against riotus Sports, Plays and games. Her Majesty was pleased by her Order in Council of the 7th of February, 1705, for the Reasons then laid before Her, to repeal several Laws of Pennsylvania, among which was one with the same Title and Contents with this before mentioned, which is lyable to the same Objection as the former, viz., that it restrains her Majesty's subjects from Innocent Sports and Diversion ..." (*Pennsylvania Archives*, 1st Series, 1: 155, as quoted by Dye, "Pennsylvania vs. the Theatre," 349; cf., Pollock 4.

✳✳✳

6 May 1709   New York
Law passed.

[Odell (1:8) indicates that on this date the Governor's Council in New York forbade play acting.]

1711

The Quaker Assembly in Pennsylvania for a third time prohibited stage plays (cf. Pollock 4, 73).

1712

Curtis (9–10) quotes a statute that was passed this year in Charleston which prohibited "bear-baiting, foot ball playing, horse-raceing, enterludes or common plays" on Sunday. Cf. *Statutes at Large of South Carolina*, 2:396.

1713

The Assembly of Pennsylvania's law prohibiting stage plays was again repealed by the British government. Cf. Pollock 4.

1714

During this year *Androboros, A B[i]ographical Farce in Three Acts*, was published in "Monoropolis," (i.e., New York). Quinn (1:6) believes that this play by Robert Hunter, governor of New York, is the first written and published in America. No evidence exists of performance.

✳✳✳

2 March 1714   Boston
Letter of complaint.
 [Chief Justice Samuel Sewall complained to Isaac Addington of Boston in a letter of this date concerning the possible acting of a play:

> There is a Rumor, as if some design'd to have a Play acted in the Council-Chamber, next Monday; which most surprises me: And as much as in me lyes, I do forbid it. The Romans were very fond of their Plays: but I never heard they were so far set upon them, as to turn their Senat-House into a Play-House. Our Town-House was built at great Cost and Charge, for the sake of very serious and important Business;

the Three Chambers above, and the Exchange below; Business of the Province, County, and Town. Let it not be abused with Dances, or other Scenical divertisements ... Let not Christian Boston goe beyond Heathen Rome in the practice of shameful Vanities....

Source: Samuel Sewall, *The Letter Book of Samuel Sewall*, 2:29–30.]

1715

On 23 and 24 September of this year, Charles and Mary Stagg, former dancers from London, entered into a contract of indenturement with a Williamsburg merchant, William Levingston, "to serve him in the Colony of Virginia in ye Arts, Professions." This contract created colonial America's oldest known company. Unfortunately, the story of the Levingston-Stagg Company is not a happy one for William Levingston, whose career spearheading the 1st Williamsburg Theatre resulted in numerous lawsuits, entanglements with servants, a defaulted mortgage, an eviction, and finally his quitting the county altogether. Early biographical information about the Staggs is a little better but scarce, indeed. A Mr. and Mrs. Stagg are advertised as dancing masters in London c. 1712, though we are not certain these are the same dancers, but a Mrs. Stagg received a benefit concert on 27 February 1712 at the Dancing Room in Picadilly. If this is the same couple, their careers went without notice until they were enjoined to travel to the colonies to open a dancing school.

1716

Sometime in the spring of 1716, William Levingston established a dancing school in Williamsburg. Rankin (12) cites a 16 March 1716 petition that granted Levingston permission from the College of William and Mary for "use of the lower Room at the South end of the Colledge [sic] for teaching the Scholars and others to dance until his own dancing school in Williamsburg be finished."

On 11 July 1716 (see entry for this date) Levingston entered into a new contract with Charles and Mary Stagg, superseding the prior (1715) terms of indenture. This new contract (*York County Records, Orders, Wills, etc,*. Book XV, 53) allowed Stagg to retain whatever profits he earned from dance instruction in return for an annual fee to Levingston. The new contract also established a professional acting company, the proceeds of which were to be divided between Stagg and Levingston: "for ye joint benefit of himself [Stagg] and ye sd Wm Levingstone." The contract outlines with great detail the proposed theatrical venture, including securing a patent from the Governor of Virginia "for ye sole privilege of Acting Comedies, Drolls or other kind of Stage Plays within any part of ye sd Colony not only for ye three years next ensueing ye date hereof but for as much longer time as ye sd Governour shall be pleased to grant ye same for ye joint benefit of ye sd Wm Levingstone or Charles Stagg...." The agreement furthered obligated Stagg and his wife to act in the plays (barring sickness), and to teach the art of acting, while prohibiting the Staggs from acting anywhere else in the colony of Virginia without the permission of Levingston, or obtaining an independent patent or license. In return, Levingston agreed to construct a playhouse "at his own proper cost ... with all convenient speed" and to share the expenses of equipping the playhouse and company with scenery, costuming, music "and other necessaries required for acting sd play."

Levingston had also apparently entered into several other contracts of indenture with other performers, as he had "at his own proper cost and charge sent to England for actors and musicians for ye better performance of ye sd plays." Working from the names of Levingston's other servants Rankin posited the identity of the company when performance records are few or absent.

***

11 July 1716   1st Williamsburg Theatre
Business agreement.
[A contract recorded at Yorktown, dated 11 July 1716, between William Levingston, merchant, and Charles and Mary Stagg, "actors," memorializes their project to build a theatre in Williamsburg and to provide actors, scenery and music out of England:

> Articles of Agreement Indented, concluded and made ye eleventh day of July in the year of our Lord one thousand seven hundred and sixteen between William Levingston of ye said County of New Kent Merchant of ye one part and Chas. Stagg of ye same county Dancing master and Mary his wife by two several indentures bearing date ye 23 and 24 days of September, 1715, were bound to ye said William Levingston to serve him in ye Colony of Virginia in ye Arts, Professions and for ye time in ye sd indentures mentioned and ye sd Chas. Stagg for his advancement

and greater profit requested for himself and his wife to be free of ye service mentioned in ye sd Indentures. These presents witnesseth that ye sd Wm Levingston hath released and acquitted and doth hereby release and acquit ye sd Chas Stagg and Mary his wife of all service claims or demands which ye sd Wm Levingston was in any ways instituted to by virtue of ye sd Indentures. And ye sd Wm Levingston doth further hereby assign and make over unto sd Charles Stagg all right, title or interest which he ye said Levinsgton might claim in any sums of money or other perquiesites or profits already due for ye sd Charles Staggs services in teaching or instructing any person or persons whatsoever in ye science of Dancing from ye time of ye sd Staggs arrival in this countrey so as ye sd Charles Stagg shall and may have and enjoy to his own use and behoof as well as the Entrance money as other ye profits arising from ye said scholars without ye Lett or interruption of ye sd Wm. Levingston. In consideration whereof ye sd Charles Stagg doth hereby convenant and agree with ye sd Wm Levingston that ye sd Charles Stagg his Exec or admr shall and will well and truly satisfy and pay unto ye sd Wm Levingston or his assings ye sum of Sixty pounds Currt money yearly during ye space of three years next ensueing ye date hereof (if ye sd Charles Stagg shall so long live) in manner and form following, that is to say Sixty Pounds currt money being ye first payment at Lady day which sall be in ye year of our Lord one thousand seven hundred and seventeen, Sixty Pounds like Money at Lady day one thousand seven hundred and eighteen, and ye other Sixty Pounds at Lady day one thousand seven hundred and nineteen. Provided always and it is ye true intent and meaning hereof that ye sd Wm Levingston and his assigns shall be and are truely obliged to abate and deduct out of ye sd respective yearly payments after ye rate of five pounds currt money for each month which ye sd charles Stagg shall be diverted from teaching to dance in consideration of his ye sd Charles Stagg being imployed in ye preparation and acting of Play for ye joint benefit of himself and ye sd Wm Levingstone. And ye sd Charles Stagg doth further covenant and agree to and withye sd Wm Levingston that ye sd Charles Stagg his Exec and Admrs shall and will within ye space of eighteen months next after ye ensealing of these presents well and truly content and pay unto ye sd Wm Levingstone or his assings ye sum of thirty five pounds seventeen shillings which is in full of all charge and Expenses which ye sd Wm Levingston hath been at for horses, ferriages, or otherways for ye greater convenience of ye sd Charles Stagg in attending at ye respected places where he teaches to dance at any time heretofore and also of all such sums of money as ye sd Wm Levingston hath advanced to ye sd Charles Stagg or his wife either in species or in goods and merchandise since ye sd Staggs arrival in Virginia. And it is further convenanted and agreed between sd parties in manner and form following, that is to say, that ye sd Wm. Levingstone and Charles Stagg shall with all convenient speed after ye ensealing of these Presents use their best endeavor to obtain a Patent or a Lycense from ye Governour of Virginia for ye sole provilege of Acting Comedies, Drolls or other kind of Stage Plays within any part of ye sd colony not only for ye three years next ensueing ye date hereof but for as much longer time Play house 5/.

Source: *York County Records, Orders, Wills, etc,*. Book XV, 53; also quoted in part in Odell (1:9), following Tyler, 224–31. Cf. Rankin 12–13.]

1718

Though only one record survives to confirm the presence of a company in Williamsburg, the Levingston-Stagg Company was undoubtedly collected and performed at least occasionally. Rankin (15) suggests the company was assembled from "indentured servants who had acquired some acting experience." He further nominates the following individuals as possible company members, as they were indentured to either Levingston or the Staggs: Mary Ansell, Nicholas Hurlston, Alice and Elizabeth Ives, Mary Peel, and Little Thomas Sellers. These names, however, are problematical, having been derived from legal and other records over a span of many years and not from performance bills. Little Thomas Sellers, for example, a servant to Stagg, is far too young in 1718, being advertised when he ran away in January of 1735 as "about 20 years of age," while Alice and Elizabeth Ives both passed away in the winter of 1722–23. Kollatz (4) notes that Levingston had two additional servants not named by Rankin who are known through court records and might also have performed in the company in some capacity: George McFarlin (aged ten on 16 May 1720), and one William Jones, whom Levingston bailed out of jail, though Rankin (16) tells us Jones was "indited for attempting to incite other servants of the community to rebel and murder their masters." Thus the company was held together by contract labor and subject to frequent strife.

In the Connecticut colony, the *Public Records of the Colony of Connecticut* (82–3) state that in this year vagrancy laws were enacted prohibiting "rogues, vagabonds or sturdy beggars" from "begging, wandering or misordering him or themselves, using unlawful games, or setting up and practicing any common plays."

✳✳✳

c. 28 May 1718   1st Williamsburg Theatre
Play not identified.
Levingston-Stagg Company?

["In order to the solemnizing His Majesty's birthday, I gave a public entertainment at my home .... These eight committeemen would neither come to my house nor go to the play which was acted on the occasion ...." Source: Hornblow (1:36), quoting a letter of Governor Spotswood of 24 June 1718 (Collection of the Virginia Historical Society, 2:284); cf. Rankin 14.]

1720

Charles Stagg, dancing master, is known to have taught dance and to have held balls in Williamsburg and the surrounding country. He visited the residence of William Byrd, where he prepared Byrd's daughters for a 20 October Ball (Byrd, *London Diary*, 464).

1721

In spite of multiple legal entanglements, the Levingston-Stagg Company played at least occasionally during the spring court and General Assembly as evidenced by the diary entries of William Byrd who attended the playhouse two nights and noted the acting was "tolerably well." Levingston was a familiar face in court this year, bringing complaints against Mary Ansell, Elizabeth Ives, and Mary Peel, in February, May, and September 1721, respectively, to contest or extend the terms of their separate indentures. On 29 May Levingston was forced to mortgage the playhouse to Archibald Blair (Kolatz 4-5; Rankin 16).

***

25 April 1721   1st Williamsburg Theatre
Levingston-Stagg Company
Play not identified.
   ["After dinner we walked to see Grymes just come to town and from thence we went to the play, which was acted tolerably well." Source: Byrd, *London Diary*, 522.]

26 April 1721   1st Williamsburg Theatre
Levingston-Stagg Company
Play not identified.
   ["The Governor invited me to dinner and I ate some pigeon and bacon. After dinner we drank a bottle of claret and then

went to the play but I stayed not above two acts." Source: Byrd, *London Diary*, 522.]

1722

The winter of 1722–23 saw the deaths of both Alice and Elizabeth Ives, both indentured to Levingston and possibly performing. Davis (1691 n. 234), surveying the inventory of clothing and dress material left at their deaths, suggests that the two "may have been wardrobe mistresses of this theatre."

1723

On 24 June of this year, William Levingston defaulted on the mortgage for the 1st Williamsburg Theatre, and Archibald Blair, the holder of the mortgage, leased the property to one Robert Faldo, though Rankin (16) speculates that "Faldo" was a legal pseudonym. Unwilling to give up his holdings, Levingston took to blows when Faldo sought to occupy his acquistion, and legal intervention was required to evict Levingston from his former lodgings.

Professional actors arrived in Philadelphia, "led by a player who had strowled hither to act as a Comedian ... chose for their Stage a place just without the verge of the City ... [then] printed bills ... [and began] to act accordingly" (Pollock 4–5).[1] The governor, Sir William Keith, apparently supported the performers, much to the displeasure of James Logan, mayor of Philadelphia, as evidenced by his remarks in a letter:

> ...after an order for a thousand pounds was presented and the Laws past, the Speaker, by appointment of the House, applied to the Governor to discourage a Player who had Strowled hither to act as a Comedian. The Governor excused himself from prohibiting it, but

---

[1] While there may be no connection between the arrival of the actors in Philadelphia and the defaulted mortgage on the playhouse in Williamsburg, it should be noted that the original terms of the Levingston-Stagg contract prohibited the Staggs only from playing anywhere else in the colony of Virginia. Thus the possibility exists that if the company continued to perform without a playhouse they would be forced to find other venues, perhaps even outside of Virginia. At present, no solid evidence supports such a thesis, but the circumstantial connection is compelling.

assured them he would take care good order should be kept, and so the man went on to publish his printed Bills, as thou wilt see by one of them inclosed, and to act accordingly.

How grievous this proves to the sober people of the place, thou wilt easily judge, but it happens at present to be more particularly so on me, for having, unfortunately, been chosen Mayor of Philadelphia for this year, there is an expectation that I should exert that authority to suppress their acting. But as they have chose for their Stage a place just without the verge of the City, and the Governor himself resorts thither, I can by no means think it adviseable to embroil myself with the Governour to no purpose, or to raise a dispute between the Corporation and him in which nothing is to be gained. (*Pennsylvania Archives*, 2d Series, 7:71–72)

1724

While no performance information has survived, contemporary reports relevant to two locations are worth noting. Hugh Jones (*Present State of Virginia*, 30–31), a contemporary observer, remarks on the location of the theatre in Williamsburg: "Not far from [the Magazine] is a large Area for a Market Place: near which is a Play House."[2] Also cited in Quinn 7.

A 1724 newspaper notice from Pennsylvania ends with the promise of "the comical humor of your old friend, Pickle Herring. There will also be several other diverting performances on the stage too large here to mention .... Prices–on the stage, 3s.; in the pit 2s.; in the gallery 1s. 6d." (*American Weekly Mercury*, 30 April–7 May 1724). This puff regarding "your old friend, Pickle Herring" suggests some level of familiarity with the clown. Further, the advertisement of the price structure requires an audience accustomed to English-style theatre seating. Therefore while this is not notice of a dramatic performance, per se, it evidences a certain level of theatrical sophistication in the absence of documented productions.

---

[2] Jones published *The Present State of Virginia* in London in 1724 but had left Virginia in 1722.

1727

On 2 February 1726/27, William Byrd II, writing from Williamsburg to John Boyle, is certainly missing theatricals: "My young gentlewomen like everything in their own county, except the retirement, they can't get the plays, the operas, & the masquerades out of their heads ..." (*The Correspondence of the Three William Byrds*, 1:361).

1728

The first mention of a company of some nature performing in Barbados appears in Daly (*First Theatre in America*, 19), following a Barbados newspaper account from 18 March 1731, which reports the names of two gentlemen who acted plays in Barbados in 1728: Mr. Vaughan and Mr. Rice. We have intermittent references from 1728 through 1732 of play titles, personnel, and prologues. The performances appear to be occasional and non-professional, but information is scant.

1729

Further information concerning performances in Bridgetown, Barbados is presented by Wright, *Revels in Jamaica* (36), following *Caribianna*, 1: 37: "Some Gentlemen were pleased to act several plays for the Diversion of themselves and their friends ...." Apparently **Sir Courtly Nice*** (John Crowne, 1685) and **The Royal Convert*** (Nicholas Rowe, 1707) were presented.

1730

Rankin (23) claims–cautiously–that a troupe was "said to have presented plays in and around Lancaster, Pennsylvania, between 1730 and 1742," though no further information has survived.

In New York, an amateur group under the direction of Dr. Joachimus Bertrand, fitted up the Revenge Meeting House and performed, as evidence suggests, a single play.

✳✳✳

23 March 1730   Revenge Meeting House, New York
Romeo and Juliet* (William Shakespeare).
   Apothecary–Dr. Bertrand.
Local amateurs.
   [Performed by a group under the direction of Dr. Joachimus Bertrand. Source: *New York Gazette* (16–23 March 1729/30).]

1731

The *New England Weekly Journal* of 8 March 1731 contains the following item of theatrical relevance:

> Truely Sir, it cannot but rejoyce the hearts of the inhabitants of New-England, to hear of the famous Mr. C. H. the great characterizer, lately arrived from Great Britain; being the first of that profession that ever inhabited this continent ....

Unfortunately, no further information has survived concerning Mr. C. H.

1732

Brown (*History of the New York Stage*, 1–2) offers the following claim regarding the presence of an acting company in New York this year:

> In September, 1732, a company of professionals arrived [in New York] from London and secured a large room in the upper part of a building near the junction of Pearl Street and Maiden Lane, which was fitted up with a platform stage and raised seats, capable of seating about four hundred people. They continued their performances for one month, acting three times each week. Early in December of the same year they resumed, having made several additions to their party.

Frustrating authority that he is, Brown was possibly working from playbills no longer extant in offering the following names of the company: Mr. R. Bessel, Miss Brenan, Mr. Centour, Mrs. Centour, Mr. Cone, Mr. Chase, Mrs. Chase, Mr. Drown, Mrs. Drown, Mr. Eastlake, and Thomas Heady (the latter being the only name actually recorded in the newspapers). Brown further claims that this company, led by Mr. Heady, played three times a week through to 31 December 1734. When they resumed in December with their additional members, they may also have moved to a new location. The New Theatre in Nassau Street opened in New York on 6 December 1732, and may not be the same site as the building described by Brown. The old site in Maiden Street may have been abandoned at this time. Henderson (*The City and the Theatre*, 16) suggests that Brown confused the two and that the Nassau Street Theatre was the same as the original Maiden Lane building. Her map (map 1, page 8), however, indicates separate sites.

Laying aside the Maiden Lane site, Henderson (14–15) further suggests that the New Theatre at Nassau was actually the second theatre in New York at the time: "A contemporary manuscript map shows a theatre or playhouse in existence on Broadway, east of the Commons." She goes on—convincingly—to defend the date of this map as no later than 1732. More importantly, Henderson (15) offers a strong argument to explain the second theatre as the political result of a two-party town:

> The existence of two theatres in 1732 may very well have represented the earliest signs of the colonial schism in loyalties, with those who sided with the governor (and the crown) going to the Theatre on Broadway and those who were aligned with Van Dam and Zengar (and local rule) going to the Theatre in Nassau Street.

The presence of a second theatre would seem to suggest a second company, though we have no material evidence to support this conjecture.

Regarding activity in Barbados, Daly (*First Theatre in America*, 19) offers two more names from a company performing there, Mr. John Snow and Miss Whiten, apparently newcomers to the island.

Rankin (16) offers this tidbit from Williamsburg: "a passing observation by William Hugh Grove in his diary in 1732–'There was a Playhouse managed by Bowes but having little to do is dropped.'"

***

16 August 1732   Barbados
The Royal Convert.
    Prologue–John Snow; Epilogue–Miss Whiten.
    [Source: Daly (19); cf. *Caribianna*, 1:380.]

December 1732   The New Theatre, New York
Cato* (Joseph Addison, 1713).
The Busy Body* (Susannah Centlivre, 1709).
The Beaux' Strategem* (George Farquhar, 1707).
   [The exact dates of performance are not known, but Rankin (24) states that this is the same company responsible for the 6 December 1732 production.]

6 December 1732   The New Theatre, New York
The Recruiting Officer* (George Farquhar, 1706).
   Worthy–Thomas Heady, barber and peruke maker.
   ["On the 6th instant the new theatre in the buildings of the honourable Rip Van Dam Esq. was opened, with the comedy called 'The Recruiting Officer.'" Source: *New York Gazette* of 4–11 December 1732; cf. *New England & Boston Gazette* (1 January 1733), providing news from New York.]

1733

Brown (*History of the New York Stage*, 2) suggests that the New York company headed by Mr. Heady performed during this year though no subsequent stage history of the city has confirmed his assertion.

※※※

15 October 1733   New York
Newspaper advertisement.
   [The following advertisement appears in the *Bradford's New York Gazette* of 8–15 October 1733:

> To be sold at reasonable rates, all sorts of household goods, viz. Beds, chairs, tables, chest of drawers, looking-glasses, andirons and pictures; as also, several sorts of druggs and medicines, also, a Negro girl about 16 years of age, has had the small-pox and is fit for town or country. Enquire of Mr. George Talbot, next door to the play-house.

Cf. Odell 1:11. Brown (*History of the New York Stage*, 2) claims that in the same paper appeared an advertisement as follows: "This evening will be performed the tragedy of 'Cato' and for three evenings next week, the following comedies will be acted, viz: 'The Recruiting Officer,' 'The Beaux' Stratagem,' and 'The Busy Body.'" The copy of the newspaper which we examined

(New York Public Library, microfilm), however, did not contain the advertisement.]

1733   Kingston, Jamaica
The Beggar's Opera.
[Hill (*Jamaican Stage*, 21, following Fitzgerald, *Book of Theatrical Anecdotes*, 124) remarks that a "company of players from England came to Jamaica and performed there."]

1734

Curtis (12), citing the *South Carolina Gazette* of 3 March 1734, states that this year Charles Shepherd[3] opened the Court Room in Charleston.

The *American Weekly Mercury* (17–24 December 1734), reprinting a London newspaper item of 1 October 1734, reports the following item regarding Montserrat, British West Indies: "A playhouse has been erected in Plymouth Town in that island."

Brown (*History of the New York Stage*, 2) suggests that the New York Company headed by Mr. Heady performed through 31 December of this year, though no subsequent stage history of the city has confirmed his assertion.

One very good piece of additional information confirms the presence of players in New York City sometime between 1732 and 1735, and that quite possibly they were a touring company. In her autobiography, *Some Account of the Fore Part of the Life of Elizabeth Ashbridge,* the young Elizabeth records the misery she has endured from having been indentured for a term of four years to a very religious and very tyrannical master who at one point nearly drove the poor girl to suicide. She had concluded to end her miserable existence with a rope

---

[3] Clark (36) lists a Charles Shepherd as a strolling theatrical manager who died in 1768, leaving a daughter of marriageable age. This Charles Shepherd had been in Ireland at least since 1761 where his name is noted in a Smock Alley playbill. If this was the man attached to Holt's Company in South Carolina in 1734–35, perhaps he was more than the building owner.

in the garret when a religious vision forestalled her plans. But she was not out of despair yet:

> But alas! I did not give up nor Comply with the heavenly Vision, as I think I may Call it, for after this I had like to have been caught in another Snare, which if I had would Probably have been my Ruin, from which I was also preserved. I was Counted a fine Singer and Dancer, in which I took great Delight, and once falling in with some of the Play house company then at New York, they took a Great fancy to me, as they said, & Perswaded [sic] me to become an Actress amongst them, & they would find means to get me from my cruel Servitude, & I should live Like a Lady—the Proposal took with me & I used no small Pains to Qualify my Self for it in Reading their Play Books, even when I should have Slept, yet was put to the Demur when I came to Consider what my Father would say who had forgiven my Disobedience in marrying and earnestly desiring to see me again had sent for me home, but my proud heart would not Consent to return in so mean a Condition; therefore I chose Bondage rather.[4]

Elizabeth arrived in New York on 15 July, 1732, and her indentureship began some two weeks later. When, exactly, her encounter with the players began she does not tell us, only that "for a while at first I was Pretty well used, but in a little time the Scale turned" (Andrews 152). The paragraph immediately following the one cited above begins: "When I had served near three years" (i.e. presumably summer 1735), which may indicate only the next eventful moment in her narrative, or frame the playhouse experience. Therefore the evidence suggests that her brush with the players took place in 1734, give or take six months.

Though the journal of Elizabeth Ashbridge offers no names or details about this company of players, she does describe them as clearly active, and if this passage does relate to 1734, then they have been in town for up to two years. She also characterizes them as "then at New York," perhaps suggesting that the company traveled, and was often or occasionally elsewhere (the West Indies?). Thus T. Alston Brown's claim that a company played in New York through 31 December 1734 is now strongly corroborated by the Ashbridge journal.

---

[4] *Journeys in New Worlds: Early American Women's Narratives*, William L. Andrews, ed., 153. We are indebted to Tom Goyens at the Williamsburg Foundation for calling this journal to our attention.

1735

This year Henry Holt, in Charleston, South Carolina, assembled one of the earliest companies in the colonies. Holt has not received the recognition he has deserved, so we offer the following biographical precis of one of the first known colonial American theatrical managers. Holt was a former dancer and actor on the London stage, listed in the *Biographical Dictionary* from 1729–34 in various roles at Drury Lane, Goodman's Field, the Haymarket, and the Great Booth on Windmill Hill. He last performed in London on 24 May 1734 and sometime in the late summer left England for America (*BD*, 7:396). He first comes to the attention of the public of Charleston, South Carolina, with a self-promoting advertisement placed in the *South Carolina Gazette*, the first week of November 1734:

> Mr. Henry Holt, lately arrived in this province, takes leave to inform the publick, that on Monday next he intends to open his Dancing Room at Mrs. Lory's in Church Street ...where his constant attendance and utmost application on Mondays and Thursdays may be depended upon by those who shall be pleased to encourage him: the said Henry Holt is, he hopes sufficiently qualified to teach, having served his time under Mr. Essex Jun. the most celebrated master in England, and danced a considerable time at both the Play-Houses. N.B. The hours of attendance are from 9 to 12 o'clock in the forenoon and from 2 to 5 in the afternoon.

Holt assembled a small company of students and quickly progressed from singing to the presentation of plays. Of this company, we have no names, not even the real name of the very popular actress from Otway's *The Orphan* who is known in print only as "Monimia," and some evidence implies that amateurs participated (see May 1735). The company performed a brief season during early 1735 at the Courtroom, the success of which led Holt to advertise in May for subscriptions. Thus by the conclusion of his first year in Charleston, Holt had established a viable theatrical market. Though Holt's name does not appear in the advertisements, which name Shepherd as the ticket agent, this type of arrangement was standard practice, so Holt was very likely the artistic director of the company. Further information concerning Holt's ventures will be continued in the headnotes for 1736, 1737, and 1739.

In Williamsburg this year (1735) two deaths cleared the way for the reopening of the Williamsburg Theatre. Quite late in the year Charles Stagg died (see 21 January 1736) who may have retained a monopoly by the terms of his original contract; while earlier in the year Alexander Blair, who owned the old Levingston property, had also passed away. His executor, John Blair, sold the playhouse to George Gilmer (i.e., Apothecary Gilmore). Gilmer becomes active in assembling an amateur troupe in 1736.

***

1735? The Court Room, Charleston
Cato.
Company not known.
   [A performance in Charleston this year of Addison's famous tragedy is implied by the publication in 1743 of an epilogue written in 1735 for the occasion. Source: *South Carolina Gazette* (5 September 1743).]

24 January 1735   The Court Room, Charleston
The Orphan* (Thomas Otway, 1680).
Holt Company.
   [Tickets: 40s. An "Occasional Prologue" for this performance appears in the *South Carolina Gazette* of 1–8 February 1735) and is reprinted in Willis 11. Source: *South Carolina Gazette* (11–18 January 1735).]

28 January 1735   The Court Room, Charleston
The Orphan.
Holt Company.
   [Source: *South Carolina Gazette* (18–25 January 1735).]

4 February 1735   The Court Room, Charleston
The Orphan.
The Adventures of Harlequin and Scaramouche*
   (Anonymous).
Holt Company.
   [Source: *South Carolina Gazette* (25 January–1 February 1735).]

7 February 1735   The Court Room, Charleston
The Orphan.
Holt Company.

[A new "Occasional Prologue" appeared in the *South Carolina Gazette* of 1–8 February 1735 and is reprinted in Willis, 12–13. An epilogue appears in the *South Carolina Gazette* of 15–22 February 1735. Source: *South Carolina Gazette* (1–8 February 1735).]

13 February 1735   Savannah, Georgia
Correspondence.
   A letter of this date to the London-based Trustees of the colony of Georgia reports a fight with weapons ("dancing") that broke out in Savannah, Georgia, over the intended introduction of plays:

> Last Night a Quarrel happened between Mr. Bush the tythingman with his Guard and Some Gentlemen who were dancing many blows were given. Dr. Tailfer had like to have had his Arm Cut off by Bush with his Dagger. Capt Dunbar and several others were Concerned. The Magistrates have heard the two parties but what has been decided I know not as yet no doubt yr Hon Board Shall have an account of the Same. The Intent of Dancing was to Introduce Acting of Plays. I am humbly of Opinion we have Scenes of Poverty Enough in reality without Inventing ways to Divert our thoughts from business & the Care of providing food for our Families ....

Source: letter to the Board of Trustees of Georgia, Allen D. Candler, quoted in Curtis, "A Note on Henry Holt," 5. Curtis speculates that the wellspring of the conversation was Holt's company in Charleston that were playing that winter.]

18 February 1735   The Court Room, Charleston
Flora, or Hob in the Well* (John Hippisley, 1729).
Holt Company.
   [Willis (14) adds as part of the evening's bill "the dance of the two Pierrots of the Pantomime of Harlequin and Scaramouche." Source: *South Carolina Gazette* (8–15 February 1735).]

25 March 1735   The Court Room, Charleston
The Spanish Friar* (John Dryden, 1680).
Holt Company.
   [Source: *South Carolina Gazette* (15–22 March 1735).]

27 March 1735   The Court Room, Charleston
The Spanish Friar.
Holt Company.

[For the benefit of the actress performing the role of Monimia. Source: *South Carolina Gazette* (8–15 February 1735).]

May 1735   Charleston
Newspaper advertisement.
[The following notice appears in the *South Carolina Gazette* of 26 April–3 May 1735:

> Any gentlemen that are dispos'd to encourage the exhibiting of plays next winter, may have a sight of the proposals for a subscription at Mr. Shepheard's in Broad-street. And any persons that are desirous of having a share in the performance thereof, upon application to Mr. Shepheard, shall receive a satisfactory answer. N.B. The subscription will be closed the last day of this month.]

15 December 1735 The Court Room, Charleston
Newspaper advertisement.
[The following item appeared in the *South Carolina Gazette* of 6–13 December 1735: "At the Court-Room on Monday the 15th December will be A Ball .... Henry Holt, Master."]

1736

Holt's subscription project for his theatre in Charleston was successful enough to open the Queen Street Theatre on 12 February, 1736, but plays alone apparently could not sustain the enterprise, so Holt supplemented the performance season with balls and dancing lessons, and expanded his school to take on one additional instructor:

> Whereas several gentlemen and ladies are desirous of having their children taught to draw: this is to inform all such persons, that their children will be diligently attended on their dancing-days, at Mr. Holt's school, and carefully instructed in the art of drawing by B. Roberts. (*South Carolina Gazette*, 27 March–3 April 1736)

By the end of the 1736 winter season, plays, dancing, and drawing aside, the new playhouse was up for sale (see 1–8 May 1736). A poem, "On the Sale of the Theatre" (see 29 May 1736), strongly suggests a rift between Shepherd and Holt. Whatever the cause, the crisis was apparently resolved, as the Holt Company was back in the theatre by November 1736, where they played until the spring of 1737.

There is also—for the period—substantial activity in Williamsburg, Virginia. Two companies, one amateur, one mixed (?), performed for "court" occasions. The first company was advertised as "Young Gentlemen of the College." These we assume to be students at William and Mary who mounted a production of *Cato* in September 1736. The second company performing in Williamsburg was composed of members from the community and perhaps several experienced actors. Rankin (17) suggests "a hybrid combination of the remnants of the Levingston-Stagg troupe joined with the community's dilettantes." Of the recorded members of this company we know of the governor's sister and son, and three names of those who assembled and performed during the General Court in August 1736 and carried their season into September: Dr. [Henry] Potter, Apothecary Gilmore, and Abraham Nichols. Of this company Hornblow (1:49–50) points out that their small repertoire was nearly identical to the short flurry of plays presented in New York in 1732, which observation Willis echoes. It should be noted, however, that little is known of both seasons and that the titles are commonplace and may simply prove to be the most popular and available plays in print.

These companies are sometimes confused (e.g., Rankin 16–17, 20), but the fact that these are indeed two separate troupes is well documented by Hornblow (1:37–38). Dr. Potter and his assembly are referred to in a contemporary letter as "the Company," while the other troupe is denominated "the Young Gentlemen of the College."

***

January 1736   Williamsburg
The Busy Body.
    Marplot–Dr. Henry Potter.
    [Source: Rankin 17, following a typescript of a letter by Gov. William Gooch (responding to an enquiry by William Byrd II) housed in the Department of Research, Colonial Williamsburg Foundation.]

21 January 1736   Williamsburg
Correspondence.
    [Sir John Randolph, writing to William Byrd II, informs us of two theatrically related news items (that Charles Stagg had recently died, and that an amateur company was performing in Williamsburg):

Upon the news of Mr. Stagg's death Madame La Baronne de Graffenriedt is in hopes to succeed to part of his business in towne. And were it nor for making my good Lady jealouse (which I would not do for the world) I would recommend her to your favour ....

We are told there is a Bristol ship arrivd in York River, if she brings any news, be so good as to communicate it to your country friends. And in case you should have nothing forreign, we should be glad of a little domestick. Which of your actors shone most in the play next to Isabinda, who I take it for granted is the Oldfields of our theatre? How came Squire Marplot off? With many a clap I suppose, tho' I fancy he would have acted more to the life in the comedy calld the Sham Doctor. But not a word of this for fear in case of sickness, he might poison in revenge.

Source: *The Correspondence of the Three William Byrds of Westover, Virginia, 1684-1776*, 471.]

12 February 1736   Queen St. Theatre, Charleston
The Recruiting Officer.
Holt Company.
   [Sufficient subscriptions were apparently raised, as the new theatre opened on this evening. Prices: boxes 30s.; pit 20s.; gallery 15s. Willis (27) reprints the "Occasional Epilogue" spoken on this evening, which was published in the *Gentleman's Magazine* 6 (1736):288. The following notice was included in the advertisement for the play in the *South Carolina Gazette* of 31 January–7 February 1736: "The doors will be open'd all the afternoon. The subscribers are desired to send to the stage-door in the forenoon to bespeak places, otherwise it will be too late." Source: *South Carolina Gazette* (24–31 January 1736).]

23 February 1736   Queen St. Theatre, Charleston
The Orphan.
Holt Company.
   [Source: *South Carolina Gazette* (14–21 February 1736).]

2 March 1736   Queen St. Theatre, Charleston
The Recruiting Officer.
Holt Company.
   ["By desire of the officers of the Troop and Foot companies." Source: *South Carolina Gazette* (21–28 February 1736).]

9 March 1736   Queen St. Theatre, Charleston
George Barnwell [i.e., **The London Merchant**]* (George Lillo, 1731).
Holt Company.

[Curtis (428) adds *The Devil to Pay* to the evening's program. Source: *South Carolina Gazette* (28 February–6 March 1736).]

16 March 1736   Queen St. Theatre, Charleston
The London Merchant.
The Devil to Pay* (Charles Coffey, 1731).
Holt Company.
   [Prices: pit and box, 25s. Source: *South Carolina Gazette* (6–13 March 1736).]

23 March 1736   Queen St. Theatre, Charleston
The Orphan.
The Devil to Pay.
Holt Company.
   [This was the close of the season. Prices: pit and boxes 25s.; gallery 15s. Source: *South Carolina Gazette* (13–20 March 1736).]

15 April 1736   Queen St. Theatre, Charleston
Newspaper advertisement.
   [The *South Carolina Gazette* of 3–10 April 1736 printed the following notice: "On Thursday April 15, 1736, at the New Theatre in Queen-street, will be a ball, to begin precisely at six o'clock, Henry Holt master."]

8 May 1736   Charleston
Newspaper advertisement.
   [The following notice appeared in the *South Carolina Gazette* of 1–8 May 1736:

> To be sold to the best bidder on Wednesday next the 12th instant at the Theatre in Queen street, one half (or the whole) of the said Theatre with the ground thereunto belonging, containing front in Church-street 57 feet, depth 119 feet, with all the scenes, cloathing, &c. N.B. The conditions of sale to be seen at the theatre upon the day of sale.]

29 May 1736   Charleston
Poem.
   [The *South Carolina Gazette* of 22–29 May 1736 published the following poem:

>   ON THE SALE OF THE THEATRE.
> How cruel Fortune, and how fickle too,
> To crop the method made for making you.
> Changes, tho' common, yet when great they prove,

Make men distrust the care of mighty Jove.
Half made in thought, (tho' not in fact) we find
You bought and sold, but left poor H--- behind.
    P.S. Since so it is, ne'er mind the silly trick,
    The pair will please when Pierrot make you sick.]

c. 12–18 August 1736   1st Williamsburg Theatre
The Recruiting Officer.
The Busy Body.

[The following item in the *American Weekly Mercury* (19–26 August 1736) establishes details concerning theatrical activity in Williamsburg:

> This being the time of our general court, the town was last week filled with an extraordinary concourse of gentlemen and ladies; who came hither to see our Governors sister and son, in company with one Dr. Potter, Apothecary Gilmore, Abraham Nicholas, a painter, and several others, put plays on the public theatre: And in acting the Recruiting Officer, and Busy-Body, they performed their parts with so much applause, that they have already got about one hundred and fifty pounds subscriptions, to encourage their entertaining the country with the like diversions at future public meetings of our general court and assembly. N.B. The terms of subscriptions are, that a ticket will be delivered for every twenty shillings subscribed.]

10 September 1736   1st Williamsburg Theatre
Cato.
Students of William and Mary College.

[The following notice appeared in the *Virginia Gazette,* 3–10 September 1736:

> This evening will be performed at the theatre, by the young gentlemen of the college, The Tragedy of Cato: And, on Monday, Wednesday, Friday next, will be acted the following comedies, by the gentlemen and ladies of this country, viz. The Busy-Body, The Recruiting-Officer, and The Beaux-Stratagem.]

13 September 1736   1st Williamsburg Theatre
The Busy Body.
Local amateurs.

[Acted by "young Gentlemen and Ladies of this Country."
Source: *Virginia Gazette* (3–10 September 1736).]

15 September 1736   1st Williamsburg Theatre
The Recruiting Officer.
Local amateurs.

[Acted by "young Gentlemen and Ladies of this Country." Source: *Virginia Gazette* (3–10 September 1736).]

17 September 1736   1st Williamsburg Theatre
The Beaux' Stratagem.
Local amateurs.

[Acted by "young Gentlemen and Ladies of the Country." Source: *Virginia Gazette* (3–10 September 1736). Davis (1287) discusses a letter relevant to this production:

> Thomas Jones on this date wrote to his wife in Caroline Country, mentioning the performances of *Cato* and *The Busy Body*, and everyone's disappointment that no 'fine lady' had been found to play Dorinda in *The Beaux' Stratagem*. Jones' postscript concludes that though it is a great secret, the 'Miss Anderson that came to town with Mrs. Carter' has been persuaded to play the part.]

20 September 1736   1st Williamsburg Theatre
The Drummer; or The Haunted House* (Joseph Addison, 1716).
Students of William and Mary College.

[Acted by "the young Gentlemen of the College." Source: *Virginia Gazette* (10–17 September 1736).]

23 October 1736   Williamsburg
Correspondence.

[Elizabeth Holloway wrote to Elizabeth Jones concerning local theatrical news: "I hear there will be no plays this Court. So my dear B[etty] Pratt will loose no diversions by being absent for heare is not nor is there likely to be anything to do." Source: Jones, papers.]

11 November 1736   Queen St. Theatre, Charleston
Cato.
Holt Company.

["Tickets to be had at Mr. Charles Shepheard's. Stage & Balcony boxes 30s. Pit & Boxes 25s. Gallery 15s. N.B. If any persons are possessed of last year's tickets, they are desired to send them in to be chang'd for new ones. No person whatsoever to be admitted behind the scenes. To begin exactly at 6 o'clock." Source: *South Carolina Gazette* (30 October–6 November 1736).]

18 November 1736   Queen St. Theatre, Charleston
Cato.
Holt Company.

[The epilogue to this performance was published in the *South Carolina Gazette* for 5 September 1743 and is reprinted in Willis (29–30). Prices: Stage & Balcony boxes 30s.; pit & boxes 25s.; gallery 10s. Source: *South Carolina Gazette* (6–13 November 1736).]

23 November 1736   Queen St. Theatre, Charleston
Flora, or Hob in the Well.
Holt Company.
   [Source: Sonneck 13.]

1 December 1736   Queen St. Theatre, Charleston
The Recruiting Officer.
Flora, or Hob in the Well.
Holt Company.
   [Source: *South Carolina Gazette* (20–27 November 1736).]

7 December 1736   Queen St. Theatre, Charleston
The Recruiting Officer.
Flora, or Hob in the Well.
Holt Company.
   ["At the desire of the Officers of the Troop and Foot Companies." Source: *South Carolina Gazette* (27 November–4 December 1736).]

15 December 1736   Queen St. Theatre, Charleston
Newspaper notice.
   [Henry Holt offered a ball at his theatre on this evening. Other balls were held on 18 and 25 May 1737. Source: *South Carolina Gazette* (27 November–4 December 1736; 16–23 April 1737; and 14–21 May 1737).]

17 December 1736   Queen St. Theatre, Charleston
Cato.
Holt Company.
   [Source: *South Carolina Gazette* (4–11 December 1736).]

1737

Holt's company in Charleston played through the winter and early spring, when, perhaps suffering from personal indiscretions (see 15 January 1737 and Introduction, "Companies"), Holt announced his intentions of quitting the province. Sometime after the end of May 1737 he settled his accounts and left for New York, thus bringing to a conclusion one of the earliest sustained attempts to establish professional theatre in the colonies, though Holt briefly reappeared in New York in 1739.

✳✳✳

11 January 1737　　　　　　Queen St. Theatre, Charleston
The Recruiting Officer.
Holt Company.
　[Source: Willis 30.]

c. 15 January 1737　　　　　Queen St. Theatre, Charleston
Newspaper advertisement.
　[The following notice appeared in the *South Carolina Gazette* of 15–22 January 1737:

> This is to give notice to all people in Charlestown or elsewhere, not to credit harbour nor entertain Mary Simmons, the wife of Isaac Simmons, which has made an elopement from her said husband, especially for the said master of the Play-house in Charleston, to employ her, being entirely against the said Mr. Simmon's request. Isaac Simmons.]

10 February 1737　　　　　　Queen St. Theatre, Charleston
Newspaper advertisement.
　[Henry Holt offered a ball at his theatre on this evening. Source: *South Carolina Gazette* (22–29 January 1737).]

c. 19 February 1737　　　　　Queen St. Theatre, Charleston
Newspaper advertisement.
　[The following notice appeared in the *South Carolina Gazette* of 19–26 February 1737:

> Henry Holt intending to leave this province, desires all persons to whom he is indebted to send in their accounts, and all persons indebted to him are desired to discharge theirs by the first of May next.]

18 May 1737　　　　　　　　Queen St. Theatre, Charleston
Newspaper advertisement.
　[Henry Holt offered a ball at his theatre on this evening. Source: *South Carolina Gazette* (16–23 April 1737).]

25 May 1737　　　　　　　　Queen St. Theatre, Charleston
Newspaper advertisement.
　[Henry Holt offered a ball at his theatre on this evening. Source: *South Carolina Gazette* (14–21 May 1737).]

26 May 1737   Queen St. Theatre, Charleston
The Recruiting Officer.
Holt Company.
   [Prices: pit and box 25s.; gallery 10s. This performance was part of a special engagement for the Masons. See review at 28 May 1737. Curtis (428) claims that "Harlequin and the Clown" was performed as an afterpiece. Source: *South Carolina Gazette* (21–28 May 1737).]

28 May 1737   Queen St. Theatre, Charleston
Review.
   [The *South Carolina Gazette* for this date contains the following review of the performance of *The Recruiting Officer* the previous evening. This commentary is an example of an early theatrical notice of the colonial period:

> On Thursday night last the Recruiting Officer was acted for the entertainment of the Ancient and honourable Society of Free and Accepted Masons, who came to the Play-house about 7 o'clock, in the usual manner, and made a very decent and solemn appearance; there was a fuller house on this occasion than ever had been known in this place before. A proper prologue and epilogue were spoke, and the Entered Apprentices and Masters songs sung upon the stage, which were joined in chorus by the Masons in the pit, to the satisfaction and entertainment of the whole audience. After the play, the Masons return'd to the lodge at Mr. Shepheard's, in the same order observed in coming to the Play-house.]

1739

Henry Holt, from Charleston, reappears in New York for a brief season during February after which he is not specifically named in the historical record. Odell (1:21–22), however, cites three pieces of evidence to suggest a lengthier season in New York in 1739 in which Holt might be involved. The first is a prologue, titled "The Second Opening of the Theatre at New York, Anno 1739," that praises the encouragement given to the new theatre; the second is a letter in the 9–16 April *New York Gazette* taking a townsman to task for his behavior on "the first night of a new Play;" and the third is correspondence that reproaches a young girl for her infatuation with plays. Thus, though we can at this point offer no titles and dates, that a more substantial offering appeared than what is recorded is highly likely.

✳✳✳

12 February 1739   Mr. Holt's Long Room, New York
Harlequin and Scaramouche; or the Spaniard Tricked*
(Anonymous).
Holt Company.
   [With a Prologue and Epilogue spoken by Master Holt. Source: *New York Gazette* (29 January–6 February 1739).]

19 February 1739   Mr. Holt's Long Room, New York
Harlequin and Scaramouche; or the Spaniard Tricked.
Holt Company.
   [Tickets: 5 shillings. "With a new prologue and epilogue address'd to the town, the epilogue to be spoken by Master Holt." Source: *New York Weekly Journal* (19 February 1739).]

21 February 1739   Mr. Holt's Long Room, New York
Harlequin and Scaramouche; or the Spaniard Tricked.
Holt company.
   [Advertised as "the last time it will be acted." Source: *New York Gazette* (13–20 February 1739).]

1740

Willis (38) claims a great fire in Charleston, South Carolina colony, this year likely destroyed the Queen St. Theatre, but this assertion cannot be true, as the structure is described as still standing in October 1741 (see entry for that date). Rankin (72) probably has the correct explanation in his claim that it was still standing when the great hurricane of 15 September 1752 leveled "over 500 buildings ... one of which was probably the old Queen Street Theatre."

Spanish Town, Jamaica: "[S]everal wealthy merchants reside there, and most Gentlemen of Estates have Houses in it, and live after a very gay manner. 'Tiz surprizing to see the Number of Coaches and chariots which are perpetually plying, besides those belonging to private Persons; they have frequent balls, and lately got a Play-House, where they retain a Set of Extraordinary Good Actors. In short, they live as if they were within the Verge of the British Court" (Leslie, *New History of Jamaica*, 20).

※※※

January 1740   Charleston
Correspondence.
[A letter of 9 January 1739/40, as printed in the *New York Gazette* (7–14 April 1740), while discussing George Whitefield, specifically mentions that "religion and virtue" can never thrive "under the shadow of a theatre" which is implied as existing at that time.]

1741

A company of some nature played at the New Theatre in New York, though no names are available and only one performance is preserved in the record, announcing a person who "never appear'd on any Stage before now." This notice might imply that the other members regularly appeared on stage.

Considerable activity occurs this year in Spanish Town, Jamaica. John Oldmixon reports that the port city "has frequent balls, and Assemblies, a Play-House, and a Company of Players" (*The British Empire in America*, 416). Both Hill and Wright note that the theatre does not appear in Oldmixon's first edition, published in 1708.

※※※

12 February 1741   New Theatre in the Broadway, New York
The Beaux' Stratagem.
  [Aimwell "to be perform'd by a Person who never appear'd on any Stage before." Prices: boxes, 5s.; pit 2s. 6d. Source: *Zenger's Journal* (9 February 1740/41).]

October 1741   Queen St. Theatre, Charleston
Newspaper advertisement.
  [The *South Carolina Gazette* of 3–10 October 1741 prints the following notice:

> To be sold the lot of land whereon the Theatre now stands in Charles-Town, together with all the buildings belonging to the same. Any persons inclinable to purchase may treat with Charles Pinckney, Esq; or James Wright.]

1742

8 November 1742   Queen St. Theatre, Charleston
Newspaper advertisement.
[A notice in the *South Carolina Gazette* of this date reads as follows: "On the ninth of December next at the (formerly) theatre in Charleston will be a ball, Henry Campbell, Master."]

1743

Evidence exists that garrison troops at Fort Anne, Nova Scotia (i.e., Annapolis Royal), performed plays during the winter of 1743–44 (Gardner 5; O'Neill 388; cf., headnote for 1744).

※※※

17 October 1743   Jamaica and New York
Newspaper advertisement.
[The following notice appeared in the *New York Gazette & Weekly Post-Boy* for this date concerning one Thomas Vernon, alias Thomas Allman, wanted for various crimes:

> about the 10th of November, 1742, ... [he] went privately on board a vessel without the usual licences, and sailed from this island for South-Carolina .... These are therefore to give notice, that if any person or persons shall apprehend the said Thomas Allman, so that he may be brought to justice, he or they shall receive one hundred pounds sterling reward .... [Note that] he for some part of the time acted as a comedian with applause ....

Allman apparently acted in Jamaica during c. 1734–42.]

1744

A single record of performance by garrison troops in Halifax, Nova Scotia, exists for this year, but apparently this is the second in a series which began late in 1743 (O'Neill 388).

※※※

6 January 1744   Garrison, Halifax, Nova Scotia
The Misanthrope* (Moliere).

Garrison soldiers.

[Lieutenant Governor Paul Mascarene translated Moliere's play. This particular performance coincided with the celebration of the birthday of Frederick, prince of Wales. The first performance apparently took place during late 1743. Source: O'Neill 388.]

1745

This year a young Irishman named John Cochran, allegedly either involved in the second Jacobite rebellion or disgruntled by his treatment in the London theatre, or both, changed his name to John Moody (perhaps after the character in *The Provoked Husband*?) and took flight to Jamaica. Traditionally it is claimed that he wandered the island and discovered a company of players performing in a ballroom. Durang (iii) records that Moody applied for a first appearance and debuted as "one of Shakespeare's heroes." His success was enough to build—by subscription—a permanent theatre. To this end he raised money and returned to London to assemble a company. Durang reports his return to the island "by winter," i.e., presumably 1746–47. Though we have no records of performance, Moody is known to have performed the roles of Hamlet, Romeo, and Lear during his early stay in Jamaica (*BD*, 10: 289). He apparently remained in Jamaica until 1749 (see headnote for that season).

In Williamsburg on 4 December 1745 George Gilmer sold the 1st Williamsburg theatre to a consortium of investors for £250, who, in turn, apparently donated the building to the city (Rankin 20–21). A few days later the following notice appeared in the *Virginia Gazette* of 12–19 December 1745: "The Play-house in Williamsburg, being, by order of the Common-Hall of the said city, to be fitted up for a Court-house, with the necessary alterations and repairs ...."

1746

In Providence, Bahamas, a company of local residents took up a subscription, built a playhouse, and offered a series of performances in the winter of 1746–47.

✻✻✻

29 November 1746   Fort   Street Playhouse, Providence, Bahamas
The Beggar's Opera* (John Gay, 1728).
Local residents.

[The *South Carolina Gazette* (29 December 1746) prints the following news about theatricals in Providence:

> We hear from Providence, that on Saturday evening the 29th of November, the Beggar's Opera was acted with applause at their play house in Fort street, by a sett of the inhabitants for the entertainment of the town: His Excellency John Tinker, Esq; (to whose only administration they owe their deliverance from Gothick rudeness and tyranny, their improvement in trade, politeness and every honest art) was pleased to honour it with his presence, and expressed a particular satisfaction at the good performance of the actors. Tickets sold for a dollar each. As their play-house was but lately finished, and set off with variety of scenes and decorations, several other plays are to be acted this winter.]

1748

January-February 1748   Annapolis
Play not identified.
Performers unknown.

[The following notice appeared in the *Boston News Letter* of 3 March 1748:

> On the Prince of Wales birth-day a play was acted by some of the gentlemen there (who gave a ball) and by those that were judges it is said to be done in an extraordinary manner, and to the acceptance of all spectators: And that the arrival of Capt. Miller with the agreeable news of Admiral Hawke's success, Mr. Cowley gave a ball; and on the 2d of February, at the desire of Capt. Winslow, the play was re-acted; after which he gave a ball.]

1749

Sometime between 1745 and 1749 John Moody, now managing the company in Jamaica, again returned to England to recruit actors. Among those who may have arrived in Jamaica around this time were David Douglass, Owen Morris, and Mary Morris.

Five pieces of evidence suggest productions of some nature performed this year in Philadelphia, but what information is known about the company or companies is particularly problematic. (1) Evidence from municipal records of 8 January (quoted in Dye, "Pennsylvania vs. the Theatre," 353) suggests the strong likelihood of a series of performances and an intent to continue to act plays in the city in January of 1749 (see entry for early January 1749). The magistrates of that city bound the players over on good behavior, which we can assume curtailed their season. (2) Further evidence comes from a letter by Edward Shippen in London to James Burd in Philadelphia in which Burd confessed to acting in a play the previous winter (see August 1749). (3) Many years later, a prologue appears in the *Pennsylvania Evening Post* of 14 September 1775, "SPOKEN BY A GREAT PERSONAGE BEFORE THE TRAGEDY OF CATO, IN THE YEAR 1749, WHEN HE PERFORMED THE PART OF PORTIUS." "Spoken by a great personage," however, does not suggest the acting of clandestine amateurs, the identity often assumed by scholars for the performers who were bound over by the magistrates. (4) Pollock (74), following the fourth piece of evidence, an entry in the "Manuscript Diary of John Smith," claims this play (i.e., *Cato*) was performed on 22/23 August 1749. Daly (*First Theatre in America*, 84) dates Smith's diary entry as 12 August 1749, recording that "Smith had been at a friend's house whose daughter was going, as one of a company, to hear the tragedy of *Cato*." (5) Finally, the fifth piece of evidence is the public notice of 26 February 1750 (see entry that date) announcing the New York arrival of "a Company of Comedians from Philadelphia," establishing a certain professional nature of the company.

Some confusion exists, however, as to whether the 8 January municipal records refer to Old Style (1749) or New Style (1750), further clouding any attempts at sorting out the period. If New Style is assumed, then the August 1749 production of *Cato* goes unaccounted for, as well as the Shippen letter's reference to the previous winter's performance. Durang (i) is among those who concur with the New Style premise, stating that "The Company [Murray-Kean] may have played during the months of December 1749–January 1750." Therefore, if the court records are dated New Style (1750), then the company appeared in January 1750, was immediately suppressed and moved to New York by mid-February, and the production of

Cato was under auspices entirely distinct from the Murray-Kean troupe.

The simpler explanation, however, is that the Shippen letter (dated August 1749) clearly refers to the previous winter (i.e., January 1749) in which a company of some nature performed a series of plays much to the displeasure of the city. They were bound over, occasionally erupting from their good behavior (i.e., *Cato*). Perhaps finding the challenges of Philadelphia too difficult, they relocated during the following winter of 1749–50, becoming the nucleus of what is now known as the Murray-Kean Company. This scenario has the added virtue of clarifying the origins of the Murray-Kean Company, who are referred to in New York as "a company of Comedians from Philadelphia."[5]

Further details on the origins of the Murray-Kean troupe are scanty. Pollock (6–7) posits that the company "was composed in part of players from the West Indies who had come north to try their fortunes." Francis Wemyss, writing in 1852, offers, "From other sources we have heard that this Old Company [the Murray-Kean Company] consisted of Amateur performers entirely except one or two Actors, who had straggled into America from Jamaica and other British West Indies islands" (*Chronology of the American Stage*, 191). Unfortunately, with the exception of James Burd, who boasted to Shippen of having acted a play in the winter of 1749, no names are known of the performers in the Philadelphia production(s). The August 1749 production of *Cato* has been traditionally attributed to the Murray-Kean Company, though there is no preserved cast list to directly support this assumption. If this was indeed their production, they most likely performed more than *Cato* in Philadelphia during late 1749, as they are known to have presented an extensive repertory (eighteen main pieces and twelve afterpieces that we know of) immediately after their arrival in New York in early 1750 and on into 1751. Incidently, when cast lists for the Murray-Kean Company become

---

[5] Pollock's explanation (6) is this: "In August 1749 a 'Company of Comedians' was in Philadelphia playing in a large warehouse owned by William Plumstead ... [who] gave *Cato* on August 22 or 23 and were still in the city in January, 1750 when the Common Council attempted to 'discourage' them. In February they went to New York."

available in New York, the name of James Burd does not appear among them.

Also at issue is the venue of the 1749 Murray-Kean troupe. Pollock (6) places the company "in a large warehouse owned by William Plumstead." Wemyss (189–190), however, claims that "the place of performance was in the neighborhood of the Luxley House, in what is called Little Duck Street." Both authorities may be referring to the same location.

Also in this year, one Mr. Stokes, formerly of Goodman's Fields Theatre, London, presented several dramatic entertainments in Charleston.

***

c. early January 1749 Philadelphia
Play not identified.
Performers unknown.
[Evidence from municipal records of 8 January (quoted in Dye, "Pennsylvania vs. the Theatre," 353) suggests the strong likelihood of a January performance:

> certain persons had lately taken upon them to act plays in this city, and as he [the Recorder] was informed, intended to make a frequent practice thereof .... Whereupon the Board unanimously requested the magistrates to take the most effectual measures for suppressing this disorder, by sending for the actors, and binding them for their good behavior, or by such other means as they should think proper.

Further evidence comes from Rankin (30), who quotes a letter from Edward Shippen in London to James Burd in Philadelphia dated August 1749: "You acquaint me of your acting a play last Winter to the satisfaction of the Spectators."]

August 1749 Plumsted's Warehouse, Philadelphia
Cato.
Murray-Kean Company?
[A prologue appears in the *Pennsylvania Evening Post* of 14 September 1775, "SPOKEN BY A GREAT PERSONAGE BEFORE THE TRAGEDY OF CATO, IN THE YEAR 1749, WHEN HE PERFORMED THE PART OF PORTIUS." The "Manuscript Diary of John Smith," for 22 August 1749 contains the following relevant entry:

> Joseph Morris and I happened in at Peacock Bigger's and drank tea there, and his daughter, being one of the company who were going to

hear the tragedy of Cato acted, it occasioned some conversation, in which I expressed my sorrow that anything of the kind was encouraged.

Cf., Pollock, 6–7.]

1 August 1749   Philadelphia
Correspondence.

[Edward Shippen, writing from London to James Burd[6] in Philadelphia, recounts theatrical news:

> You acquaint me of your acting a play last Winter to the Satisfaction of all Spectators .... I am glad that Spirit is kept up, because it is an amusement the most useful of any to Young People and I heartily wish it would spread to ye younger sort, I mean School Boys.

Source: Lewis 15–16.]

1 December 1749   Mrs. Blythe's Court-Room, Charleston
Plays not identified.
Mr. Stokes.

[The following notice suggesting the performance of theatricals appeared in the *South Carolina Gazette* of 20–27 November 1749:

> At the Court-Room at Mrs. Blythe's, several dramatick entertainments will be performed, by Mr. Stokes, who for several years acted on the stages in Dublin, Edinburgh and Goodman's-Fields. The performer will submit to the generosity of the company, what recompence he may merit, when they see his performances.]

---

[6] James Burd, the recipient of the Shippen letter was a young merchant of Philadelphia, Shippen's son-in-law, and one of four directors of the Philadelphia Assembly, a newly formed social club that met regularly to sing, dance, and, apparently, to perform and to sponsor theatricals. So, speculatively at least, the cast lists of play could be drawn from the Philadelphia Assembly membership, which may suggest Philadelphia hosted both amateur productions and the Murray-Kean Company. Also of note, in the following year Burd's business ventures prompted him to take over a contract on a new ship to transport merchandise. Completed in 1750, the ship was named after Burd's youngest daughter, Sally, i.e., the "Charming Sally," which regularly transported theatrical personnel during the colonial period (Nixon 10, 15).

1750

A company of comedians arrived in New York from Philadelphia in February 1750 (see 26 February 1750). Though we have no cast lists for the New York performances of this year, the benefits at the beginning of 1751 reveal this to be the Murray-Kean Company, headed by Walter Murray and Thomas Kean. This early colonial company played from March to July 1750, when, after a brief recess, they continued an extraordinary fall season from September 1750 well into July of 1751. Though newspaper notices appeared only once a week, the company almost certainly performed more often. From the 1751 benefit season, the names of the following members of the Murray-Kean Company for 1750 are recorded: Miss Nancy George, Mr. Jago, Thomas Kean, Mrs. Leigh, Mr. Marks, Mr. Moore, Walter Murray, Dick Murray, Mrs. "Widow" Osborne, Miss Osborne, Mr. Scott, Mr. Taylor, Mrs. Taylor, John Tremaine, and Charles Somerset Woodham. While there is no preserved record for Mr. Leigh (or Lee), a Mrs. Leigh occupied a minor role in the company (cf. headnote for 1751), and Leigh himself was likely in residence.

Sometime in March, a tumult at a coffee house in Boston occurred over an amateur production of *The Orphan*, quickly resulting in legislation prohibiting acting in that commonwealth. This clandestine production apparently inspired at least one individual to attempt an original play. Frank Pierce Hill (119) lists a farce in three acts, *The Suspicious Daughter*, written by T. T. Jr. of Boston, and printed in 1751.

Fowler (55) reports that in 1750 John Moody proposed to erect a regular theatre in Kingston, Jamaica.

***

8 January 1750   Philadelphia
Law passed.
   [The Common Council condemns public performance of theatricals. Source: Rankin 31.]

26 February 1750   First Nassau St. Theatre, New York
Newspaper notice.
Murray-Kean Company

["Last week arrived here a Company of Comedians from Philadelphia, who, we hear, have taken a convenient Room for their Purpose, in one of the Buildings lately belonging to the Hon. Rip Van Dam, esq; deceased, in Nassau St; where they intend to perform as long as the season lasts." Source: *New York Gazette & Weekly Post-Boy* (6 March 1749/50).]

March 1750   Coffee House, State St., Boston
The Orphan.
Local amateurs.

[Clapp (2) relates that this production occurred "at the Coffee House in State Street, by two young Englishmen assisted by some volunteer comrades from the town. Such an innovation was looked upon with horror." Willard (4) claims "the eagerness of the public to witness the performance occasioned a serious disturbance at the door." This performance by amateurs in a coffee-house in State St. caused the authorities to enact a law in April 1750 forbidding acting in the commonwealth (Odell, 1:33; following Clapp, *History of the Boston Stage*).]

5 March 1750   First Nassau St. Theatre, New York
Richard III* (Shakespeare; as adapted by Colley Cibber, 1700).
Murray-Kean Company.

[This evening marked the opening of this theatre. Source: *New York Gazette & Weekly Post-Boy* (26 February 1749/50).]

12 March 1750   First Nassau St. Theatre, New York
Richard III.
The Beau in the Suds* (Charles Coffey, 1730).
Murray-Kean Company.

[Coffey's play is also known as *The Female Parson*. Source: *New York Gazette & Weekly Post-Boy* (12 March 1749/50).]

17 March 1750   First Nassau St. Theatre, New York
The Spanish Friar.
Murray-Kean Company.

[Source: *New York Gazette & Weekly Post-Boy* (12 March 1749/50).]

20 March 1750   First Nassau St. Theatre, New York
The Spanish Friar.
Murray-Kean Company.

[Source: *New York Gazette & Weekly Post-Boy* (19 March 1749/50).]

27 March 1750   First Nassau St. Theatre, New York
The Orphan.
Murray-Kean Company.
  ["For the Benefit of the Charity School in this City." Source: *New York Gazette & Weekly Post-Boy* (26 March 1749/50).]

2 April 1750   First Nassau St. Theatre, New York
The Orphan.
The Beau in the Suds.
Murray-Kean Company.
  [Some confusion exists over the precise program. The *New York Weekly Post-Boy* of this date announces *The Beaux' Stratagem* and *The Mock Doctor* for this evening, but the playbill, the more reliable source, announces the above program. Source: playbill in the Harvard Theatre Collection, reproduced in Odell (opposite 1:34) and thought to be the oldest surviving New York playbill. Cf. *New York Gazette & Weekly Post-Boy* (2 April 1750).]

16 April 1750   First Nassau St. Theatre, New York
The Beaux' Stratagem.
Murray-Kean Company.
  [Source: *New York Gazette & Weekly Post-Boy* (9 April 1750).]

20 April 1750   Boston
Law passed.
  [The *Boston Evening Post* of 23 April 1750 reports that on 20 April the General Court passed "an Act to prevent Stage-Plays, and other Theatrical Entertainments," which was not repealed until 1793. A portion of the act reads as follows:

> For preventing and avoiding the many and great mischiefs which arise from public stage-plays, interludes and other theatrical entertainments, which not only occasion great and unnecessary expenses, and discourage industry and frugality, but likewise tend generally to increase immorality, impiety, and a contempt of religion.
>   Section 1.–Be it enacted by the Lieutenant Governor, Council and House of Representatives, that from and after the publication of this act, no person or persons whosoever shall or may, for his or their gain, or for any valuable consideration, let or suffer to be used and improved, any house house, room, or place whatsoever, for

acting or carrying on any stage-plays, interludes, or other theatrical entertainments, on pain of forfeiting and paying for each and every day or time such house, room, or place shall be let, or improved, contrary to this act, twenty pounds.

Section 2. - And be it further enacted, that if at any time or times whatsoever, from and after the publication of this act, any person or persons shall be present, as an actor or spectator of any stage-play, interlude, or theatrical entertainment in any house, room, or place where a greater number of persons than twenty shall be assembled together, every such person shall forfeit and pay, for every time he or they shall be present as aforesaid, five pounds. The forfeitures and penalties aforesaid to be one half to his Majesty for the use of the Government, the other half to him or them that shall inform or sue for the same; and the aforesaid forfeitures and penalties may likewise be recovered by presentment of the grand jury, in which case the whole of the forfeitures shall be to his Majesty for the use of this Government.

Source: *Boston Evening Post* (23 April 1750); cf. Clapp, *History of the Boston Stage*, 2.]

23 April 1750   First Nassau St. Theatre, New York
The Beaux' Stratagem.
The Mock Doctor* (Henry Fielding, 1732).
Murray-Kean Company.
    [Source: *New York Gazette & Weekly Post-Boy* (23 April 1750).]

30 April 1750   First Nassau St. Theatre, New York
Richard III.
The Mock Doctor.
Murray-Kean Company.
    [Source: Odell 1: 34.]

7 May 1750   First Nassau St. Theatre, New York
The London Merchant.
Murray-Kean Company.
    [Source: *New York Gazette & Weekly Post-Boy* (7 May 1750).]

28 May 1750   First Nassau St. Theatre, New York
The Constant Couple* (George Farquhar, 1699).
The Lying Valet* (David Garrick, 1741).
Murray-Kean Company.
    [At which "the two Moor Princes will be present." Source: *New York Gazette & Weekly Post-Boy* (28 May 1750).]

4 June 1750   First Nassau St. Theatre, New York
The Twin Rivals* (George Farquhar, 1702).
The Lying Valet.
Colin and Phoebe* (Anonymous).
Murray-Kean Company.
   [Source: *New York Gazette & Weekly Post-Boy* (4 June 1750).]

16 July 1750   First Nassau St. Theatre, New York
Play not identified.
Murray-Kean Company.
   ["The Heat, having prevented the Play last Thursday Night, it is designed to be presented this Evening." Source: *New York Gazette & Weekly Post-Boy* (16 July 1750).]

23 July 1750   First Nassau St. Theatre, New York
Love for Love* (William Congreve, 1695).
The Stage Coach* (George Farquhar, 1704).
Murray-Kean Company.
   [Being "the last night of playing this season." Source: *New York Gazette & Weekly Post-Boy* (23 July 1750).]

13 September 1750   First Nassau St. Theatre, New York
The Recruiting Officer.
Murray-Kean Company.
   [This evening was the start of the new season. Source: *New York Gazette & Weekly Post-Boy* (10 September 1750).]

20 September 1750   First Nassau St. Theatre, New York
Cato.
Murray-Kean Company.
   [Source: *New York Gazette & Weekly Post-Boy* (24 September 1750). A review of this production appeared in the *New York Gazette & Weekly Post-Boy* of 24 September 1750:

> Thursday Evening last, the Tragedy of CATO, was play'd at the Theatre in this City, before a very numerous Audience, the greater part of whom were of Opinion, that it was pretty well perform'd: As it was the fullest Assembly that has appear'd in that House, it may serve to prove, that the Taste of this Place is not so much vitiated, or lost to a Sense of Liberty, but that they can prefer a Representation of Virtue, to those of a loose Character.]

24 September 1750   First Nassau St. Theatre, New York
The Recruiting Officer.

Murray-Kean Company.
[Source: *New York Gazette & Weekly Post-Boy* (24 September 1750).]

2 October 1750 First Nassau St. Theatre, New York
The Spanish Friar.
Murray-Kean Company.
[With "a Pantomime entertainment." Source: *New York Gazette & Weekly Post-Boy* (1 October 1750).]

8 October 1750 First Nassau St. Theatre, New York
The Beaux' Stratagem.
The Lying Valet* (David Garrick, 1741).
Murray-Kean Company.
[Source: *New York Gazette & Weekly Post-Boy* (8 October 1750).]

15 October 1750 First Nassau St. Theatre, New York
Cato.
Murray-Kean Company.
[With "a Pantomime." Source: *New York Gazette & Weekly Post-Boy* (15 October 1750).]

22 October 1750 First Nassau St. Theatre, New York
Amphitryon; or, The Two Sosias* (John Dryden, 1690).
Murray-Kean Company.
[Source: *New York Gazette & Weekly Post-Boy* (22 October 1750).]

29 October 1750 First Nassau St. Theatre, New York
Amphitryon.
Murray-Kean Company.
[Also "a Pantomime ... with some new Additions." Source: *New York Gazette & Weekly Post-Boy* (29 October 1750).]

5 November 1750 First Nassau St. Theatre, New York
Sir Harry Wildair* (George Farquhar, 1701).
Murray-Kean Company.
[With "the Pantomime." The advertisement also reports that "The Play-House is new floor'd and made very warm." Source: *New York Gazette & Weekly Post-Boy* (5 November 1750).]

12 November 1750 First Nassau St. Theatre, New York
George Barnwell [i.e., *The London Merchant*].

The Beau in the Suds.
Murray-Kean Company.
   [Source: *New York Gazette & Weekly Post-Boy* (12 November 1750).]

19 November 1750   First Nassau St. Theatre, New York
A Bold Stroke for a Wife* (Susanna Centlivre, 1718).
Murray-Kean Company.
   [The advertisement again announces that "The House being new floor'd, is made warm and comfortable; besides which, Gentlemen and Ladies may cause their Stoves to be brought," to which Odell (1: 37) adds, "foot-stoves, of course." Source: *New York Gazette & Weekly Post-Boy* (19 November 1750).]

3 December 1750   First Nassau St. Theatre, New York
The Beggar's Opera.
The Mock Doctor.
Murray-Kean Company.
   [Source: *New York Gazette & Weekly Post-Boy* (3 December 1750).]

10 December 1750   First Nassau St. Theatre, New York
The Beggar's Opera.
The Beau in the Suds.
Murray-Kean Company.
   [Source: *New York Gazette & Weekly Post-Boy* (10 December 1750).]

17 December 1750   First Nassau St. Theatre, New York
A Bold Stroke for a Wife.
The Lying Valet.
Murray-Kean Company.
   [Source: Odell 1:38.]

31 December 1750   First Nassau St. Theatre, New York
The Fair Penitent* (Nicholas Rowe, 1703).
The Lying Valet.
Murray-Kean Company.
   [Source: *New York Gazette & Weekly Post-Boy* (31 December 1750).]

1751

Though the names of the personnel are not available, nonetheless, a company performed in Barbados. The best guess is still Rankin's assumption (45) that this is the Moody Jamaican Company touring the islands. This company is known to have been in Kingston, Jamaica, and the principal identified members are William Daniels, Mrs. Daniels, Mr. Donald, David Douglass, Miss Hamilton, Mr. Kershaw, Mrs. Kershaw, John Moody, Owen Morris, Mrs. Morris, Mr. Smith, and Mrs. Smith.

The Murray-Kean Company continued their New York season until July 1751, after which Thomas Kean intended to retire from the stage to pursue a writing career, as announced in the *New York Gazette & Weekly Post-Boy* of 22 April 1751. His retirement was short-lived as he rejoined the company when it traveled to Williamsburg in the fall (see 24 October). John Tremain remained in New York to take up cabinet making. He returned to the stage occasionally, with Robert Upton (1752), and later for David Douglass (1762), but only in New York engagements. Other members who also likely remained in New York were "Widow" Henrietta Osborne and her daughter, Miss Osborne, and Mr. and Mrs. Leigh. The Osbornes, John Tremaine (and his wife), and Mr. Leigh later appeared with the Upton Company, after Robert Upton arrived in New York in November or December of 1751. The known members of the Murray-Kean Company included Mrs. Davis, Nancy George, Jago, Thomas Kean, [Mr. Leigh?], Mrs. Leigh, Mr. Marks, Mr. Moore, Dick Murray, Walter Murray, Miss Osborne, "Widow" Osborne, Mr. Scott, Smith, Miss Taylor, Mr. Taylor, Mrs. Taylor, John Tremaine, and Charles Woodham.

Some details have also survived concerning the New York Nassau Street venue used in 1751 by the Murray-Kean Company. A notice in the *New York Gazette & Weekly Post-Boy* of 21 January 1750/51 comments that for a benefit performance, 161 pit tickets were printed, 10 for the boxes, and 121 for the gallery, for a total of 292 (see Introduction, "Company Finances").

Robert Upton is, frankly, a bit of a mystery. In his public letter of 2 July 1753 (see entry under that date) Hallam claimed Upton was sent over from London by him as an advance agent in October of 1750. Upton does not appear in the record until

January 1752, though we can safely assume that the "new company of comedians" advertised as playing the last week of December, 1751, was his (see 26 December 1751). Daly (10) claims that Upton "in all probability came from Jamaica, in a vessel which had arrived a short time before [i.e., in December 1751]." Rankin (33), however, assumes Upton had been in the Murray-Kean Company almost the entire year, at least since Kean's benefit night of 15 January 1751. Rankin, as does Odell, nominates Upton as the advertised "gentleman lately from London" who performed a Harlequin dance, an assumption replicated by Durnam (356). Neither Upton's nor his wife's name, however, appears on any cast lists or benefits for the entire 1751 Murray-Kean season. Further, when Upton did advertise his benefit with his own new company on 20 January 1752, he referred to himself as "an absolute stranger" to the town, hardly possible if he had debuted a year earlier and had played the season through. His wife, Mrs. Upton, enjoyed a benefit a month later and also billed herself as a stranger. Therefore in this instance we are following Daly in assuming that Upton arrived in New York sometime in November or December 1751, pieced together a company from ex-Murray-Kean players and opened as a "new company" on 26 December 1751. If he did indeed sail from London in 1750, his whereabouts during that interim year are unknown.

After the Murray-Kean Company adjourned for the season in New York (July 1751), the remaining company members organized a subscription to build a theatre in Williamsburg, the Second Williamsburg Theatre, which they opened on 21 October 1751. A notice (signed by Charles Woodham, Walter Murray, and Thomas Kean) appeared in the *Virginia Gazette* stating that the company have "a greater Expence than they first expected" and requesting subscribers to assist them (see 24 October 1751). Apparently they did not meet with the reception they had expected, as less than one month after opening the theatre in Williamsburg we find them playing in Norfolk. Dormon (*Theater in the Ante Bellum South*, 8–9) claims that the company also played Suffolk before returning to Williamsburg in December, though we have found no record of their performances at that location. Once back in Williamsburg, they soon after announced their intent to travel to Petersburg, suggesting a continuing lukewarm reception in the colonial capital.

Evidence remains of a student theatrical in November 1751 at the College of William and Mary, Williamsburg, this year, though the performance was apparently interrupted.

※※※

7 January 1751   First Nassau St. Theatre, New York
A Bold Stroke for a Wife.
The Devil to Pay.
Murray-Kean Company.
   [Benefit Murray. Announced but postponed. Source: *New York Gazette & Weekly Post-Boy* (31 December 1750).]

8 January 1751   First Nassau St. Theatre, New York
A Bold Stroke for a Wife.
The Devil to Pay.
Murray-Kean Company.
   [Benefit Murray. Source: *New York Gazette & Weekly Post-Boy* (7 January 1751).]

14 January 1751   First Nassau St. Theatre, New York
The Beggar's Opera.
Miss in Her Teens.
Murray-Kean Company.
   [Announced but postponed. The *New York Gazette & Weekly Post-Boy* of 14 January 1751 contains the following notice: "By reason of the weather, 'tis thought proper to postpone The Beggars Opera, with the farce, call'd Miss in her Teens, for the benefit of Mr. Kean, 'till to morrow evening."]

15 January 1751   First Nassau St. Theatre, New York
The Beggar's Opera.
Miss in her Teens* (David Garrick, 1747).
Murray-Kean Company.
   [Benefit Kean. A notice in The *New York Gazette & Weekly Post-Boy* of 7 January 1751 mentions a series of dances "all by a gentleman lately from London," which Rankin (33) claims was the first appearance of Robert Upton. See also the related notice in the entry for 21 January 1751. Source: *New York Gazette & Weekly Post-Boy* (14 January 1751).]

21 January 1751   First Nassau St. Theatre, New York
The Recruiting Officer.

Miss in Her Teens.
Murray-Kean Company.
[Benefit Tremain. Source: *New York Gazette & Weekly Post-Boy* (21 January 1751).]

21 January 1751   First Nassau St. Theatre, New York
Newspaper notice.
Murray-Kean Company.
[The following notice relates to Thomas Kean's benefit on 15 January 1751:

> Whereas several reports have been unkindly spread, that Mr. Kean, on his Benefit Night on Monday last, had caused a greater Number of Tickets to be printed than the House would hold; this is to certify that (according to be [sic] best of my Knowledge) there were but 161 Pit Tickets, 10 Boxes, and 121 Gallery Tickets printed in all, and it is well known that as large a Number have been in the house at one Time. *James Parker.*
>
> N.B. Tho' it was then determined not to receive any Money at the Door, it was afterwards found to be a Measure impracticable to be followed without great offence; and such whose Business could not permit to come in Time, have since had their Money Return'd.
>
> Whereas it has been reported that Mrs. Taylor in playing her Part at my Benefit, endeavour'd to perform it in a worse manner than she was capable, and that it was done on Account of a falling-out between us: This is therefore to certify, that there was no such Difference between her and me; and that I believe her being out so much in her Part, was owing to her not getting the Part in Time. THOMAS KEAN.]

28 January 1751   First Nassau St. Theatre, New York
Cato.
The Devil to Pay.
Murray-Kean Company.
[Benefit Scott. Source: *New York Gazette & Weekly Post-Boy* (28 January 1751).]

4 February 1751   First Nassau St. Theatre, New York
Love for Love.
The Devil to Pay.
Murray-Kean Company.
[First benefit for Mrs. Taylor. Source: *New York Gazette & Weekly Post-Boy* (28 January and 4 February 1751).]

11 February 1751   First Nassau St. Theatre, New York
The Beaux' Stratagem.
Miss in her Teens.
Murray-Kean Company.

[Benefit Miss Osborne. Postponed. Source: *New York Gazette & Weekly Post-Boy* (4 February 1751).]

12 February 1751   First Nassau St. Theatre, New York
The Beaux' Stratagem.
Miss in her Teens.
Murray-Kean Company.
[Benefit Miss Osborne. Source: *New York Gazette & Weekly Post-Boy* (4 February 1751).]

18 February 1751   First Nassau St. Theatre, New York
The Beggar's Opera.
Damon and Phillida* (Henry Carey, 1729).
Murray-Kean Company.
[Benefit Woodham. Source: *New York Gazette & Weekly Post-Boy* (18 February 1751).]

25 February 1751   First Nassau St. Theatre, New York
Richard III.
   Richard–Kean.
Damon and Phillida.
Murray-Kean Company.
[Second benefit for Mrs. Taylor. "As there wasn't much Company at Love for Love, the Managers took the Profit arising by that Night, to themselves, and gave Mrs. Taylor another benefit; who hopes that the Ladies and Gentlemen that favour'd the other Benefits, will be so kind as to favour hers with their Company." Source: *New York Gazette & Weekly Post-Boy* (25 February 1751).]

4 March 1751   First Nassau St. Theatre, New York
The Fair Penitent.
The Lying Valet.
Murray-Kean Company.
[*A Bold Stroke for a Wife* and *Damon and Phillida* were originally announced for the benefit of Miss Nancy George in the *New York Gazette & Weekly Post-Boy* of 25 February 1751, but in fact, were not performed. Cf. Odell 1:40. In spite of the new program, not recorded in Odell, Miss George met with disappointment and was given another evening on 11 March 1751. Source: *New York Gazette & Weekly Post-Boy* (4 and 11 March 1751).]

11 March 1751   First Nassau St. Theatre, New York
The Orphan.

The Mock Doctor.
Murray-Kean Company.
 [Second benefit for Nancy George. "The play design'd last week for the Benefit of Miss George, having been attended with bad weather, and other Disappointments, the Company took that Night to themselves, and agreed to give her a Benefit this Evening." Source: *New York Gazette & Weekly Post-Boy* (11 March 1751).]

18 March 1751　　　First Nassau St. Theatre, New York
The Fair Penitent.
The Lying Valet.
Murray-Kean Company.
 [Source: *New York Gazette & Weekly Post-Boy* (18 March 1751).]

26 March 1751　　　First Nassau St. Theatre, New York
The Committee* (Sir Robert Howard, 1662).
Damon and Phillida.
Murray-Kean Company.
 [Source: *New York Gazette & Weekly Post-Boy* (25 March 1751).]

1 April 1751　　　First Nassau St. Theatre, New York
The Committee.
Damon and Phillida.
Murray-Kean Company.
 [Source: *New York Gazette & Weekly Post-Boy* (1 April 1751).]

16 April 1751　　　First Nassau St. Theatre, New York
The Spanish Friar.
The Virgin Unmasked* (Henry Fielding, 1735).
Murray-Kean Company.
 [Fielding's play is also known by *An Old Man Taught Wisdom*. Source: *New York Gazette & Weekly Post-Boy* (15 April 1751).]

22 April 1751　　　First Nassau St. Theatre, New York
The Busy Body.
The Virgin Unmasked.
Murray-Kean Company.
 [Source: *New York Gazette & Weekly Post-Boy* (22 April 1751).]

146   THE COLONIAL AMERICAN STAGE

29 April 1751   First Nassau St. Theatre, New York
The Busy Body.
The Virgin Unmasked.
Murray-Kean Company.

[A "farewell benefit" for Thomas Kean was announced in the *New York Gazette & Weekly Post-Boy* of 22 April 1751 as follows:

> Mr. Kean, by the Advice of several Gentlemen in town, who are his Friends, having resolv'd to quit the Stage, and following his Employment of Writing (wherein he hopes for encouragement;) and Mr. Murray having agreed to give him a Night, clear of all Expences, for his half of the Cloaths, Scenes, &c. belonging to the Play House; it is resolved, that for the Benefit of said Kean, by his Excellency's Permission, on Monday the 29th of this month will be perform'd King Richard the III: the part of Richard to be perform'd by Mr. Kean; being the last Time of his appearing on the Stage.

Why Kean altered the program from *Richard III* to *The Busy Body* is not known, but, in fact, Kean later returned to acting by at least 17 April 1752. Source: *New York Gazette & Weekly Post-Boy* (29 April 1751).]

6 May 1751   First Nassau St. Theatre, New York
Sir Harry Wildair.
Damon and Phillida.
Murray-Kean Company.

[Benefit Master Dick Murray. Source: *New York Gazette & Weekly Post-Boy* (29 April 1751).]

13 May 1751   First Nassau St. Theatre, New York
The Beggar's Opera.
The Virgin Unmasked.
Murray-Kean Company.

[Second benefit for Tremain and Scott. The players apparently had a difficult time procuring scripts, as made clear in the following notice appended to their usual notice: "If any gentleman or lady, has the farce call'd The Intriguing Chambermaid, and will lend it a while to the players, it will be thankfully acknowledged." Source: *New York Gazette & Weekly Post-Boy* (6 May 1751).]

20 May 1751   First Nassau St. Theatre, New York
The Busy Body.
Hob in the Well.
Murray-Kean Company.

THE COLONIAL AMERICAN STAGE 147

[Second benefit for Woodham. Source: *New York Gazette & Weekly Post-Boy* (20 May 1751).]

23 May 1751   First Nassau St. Theatre, New York
Sir Harry Wildair.
Hob in the Well.
Murray-Kean Company.

[Benefit Moore and Marks. Source: *New York Gazette & Weekly Post-Boy* (20 May 1751).]

3 June 1751   First Nassau St. Theatre, New York
The Distrest Mother* (Ambrose Phillips, 1712).
The Walking Statue, or the Devil in the Wine Cellar* (Aaron Hill, 1710).
Murray-Kean Company.

[Second benefit for Miss Taylor and Miss Osborne; there is no record of Miss Taylor's first benefit. Source: *New York Gazette & Weekly Post-Boy* (27 May 1751).]

6 June 1751   First Nassau St. Theatre, New York
The Distrest Mother.
The Walking Statue.
Murray-Kean Company.

[The play is advertised as "for the Benefit of Mr. Jago, and he humbly begs all Gentlemen and Ladies would be so kind as to favour him with their company as he never had a Benefit before, and is just come out of Prison." Source: *New York Gazette & Weekly Post-Boy* (3 June 1751).]

13 June 1751   First Nassau St. Theatre, New York
George Barnwell [i.e., *The London Merchant.*]
Devil upon Two Sticks* (Charles Coffey, 1729).
Murray-Kean Company.

[Benefit Mrs. Davis, "to enable her to buy off her time." Source: *New York Gazette & Weekly Post-Boy* (10 June 1751).]

17 June 1751   First Nassau St. Theatre, New York
The Distrest Mother.
Beau in the Suds.
Murray-Kean Company.

[Benefit "Widow Osborne." Source: *New York Gazette & Weekly Post-Boy* (10 June 1751).]

20 June 1751   First Nassau St. Theatre, New York
The Recruiting Officer.

Beau in the Suds.
Murray-Kean Company.
   [Benefit Mrs. Leigh. Source: *New York Gazette & Weekly Post-Boy* (17 June 1751).]

27 June 1751   First Nassau St. Theatre, New York
The Distrest Mother.
Beau in the Suds.
Murray-Kean Company.
   [Second benefit for "Widow" Osborne, "having been disappointed of her Benefit." Source: *New York Gazette & Weekly Post-Boy* (24 June 1751).]

8 July 1751   First Nassau St. Theatre, New York
The Recruiting Officer.
Damon and Phillida.
Murray-Kean Company.
   [Last performance of the season. Benefit Smith. Source: *New York Gazette & Weekly Post-Boy* (8 July 1751).]

29 August 1751   Williamsburg, Virginia colony
Newspaper notice.
   [The following notice appeared in the *Virginia Gazette* on this date:

> By permission of his Honour the President, whereas the Company of Comedians that are in New-York intend performing in this city; but there being no room suitable for a play-house, 'tis proposed that a theatre shall be built by way of subscription: Each subscriber, advancing a pistole, to be entitled to a box ticket, for the first night's diversions. Those gentlemen and ladies who are kind enough to favour this undertaking, are desired to send their subscription money to Mr. Finnie's, at the Raleigh, where tickets may be had. N.B. The house to be completed by October court.

Cf. Hughes 15.]

6 October 1751   Williamsburg
Diary entry.
Murray-Kean Company.
   [John Blair records that the actors (of the Murray-Kean Company) have found lodging: "Hear the Actors are Dispers'd." Source: Blair, "Diary," 3, 147.]

21 October 1751   2nd Williamsburg Theatre, Williamsburg
Richard III.

Murray-Kean Company.
[Prices: box 7s. 6d.; pit 5s. 9d.; gallery 3s. 9d. Source: *Virginia Gazette* (17 October 1751).]

24 October 1751   2nd Williamsburg Theatre, Williamsburg
Newspaper notice.
[The following notice appears in the *Virginia Gazette* of this date:

> The Company of Comedians having been at a greater expence than they at first expected in erecting a theatre in the city of Williamsburg, and having an immediate occasion for the money expended in that particular, in order to procure proper scenes and dresses, humbly hope that those gentlemen who are lovers of theatrical performances, will be kind enough to assist them, by way of subscription, for the payment of the house and lots, each subscriber to have a property therein, in proportion to the sum subscribed. As the money is immediately wanted, we hope the gentlemen will be kind enough to pay it as they subscribe, into the hands of Messrs. Mitchelson and Hyndman, who have obliged us so far as to receive the same, and to whom deeds will be delivered, on the subscription being compleated, for the purpose above mentioned. Which shall be gratefully acknowledged, by their most obliged humble servants, Charles Somerset Woodham, Walter Murray, Thomas Kean.]

November 1751   College of William and Mary, Williamsburg
Cato.
Students of the college.
[John Blair records in his diary the following information relating to a student production at the college:

> This evening Mr. Pre[s]ton to prevent the young gentlemen of the college from playing at a rehearsal in the dormitory, how they could act Cato privately among themselves, did himself, they say, act the Drunken Peasant; but his tearing down the curtains is to me very surprising.

Source: Blair, "Diary," quoted in Davis 1301.]

15 November 1751   Barbados
George Barnwell [i.e., *The London Merchant*].
[George Washington "was treated with a play ticket by Mr. Carter to see the tragedy of *George Barnwell* acted; the character of Barnwell and several others was said to be well performed. There was Music adapted and regularly conducted by Mr. ...." Source: Ford 6–7.]

18 November 1751 Capt. Newton's Great Room, Norfolk, Virginia colony

The Recruiting Officer.
Murray-Kean Company.
    [Rankin (38) claims that this performance took place on 17 November, but that date fell on a Sunday. Source: *Virginia Gazette* (14 November 1751).]

19 December 1751 Williamsburg
Newspaper advertisement.
Murray-Kean Company.
    [The *Virginia Gazette* of this date prints the following notice: "Williamsburg, December 17, 1751. The company of comedians intend to be at Petersburg by the middle of next month, and hope that the gentlemen and ladies who are lovers of theatrical entertainment, will favour them with their company."]

26 December 1751 First Nassau St. Theatre, New York
Othello (William Shakespeare).
Lethe* (David Garrick, 1740).
Upton Company.
    [Box 5s.; pit 4s.; gallery 2s. To begin at 6 o'clock. Source: *New York Gazette & Weekly Post-Boy* (23 December 1751).]

30 December 1751 First Nassau St. Theatre, New York
Othello.
Lethe.
Upton Company.
    [Source: *New York Gazette & Weekly Post-Boy* (30 December 1751).]

1752

In 1752 three companies played on the continent. The first was under the management of Robert Upton, who began in New York with several ex-members of the Murray-Kean Company. This "new company" aborted its brief season by March, 1752, after which Upton shipped back to England. This temporary ensemble consisted of the following known members: Mr. Fitzgerald, Mr. James, Mr. Leigh, Mrs. Leigh, Miss Osborne, "Widow" Osborne, Mr. Petty, John Tremaine, Mrs. Tremaine, Robert Upton, and Mrs. Upton.

The Murray-Kean Company (renaming itself the Annapolis Company as of 20 August) played in and around Williamsburg and Annapolis for the full year, in sites such as Fredericksburg, Hobbes Holes, Petersburg, Upper Marlborough, Port Tobacco, and Piscataway.[7] Because these performances were seldom advertised in newspaper notices, the names of few company members are recorded: Mrs. Beccely, Mr. Eyanson, Mr. Herbert (from the theatre in Williamsburg), Miss Osborne, Thomas Kean, Walter Murray, Charles Woodham, and Mr. Wynell (from the theatre in Williamsburg). Equally scanty are the records of their repertory, as regular newspaper notices did not begin until April 1752 with the advent of the benefits. After 16 December 1752, we hear no more of the company, though several members later appeared in the Hallam Company.[8]

The famous Hallam Company arrived in the summer of 1752, but some dispute exists about the exact date of their appearance. In a public letter of 2 July 1753 (see entry for that date) Lewis Hallam, Sr. claimed that the company arrived on 28 June 1752. Durang (2), relying on reminiscences of Lewis Hallam Jr., concurs that they left London the early part of May and "made the Capes of Virginia in six weeks." Rankin (50), however, offers evidence that their ship, the *Charming Sally*, arrived 2 June 1752, and that the company spent the summer gaining permission to play as well as refitting the theatre at Williamsburg. The minutes from a 13 June town council meeting in Williamsburg (see entry for that date), however, reveal that by this date "several Comedians were lately arrived and others daily expected," indicating both a variation in arrival dates and the fact that the company arrived in at least two waves. These minutes further reveal that the initial petition to perform was denied, but the governor afterward relented and permission was secured. The company certainly commenced playing in September 1752 and consisted of William Adcock, Mrs. Adcock, Thomas Clarkson, Mrs. Clarkson, Mr. Lewis Hallam, Lewis Hallam Jr., Mrs. Hallam, Miss Hallam, Mr. Herbert, Patrick Malone, Miss Palmer,

---

[7] Sherman (*Comedies Useful*, 9) also places the company in Norfolk and Tappahannock but provides no documentation.

[8] Seilhamer (1:30) claims that this company existed for twenty years, but he has erroneously conflated records of several separate companies.

William Rigby, Mrs. Rigby, John Singleton, and Mr. Wynell. Sometime during this year Miss Palmer becomes Mrs. Adcock. What had happened to the previous Mrs. Adcock is not known.

Though performance records are slight, a letter dated 1752 from George Gilmer to Walter King states that "when Court was in session, they played practically every night ... [while] at other times, they performed three evenings a week" (Gilmer Letter Book, 1752, quoted in Land 48; cf. "Original Letters," 240–41). Dunlap (8) reported from conversations with Hallam Jr. a list of plays that the Hallam Company rehearsed prior to leaving England which may well have constituted the company's repertory: *The Fair Penitent, The Beaux' Stratagem, Jane Shore, The Recruiting Officer, King Richard III, The Careless Husband, The Constant Couple, Hamlet, Othello, Theodosius, The Provoked Husband, Tamerlane, The Inconstant, Woman's a Riddle, The Suspicious Husband, The Conscious Lovers, George Barnwell, The Committee,* and *The Twin Rivals.* The afterpieces included *Lethe, The Lying Valet, Miss in Her Teens, The Mock Doctor, The Devil to Pay, Hob in the Well, Damon and Phillida,* and *The Anatomist.*

During the summer of 1752 while the Hallams were securing a theatre in Williamsburg, the Murray-Kean Company was building a permanent brick theatre in Annapolis. Durang (iii) offers the following anecdotal suggestion: "We think that Mr. Hallam (Lewis Hallam, Jr.) said that while the Williamsburg theatre was preparing, some of their company went to Annapolis, to assist an amateur corps [Murray-Kean]. The report of these actors, on their return to Hallam, led him afterwards to Annapolis." Certainly by December of 1752, Herbert and Wynell had left the Hallam Company and had joined (or rejoined?) the Murray-Kean Company.

The *Cambridge Guide to African and Caribbean Theatre* (153) states (though offering no evidence) that a company in Barbados performed this year at Marshall's Great Room, Bridgetown.

In September 1752 the Georgian Calendar was corrected by an act of Parliament; this recalibration of the calendar explains the many dating incongruities in various scholarly accounts (e.g., Hornblow 1:83).

The Colonial American Stage

***

6 January 1752   First Nassau St. Theatre, New York
The Provoked Husband* (John Vanbrugh and Colley Cibber, 1728)
Lethe.
Upton Company.
   [Source: *New York Gazette & Weekly Post-Boy* (6 January 1752).]

13 January 1752   First Nassau St. Theatre, New York
The Fair Penitent.
The King and the Miller of Mansfield* (Robert Dodsley, 1737).
Upton Company.
   [The following notice appears in the *New York Gazette & Weekly Post-Boy* of this date:

> Mr. Upton (to his great disappointment) not meeting with encouragement enough to support the company for the season, intends to shorten it, by performing 5 or 6 plays only, for benefits, and begins with his own on Monday the 20th instant.

   Source: *New York Gazette & Weekly Post-Boy* (13 January 1752).]

20 January 1752   First Nassau St. Theatre, New York
Tunbridge Walks* (Thomas Baker, 1703).
The Lying Valet.
Upton Company.
   [Benefit Upton. The following notice appears in the *New York Gazette & Weekly Post-Boy* of this date:

> As Mr. Upton is an absolute stranger, if, in his application, he should have omitted any gentleman or lady's house, or lodging, he humbly hopes they'll impute it to want of information, not of respect.

Source: *New York Gazette & Weekly Post-Boy* (20 January 1752).]

23 January 1752   First Nassau St. Theatre, New York
Richard III.
   Richard–Upton.
Lethe.
Upton Company.

[Benefit Tremain. Source: *New York Gazette & Weekly Post-Boy* (20 January 1752).]

27 January 1752   First Nassau St. Theatre, New York
A Bold Stroke for a Wife.
The King and the Miller of Mansfield.
Upton Company.
   [Benefit Leigh. Source: *New York Gazette & Weekly Post-Boy* (27 January 1752).]

29 January 1752   First Nassau St. Theatre, New York
Othello.
The King and the Miller of Mansfield.
Upton Company.
   [Benefit Miss Osborne. Source: Odell 1:45.]

17 February 1752   First Nassau St. Theatre, New York
Richard III.
Sir John Cockle at Court* (Robert Dodsley, 1738).
Upton Company.
   [Benefit "Widow" Osborne. The afterpiece is the sequel to *The King and the Miller of Mansfield.* Source: *New York Gazette & Weekly Post-Boy* (17 February 1752).]

20 February 1752   First Nassau St. Theatre, New York
Venice Preserved* (Thomas Otway, 1682).
      Jaffier–Upton; Pierre–Petty; Priuli–Leigh; "Bidamar" [i.e., Bedamore]–Fitzgerald; Renault–Tremain; Eliot–James; Belvidera–Mrs. Upton.
Miss in Her Teens.
Upton Company.
   [Advertised as "absolutely the last Time of playing here . . . for the benefit of Mrs. Upton," but see 4 March 1752. Source: *New York Gazette & Weekly Post-Boy* (17 February 1752); a playbill in the Harvard Theater Collection is reproduced in Odell (opp. 1:50).]

2 March 1752   First Nassau St. Theatre, New York
The Fair Penitent.
The Honest Yorkshireman* (Henry Carey).
Upton Company.
   [Source: *New York Gazette & Weekly Post-Boy* (2 March 1752).]

4 March 1752   First Nassau St. Theatre, New York
The Fair Penitent.
    Lavinia–Mrs. Tremain.
The Honest Yorkshireman.
Upton Company.
    [The following notice appeared in the company's advertisement for this performance:

> The play for this night, as usual; and on Wednesday (which will certainly be the last night of attempting to play here; the vessel in which Mr. Upton goes, sailing the latter end of the week) will be acted ... and a farewell epilogue, adapted to the occasion, by Mr. Upton.

A few days later Robert Upton sailed for England. Source: *New York Gazette & Weekly Post-Boy* (2 March 1752).]

15 April 1752   New Theater, Williamsburg, Virginia colony
Play not idenitified.
Murray-Kean Company.
    [The dour Colonel Carter found himself in the playhouse this evening, much against his inclination and taste. Though he did not specify the play, he may be implying that it was Aaron Hill's *The Walking Statue*, a popular comedy:

> We waited upon the Governor to know when he would appoint to receive our address, and he told us he would send word tomorrow. From thence Charles Carter and the Attorney dragged me to the Play, and there I was surfeited with Stupidity and nonsence delivered from the mouths of Walking Statues.

Source: Carter, *Diary*, 1:103.]

24 April 1752   New Theater, Williamsburg, Virginia colony
The Constant Couple.
    Sir Harry Wildair–Kean; Colonel Standard–Murray; Angelica–Mrs. Beccely.
The Lying Valet.
Murray-Kean Company.
    [Benefit Mrs. Beccely. Source: *Virginia Gazette* (17 April 1752).]

30 April 1752   Williamsburg, Virginia colony
Newspaper advertisement.
    [The *Virginia Gazette* for this date carries the following notice:

The Company of Comedians, from the New Theatre at Williamsburg, propose playing at Hobbs's-Hole, from the 10th of May to the 24th; from thence they intend to proceed to Fredericksburg, to play during the continuance of June Fair. We therefore hope, that all gentlemen and ladies, who are lovers of theatrical entertainments, will favour us with their company.]

2 June 1752   Fredericksburg, Virginia colony
Play not identified.
Murray-Kean Company?

[George Washington records in his *Diary* that he and his brother attended this performance and paid "1/3" for admission. Dunlap (20–21) suggests the play may have been *Richard III*. Source: Ford, 9]

12 June 1752   Williamsburg
Newspaper advertisement.
Hallam Company.

[The *Virginia Gazette* for this date carries the following announcement:

This is to inform the public, that Mr. Hallam, from the new theatre in Goodmans Fields, London, is daily expected here with a select Company of Comedians; the scenes, cloaths, and decorations are all entirely new, extremely rich, and finished in the highest taste, the scenes being painted by the best hands in London, are excell'd by none in beauty and elegance, so that the ladies and gentlemen may depend on being entertain'd in as polite a manner as at the theatres in London, the company being perfect in all the best plays, opera's, farces, and pantomimes, that have been exhibited in any of the theatres for these ten years past.]

13 June 1752   Williamsburg
Government hearing.
Hallam Company.

[The following minutes from a meeting of the Executive Council of Williamsburg make clear that anti-theatrical forces sought to prevent the Hallam Company from performing in that city:

The Governor acquainting the Council that he had been informed several commedians were lately arrived, and others daily expected, and desiring their Advice, whether he should grant them a permission to act Plays, It was the advice of the Board that his Honour would not permit them to act or exhibit any plays or theatrical entertainment in this Government.

Source: Hall 4:404.]

THE COLONIAL AMERICAN STAGE 157

22 June 1752   New Theatre, Annapolis
The Beggar's Opera.
The Lying Valet.
Murray-Kean Company.

["By permission of his honour the President." Prices: box–10s., pit–7s. 6d. The *Maryland Gazette* of 18 June 1752 contains the following notice:

> N.B. The Company immediately intend to Upper Marlborough, as soon as they have done performing here, where they intend to play as long as they meet with encouragement, and so on to Piscataway, and Port Tobacco. And hope to give satisfaction to the gentlemen and ladies in each place, that will favour them with their company.

Source: *Maryland Gazette* (18 June 1752).]

28 June 1752   Yorktown, Virginia colony
Newspaper notice.

[Lewis Hallam claims that the company on this date arrives in Yorktown after arriving from London. Source: Hallam letter, 2 July 1753 (see entry for that date).]

30 June 1752   Williamsburg
Correspondence.

[Dr. George Gilmer relates some theatrical news in a letter to Dr. Thomas Walker, member of the Assembly:
> I have nothing to trouble you with only the arrival of Hallam and his Company .... The Governor and Council, because you would not pass a bill for suppressing ordinaries and players, have made an order that no player should act here; which is likely to prove the utter ruin of a set of idle wretches, arrived in Lee, at about 1000 expense.

Source: Gilmer Letter Book, 30 June 1752; quoted in Land 43.]

6 July 1752   New Theatre, Annapolis
The Busy Body.
The Lying Valet.
Murray-Kean Company.

[The *Maryland Gazette* of 2 July 1752 contains the following notice: "N.B. As the company have now got their hands, cloaths, &c. compleat, they now confirm their resolution of going to Upper Marlborough, as soon as ever encouragement fails here." Source: *Maryland Gazette* (2 July 1752).]

13 July 1752   New Theatre, Annapolis
The Beaux Stratagem.

The Virgin Unmasked.
Murray-Kean Company.
   [Prices: box 10s.; pit 7s. 6d.; gallery 5s. Source: *Maryland Gazette* (9 July 1752).]

20 July 1752   New Theatre, Annapolis
The Recruiting Officer.
The Beau in the Suds.
Murray-Kean Company.
   [Source: *Maryland Gazette* (16 July 1752).]

21 July 1752   New Theatre, Annapolis
The Recruiting Officer.
The Mock Doctor.
Murray-Kean Company.
   [Source: Seilhamer 1:33; Sonneck 18.]

27 July 1752   New Theatre, Annapolis
The London Merchant.
Damon and Phillida.
Murray-Kean Company.
   [Source: *Maryland Gazette* (23 July 1752).]

31 July 1752   New Theatre, Annapolis
A Bold Stroke for a Wife.
The Beau in the Suds.
Murray-Kean Company.
   [Source: *Maryland Gazette* (30 July 1752).]

3 August 1752   New Theatre, Annapolis
The Drummer.
The Devil to Pay.
Murray-Kean Company.
   [Source: *Maryland Gazette* (30 July 1752).]

20 August 1752   New   Theatre, Upper Marlborough,
                      Maryland colony
The Beggar's Opera.
The Lying Valet.
Annapolis Company.
   [As of this date the Murray-Kean Company renamed itself "The Annapolis Company." Source: *Maryland Gazette* (13 August 1752).]

THE COLONIAL AMERICAN STAGE   159

21 August 1752   Williamsburg, Virginia colony
Newspaper notice.
Hallam Company.
[The *Virginia Gazette* for this date carries a notice concerning the preparations of the Hallam Company, the first fully professional, London-outfitted company to operate in the colonies, and their new theatre:

> We are desired to inform the publick, that as the Company of Comedians, lately from London, have obtain'd his honour the Governor's permission, and have, with great expence, entirely altered the play-house at Williamsburg to a regular theatre, fit for the reception of ladies and gentlemen, and the execution of their own performances, they intend to open on the first Friday in September next, with a play, call'd The Merchant of Venice, (written by Shakespear) and a farce, call'd The Anatomist, or, Sham Doctor. The ladies are desired to give timely notice to Mr. Hallam, at Mr. Fisher's, for their places in the boxes, and on the day of performance to send their servants early to keep them, in order to prevent trouble and disappointment.]

3–13 September 1752
Calendar change.
[The absence of these dates reflects the implementation of the Georgian calendar. See discussion in the headnote for this season.]

14 September 1752 New   Theatre, Upper Marlborough,
                    Maryland colony
The Beggar's Opera.
The Lying Valet.
Annapolis Company.
[Prices: pit 7s. 6d.; gallery 5s. "By permission of his honour the President, at the New Theatre, in Upper Marlborough, by the company of comedians from Annapolis." Source: *Maryland Gazette* (27 August 1752).]

15 September 1752 Second Williamsburg Theatre,
                    Williamsburg
The Merchant of Venice* (William Shakespeare).
   Shylock–Malone; Bassanio–Rigby; Antonio–Clarkson; Gratiano–Singleton; Salanio and Duke–Herbert; Salarino and Gobbo–Wynell; Launcelot and Tubal–Hallam; Servant to Portia–Master Lewis Hallam (first appearance on any stage); Nerissa–Miss Palmer; Jessica–Miss Hallam; Portia–Mrs. Hallam.
The Anatomist* (Edward Ravenscroft, 1696).

Monsieur le Medicin–Rigby; Beatrice–Mrs. Adcock.
Hallam Company.
   [This is the first performance of the Hallam Company from London. Prices for the theatre were as follows: box, 7s. 6d.; pit, 5s. 9d.; gallery, 3s. 9d. The occasional prologue spoken by Rigby marking the opening of the theatre appears in the *Virginia Gazette* (22 September 1752) and is reprinted by Ford (12–14) and Odell (1:53–54). Sources: *Virginia Gazette* (28 August 1752); playbill in the New York Public Library.]

2 October 1752   New Theatre, Annapolis
The Constant Couple.
The Lying Valet.
Annapolis Company.
   [Source: *Maryland Gazette* (28 September 1752).]

21 October 1752   New Theatre, Annapolis
Cato.
Miss in Her Teens.
Annapolis Company.
   [Benefit Eyanson. Prices: box, 10s.; pit 7s. 6d.; gallery, 5s. Source: *Maryland Gazette* (19 October 1752).]

26 October 1752   Chester Town, Maryland colony
The Beggar's Opera.
The Lying Valet.
Annapolis Company.
   [Source: *Maryland Gazette* (19 October 1752).]

9 November 1752   Second Williamsburg Theatre, Williamsburg
Othello.
Harlequin Collector.
Hallam Company.
   [This evening the Chief of the Cherokee nation and his family were

> entertained, at the theatre, with the play, (the tragedy of Othello) and a pantomime performance, which gave them great surprize, as did the fighting with naked swords on the stage, which occasioned the Empress to order some about her to go and prevent their killing one another ....

The next evening Lewis Hallam presented to the city, on the occasion of His majesty's birthday, a display of fireworks (see

New York Gazette & Weekly Post-Boy for 22 January 1753).
Source: *Maryland Gazette* (14 December 1752).]

1 December 1752   Second Williamsburg Theatre, Williamsburg
Actor assaulted.
Hallam Company.
[The *Pennsylvania Gazette* of 20 February 1753 reprints a notice from the *Virginia Gazette* of 8 December 1752 which reports that a servant of the company was surprised and assaulted in the playhouse:

> Williamsburg, December 8. Last Friday night about 11 o'clock, the play-house in this city was broke open by one white man and two Negroes, who violently assaulted and wounded Patrick Malony, servant to the company, by knocking him down, and throwing him upon the iron-spikes,[9] one of which run into his leg, by which he hung for a considerable time, till he was relieved by some Negroes: The villains that perpetrated this horrid fact escaped, but a reward is offered for apprehending them, and as the aforesaid Patrick Malony continues dangerously ill of his wounds, it is hoped they will be taken and brought to justice.]

11 December 1752 New Theatre, Annapolis
Richard III.
   Richard–Wynell; Richmond–Herbert (both from the theatre in Williamsburg).
Miss in Her Teens.
Annapolis ccompany.
   ["N.B. The house is intirely lined thoughout, fit for the reception of ladies and gentlemen; and they have also raised a porch at the door, that will keep out the inclemency of the weather." Source: *Maryland Gazette* (7 December 1752).]

13 December 1752 New Theatre, Annapolis
The Constant Couple.

---

[9] The use of spikes to separate seating areas in theatres was common during the colonial era, and they were quite dangerous, as expressed in the following Dublin news which appeared in the *Virginia Gazette* of 28 November 1771: "Letters from Dublin mention that a certain theatrical performer there, having some words with one of the carpenters on the stage during the time of rehearsal, suddenly knocked him over the orchestra, and the man falling upon the spikes, was so terribly wounded that he died soon after. The offender was secured and committed to jail."

Principal parts performed by Herbert, Kean, Wynell, and Miss Osborne
The Anatomist.
Annapolis Company.
   [Source: *Maryland Gazette* (7 December 1752).]

16 December 1752   New Theatre, Annapolis
Richard III.
   Richard–Wynell; Richmond–Herbert (both from the theatre in Williamsburg).
The Lying Valet.
Annapolis Company.
   [Benefit for the Talbot County charity school. Source: *Maryland Gazette* (14 December 1752).]

1753

Lewis Hallam's public letter published in the *New York Mercury* (see 2 July 1753) states that the company had "lately arrived [in New York] from Virginia ...[and] were there eleven months." On the basis of this letter it has been assumed that they played through the spring of 1753 in and around Williamsburg, for which the only evidence to support this inference is a single known performance on 20 June 1753. Durnam (11), following Rankin (58), takes Hallam at his word, that the company had in fact arrived in New York from Virginia. Indeed Durnam has the company "arriving about July 2" by coastal packet. Evidence of a more complex route, however, appears in other sources. Daly (12) claims that after Virginia the company traveled to Annapolis before they played in New York. Durang (iii), again relying on the memory of Lewis Hallam Jr., more specifically claims that after the Hallam company left Williamsburg they followed the route the Murray-Kean Company had taken the previous year: "after the Williamsburg season Hallam and his corps went to Annapolis .... There they performed all their stock plays with success and profit. They then visited all the other settlements of wealth in the Colony of Maryland, viz: Port Tobacco, Upper Marlborough, Piscataway, etc." Hallam, Jr.'s recollection concurs with the statement made by Hallam Sr. in a public letter of 2 July 1753 that the company had traveled to New York "by sea *and land* five hundred Miles" (emphasis added). If the Hallam Company in 1753 followed the Murray-Kean Company route from 1752, perhaps the season in Williamsburg was not as long (or as successful) as claimed in his 2 July 1753 letter.

Upon arrival in New York, the Hallam Company were obliged to rebuild the theatre in Nassau Street (see the *New York Gazette & Weekly Post-Boy* for 17 September 1753). Hornblow (91) claims that in New York the Hallam Company played three nights a week from 17 September 1753 until 18 March 1754 and had a repertory of 21 plays. Advertisements, unfortunately, announced plays only once in the week. While no cast list is available for the spring season, by September the company in New York consisted of the following known members: William Adcock, Mrs. Adcock, Mrs. Becceley, Charles Bell, Thomas Clarkson, Mrs. Clarkson, Mr. Lewis Hallam, Lewis Hallam Jr., Mrs. Hallam, Miss Hallam, Patrick Malone, Mr. Miller, William Rigby, Mrs. Rigby, and John Singleton.

The Carribean area provides some information during this year. Slight evidence exists for a company playing in Barbados, as revealed in a newspaper entry of 21 May 1753; and Hill (21–23) offers a Jamaican indenture dated 4 May 1753 which lists "the Old Playhouse in Harbour street."

✳✳✳

21 May 1753   Barbados
Newspaper notice.
   [The *Barbados Gazette* of 30 May 1753 contains the following item: "Lost, out of the holster of a saddle, on Monday night last, at the Playhouse, a silver mounted pistol."]

2 July 1753   New York
Newspaper notice.
Hallam Company.
   [The following letter appears in the *New York Mercury* of this date:

> The case of the London company of comedians, lately arrived from Virginia, humbly submitted to the consideration of the publick; whose servants they are, and whose protection they intreat. As our expedition to New-York seems likely to be attended with a very fatal consequence, and ourselves haply censur'd for undertaking it, without assurance of success; we beg leave, humbly to lay a true state of our case before the worthy inhabitants of this city; if possible endeavour to remove those great Obstacles which at present lie before us, and great very sufficient Reasons for our Appearance in this Part of the World, where we all had

the most sanguine Hopes of meeting a very different Reception; little imagining, that in a city, to all appearance so polite as this, the muses would be banish'd, the works of the immortal Shakespear, and other the greatest geniuses England ever produc'd, deny'd admittance among them, and the instructive and elegant entertainment of the stage utterly protested against; When, without Boasting, we may venture to affirm, that we are capable of supporting its Dignity with proper Decorum and Regularity .... In the infancy of this scheme, it was proposed to Mr. William Hallam, now of London to collect a company of comedians, and send them to New-York, and the other colonies of America. Accordingly he assented, and was at vast Expense to procure Scenes, Cloaths, People, &c. &c. In October 1750 [recte 1751?], sent over to this Place, Mr. Robert Upton, in order to obtain Permission to perform, erect a Building, and settle every Thing against our Arrival; for which Service, Mr. Hallam advanc'd no inconsiderable Sum. But Mr. Upton, on his Arrival, found here that Sett of Pretenders, with whom he join'd, and unhappily for us, quite neglected the Business he was sent about from England; for we never heard from him after. Being thus deceiv'd by him, the Company was at Stand, till April 1752, when by the Persuasion of several Gentlemen in London, and Virginia Captains, we set sail on Board of Mr. William Lee, and arrived after a very expensive and tiresome Voyage, at York River, on the 28th of June following: Where we obtain'd Leave of his Excellency the Governor, and perform'd with universal Applause, and met with the greatest Encouragement; for which we are bound by the strongest Obligations, to acknowledge the many and repeated Instances of their Spirit and Generosity. We were there eleven months before we thought of removing; and then asking advice, we were again persuaded to come to New-York, by several gentlemen, &c. whose names we can mention, but do not think proper to publish: They told us, that we should not fail of a genteel and favourable reception; that the inhabitants were generous and polite, naturally fond of diversions rational, particularly those of the theatre: Nay, they even told us, there was a very fine play-house building, and that we were really expected. This was Encouragement sufficient for us, as we thought, and came firmly assured of Success; but how far our Expectations are answered, we shall leave to the Candid to determine, and only beg Leave to add, That as we are a People of no Estates, it cannot be supposed that we have a Fund sufficient to bear up against such unexpected Repulses. A Journey by sea and land five hundred Miles is not undertaken without Money. Therefore, if the worthy magistrates would consider this in our favour, that it must rather turn out a publick advantage and pleasure, than a private injury; They would, we make no doubt, grant permission, and give us an opportunity to convince them, we were not cast in the same mould with our theatrical predecessors; or that in private life or publick occupation, we have the least affinity to them.]

12 July 1753   Philadelphia
Newspaper item.
Hallam company.

[The *Pennsylvania Gazette* of this date records that William Hallam has booked passage for London.]

17 July 1753   New York
Correspondence.
Hallam Company.
[Young (1:13) prints the following contemporary letter:

> We are to have the diversions of the Stage the Season. There are Several actors from some part of Europe who after much Solissitation [sic] have at last obtained leave of his Excellency to perform. They talk of building a house for that purpose and have offered themselves to Subscribe £100 for the Encouragement of it. This is a Melancholy Story among considerate persons that so Small aplace [sic] as this Should Encourage the toleration of such publick diversions. People are dayly murmuring at the badness of the times as tho' they were actually concerned for their Interest but their conduct proves a contradiction [sic] to it. For men in every Profession are ever fond of some party of pleasure or other and as if they had not room enough to Spend their money that way they must for all put themselves under greater temptations in going to the play house. This I speak with regard to those who are Scarcely above want. These sort of people are the most fond of it which makes the Toleration of Publick Diversions the greater Nuisance to a Place Especially as it Contains So few Inhabitants.

Source: Mathew Clarkson to "Dear John," New York Historical Society, quoted in Young 1:13.]

17 September 1753   Second Nassau St. Theatre, New York
Newspaper notice.
Hallam Company.
[The *New York Gazette & Weekly Post-Boy* of this date contains the following notice concerning the Hallam Company:

> The Company of Comedians who arrived here the past Summer, having obtained Permission from the Proper Authority to Act, have built a very fine, large and commodious New Theatre in the place where the old One stood, and having got it in good order design to begin this Evening. As they propose to tarry here but a short Time, we hear they design to perform three Times a Week.]

17 September 1753   Second Nassau St.Theatre, New York
The Conscious Lovers* (Richard Steele, 1722).
    Young Bevil–Rigby; Sealand–Malone; Sr. John Bevil–Bell; Myrtle–Clarkson; Cimberton–Miller; Humphrey–Adcock; Daniel–Master L. Hallam; Tom–Singleton; Phyllis–Mrs. Becceley; Mrs. Sealand–Mrs. Clarkson; Lucinda–Miss Hallam; Isabella–Mrs. Rigby; Indiana–Mrs. Hallam.

Damon and Phillida ? (See below.)
   Arcas–Bell; Orgon–Rigby; Corydon–Clarkson; Cymon–Miller; Damon–Adcock; Phillida–Mrs. Becceley.
Hallam Company.

[The afterpiece and cast, which are not advertised, are suggested by Dunlap (24). To begin at 6 o'clock. Prices: Box–8s.; Pit–6s.; Gallery–3s. Source: *New York Mercury* (17 September 1753).]

19 September 1753   Second Nassau St. Theatre, New York
The Conscious Lovers.
Hallam Company.

[Odell reprints a fine letter written by Philip Schuyler of 21 September 1753 to a relative in Albany evidencing actual performance practices and details of this production:

> The schooner arrived at Ten Eyck's wharf on Wednesday, at one o'clock, and the same evening I went to the play with Phil. You know I told you before I left home that if the players should be here I should see them, for a player is a new thing under the sun in our good province. Phil's sweetheart went with us. She is a handsome brunette from Barbadoes, has an eye like that of a Mohawk beauty, and appears to possess a good understanding. Phil and I went to see the grand battery in the afternoon, and to pay our respects to the governor, whose lady spent a week with us last spring, and we bought our play tickets for eight shillings apiece, at Parker and Weyman's printing-office, in Beaver Street, on our return. We had tea at five o'clock, and before sundown we were in the Theatre, for the players commenced at six. The room was quite full already. Among the company were your cousin Tom and Kitty Livingston, and also Jack Watts, Sir Peter Warren's brother-in-law. I would like to tell you about the play, but I can't now for Billy must take this to the wharf for Captain Wynkoop in half an hour. He sails this afternoon.
>
> A large green curtain hung before the players until they were ready to begin, when, on the blast of a whistle, it was raised, and some of them appeared and commenced acting. The play was called The Conscious Lovers, written you know, by Sir Richard Steele, Addison's help in writing the Spectator. Hallam, and his wife and sister, all performed, and a sprightly young man named Hulett played the violin and danced merrily. But I said I could not tell you about the play, so I will forbear, only adding that I was no better pleased than I should have been at the club, where, last year, I went with cousin Stephen, and heard many wise sayings which I hope profited me something.

Source: Odell 1:58–59.]

24 September 1753   Second Nassau St. Theatre, New York
Tunbridge Walks.

Woodcock–Malone; Reynard–Rigby; Loveworth–Miller; Captain Squibb–Hallam; Maiden–Singleton; Hilaria–Mrs. Hallam; Belinda–Mrs. Becceley; Mrs. Goodfellow–Mrs. Rigby; Penelope–Mrs. Clarkson; Lucy–Miss Hallam.
Hallam Company.
[Source: *New York Gazette & Weekly Post-Boy* (24 September 1753).]

1 October 1753   Second Nassau St. Theatre, New York
The Constant Couple.
Sir Harry Wildair–Singleton; Col. Standard–Rigby; Vizard–Miller; Smuggler–Malone; Clincher Sr.–Hallam; Clincher Jr.–Clarkson; Dicky–L. Hallam; Errand–Bell; Constable–Adcock; Lady Lurewell–Mrs. Hallam; Lady Darling–Mrs. Rigby; Angelica–Mrs. Becceley; Parley–Miss Hallam; Porter's wife–Mrs. Clarkson.
The Anatomist.
M. le Medicin–Rigby; Old Gerald–Clarkson; Young Gerald–Adcock; Crispin–Hallam; Martic–Bell; Beatrice–Mrs. Hallam; Doctor's wife–Mrs. Rigby; Angelica–Mrs. Clarkson; Waiting maid–Miss Hallam.
Hallam Company.
[Source: *New York Mercury* (1 October 1753).]

8 October 1753   Second Nassau St. Theatre, New York
The Conscious Lovers.
As 17 September 1753.
The Virgin Unmasked.
Goodwill–Clarkson; Blister–Malone; Coupée–Singleton; Quaver–Adcock; Wormwood–Miller; Thomas–Bell; Lucy–Miss Hallam.
Hallam Company.
[Prices: box, 6s.; pit, 5s.; gallery, 3s. "The company intend to play on Mondays, Wednesdays, and Fridays." Source: *New York Gazette & Weekly Post-Boy* (8 October 1753).]

22 October 1753   Second Nassau St. Theatre, New York
Love for Love.
Sir Sampson–Malone; Valentine–Rigby; Scandal–Bell; Tattle–Singleton; Ben–Hallam; Foresight–Clarkson; Jeremy–Miller; Angelica–Mrs. Hallam; Mrs. Foresight–Mrs. Rigby; Mrs. Frail–Mrs. Adcock; Miss Prue–Miss Hallam; Nurse–Adcock.
Tom Thumb* (Henry Fielding, 1730).

Tom Thumb–Master A. Hallam; King Arthur–Singleton; Lord Grizzle–Rigby; Noodle–Miller; Doodle–Bell; Bailiff–Clarkson; Follower–Malone; Queen Dollalolla–Hallam; Huncamunca–Adcock; Cleora–Miss Hallam.
Hallam Company.
[Source: *New York Mercury* (22 October 1753).]

29 October 1753   Second Nassau St. Theatre, New York
The London Merchant.
Thorowgood–Malone; Uncle–Adcock; Barnwell–Bell; Trueman–Rigby; Blunt–Miller; Maria–Mrs. Becceley; Millwood–Mrs. Hallam; Lucy–Mrs. Adcock.
The Lying Valet.
Sharp–Singleton; Gayless–Adcock; Justice Guttle–Malone; Beau Trippet–Bell; Dick–Miller; Melissa–Mrs. Adcock; Kitty–Miss Hallam; Mrs. Gadabout–Mrs. Rigby; Mrs. Trippet–Mrs. Clarkson.
Hallam Company.
[Source: *New York Mercury* (29 October 1753).]

5 November 1753   Second Nassau St. Theatre, New York
The Distrest Mother.
Pyrrhus–Singleton; Orestes–Rigby; Pylades–Bell; Phoenix–Clarkson; Cleone–Miss Hallam; Cephisa–Mrs. Rigby; Andromache–Mrs. Hallam; Hermione–Mrs. Adcock.
Flora, or Hob in the Well.
Hob–Hallam; Sir Thomas–Clarkson; Friendly–Adcock; Dick–Master Lewis Hallam; Old Hob–Miller; Flora–Mrs. Becceley; Betty–Miss Hallam; Hob's mother–Mrs. Clarkson.
Hallam Company.
[Prices: box, 6s.; pit, 4s.; gallery, 2s. Source: *New York Mercury* (5 November 1753).]

12 November 1753   Second Nassau St. Theatre, New York
Richard III.
Richard–Rigby; King Henry–Hallam; Prince Edward–Master L. Hallam; Duke of York–Master A. Hallam; Richmond–Clarkson; Buckingham–Malone; Norfolk–Miller; Stanley–Singleton; Lieu-tenant–Bell; Catesby–Adcock; Queen Elizabeth–Mrs. Hallam; Lady Anne–Mrs. Adcock; Duchess of York–Mrs. Rigby.
The Devil to Pay.
Sir John–Adcock; Jobson–Malone; Butler–Miller; Footman–Singelton; Cook–Bell; Coachman–Rigby; Conjurer–

Clarkson; Lady Loverule–Mrs. Adcock; Nell–Mrs. Becceley; Lettice–Mrs. Clarkson; Lucy–Mrs. Love.
Hallam Company.
[Box 6s.; pit 4s.; gallery 2s. Source: playbill in the Harvard Theatre Collection, reproduced in Odell (opp. 1:68); *New York Mercury* (12 November 1753).]

19 November 1753   Second Nassau St. Theatre, New York
The Beggar's Opera.
Peachum–Hallam; Lockit–Malone; Macheath–Adcock; Filch–Miller; Mat of the Mint–Bell; Wat–Singleton; Ned–Hulett; Mrs. Peachum–Mrs. Adcock; Polly–Mrs. Becceley; Lucy–Mrs. Clarkson; Mrs. Coaxer–Miss Hallam; Diana Trapes–Mrs. Adcock; Mrs Vixen–Mrs. Rigby; Jenny Diver–Mrs. Love; Moll Brazen–Clarkson.
The Lying Valet.
Hallam Company.
[Source: *New York Gazette & Weekly Post-Boy* (19 November 1753).]

26 November 1753   Second Nassau St. Theatre, New York
The Committee.
Careless–Singleton; Blunt–Bell; Day–Malone; Abel–Clarkson; Obadiah–Miller; Teague–Hallam; Bailiff–Adcock; Bookseller–Hulett; Arabella–Mrs. Becceley; Mrs. Day–Mrs. Adcock; Ruth–Mrs. Hallam; Mrs. Chat–Mrs. Clarkson.
The Anatomist.
As 1 October 1753, but Beatrice–Mrs. Adcock.
Hallam Company.
[Source: *New York Mercury* (26 November 1753).]

30 November 1753   Second Nassau St. Theatre, New York
The Spanish Friar.
Father Dominic–Hallam; Torismond–Rigby; Bertran–Miller; Alphonso–Bell; Lorenzo–Singleton; Raymond–Clarkson; Pedro–Adcock; Gomez–Malone; Leonora–Mrs. Becceley; Teresa–Miss Hallam; Elvira–Mrs. Hallam.
The Stage Coach.
Hallam Company.
[Source: playbill in the Long Island Historical Society.]

3 December 1753   Second Nassau St. Theatre, New York
The Careless Husband* (Colley Cibber, 1704).

Sir Charles–Miller; Foppington–Singleton; Morelove–Rigby; Lady Betty–Mrs. Hallam; Lady Easy–Mrs. Adcock; Lady Graveairs–Mrs. Becceley; Edging–Miss Hallam.

Lethe.
Aesop–Clarkson; Charon–Bell; Mercury–Adcock; Old Man–Malone; Fine Gentleman–Singleton; Tattoo–Miller; Frenchman–Miller; Drunken Man–Hallam; Fine Lady–Mrs. Becceley; Mrs. Tattoo–Mrs. Adcock.

Hallam Company.

[Source: *New York Gazette & Weekly Post-Boy* (3 December 1753).]

10 December 1753   Second Nassau St. Theatre, New York
The Beaux' Stratagem.
Aimwell–Adcock; Archer–Singleton; Freeman–Bell; Sullen–Rigby; Foigard–Hallam; Boniface–Miller; Gibbet–Clarkson; Scrub–Malone; Mrs. Sullen–Mrs. Hallam; Dorinda–Mrs. Becceley; Lady Bountiful–Mrs. Rigby; Cherry–Miss Hallam; Gipsy–Mrs. Clarkson.

Harlequin Collector; or, The Miller Deceived* (Anonymous).
Harlequin–Miller; Clown–Hallam; Miller–Singleton; Columbine–Mrs. Hallam; unspecified–Adcock; Mrs. Adcock; Mrs. Rigby; Miss Hallam.

Hallam Company.

[Source: *New York Mercury* (10 December 1753).]

17 December 1753   Second Nassau St. Theatre, New York
The Fair Penitent.
Sciolto–Malone; Altamont–Clarkson; Horatio–Rigby; Lothario–Singleton; Rossano–Adcock; Calista–Mrs. Hallam; Lavinia–Mrs. Adcock; Lucilla–Mrs. Rigby.

Lover's Quarrel (Att. Thomas King).
Carlos–Bell; Sancho–Hallam; Leonora–Mrs. Becceley; Jacinta–Mrs. Adcock.

Hallam Company.

[Source: *New York Mercury* (17 December 1753).]

20 December 1753 Second Nassau St. Theatre, New York
Love for Love.
As 22 October 1753, except Buckram–Adcock; Nurse–Mrs. Clarkson.

Flora, or Hob in the Well.
As 5 November 1753.

Hallam Company.

[Benefit for the poor. The "last Time of performing till the Holidays." Source: playbill in the Harvard Theatre Collection.]

26 December 1753 Second Nassau St. Theatre, New York
The Twin Rivals.
   Elder Wou'd Be–Rigby; Younger Wou'd Be–Clarkson; Richmore–Bell; Trueman–Singleton; Subtleman–Miller; Balderdash & Alder-man–Malone; Clearaccount–Adcock; Teague–Hallam; Frisure–Master L. Hallam; Constance–Mrs. Hallam; Aurelia–Mrs. Becceley; Mrs. Midnight–Mrs. Adcock; Mrs. Clearaccount–Mrs. Rigby; Maid–Mrs. Clarkson.
Damon and Phillida.
   As 17 September 1753.
Hallam Company.
   [Source: *New York Gazette & Weekly Post Boy* (24 December 1753).]

27 December 1753   Second Nassau St. Theatre, New York
The Conscious Lovers.
Hallam Company.
   [A special performance for the Masons. Epilogue spoken by Mrs. Hallam. Not recorded in Odell. Source: *New York Gazette & Weekly Post Boy* (31 December 1753).]

1754

Further evidence of a company touring the West Indies comes from Jamaica. Errol Hill (21–23) offers two references to this company. Following Wright (41) he reprints a segment of the tax rolls of Kingston from 1754 listing the Comedians as "tenants of the King's Store in Harbour Street for which they paid £120 a year in rent," and notes a production advertisement for 1 July of 1754, "at the New Theatre in Harbour Street."

The Hallam Company continued in New York through the winter 1753–54 (as noted in the head note to the season of 1753). The company is known to have included the following performers: Mr. Adcock, Mrs. Adcock, Charles Bell, Mrs. Becceley, Mr. Clarkson, Mrs. Clarkson, Adam Hallam, Miss Helen Hallam, Lewis Hallam, Jr., Mrs. Hallam, Lewis Hallam, Sr., Mr. Hulett, Mr. Love, Mrs. Love, Patrick Malone, [Mrs. Malone?], Mr. Miller, Mr. Rigby, Mrs. Rigby, and John Singleton. When company departed southward in April,

Charles Love and Mrs. Love remained in New York and opened a music school.

Sometime after January 14, Patrick Malone was dispatched to Philadelphia as an advance agent of the company to secure permission to play in that city. After negotiations, petitions and counter-petitions, the company was granted permission for a short season of twenty-four performances with several provisos: (1) that nothing indecent or immoral be performed; (2) that one night's benefit be donated to the poor; and (3) that the management should give bonds for the payment of all debts and contracts entered into by the company. The company opened in Philadelphia 15 April 1754 and performed three nights a week in a season that was later extended into June, though of the 24 possible performances, only six are documented. At the conclusion of the season William Hallam visited the company from London and sold his shares of the organization to his brother and withdrew—at least temporarily (see headnote for 1758)—from the business. The "New Theatre" is actually a remodeled version of Plumsted's Warehouse.[10]

The Hallam Company's whereabouts for summer 1754 are unknown. Pollock (13) errs when he claims the company left for the West Indies after their Philadelphia season. The company next traveled to Charleston, South Carolina colony, where they apparently built a new theatre and were playing by 7 October and continued into 1755. The company consisted of the following known members: Mr. Adcock, Mrs. Adcock, Charles Bell, Mrs. Becceley, Mr. Clarkson, Mrs. Clarkson, Lewis Hallam, Mrs. Hallam, Lewis Hallam Jr., Miss Helen Hallam, Mr. Hulett, Mrs. Love, Mr. Patrick Malone, Mr. Miller, Mr. Rigby, Mrs. Rigby, and Mr. John Singleton.

This year also yields the first evidence of students at Yale College initiating what was a continuing though illegal theatrical tradition extending through 1773.

✳✳✳

7 January 1754   Second Nassau St. Theatre, New York
The Drummer.

---

[10] An image of this venue is reproduced in Young 6.

Sir George–Bell; Tinsel–Miller; Fantome–Adcock; Vellum–Malone; the Butler–Clarkson; the Coachman–Singleton; the Gardener–Hallam; Lady Trueman–Mrs. Becceley; Abigail–Mrs. Adcock.
Lethe.
   As 3 December 1753.
Hallam Company.
   [Source: *New York Gazette & Weekly Post-Boy* (7 January 1754).]

14 January 1754   Second Nassau St. Theatre, New York
King Lear* (William Shakespeare; adap. by Nahum Tate, 1681).
   Lear–Malone; Gloster–Bell; Kent–Hallam; Edgar–Singleton; Bastard–Clarkson; Cornwall–Miller; Albany–Adcock; Burgundy–Hulett; Usher–Rigby; Attendant–Master L. Hallam; Page–Master A. Hallam; Goneril–Mrs. Becceley; Regan–Mrs. Adcock; Cordelia–Mrs. Hallam; Aranthe–Mrs. Rigby.
Damon and Phillida.
   As 17 September 1753.
Hallam Company.
   [Source: *New York Gazette & Weekly Post-Boy* (14 January 1754).]

21 January 1754   Second Nassau St. Theatre, New York
Woman is a Riddle* (Christopher Bullock, 1716).
   Manly–Bell; Courtwell–Singleton; Vainwit–Hallam; Vulture–Rigby; Aspin–Miller; Butler–Adcock; Lady Outside–Mrs. Hallam; Miranda–Mrs. Adcock; Clarinda–Mrs. Clarkson; Betty–Mrs. Rigby; Necessary–Miss Hallam.
The Devil to Pay.
   As 12 November 1753.
Hallam Company.
   [Source: *New York Gazette & Weekly Post-Boy* (21 January 1754).]

28 January 1754   Second Nassau St. Theatre, New York
Romeo and Juliet.
   Romeo–Rigby; Paris–Adcock; Montague–Hallam; Capulet–Bell; Mercutio–Singleton; Tybalt–Malone; Friar–Clarkson; Balthazar–Master L. Hallam; Benvolio–Miller; Juliet–Mrs. Hallam; Lady Capulet–Mrs. Rigby; Nurse–Mrs. Adcock.
The Anatomist.
   As 26 November 1753.
Hallam Company.

[Benefit Clarkson. Odell (1:66) suggests that this is David Garrick's version of *Romeo and Juliet*. Source: *New York Gazette & Weekly Post-Boy* (28 January 1754).]

4 February 1754   Second Nassau St. Theatre, New York
The Gamester* (Edward Moore and David Garrick, 1753).
   Beverley–Rigby; Lewson–Miller; Stukely–Singleton; Jarvis–Hallam; Bates–Bell; Dawson–Clarkson; Waiter–Adcock; Mrs. Beverley–Mrs. Hallam; Charlotte–Mrs. Becceley; Lucy–Mrs. Clarkson.
Lethe.
   As 3 December 1753.
Hallam Company.
   [Benefit Rigby. Source: *New York Gazette & Weekly Post-Boy* (4 February 1754); playbill in the Harvard Theatre Collection.]

11 February 1754   Second Nassau St. Theatre, New York
The Earl of Essex* (Henry Jones, 1753).
   Essex–Rigby; Southampton–Bell; Burleigh–Singleton; Raleigh–Miller; Lieutenant–Adcock; Queen Elizabeth–Mrs. Adcock; Countess of Rutland–Mrs. Hallam; Countess of Nottingham–Mrs. Becceley.
The King and the Miller of Mansfield.
   King–Singleton; Miller–Hallam; Dick–Bell; Lurewell–Clarkson; Keepers–Miller and Adcock; Courtiers–Rigby and Hulett; Peggy–Mrs. Clarkson; Phebe–Mrs. Rigby; Margery–Mrs. Adcock; Kate–Miss Hallam.
Hallam Company.
   [Benefit Mrs. Becceley. Source: *New York Gazette & Weekly Post-Boy* (11 February 1754).]

18 February 1754   Second Nassau St. Theatre, New York
The Suspicious Husband* (Benjamin Hoadly, 1747).
   Strictland–Rigby; Frankly–Singleton; Bellamy–Bell; Ranger–Miller; Meggot–Clarkson; Tester–Master L. Hallam; Simon–Hulett; Buckle–Adcock; Mrs. Strictland–Mrs. Becceley; Clarinda–Mrs. Hallam; Jacintha–Mrs. Adcock; Lucetta–Miss Hallam; Landlady–Mrs. Rigby; Milliner–Mrs. Clarkson; Maid–Mrs. Love.
Harlequin Skeleton, or, The Miller Deceived* (Anonymous).
Hallam Company.
   [Benefit Miller. Prices: box, 6s.; pit, 4s.; gallery, 2s. Source: *New York Mercury* (18 February 1754).]

25 February 1754   Second Nassau St. Theatre, New York
The Albion Queens* (John Banks; adap. by Jo Haines?, 1704).
   Norfolk–Singleton; Morton–Miller; Cecil–Bell; Gifford–Clarkson; Page–Master L. Hallam; Queen Elizabeth–Mrs. Adcock; Mary, Queen of Scots–Mrs. Hallam.
The Virgin Unmasked.
Hallam Company.
   [Benefit Mrs. Hallam. Source: *New York Mercury* (25 February 1754).]

4 March 1754   Second Nassau St. Theatre, New York
Jane Shore* (Nicholas Rowe, 1714).
   Gloster–Hallam; Dumont–Singleton; Hastings–Rigby; Ratcliff–Miller; Belmour–Bell; Catesby–Adcock; Jane Shore–Mrs. Hallam; Alicia–Mrs. Adcock.
Harlequin Skeleton.
   Harlequin–Rigby.
Hallam Company.
   [Benefit Mrs. Rigby. Source: *New York Mercury* (4 March 1754).]

11 March 1754   Second Nassau St. Theatre, New York
Romeo and Juliet.
   As 28 January, but Benvolio and Friar John–Miller; Tybalt and Friar Lawrence–Clarkson.
The Stage Coach.
   Macahone–Hallam; Sir Nicodemus–Miller; Basil–Bell; Michar–Clarkson; Fetch–Rigby; Jolt–Adcock; Landlord–Singleton; Isabella–Mrs. Clarkson; Dolly–Miss Hallam.
Hallam Company.
   [Benefit Miss Hallam and her brothers. Source: *New York Gazette & Weekly Post-Boy* (11 March 1754).

18 March 1754   Second Nassau St. Theatre, New York
The Beggar's Opera.
   As 19 November 1753, but Filch–Hulett; Mimming Ned–Singleton; Walt Dreary–Rigby.
The Devil to Pay.
Hallam Company.
   [Benefit Mr. and Mrs. Love. Source: *New York Gazette & Weekly Post-Boy* (18 March 1754).]

25 March 1754   Second Nassau St. Theatre, New York
The Gamester.
Hallam Company.

[The program is advertised as including "a new Harlequin entertainment." "Lewis Hallam, Comedian, intending for Philadelphia, begs the favour of those that has [sic] any demands upon him, to bring in their accounts, and receive their money." Source: *New York Gazette & Weekly Post-Boy* (25 March 1754).]

26 March 1754   Philadelphia
Permission to perform.
Hallam Company.

[The *Pennsylvania Gazette* of this date contains the following notice: "And indeed I have heard, that one express condition of the permission lately granted for the acting a few plays here, is, that nothing indecent, nothing even in its tendency immoral, shall be exhibited." The Hallam Company secured from Governor Hamilton permission to open a theatre and cause 24 plays with their attendant afterpieces to be performed (Pollock 8, following Dunlap 15–17). This short season was later extended for six additional nights by Governor Hamilton (Pollock 9).]

15 April 1754   New Theatre in Water St., Philadelphia
The Fair Penitent.
   As 17 December 1753, but Servant–Master L. Hallam.
Miss in Her Teens.
   Fribble–Singleton; Flash–Clarkson; Jasper–Rigby; Loveit–Adcock; Puff–Miller; Tagg–Adcock; Biddy–Miss Hallam.
Hallam Company.

[This is the Hallam Company's first appearance in Philadelphia. The Prologue (spoken by Rigby) and Epilogue (spoken by Mrs. Hallam) appear in the *Pennsylvania Gazette* of 25 April 1754. Source: *Pennsylvania Gazette* (11 April 1754).]

April-May 1754   Philadelphia
Theatrical activity.
Hallam Company.

[The Account Book of the Philadelphia printers Franklin and Hall records the publication of thirteen different playbills printed between 12 April and 27 May 1754. Source: Wolf 99.]

27 May 1754   New Theatre in Water St., Philadelphia
Tunbridge Walks.
   As 24 September 1753.
The Country Wake, or, Hob in the Well.
   As 5 November 1753.

Hallam Company.
[Benefit Lewis Hallam. Source: playbill in the Historical Society of Pennsylvania.]

10 June 1754   New Theatre in Water St., Philadelphia
The Gamester.
Beverly–Rigby; Lewson–Miller; Jervis–Hallam; Bates–Bell; Dawson–Clarkson; Waiter–Master L. Hallam; Stukely–Singleton; Charlotte–Mrs. Becceley; Lucy–Mrs. Clarkson; Mrs. Beverly–Mrs. Hallam.
Miss in Her Teens.
Fribble–Singleton; Flash–Clarkson; Biddy–Miss Hallam.
Hallam Company.
[Prices: boxes 6s., pit 4s., gallery 2s. 6d. Benefit Miss Hallam and her two brothers. Governor Hamilton granted the company six additional performances. Source: *Pennsylvania Gazette* (6 June 1754); playbill in the Historical Society of Pennsylvania.]

12 June 1754   New Theatre in Water St., Philadelphia
Tamerlane* (Nicholas Rowe, 1701).
Tamerlane–Singleton; Axalla–Bell; Stratocles–Miller; Omar–Clarkson; Haly–Master L. Hallam; Moneses–Rigby; Prince of Tanais–Adcock; Bajazet–Malone; Dervise–Hallam; Arpasia–Mrs. Hallam; Selima–Mrs. Becceley.
A Wife Well Managed* (Susannah Centlivre, 1715).
Hallam Company.
[Benefit Adcock. Source: *Pennsylvania Gazette* (6 June 1754).]

19 June 1754   New Theatre in Water St., Philadelphia
The Careless Husband.
Harlequin Collector.
Hallam Company.
[Originally announced for 17 June but postponed. Nearly £100 was raised for the benefit of the Charity School of Philadelphia. "Charity Prologue" as it appeared in the *Pennsylvania Gazette* of 20 June 1754 is reprinted in Seilhamer 1:70–71. Source: *Pennsylvania Gazette* (13 and 20 June 1754).]

24 June 1754   New Theatre in Water St., Philadelphia
The Provoked Husband.
Miss in Her Teens.
Hallam Company.

[Last night of the season. The "Farewell Epilogue," which appeared in the *Pennsylvania Gazette* of 27 June 1754, is reprinted in Seilhamer 1: 72–73; a parody of the epilogue is also reprinted by Seilhamer 1:73–74. Source: *Pennsylvania Gazette* (27 June 1754).]

1 July of 1754   The New Theatre in Harbour Street, Kingston, Jamaica
The Orphan.
Tom Thumb the Great.
West Indian Company.
[Benefit for Master Marsh. Source: *Jamaican Courant* 22–29 June 1754.]

September 1754   Princeton College, New Jersey
Tamerlane.
Students of Princeton College.
[Ezra Stiles reported that during a visit to the "College at Newark, New Jersey" (i.e., Princeton) he "went to prayers, after which 2 young gentlemen of the college acted Tambourlane and Bajazet &c." Source: Stiles, "Extracts," 7:340.]

7 October 1754   New Theatre, Charleston
The Fair Penitent.
Hallam Company.
[The location of this venue is not known. Rankin (72) suggests that a hurricane of 15 September 1752 had destroyed the original Queen St. Theatre. Prices: stage box, 50s; front and side boxes, 40s.; pit, 30s.; gallery, 20s. Source: *South Carolina Gazette* (3 October 1754).]

17 October 1754   New Theatre, Charleston
A Bold Stroke for a Wife.
The Mock Doctor.
Hallam Company.
[Willis (39) dates this performance as 13 October 1754. Source: *South Carolina Gazette* (10 October 1754).]

24 October 1754   New Theatre, Charleston
The Orphan.
Hallam Company.
[Willis (39) dates this performance as 17 October 1754, while Curtis (429) claims it took place on 25 October. Source: *South Carolina Gazette* (17 October 1754).]

7 November 1754   New Theatre, Charleston
Cato.
Hallam Company.
   [Willis (41) dates this performance as 6 November 1754; Curtis (429) states that it was presented on 2 November. Source: *South Carolina Gazette* (31 October 1754).]

11 November 1754 New Theatre, Charleston
George Barnwell [i.e., *The London Merchant*].
Hallam Company.
   [Source: Manigault, "Extracts of the Journal," 59.]

13 November 1754 New Theatre, Charleston
The Recruiting Officer.
The King and the Miller of Mansfield.
Hallam Company.
   [The *South Carolina Gazette* for 7 November 1754 refers to 13 November as "Thursday," but in 1754 13 November fell on a Wednesday. It is possible that all of the performance dates for October and November 1754 are incorrect. Source: *South Carolina Gazette* (7 November 1754).]

25 November 1754 New Theatre, Charleston
The London Merchant [i.e., *The London Merchant*].
Hallam Company.
   [Source: Willis 40, 41; Manigault, "Extracts of the Journal," 59.]

1 December 1754   New Theatre, Charleston
Play not identified.
Hallam Company.
   ["Went to the play." Source: Manigault, "Extracts of the Journal," 59.]

27 December 1754   New Theatre, Charleston
The Distressed Mother.
Hallam Company.
   ["Went to the Play." Source: Willis 41; Manigault, "Extracts of the Journal," 59.]

December 1754–January 1755   Amity, Connecticut colony
Play unidentified.
Yale students.
   [Bloom (8) provides evidence from 2 July 1755 that the students of Yale performed a play about seven months earlier:

Whereas it appears that sometime last winter, Stoddard 2, Strong 2, Lyman 1, Clark, Martin, Noble 2, Smith 1, Reaves, and Wright went up to Amity, and there publicly acted a play–which is contrary to the express orders of the President heretofore several times given .... It is therefore considered by the President with the advice of the Tutors, that the said Lyman, Martin, Clark, Noble, Reaves and Wright to be fined 20'/Old Tenr each .... And whereas the said Strong voluntarily came before the president and Tutors and said that upon consideration he was sensible it was wrong, it is thereon considered that said Strong shall be fined 10 /only. And whereas in order to act this play, said Stoddard and Smith dressed themselves in women's apparel which is contrary to the Laws of God, the Laws of this colony as well as the Laws of this college, it is thereupon considered that the said Stoddard and Smith be publickly admonished.]

1755

The Hallam Company opened the year in Charleston, though records are scanty. Quinn (1:12–13) claims that sometime in the year, part or all of the company traveled to Jamaica, remaining there until 1758. Apart from the Hallams, none of the names of the company appears in Jamaica, nor do we hear from them on the continent. The Adcocks, the Clarksons, the Rigbys, Miller, all disappear from the record, though Patrick Malone does resurface during the 1767 season. Lewis Hallam, Sr. died in Jamaica in 1756. When the Douglass Company appeared in New York in 1758, the *New York Mercury* of 16 October 1758 remarked, "some part of [the company] ... were here in the year 1753."

A company continued to perform in Barbados, Jamaica, and the West Indies. Wright (39) offers the following names as (presumably) still playing: David Douglass, Owen Morris, Mary Morris, William Daniels, Miss Hamilton, Mr. Kershaw, Mr. Smith, and Mrs. Smith. When David Douglass ventured to New York in 1758 he carried with him letters of recommendation from the Governor of the Danish West Indies, implying at some point prior to his arrival on the continent that his company played across the West Indian islands.

※※※

early January 1755 New Theatre, Charleston
Play unidentified.
Hallam Company.

[This performance is known because of a newspaper entry recording the presence of the Masons this evening. Source: *South Carolina Gazette* (9 January 1755); Cohen 94.]

7 January 1755   New Theatre, Charleston
Play not identified.
Hallam Company.
   ["I went to the play." Source: Manigault, "Extracts of the Journal," 59.]

27 January 1755   New Theatre, Charleston
Play unidentified.
Hallam Company.
   ["I went to the play." Source: Manigault, "Extracts of the Journal," 59; Willis (42).]

1756

William Daniels, actor and printer in Jamaica, dies. Charles Woodham, once of the Murray-Kean Company, succeeds Daniels as a printer in Jamaica, evidencing the island residency of both (Wright 33–34).

Given the paucity of evidence for this year, we offer a retrospective of theatrical activity in Jamaica during the Seven Years' War of 1755–1763. Edward Long was resident in Jamaica during the war and offers the following relevant detail concerning life on the island: "In the lower part of the town is a very pretty theatre, exceedingly well contrived and neatly furnished. Dramatical performances were exhibited here during the last war, at which time there was considerable quantity of prize money in circulation, but in time of peace, the town in not able or not disposed to support so costly an amusement" (*History of Jamaica* [London 1774], 2:117; quoted in Hill 25). As the company left in 1758, Long is referring here to the opening years of the conflict.

The students at Yale College provide the only entries for this year.

❋❋❋

16 January 1756   New Haven, Connecticut colony
Play unidentified.

Yale students.

[Bloom documents clandestine theatrical activity by students at Yale College (19).]

May 1756   Grosvenor's Tavern, Pomfret, Connecticut colony

Play unidentified.
Yale students.

[Bloom (26) documents clandestine theatrical activity by students at Yale College while on vacation, from the records of a meeting of 18 June 1756:

> whereas it has been oftentimes declared that the Actings of Plays by the students of this College is of very bad tendency to corrupt the morals of this seminary of Religion and learning and of mankind in general, and yet it appears that Craft, Chandler 2, Pain, Sabin Grosvenor, Sumner 2, Weld and Nide in May last publickly acted a Play at the Tavern in Pomfret before a great Number of Spectators, and gave previous Notice of it in the neighboring Towns, many days before.]

1757

In Jamaica Teresa Constantia Phillips served as Mistress of the Revels in Jamaica during 1757–58 (Wright 25–26), a position that clearly evidences ongoing theatrical activity.

Few records exist of theatrical activity this year. Students of the College of Philadelphia arranged four performances of one play. Odell (1:108) claims that *Alfred* was first performed in 1756 and repeated in early 1757.
In Albany, a garrison of bored British soldiers fitted up a playhouse and performed at least two plays, much to the annoyance of the local clergy (cf. Odell 1:104–5).

Durnam (12) claims that the Hallam-Douglass Company returned to New York and opened their season 28 December 1757, but this is clearly a misdate for 1758.

※※※

1757   Jamaica
Newspaper item.

[Ten years after the fact, the *New Hampshire Gazette* of 30 January 1767 contains an anecdote of the celebrated Teresa

Constantia Phillips, during her residence in Jamaica. Part of the accounts runs as follows: "In the year 1757, or 1758, she was appointed mistress of the revels in that island, which gave her power over players there, which entitled her to a place on the stage every time they played, and a benefit every season, by which she generally got 100 guineas."]

1757   Albany, New York colony
The Beaux' Stratagem.
The Recruiting Officer.
British army officers.

[Odell (1:105) quotes Mrs. Anne Grant's *Memoirs* (1808) as remarking that army officers stationed in Albany for their amusement fitted up a theatre and "preparations [were] made for the acting of a play .... The play [i.e., *The Beaux' Stratagem*] ... was acted in a barn, and pretty well attended...." The officers later also presented *The Recruiting Officer.* Phelps (16) situates this activity c. 1760.]

20 January 1757   College of Philadelphia, Pennsylvania colony
The Masque of Alfred the Great* (James Thomson, 1740 ; adap. by David Mallet, 1751).
Students of the College of Philadelphia.
Alfred–Mr. Duche Jr.
[The prologue for this performance appears in the *Pennsylvania Gazette* of this date. Source: *Pennsylvania Gazette* (20 January 1757).]

27 January 1757   College of Philadelphia, Pennsylvania colony
The Masque of Alfred.
Students of the College of Philadelphia.
Alfred–Mr. Duche Jr.
[Source: *Pennsylvania Gazette* (27 January 1757).]

3 February 1757   College of Philadelphia, Pennsylvania colony
The Masque of Alfred.
Students of the College of Philadelphia.
Alfred–Mr. Duche Jr.
[Source: *Pennsylvania Gazette* (3 February 1757).]

10 February 1757   College of Philadelphia, Pennsylvania colony

The Masque of Alfred.
Students of the College of Philadelphia.
   Alfred–Mr. Duche Jr.
   [Young ladies also appeared in the performance. Source: *Pennsylvania Gazette* (10 February 1757). A lengthy review by "J. Duche" and the prologue appear in the *New Hampshire Gazette* of 18 March 1757, a portion of which we here reprint:

> With Regard to the young Gentlemen who so lately entertained the Town with this Performance, the Applause they met with, from crouded and discerning Audiences, during the several Nights of its Representation, is the best proof of their Merit, as it will be their justest Praise and highest Encouragement ....
>
> The Kindness of the Gentlemen who politely obliged us with the instrumental Parts of the Music is to be acknowledged. As to the young Ladies, who were so great an Ornament to the whole Representation, by their performance of the vocal parts, the most grateful acknowledgments have been already made to them by some of those young favourites of the muses, on whom they conferred so great an obligation, and therefore such acknowledgments ought not to be separated from this account.
>
> All I shall say is, that as the engaging condescension of these ladies conferred an obligation on their friends, it did honour to their education. For to see a number of young proficients in music and oratory, capable of representing to advantage, in all the complexity of its parts, so difficult and beautiful a performance as that of Alfred, would be an honor to the taste and improvement of any country. And it must be doubly so to see these talents and improvements reserved for the most exalted subjects, and bestowed for none but the noblest purposes!

Additional commentary and another prologue appear in the *New Hampshire Gazette* of 25 March 1757.]

1758

After Lewis Hallam's demise in 1756, the widowed Mrs. Hallam inherited one-half of her deceased husband's shares in the company and then married David Douglass in Jamaica. The will of William Hallam indicates that in spite of selling his share of the American theatrical venture to his brother, Lewis, in 1754, by 1756, after Lewis Hallam's death, William is again part owner and probably part manager of a company playing in the West Indies (see Myers and Brodowski). Perhaps William Hallam inherited the other half of his brother's company shares and the stock scenery. We do know that William left London after 1756 to join the company and that he died in Tortola, West Indies, in August of 1758, where his will was witnessed by Lewis Hallam Jr. and John Harman, both actors in the Hallam Company (see August 1758). We offer that Douglass acquired by marriage the shares left to Lewis Hallam's widow and then purchased outright William Hallam's shares upon his death, thus becoming chief share holder and de facto manager. We also assume that the newly combined Hallam-Douglass Company was very active in the islands during this interim, though few records exist to document their performances.

Rankin (77) suggests that "near the middle of October" the reorganized Hallam-Douglass Company disembarked in New York. Durang (v) concurs that the company had been roving among the islands since their departure. We do not have cast lists for the brief New York season, but the following members named in playbills of spring 1759 are assumed to have traveled to New York from Jamaica: David Douglass, Mrs. Douglass, Lewis Hallam, Jr., Adam Hallam, Miss Helen Hallam, Catherine Harman, Mr. Horne, Mrs. Love, Owen Morris, Mary Morris, Mr. Reed, Mr. Tomlinson, and Mrs. Tomlinson.

Like the Lewis Hallam Company in 1753, the Douglass Company was initially denied permission to play in New York. Like Hallam, Douglass offered an open letter claiming hardship, airing their expenses, their adversity, etc. and requesting permission to play just so much as to defray their travel expenses out of the colony. After a lengthy dispute that involved opening a Histrionic Academy, and later an apology for the subterfuge, they were granted permission for a brief season (see 6 November and 11 December 1758).

There is—curiously—also a company of players at Fort Cumberland. Who this company is and what they are doing on the frontier is unknown. Odell (1:106) suggests these are garrison players, a practice that no doubt was carried out much more frequently than recorded.

Evidence from this year confirms further student theatricals at Harvard College.

※※※

ca. 10 January 1758   Fort Cumberland, the frontier
Diary entry.

[George Washington records in his *Diary* the following item: "By Cash gave the Players at Fort Cumb^d" £1. Whether this entry refers to payment made to a professional troupe or to amateurs is not established. Source: Ford 18.]

22 June 1758   Harvard College, Cambridge,
                 Massachusetts colony

The Roman Father* (William Whitehead, 1750).
Students of Harvard College.

[Source: Odell 1:108; following the diary of Dr. Nathaniel Ames. Cf. *Records of the Massachusetts Colonial Society*, 48:295.]

3 July 1758   Harvard College, Cambridge,
                Massachusetts colony

Cato.
Students of Harvard College.

[Source: Odell 1:108; following the diary of Dr. Nathaniel Ames. Cf., *Records of the Massachusetts Colonial Society*, 48.295.]

3 July 1758   Kingston, Jamaica
The Constant Couple.
Company unknown.

[The *Boston Evening Post* (2 October 1758) reports a letter from Kingston, dated 8 July 1758:

> On Monday last was celebrated at St. Jago de la Vega, by the brethren of the Ancient and Honourable Society of Free and Accepted Masons, the annual feast of St. John the Baptist. In the forenoon of that day, the brethren, to the number of 73 assembled at the house of Brother Curtis, and from thence proceeded to the church, where an excellent sermon, suitable to the occasion, was preached by their Rev. Brother Anthony Davis; after which they returned in the same order, to Brother Curtis's, where an elegant entertainment was prepared; and having finished the necessary business of the day, went in a body to the house of Brother Bankes, where the comedy of the Constant Couple was performed for the benefit of that brother.]

August 1758   Tortola, West Indies
Will.

[William Hallam's will provides useful information concerning the affairs of the American Company.

Tortola

In the name of God Amen the second day of August one thousand seven hundred and fifty eight I William Hallam late of the city of London but now of the island of Tortola being very sick and weak in body but of perfect mind and memory ... do make and ordain this my last will and Testament ... I give and bequeath in the manner following Vizt. Item I give and bequeath unto my well beloved wife Ann Hallam and my two daughters Ann and Mary Hallam all and every one of my Clothes and Scenes belonging or in any wise appertaining to the Stage also all the money that is now due or that may become due and owing unto me by Bonds Notes of hand Book debts or otherwise and wheras my Wife Ann Hallam not being capable to manage or Carry on the affairs of the Stage, I do therefore consitute nominate and appoint my Trusty and well beloved friend John Harman my whole and sole Executor to this my last will and Testament....

Wm. Hallam (Signature)

Source: Myers and Brodowski 8.]

16 October 1758   New York
Newspaper notice.
Douglass Company.

[The *New York Mercury* of this date contains the following item: "Friday last arrived here from the West Indies a Company of Comedians; some part of which were here in the year 1753."]

6 November 1758   New York
Newspaper notice.
Douglass Company.

[The following notice appears in the Gaine's *New York Mercury* of 6 November 1758:

Mr. Douglass, who came here with a company of comedians, having apply'd to the gentlemen in power for permission to play, has (to his great mortification) met with a positive and absolute denial: He has in vain represented, that such are his circumstances, and those of the other members of his company, that it is impossible for them to move to another place; and tho' in the humblest manner he begg'd the magistrates wou'd indulge him in acting as many plays as would barely defray the expences he and the company have been at, in coming to this city, and enable them to proceed to another; he has been unfortunate enough to be peremptorily refused it. As he has given over all thoughts of acting, he begs leave to inform the publick, that in a few days he will open an Histrionic academy, of which proper notice will be given in this paper.

Cf. Odell 1:75.]

11 December 1758 New York
Newspaper notice.
Douglass Company.

[The *New York Mercury* of this date contains the following item:

> Whereas I am informed, that an advertisement of mine, which appeared some time ago in this paper, giving notice that I would open an Histrionic Academy, has been understood by many, as a declaration that I proposed under that colour, to act plays, without the consent of the magistracy: This is therefore to inform the publick, that such a construction was quite foreign to my intent and meaning, that so vain, so insolent a project never once entered into my head; It is an impeachment of my understanding to imagine, I would dare, in a publick manner, to aim at an affront on gentlemen, on whom I am dependent for the only means that can save us from utter ruin. All that I proposed to do was, to deliver dissertations on subjects, moral, instructive and entertaining, and to endeavour to qualify such as would favour me with their attendance, to speak in publick with propriety. But as such an undertaking might have occasioned an inquiry into my capacity, I thought the publick would treat me with greater favour, when they were informed that I was deprived of any other means of getting my bread; nor would that have done any more than barely supplied our present necessities. The expenses of our coming here, our living since our arrival, with the charge of building, etc. (which let me observe, we had engaged for before we had any reason to apprehend a denial) amount to a sum that would swallow up the profits of a great many nights acting, had we permission. I shall conclude with humbly hoping, that those gentlemen who have entertained an ill opinion of me, from my supposed presumption, will do me the favour to believe, that I have truly explained the advertisement, and that I am, to them, and the publick, a very humble, and very devoted servant, David Douglass.   Decemb. 8, 1758.]

28 December 1758 Cruger's Wharf Theatre, New York
Jane Shore.
The Mock Doctor.
Douglass Company.

[The Douglass company is given permission to perform for thirteen nights. Source: *New York Mercury* (28 December 1758).]

1759

The Douglass Company were in New York at the beginning of the year. After the debacle with the authorities of that city, they were granted permission to perform a brief season which concluded on 7 February 1759. After New York, the whereabouts of the company are unknown until late spring when they opened a season in Philadelphia. Rankin (79) suggests this "may have been the year they visited Perth Amboy." Dunlap, who was born in Perth Amboy, recollects those who knew the Douglass Company in that city, but no substantive evidence exists to document their performances, if they did indeed play there. Durang (1: xix, 24) puts the company in Providence, Rhode Island colony, sometime in 1759, and, as it was prior to their opening at Philadelphia, it would have to be the spring. Durang claims that "when the American Company first played at Providence, Rhode Island, in 1759, they found Mr. Snyder there [a scene painter]. Mr. Douglass engaged him to paint scenery for the new Southwark theatre, which he did not complete until sometime afterward." Since Douglass did not open the Southwark Theatre until 25 June, this could put the company in Providence for a short spring season; unfortunately we have no calendar dates to document a possible sojourn into Rhode Island at this date. Willard (12) and Rankin (99) both assert that Providence first saw professional actors in 1762. Furthermore, we know that Douglass engaged one William Williams of Philadelphia to paint scenery for the opening of the Southwark Theatre. It should also be noted that when the Douglass Company opened in Newport, Rhode Island, in September of 1761, they attracted quite a lot of press, protests, and town meetings. A quiet introduction of actors into New England in 1759 seems unlikely and therefore, until evidence arises, we must cautiously set Durang aside on this assertion.

In Philadelphia we find the first complete Douglass Company cast lists. The roster consisted of Adam Allyn, David Douglass, Mrs. Douglass, Adam Hallam, Lewis Hallam, Jr., Miss Nancy Hallam, Mr. Harman, Mrs. Harman, Mr. Horne, Mrs. Love, Owen Morris, Mr. John Palmer (a major performer from London, who joins the company in time for the benefit season and is promptly rewarded with one), Mr. Reed, Mr. Scott (from the 1751 Murray-Kean Company?), Mr. Tomlinson, and Mrs. Tomlinson. Also George Abbington, a dancing master, occasionally performed (e.g., 21 December 1759). Charles Love and his wife later rejoined the company in New York, Mrs. Love to act and Charles to supply music, as the afterpiece cast lists indicate.

In Philadelphia the Douglass company again met with resistance. Soon after the players arrived circa late May and made known their intention of building a playhouse, motions were underway to suppress their activity. The General Assembly of Pennsylvania met and on 31 May passed an act "for the more effectual Suppressing of Lotteries and Plays" (Dormon 14) which carried a £500 fine for anyone attempting to perform a play. In deference to the players, the Governor, William Denny, delayed the effective date of this act to 1 January 1760. This strategy allowed the Douglass company to build a new playhouse, just outside the city limits, and to perform a substantial season from 25 June to 28 December 1759, finishing the year with a civic benefit. Like other previous Pennsylvania referenda, this latest prohibition against the theatre was also repealed in England, 8 September 1759, but ironically the news did not reach Philadelphia until after the company had departed (cf. Durang v, n. a).

William Williams, a painter in Philadelphia, supplied the company with new scenes for the Philadelphia season. Williams is the first known American scenographer.

Boston newspapers reprint the act prohibiting stage plays, which is perhaps a reaction against theatricals being presented by the students of Harvard College.

From the diary of Nathaniel Knapp we learn of two performances in Nova Scotia in March and May of this year (O'Neill 388).

※※※

1 January 1759   Cruger's Wharf Theatre, New York
The Inconstant* (George Farquhar, 1702).
The Mock Doctor.
Douglass Company.
   [Prices: box, 8s.; pit, 5s.; gallery, 2s. Play to begin at 6:00. Source: *New York Mercury* (1 January 1759).]

3 January 1759   Cruger's Wharf Theatre, New York
The Orphan.
Douglass Company.
   [Source: *New York Mercury* (1 January 1759).]

5 January 1759   Cruger's Wharf Theatre, New York
The Spanish Friar.
Douglass Company.

[Source: *New York Mercury* (1 January 1759).]

8 January 1759   Cruger's Wharf Theatre, New York
The Recruiting Officer.
Lover's Quarrel.
Douglass Company.
   [The prologue (by Singleton, spoken by Master Lewis Hallam) and epilogue (by Adam Thomson, spoken by Mrs. Douglass) presented upon the opening of the theater on 28 December 1758 appeared in the *Mercury* of this date, and the epilogue is reprinted by Seilhamer 1:96–98. Source: *New York Mercury* (8 January 1759).]

10 January 1759   Cruger's Wharf Theatre, New York
Othello.
Douglass Company.
   [Source: *New York Mercury* (8 January 1759).]

12 January 1759   Cruger's Wharf Theatre, New York
The Beaux' Stratagem.
Douglass Company.
   [Source: *New York Mercury* (8 January 1759).]

15 January 1759   Cruger's Wharf Theatre, New York
Venice Preserved.
The Stage Coach.
Douglass Company.
   [Source: *New York Mercury* (15 January 1759).]

24 January 1759   Cruger's Wharf Theatre, New York
Douglas* (John Home, 1756).
Lethe.
Douglass Company.
   [Source: *New York Mercury* (22 January 1759).]

26 January 1759   Cruger's Wharf Theatre, New York
Tamerlane.
Douglass Company.
   [Source: *New York Mercury* (22 January 1759).]

29 January 1759   Cruger's Wharf Theatre, New York
The Drummer.
Damon and Phillida.
Douglass Company.

[Source: *New York Mercury* (29 January 1759).]

7 February 1759   Cruger's Wharf Theatre, New York
Richard III.
Damon and Phillida.
Douglass Company.
["Positively the last Time of acting in this City." Source: *New York Mercury* (5 February 1759).]

9 March 1759   Louisburg, Nova Scotia
Play not identified.
Company not known.
[Nathaniel Knapp records the following entry which indicates a performance took place on this date: "At night went to ye play acting." Source: O'Neill 388.]

20 April 1759   Harvard College, Cambridge
The Drummer.
Students of Harvard College.
[Source: Odell 1:108; following the diary of Dr. Nathaniel Ames. Cf. *Records of the Massachusetts Colonial Society*, 48:295.]

7 May 1759   Louisburg, Nova Scotia
Play not identified.
Company not known.
[Nathaniel Knapp records the following entry which indicates a performance took place on this date: "and had Play Day today." Source: O'Neill 388.]

31 May 1759   Pennsylvania colony
Law passed.
[The Commonwealth of Pennsylvania passes a law forbidding plays, with a penalty of £500 for violation (Hornblow 24). This act was later modified to allow a short season during 25 June through 28 December 1759 (Quinn 1:14).]

25 June 1759   Society Hill Theatre, Philadelphia
Tamerlane.
  Tamerlane–Harman; Bajazet–Hallam; Moneses–Douglass; Axalla–Reed; Omar–Tomlinson; Prince of Tanais–Horne; Dervise–Morris; Haly–A. Hallam; Arpasia–Mrs. Douglass; Selima–Mrs. Harman.
The Virgin Unmasked.
  Miss Lucy–Mrs. Harman.

Douglass Company.
[The opening night of the season. Prices: box, 7s.6d.; pit and gallery, 3s. Source: *Pennsylvania Gazette* (21 June 1759).]

29 June 1759   Society Hill Theatre, Philadelphia
Richard III.
   King Henry–Douglass; Duke of York–Miss Nancy Hallam; Richmond–Hallam; Catesby–Tomlinson; Oxford–Horne; Prince Edward–A. Hallam; Richard–Harman; Buckingham–Reed; Stanley–Morris; Lady Anne–Mrs. Harman; Queen Elizabeth–Mrs. Douglass; Duchess of York–Mrs. Love.
Lethe.
Douglass Company.
   [Source: *Pennsylvania Gazette* (28 June 1759).]

6 July 1759   Society Hill Theatre, Philadelphia
The Provoked Husband.
   Townly–Douglass; Squire Richard–Morris; Basset–Reed; Sir Francis–Harman; Manly–Hallam; Moody–Tomlinson; Constable–Horne; Lady Grace–Mrs. Harman; Miss Jenny–Mrs. Harman; Lady Townly–Mrs. Douglass; Lady Wronghead–Mrs. Love; Myrtilla–Mrs. Tomlinson.
A Wonder, an Honest Yorkshireman!
Douglass Company.
   [Source: *Pennsylvania Gazette* (5 July 1759).]

13 July 1759   Society Hill Theatre, Philadelphia
Douglas.
   Randolph–Douglass; Glenalvon–Reed; Douglas–Hallam; Old Norval–Harman; Lady Randolph–Mrs. Douglass; Anna–Mrs. Harman.
The Mock Doctor.
Douglass Company.
   [Source: *Pennsylvania Gazette* (12 July 1759).]

20 July 1759   Society Hill Theatre, Philadelphia
The Recruiting Officer.
   Ballance–Reed; Plume–Hallam; Brazen–Harman; Worthy–Morris; Kite–Douglass; Bullock–Tomlinson; Constable–Horne; Recruits–Allyn and Harman; Melinda–Mrs. Harman; Sylvia–Mrs. Douglass; Rose–Mrs. Love; Lucy–Mrs. Tomlinson.
The Adventures of Half an Hour* (Christopher Bullock, 1716).

Douglass Company.
[Source: *Pennsylvania Gazette* (19 July 1759).]

27 July 1759 Society Hill Theatre, Philadelphia
Hamlet (William Shakespeare).
Claudius–Tomlinson; Hamlet–Hallam; Polonius–Harman; Horatio–Morris; Laertes–Reed; Guildenstern–Horne; Osrick–A. Hallam; Marcellus–Allyn; Grave-diggers–Harman and Allyn; Ghost–Douglass; Gertrude–Mrs. Douglass; Ophelia–Mrs. Harman; Player Queen–Mrs. Love.
The Stage Coach.
Douglass Company.
[Source: *Pennsylvania Gazette* (26 July 1759).]

3 August 1759 Society Hill Theatre, Philadelphia
The Drummer.
Truman–Reed; Fantom–Morris; Tinfall–Hallam; Vellum–Harman; Butler–Tomlinson; Coachman–Douglass; Gardner–Allyn; Lady Tru-man–Mrs. Douglass; Abigail–Mrs. Harman.
The Anatomist, or The Sham Doctor.
Douglass Company.
[Source: *Pennsylvania Gazette* (2 August 1759).]

10 August 1759 Society Hill Theatre, Philadelphia
Theodosius, or The Force of Love* (Nathaniel Lee, 1680).
Theodosius–Reed; Varamnes–Allyn; Marcian–Hallam; Atticus–Harman; Leontine–Tomlinson; Lucius–Douglass; Aranthes–Morris; Pulcheria–Mrs. Harman; Athenais–Mrs. Douglass; Marina–Mrs. Tomlinson; Flavilla–Mrs. Love.
Lethe.
Douglass Company.
[Source: *Pennsylvania Gazette* (9 August 1759).]

17 August 1759 Society Hill Theatre, Philadelphia
George Barnwell [i.e., *The London Merchant*].
Thorowgood–Douglass; Uncle–Morris; Barnwell–Hallam; Truman–Reed; Blunt–Harman; Millwood–Mrs. Douglass; Marcia–Mrs. Love; Lucy–Mrs. Harman.
Harlequin Collector.
Douglass Company.
[Source: *Pennsylvania Gazette* (16 August 1759).]

24 August 1759 Society Hill Theatre, Philadelphia
The Beggar's Opera.

Macheath–Harman; Peachum–Tomlinson; Lockit–Scott; Mat of the Mint–Reed; Beggar–Morris; Player–Douglass; Harry–Horne; Filch–A. Hallam; Jemmy Twitcher–Allyn; Polly–Mrs. Love; Lucy–Mrs. Harman; Mrs. Peachum–Mrs. Harman; Mrs. Coaxer–Mrs. Douglass; Mrs. Slammekin–Mrs. Tomlinson.
Lethe.
Douglass Company.
[Source: *Pennsylvania Gazette* (23 August 1759).]

31 August 1759   Society Hill Theatre, Philadelphia
The Fair Penitent.
Sciolto–Tomlinson; Altamount–Reed; Lothario–Harman; Horatio–Hallam; Rossano–Morris; Calista–Mrs. Harman; Lavinia–Mrs. Douglass; Lucilla–Mrs. Love.
The School Boy* (Colley Cibber, 1702).
Douglass Company.
[Source: *Pennsylvania Gazette* (30 August 1759).]

7 September 1759   Society Hill Theatre, Philadelphia
Douglas.
Douglass Company.
[Source: *Pennsylvania Gazette* (6 September 1759).]

14 September 1759   Society Hill Theatre, Philadelphia
Hamlet.
As 27 July, but Player King–Scott.
The Adventures of Half an Hour.
Douglass Company.
[Source: *Pennsylvania Gazette* (13 September 1759).]

21 September 1759 Society Hill Theatre, Philadelphia
The Recruiting Officer.
As 20 July 1759, but Constable–Allyn; Recruits–Tomlinson and Allyn.
The Stage Coach.
Douglass Company.
[Seilhamer (1:103) incorrectly dates this performance as 26 September. Source: *Pennsylvania Gazette* (20 September 1759).]

28 September 1759 Society Hill Theatre, Philadelphia
King Lear.
Lear–Harman; Gloster–Scott; Kent–Tomlinson; Edgar–Hallam; Bastard–Reed; Cornwall–Horne; Albany–Morris;

Burgundy–Douglass; Usher–Allyn; Goneril–Mrs. Love; Regan–Mrs. Harman; Cordelia–Mrs. Douglass.
Douglass Company.
[An unnamed farce was also performed. Source: *Pennsylvania Gazette* (27 September 1759).]

5 October 1759   Society Hill Theatre, Philadelphia
The Provoked Husband.
As 6 July 1759, but Manly–Allyn; Sir Francis–Scott; Townly–Douglass.
The Toy Shop* (Robert Dodsley, 1735).
Douglass Company.
[Source: *Pennsylvania Gazette* (4 October 1759).]

11 October 1759   New York
Marriage.
[Lewis Hallam Jr. married Sarah Perry in New York on this date. Myers and Brodowski suggest Hallam left the company in Philadelphia sometime after 28 September to marry in New York, returning by 26 October. Source: Myers and Browdoski 9.]

12 October 1759   Society Hill Theatre, Philadelphia
The Provoked Husband.
As 5 October 1759.
Douglass Company.
[Source: *Pennsylvania Gazette* (11 October 1759).]

26 October 1759   Society Hill Theatre, Philadelphia
Macbeth* (William Shakespeare; adap. by William Davenant, 1673).
Duncan–Harman; Malcolm–Reed; Donaldbaine–A. Hallam; Lenox–Morris; Macbeth–Hallam; Banquo–Scott; Macduff–Douglass; Seyton–Tomlinson; Flean–Miss Nancy Hallam; Lady Macbeth–Mrs. Douglass; Lady Macduff–Mrs. Love; Hecate–Mrs. Harman; Witches–Allyn, Harman, and Tomlinson.
Douglass Company.
[Prices: box 7s.; pit 5s.; gallery 3s. "Days of playing, Mondays, Wednesdays, and Fridays." Source: *Pennsylvania Gazette* (25 October 1759).]

2 November 1759   Society Hill Theatre, Philadelphia
Romeo and Juliet.

Romeo–Hallam; Mercutio–Harman; Montague–Douglass; Capulet–Tomlinson; Friar Laurence–Scott; Paris–Horne; Tybalt–Reed; Apothecary–Allyn; Lady Capulet–Mrs. Love; Juliet–Mrs. Douglass; Nurse–Mrs. Harman.
Miss in Her Teens.
Douglass Company.
[Benefit Douglass. Cast from Seilhamer (1:105). Source: *Pennsylvania Gazette* (1 November 1759).]

9 November 1759   Society Hill Theatre, Philadelphia
The Beggar's Opera.
As 24 August 1759, but Filch–Allyn; Beggar–Tomlinson; Diana Trapes–Mrs. Harman; Moll Brazen–Mrs. Douglass.
Harlequin Collector.
Harlequin–Hallam; Miller–Allyn; Clown–Douglass; Conjurer–Harman; Doctor–Tomlinson; Columbine–Mrs. Douglass.
Douglass Company.
[Benefit Mrs. Love. Source: *Pennsylvania Gazette* (8 November 1759).]

16 November 1759   Society Hill Theatre, Philadelphia
Theodosius.
As 10 August 1759, but Theodosius–Douglass; Lucius–Horne.
The Lying Valet.
Douglass Company.
[Benefit Scott. Source: *Pennsylvania Gazette* (15 November 1759).]

23 November 1759   Society Hill Theatre, Philadelphia
The Provoked Husband.
As 5 October 1759, but Townly–Hallam; Constable–not listed.
Harlequin Collector.
Douglass Company.
[Benefit Hallam. The pantomime features a new scene advertised under the title *Harlequin Statue.* Source: *Pennsylvania Gazette* (22 November 1759).]

1 December 1759   Society Hill Theatre, Philadelphia
Macbeth.
Macbeth–Palmer; Lady Macbeth–Mrs. Douglass.
The Stage Coach.
Douglass Company.

[Benefit Allyn. This is Palmer's first appearance. Source: *Pennsylvania Gazette* (29 November 1759).]

7 December 1759   Society Hill Theatre, Philadelphia
The Suspicious Husband.
   Strickland–Palmer; Frankly–Douglass; Bellamy–Morris; Ranger–Hallam; Tester–Tomlinson; Maggot–Reed; Buckle–Horne; Chairman–Scott; Mrs. Strickland–Mrs. Harman; Jacintha–Mrs. Love; Lucetta–Mrs. Tomlinson; Clarinda–Mrs. Douglass.
The Virgin Unmasked.
   Miss Lucy–Mrs. Harman.
Douglas Company.
   [Benefit Adam Hallam. Source: *Pennsylvania Gazette* (6 December 1759).]

14 December 1759   Society Hill Theatre, Philadelphia
The Gamester.
   Beverly–Hallam; Jarvis–Tomlinson; Lewson–Harman; Bates–Morris; Stukely–Palmer; Dawson–Allyn; Mrs. Beverly–Mrs. Douglass; Charlotte–Mrs. Harman.
The School Boy.
Douglass Company.
   [Benefit Reed. Source: *Pennsylvania Gazette* (13 December 1759).]

21 December 1759   Society Hill Theatre, Philadelphia
Romeo and Juliet.
   As 2 November 1759, but Romeo–Palmer; Benvolio–Morris; Mercutio–Hallam.
Harlequin Collector.
Douglass Company.
   [Benefit Palmer. "By particular desire, dancing by Mr. Abbington." Source: *Pennsylvania Gazette* (20 December 1759).]

27 December 1759   Society Hill Theatre, Philadelphia
George Barnwell [i.e., *The London Merchant*].
   As 17 August 1759, but Trueman–Tomlinson.
Lethe.
   Lord Chalkstone–Allyn.
Douglass Company.
   [In this performance of *Lethe,* Garrick's new addition of the character of Lord Chalkstone was first introduced in the colonies. "Towards the raising a Fund for purchasing an

THE COLONIAL AMERICAN STAGE   199

Organ to the College-Hall in this City, and instructing the Charity Children in Psalmody." Source: *Pennsylvania Gazette* (27 December 1759).]

27 December 1759   Boston
Law passed.

[The *Boston News Letter* of this date reprints the following prohibition against acting:

> At the desire of a number of the principal inhabitants of this town the following Act of the Province (now in force) is here inserted, viz. An Act to prevent State-Plays and other Theatrical Entertainments. For preventing and avoiding the many and great mischiefs which arise from publick stage plays, interludes and other theatrical entertainments, which not only occasion great and unnecessary expences, and discourage industry and frugality, but likewise tend generally to encrease immorality, impiety, and a contempt of religion: Be it enacted by the Lieutenant-Governour, Council and House of representatives, That from and after the publication of this act no person or persons whosoever shall or may for his or their gain, or for any price or valuable consideration, let or suffer to be used and improved, any house, room or place whatsoever, no acting or carrying on any stage-plays, interludes or other theatrical entertainments, on pain of forfeiting and paying for each and every day or time such house. room or place shall be let used or improved contrary to this act, twenty pounds. And be it further enacted, That if at any time or times whatsoever, from and after the publication of this Act, any person or persons shall be present as an actor in or spectator of any stage-play, interlude, or theatrical entertainment in any house, room or place where a greater number of persons than twenty shall be assembled together, every such person shall forfeit and pay for every time he or they shall be present as aforesaid five pounds. The forfeitures and penalties aforesaid to be one half to his Majesty for the use of the government, the other half to him or them that shall inform and sue for the same. And the aforesaid forfeitures and penalties may likewise be recovered by presentment of the Grand Jury; in which case the whole forfeiture shall be to his Majesty for the use of this government.]

28 December 1759   Society Hill Theatre, Philadelphia
Hamlet.
Douglass Company.

[Benefit for the Pennsylvania Hospital. "Thus ended ...the brilliant season of June 25 to December 28, 1759. We have record of twenty-eight performances having been given this season, of a probable eighty" (Pollock 83). Source: *Pennsylvania Gazette* (27 December 1759).]

1760

After the Douglass Company departed Philadelphia, they began the new year playing in Chestertown, Maryland colony, while awaiting the completion of a new theatre in Annapolis. The company consisted of the following known returning members: David Douglass, Mrs. Douglass, Adam Hallam, Lewis Hallam Jr., Owen Morris, Mary Morris, Mr. Palmer, and Mr. Scott. Besides these several new members appeared: Miss Dowthwaite and her mother, Mrs. Dowthwaite, Miss Crane, and Walter Murray. Though he announces himself "being the first time appearing on this stage" (see 20 March 1760), this was indeed the same Walter Murray from the Murray-Kean Company, whose whereabouts are unknown since 1752.

After the 1759 Philadelphia engagement, several names have disappeared from the record, and the company's personnel becomes less stable. Adam Allyn, Nancy Hallam, Mr. Harman, Mrs. Harman, Mr. Horne, Mrs. Love, Mr. Reed, Mr. Tomlinson, and Mrs. Tomlinson, some of whom may have been recruited in Philadelphia, played there and remained behind when the company moved south. Subsequent double-casting in Upper Marlborough may also indicate the company's personnel had diminished, though a Mr. Sturt was added to the company at that time.

The Douglass Company played Annapolis through the spring, after which they traveled to Upper Marlborough where they entertained well into summer (cf. Seilhamer 1:121). During the summer, Douglass had made arrangements to have built a new playhouse in Williamsburg,[11] and by October the company began performances in that venue; what little evidence survives indicates a substantial season.

In spite of the December 1759 reprint of the Act to Prevent Stage Plays, clandestine theatrical activity in Boston is recorded for this year. Unfortunately, the record is ambiguous as to whether a January or March performance of *Cato* was presented by local amateurs. The *Boston Post-Boy* of 7 January 1760 records the following item (and an intended

---

[11] The site of this structure was excavated during 2000–2001 by researchers of the Colonial Williamsburg Foundation.

prologue) suggesting either a January performance or perhaps none at all:

> The gentlemen who had proposed to amuse themselves, and their friends, by the representation of a play, wish the wise men of Boston to understand that the piece they had made choice of for that purpose was Mr. Addison's Cato, and that they are very sorry they should have been suspected to be promoters of vice, impiety, immorality, &c.

The *Maryland Gazette* of 27 March 1760, however, implies that a performance actually took place at a later date in reprinting a letter from a "late Boston Paper" which offers an account of a company of gentlemen who "amused themselves and their friends by a representation of ...*Cato*."

***

early 1760   Chestertown, Maryland colony
Newspaper notice.
Douglass Company.
  [As indicated by a notice in *Maryland Gazette* of 7 February 1760 (see entry for that date), the Douglass troupe is apparently performing in this provincial location.]

7 February 1760   Annapolis
Newspaper notice.
  ["By permission of his Excellency the Governor, a Theatre is erecting in this city, which will be opened soon by a Company of Comedians, who are now at Chester-Town." Source: *Maryland Gazette* (7 February 1760).]

3 March 1760   The New Theatre, Annapolis
The Orphan.
Lethe.
Douglass Company.
  [This is the opening night of this season. A review of this performance, the Prologue (spoken by Douglass), and the Epilogue (spoken by Mrs. Douglass) appear in the *Maryland Gazette* for 6 March 1760 (see entry for that date). Source: *Maryland Gazette* (6 March 1760).]

6 March 1760   Annapolis
Theatrical review.
Douglass Company.

[This day the following review of the 3 March 1760 program was published:

> Monday last the theatre in this city was open'd, when the tragedy of the Orphan, and Lethe (a dramatic satire) were perform'd, in the presence of his Excellency the Governor, to a polite and numerous audience, who all express'd a general satisfaction. The principal character, both in the play and entertainment, were perform'd with great justice, and the applause which attended the whole representation, did less honour to the abilities of the actors than to the taste of their auditors.

The review is reprinted by Quinn (1:14); cf. Seilhamer 1:114. Source: *Maryland Gazette* (6 March 1760).]

6 March 1760   The New Theatre, Annapolis
The Recruiting Officer.
Miss in Her Teens.
Douglass Company.
  [Source: *Maryland Gazette* (6 March 1760).]

8 March 1760   The New Theatre, Annapolis
Venice Preserved.
   Duke–Morris; Priuli–Douglass; Jaffier–Palmer; Pierre–Hallam; Renault–Scott; Conspirators–A. Hallam, Douglass, and Mrs. Morris; Belvidera–Mrs. Douglass.
The Mock Doctor.
Douglass Company.
  [Prices: box 10s.; pit 7s.6d.; gallery 5s. Source: *Maryland Gazette* (6 March 1760).]

10 March 1760   The New Theatre, Annapolis
Richard III.
The King and the Miller of Mansfield.
Douglass Company.
  [Source: *Maryland Gazette* (13 March 1760).]

13 March 1760   The New Theatre, Annapolis
The Provoked Husband.
The Stage Coach.
Douglass Company.
  [Source: *Maryland Gazette* (13 March 1760).]

15 March 1760   The New Theatre, Annapolis
The Fair Penitent.

Sciolto–Scott; Altamount–Hallam; Horatio–Palmer; Lothario–Douglass; Rossano–Morris; Calista–Mrs. Douglass; Lavinia–Mrs. Morris; Lucilla–Miss Dowthwaite.
The Anatomist.
Douglass Company.
[Source: *Maryland Gazette* (13 March 1760).]

20 March 1760   The New Theatre, Annapolis
The Beaux' Stratagem.
Aimwell–Murray, "being the first time of his appearing on this stage."
Lethe.
Douglass Company.
[Source: *Maryland Gazette* (20 March 1760).]

22 March 1760   The New Theatre, Annapolis
The London Merchant.
Thorowgood–Douglass; Barnwell–Hallam; Trueman–Morris; Uncle–Murray; Blunt–Scott; Millwood–Mrs. Douglass; Maria–Mrs. Morris; Lucy–Miss Crane.
The Lying Valet.
Douglass Company.
[Source: *Maryland Gazette* (20 March 1760).]

24 March 1760   The New Theatre, Annapolis
The Busy Body.
The Mock Doctor.
Douglass Company.
[Source: *Maryland Gazette* (15 May 1760).]

27 March 1760   The New Theatre, Annapolis
The Revenge* (Edward Young, 1721).
The Lying Valet.
Douglass Company.
[Source: *Maryland Gazette* (27 March 1760).]

29 March 1760   The New Theatre, Annapolis
A Bold Stroke for a Wife.
Sir Philip–Murray; Periwinkle–Palmer; Tradelove–Morris; Prim–Scott; Fainwell–Douglass; Freeman–Hallam; Sackbut–Scott; Quak-ing Boy–A. Hallam; Mrs. Lovely–Mrs. Douglass; Mrs. Prim–Mrs. Morris; Betty–Mrs. Dowthwaite; Masked Lady–Miss Dowthwaite.
Damon and Phillida.
Douglass Company.

["Being the last time of acting 'til the Easter Holidays."
Source: *Maryland Gazette* (27 March 1760).]

7 April 1760   The New Theatre, Annapolis
Romeo and Juliet.
   Romeo–by a young gentleman for his diversion.
The Stage Coach.
Douglass Company.
   [Originally advertised in the *Maryland Gazette* (3 April 1760) for this evening but apparently rescheduled were the following plays and casts:
   Othello.
      Duke–Murray; Brabantio–Scott; Othello–Douglass; Cassio–Hallam; Iago–Palmer; Rodorigo–A. Hallam; Montano–Morris; Desdemona–Mrs. Douglass; Amelia–Miss Crane.
   The Honest Yorkshireman.
Source: the revised source for this and other subsequent variations and unadvertised performances for this season is a summary of the offerings published in the *Maryland Gazette* for 15 May 1760.]

8 April 1760   The New Theatre, Annapolis
The Provoked Husband.
The Honest Yorkshireman.
Douglass Company.
   [Source: *Maryland Gazette* (15 May 1760).]

9 April 1760   The New Theatre, Annapolis
Othello.
   Cast not listed, but see 7 April 1760.
The Devil to Pay.
Douglass Company.
   [Source: *Maryland Gazette* (15 May 1760).]

10 April 1760   The New Theatre, Annapolis
The Constant Couple.
   Sir Harry Wildair–Hallam; Col. Standard–Douglass; Alderman Smuggler–Morris; Beau Clincher–Palmer; Clincher, Junior–Murray; Vizard–Scott; Dickey–A. Hallam; Lady Lurewell–Mrs. Douglass; Angelica–Mrs. Morris; Lady Darling–Miss Crane; Parley–Miss Dowthwaite.
The King and the Miller of Mansfield.
Douglass Company.

[Seilhamer (1:114) and Sonneck (30) incorrectly report the afterpiece as *The Devil to Pay*. Source: *Maryland Gazette* (10 April 1760).]

11 April 1760   The New Theatre, Annapolis
Romeo and Juliet.
Miss in Her Teens.
Douglass Company.
   [Source: *Maryland Gazette* (15 May 1760).]

12 April 1760   The New Theatre, Annapolis
The Suspicious Husband.
The Mock Doctor.
Douglass Company.
   [Source: *Maryland Gazette* (15 May 1760).]

14 April 1760   The New Theatre, Annapolis
Richard III.
Hob in the Well.
Douglass Company.
   [Benefit Douglass. Source: *Maryland Gazette* (15 May 1760).]

15 April 1760   The New Theatre, Annapolis
The Fair Penitent.
The Lying Valet.
Douglass Company.
   [Benefit Palmer. Source: *Maryland Gazette* (15 May 1760).]

16 April 1760   The New Theatre, Annapolis
Venice Preserved.
The Devil to Pay.
Douglass Company.
   [Benefit Murray. Source: *Maryland Gazette* (15 May 1760).]

17 April 1760   The New Theatre, Annapolis
The Provoked Husband.
   Lord Townley–Palmer; Manley–Hallam; Sir Francis Wronghead–Scott; Squire Richard–A. Hallam; Count Bassett–Morris; John Moody–Douglass; Lady Townly–Mrs. Douglass; Lady Grace–Miss Crane; Lady Wronghead–Mrs. Morris; Miss Jenny–Miss Dowthwaite; Myrtilla–Mrs. Dowthwaite.
The Honest Yorkshireman.
Douglass Company.

[Benefit Mrs. Douglass. Source: *Maryland Gazette* (17 April 1760).]

19 April 1760   The New Theatre, Annapolis
The Revenge.
Lethe.
Douglass Company.
   [Benefit Lewis Hallam. Source: *Maryland Gazette* (15 May 1760).]

22 April 1760   The New Theatre, Annapolis
The Beaux' Stratagem.
The Lying Valet.
Douglass Company.
   [Benefit Mrs. and Miss Dowthwaite. Source: *Maryland Gazette* (15 May 1760).]

23 April 1760   The New Theatre, Annapolis
The Orphan.
Lethe.
Douglass Company.
   [Benefit Miss Crane. Source: *Maryland Gazette* (15 May 1760).]

24 April 1760   The New Theatre, Annapolis
The Constant Couple.
   As 10 April 1760.
The Honest Yorkshireman.
Douglass Company.
   [Benefit Morris. Source: *Maryland Gazette* (24 April 1760).]

1 May 1760   The New Theatre, Annapolis
Douglas.
   Lord Randolph–Scott; Glenalvon–Douglass; Douglas–Hallam; Norval–Morris; Officer–Murray; Lady Randolph–Mrs. Douglass; Anna–Miss Crane.
The Virgin Unmasked.
Douglass Company.
   [Benefit Adam Hallam. Apparently postponed. Seilhamer (1:115) dates this performance as 5 May 1760. Source: *Maryland Gazette* (1 May 1760).]

5 May 1760   The New Theatre, Annapolis
Douglas.
   As advertised for 1 May 1760.

The Virgin Unmasked.
Douglass Company.
  [Benefit Adam Hallam. Source: *Maryland Gazette* (15 May 1760).]

8 May 1760   The New Theatre, Annapolis
The Jew of Venice; or, The Female Lawyer* (Lord Landsdowne, 1701).
  Bassanio–Douglass; Antonio–Scott; Gratiano–A. Hallam; Lorenzo–Morris; Shylock–Hallam; Duke–Murray; Portia–Mrs. Douglass; Nerissa–Miss Crane; Jessica–Mrs. Morris.
Lethe.
Douglass Company.
  [Benefit Mrs. Morris. Seilhamer (1:115) incorrectly identifies the mainpiece as Shakespeare's *The Merchant of Venice*. Source: *Maryland Gazette* (8 May 1760).]

12 May 1760   The New Theatre, Annapolis
The Gamester.
The Toy Shop.
Douglass Company.
  [Benefit Scott. The last evening of the season. The Epilogue (spoken by Mrs. Douglass) is published in *The Maryland Gazette* for 15 May 1760. Source: *Maryland Gazette* (15 May 1760).]

22 May 1760   Upper Marlborough, Maryland
Douglas.
  As 5 May 1760.
Lethe.
Douglass Company.
  [Source: *Maryland Gazette* (15 May 1760).]

26 May 1760   Upper Marlborough, Maryland
The Provoked Husband.
  As 17 April 1760, but Lord Townley–Douglass; John Moody–Murray.
The Virgin Unmasked.
Douglass Company.
  [Source: *Maryland Gazette* (22 May 1760).]

2 June 1760   Upper Marlborough, Maryland
The Beaux' Stratagem.
  Aimwell–Murray; Archer–Hallam; Sullen–Douglass; Gibbet–Morris; Scrub–A. Hallam; Foigard–Douglass; Free-

man–Morris; Boniface–Scott; Mrs. Sullen–Mrs. Douglass; Dorinda–Miss Crane; Lady Bountiful–Mrs. Dowthwaite; Cherry–Mrs. Morris; Gipsey–Miss Dowthwaite.
Miss in Her Teens.
Douglass Company.
[Source: *Maryland Gazette* (29 May 1760).]

9 June 1760   Upper Marlborough, Maryland
Richard III.
Richard–Hallam; King Henry–Murray; Prince Edward–A. Hallam; Duke of York–Miss S. Dowthwaite; Richmond–Douglass; Stanley–Morris; Lieutenant–Sturt; Tressell–Douglass; Norfolk–Scott; Lady Anne–Mrs. Morris; Duchess of York–Miss Crane; Queen Elizabeth–Mrs. Douglass.
The King and the Miller of Mansfield.
Douglass Company.
[Source: *Maryland Gazette* (5 June 1760).]

16 June 1760   Upper Marlborough, Maryland
The Revenge.
Don Alonzo–Douglass; Don Carlos–Scott; Don Alvarez–Morris; Don Manuel–Murray; Zanga–Hallam; Leonora–Mrs. Douglass; Isabella–Mrs. Morris.
The Devil to Pay.
Douglass Company.
[Source: *Maryland Gazette* (12 June 1760).]

19 June 1760   Upper Marlborough, Maryland
Romeo and Juliet.
Romeo–Hallam; Prince–Douglass; Montague–Murray; Capulet–Sturt; Mercutio–Douglass; Benvolio–Morris; Friar Lawrence–Scott; Peter–A. Hallam; Juliet–Mrs. Douglass; Lady Capulet–Miss Crane; Nurse–Mrs. Morris.
Douglass Company.
[Source: *Maryland Gazette* (19 June 1760); cf. Black 33.]

24 June 1760   Upper Marlborough, Maryland
The Gamester.
Beverly–Hallam; Lewson–Scott; Stukely–Douglass; Jarvis–Morris; Bates–Sturt; Dawson–Murray; Mrs. Beverly–Mrs. Douglass; Charlotte–Mrs. Morris; Lucy–Miss Crane.
Lethe.
Douglass Company.
[Source: *Maryland Gazette* (19 June 1760).]

1 July 1760   Upper Marlborough, Maryland
Romeo and Juliet.
   As 19 June 1760.
The King and the Miller of Mansfield.
Douglass Company.
   ["With the funeral procession of Juliet to the monument of the Capulets; and a Solemn Dirge: As perform'd at the Theatre-Royal in Covent-Garden." Source: *Maryland Gazette* (26 June 1760).]

8 October 1760   New Theater, Williamsburg, Virginia colony
Plays unidentified.
Douglass Company.
   [While no specific play titles are indicated, George Washington records in his *Diary* that he spent £7.10.3 on "Play Tickets" while in Williamsburg. This unusually large collective figure suggests multiple dramatic performances at this venue, via either single night ticket purchases or possibly a subscription fee. Source: Ford 19.]

c. 30 October 1760 Williamsburg
Plays unidentified.
Douglass Company.
   [A letter from Mrs. Maria Taylor Byrd dated 5 November 1760 complains much of the sickness in Virginia that fall before offering this note: "Mrs. Peter Randolph came here last week and carry'd your niece to town with her to see plays." Source: *The Correspondence of the three William Byrds of Westover, Virginia, 1684–1776,* 708.]

1761

We do not have a complete roster of the Douglass Company before their New York stint beginning on 26 November of this year. At that time members included Adam Allyn, Mrs. Allyn, Mrs. Crane (formerly Miss Crane?), David Douglass, Mrs. Douglass, Lewis Hallam Jr., Adam Hallam, Mrs. Hallam, Owen Morris, Mary Morris, Mr. Quelch, Mr. Reed, Mr. Sturt, Mr. Tomlinson, and John Tremaine. Members from the 1760 season Mrs. Dowthwaite and her daughter, no longer appear, nor does Walter Murray. The Allyns, Reed, and Tomlinson performed with the company during the 1759 season that began in New York and ended in Philadelphia. Apparently these irregulars returned to New York, and when the company returned to that city 1761, supplemented their incomes by acting in the evening. It will also be remembered that John Tremaine, who played with the Murray-Kean Company and the Upton Company in New York, had previously "retired" from the stage in 1752. The Mrs. Hallam who joins the company this year is Lewis Hallam Jr.'s new wife, Sarah Hallam.

The company began the year in Williamsburg where they had been playing in the fall of 1760. No evidence exists to suggest precisely when this engagement was concluded though they were certainly gone by early June. When the company traveled to Newport, Rhode Island colony, they carried with them a letter of recommendation from the Governor of the colony of Virginia dated 11 June 1761 which stated that the company had been in Virginia "for near a twelvemonth" (see 11 August 1761). Presumably they gathered the recommendation for their travels north in the summer, anticipating that such credentials might prove efficacious. Some dispute among scholars has arisen, however, in regard to this June 11 letter. Rankin (93) suggests that the company traveled without the document, and when it was needed a "representative rushed southward to rectify this oversight." Rankin's explanation is based upon a handbill advertising a series of *Moral Dialogues* (i.e., *Othello*) to be delivered by the Douglass Company in Newport 10 June, though no year is specified on the handbill. This ambiguity proves to be the critical point.

From this handbill Rankin (and others) have surmised that the Douglass Company arrived in Rhode Island in the spring, encountered opposition, sent "a representative southward" for their character letter, while proceeding with the subterfuge of *Moral Dialogues*. The printed cast list of the *Dialogues*, however, requires all the principals of the company, leaving only four minor actors unaccounted for: Mr. Reed, Mr. Sturt, Mr. Tomlinson, and John Tremaine. Three of these four were not even members of the company in Williamsburg (Tremaine, Tomlinson, Reed all remained in New York at that time), and therefore none was a likely representative to the governor of Virginia. The fourth, Sturt–a minor actor–possibly performed in Williamsburg, but had only joined the company in Upper Marlborough less than a year before. Presumably Douglass would not have entrusted such important business to such a minor member. In fact, the likelihood of Douglass ever leaving Virginia without a character letter for a completely new location is highly improbable as such letters were routinely required. Perhaps the issue is not as complex as Rankin argues. The complications evaporate if the undated handbill refers to a 1762 rather than a 1761 production of the *Moral Dialogues*.

We offer, therefore, that the Douglass Company arrived in Rhode Island in early summer 1761, perhaps July, with their letter of character in hand dated from Virginia, 11 June 1761. Douglass made known his plans to open a theatre in Newport, and immediately a faction of the town assembled to prohibit the players (see 1 August). Douglass pleaded publicly, offered his recommendations, and in spite of the opposition (see 11 August) built his theatre, which Seilhamer (1:125) states "stood at Easton's Point, near Dyer's Gate, in the north part of town." The theatre opened on 2 September, the opposition subsided (see 10 September), and the town supported a two-month season, culminating with two performances for the benefit of the poor. The opposition arose once again during late spring and early summer 1762 when the Douglass Company returned to Rhode Island (see headnote for 1762). It is to this season (i.e., 1762), therefore, that the undated handbill which announces the *Moral Dialogues* belongs.

At the same time (August 1761) Douglass was also engaged with the Lieutenant Governor of New York to secure permission to build a theatre and perform that winter. From Newport the Douglass Company returned to New York in early November where they built the Chapel Street Theatre, which opened on 18 November, and played out the year.

✱✱✱

March 1761   New Theater, Williamsburg, Virginia colony
Play not identified.
Douglass Company.
   [George Washington records in his *Diary* that he spent £2.7.6 on "Play Tickets" while in Williamsburg. Source: Ford 19.]

1 August 1761   Newport, Rhode Island colony
Governmental meeting.
Douglass Company.
   [Willard (6) states that on this date

a special town meeting was called at the request of a number of freemen, by warrant of the town council, and it being put to vote whether the freemen 'were for allowing plays to be acted in town or not, it was voted, not.' The players, notwithstanding this intimation of the popular will, prepared a temporary theatre, and gave their initial performance on the 7th [*recte* 2nd] of September.]

11 August 1761   Newport, Rhode Island colony
Newspaper notice.
Douglass Company.

[The *Newport Mercury* of this date reprints the following notice:

> The company of comedians propose to entertain the town for a short time with theatrical performances. As they have been at considerable expense, they humbly hope that the inhabitants will grant them their protection; and, if they are so happy as to meet with encouragement, they propose to give a benefit night for the support of the poor. The following recommendation, copied from the original was signed by the Governor, Council, and near one hundred of the principal gentlemen of Virginia:
>
> Williamsburg, June 11, 1761.
> The company of comedians under the direction of David Douglass have performed in this colony for near a twelvemonth; during which time they have made it their constant practice to behave with prudence and discretion in their private character, and to use their utmost endeavours to give general satisfaction in their public capacity. We have therefore thought proper to recommend them as a company whose behaviour merits the favour of the public, and who are capable of entertaining a sensible and polite audience.]

22 August 1761   New York
Newspaper notice.
Douglass Company.

[The following item appeared in the *Connecticut Gazette* of this date: "New-York, August 17. Last week his honour the Lieutenant Governor was pleased to give Mr. Douglass permission to build a theatre, to perform in this city the ensuing winter."]

2 September 1761   The Theatre, Newport, Rhode Island colony
The Fair Penitent.
Lethe.
Douglass Company.

[Source: *Boston Gazette* (21 September 1761).]

4 September 1761   The Theatre, Newport, Rhode Island colony
Jane Shore.
The Toy Shop.
Douglass Company.
   [Source: *Boston Gazette* (21 September 1761).]

7 September 1761   The Theatre, Newport, Rhode Island colony
The Provoked Husband.
The King and the Miller of Mansfield.
Douglass Company.
   [About £50 was raised for "the benefit of the poor." Source: (New York) *Parker's Gazette* (1 October 1761); *Boston Gazette* (21 September 1761).]

8 September 1761   The Theatre, Newport, Rhode Island colony
The Provoked Husband.
The King and the Miller of Mansfield.
Douglass Company.
   [Source: *Boston Gazette* (21 September 1761).]

9 September 1761   The Theatre, Newport, Rhode Island colony
George Barnwell [i.e., *The London Merchant*].
The Mock Doctor.
Douglass Company.
   [Source: *Boston Gazette* (21 September 1761).]

10 September 1761 Newport, Rhode Island colony
Newspaper notice.
Douglass Company.
   [The *Boston Gazette* of 21 September 1761 contains the following extract of a letter from Newport, dated 10 September 1761:

> As to the opposition and clamour against the Play-House erected here, it was much too vehement to continue, and, like the snow or hail of midsummer, melted gradually away. The house was open'd on the second of the month with the Fair Penitent, and Aesop in the Shades: and I cannot think you ever saw the Royal houses of Drury and Covent Garden fuller (without being crowded) or any audience there more deeply attentive or better pleased. On the evening of the fourth Jane Shore with the Toy-Shop were perform'd to the highest satisfaction of a very full house. On Monday and Tuesday last the Provok'd Husband with the Miller of Mansfield were perform'd with the greatest applause. Last evening George Barnwell with the Mock Doctor were exhibited before a great many of our General Assembly, and as many others as then could be admitted, and I can assure you that the audience were greatly mov'd and affected with the distress and fate of the unhappy

hero of that very moral and virtuous entertainment. Upon the whole I not only invite you here on this occasion, but encourage you to give all your friends ample assurances that the Company of Comedians here, more than verify their just letters of credence from Virginia, and are indeed capable of entertaining a very polite and sensible audience.]

21 September 1761 Newport, Rhode Island colony
Newspaper notice.
Douglass Company.

[The *Boston Gazette* of this date prints a long and scathing letter dated 18 September 1761 which disparagingly refers to the benefit of 7 September, of which the "motives are so obvious that he who runs may read them." The benefit, the writer argues, was "artfully contriv'd to accomplish the design [i.e., of establishing a theatre], in opposition to the avow'd sentiments of the town, and 'tis needless to mention the indefatigable measures pursued, to draw persons of every rank into the game." This ruse was accomplished when the "comedians complimented the house [i.e., the House of Representatives] with tickets, the lure took, and it was accordingly adjourn'd by Mr. Speaker, and the play-house attended by the major part of the members .... To oppose vice, luxury, and debauchery, is for the publick good, but to offer robbery for burnt offerings, is an empty sacrifice." The author concludes as follows:

> However well the pretended charity has been adapted, a theater is in no respect adapted to the state and circumstances of this poor, small town.—Can any man in his senses, not abandon'd to pleasure, think a place so young can throw away three or four thousand pounds a week at a play-house, or can he probably imagine, that a thousand pounds given to the poor to still, what is term'd a popular clamour, can be an equivalent for the loss of £30,000 consum'd in the short space of eight of ten weeks, besides a great loss of time.—To all such charities, may not the following maxim be justly applied, he steals the goose and gives the giblets in alms.]

27 October 1761   The Theatre, Newport, Rhode Island colony
Newspaper notice.
Douglass Company.

[A violent storm "came near spoiling the entertainment." Source: *Newport Mercury* (27 October 1761).]

31 October 1761   The Theatre, Newport, Rhode Island colony
Douglas.
Douglass Company.

THE COLONIAL AMERICAN STAGE 215

[Second benefit for the poor. A review of this performance appeared in the *Newport Mercury* for 3 November 1761:

> On Friday evening last, the company of comedians finished their performances in this town by enacting the tragedy of "Douglas" for the benefit of the poor. This second charity is undoubtedly intended as an expression of gratitude for the countenence and favour the town has shown them, and it can not without an uncommon degree of malevolence be ascribed to an interested or selfish view, because it is given at a time when the company are just leaving the place, and conseqently can have neither hopes nor fears from the publick. In return for this generosity it ought in justice to be told that the behavior of the company has been irreproachable; and with regard to their skill as players, the universal pleasure and satisfaction they have given is their best and most honourable testimony. The character they brought from the governor and gentlemen of Virginia has been fully verified, and therefore we shall run no risk in pronouncing that "they are capable of entertaining a sensible and polite audience."

Source: *Newport Mercury* (3 November 1761).]

18 November 1761   Chapel St. Theatre, New York
The Fair Penitent.
Lethe.
Douglass Company.
   [The Chapel St.Theatre opened with this performance. Prices: Box, 8s.; pit, 5s.; gallery, 3s. The play begins at 6:00. Source: *New York Mercury* (16 November 1761).]

23 November 1761   Chapel St. Theatre, New York
The Provoked Husband.
The King and the Miller of Mansfield.
Douglass Company
   [Source: *New York Mercury* (23 November 1761).]

26 November 1761   Chapel St. Theatre, New York
Hamlet.
   Hamlet–Hallam; Claudius–Douglass; Horatio–Reed; Ghost–Quelch; Polonius–Morris; Laertes–Allyn; Marcellus–A. Hallam; Guildenstern–Sturt; Lucianus–Tomlinson; Francisco–Tremain; Grave-diggers–Quelch and Tomlinson; Gertrude–Mrs. Douglass; Ophelia–Mrs. Morris; Player Queen–Mrs. Hallam.
A Wonder! An Honest Yorkshireman.
   Gaylove–Quelch; Blunder–Allyn; Slango–A. Hallam; Muckworm–Morris; Sapscull–Sturt; Arabella–Mrs. Morris; Combrush–Mrs. Douglass.

Douglass Company.
   [Source: Odell 1:82–83, following a now lost playbill, the details of which were preserved by Ireland.]

1 December 1761   Chapel St. Theatre, New York
The Suspicious Husband
   Strickland–Douglass; Frankly–Quelch; Bellamy–Morris; Ranger–Hallam; Meggot–Allyn; Buckle–Sturt; Tester–Tomlinson; Simon–Tremain; Clarinda–Mrs. Douglass; Mrs. Strickand–Mrs. Hallam; Jacintha–Mrs. Morris; Lucetta–Mrs. Allyn; Landlady–Mrs. Crane; Milliner–Mrs. Allyn.
Damon and Phillida.
   Damon–Sturt; Arcas–Reed; Corydon–Morris; Mopsus–Quelch; Cymon–Tomlinson; Phillida–Mrs. Morris.
Douglass Company.
   [Odell (1:83) located the cast lists in the *New York Mirror* of 25 November 1837. Source: *New York Mercury* (30 November 1761).]

4 December 1761   Chapel St. Theatre, New York
Tamerlane.
The Toy Shop.
Douglass Company.
   [Prices: boxes 8s.; pit 5s.; gallery 3s. Source: *New York Gazette & Weekly Post-Boy* (3 December 1761).]

7 December 1761   Chapel St. Theatre, New York
The Constant Couple.
   Sir Harry Wildair–Hallam; Lady Lurewell–Mrs. Douglass.
The Virgin Unmasked.
Douglass Company.
   [Source: *New York Mercury* (7 December 1761).]

14 December 1761 Chapel St. Theatre, New York
The Conscious Lovers.
The Mock Doctor.
Douglass Company.
   [Source: *New York Mercury* (14 December 1761).]

18 December 1761 Chapel St. Theatre, New York
Henry IV, Part 1* (William Shakespeare).
   King Henry–Quelch; Hotspur–Hallam; Falstaff–Douglass.
Flora, or Hob in the Well.
   Hob–Quelch; Flora–Mrs. Hallam.
Douglass company.

[Source: *New York Gazette & Weekly Post-Boy* (17 December 1761).]

21 December 1761   Chapel St. Theatre, New York
Douglas.
The Devil to Pay.
Douglass company.
   [Source: *New York Mercury* (21 December 1761).]

26 December 1761   Chapel St. Theatre, New York
George Barnwell [i.e., *The London Merchant*].
   Millwood–Mrs. Douglass.
Lethe.
Douglass Company.
   [Source: Odell 1:84.]

28 December 1761   Chapel St. Theatre, New York
The Gamester.
The Devil to Pay.
Douglass Company.
   [This performance was presented

by particular Desire, and for the Entertainment of the Master, Wardens, and the rest of the Brethren of the Ancient and Honourable Society of Free and Accepted Masons ... An occasional prologue to be spoken by Mr. Douglass in the character of a Master Mason .... After the play, the original epilogue, and after the farce, a Mason's epilogue, by Mrs. Douglass.

Source: *New York Mercury* (28 December 1761).]

28 December 1761   New York
Newspaper notice.
Douglass Company.
   [The *New York Mercury* of this date prints a rebuttal by Douglass of charges that the company have made exorbitant profits (cf., Hughes 33; Odell 1:84–86). Herewith a portion of Douglass's remarks:

The unchristian-like temper of this declaimer, is not more evident in any thing, than in the very ungenerous manner in which he treats the characters of the company of comedians now here. He gives them the vilest epithets, without perhaps being acquainted in the least with one of them, or having given himself the trouble to enquire about them; if he had, I am certain he could not have learnt any thing in their behaviour which could give any ground for such base and abusive language. Mr. Douglass, the director of the company, is of a good family, and has a genteel and liberal education; and if we may judge from behaviour, conduct, and conversation, has better pretentions to the name of a gentleman in every sense of the word, than he who so politely and generously lavishes the appellation of vagrant and stroller on him.

    I cannot conclude without taking notice of one other glaring instance of this pious gentleman's little regard to candour or truth; he tells us the expence of the Play-House to the public for the season will amount to £6000, by which he certainly intends to make the credulous believe, that the comedians will carry away that sum from the city. They have as yet permission to act but for two months from their beginning. They act but twice a week, which will be 16 plays in the two months. The greatest sum they have received any night was about £180; they cannot get more, for the house will not hold a larger audience than they then had; but at a medium we may set them down at £120 a night, which for 16 nights amounts to £1920. The current expence of these 16 nights will amount to £250; the house cost them not less than £650, and they have laid out about £400 in scenes and cloaths, which sums, amounting to £1300, all expended by them in this city, when deducted from the other, leaves £620, out of which they are to pay for their lodging, washing, and diet, for a much longer time than they have acted. What shall we now think of this terrible tax upon the publick of £6000?]

1762

The Douglass Company continued a lively winter 1761–62 New York season where they concluded with charity benefits at the end of April. The company consisted of the following known players: Adam Allyn, Mrs. Allyn, Mrs. Crane, David Douglass, Mrs. Douglass, Adam Hallam, Lewis Hallam Jr., Mrs. Hallam, Owen Morris, Mary Morris, Mr. Quelch, Mr. Reed, Mr. Sturt, Mr. Tomlinson, and Mr. Tremaine. When the company left New York several local actors remained behind, namely Mr. Reed, Mr. Tomlinson, and Mr. Tremaine.

Douglass, sensing that fresh markets were needed, attempted to open new territory in Portsmouth, New Hampshire colony, during late spring and early summer of this year. He petitioned the government of that colony for permission to build and operate a playhouse, but despite the support of some forty citizens, who argued that plays were invaluable to "a civil and well regulated society," more than two hundred opposing citizens carried the day. On 5 June 1762 the House of Representatives passed an order denying Douglass's request (see entry for that date). Douglass returned to Portsmouth in 1769, no doubt hoping that the climate of opposition had subsided, but again was unsuccessful. In fact, Portsmouth did not welcome a theatrical presence until 1772, when a Mr. Morgan temporarily established a small troupe (see headnote for 1772).

Failing in New Hampshire, Douglass carried his company back to Newport, Rhode Island colony, where the opposition seemed to have the upper hand this year, as the only evidence of performance in Newport is the subterfuge of *Othello* presented as a "moral dialogue." Blake (21) states that they gave several performances in the large room of an inn, which we suggest is the King's Arm Tavern, that is, where the *Moral Dialogues* are announced for performance. The fact that the company performed in the King's Arm Tavern instead of the new theatre erected during September 1761 is problematic. The traditional account maintains that a violent storm on 27 October 1761 destroyed several buildings in Newport, including serious damage to the theatre (see entry for that date; cf. Seilhamer 1:125; Rankin 95). As the company performed in that theatre on 31 October 1761, however, another explanation is required. We suggest that the company performed in the King's Arms Tavern as a part of the subterfuge for avoiding the anti-theatrical opposition. The company left little record of their brief and troubled stay in Newport and moved on to Providence.

By July the record is far more solid. The company solicited Providence, Rhode Island colony, for permission to play where again the citizenry voted to prohibit stage plays (see 19 July). Douglass temporarily ignored the opposition and evaded the law by using the "concert" strategy similar to that employed by unlicensed managers such as Samuel Foote in London to evade the Licensing Act, i.e., by charging for music and then offering plays "gratis." A notice in the *Boston Evening Post* of 16 August 1762 reads "'N.B. There will be a concert every day this week, except Saturday," meaning that in employing the concert format, they were performing daily, though details have survived for only a few of the dates. The device was apparently successful enough to draw sufficient clientele, for by August, Douglass had built a theatre by subscription (see 23 August). The opposition remained active drafting a petition to oppose the theatre and presenting it to the General Assembly where it found favor (see 24 August). Douglass, deterred in Rhode Island, abandoned the colony. We know nothing of the company's whereabouts until November finds them again

220   THE COLONIAL AMERICAN STAGE

playing in Williamsburg, which may again have hosted a solid season but has left little evidence.

Also this year we hear for the first time of theatrical activity in Cuba (see December 1762).

※※※

1 January 1762   Chapel St. Theatre, New York
The Beggar's Opera.
    Macheath–Quelch; Peachum–Tuckey; Polly–Mrs. Hallam; Lucy–Mrs. Morris.
Douglass Company.
    [Source: *New York Mercury* (31 December 1761).]

4 January 1762   Chapel St. Theatre, New York
Venice Preserved.
The Lying Valet.
Douglass Company.
    ["A prologue and epilogue, in vindication of dramatic entertainments, to be spoken by Mr. Hallam and Mrs. Douglass" appear in the *New York Mercury* of 11 January 1762. Prices: boxes 8s.; pit 5s.; gallery 3s. "The doors to be open'd at four, and the play to begin precisely at six o'clock." Source: *New York Mercury* (4 January 1762).]

7 January 1762   Chapel St. Theatre, New York
Cato.
    Cato–Douglass; Sempronius–Hallam; Marcia–Mrs. Douglass; Lucia–Mrs. Morris. Prologue spoken by Quelch.
The Honest Yorkshireman.
Douglass Company.
    [Source: *New York Gazette & Weekly Post-Boy* (7 January 1762).]

11 January 1762   Chapel St. Theatre, New York
Romeo and Juliet.
Douglass Company.
    [Source: *New York Mercury* (11 January 1762).]

20 January 1762   Chapel St. Theatre, New York
The Recruiting Officer.
Harlequin Collector.
Douglass Company.
    [Source: *New York Mercury* (18 January 1762).]

25 January 1762   Chapel St. Theatre, New York
Othello.
The Lying Valet.
Douglass Company.
   ["For the Benefit of the Poor." *New York Mercury* (1 February 1762) prints the complete accounts for this benefit, which are summarized as follows:

		£	s	d
Box	116@8s	46	8	
Pit	146@5s	36	10	
Gallery	90@3s	13	10	
Cash at door		36	12	6
Totals	352 tickets	133		6

Charges.
To candles, 26lb. spermacete, at 3s 6d, and 14 lb. Tallow, at 12d.
             5   5   0
To musick, Messrs. Harrison   and Van Dienval, at 36s
             3 12   0
To the front door keeper, 16s. Stage door keeper, 8s.
             1   4   0
To the assistants, 13s. bill-sticker, 4s.
             0 17   0
To the men's dresser, 4s, the stage-keeper, 32s.
             1 16   0
To the drummer, 4s.   4
Wine in the 2d act, 2s6d.   0   6   6
To H. Gaine, for two sets of bills, advertisements, and commissions,
             5 10   0
                            ———————
                            18 10   6

Balance   £114 10   0

Source: *New York Mercury* (25 January 1762); cf. discussion in Odell 1:87–88.]

1 February 1762   Chapel St. Theatre, New York
Richard III.
   Richard–Douglass; Richmond–Hallam; King Henry–Allyn; Prince Edward–A. Hallam; Duke of York–"a young Master, for his Diversion;" Buckingham–Tomlinson; Stanley–Morris; Lieutenant–Sturt; Catesby–Reed; Tressel–Hallam; Duchess–Mrs. Crane; Anne–Mrs. Morris; Queen Elizabeth–Mrs. Douglass.
Lethe.
   Chalkstone–Allyn;   Aesop–Douglass;   Fine Gentleman– Hallam; Mercury–Sturt; Frenchman–Allyn; Charon–Tom-

linson; Old Man–Morris; Tatoo–Reed; Bowman–Tomlinson; Drunken Man–Hallam; Mrs. Riot–Mrs. Douglass.
Douglass Company.
[Benefit Mrs. Douglass. Source: *New York Gazette & Weekly Post-Boy* (28 January 1762).]

4 February 1762   Chapel St. Theatre, New York
Theodosius.
Varanes–Hallam; Theodosius–Morris; Marcian–Douglass; Lucian–Reed; Atticus–Sturt; Leontine–Tomlinson; Aranthes–A. Hallam; Pulcheria–Mrs. Morris; Marina–Mrs. Hallam; Flavilla–Mrs. Allyn; Julia–Mrs. Crane; Athenais–Mrs. Douglass.
The Virgin Unmasked.
Goodwill–Morris; Coupée–A. Hallam; Quaver–Tomlinson; Mr. Thomas–Reed; Miss Lucy–Mrs. Morris.
Douglass Company.
[Benefit Mrs. Morris. "With a view of the inside of the temple in its original splendor, at the first institution of the Christian religion at Constantinople: The vision of Constantine the Great, a bloody cross in the air, and these words in golden characters, In Hoc Signo Vinces." Source: *New York Gazette & Weekly Post-Boy* (4 February 1762).]

8 February 1762   Chapel St. Theatre, New York
The Committee.
Damon and Phillida.
Douglass Company.
[Benefit A. Hallam. Announced but postponed due to the indisposition of Mrs. Morris. Source: Odell 1:89.]

10 February 1762   Chapel St. Theatre, New York
The Committee.
Damon and Phillida.
Douglass Company.
[Benefit A. Hallam. Announced but postponed due to the indisposition of Mrs. Morris Source: *New York Gazette & Weekly Post-Boy* (8 February 1762).]

11 February 1762   Chapel St. Theatre, New York
Newspaper notice.
[The following notice appeared in the *New York Gazette & Weekly Post-Boy* of this date:

Mr. A. Hallam is sorry to acquaint the town that he is under the disagreeable necessity of again postponing his play till Monday next, when it will certainly be acted, as another performer will be ready in the character of Mrs. Day, should Mrs. Morris's indisposition continue.

The play in question is *The Committee*.]

15 February 1762   Chapel St. Theatre, New York
The Committee.
    Teague–Hallam; Ruth–Mrs. Douglass; Mrs. Day–Mrs. Morris.
Damon and Phillida.
Douglass Company.
    [Benefit Adam Hallam. Source: *New York Gazette & Weekly Post-Boy* (11 February 1762).]

18 February 1762   Chapel St. Theatre, New York
Douglas.
    Young Norval–Hallam; Randolph–Douglass; Glenalvon–Reed; Old Norval–Morris; Officer–Tomlinson; Attendant–Tremain; Lady Randolph–Mrs. Douglass.
Harlequin Collector.
    Harlequin–Hallam; Miller–Allyn; Magician–Sturt; Anatomist–Morris; Porter–Tomlinson; Clown–Douglass; Columbine–Mrs. Douglass.
Douglass Company.
    [Benefit Douglass. Source: *New York Gazette & Weekly Post-Boy* (18 February 1762).]

22 February 1762   Chapel St. Theatre, New York
A Bold Stroke for a Wife.
The King and the Miller of Mansfield.
Douglass Company.
    [Benefit Allyn. Source: *New York Gazette & Weekly Post-Boy* (22 February 1762).]

1 March 1762   Chapel St. Theatre, New York
Romeo and Juliet.
Douglass Company.
    [Benefit Quelch. Announced but postponed. Source: *New York Gazette & Weekly Post-Boy* (25 February 1762).]

4 March 1762   Chapel St. Theatre, New York
Romeo and Juliet.

Romeo–Hallam; Prince–Douglass; Paris–Tomlinson; Montague–Sturt; Capulet–Morris; Mercutio–Douglass; Benvolio–A. Hallam; Tybalt–Reed; Friar Laurence–Allyn; Friar John–Tremain; Lady Capulet–Mrs. Allyn; Juliet–Mrs. Douglass; Nurse–Mrs. Morris. Vocal parts in the funeral procession: Mrs. Morris, Quelch, Sturt, Tremain, and Mrs. Allyn.
Douglass Company.
[Benefit Quelch. Seilhamer (1:131) assigns this play to 1 March 1762; however, the play was announced for that date but was postponed. Source: *New York Gazette & Weekly Post-Boy* (1 March 1762).]

8 March 1762   Chapel St. Theatre, New York
Love for Love.
Harlequin Collector.
Douglass Company.
[Benefit Hallam. Announced but postponed. Source: *New York Gazette & Weekly Post-Boy* (8 March 1762).]

15 March 1762   Chapel St. Theatre, New York
Love for Love.
Ben–Hallam; Valentine–Douglass; Angelica–Mrs. Douglass.
Harlequin Collector.
Harlequin–Hallam; Clown–Douglass.
Douglass Company.
[Benefit Hallam. Originally announced for 8 March but postponed until this date. Source: *New York Gazette & Weekly Post-Boy* (11 March 1762).]

22 March 1762   Chapel St. Theatre, New York
The Beaux' Stratagem.
Archer–Hallam; Aimwell–Douglass; Scrub–A. Hallam; Mrs. Sullen–Mrs. Douglass.
Flora.
Hob–Allyn; Flora–Mrs. Hallam.
Douglass Company.
[Benefit Morris. *Richard III* had originally been announced for this benefit. Source: *New York Gazette & Weekly Post-Boy* (18 March 1762).]

29 March 1762   Chapel St. Theatre, New York
The Inconstant.
Young Mirabel–Hallam; Old Mirabel–Morris; Bisarre–Mrs. Hallam.
Miss in Her Teens.

Flash–Hallam; Loveit–Tomlinson; Biddy–Mrs. Hallam.
Douglass Company.
　　[Benefit Mrs. Hallam. The afterpiece advertised as "not acted here these eight years." Source: *New York Gazette & Weekly Post-Boy* (25 March 1762).]

April 1762　　　　　Milford, Connecticut colony
Play unidentified.
Students of Yale.
　　[Bloom (31) documents clandestine theatrical activity by students at Yale College. The records of the college indicate that Ingersal and "a number of Scholars and others went to the Tavern and acted a Play and had a mixed dance.... Ingersal shall be fined three shillings."]

12 April 1762　　　　Chapel St. Theatre, New York
Hamlet.
　　Hamlet–Hallam; Ghost–Tomlinson; Queen–Mrs. Douglass.
The Devil to Pay.
　　Jobson–Tomlinson; Nell–Mrs. Morris.
Douglass Company.
　　[Benefit Tomlinson. Source: *American Chronicle* (12 April 1762).

19 April 1762　　　　Chapel St. Theatre, New York
The Distrest Mother.
　　Orestes–Hallam; Pylades–Reed; Phoenix–Tomlinson; Pyrrhus–Douglass; Hermione–Mrs. Morris; Cephisa–Mrs. Allyn; Cleone–Mrs. Hallam; Andromache–Mrs. Douglass.
The Mock Doctor.
　　Gregory–Douglass; Sir Jasper–Morris; Leander–Sturt; Helebore–Tremain; Robert–A. Hallam; Harry–Tomlinson; Davy–Allyn; James–Reed; Charlotte–Mrs. Crane; Dorcas–Mrs. Morris.
Douglass Company.
　　[Benefit Reed. Source: *New York Gazette & Weekly Post-Boy* (19 April 1762).]

26 April 1762　　　　Chapel St. Theatre, New York
The Committee.
　　As 15 February 1762.
A Wonder! An Honest Yorkshireman.
　　Gaylove–Quelch; Arabella–Mrs. Morris.
Douglass Company.

[Benefit for the Charity School. Source: *New York Gazette & Weekly Post-Boy* (26 April 1762).]

3 May 1762   Chapel St. Theatre, New York
Newspaper notice.
Douglass Company.

[The following item appeared in the *New York Mercury* of this date:

> A Pistole Reward, WILL be given to whoever can discover the Person who was so very rude to throw Eggs from the Gallery, upon the Stage last Monday, by which the Cloaths of some Ladies and Gentlemen in the Boxes were spoiled, and the Performance in some Measure interrupted. DAVID DOUGLASS.]

3 June 1762   Portsmouth, New Hampshire colony
Petitions.

[The following two petitions relevant to the Douglass Company were recorded on this date:

> Petition for a Playhouse at Portsmouth.
> Province of New Hampshire.
> To his Excellency Benning Wentworth Esq. Governor and Commander-in-Chief in and over his Majesty's Province of New Hampshire: The Petition of sundry of the Inhabitants of Portsmouth, in the Province of New Hampshire — humbly shews:
> That the subscribers understand that there has been a proposal made by one of the actors of the plays, sometime since at Newport, but more lately at New York, to erect a playhouse here something hence; and that there is a petition presented to your Excellency to inhibit and prevent the same, Now your petitioners, being informed that the said actors act no obscene or immoral plays, but such as tend to the improvement of the mind and informing the judgement in things proper to be known, in a civil and well regulated society: Your Petitioners pray your Excellency not to discourage, but rather forward the same; and your petitioners as in duty bound shall ever pray, &c. Signed June 3rd, 1762.

Forty-five signatures follow. Source: *Provincial Papers–New Hampshire*, 6:832.

> Petition Against a Playhouse at Portsmouth.
> To his Excellency Benning Wentworth Esq. Governor and Commander-in-Chief in and over his Majesty's Province of New Hampshire, and the Honorable his Majesty's Council for said Province:
> Humbly shews, sundry of the freeholders and other Inhabitants of the Town of Portsmouth, in said Province—That your petitioners have been informed that a motion has been made of liberty for a number of plays to exhibit sundry entertainments of the stage in this town, which

your petitioners apprehend would be of very pernicious consequences, not only to the morals of the young people, (even if there should be no immoral exhibitions) by dissipating their minds, and giving them an idle turn of attachment to pleasure and amusement, with other ill effects, which there is the greatest reason to fear from such entertainments in a place where they are a novelty. Add to this, that such a time of general distress, where in the people here have lately suffered for want of the necessaries of life, and which is not yet entirely over, is more peculiarly improper for such amusements, which are always destructive to a new country, but especially at a season when there is the utmost need to raise and promote a spirit of industry: Wherefore, for these and many other reasons, your petitioners humbly pray that no such liberty may be granted: and if assumed, that they may be restrained, and your petitioners shall ever pray, &c.

Forty signatures follow. Source: *Provincial Papers–New Hampshire*, 6:833.]

5 June 1762   Portsmouth, New Hampshire colony
Governmental action.
Douglass Company.
   [On this date, acting on David Douglass's earlier petition for approval of his plan to establish a theatre in Portsmouth, the House of Representatives of New Hampshire denied Douglass's request and passed a measure to prevent the acting of plays in in the colony. Source: "Attempt to Establish a Play-House in New Hampshire, 1762."]

10 June [1762 ?]   King's Arms Tavern, Newport, Rhode Island colony
"Moral Dialogues, in five parts."
   Othello–Douglass; Iago–Allyn; Cassio–Hallam; Brabantio–Morris; Roderigo–Quelch; Desdemona–Mrs. Morris; Amelia–Mrs. Douglass.
Douglass Company.
   [These "Dialogues" were, in fact, the five acts of *Othello*. Source: Seilhamer 1:123ff.; from a playbill now lost; cf. Blake 23, Willard 8.]

19 July 1762 Providence, Rhode Island colony
Governmental action.
Douglass Company.
   [It was voted and resolved at a town meeting "that actors should not be permitted to exhibit stage-plays." Source: Blake 30.]

10 August 1762   Providence, Rhode Island colony
The Fair Penitent.
   Lothario–Hallam; Horatio–Douglass; Sciolto–Allyn; Rossano–A. Hallam; Altamont–Quelch; Calista–Mrs. Douglass; Lavinia–Mrs. Morris; Lucilla–Mrs. Hallam.
Damon and Phillida.
   Damon–Sturt; Mopsus–Quelch; Corydon–Morris; Arcas–Allyn; Cymon–A. Hallam; Phillida–Mrs. Morris.
Douglass Company.
   [The plays were performed "gratis" between the parts of a musical concert. "N.B. There will be a concert [i.e., plays] on Friday, and on every day next week, except Saturday." Source: *Newport Mercury* (10 August 1762).]

12 August 1762   The New School House, Providence, Rhode Island colony
The Fair Penitent.
   As 10 August 1762.
Damon and Phillida.
   As 10 August 1762.
Douglass Company.
   [The plays were performed "gratis" between the parts of a musical concert. Source: *Boston Evening Post* (9 August 1762).]

17 August 1762   The New School House, Providence, Rhode Island colony
Cato.
   Cato–Douglass; Semphonis–Hallam; Lucius–Quelch; Syphax–Allyn; Portius–Morris; Marcus–A. Hallam; Marcia–Mrs. Douglass; Lucia–Mrs. Morris.
The Lying Valet.
   Sharp–Quelch; Cuttle–Douglass; Dick–Hallam; Gayless–Morris; Beau Trippet–Allyn; Mrs. Trippet–Mrs. Allyn; Miss Trippet–Mrs. Hallam. Melissa–Mrs. Morris; Kitty Pry–Mrs. Douglass; Mrs. Gadabout–Mrs. Crane.
Douglass Company.
   [Performed "gratis" between the parts of a musical concert. Source: *Boston Evening Post* (16 August 1762).]

23 August 1762   Providence, Rhode Island colony
Governmental action.
   [The following petition, reprinted by Blake (30–31) was presented to the General Assembly of the Colony of Rhode Island:

The Petition of us, the subscribers, inhabitants of the County of Providence, humbly sheweth that a number of stage-players have lately appeared, and a play-house has lately been built in the town of Providence, that the inhabitants of said town being legally called by warrant did, at their late town meeting, by a large majority, pass a vote that no stage-plays be acted in said town; yet the actors, in defiance of said vote, and in defiance of the public authority of said town have begun, and are now daily continuing to exhibit stage plays and other theatrical performance, which has been, and still is, the occasion of great uneasiness to many people in this Colony. . . Wherefore your petitioners pray that you will take this matter into your consideration, and make some effectual law to prevent any stage-plays, comedies, or theatrical performances being acted in the Colony for the future.

Cf., *Rhode Island Colonial Records, 1757–1769*, 6:324–26.]

24 August 1762   Providence
Legislative action.
    [The petition of 23 August to suppress plays "was presented to the General Assembly on the 24th of August and immediately found favour in both Houses." Source: *Rhode Island Colonial Records, 1757–1769*, 6: 324–26; cf., Willard 14.]

24 August 1762   New School House, Providence, Rhode Island colony
The Distrest Mother.
    Pyrrhus–Quelch; Orestes–Hallam; Pylades–A. Hallam; Phoenix–Douglass; Andromache–Mrs. Douglas; Hermione–Mrs. Morris; Cephisa–Mrs. Allyn; Cleone–Mrs. Hallam.
Harlequin Collector.
    Harlequin–Hallam; Anatomist–Morris; Clown–Douglass; Miller–Allyn; Magician–Sturt; Columbine–Mrs. Hallam.
Douglass Company.
    [Performed "gratis" between the parts of a musical concert. Source: *Boston Evening Post* (23 August 1762).]

November 1762   New Theater, Williamsburg, Virginia colony
Play not identified.
Douglass Company.
    [George Washington records in his *Diary* that he spent £2.18.3 on "Play Tickets" while in Williamsburg. Source: Ford 19.]

December 1762   Havana, Cuba
The Fair Penitent.
A company of army officers.

[The *Boston Post-Boy* of 28 February 1763 prints the following extract of a December 1762 letter: "We open a theatre to-morrow night, which exhibits once a week, Captain ----- and some others, chief actors and managers." The *Pennsylvania Gazette* (27 November 1762), however, provides more details in reprinting of an extract of a letter from a gentleman in Havana:

> Thursday next is appointed to celebrate the Birth of the Prince of Wales, when there is to be a triple discharge of all the artillery in this place, and the evening is to be concluded with the play of the Fair Penitent, by the officers of the army, in a theatre built for that purpose ...."]

1763

Though no preserved cast lists are known, almost certainly the troupe playing in and around Williamsburg throughout the winter of 1762–63 was the Douglass Company. The records of this season are slight, indeed, and are primarily derived from George Washington's journal, which, regrettably, records payments for tickets but not play titles. After the Williamsburg season, the exact whereabouts of the company during the summer are unknown, though when they arrive in Charleston in November, they have apparently changed their name, being announced as "the American Company" (see 5 November), a title they would retain for the duration of their appearances in the colonies. In the same announcement several members of the company are named: David Douglass, Mrs. Douglass, Lewis Hallam Jr., Mrs. Harman, and Mr. Quelch.

By early December they have rebuilt the theatre on Queen Street in Charleston and opened a winter season. Though no cast lists are preserved from this season, besides those named in the 5 November announcement, several long-standing members who are listed in the spring playbills can be assumed to be in the company: Adam Allyn, Mrs. Allyn, Mrs. Crane, Adam Hallam, Mary Morris, and Owen Morris.

A further clandestine performance is known to have taken place in Boston (see 1 December).

***

20 January 1763   Petersburg, Virginia colony
Correspondence.
[Davis (1:291) quotes a letter the young Thomas Jefferson wrote to his friend John Page on this date: "I have some

thoughts of going to Petersburg if the actors go there in May." Source: Jefferson, *Papers*, 1: 7.]

26 April 1763   New Theater, Williamsburg, Virginia colony
Douglass Company.
    [George Washington records in his *Diary* that he spent 5s. on a "Play Ticket" for this date while in Williamsburg. Source: *Papers*, 7:190.]

29 April 1763   New Theater, Williamsburg, Virginia colony
Douglass Company.
    [George Washington records in his *Diary* that he spent 10s. on "Play Tickets" for this date while in Williamsburg. Source: *Papers*, 7:190.]

2 May 1763   New Theater, Williamsburg, Virginia colony
Douglass Company.
    [George Washington records in his *Diary* that he spent 12s. 6d. on "Play Tickets" for this date while in Williamsburg. Source: *Papers*, 7:209.]

3 May 1763   New Theater, Williamsburg, Virginia colony
Douglass Company.
    [George Washington records in his *Diary* that he spent 8s. 9d. on a"Play" for this date while in Williamsburg. Source: *Papers*, 7:209.]

5 May 1763   New Theater, Williamsburg, Virginia colony
Douglass Company.
    [George Washington records in his *Diary* that he spent 5s. on a "Play Ticket" for this date while in Williamsburg. Source: Ford 19.]

7 September 1763   Charleston
Newspaper notice.
    [Curtis (61) reprints evidence in the short-lived South Carolina newspaper, *Star and Public Advertiser*, of 7 September 1763 accusing "malicious and evil-disposed persons [having] cut and destroyed the scenes and furniture of the [play]house," evidencing the continuing presence of the theatre. The Douglass Company soon thereafter refitted this building for the opening of their winter season.]

5 November 1763   Queen St. Theatre, Charleston
Newspaper notice.

American Company.

[The *South Carolina Gazette* of this date announces the arrival of the Douglass Company, now having renamed itself the American Company, a title it would retain for the duration of the colonial period and again after the Revolution:

> A company of Comedians arrived here last Monday from Virginia who are called the American Company and were formerly under the direction of Mr. Lewis Hallam, till his death. Amongst the principal performers we hear are Mr. David Douglass (the present manager, married to Mrs. Hallam), Mr. Lewis Hallam, Jr., Mr. Quelsh, Mrs. Douglass, Mrs. Harman, etc. They have performed several years with great applause and in their private capacities acquired the best of characters. A theatre is already contracted for 75 feet by 35, to be erected near where that of Messrs. Holliday and Comp. formerly stood and intended to be opened the 5th of December next.]

1 December 1763   Boston
The Orphan.
Company unknown.

[The *Boston Evening Post* of 5 December 1763 contains the following item:

> It is said–that the ORPHAN on Thursday night last, was neither a credit to the actors or the company; and, notwithstanding the effect it had on some of the ladies, the characters were taken off in such a dull and insipid manner, that none but weak minds could be affected therewith;–and that the actors are in no danger of incurring the penalties in the law for preventing theatrical entertainments, as this could not be any ways denominated entertaining.]

12 December 1763   Queen St. Theatre, Charleston
The Mourning Bride* (William Congreve, 1697).
American Company.
[Source: Manigault, "Extracts of the Journal," 206.]

14 December 1763   Queen St. Theatre, Charleston
The Suspicious Husband.
Lethe.
American Company.
[Source: *Georgia Gazette* (29 December 1763).]

16 December 1763   Queen St. Theatre, Charleston
The Gamester.
Wives Metamorphosed [i.e., *The Devil to Pay*].
American Company.

["We hear they intend to perform every Monday, Wednesday and Friday." Source: *South Carolina Gazette* (10–17 December 1763).]

17 December 1763 Queen St. Theatre, Charleston
Newspaper notice.
[The *South Carolina Gazette* of this date comments on the elegance of the new theatre:

> The New Theatre in this town, which is elegantly finished, was opened on Wednesday evening, with the Suspicious Husband, and Lethe: Yesterday evening the company performed the Gamester and Wives Metamorphosed; and on Monday next, they present the Provoked Husband with Damon and Phillida.

Source: *South Carolina Gazette* (10–17 December 1763).]

19 December 1763 Queen St. Theatre, Charleston
The Provoked Husband.
Damon and Phillida.
American Company.
   [Source: *South Carolina Gazette* (10–17 December 1763).]

22 December 1763 Queen St. Theatre, Charleston
The Mourning Bride.
American Company.
   [Source: Curtis 430.]

27 December 1763 Queen St. Theatre, Charleston
The Beaux' Stratagem.
American Company.
   [Source: Cohen 117; *South Carolina Gazette* (31 December 1763).]

1764

During the spring the American Company continued their season in Charleston, and fortunately, advertised more complete cast listings. Known members included the following personnel: Adam Allyn, Mrs. Allyn, Mr. Barry, Miss Cheer, Mrs. Crane, David Douglass, Mrs. Douglass, Mr. Emmet, Mr. Furell, Adam Hallam, Lewis Hallam Jr., Mrs. Harman, Mr. Morris, Mrs. Morris, and Mr. Quelch.

At the close of the 1764 Charleston season, Douglass embarked for London where he arrived in early July to replenish his supply of actors, scenes, scripts, etc. (see 5 July 1764). An epidemic of smallpox may have shortened the theatrical season. The company probably returned to the West Indies, as a reference from 31 October 1765 refers to Douglass joined by the company in Barbados.

***

7 January 1764   Queen St. Theatre, Charleston
Douglas.
American Company.
  [Source: Manigault, "Extracts of the Journal," 206.]

13 January 1764   Queen St. Theatre, Charleston
Douglas.
American Company.
  [Source: Curtis 430.]

1 February 1764   Charleston
Correspondence.
  [Alexander Garden wrote to David Colden, son of New York Governor Cadawallader Colden, the following letter describing theatrical activities and finances in Charleston at this time:

> Sir — Your favour of Janry 26th 1763 was sent to me some time in November by Mr. Douglass. I was then confined to my room & had been for many weeks, as soon as I was able to see Company I begged Mr. Douglass to favour me with his & found him perfectly answer the Character which you draw of him. You may depend on this that I will not omit any opportunity to shew Every service in my power to him or any person whose acquaintance you are so obliging as to offer me.
>   He has met with all imaginable Success in this place since their theatre was opened, which I think was the first Wednesday of December, since which time they have performed thrice a week & Every night to a full nay a Crowded house. Hitherto they can't possibly have made less than £110 sterling [per] night at a medium for some nights they have made between 130 and 140 sterling in one night & I believe never under 90 £ sterling & that only one or two rainy evenings. This will shew you how much the people here are given to gaiety, when you compare this place in numbers of Inhabitants to York which is at Least double if not Treble in number to us. Mr. Douglass has made a valuable acquisition in Miss Cheer who arrived here from London much about the time that Mr. Douglass arrived with his company. Soon after that, she agreed to go on the stage where she has since appeared in some Chief Characters with great applause particularly Monimia in the

Orphan and Juliet of Shakespeare and Hermione of the Distrest Mother. Her fine person, her youth, her Voice, & Appearance &c conspire to make her appear with propriety—Such a one they much wanted as Mrs. Douglass was their Chief actress before & who on that account had always too many Characters to appear in.

Source: Colden 6: 281–82.]

3 February 1764   Queen St. Theatre, Charleston
George Barnwell; or, The London Merchant.
American Company.
 [Source: Manigault, "Extracts of the Journal," 206.]

13 February 1764   Queen St. Theatre, Charleston
The Conscious Lovers.
American Company.
 [Source: Manigault, "Extracts of the Journal," 206.]

24 February 1764   Queen St. Theatre, Charleston
Jane Shore.
American Company.
 [Source: Manigault, "Extracts of the Journal," 206.]

27 February 1764   Queen St. Theatre, Charleston
Love for Love.
American Company.
 [Source: Manigault, "Extracts of the Journal," 206.]

19 March 1764   Queen St. Theatre, Charleston
The Jealous Wife* (George Colman Sr., 1761).
American Company.
 [Curtis (430) dates this performance as 17 March 1764. Source: Manigault, "Extracts of the Journal," 207.]

26 March 1764   Queen St. Theatre, Charleston
The Orphan of China* (Arthur Murphy, 1759).
 Timurkan–Allyn; Octar–Emmet; Zamti–Douglass; Etan–Hallam; Hamet–A. Hallam; Morat–Morris; Orasming–Furell; Zimventi–Barry; Mirvan–Morris; Mandane–Mrs. Douglass.
The Anatomist.
 Old Gerrald–Morris; Young Gerrald–Douglass; Mons. le Med'cine–Allyn; Martin–A. Hallam; Crispin–Hallam; Simon–Furell; Doctor's Wife–Mrs. Crane; Angelica–Mrs. Morris; Beatrice–Mrs. Douglass; Waiting Woman–Mrs. Allyn.
American Company.

[Benefit Morris. Prices: boxes, 40s.; pit, 30s.; gallery, 20s. "To begin exactly at half past six o'clock." Hughes (35) misdates this performance as 10 March 1764. Source: *South Carolina Gazette* (10–17 March 1764).]

29 March 1764   Queen St. Theatre, Charleston
Theodosius.
American Company.
[Source:Manigault, "Extracts of the Journal," 207.]

2 April 1764   Beekman St. Theatre, New York
Newspaper notice.
[The following item appears in the *New York Gazette* of this date: "To Be Let, The Play-House at the upper end of Beekman's Street, very convenient for a store, being upwards of 90 feet in length, nigh 40 feet wide. Enquire of William Beekman."]

9 April 1764   Queen St. Theatre, Charleston
The Mourning Bride.
American Company.
[Source: Manigault, "Extracts of the Journal," 207.]

12 April 1764   Queen St. Theatre, Charleston
Romeo and Juliet.
American Company.
[Source: Manigault, "Extracts of the Journal," 207.]

25 April 1764   Queen St. Theatre, Charleston
A Wonder! A Woman Keeps a Secret!* (Susanna Centlivre, 1718).
Don Felix–Hallam; Don Lopez–Morris; Frederick–A. Hallam; Don Pedro–Emmet; Col. Britton–Furell; Gibby–Barry; Lissardo–Allyn; Juliet–Miss Cheer; Isabella–Mrs. Crane; Flora–Mrs. Morris; Inis–Mrs. Harman.
An unspecified farce.
American Company.
[Benefit Mrs. Crane and Mr. Barry. "Being the last Benefit." Source: *South Carolina Gazette* (24–31 March 1764).]

10 May 1764 Queen St. Theatre, Charleston
King Lear.
American Company.
[Source: Manigault, "Extracts of the Journal," 207.]

5 July 1764   New York
Newspaper notice.
[The *New York Post-Boy* of this date reprints the following item from an unspecified London source:

> A gentleman is just arrived in town [i.e., London] from Carolina, in order to engage a select company of players of both sexes, for the new theatre open'd last winter in Charles-Town, with great applause.--New scenes, machinery, and abundance of other playhouse decorations, are now shipping for the same place.

This letter very likely refers to David Douglass in London. His presence there, to assemble a company, explains the gap in the record until late October 1765.]

1765

In the absence of a professional company, in New York, only two productions are known for the spring of this year. Though we have little hard evidence about this "company" beyond a benefit performance for Mr. Tomlinson and a cameo for a Mr. Walsh, the nature of these performances is worth speculating that this may in fact be two separate companies–an amateur troupe under the direction of Tomlinson and a garrison company under Captain Walsh.

Tomlinson, who is the recipient of the 4 March benefit, played with the American Company in 1759-60, and again when the company returned to New York in 1762, and later accompanied Douglass when he opened in Philadelphia in the fall of 1765. Therefore, perhaps the "Company of Young Gentlemen" is a group of amateurs recruited by Tomlinson who profited from the evening's program. As for the 4 April production for the benefit of the prisoners, this company might have been officers from the city garrison under the command of a Captain Walsh (alone whose named is advertised), and no mention is made of a "Company of Young Gentlemen" as in the 4 March notice. Odell (1:93), however, speculates that both performances were undertaken by garrison officers.

In May of 1765 a summer resort opens in New York City, the Vauxhall. Primarily a musical establishment, the Vauxhall nonetheless later hosted many of the talents of the American Company during summer recesses.

Once again a clandestine performance is reported in Boston during March (see 13 March 1765), and a religious play was presented at Harvard in November (see 20 November 1765).

For most of 1765 the American Company was in the West Indies (certainly Barbados). Sometime in mid October, David Douglass returned to Charleston from a recruitment trip in London. He carried back with him several new members, especially advertising his new singers, Thomas Wall (who advertised to teach guitar in Charleston) and Miss Wainwright. Douglass also intended to bring with him from London new scenery, painted, we are told, by Doll. Unfortunately, the divided company had trouble reassembling, as Douglass relates in an important and previously unknown broadside of 4 November 1765 (see entry for that date). Many of his major performers and the new scenery, all intended for Charleston by October 1765, did not arrive for the 1765–66 season in that city.

And, finally, attention to the market potential of the colonial circuit is made evident by a published London rumor early in the year that a patent was to be issued for a company in New York (see 6 May 1765).

***

4 March 1765   Chapel St. Theater, New York
The Fair Penitent.
The Lying Valet.
Local performers.
 [Benefit Tomlinson. Performed by "a Company of Young Gentlemen." Source: *New York Mercury* (4 March 1765).]

13 March 1765   Boston
The Orphan.
 [A clandestine performance. Source: *Diary of John Rowe* as published in the *Proceedings of the Massachusetts Historical Society*, 10: 28. Cf. Bonawitz (17), who provides the following comments from it: "miserably performed; about 210 persons were there."]

10 April 1765   Chapel St. Theater, New York
George Barnwell [i.e., *The London Merchant*].

Captain O'Blunder; or, The Brave Irishman* (Thomas Sheridan; adap. unknown, 1737).
Army officers.
O'Blunder–Walsh.
[Presented "for the benefit of the Prisoners in the New Gaol." Source: *New York Gazette & Weekly Post-Boy* (4 April 1765).]

6 May 1765   New York
Notice of possible patent.

[The *New York Gazette & Weekly Post-Boy* of 6 May 1765 reprints the following item from an unspecified London source: "London, Feb. 12. We hear a patent will soon be made out, in favor of an eminent English actor, who intends to establish a play house in New York." A similar notice appears in the *Boston Gazette* of 6 May 1765, with the following addition: "God prevent it ever being established."]

31 October 1765   Charleston
Newspaper notice.
American Company.

[The *South Carolina & American General Gazette* of 23–31 October 1765 contains the following item:

> On Friday last, Mr. Douglass, director of the Theatre in this town, arriv'd from London with a reinforcement to his company. We hear he has engaged some very capital singers from the theatres in London, with a view of entertaining the town this winter with English operas. It is imagined, when he is joined by the company from Barbados, that our theatrical performance will be executed in a manner not inferiour to the most applauded in England. The scenes and decorations, we are informed, are of a superiour kind to any that have been seen in America, being designed by the most eminent maker in London.

The *South Carolina Gazette* of 19–31 October 1765 carries a similar notice with interesting variations:

> In the Carolina Packet, Capt. Robson, from London, Mr. Douglass, Manager of the American Company of Comedians is returned, who, we hear, has brought over, at a great expense, a most excellent set of scenes done by Mr. Doll, principal scene painter to Covent-Garden House, and collected some very eminent performers from both the theatres in London, particularly in the Singing-Way, so that the English Comic Opera, a species of entertainment that has never yet appeared properly on this side of the water, is likely to be performed here this winter to great advantage.]

early November 1765   Charleston
Notice of opening of season.
American Company.

["On Monday the 11th instant ...I propose to open it [i.e., the theatre] with a Play and a Farce, which will be expressed in the bills of the Day. David Douglass." Source: "Proposal;" cf. Cohen 109.]

4 November 1765   Charleston
Printed broadside.

[David Douglass offered the following explanation to the people of Charleston concerning the status of the company then under his direction:

To the Public:

A sense of past favours, and an ambition of convincing my friends that they were not thrown away, but conferred upon a heart truly grateful that pants for an opportunity of acknowledging them, were my motives for planning an Entertainment this winter, which, I flattered myself, would not have been altogether unworthy the attention of so respectable and judicious an audience as the ladies and gentlemen of Carolina compose: To that end, I collected in London, some Performers, who, when joined to the company now at Barbados, would have enabled me to execute my Entertainments with a superiour degree of excellence to any that have hitherto appeared in America; and it was my pride to produce them first in this town, where my former labours had met with such distinguished, such uncommon marks of approbation.

I had also employed the proper artificers to refit the Theatre, and make such commodious and elegant alterations, the construction of it would admit.

The new scenes I have brought over with me, with those in the possession of the company at Barbados, as they would have given a diversity, so they would have been a considerable improvement to our representations.

But these flattering hopes, in which I fondly indulged myself, are now at an end: I received, on Friday, letters from Barbados, which to my utter astonishment, inform me, that the company cannot possibly leave that island before the end of March! Notwithstanding I had taken every previous measure necessary as I thought, to effect a junction here by October.

Great as this disappointment must be to a person in my situation, in regard to the expences I have been at, I feel more concern to find myself obliged to baulk the expectations [the town?] had conceived, from my declarations, of an Entertainment. Than [torn; missing text] ... my own particular interest may sustain.

Under these circumstances I would have embarked immediately for Barbados, had there been an opportunity; but none offering at this time, I must have contented myself with waiting until I could have procured a vessel, and consequently given over all thoughts of performing here this winter, had not some ladies and gentlemen insisted upon my opening the Theatre with the little strength I have brought from London with me, and presenting such pieces as the thinness of my company will permit me to exhibit [torn]; in order, as they very politely observed, to enable me to defray some part of the expence I have incurred: It was to no purpose that I urged, the [contemptible?] light I might stand in with many, for presuming to treat the publick with plain dishes after having giving them so sumptuous a bill of fare I was obliged to submit, as there is nothing a Carolina audience can ask, that I dare refuse.

Therefore, considering myself once more listed under the banners of the publick, I shall proceed with the utmost dispatch to refit the Theatre, which I hope will be in proper order to receive an audience on Monday the 11th instant; when, by permission of his Honour the Lieutenant-Governor, I propose to open it, with a Play and Face, which will be expressed in the bills for the day.

And, that I may demonstrate my inclinations to remove every cause of complaint, I shall voluntarily reduce the prices of the tickets from the accustomed rated of forty, thirty and twenty shillings (which I find there are some objections to) to thirty-five, twenty-five, and fifteen; which, I am confident, if properly considered, will be acknowledged to be as low as we can possibly perform for.

I have the honour to be the Publick's
Most obedient,
Mot devoted, and
Most humble servant
D. Douglass

[Source: Douglass, "To the Public."]

11 November 1765   Queen St. Theatre, Charleston
Play not identified.
American Company.
   [This date perhaps marked the opening of the theatre. See previous entry.]

13 November 1765   Queen St. Theatre, Charleston
Musical concert.
   [Performers: Miss Wainright; Miss Hallam. Tickets: two dollars. Source: *South Carolina Gazette* (19–31 October 1765).]

20 November 1765   Harvard College, Cambridge
Play not identified
Faculty of Harvard College.
   [A religious drama was performed by the faculty of the college on this date. Source: *Proceedings of the Massachusetts Historical Society*, 3:230. Cf. Bonawitz 17.]

1766

The American Company—though far from fully assembled—continued their winter season in Charleston, with several new members and, more importantly, new plays and afterpieces. They remained in Charleston until mid-April.

After a final benefit for the poor, Douglass presented George Stevens's *Lecture on Heads,* a one-man program which he (and several others) performed frequently in subsequent years. These "lectures" appear only when a full company is no longer available, strongly suggesting that the company has dispersed. Indeed, the whereabouts of the American Company during the summer of 1766 are unclear until they reassembled in Philadelphia in the fall. Though Douglass leads his subscribers to believe that he is the first to present the *Lecture* in the colonies, in point of fact, a student at Joseph Garner's school in Philadelphia was the first person known to have delivered the *Lecture* in the colonies on 15 February 1766 (Kahan 111); indeed, Garner himself had earlier performed the *Lecture* (see 17 April 1766), a program he would repeat from time to time in subsequent months.

Parts of the American Company are performing in the West Indies until the fall of this year, as now known by evidence from Douglass's letter of 4 November 1765. He later further announced in the *South Carolina Gazette* that he was about "to depart this province," however, not the continent itself (see 6 May 1766). Douglass may have traveled to Philadelphia to secure permission for performances and to oversee construction of a new theatre (i.e., the Southwark Theatre; see 31 July 1766), where the company opened in early November.

The known members of the American Company in Charleston included David Douglass, Mrs. Douglass, Mr. Emmet, Miss Hallam, Mrs. Osborne, Mr. Wall, Miss Wainwright, and William Verling. Recently recruited by Douglass from London were Mrs. Osborne, Miss Nancy Hallam, Miss Wainwright, and Mr. Thomas Wall ("from the theatre Royal Drury Lane"), who offered in the papers of Charleston to teach ladies and gentlemen to play upon the guitar. Mrs. Osborne, it will be remembered, played in the original Murray-Kean Company, next with Robert Upton during 1751–52, then rejoined the Murray-Kean troupe in 1752. She apparently played in Jamaica sometime in the 1750's, where she met John Moody, later traveling with him to London in 1758 or 1759. According to the *Memoirs* of Tate Wilkinson (2:96–97), John Moody arrived from Jamaica in London in 1759 with a very pregnant Widow Osborne. Moody was described as "godfather–or some kind of a father–which, he knows best." Wilkinson may have postdated her arrival, for, according to Highfill (11:121–22), Mrs. Osborne appeared in Portsmouth, England, a year earlier, during the summer of 1758, and performed in London and the English provincial circuit at least until February 1764. The much-traveled Mrs. Osborne returned to the colonies sometime after spring of 1764. Her temperament had apparently not improved, as she announced her return to Europe at the end of the 1766 Charleston season.

Major problems plague the 1765–66 Charleston season. Many key performers in the company are absent, being still in Barbados (see entry for 4 November 1765). Noticeably missing from the cast lists and benefits are the names of several stable members, such as Owen and Mary Morris, Mr. and Mrs. Allyn, and Lewis and Adam Hallam, whose roles are apparently reassigned during the spring season (e.g., *The Gamester*, 6 March). Furthermore, after the company's Charleston season was concluded, Douglass apparently remained behind in that city nearly two months. The whereabout of the balance of his company through late spring is unknown.

Exactly when the rest of the company arrived from Barbados is also not known. After 3 April the company may have reassembled, while Douglass remained behind to await his recruits. Whatever the explanation, Douglass would certainly have been among the "Company of Stage Players" who arrived in Philadelphia sometime in June (see 27 June 1766) to secure permission to play. When the new Southwark Theatre opened in Philadelphia in November 1766, the American Company included the following known members: Adam Allyn, Margaret Cheer, David Douglass, Mrs. Douglass, Miss Dowthwaite, James Godwin, Lewis Hallam, Mrs. Harmon, Mr. Mathews, Owen Morris, Mary Morris, Mr. Tomlinson, Anna Tomlinson, Miss Wainwright, Thomas Wall, and Stephen Woolls. Neither Mr. Emmet and Mr. Verling, nor Mrs. Osborne, from Charleston, appeared with the company in Philadelphia. The new members include singer-actors Miss Cheer and Stephen Woolls and dancer James Godwin, whose special talents allowed the premieres of at least a half-dozen new musicals during the 1766–67 season.

1766 presents yet another problem—the identity of the company performing at the Chapel St. Theatre in New York during the Stamp Act riots (see 5 May). Rankin (109) demonstrates that in the spring of 1766, strollers had "arrived" in New York with permission to act, but that the Stamp Act mobs proved hostile. He suggests, and we tentatively concur, that these strollers are Tomlinson's Company, "perhaps returning from a tour of the rural areas." Odell (1:95), less certain, points out that whoever they were, that the company was recognized enough to have "secured the permission of authority to act." It should also be noted the company had resources sufficient to undertake a full production, which was announced for 9 April, but later postponed.

When the performance did occur, 5 May 1766, the hostility had not yet subsided, a riot ensued, and the Chapel Street Theatre was partially burned. This act may not have reflected the hostility toward the players so much as toward the Governor, Cadwallader Colden, which reached such a pitch that mobs destroyed everything associated with Colden, including the Chapel Street Theatre, owned by Philip Miller, a friend of the governor's.

✳✳✳

17 January 1766   Queen St Theatre, Charleston
The Distrest Mother.
American Company.
   [Source: Willis 51.]

31 January 1766   Queen St. Theatre, Charleston
Douglas.
American Company.
   [Source: Willis 51.]

10 February 1766   Queen St. Theatre, Charleston
Love in a Village* (Isaac Bickerstaffe, 1762).
American Company.
   [Source: Willis 51.]

15 February 1766   Christ Church School House, Philadelphia
Lecture on Heads.
Joseph Garner.
   [Source: Kahan 111–12.]

27 February 1766   Queen St. Theatre, Charleston
The Constant Couple.
The Mock Doctor.
   Mock Doctor–Douglass; Dorcas–Miss Wainwright.
American Company.
   [Benefit Mrs. Osborne. Source: *South Carolina Gazette* (25 February 1766).]

3 March 1766   Queen St. Theatre, Charleston
Play unidentified.
American Company.
   [A letter in the *South Carolina Gazette* of 4 March 1766 begins, "I was at the play last night, and with infinite pleasure heard the Gamester and the Oracle [are to be] given out for Mrs. Douglass's benefit" (i.e., on 6 March 1766; see below).]

6 March 1766   Queen St. Theatre, Charleston
The Gamester.
   Beverley–Verling; Stukely–Douglass; Lewson–Wall; Jarvis–Emmet; Charlotte–Mrs. Osborne; Lucy–Miss Hallam; Mrs. Beverley–Mrs. Douglass.
The Oracle* (Susannah Cibber, 1752).
   Oberon–Wall; Cinthia–Miss Hallam; Fairy Queen–Mrs. Douglass; the Statue's Dance–Mrs. Osborne.
American Company.
   [Benefit Mrs. Douglass. "The prologue and epilogue, by Mr. and Mrs. Douglass." The afterpiece advertised as "never acted in America." Source: *South Carolina Gazette* (4 March 1766).]

13 March 1766   Queen St. Theatre, Charleston
The Provoked Husband.
The Lying Valet.
American Company.
   [Benefit Emmet. Source: *South Carolina Gazette* (11 March 1766).]

20 March 1766   Queen St. Theatre, Charleston
The Way to Keep Him* (Arthur Murphy, 1760).
The Brave Irishman.
American Company.
   [Benefit Verling. The mainpiece is advertised as "never acted in America." The newspaper advertisement contains the following information:

After the play, an occasional epilogue, written and to be spoken by Mr. Verling, in the character of a Master Mason .... As the play to be acted on Thursday the 20th instant, is for the benefit of our brother Mr. William Verling, the members of Solomon's Lodge, with those of the several lodges in Charlestown, also all transient brethren, are requested to meet at the house of Mr. Robert Dillon, at half after four in the afternoon of said day, thence to proceed in procession to the theatre. By order of the Master, I. de Costa, Secry.

Source: *South Carolina Gazette* (18 March 1766).]

31 March 1766   Christ Church School House, Philadelphia
Lecture on Heads.
Joseph Garner.
   [Source: Kahan 111–12.]

2 April 1766   Christ Church School House, Philadelphia
Lecture on Heads.
Joseph Garner.
   [Source: Kahan 111–12.]

3 April 1766   Queen St. Theatre, Charleston
The School for Lovers* (William Whitehead, 1762).
The Oracle.
American Company.
   [Benefit Miss Hallam. The mainpiece is advertised as "never acted in America." "Positively the last night this season." Source: *South Carolina Gazette* (1 April 1766).]

4 April 1766 New York
Journal entry.
   [Montressor records for this day news relating to the arrival of what may be Tomlinson's Company:

   A Grand meeting of the Sons of Liberty to settle matters of moment, amongst the many whether they shall admit the strollers, arrived here to act, tho the General[12] has given them permission.... Some stamps as tis said found in the Streets were publickly burned at the Coffeehouse together with some play bills, all to prevent Their spirits to flag.

Source: Montressor 362; cf. Rankin 109.]

4 April 1766   Christ Church School House, Philadelphia
Lecture on Heads.

---

[12] I.e., General Gage, military governor of New York.

Joseph Garner.
[Source: Kahan 111–12.]

9 April 1766   Chapel St. Theatre, New York
The Twin Rivals.
Tomlinson's Company?
[Announced but postponed; see 5 May 1766. Source: *New York Gazette & Weekly Post Boy* (3 April 1766).]

15 April 1766   Queen St. Theatre, Charleston
Newspaper notice.
[The *South Carolina Gazette* of this date contains a lengthy notice of Douglass's intention to present a series of *Lectures upon Heads* by subscription:

> Mr. Douglass returns the public his most sincere thanks for the many favours he received this winter as an actor; he assures them, he will ever retain a most grateful sense of the obligations he has to this province, which have so amply rewarded his imperfect, though well-meant, attempts to contribute to their entertainment. He purchased, when in London, a genuine copy of the Lectures on Heads written by Mr. Stevens, and provided himself with the necessary apparatus for delivering it; He has made some alterations and improvements, which he flatters himself will be a considerable advantage to it, as many strokes of satire have escaped the author, which Mr. Douglass imagines to be directed at, rather, improper objects, and in some places the sense was so obscure, that it was absolutely necessary to elucidate it, in order to convey with precision, his meaning to the audience. In this state he intends to exhibit it to the town: But as an undertaking of this kind, is wholly new in this part of the world, and the success uncertain, he is advised by his friends, (that he may be enabled to form a judgement of the encouragement it is likely to meet with, before he engages in any further expence) to propose a subscription, for three nights only, at three pounds for the three nights. As soon as a competent number have subscribed tickets will be issued, and proper notice given of the night on which he will deliver the lecture.
>
> Subscriptions are taken in at Mr. Douglass's lodgings in Queen-street, and at Mr. Wells's shop on the bay. Charles-Town, April 14, 1766.]

16 April 1766   Queen St. Theatre, Charleston
Cato.
Miss in Her Teens.
American Company.
[Benefit for the poor. Source: *South Carolina Gazette* (15 April 1766).]

17 April 1766   Christ Church School House, Philadelphia
Lecture on Heads.
Joseph Garner.
["This evening will be continued the lecture upon Heads."
Source: *Pennsylvania Gazette* (17 April 1766).]

28 April 1766   Assembly Room, Lodge Alley, Philadelphia
Lecture on Heads.
Joseph Garner.
[The *Pennsylvania Journal* of 24 April 1766 prints the following notice regarding the activities of Mr. Garner:

> By particular desire of several gentlemen and ladies on Monday and Tuesday the 28th and 29th inst. and on Monday and Tuesday the 5th and 6th of May, will be a concert of music on each of the above evenings, the much applauded Lecture on Heads began and completely finished on the two first evenings; and continued on the two last, if desired, by Master Joseph Redman: with several orations by some of the children of Christ Church School. As these are to be the last publick evenings this season, Mr. Garner is determined to tender every particular of each entertainment as agreeable as possible. Tickets at half a dollar each, may be had at his house in Laetitia Court, at the coffee-house and at the school. To begin each evening at half after seven o'clock. Note, each ticket admits the bearer two evenings.]

29 April 1766   Assembly Room, Lodge Alley, Philadelphia
Lecture on Heads.
Joseph Garner.
[Source: *Pennsylvania Journal* (24 April 1766).]

30 April 1766   Queen St. Theatre, Charleston
Lecture on Heads.
David Douglass.
[Source: *South Carolina Gazette* (3 April 1766).]

5 May 1766   Chapel St. Theatre, New York
The Twin Rivals.
The King and the Miller of Mansfield.
Tomlinson's Company?
[Originally announced for 9 April 1766 but postponed. Source: *New York Mercury* (5 May 1766); cf. Daly 15. An account of a riot which transpired this evening and which left the theatre badly burned appears in the *New York Gazette* of 12 May 1766 (cf. Odell 1:94):

> Our Grand Theatre in Chapel-Street on Monday night last had a grand Rout. When the Audience were fixed, (agreeable to the Assurance of

performing the Play of the Twin-Rivals) about the Middle of the first Scene a more grand Rout instantly took Place both Out and In the House, for by the usual English Signal of one Candle, and an Huzza on both Sides, the Rivals began in earnest, and those were best off who got out first, either by jumping out of Windows, or making their Way through the Doors, as the Lights were extinguished, and both Inside and Outside soon torn to Pieces and burnt by Persons unknown about Ten and Eleven a Clock at Night, to the Satisfaction of Many at this distressed Time, and to the great Grievance of those less inclined for the Publick Good. Thus ended the Comedy, in which a Boy unhappily had his Skull fractured, his Recovery doubtful; others lost their Caps, Hats, Wigs, Cardinals and Cloaks Tails of Smocks torn off (thro' a Mistake) in the Hurry; and a certain He (who was to act the Part of Mrs. Mandrake) being caught in the She-Dress, was soon turn'd topsey-turvey, and whipped for a considerable Distance.

Another account appears in the *Post-Boy* of 8 May 1766. The *Maryland Gazette* of 22 May 1766 offers yet further details of the riot:

New-York, May 8. The play advertised to be acted on last Monday evening, having given offence to many of the inhabitants of this city, who thought it highly improper that such entertainments should be exhibited at this time of public distress, when great numbers of poor people can scarce find means of subsistence, whereby many persons might be tempted to neglect their business, and squander that money, which is necessary to the payment of their debts, and support of their families, a rumour was spread about town, on Monday, that if the play went on, the audience would meet with some disturbance from the multitude. This prevented the greatest part of those who intended to have been there from going: however many people came, and the play began; but soon interrupted by the multitude who burst open the doors, and entered with noise and tumult. The audience escaped in the best manner they could; many lost their hats and other parts of dress. A boy had his skull fractured, and was yesterday trepanned, his recovery is doubtful; several others were dangerously hurt; but we have heard of no lives lost. The multitude immediately demolished the house, and carried the pieces to the common, where they consumed them in a bonfire.]

5 May 1766   New York
Journal entry.

[Capt. Montressor records the following narrative in his journal which relates the destruction of the playhouse and related events:

This evening a play was acted by permission of our Governor, to be performed by a company of comedians or Strollers, notwithstanding the Sons of Liberty without any Reason given pulled down the Playhouse the beginning of the 2nd act, put out all the lights, then began picking of pockets, stealing watches, throwing brick Bats, sticks and bottles and glasses, crying out Liberty, Liberty, then proceeded to the Fields or Common and burnt the materials. One boy Killed and Many people hurt in this Licentious affair.

Source: Montressor 364.]

5 May 1766   Assembly Room, Lodge Alley, Philadelphia
Lecture on Heads.
Joseph Garner.
   [Source: *Pennsylvania Journal* (24 April 1766).]

6 May 1766   Assembly Room, Lodge Alley, Philadelphia
Lecture on Heads.
Joseph Garner.
   [Source: *Pennsylvania Journal* (24 April 1766).]

6 May 1766   Queen St. Theatre, Charleston
Lecture on Heads.
David Douglass.
   [Prices: boxes and pit, 20s.; gallery, 15s. "David Douglass, intending to depart this province very soon, desires the favour of those who are indebted to him to discharge their accounts, and those who have demands on him to come and receive payment." Source: *South Carolina Gazette* (6 May 1766).]

8 May 1766   Queen St. Theatre, Charleston
Lecture on Heads.
David Douglass.
   [Source: Curtis 431.]

30 May 1766 Charleston
Newspaper notice.
   [The following item appears in the *South Carolina & American General Gazette* of 23–30 May 1766 establishing Douglass's presence in Charleston at this date: "Found some time ago in the Theatre, a man's Blue Cloak. The owner may have it by applying to David Douglass, and paying for this advertisement."]

27 June 1766   Philadelphia
Petition.
   [The following petition was presented by Quakers opposed to the erection of a new theatre in this city:

> Remonstrances Against Erecting a Theatre, and Theatrical Performances in Philadelphia 1766–1767

> To John Penn Esquire, Lieutenant Governor of the Province of Pennsylvania and Counties of Newcastle, Kent and Sussex on Delaware. The Address of the People called Quakers in Philadelphia, Respectfully sheweth—That we have, with real concern, heard that a Company of Stage Players are lately arrived in this City, with Intention to exhibit Plays, which we conceive, if permitted, will tend to subvert the good Order, Morals and Prosperity we desire may be preserved among us.
> We therefore esteem it our Duty earnestly to solicit the Governor that he would be pleased to prohibit those ensnaring and irreligious Entertainments; that the destructive Consequences arising from them to the Youth and others, which heretofore have been very evident, may be prevented .... Signed in and on Behalf of our Monthly Meeting held in Philadelphia the 27th: 6 month: 1766.

Source: "Notes and Queries," 23: 267–68.]

4 July 1766   Assembly Room, Lodge Alley, Philadelphia
Lecture on Heads.
Joseph Garner.
[Source: Kahan: 111–12.]

17 July 1766   Philadelphia
Newspaper notice.
[A lengthy anti-theatrical protest was published in the *Pennsylvania Journal* of this date, a portion of which reads as follows:

> These are the motives which lead them to wish, that no provocatives to any species of vice, luxury and effeminacy may be admitted among us; and in particular they hope that the introduction of plays and players may be timeously and effectually prevented. This is a species of diversion which always has been disagreeable to the virtuous, the learned and the religious of almost all countries.]

31 July 1766   Philadelphia
Newspaper notice.
[An anti-theatrical letter in the *Pennsylvania Journal* of this date mentions the Southwark Theatre, which eventually opened in the fall of 1766: "They for sooth are going to build a playhouse in Philadelphia." Another section of the letter complains that the performers are

> endeavouring to fill the minds of ancient people, with the follies of those of sixteen, and to make the young of both sexes go wild, and perhaps make many an honest parent's heart ache, the sure effects of all gaming houses, midnight dances, public shows, and especially the head and crown of them all, playhouses, which tend to draw people's minds from everything that is profitable, here or hereafter, and tho'

they pretend to lash and expose every vice and folly, they take care to do it in such a manner, that (young) people (especially) gradually and imperceptibly, become enamoured with those very vices they pretend to expose ....

Durang (6) publishes numerous examples of the anti-theatrical sentiments of this year.]

30 October 1766   Philadelphia
Newspaper notice.

[The *Pennsylvania Journal* of this date contains the following notice: "We hear the new theatre in Southwark will be opened on Monday, the tenth of November." The first confirmed performance took place on 14 November 1766, but the advertisement for that evening does not state that this was the opening night, as is typically the practice.]

14 November 1766   Southwark Theatre, Philadelphia
The Provoked Husband.
Thomas and Sally* (Isaac Bickerstaffe, 1760).
American Company.

[This may well be opening night for this theatre. The program was announced for 12 November but postponed. Prices: box 7s. 6d.; pit 5s.; gallery 3s. Source: *Pennsylvania Journal* (13 November 1766).]

17 November 1766   Southwark Theatre, Philadelphia
The Distrest Mother.
The Lying Valet.
American Company.
   [Source: *Pennsylvania Journal* (13 November 1766).]

19 November 1766   Southwark Theatre, Philadelphia
The Wonder.
The Citizen* (Arthur Murphy, 1761).
American Company.
   [Source: *Pennsylvania Journal* (13 November 1766).]

21 November 1766   Southwark Theatre, Philadelphia
Douglas.
   Douglas–Hallam; Lord Randolph–Douglass; Glenalvon–Wall; Old Norval–Morris; Anna–Mrs. Harman.
Catherine and Petruchio* (David Garrick, 1756).
   Petruchio–Hallam; Catherine–Miss Cheer.
American Company.
   [Source: *Pennsylvania Gazette* (20 November 1766).]

24 November 1766 Southwark Theatre, Philadelphia
The School for Lovers.
American Company.
  [Source: *Pennsylvania Gazette* (20 November 1766).]

26 November 1766 Southwark Theatre, Philadelphia
Jane Shore.
American company.
  [Source: *Pennsylvania Gazette* (20 November 1766).]

28 November 1766 Southwark Theatre, Philadelphia
The Beggar's Opera.
  Macheath–Woolls; Peachum–Allyn; Lockit–Tomlinson; Filch–Wall; Twitcher–Matthews; Beggar–Morris; Lucy–Mrs. Morris; Polly–Miss Wainwright; Mrs. Peachum–Mrs. Harman; Mrs. Slammekin–Miss Dowthwaite; Moll Brazen–Douglass.
The Old Maid* (Arthur Murphy, 1761).
  Cleremont–Hallam; Heartly–Morris; Cape–Douglass; Harlow–Allyn; Old Maid–Mrs. Harman; Mrs. Harlow–Miss Cheer; Trifle–Mrs. Morris.
American Company.
  [Source: *Pennsylvania Gazette* (27 November 1766).]

5 December 1766   Southwark Theatre, Philadelphia
Richard III.
  Richard–Hallam; Richmond–Douglass; King Henry–Morris; Buckingham–Wall; Prince Edward–Godwin; Stanley–Allyn; Ratcliffe–Woolls; Catesby–Tomlinson; Duke of York–Miss Dowthwaite; Lady Anne–Miss Cheer; Queen Elizabeth–Mrs. Douglass; Duchess of York–Mrs. Harman.
The Oracle.
  Oberon–Wall; Cinthia–Miss [Nancy] Hallam; Fairy Queen–Mrs. Douglass.
American Company.
  [Source: *Pennsylvania Gazette* (4 December 1766).]

12 December 1766 Southwark Theatre, Philadelphia
The Merchant of Venice.
  Shylock–Hallam; Antonio–Tomlinson; Launcelot–Morris; Salanio–Wall; Bassanio–Douglass; Gratiano–Allyn; Lorenzo–Woolls; Portia–Miss Cheer; Jessica–Miss Wainwright; Nerissa–Mrs. Harman.
The King and the Miller of Mansfield.

American Company.
[Source: *Pennsylvania Gazette* (11 December 1766).]

19 December 1766   Southwark Theatre, Philadelphia
The Constant Couple.
   Sir Harry–Hallam; Clincher–Allyn; Smuggler–Morris; Dickey–Woolls; Standard–Douglass; Young Clincher–Wall; Vizand–Tomlinson; Lady Darling–Mrs. Tomlinson; Mob's wife–Mrs. Harman; Angelica–Miss Cheer; Parley–Miss Wainwright; Lady Lurewell–Mrs. Douglass.
The Devil to Pay.
   Sir John–Woolls; Jobson–Tomlinson; Butler–Morris; Footman–Wall; Coachman–Allyn; Doctor–Douglass; Lucy–Mrs. Tomlinson; Nell–Mrs. Morris; Lady Loverule–Mrs. Harman; Lettice–Miss Dowthwaite.
American Company.
[Source: *Pennsylvania Gazette* (18 December 1766).]

26 December 1766   Southwark Theatre, Philadelphia
Theodosius.
   Varanes–Hallam; Theodosius–Morris; Marcian–Douglass; Atticus–Tomlinson; Leontine–Allyn; Aranthes–Wall; Lucius–Woolls; Pulcheria–Mrs. Harman; Marina–Miss Hallam; Flavilla–Miss Wainwright; Julia–Miss Dowthwaite; Delia–Mrs. Tomlinson; Athenais–Miss Cheer.
Lethe.
   Drunken Man–Hallam; Frenchman–Allyn; Mercury–Woolls; Old Man–Morris; Fine Gentleman–Wall; Charon–Tomlinson; Aesop–Douglass; Mrs. Tatoo–Mrs. Harman; Mrs. Riot–Miss Wainwright.
American Company.
[Source: *Pennsylvania Gazette* (25 December 1766).]

1767

The American Company continued to enjoy an enormously successful engagement season in Philadelphia which extended into July. Pollock (100) remarks of this season, "we know of at least fifty-nine performances, which were given, of a probable hundred." After a summer recess, they continued in this city. During July or early August, Douglass and Woolls toured the *Lecture on Heads* to New York, hostilities having apparently subsided. At this time Douglass began securing permission to play a winter season in New York and to arrange for the building of the John St. Theater (cf., Hornblow 124). Other members of the company—or perhaps even the full troupe—performed a short summer season in a new city: Bristol, Rhode Island. Though the names of the company are not recorded, it is nonetheless a testament to the perseverance of Douglass that he was finally able to establish a theatre in this reluctant colony (see 27 August 1767).

The American Company in early 1767 included the following members: Adam Allyn, Mr. Broadbelt, Margaret Cheer, David Douglass, Mrs. Douglass, James Godwin, Samuel Greville, Lewis Hallam Jr., Nancy Hallam, Mrs. Harman, Mr. Mathews, Owen Morris, Mrs. Morris, Mr. Platt, Mr. Tomlinson, Mrs. Tomlinson, Miss Wainwright, Thomas Wall, Mrs. Wall, and Stephen Woolls. Both Godwin and Matthews also performed as dancers. Samuel Greville was a student at Princeton, whom Hughes (38) tells us "deserted college for the stage." Rankin (113) has more to say about this young recruit. He tried out on 2 January as Moneses in *Tamerlane* and on 9 January as Horatio in *Hamlet*, and then was accepted into the company. Durnam (16) lists Broadbelt as the business manager of the American Company, c. 1767; his exact function is unknown, though he certainly made stage appearances and received benefits in 1767. Mrs. Wall is listed as a cast member this year. She may have traveled with her husband in October 1765 and took to the stage later, or Thomas Wall may have made the most of his time in the colonies. About Platt, nothing is known.

When the company resumed in Philadelphia in October 1767, they boasted the following new personnel: Patrick Malone, Mr. Roberts, John Henry, and several Ms. Storers. Mr. Malone, it will be remembered—if this is indeed the same Mr. Malone—played with the original Hallam Company during 1752–54. His whereabouts in the ensuing years are unknown. Mr. Roberts appeared with the company beginning in October 1767.

John Henry, Miss Ann Storer, Maria Storer, and Fanny Storer all joined the American Company from Jamaica. Wright (51) claims they were billed as "from the Theatre in Jamaica," where Henry and the Storers had played since 1762. In September 1767 Henry and his wife (formerly Jane Storer), traveled from Jamaica with scenery and costumes. Accompanying them were three Storer sisters, Ann, Fanny, Maria, and their mother, as well as two children of the Henrys.

The ship caught fire off the coast of Newport, Rhode Island colony, and the two children and their mother, Mrs. Henry, perished (see 27 August 1767). The newspapers originally reported the victim as "the young Mrs. Hallam," but this was not true. Hornblow (1:24) incorrectly antedates Henry's debut as 1766, an error followed by Wright (51).

The company played in Philadelphia until the end of November, after which they crossed to New York, where they opened the John St. Theater on 7 December 1767. An unfortunate accident befell the company as they traveled, when Mrs. Morris and her maid died in a ferry accident (see early December 1767).

William Verling, who had left the American Company in Charleston in the spring of 1766, arrived in Williamsburg in January 1767 and began performing. Presumably he assembled a company, but we hear nothing else from him for the year beyond two performances in early January of the *Lecture on Heads*, pirated from Douglass. Also Joseph Garner continues to present the *Lecture* from time to time in Philadelphia.

Boston enjoyed more clandestine theatrical activity which generated no end of press debates speculating on why plays were being performed at "unseasonable hours." In later reports (see 20 March 1769) it was claimed that these amateurs were tradesmen performing at night for the purpose of making assignations.

In Hampton, Virginia, though we have no precise data, the young gentlemen of Rev. Warrington's school apparently performed *Cato*.[13]

And, finally, a new company appears in March of this year, announcing themselves as from Sadler's Wells, London, and headed by a Mr. Bayly. Little is known of this troupe, which interspersed short dramatic pieces at the Orange Tree, Golden Hill, New York, with other sorts of entertainments, such as balancing acts, puppet shows, and sleight of hand tricks. The following names appear in the newspaper notices: Mr. Bayly, Mrs. Bayly, Mr. Hymes, Mr. Martin, Mr. Shaw, and Mr. Tea.

---

[13] See Vernon Jones, "The Theatre in Colonial Virginia," *The Reviewer* 5 (Jan. 1925), p. 87.

                    THE COLONIAL AMERICAN STAGE   257

✳✳✳

2 January 1767   Southwark Theatre, Philadelphia
Tamerlane.
   Bajazet–Hallam; Tamerlane–Douglass; Axalla–Wall; Dervise–Morris; Omar–Tomlinson; Zama–Platt; Prince of Tanais–Allyn; Mirvan–Woolls; Haly–Godwin; Selima–Miss Cheer; Arpasia–Mrs. Douglass.
The Oracle.
   As 5 December 1766.
American Company.
   [Source: *Pennsylvania Journal* (1 January 1767).]

9 January 1767   Southwark Theatre, Philadelphia
Hamlet.
   Hamlet–Hallam; Claudius–Douglass; Horatio–"A Young Gentleman" (his second appearance); Laertes–Wall; Polonius–Morris; Ghost–Tomlinson; Player King–Allyn; Ostric–Godwin; Rosencranz–Woolls; Bernardo–Platt; Grave Diggers–Morris and Tomlinson; Player Queen–Mrs. Harman; Ophelia–Miss Cheer; Gertrude–Mrs. Douglass.
The Mock Doctor.
   Mock Doctor–Allyn; Sir Jasper–Morris; Leander–Woolls; Squire Robert–Wall; James–Platt; Harry–Godwin; Helebore–Tomlinson; Charlotte–Mrs. Wall; Dorcas–Mrs. Morris.
American Company.
   [Source: *Pennsylvania Journal* (8 January 1767).]

13 January 1767   Great Room of the Rawleigh Tavern, Williamsburg
Lecture on Heads.
William Verling.
   ["The celebrated Lecture on Heads, so much admired and applauded by all who have heard it performed, will be delivered . . . at 6 o'clock in the evening, in the Great room of the Rawleigh Tavern, by Mr. William Verling, who is just arrived in this city. He does not intend to Exhibit but these two Nights." Source: *Virginia Gazette* (8 January 1767).]

14 January 1767   Philadelphia
Correspondence.
   [From a letter by Margaret Shippen we learn of burglars working in Philadelphia whose victims included the American Company and of other theatrical news:

> The same two fellows [burglars] and Consiglio and Bowman went into a tavernkeeper's house and carried off a mahogany chest full of player's cloaths from a room up two pair of stairs while the family were at supper.
>
> Uncle J.S. made me a present of a ticket to see the play. Mr. Hallam is the best actor according to the common opinion, but I am fonder of Mr. Allyn. Miss Cheer and Miss Wainwright are the best Actresses. The latter is the best woman singer and Mr. Wools is their excellent man singer. James Godwin who used to be Mr. Tioli's dancing boy dances and acts upon the stage. They say he gets £4 per week.

Source: Walker, "Life of Margaret Shippen, wife of Benedict Arnold," 409–10.]

14 January 1767   Great Room of the Rawleigh Tavern, Williamsburg
Lecture on Heads.
William Verling.

[See 13 January 1767. Source: *Virginia Gazette* (8 January 1767).]

15 January 1767   Academy in Second Street, Philadelphia
Lecture on Heads.
Joseph Garner.

[The *Philadelphia Gazette* of 8 January 1767 contains the following notice of Mr. Garner's activities:

> Mr. Garner, from frequent solicitations, and a readiness to contribute, as much as in his power, to alleviate the deep distresses of many indigent families and prisoners in this city, many of whom the inclemency of the season, and want of the common means of supporting life, have reduced to unutterable calamities, proposes to have four public evenings for the benefit of those indigent persons, viz. on Thursday the 15th, Tuesday the 20th, Thursday the 22nd, and Tuesday the 27th instant. —On these evenings will be exhibited the celebrated Lecture on Heads, several orations by the students of this Academy, and a concert of vocal and instrumental music, by some gentlemen, whose benevolence leads them to offer themselves upon this occasion. The distribution of these collections will be by Mr Andrew Bankson's, Mr. Fleeson's, at the London Coffee House, and at the above Academy. N.B. On Sunday evening, the 11th inst. will be read, a discourse on this charitable motive, and two celebrated anthems performed vocally and instrumentally. There will be a collection made for the more immediate relief of the poor; and tickets for said evening delivered gratis, at the Academy only.]

16 January 1767   Southwark Theatre, Philadelphia
The Orphan of China.

Zamti–Douglass; Zaphimri–Hallam; Timurkan–Allyn; Hamet–Wall; Mirvan–Morris; Octar–Tomlinson; Orasming–Greville; Zimventri–Woolls; Messenger–Godwin; Mandane–Mrs. Douglass.
The Devil to Pay.
As 19 December 1766.
American Company.
[Source: *Pennsylvania Gazette* (15 January 1767).]

20 January 1767   Academy in Second Street, Philadelphia
Lecture on Heads.
Joseph Garner.
["For the benefit of ... indigent persons." Source: *Philadelphia Gazette* (8 January 1767).]

22 January 1767   Philadelphia
Performance review.
American Company.
[A lengthy letter appears in the *Pennsylvania Gazette* of this date, which is challenged in the 29 January 1767 issue. The author presents a highly positive critique of the company, especially praising Miss Cheer and Woolls. Also mentioned is a performance of *Love in a Village* for which no date is specified:

> As the practice prevails in our mother country, I hope you will have no objections against inserting in your paper, the observations that any gentleman may decently make concerning the actors on our little theatre here. I do not wholly rely upon my own delicacy of judgement in the following remarks, for I have gathered and compared the sentiments of many others, who have had good opportunities of improving their taste of both Plays and Players. The practice of altering the author's expressions is universally condemned by all men of sense, and leaves no excuse for the vanity or neglect of the actor; and I hope this little hint will be sufficient to guard our actors against any thing of the like nature for the future; for they ought to consider, that one indecent, unguarded, ill judged expression, will do them inconceivable mischief in this country, and that no one advantage can arise from taking such a liberty, but if they clearly avoid this rock, and are prudent in the choice of plays, the rational entertainment, must, and will succeed, agreeable to the highest wishes of those who are concerned in it.
> I am sorry Mr. Hallam, who is genteel in his person and action, could not take copy from the inimitable Garrick, and speak plain English, whenever he assumes a character that may be supposed to understand the language. There is no necessity of destroying the least articulate beauty of language, thro' fury, eagerness, or passion; Miss Cheer never loses the sweetest accent, or faulters in the cleverness of

expression, from any or all those causes, though I believe she is equally delicate, and capable of feeling the force of passion.

I am not alone, when I pronounce her one of the best players in the Empire; she appears to me, from that ease of behaviour which always shines through every action, to have been much among people of fashion, for she well fits the highest character she ever assumes.

I must beg leave to inform the public, that the pleasing Love in a Village is done here beyond expectation, and must give real delight to every person void of ill-nature. —Miss Wainwright is a very good singer, and her action exceeds the famous Miss Brent. Mr. Hallam exceeds every thing in the character of Hodge; and Mr. Woolls almost equals Beard in Hawthorn. Miss Hallam deserves universal applause and encouragement. I could wish to see the house better filled whenever this justly applauded entertainment is exhibited.]

22 January 1767   Academy in Second Street, Philadelphia
Lecture on Heads.
Joseph Garner.
["For the benefit of ... indigent persons." Source: *Philadelphia Gazette* (8 January 1767).]

23 January 1767   Southwark Theatre, Philadelphia
The Beaux' Stratagem.
    Archer–Hallam; Aimwell–Douglass; Sullen–Wall; Foigard–Allyn; Freeman–Greville; Scrub–Morris; Gibbet–Woolls; Boniface–Tomlinson; Hounslow–Godwin; Bagshot–Platt; Dorinda–Miss Hallam; Lady Bountiful–Mrs. Harman; Mrs. Sullen–Miss Cheer; Gipsey–Mrs. Wall.
The Upholsterer* (Arthur Murphy, 1757).
American Company.
    [Source: *Pennsylvania Gazette* (22 January 1767).]

26 January 1767   Southwark Theatre, Philadelphia
The Mourning Bride.
    Osmyn–Hallam; King–Douglass; Gonzales–Morris; Garcia–Wall; Heli–Tomlinson; Selim–Godwin; Alonzo–Greville; Perez–Allyn; Mutes–Woolls and Platt; Almeria–Miss Cheer; Attendants to Almeria–Miss Wainwright and Miss Hallam; Zara–Mrs. Douglass; Attendants to Zara–Mrs. Tomlinson and Mrs. Wall; Leonora–Mrs. Harman.
High Life Below Stairs* (James Townley, 1759).
    Lovel–Hallam; Freeman–Douglass; Lord Duke–Godwin; Kingston–Allyn; Coachman–Woolls; Tom–Tomlinson; Philip–Morris; Chloe–Platt; Cook–Mrs. Harman; Kitty–Miss Cheer; Lady Charlotte–Miss Wainwright.
American Company.
    [Source: *Pennsylvania Chronicle* (26 January 1767).]

27 January 1767   Academy in Second Street, Philadelphia
Lecture on Heads.
Joseph Garner.
["For the benefit of ... indigent persons." Source: *Philadelphia Gazette* (8 January 1767).]

29 January 1767   Southwark Theatre, Philadelphia
Newspaper letter.
The *Philadelphia Gazette* of this date reacts to the theatrical criticism of the American Company which had appeared in that same paper on 22 January 1767:

> I am led to these reflections, from seeing an essay of this sort, in the last week's Gazette, but as it is extremely difficult for a man at all times to be so awake to common sense, or distinguishing understanding, as to judge truly of his own abilities, I shall remark, that this gentleman, who professes delicacy of judgement, (as he terms it) has been deficient in two things.—He does not appear to have considered the character he assumed to himself, nor has he examined the subjects he write upon. He tells us, that he is "sorry Mr. Hallam, who is genteel in his person and action, does not take copy from the inimitable Garrick, and speak plain English, whenever he assumes a character that may be supposed to understand the language." True it is, with all his merit, there is much fault to be found with Mr. Hallam's method of articulating. —He has begun, and continues, in a bad habit of speaking; he seems to suck in, or at least not to utter the first letters of the words he speaks; on which (in many instances) the true pronouncing sound of them depends; and indeed it is from this circumstance alone (which has escaped our author's observation) that people, in general, have concluded, that he either has not had an opportunity of observing Mr. Garrick's expression; or if he has, that he is not improved   by it. Besides, as the Atlantic, at present, deprives him of the opportunity and advantage which might result from his endeavouring to copy from that unequalled Roscius, we shall be glad to know, how is he to do it without an interview? If our author means only to let Mr. Hallam know that Mr. Garrick spoke good English; Mr. Hallam certainly understood that before; but if he thinks that telling him only, will instruct him to speak with propriety, he may be said to equal Bayes in the Rehearsal—he parades—to do nothing at all. In touching upon the character of the justly celebrated and much admired Miss Cheer, he first pays her the compliment of being equally delicate with Mr. Hallam, whose merit (except in this comparison) we acknowledge— and then he pronounces her one of the best players in the Empire.
>
> Does he mean the Empire of the American Theatre, or what Empire? For here the author has left us a little in the dark. He then goes on to remark the excellency of Miss Wainwright, as a singer, and tells us, that her action exceeds that of the famous Miss Brent; but as we never knew that lady to appear properly in the character of an actress, we shall, in this case, also be glad to know what sort of action he alludes to. As to Mr. Wooll's approved performances, not only in Hawthorne, but in many other instances; as well as Miss Hallam,

deserving universal applause and encouragement, we readily subjure to; nor can we think otherwise but the American Company, in general, deserve great commendation.

But, notwithstanding this, I presume to think that they may receive just and sufficient applause, without drawing into comparison the characters of the most eminent in their profession; for this, like bestowing the epithet of beautiful, upon a tolerable handsome woman, must prove as real a disadvantage, and will, in the eyes of gentlemen and ladies of taste, who have seen a Garrick and a Cibber, as the injudicious friend would intend to do them service.]

30 January 1767   Southwark Theatre, Philadelphia
King Lear.
    Lear–Hallam; Edgar–Douglass; Bastard–Wall; Gloster–Morris; Albany–Allyn; Cornwall–Greville; Kent–Tomlinson; Burgundy–Wall; Usher–Godwin; Goneril–Mrs. Wall; Regan–Mrs. Harman; Cordelia–Miss Cheer; Arante–Mrs. Tomlinson.
The Citizen.
American Company.
    [Source: *Pennsylvania Gazette* (29 January 1767).]

2 February 1767   Southwark Theatre, Philadelphia
Cato.
    Cato–Douglass; Sempronius–Hallam; Portius–A Gentleman (his first appearance); Juba–Wall; Syphax–Allyn; Marcus–Godwin; Lucius–Tomlinson; Decius–Woolls; Marcia–Miss Cheer; Lucia–Mrs. Harman.
The Reprisal* (Tobias Smollett, 1757).
    Champignon–Allyn; O'Clabber–Morris; M'Claymore–Douglass; Block–Hallam; Lyon–Broadbelt; Heartly–Greville; Brush–Wall; Hallyard–Woolls; Sailors–Tomlinson, Godwin, and Platt; Miss Harriet–Miss Hallam.
American Company.
    [Source: *Pennsylvania Chronicle* (2 February 1767); cf. Hiltzheimer 13.]

5 February 1767   Assembly Room, Lodge Alley, Philadelphia
Musical concert.
Members of the American Company.
    Vocal parts: Miss Hallam, Woolls, Miss Wainwright, and others.
    [The following notice appears:

Mr. Garner, having made an application to Mr. Douglass, for his assistance in relieving the distresses of many indigent persons, he became immediately touch'd; but having nothing in his power, at this critical juncture, to contribute to their present relief, yet to evince his future intent of embracing the earliest opportunity, and for the present, the deepest concern that he could not immediately exert his desired benevolence, has been so humane as to prevail with Mr. Woolls, Miss Wainwright, Miss Hallam, and others, to attend at the Assembly Room in Lodge Alley, on Thursday the 5th instant.

Price: 5s. Source: *Pennsylvania Chronicle* (26 January–2 February 1767).]

6 February 1767   Southwark Theatre, Philadelphia
The Orphan of China.
   As 16 January 1767, except Timurkan–A Gentleman (being his second appearance); Octar–Allyn; Morat–Tomlinson; Arsace–Mrs. Tomlinson.
High Life Below Stairs.
American Company.
   [Source: *Pennsylvania Gazette* (5 February 1767).]

9 February 1767   Southwark Theatre, Philadelphia
The Miser* (Henry Fielding, 1733).
   Miser–Allyn; Frederick–Douglass; Cleremont–Wall; James–Tomlinson; Decoy–Morris; Sattin–Greville; Spartile–Woolls; Furnish–Platt; Bubbleboy–Godwin; Ramillie–Hallam; Harriet–Miss Hallam; Mrs. Wisely–Mrs. Tomlinson; Laffet–Mrs. Harman; Wheedle–Mrs. Wall; Mariana–Miss Cheer.
The Reprisal.
American Company.
   [Source: *Pennsylvania Chronicle* (9 February 1767).]

13 February 1767   Southwark Theatre, Philadelphia
Romeo and Juliet.
   Romeo–Hallam; Mercutio–Douglass; Capulet–Morris; Montague–Tomlinson; Friar Laurence–Allyn; Escalus–Broadbelt; Tibalt–Wall; Paris–Woolls; Benvolio–Godwin; Balthazar–Greville; Friar John–Platt; Nurse–Mrs. Harman; Lady Capulet–Mrs. Douglass; Juliet–Miss Cheer.
Catherine and Petruchio.
   As 21 November 1766.
American Company.
   [Source: *Pennsylvania Gazette* (12 February 1767); cf. Hiltzheimer 13).]

16 February 1767   Southwark Theatre, Philadelphia
The Conscious Lovers.

Young Bevil–Hallam; Sealand–Douglass; Myrtle–Wall; Cimberton–Allyn; Sir John–Broadbelt; Tom–Morris; Humphrey–Tomlinson; Daniel–Godwin; Isabella–Mrs. Douglass; Phillis–Mrs. Harman; Lucinda–Miss Hallam; Indiana–Miss Cheer.
Damon and Phillida.
American Company.
[Source: *Pennsylvania Chronicle* (16 February 1767).]

20 February 1767   Southwark Theatre, Philadelphia
The Inconstant.
Young Mirabel–Hallam; Duretete–Douglass; Durgard–Wall; Old Mirabel–Morris; Petit–Tomlinson; First Bravo–Allyn; Second Bravo–Broadbelt; Third Bravo–Woolls; Fourth Bravo–Greville; Oriana–Mrs. Harman; Lamorce–Miss Wainwright; Bisarre–Miss Cheer.
Thomas and Sally.
Squire–Woolls; Sailor–Wall; Dorcas–Miss Cheer; Sally–Miss Wainwright.
American Company.
[Source: Some confusion exists concerning this evening's program. The *Pennsylvania Gazette* (19 February 1767) offers the above bill (also cited by Pollock [91]), while Rankin (116), presumably following the *Pennsylvania Journal* (but not offering an exact citation), claims that *Love for Love* was presented.]

23 February 1767   Southwark Theatre, Philadelphia
George Barnwell [i.e., *The London Merchant*].
Barnwell–Hallam; Thorowgood–Douglass; Trueman–Morris; Uncle–Allyn; Blunt–Tomlinson; Maria–Miss Hallam; Lucy–Mrs. Harman; Millwood–Miss Cheer.
The Mayor of Garratt* (Samuel Foote, 1763).
Sturgeon–Hallam; Mug–Hallam; Sneak and Lint–Wall; Jollup–Tomlinson; Bruin–Douglass; Crispin–Morris; Roger–Godwin; Snuffle–Platt; First Mob–Woolls; Second Mob–Matthews; Third Mob–Broadbelt; Fourth Mob–Allyn; Mrs Bruin–Mrs. Harman; Mrs. Sneak–Miss Cheer.
American Company.
[Source: *Pennsylvania Chronicle* (23 February 1767).]

27 February 1767   Southwark Theatre, Philadelphia
Love for Love.
Valentine–Douglass; Sir Sampson–Tomlinson; Ben–Hallam; Foresight–Morris; Scandal–Allyn; Tattle–Wall; Jeremy–Godwin; Buckram–Greville; Miss Prue–Miss Cheer; Angeli-

ca–Miss Hallam; Mrs. Frail–Mrs. Douglass; Mrs. Foresight–Mrs. Wall; Nurse–Mrs. Harman.
Damon and Phillida.
Damon–Woolls; Mopsus–Hallam; Cimon–Wall; Orcas–Allyn; Corydon–Morris; Phillida–Miss Wainwright.
American Company.
[The advertisement announces that regarding Congreve's play, the "Reviver ... has taken the Freedom to ... expunge every Passage that might be offensive either to Decency or good Manners." Source: *Pennsylvania Gazette* (26 February 1767).]

3 March 1767   Southwark Theatre, Philadelphia
The Provoked Husband.
Townly–Hallam; Manly–Douglass; Wronghead–Morris; Richard–Allyn; Barret–Wall; Moody–Tomlinson; Lady Grace–Mrs. Douglass; Lady Wronghead–Mrs. Harman; Miss Jenny–Miss Hallam; Mrs. Motherly–Miss Wainwright; Myrtilla–Mrs. Wall; Lady Townly–Miss Cheer; Trusty–Mrs. Morris.
Harlequin Collector.
Harlequin–Hallam; Skeleton–Matthews; Porter–Morris; Baboon–Wall; Miller's Men–Broadbelt and Appleby; Doctor–Douglass; Clown–Tomlinson; Columbine–Miss Cheer; Hay-Makers–Woolls, Wall, Godwin, Broadbelt, Matthews, Mrs. Harman, Miss Hallam, Miss Wainwright, Mrs. Wall, Mrs. Morris, &c.
American Company.
[Source: *Pennsylvania Chronicle* (2 March 1767).]

5 March 1767   Southwark Theatre, Philadelphia
The Miser.
As 9 February 1767, but Mrs. Wisely–Mrs. Douglass.
Harlequin Collector.
As 3 March 1767, but Clown–Morris; Porter–Tomlinson.
American Company.
[Source: *Pennsylvania Gazette* (5 March 1767).]

9 March 1767   Boston
Anti-theatrical activity.
[The *Boston Evening Post* of this date prints the following letter objecting to recent local interest in theatrical performances:

> To all whom it may concern. Is it not surprising that such a number of lads should be encouraged to act in characters unbecoming their callings? Does it not tend to take their minds off from their business,

and instead of making them good taylors, shoemakers, &c. render them nothing more than strolling players? Is it not detrimental to their master's interest, as well as their own health, to have their shews at such unseasonable hours, when so many children are obliged to steal from their homes to be of the party? ... I am a friend to family order, and a sufferer by such performances. [Signed] S. B.]

9 March 1767   Southwark Theatre, Philadelphia
All for Love* (John Dryden, 1677).
  Marc Antony–Hallam; Ventidius–Douglass; Dolabella–Wall; Alexas–Morris; Serapion–Tomlinson; Neyris–Woolls; Octavia–Mrs. Douglass; Charmion–Miss Wainwright; Cleopatra–Miss Cheer; Iras–Mr. Wall; Antonius and Agrippine–Master Hallam and Miss Tomlinson.
Harlequin Collector.
  As 5 March 1767.
American Company.
  [Source: *Pennsylvania Chronicle* (9 March 1767).]

14 March 1767   Southwark Theatre, Philadelphia
Love Makes a Man* (Colley Cibber, 1700).
  Clodio–Hallam; Carlos–Douglass; Don Lewis–Morris; Antonio–Allyn; Charino–Tomlinson; Don Duart–Wall; Governor–Greville; Monsieur–Godwin; Priest–Woolls; Page–Miss Dowthwaite; Lawyer–Platt; Louise–Mrs. Douglass; Elvira–Miss Wainwright; Honoria–Mrs. Wall; Angelina–Miss Cheer.
The Deuce is in Him* (George Colman Sr., 1763).
  Tamper–Hallam; Belford–Douglass; Prattle–Wall; Mademoiselle Florival–Mrs. Harman; Bell–Miss Wainwright; Emily–Miss Hallam.
American Company.
  [Source: *Pennsylvania Gazette* (12 March 1767).]

17 March 1767   Southwark Theatre, Philadelphia
Richard III.
  As 5 December 1766.
The Brave Irishman.
American Company.
  [Source: *Pennsylvania Chronicle* (16 March 1767).]

19 March 1767   Southwark Theatre, Philadelphia
Love in a Village.
  Woodcock–Douglass; Hawthorn–Woolls; Young Meadows–Wall; Hodge–Hallam; Sir William–Morris; Eustace–Allyn; Lucinda–Miss Hallam; Margery–Mrs. Harman; Mrs. Wood-

cock–Mrs. Douglass; Rosetta–Miss Wainwright; Servants–Tomlinson, Greville, Platt, Wall, etc.
The Mayor of Garratt.
American Company.

[*Love in a Village* is advertised "the Fourth Night," but the present entry is the first confirmed performance in that city. Theatrical criticism in the *Pennsylvania Gazette* of 22 January 1767 (see entry for that date) makes clear that *Love in a Village* had already been staged in Philadelphia. *The Mayor of Garratt* is advertised as "the Third Night." Source: *Pennsylvania Gazette* (19 March 1767).]

19 March 1767   The Orange Tree, Golden Hill, New York City
Non-theatrical performance.
Bayly Company.

[The *New York Journal* of 12 March 1767 prints the following notice of the Bayly Company's activities:

> For the benefit of the poor, on Thursday next, the 19th inst. in a commodious room, which is now fitted up in theatrical manner, for the accommodation of ladies and gentlemen, at the sign of the Orange tree, on Golden-Hill,—will be presented the noted Bayly's performances, by dexterity of hand, with a variety of curious balances, by the noted Hymes, lately arrived from Sadler's-Wells; with the facetious humours of Mr. Punch, his family, and company of artificial commedians three feet high; a view of the sea, with ships, mermaids, fish, sea monsters, etc. which is allowed the most natural curiosity of the kind ever seen; and a court of twenty-five figures, or assembly of maids and bachelors.
>
> Boxes 4s.–Front seats 3s.–Second seats 2s.–Back seats 1s.–for children. N.B. They continue their performances every evening, Sundays excepted. Any set company may have a private performance at two o'clock, any day, on giving four hours notice.]

23 March 1767   Southwark Theatre, Philadelphia
The Earl of Essex.
   Essex–Halam; Southampton–Douglass; Burleigh–Morris; Raleigh–Tomlinson; Lieutenant–Woolls; Queen Elizabeth–Mrs. Douglass; Countess of Rutland–Miss Cheer; Countess of Nottingham–Miss Hallam; Lords and Ladies, etc.–Greville, Godwin, Platt, Miss Wainwright, Mrs. Morris, Mrs. Tomlinson, Mrs. Wall, etc.
Harlequin Collector.
American Company.
   [Source: *Pennsylvania Chronicle* (23 March 1767).]

28 March 1767   Southwark Theatre, Philadelphia
Macbeth.

Macbeth–Hallam; Macduff–Douglass; Duncan–Allyn; Banquo–Morris; Lennox–Wall; Seyton–Tomlinson; Malcolm–Godwin; Flean–Miss Dowthwaite; Donaldbain–Platt; Officer–Greville; First Murderer–Matthews; Hecate–Mrs. Harman; Lady Macduff–Mrs. Douglass; Lady Macbeth–Miss Cheer; Attendant–Mrs. Morris; Witches–Mrs. Harman, Miss Wainwright, and Mrs. Tomlinson.

The Oracle.
As 5 December 1766, but Dance–Godwin.
American Company.
[Source: *Pennsylvania Journal* (26 March 1767).]

30 March 1767   Southwark Theatre, Philadelphia
Macbeth.
As 28 March, but Malcolm–Greville.
The Lying Valet.
American Company.
[Source: *Pennsylvania Chronicle* (30 March 1767).]

30 March 1767   Boston
The Fair Penitent.
Company unknown.

[The following item appeared in the *Boston Gazette* of 13 April 1767:

Mr. B. S. in the Evening-Post of the 6th inst. with a good deal of candour and judgment, pointed out the consequence of acting plays at such unseasonable hours. Whether he be intirely ignorant of the real cause that obliges them to be performed at such a time of night, or 'chuses not to mention it, "it is not for me to determine." The law that put a stop to these credible gentlemen who entertained their friends with a noble and decent comedy or tragedy; is that which obliges them to perform at such hours, and not an account of assignations (as he is pleased to suppose). Mr. B. S. would do well to consider before he throws out any further reactions against the present performers, whether nature has confin'd the theatrical genius to credible persons (like himself) exclusive of those of a more insignificant character; and why a "Bungler or cobler in one business, may not shine conspicuous in another." "Many in many parts are know t' excell; / But 'tis too hard for one to act all well." Had the present actors an opportunity of seeing a play well exhibited, I am confident some of them might make as considerable a figure as any of those credible gentlemen, or even Mr. B. S. himself; and I think the best way of his convincing the world that he is not a bungler nor cobler, would be to leave off writing, and display his genius; and those credible gentlemen, by entertaining the town with another noble and decent comedy or tragedy.

On the 30th of last month, "The Fair Penitent" made an appearance in Boston; she then look'd very beautiful, and with her attendants made a very brilliant figure (her metamorphosis and all things considered): But as there was a great deal of nonsensical talk about her, and many impertinent things said of her, besides an inexplicable hypocritical fellow wrote such a [non-sense] performance in the "Evening-Post," that she left the town immediately (dismissing her attendants at Boston) and went to Cambridge, where a number of grand young gentlemen (who had before enter'd into her service) immediately waited upon her, and invited her about a mile and a half from the town, where they most barbarously murder'd her before a number of grand spectators.—Oh! cruel butchery.—worse than "Coblers and Bunglers." N.B. It is said her beauty decay'd before she got to Cambridge, and her behaviour quite alter'd.]

2 April 1767   Southwark Theatre, Philadelphia
The Gamester.
   Beverly–Hallam; Stukely–Douglass; Jarvis–Morris; Lewson–Wall; Bates–Tomlinson; Dawson–Allyn; Lucy–Miss Wainwright; Charlotte–Mrs. Harman; Mrs. Beverly–Miss Cheer; Epilogue–Miss Cheer.
The Witches, or Harlequin Restored* (James Love, 1762).
   Harlequin–Hallam; Statuary–Douglass; Pantaloon–Morris; Petit Maitre–Allyn; Constable–Broadbelt; Mercury–Woolls; Necromancer–Woolls; Valet–Wall; Periot–Tomlinson; Cook–Mrs. Harman; Colombine–Miss Cheer; Witches–Broadbelt, Matthews, Miss Wainwright, Mrs. Harman, Mrs. Tomlinson, and Mrs. Wall.
American Company.
[Source: *Pennsylvania Gazette* (2 April 1767).]

2 April 1767   The Orange Tree, Golden Hill, New York City
Non-theatrical performance.
Bayly Company.
   [The *New York Journal* of this date prints the following notice of the Bayly Company's further activities:

> For the benefit of the prisoners. This evening the second of April in a commodious room, which is now fitted up in a theatrical manner, for the accommodation of ladies and gentlemen, at the sign of the Orange tree, on Golden-Hill,—will be presented the noted Bayly's performances, by dexterity of hand: When besides his usual performances, he will exhibit several others, never attempted before. Secondly, by Mr. Hymes, will be exhibited several curious balances (besides the usual) not yet shewn by him. Mr. Punch likewise begs leave to inform the public, that by him, his merry family, and company of artificial commedians three feet high, several diverting drolls, burlettas, etc. etc. With the curious performances of his artificial posture-master; and a grand court of twenty-eight figures, or old maids and bachelors assembly. To conclude with a view of the sea, with ships sailing, fish, etc. etc. swimming. Care has been taken to divide the seats properly, according to their different prices.

Boxes 3s.9d.–front seats 3s.–second seats 2s–back seats 1s. Ladies and gentlemen may be assured the strictest decency and modesty will be observed in the performances. Tickets to be had at the place of performance.—The doors to be opened at 6, and to begin at 7 o'clock in the evening. They continue their performances Monday, Tuesday, Thursday, and Saturday evenings, for a few weeks longer. Any set company may have a private performance, at two or three o'clock, any day, giving four hours notice.]

4 April 1767   The Orange Tree, Golden Hill, New York
Non-theatrical performance.
Bayly Company.
[For the benefit of the prisoners. Source: *New York Journal* (26 March 1767).]

6 April 1767   Boston
Anti-theatrical activity.
[The *Boston Evening Post* of this date prints a long letter which present a complaint against recent theatrical activity:

> ... acting of plays and tragedies in this town is now practiced with impunity.... P.S. It is apprehended that when the American Company of Comedians, who are now at New York or Philadelphia, hear there is so great an inclination for such entertainments in this place, they will endeavor to introduce themselves, and certainly with more justice than these bunglers and coblers in every business.]

7 April 1767   Southwark Theatre, Philadelphia
Romeo and Juliet.
    As 13 February 1767.
Lethe.
American Company.
[Source: *Pennsylvania Chronicle* (6 April 1767); playbill in the New York Public Library.]

9 April 1767   Southwark Theatre, Philadelphia
Hamlet.
    As 9 January 1767, but Horatio–Greville.
The Witches, or Harlequin Restored.
    As 2 April 1767.
American Company.
[Source: *Pennsylvania Gazette* (9 April 1767).]

14 April 1767   The Orange Tree, Golden Hill, New York City
The Enchanted Lady of the Grove* (Anonymous).
Harlequin and the Miller* (Anonymous).
Bayly Company.

Miller–Bayly; Harlequin–Tea.
[Benefit Bayly. Prices: boxes, 4s.; front seats 3s.; second seats 2s. To begin at 7 o'clock. "The Tuesday following will be for the benefit of Mr. Tea." Source: *New York Journal* (9 April 1767).]

20 April 1767   Southwark Theatre, Philadelphia
The Morning Bride.
The Contrivances* (Henry Carey, 1715).
American Company.
[Forrest's *The Disappointment* was announced in the *Pennsylvania Chronicle* of 13 April 1767 for this date but was withdrawn as announced in the *Gazette* of 16 April 1767. Pollock (95–96) remarks that this "was the first American play announced for production." Source: *Pennsylvania Gazette* (16 April 1767).]

21 April 1767   The Orange Tree, Golden Hill, New York City
Play not identified.
Bayly Company.
[A benefit for Mr. Tea on this date is implied by a notice in the *New York Journal* of 9 April 1767.]

24 April 1767   Southwark Theatre, Philadelphia
The Prince of Parthia* (Thomas Godfrey).
     Possible cast: Arsaces–Hallam; Artabanes–Douglass; Gotarzes–Wall; Bethas–Morris; Barzaphernes–Allyn; Vardanes–Tomlinson; Lysias–Broadbelt; Phraates–Greville; Thermusa–Mrs. Douglass; Edessa–Mrs. Morris; Cleone–Miss Wainwright; Evanthe–Miss Cheer.
The Contrivances.
American Company.
[Cast suggested by Seilhamer (1:194). Pollock (96) remarks that this is "the first American drama to be professionally produced on the American stage." The play was advertised in the following manner:

> By authority. Never performed before. By the American Company. At the new theatre, in Southwark, on Friday, the twenty-fourth of April, will be presented, a tragedy written by the late ingenious Mr. Thomas Godfrey, of this city, called The Prince of Parthia.

Source: *Pennsylvania Journal* (23 April 1767).]

27 April 1767   Southwark Theatre, Philadelphia
A Bold Stroke for a Wife.

The Devil to Pay.
American Company.
　[Source: *Pennsylvania Chronicle* (27 April 1767).]

30 April 1767　　The Orange Tree, Golden Hill, New York City
The Enchanted Lady of the Grove.
Harlequin's Escape.
　Pantaloon–by a gentleman; Spaniard–Bayly; Harlequin–by a gentleman; Clown–Tea.
Harlequin and the Miller.
　Miller–Bayly; Harlequin–Tea.
Bayly Company.
　["Mr. Bayly begs leave to inform those ladies and gentlemen, that please to honour him with their company, that he continues his performances every Monday, Tuesday, Thursday, and　Saturday evenings; for a fortnight longer. Different performances every evening, and good musick."
Source: *New York Journal* (30 April 1767).]

1 May 1767　　Southwark Theatre, Philadelphia
All for Love.
Flora, or Hob in the Well.
American Company.
　[Source: *Pennsylvania Gazette* (30 April 1767).]

4 May 1767　　Southwark Theatre, Philadelphia
A Bold Stroke for a Wife.
The Apprentice* (Arthur Murphy, 1756).
American Company.
　[Source: *Pennsylvania Chronicle* (4 May 1767).]

5 May 1767　　The Orange Tree, Golden Hill, New York City
The Enchanted Lady of the Grove.
Harlequin's Escape.
　As 30 April 1767.
Harlequin and the Miller.
　Miller–Bayly; Harlequin–Tea.
Bayly Company.
　[Benefit Bayly. Source: *New York Journal* (30 April 1767).]

7 May 1767　　The Orange Tree, Golden Hill, New York City
Play not identified.
Bayly Company.
　[A benefit for Mr. Tea on this date is implied by a notice in the *New York Journal* of 30 April 1767.]

7 May 1767   Southwark Theatre, Philadelphia
The Jealous Wife.
    Oakly–Hallam; Major Oakly–Douglass; Charles–Wall; Beagle–Allyn; Russet–Morris; Trinket–Hallam; Tom–Woolls; O'Cutter–Allyn; John–Tomlinson; William–Matthews; Mrs. Oakly–Miss Cheer; Lady Freelove–Mrs. Douglass; Harriet–Miss Hallam; Toilet–Mrs. Harman; Betty–Miss Wainwright.
The Lying Valet.
    Lying Valet–Hallam; Gayless–Wall; Tripper–Allyn; Guttle–Tomlinson; Cook–Morris; Melissa–Miss Cheer; Mrs. Gadabout–Mrs. Tomlinson; Mrs. Tripper–Mrs. Wall; Kitty–Mrs. Harman.
American Company.
    [Benefit Miss Cheer. Source: *Pennsylvania Gazette* (7 May 1767).]

11 May 1767   Southwark Theatre, Philadelphia
The Committee.
    Teague–Allyn; Careless–Douglass; Blunt–Hallam; Committee-Men–Wall and Greville; Abel–Woolls; Bayliff–Platt; Soldier–Matthews; Ruth–Miss Cheer; Arabella–Miss Hallam; Mrs. Chat–Mrs. Tomlinson.
The Spirit of Contradiction* (John Rich, 1760).
    Randal–Hallam; Steer–Douglass; Lovewell–Wall; Partlet–Morris; Ruin–Allyn; Miss Harriet–Miss Wainwright; Betty–Mrs. Morris; Mrs. Partlet–Mrs. Harman.
The Picture of a Playhouse [;or, Bucks Have at Ye All]*
    (Thomas King, 1760).
American Company.
    [Benefit Douglass. Source: *Pennsylvania Chronicle* (11 May 1767).]

14 May 1767   Southwark Theatre, Philadelphia
Romeo and Juliet.
    As 13 February 1767, but Benvolio and Balthasar–Greville; Nurse–Mrs. Morris.
The Reprisal.
American Company.
    [Benefit Mrs. Morris. Source: *Pennsylvania Journal* (14 May 1767).]

18 May 1767   Southwark Theatre, Philadelphia
The Drummer.
    Tinfil–Hallam; Sir George–Douglass; Vellum–Allyn; Fantome–Tomlinson; Gardener–Morris; Butler–Wall; Coach-

man–Greville; Lady Truman–Miss Cheer; Abigail–Mrs. Harman.
Catherine and Petruchio.
Petruchio–Hallam; Horentio–Douglass; Gumio–Morris; Baptista–Tomlinson; Biondello–Wall; Music Master–Allyn; Peter–Woolls; Catherine–Miss Cheer; Bianca–Mrs. Wall; Curtis–Mrs. Harman.
American Company.

[Benefit Mrs. Harman. Source: *Pennsylvania Chronicle* (18 May 1767).]

18 May 1767   The Orange Tree, Golden Hill, New York City
The Orphan.
By ladies and gentlemen for their amusement.
Harlequin Statue.
Bayly Company.
Panteloon–Shaw; Harlequin–Martin; Clown–Tea; Colombine–Mrs. Bayly.
[Benefit Bayly. Boxes, 6s.; pit 5s.; gallery 3s. The notice presents the following further details:

> A good band of musick will be provided, with scenes and decorations, incident to the play. Ladies and gentlemen are desired to send for tickets soon, as no more will be sold than the house can conveniently contain.–Tickets to be had of Mr. Bayly, at the place of performance. The door will be opened at four and begin positively at seven o'clock. Vivant Rex et Regina.   He continues to perform his usual entertainments, every Monday, Tuesday, Thursday and Saturday. Boxes 3s.–Fronts 2s.–Backs 1s.

Source: *New York Journal* (14 May 1767).]

21 May 1767   Southwark Theatre, Philadelphia
The Beaux' Stratagem.
As 23 January 1767, but Hounslow–Matthews; Cherry–Mrs. Morris.
Don Quixote in England* (Henry Fielding, 1734).
Don Quixote–Hallam; Sancho–Morris; Guzzel–Douglass; Sir Thomas–Tomlinson; Squire Badge–Wall; Fairlove–Greville; John–Allyn; Cook–Woolls; Jezebel–Mrs. Morris; Dorothea–Miss Wainwright.
American Company.

[Benefit Morris. This version of the afterpiece may be that of a London adaptation from 1752. Source: *Pennsylvania Journal* (21 May 1767).]

25 May 1767   Southwark Theatre, Philadelphia
Cymbeline* (William Shakespeare).
   Posthumous–Hallam; Cymbeline–Allen; Jachimo–Douglass; Bellarius–Morris; Cloten–Wall; Guiderius–Greville; Luciers–Tomlinson; Pisanio–Mrs. Harman; Arviragus–Woolls; Philario–Morris; Doctor–Platt; Lords–Tomlinson, Platt, Matthews, etc.; Imogen–Miss Cheer; Queen–Mrs. Douglass; Helen–Mrs. Tomlinson; Ladies–Mrs. Morris, Mrs. Wall, Miss Wainwright, etc.
The Mayor of Garratt.
   As 23 February 1767, but Roger, Snuffle, and the Mobs are omitted in the bill.
American Company.
   [Benefit Hallam. Source: *Pennsylvania Chronicle* (25 May 1767).]

28 May 1767   Southwark Theatre, Philadelphia
Love in a Village.
   As 19 March 1767.
High Life below Stairs.
American Company.
   [Notices advertise this performance as "the fifth night" of *Love in a Village* this season, but we have been able to identify in the extant newspapers only two prior performances and a rumor of a third. Benefit Woolls. Source: *Pennsylvania Journal* (28 May 1767).]

1 June 1767   Southwark Theatre, Philadelphia
The Revenge.
Tom Thumb the Great.
American Company.
   [Benefit Wall. Source: *Pennsylvania Chronicle* (1 June 1767).]

4 June 1767   Southwark Theatre, Philadelphia
The Country Lasses* (Charles Johnson, 1715).
   Modely–Hallam; Heartwell–Douglass; Sir John–Allyn; Freehold–Morris; Lurcher–Wall; Vulture–Tomlinson; Sneak–Woolls; Long-bottom–Greville; Carbuncle–Broadbelt; Shacklefigure–Platt; Country Man–Matthews; Flora–Miss Wainwright; Aura–Miss Cheer.
The Chaplet* (Moses Mendez, 1749).
   Damon–Woolls; Palemon–Wall; Pastora–Mrs. Harman; Laura–Miss Wainwright.
American Company.

[Benefit Miss Wainwright Source: *Pennsylvania Journal* (4 June 1767).]

8 June 1767   Southwark Theatre, Philadelphia
Coriolanus* (James Thomson, 1749).
The Contrivances.
American Company.
   [Benefit Tomlinson. Source: *Pennsylvania Chronicle* (8 June 1767).]

12 June 1767   Southwark Theatre, Philadelphia
The School for Lovers.
Neck or Nothing* (David Garrick, 1766).
American Company.
   [This program was announced "for Miss Hallam's benefit, but postponed on account of the weather." Source: *Pennsylvania Journal* (11 June 1767); for cancellation news, see the *Pennsylvania Chronicle* (15 June 1767).

15 June 1767   Southwark Theatre, Philadelphia
The Miser.
   As 9 February 1767, but Decoy and Bubbleboy–Morris; Mrs. Wisely–Mrs. Douglass.
The Double Disappointment* (Moses Mendez, 1746).
American Company.
   [Benefit Allyn. Source: *Pennsylvania Chronicle* (15 June 1767).]

18 June 1767   Southwark Theatre, Philadelphia
The Roman Father.
   Roman Father–Hallam; Publius–Douglass; Tubullus–Allyn; Valerius–Wall; First Citizen–Morris; Second Citizen–Greville; Third Citizen–Woolls; Fourth Citizen–Platt; Valeria–Mrs. Douglass; Horatia–Miss Cheer.
Neck or Nothing.
American Company.
   [Benefit Mrs. Douglass. Source: *Pennsylvania Gazette* (18 June 1767).]

22 June 1767   Southwark Theatre, Philadelphia
The Merchant of Venice.
The Lying Valet.
American Company.
   [Benefit Mrs. Tomlinson. Source: *Pennsylvania Chronicle* (15–22 June 1767).]

25 June 1767   Southwark Theatre, Philadelphia
The Wonder! A Woman Keeps a Secret.
The Citizen.
American Company.
[Benefit Greville. Source: *Pennsylvania Gazette* (25 June 1767).]

29 June 1767   Southwark Theatre, Philadelphia
Cymbeline.
Neck or Nothing.
American Company.
[Rescheduled benefit of Miss Hallam. Source: *Pennsylvania Chronicle* (29 June 1767).]

2 July 1767   Southwark Theatre, Philadelphia
The Gamester.
   As 2 April 1767 but Bates–Broadbelt.
The Reprisal.
American Company.
[Benefit Broadbelt. Source: *Pennsylvania Gazette* (2 July 1767).]

6 July 1767   Southwark Theatre, Philadelphia
The Constant Couple.
The Apprentice.
American Company.
[The last night of the season. Benefit Mrs. Wall. Source: *Pennsylvania Chronicle* (6 July 1767).]

15 July 1767   Mr. Burns's Assembly Room, New York
Lecture on Heads.
David Douglass.
[With vocals by Woolls. Price: one dollar. Source: *New York Gazette* (6–13 July 1767).]

17 July 1767   Mr. Burns's Assembly Room, New York
Lecture on Heads.
David Douglass.
[The following notice appears concerning Douglass's program:

> Mr. Douglass will deliver a lecture on Heads. A syllabus of which follows; Part Ist. Introduction–Alexander–Cherokee–Quack–Doctor–Arms–Cuckold–Cornucopia–Lawyer–Oration in Praise of Law–Case, Daniel versus Dishclout–Journey Man's Jemmy–Sir Sanguish Lispey–Frizzl'd Bob–Jockey–Nobody–Arms of Nobody, Somebody, any

Body, and every Body–Fate of Esteem, Generosity, Friendship, Gratitude, Common Sense, and Public Spirit–Genealogy of Genius–Sciences–Honesty–Flattery. Part IId. Physical Wig–Dissertation on Sneezing and Snuff taking–Blood–Woman of the Town–Tea Table Critic–Stock Jobber–Alderman Double Chin the Politician and Turtle-Eater–Gambler–his Funeral–his Monument–Anecdote of a Landlord and a Soldier–Yorick–Methodist. Part IIId. Riding Hood–Ranelagh Hood–Billingsgate–Laughing, and crying Philosophy–Origin of Ladies Bonnets, Pompoons, Egrette's, and Curtain Lectures–Night Rail–Check Wrapper–Face painting exploded–Young Wife and Old Maid contrasted–Old Bachelor–Quaker Man and Woman–Nevernois Hat–Englishman and Frenchman–Virtuoso–Learn'd Critic. Between the parts, and at the end of the lecture, singing by Mr. Woolls.

Source: *New York Journal* (16 July 1767).]

21 July 1767   Mr. Burns's Assembly Room, New York
Lecture on Heads.
David Douglass.
   [With vocals by Woolls. "Mr. Douglass proposes to deliver the Lecture on Tuesdays and Fridays, for the short time he has to stay in town." Price: one dollar. Source: *New York Gazette* (13–20 July 1767).]

28 July 1767   Mr. Burns's Assembly Room, New York
Lecture on Heads.
David Douglass.
   ["The price for admission, having been objected to as rather too high, the Exhibitor, by the advice of his friends, has lower'd it to Half a Dollar. The fourth night." Source: *New York Gazette* (20–27 July 1767).]

31 July 1767   Mr. Burns's Assembly Room, New York
Lecture on Heads.
David Douglass.
   [Singing by Woolls. Source: *New York Journal* (30 July 1767).]

4 August 1767   Mr. Burns's Assembly Room, New York
Lecture on Heads.
David Douglass.
   [Singing by Woolls. "The last night." Source: *New York Mercury* (3 August 1767).]

6 August 1767   Mr. Burns's Assembly Room, New York
Lecture on Heads.
David Douglass.

["Positively the last night." Source: *New York Gazette & Weekly Post Boy* (6 August 1767).]

26 August 1767   Newport, Rhode Island
Death of performer.
American Company.

[The *Boston Gazette* of 31 August 1767 contains the following item about the death of "young Mrs. Hallam" (*recte*, Mrs. Henry):

> We hear from Newport, Rhode-Island, that about 10 o'clock last Wednesday night as Capt. Malbone in a large brig belonging to that place, was coming in deep laden with a valuable cargo from Jamaica, and within about a league of the light house there, a Negro fellow on board went betwixt decks with intent to steal a bucket of rum out of one of the hogsheads, and having a candle with him, it unhappily catched on fire whilst he was drawing & soon set the vessel in flames, by which melancholy accident three women & two children, who were in the cabin, perished, the rest of the people on board with great difficulty saved themselves in the boat.–One of the women that perished is said to be young Mrs. Hallam, an actress, who with other comedians were returning from Jamaica.

The unfortunate casualty of the fire was not Mrs. Hallam, as reported, but Mrs. Henry (John Henry's wife) and their two children.]

27 August 1767   New York
Anti-theatrical commentary.
American Company.

[The *New York Gazette & Weekly Post-Boy* of this date contains a lengthy letter from Bristol, England lamenting the recent establishment of theatrical performers in that city. The following excerpt exemplifies the continuing uneasiness of some colonists and documents the ongoing attempts to rally public support against playhouses and players:

> The late introduction of plays into the city of Bristol, which, by the care of its corporation and magistrates, was never suffered till within these very few years, has given great uneasiness to their sober inhabitants, on account of the many dangers which attend these entertainments, and has occasioned many pieces to be published there, to discourage the future continuance of them in that city; one of which I now send you, and hope you will think it worthy a place in your paper. I think most of the arguments and reasons there laid down, may be well applied to the state of any of our cities, where there is an appearance of the evils therein represented, and may be no bad consideration for the inhabitants of this, if there be truth in the report of a play-house

going to be erected here, at a time when near one quarter of the inhabitants are under the most distressing circumstances.

Now the hurry of play-nights is over, and the company who lately entertained the town are gone, it may be proper for the inhabitants, as merchants and tradesmen, to cast up the accompt, in order to judge the propriety of countenancing such visitors in the future. And it may be reasonably hoped, that those who have entered so deeply into the scheme, as to be share-holders in the play-house (if on a candid and publick spirited review of its consequences, they see it tends to ruin the town) will not suffer private interest to outweigh every other consideration; but like noble minds, chearfully give up their plan of theatric profit, rather than be chargeable with a lucrative confederacy against the laws of the land, and against the prosperity and domestic happiness of their fellow-citizens. If the estimate of the sum received by the players, on their first essay in this city, according to common report, be true, it amounted to four thousand pounds and upwards, in about 15 weeks; which is nearly at the rate of three hundred pounds a week for that time. An amazing expence!]

9 September 1767   Southwark Theatre, Philadelphia
Lecture on Heads.
Douglass and Hallam.
["Between the parts of the lecture, singing by Mr. Wools and Miss Hallam, accompanied by the band of his Majesty's Eighteenth Regiment." Prices: box, 5s.; pit, 3s.; gallery, 2s. Source: *Pennsylvania Chronicle* (31 August–7 September 1767).]

24 September 1767 Southwark Theatre, Philadelphia
Lecture on Heads.
Douglass and Hallam.
[The lecture "with a dissection of the Hearts of a British Sailor, and his Agent for Prize-Money. Between the parts, and after the lecture, the following entertainments, viz. A humorous Scene of a Drunken Man, by Mr. Hallam. Singing by Mr.Woolls, Miss Hallam, and Miss Wainwright. Accompanied by a band of music. To conclude with a Picture of a Play-House, or Bucks have at ye all, by Mr. Hallam." Prices: boxes 5s.; pit 3s.; gallery 2s. Source: *Pennsylvania Gazette* (24 September 1767).]

6 October 1767   Southwark Theatre, Philadelphia
The Roman Father.
The Roman Father–Hallam; Publius Horatius–Henry (from the Theatre in Jamaica); Tullus Hostilius–Douglass; Valerius–Wall; Citizens–Morris, Tomlinson, Woolls, and Roberts; Valeria–Mrs. Douglass; Horatia–Miss Cheer.

Miss in Her Teens.
   Capt. Flash–Hallam; Capt. Lint–Tomlinson; Fribble–Allyn; Jasper–Woolls; Puff–Morris; Miss Biddy Bellair–Miss Storer; Tag–Miss Wainwright.
American Company.
   [Source: *Pennsylvania Chronicle* (5 October 1767).]

9 October 1767   Southwark Theatre, Philadelphia
The Jealous Wife.
   As 7 May 1767, but Charles–Henry; Lord Trinket–Wall; (Part of William not mentioned).
The Witches, or Harlequin Restored.
   As 2 April 1767, but Matthews's name omitted.
American Company.
   [Source: *Pennsylvania Gazette* (8 October 1767).]

12 October 1767   Southwark Theatre, Philadelphia
Hamlet.
The Citizen.
American Company.
   [Source: *Pennsylvania Chronicle* (5–12 October 1767).]

16 October 1767   Southwark Theatre, Philadelphia
Romeo and Juliet.
The Mayor of Garratt.
American Company.
   [Source: *Pennsylvania Gazette* (15 October 1767).]

19 October 1767   Southwark Theatre, Philadelphia
The Beaux' Stratagem.
High Life Below Stairs.
American Company.
   [Source: *Pennsylvania Chronicle* (12–19 October 1767).]

23 October 1767   Southwark Theatre, Philadelphia
The Gamester.
Harlequin Restored; or, The Miller Deceived* (Anonymous).
American Company.
   [Source: *Pennsylvania Gazette* (22 October 1767).]

26 October 1767   Southwark Theatre, Philadelphia
Love in a Village.
The Oracle.
American Company.
   [Source: *Pennsylvania Chronicle* (19–26 October 1767).]

30 October 1767   Southwark Theatre, Philadelphia
The Wonder! A Woman Keeps a Secret.
The Devil to Pay.
American Company.
   [Source: *Pennsylvania Gazette* (29 October 1767).]

2 November 1767   Southwark Theatre, Philadelphia
Venice Preserved.
   Pierre–Hallam; Jaffier–Henry; Priuli–Douglass; Renault–Morris; Bedamar–Wall; Duke–Tomlinson; Spinosa–Malone; Eliot–Greville; Theodore–Wools; Durand–Roberts; Officer–Allyn; Attendants–Mrs. Morris, Mrs. Tomlinson; Belvidera–Miss Cheer.
Neck or Nothing.
   Slip–Hallam; Belford–Wall; Martin–Morris; Mr. Stockwell–Tomlinson; Sir William–Allyn; Mrs. Stockwell–Mrs. Douglass; Miss Nancy Stockwell–Miss Hallam; Jenny–Miss Wainwright.
American Company.
   ["Not acted these eight years." Source: *Pennsylvania Chronicle* (26 October–2 November 1767).]

9 November 1767   Southwark Theatre, Philadelphia
King Lear.
The King and the Miller of Mansfield.
American Company.
   [Source: Seilhamer 1:197.]

13 November 1767   Southwark Theatre, Philadelphia
Theodosius.
The Chaplet.
American Company.
   [Source: *Philadelphia Gazette* (12 November 1767).]

17 November 1767 Philadelphia
Correspondence.
   [From a letter by Margaret Shippen we learn the following theatrical news:

> The players must soon leave off here and will not be again permitted to act these two years. They are going to New York but it is believed that the Opposition will be strong enough to prevent their acting there.

Source: Walker, "Life of Margaret Shippen, Wife of Benedict Arnold," 410.]

19 November 1767　　　　Southwark Theatre, Philadelphia
The Clandestine Marriage* (David Garrick and George Colman Sr., 1766).
Lord Ogleby–Hallam; Sir John Melvil–Douglass; Lovewell–Henry; Sterling–Morris; Canton–Allyn; Brush–Wall; Serjeant Flower–Tomlinson; Traverse–Malone; Truman–Greville; Mrs. Heidelberg–Mrs. Douglass; Fanny–Miss Hallam; Betty–Miss Storer; Chambermaid–Miss Wainwright; Trusty–Mrs. Morris; Miss Sterling–Miss Cheer.
The Brave Irishman.
American Company.
[Source: *Pennsylvania Journal* (19 November 1767).]

23 November 1767　　　　Southwark Theatre, Philadelphia
The Clandestine Marriage.
The Lying Valet.
American Company.
["A farewell epilogue, address'd to the ladies, will be spoken by Mrs. Douglass." Source: *Pennsylvania Chronicle* (16–23 November 1767).]

early December 1767　　　New York
Death of performer.
[The *New York Gazette* of 30 November–7 December 1767 contains the following item:

> Since our last, a melancholy accident happened at the Ferry at Kill-Vankull, at crossing the river, in one of the common scows from Staten Island to Bergen, being the New-Blazing Star Stage Road, occasioned by some mismanagement in approaching the shore, whereby two persons were unfortunately drowned;–we hear belonging to the Play-House, Mrs. Morris, and her maid.

Cf. Odell 1:117.]

7 December 1767　　　　John St. Theatre, New York
The Beaux Stratagem.
Archer–Hallam; Aimwell–Henry; Sullen–Tomlinson; Freeman–Malone; Foigard–Allyn; Gibbet–Woolls; Scrub–Wall; Boniface–Douglass; Dorinda–Miss Hallam; Lady Bountifull–Mrs. Harman; Cherry–Miss Wainwright; Gipsey–Mrs. Wall; Mrs. Sullen–Miss Cheer.
Lethe.
Aesop–Douglass; Drunken Man–Hallam; Frenchman–Allyn; Fine Gentleman–Wall; Mercury (with songs)–Woolls; Charon–Tomlinson; Mr. Tattoo–Malone; Mrs. Tattoo–Mrs.

Hallam; Mrs. Riot (with a song in character)–Miss Wainwright.
American Company.

[The opening night of this theatre. Prices: boxes 8s.; pit 5s.; gallery 3s. Source: *New York Gazette* (30 November–7 December 1767).]

11 December 1767 John St. Theatre, New York
The School for Lovers.
Sir John Dorilant–Douglass; Modely–Hallam; Bellmour–Wall; Steward–Tomlinson; Celia–Miss Hallam; Lady Beverly–Mrs. Harman; Araminta–Miss Cheer. The epilogue between Mr. Hallam and Miss Cheer.
The Mayor of Garratt.
Major Sturgeon and Matthew Mugg–Hallam; Jerry Sneak and Lint–Wall; Bruin–Douglass; Sir Jacob Jollup–Tomlinson; Crispin Heel Tap–Henry; Roger–Malone; Snuffle–Roberts; Mrs. Bruin–Mrs. Harman; Mrs. Sneak–Miss Wainwright. To conclude with a country dance by the characters.
American Company.

[Source: *New York Gazette & Weekly Post-Boy* (10 December 1767).]

14 December 1767 John St. Theatre, New York
Richard III.
King Richard–Hallam; King Henry–Morris; King Edward–Wall; Duke of York, by a young master; Earl of Richmond–Henry; Duke of Buckingham–Douglass; Lord Stanley–Allyn; Tressel–Malone; Catesby–Tomlinson; Ratcliff–Woolls; Blunt–Greville; Forest–Roberts, Lady Ann–Miss Cheer; Duchess of York–Mrs. Harman; Queen Elizabeth–Mrs. Douglass.
The Oracle.
Oberon–Wall; Fairy Queen–Mrs. Douglass; Cinthia (with a song)–Miss Hallam.
Harlequin's Vagaries* (Anonymous).
Principal characters: Hallam, Morris, and Miss Cheer.
American Company.

[Attending this performance were "the ten Indian warriors that arrived here last Friday, from South-Carolina." Source: *New York Mercury* (14 December 1767).]

18 December 1767 John St. Theatre, New York
The Clandestine Marriage.

Lord Ogleby–Hallam; Sir John Melvil–Douglass; Lovewell–Henry; Sterling–Morris; Canton–Allyn; Brush–Wall; Serjeant Flower–Tomlinson; Traverse–Malone; Trueman–Greville; Mrs. Heidelberg–Mrs. Douglass; Miss Fanny–Miss Hallam; Betty–Miss Storer; Chambermaid–Miss Wainwright; Trusty–Mrs. Tomlinson; Miss Sterling–Miss Cheer.

The Old Maid.
Captain Cape–Douglass; Young Clerimont–Wall; Harlow–Allyn; Hearty–Morris; Mrs. Harlow–Miss Cheer; The Old Maid–Mrs. Harman.

American Company.

[Source: *New York Gazette & Weekly Post-Boy* (17 December 1767).]

21 December 1767 John St. Theatre, New York
Hamlet.
Hamlet–Hallam; Claudius–Douglass; Polonius–Morris; Horatio–Henry; Laertes–Wall; Ghost–Tomlinson; Osrick–Allyn; Marcellus–Greville; Player King–Malone; Priest–Woolls; Grave-diggers–Morris and Tomlinson; Queen–Mrs. Douglass; Player Queen–Miss Storer; Ophelia–Miss Cheer.

Thomas and Sally.
Squire–Woolls; Sailor–Wall; Dorcas–Mrs. Harman; Sally–Miss Cheer.

American Company.

[Source: *New York Mercury* (21 December 1767).]

28 December 1767 John St. Theatre, New York
Cymbeline.
Leonatus Posthumus–Hallam; Jachimo–Douglass; Cymbeline–Allyn; Cloten–Wall; Bellarius–Henry; Guiderius–Greville; Arviragus–Woolls; Caius Lucius–Tomlinson; Pisanio–Morris; Philario–Malone; Doctor–Roberts; Queen–Mrs. Douglass; Helen–Mrs. Tomlinson; Imogen–Miss Cheer.

Damon and Phillida.
Damon–Woolls; Mopsas–Hallam; Cymon–Wall; Arcas–Allyn; Corydon–Morris; Phillida–Miss Wainwright.

American Company.

[The play was presented "at the particular desire of the Brethren composing the St. John's, Trinity, Union, and King Solomon's Lodges, of Free and Accepted Masons." Source: *New York Gazette* (14–21 December 1767).]

28 December 1767 John St. Theatre, New York
Fatal accident at the theatre.

[A notice in the *Boston Evening Post* of 18 January 1768 describes a fatal accident at the theatre:

> On Monday the 28th December one John Abrahams, a carpenter, who was at work on the Play-House, going out upon a shed to hang a window, his foot slip'd, & he fell about 28 feet into the yard, whereby his thigh, hip, arm, shoulder, and other bones were broken, and otherwise terribly bruised. He had the best assistance, but the bones could not be set, and he died the next night.]

30 December 1767   New City Hall, New York
The Mourning Bride.
The Upholsterer, or What News?
American Company.
   ["For the benefit of the debtors in the New City Jail." Source: *New York Gazette* (14–21 December 1767).]

1768

Four companies are known to have played in the colonies this year, as well as the company touring the West Indies: the Virginia Company (managed by William Verling); the American Company (managed by David Douglass); a third company in North Carolina and Nova Scotia managed by a Mr. Mills, and Bayly's Company in Charleston.

William Verling and his wife, Elizabeth Conner, assembled a company and began playing in and around Norfolk, Virginia, sometime prior to January 1768. They called themselves The Virginia Company, and later, the New American Company. Known members included Christopher Bromadge, Thomas Charlton, Mrs. Dowthwaitte and her daughter, Miss Dowthwaitte, Mr. Farrell, Mrs. Farrell, James Godwin (a dancer from the American Company), Sarah Jones, Mr. Leavie, Mr. Mallory, Henrietta Osborne, Charles Parker, Mrs. Parker, William Verling, George Walker, and a Miss Yapp. Several names will be recognizable from their work with the American Company. William Verling had acted with Douglass in 1766, Godwin in 1767, Mrs. Dowthwaitte in 1760, her daughter Miss Dowthwaitte from 1760 and more recently in 1766, and the frequent-flyer Henrietta Osborne (who earned the dubious distinction of playing with and leaving every professional company that toured the colonies). The Parkers, Seilhamer tells us (1:237), are introduced as "from the Theatre in Jamaica."

Though we have notice of only two nights of their programs from January to March, the Virginia Company played in Norfolk. Regarding the performance facilities in this village, very little information has survived, but we learn from *The Lower Norfolk County Virginia Antiquary* (2: 102) the following: "The theatre was quite well patronized before the Revolution. The theatre building was a wooden structure that had originally been built for a pottery. It stood in the rear of a lot on the south side of Main Street, somewhere about King's Lane, on the river margin."

After Norfolk the Virginia Company traveled to the Old Theatre in Williamsburg, where they opened on 31 March and played through the June Court session. The company is known to have included the following members: Mr. Bromadge, Mr. Charlton, Miss Dowthaitte, Mrs. Dowthaitte, Mr. Farrell, Mr. Godwin, Mr. Leavie, Mrs. Osborne, Mr. Parker, Mrs. Parker, William Verling, Mr. Walker, and Miss Yapp. Rankin (145 n. 3) offers court evidence that many members of the company were detained for debts, left bonds, and, worse, may very well have absconded with a slave (see 30 June). The company cautiously dropped out of sight until September, when we find them playing in Alexandria, Virginia colony. Sometime after 6 October they again disappear, though records in early 1769 indicate they are still touring Virginia (see 12 January 1769).

At the beginning of 1768 the American Company was playing in New York where their season carried them well into June. After a summer recess, they reappeared in Philadelphia in September, where they were originally to play for one month only. Apparently an extension was granted, as the company played in Philadelphia until January 1769. The American Company in New York included Adam Allyn (died in February 1768), Mr. Byerley, Margaret Cheer, Mr. Darby, David Douglass, Mrs. Douglass, Samuel Greville, Lewis Hallam Jr., Nancy Hallam, Mrs. Harman, John Henry, Patrick Malone, Owen Morris, Mr. Raworth, Mr. Roberts, Ann Storer, Fanny Storer, Maria Storer, Mr. Tomlinson, Mrs. Tomlinson, Miss Wainwright, Thomas Wall, Mrs. Wall, and Stephen Woolls. Sometime after the New York season, Miss Margaret Cheer married nobility, but her new title, Lady Rosehill, did not keep her from the stage, as she returned for the winter season in Philadelphia. Sometime after the opening of the Southwark theatre in Philadelphia, Mr. Byerley joined the company. Debts notwithstanding, Charles Parker and his wife, who played with Verling's Company earlier in the year, had joined the American Company by December 1768.

A third company also performed in the colonies this year, managed by a Mr. Mills. This ensemble assayed North Carolina for six months during this year, possibly playing at New Bern, Wilmington, and Halifax, as a new theatre is announced at the latter site in 1769. They next petitioned the Governor of Rhode Island for permission to play in that colony (see 15 June 1768), though no response has survived. When the young actor Henry Giffard, while playing in North Carolina, solicited the governor of that colony for a letter of character, he left a forwarding address of Providence, Rhode Island colony, where the company had applied to play next.[14] Rankin (141) suggests that several members of Verling's Virginia Company may have come from this little-known ensemble, but this surmise is in error, as the dates of performance of the two companies overlapped during spring of 1768. If Mr. Mills did indeed carry Giffard and the rest of his company to Rhode Island, the newspapers of Providence make no mention of actors performing in that colony. Davis (1294), following Rankin, assumes that the company broke up after their North Carolina engagement, but new evidence reveals quite a different course of events.

The Mills Company, whatever their fate in Rhode Island, next appeared in Halifax, Nova Scotia, in early August 1768, where they had obtained permission to perform at "the Theatre," a space that Bains (36) suggests was an assembly room in the Pontiac Inn. Though they did not open their season until 26 August, the presence of players in the small town was felt throughout the month. Debates over the legitimacy of theatre filled the pages of the *Nova Scotia Gazette* from 11 August onward, a trend that usually occurs with the first appearance of a professional acting company in a new locale. Theatricus and Anti-Thespis argued it out in print, while Mills readied his theatre and Giffard prepared his prologues. From the advertisements for the Halifax engagement we are able to derive for the first time the following personnel list for Mr. Mills's company: Mr. Mills, Mrs. Mills, Mr. Giffard, Mrs. Giffard, Mr. Farrel, Mr. Leggitt, Mr. Platt, Mr. Horner, and Mr. Phillips. Mr. Farrel, who is known to have been with the

---

[14] Giffard is described by Governor William Tryon in this reference letter as "the best player on the American stage" (see 11 June 1768).

Verling Company in June, rejoined the Mills company in late September. He was announced on 30 September 1768 as "being the first time of his appearance here," suggesting he had performed with the company in North Carolina. Mr. Leggitt was also announced on 30 September and remained with the company throughout October. It will be remembered that Mr. Platt played briefly with the American Company in 1767.

Also of note, the 1 September advertisement announces the troupe as "The American Company," a device designed to capitalize on the fame of David Douglass. Despite their excellent documentation of the company's activities in Halifax, both C. B. Fergussan (421–22) and Y. S. Bains (passim) fail to recognize that the company performing there was not the true American Company, who were in Philadelphia as of October 1768. Further, the cast lists clearly indicate that Mills was masquerading his own company under the title of their more famous counterparts. While in Halifax, the company played twice a week, until 28 October 1768, after which nothing further is heard of Mr. Mills and his company.

The Bayly Company reappears in March, this time in Charleston at the Bacchus on the Bay Theatre, where they play at least through May, and then again in December.

Regarding Jamaica, an ongoing company is implied by the fact that many performers appearing in the colonies are announced as "from the theatre in Jamaica" (e.g., the Henrys, Parkers, Storers, etc.). Wright (46) cites evidence that the future naval hero John Paul Jones debuted in Jamaica this year as Bevil in *The Conscious Lovers*.

※※※

1 January 1768 John St. Theatre, New York
The Busy Body.
    Marplot–Hallam; Sir George Airy–Henry; Sir Francis Gripe–Morris; Charles–Wall; Sir Jealous Traffic–Douglass; Whisper–Allyn; Butler–Greville; Isabinda–Miss Hallam; Patch–Mrs. Harman; Scentwell–Mrs. Tomlinson; Miranda–Miss Cheer.
The Deuce is in Him.
    Col. Tamper–Hallam; Major Belford–Douglass; Prattle–Wall; Bell–Miss Wainwright; Mademoiselle Florival–Mrs. Harman; Emily–Miss Hallam.

American Company.
[Presented "by command of Lady Moore" (i.e., wife of the governor). Source: *New York Gazette & Weekly Post-Boy* (31 December 1767).]

4 January 1768   John St. Theatre, New York
Romeo and Juliet.
   Romeo–Hallam; Mercutio–Douglass; Escalius–Greville; Fryar Lawrence–Allyn; Paris–Woolls; Capulet–Morris; Montague–Tomlinson; Benevolio–Wall; Tybalt–Henry; Fryar John–Roberts; Lady Capulet–Mrs. Douglass; Nurse–Mrs. Harman; Juliet–Miss Cheer.
Miss in her Teens.
   Captain Flash–Henry; Fribble–Allyn; Capt. Lovit–Wall; Puff–Morris; Jasper–Woolls; Tag–Wainwright; Miss Biddy–Miss Hallam.
American Company.
[Source: *New York Mercury* (4 January 1768).]

8 January 1768   John St. Theatre, New York
The Gamester.
   Beverly–Hallam; Stukely–Douglass; Lewson–Wall; Jarvis–Morris; Dawson–Allyn; Bates–Tomlinson; Charlotte–Miss Hallam; Mrs. Beverly–Miss Cheer.
Catharine and Petruchio.
   Petruchio–Hallam; Baptista–Tomlinson; Hortensio–Douglass; Biondell–Wall; Music Master–Allyn; Tailor–Henry; Grumio–Morris; Bianca–Miss Storer; Curtis–Mrs. Harman; Catharine–Miss Cheer.
American Company.
[Source: *New York Journal* (7 January 1768).]

11 January 1768   John St. Theatre, New York
Love in a Village.
   Justice Woodcock–Douglass; Hawthorn–Woolls; Young Meadows–Wall; Sir William–Morris; Eustace–Henry; Hodge–Hallam; Lucinda–Miss Hallam; Mrs. Deborah Woodcock–Mrs. Douglass; Margery–Mrs. Harman; Rosetta–Miss Wainwright; Servants at the statue–Tomlinson, Malone, Greville, Wall, Mrs. Tomlinson, Miss Storer, &c.&c.
The Contrivances.
   Rovewell–Woolls; Argus–Morris; Hearty–Allyn; Robin–Tomlinson; Betty–Mrs. Harman; Arethusa–Miss Wainwright.
American Company.

[Source: *New York Gazette & Weekly Post-Boy* (11 January 1767).]

14 January 1768   Mr. Burns's Long Room, New York
A musical concert.
Members of the American Company.
[While this performance is non-theatrical, it included several members of the American Company, who attempted to raise funds "for the benefit of the poor debtors in gaol": Miss Wainwright, Miss Hallam, and Mr. Woolls. Source: *New York Journal* (14 January 1768).]

15 January 1768   John St. Theatre, New York
The Earl of Essex.
   Essex–Hallam; Southampton–Douglass; Burleigh–Tomlinson; Lieutenant–Woolls; Queen Elizabeth–Mrs. Douglass; Countess of Nottingham–Miss Storer; Countess of Rutland–Miss Cheer.
The Witches; or, Harlequin Restored.
   Harlequin–Hallam; Pantaloon–Morris; Petit-Maitre–Allyn; Monsieur–Roberts; Pierot–Tomlinson; Necromancer–Woolls; Witches–Miss Wainwright, Miss Storer, Mrs. Harman, Mrs. Wall, Mrs. Tomlinson, etc.; Colombine–Miss Cheer.
American Company.
[Source: *New York Journal* (14 January 1768).]

18 January 1768   John St. Theatre, New York
The Wonder! A Woman Keeps a Secret.
   Don Felix–Hallam; Col. Briton–Wall; Gibby–Douglass; Don Lopez–Morris; Don Pedro–Tomlinson; Lissardo–Allyn; Frederic–Woolls; Isabella–Miss Hallam; Flora–Miss Wainwright; Inis–Miss Harman; Violante–Miss Cheer.
The Witches; or, Harlequin Restored.
   As 15 January 1768.
American Company.
[Source: *New York Gazette & Weekly Post-Boy* (18 January 1767).]

19 January 1768   Norfolk, Virginia colony
Play not identified.
Virginia Company.
[This performance is known by the publication of a prologue spoken by Mrs. Osborne "on her benefit night." Source: *Williamsburg Virginia Gazette* (4 February 1768).]

22 January 1768   John St. Theatre, New York
A Bold Stroke for a Wife.
   Col. Feignwell–Hallam; Obadiah Prim–Allyn; Sir Philip–Douglass; Tradelove–Henry; Periwinkle–Morris; Freeman–Wall; Simon Pure–Woolls; Sackbut–Tomlinson; Mrs. Prim–Mrs. Douglass; Betty–Miss Wainwright; Masqu'd Lady–Mrs. Wall; Ann Lovely–Miss Cheer.
The Reprisal.
   Ben Block–Hallam; Mons. Champignion–Allyn; Lieut. O'Clabber–Morris; Ensign McClayhoure–Douglass; Hearly–Greville; Brush–Wall; Halliard (with a song)–Miss Hallam, etc.
American Company.
   [Source: *New York Journal* (21 January 1768).]

25 January 1768   John St. Theatre, New York
King Lear.
   King Lear–Hallam; Edgar–Douglass; Bastard–Henry; Kent–by a Gentleman (being his first appearance on any stage); Gloster–Morris; Albany–Allyn; Cornwall–Greville; Burgundy–Malone; Officer–Tomlinson; Gentleman Usher–Wall; Goneril–Miss Wainwright; Regan–Miss Storer; Cordelia–Miss Cheer.
Hob in the Well.
   Hob–Allyn; Sir Thomas–Morris; Friendly–Woolls; Dick–Greville; Old Hob–Tomlinson; Country men and women–Wall, Malone, Roberts, Mrs. Tomlinson, Miss Storer, Miss F. Storer, &c.; Hob's Mother–Mrs. Harman; Betty–Mrs. Wall; Flora–Miss Hallam.
American Company.
   ["For the future, the days of performance will be Monday and Thursday." Source: *New York Gazette & Weekly Post-Boy* (25 January 1768).]

28 January 1768   John St. Theatre, New York
The Merchant of Venice.
   Shylock–Hallam; Bassanio–Douglass; Antonio–Tomlinson; Gratiano–Allyn; Duke–Greville; Lorenzo–Woolls; Salario–Wall; Solarino–Malone; Gobbo–Raworth; Tubal–Henry; Launcelet–Morris; Jessica–Miss Wainwright; Nerissa–Mrs. Harman; Portia–Miss Cheer.
The Witches; or, Harlequin Restored.
   Cast as 15 January 1768.
American Company.
   [Source: *New York Journal* (28 January 1768).]

1 February 1768   John St. Theatre, New York
The Suspicious Husband.
Ranger–Hallam; Strickland–Douglass; Frankly–Wall; Bellamy–Morris; Jack Meggot–Allyn; Tester–Tomlinson; Buckle–Woolls; Simon–Greville; Mrs. Strickland–Miss Storer; Jacintha–Miss F. Storer; Lucetta–Miss Wainwright; Landlady–Mrs. Harman; Milliner–Mrs. Wall; Maid–Mrs. Tomlinson; Clarinda–Miss Cheer.
The Devil to Pay.
Sir John Loverule–Woolls (in which character he will sing the Early Horn); Jobson–Tomlinson; Butler–Morris; Doctor–Malone; Foot-man–Wall; Lady Loverule–Mrs. Harman; Lucy–Mrs. Wall; Lettice–Mrs. Tomlinson; Nell–Miss Wainwright.
American Company.
[Source: *New York Gazette & Weekly Post-Boy* (1 February 1768).]

4 February 1768   John St. Theatre, New York
George Barnwell [i.e., *The London Merchant*].
George Barnwell–Wall; Thorowgood–Douglass; Uncle–Allyn; Trueman–Morris; Blunt–Tomlinson; Maria–Miss Hallam; Lucy–Mrs. Harman; Millwood–Miss Cheer,
Catherine and Petruchio.
Petruchio–Hallam; Babtista–Tomlinson; Hortentio–Douglass; Biondello–Wall; Musick Master–Allyn; Taylor–Henry; Grumio–Morris; Bianca–Miss Storer; Curtis–Mrs. Harman; Catherine–Miss Cheer.
American Company.
[Source: *New York Journal* (4 February 1768).]

4 February 1768   Norfolk, Virginia colony
Play not identified.
Virginia Company.
[Source: Hornblow 1:131.]

8 February 1768   John St. Theatre, New York
Love in a Village.
As 11 January 1768.
High Life Below Stairs.
Lovel–Hallam; Freeman–Henry; Lord Duke–Wall; Sir Harry–Allyn; Philip–Morris; Coachman–Woolls; Kingston–Tomlinson; Robert–Greville; Tom–Malone; Cloe–Roberts; Lady Bab–Miss Wainwright; Lady Charlotte–Miss Hallam; Cook–Mrs. Harman; Kitty–Miss Storer.
American Company.

[Source: *New York Gazette & Weekly Post-Boy* (8 February 1768).]

11 February 1768   John St. Theatre, New York
The Orphan.
   Chamont–Hallam; Castalio–Henry; Polydore–Wall; Acasto–Morris; Chaplain–Tomlinson; Ernesto–Allyn; Page–Miss M. Storer; Serina–Miss Storer; Florella–Mrs. Harman; Monimia–Miss Cheer.
Harlequin Collector; or, The Miller Deceived.
   Harlequin–Hallam; Clown–Morris; Miller–Allyn; Magician–Woolls; Baboon–Wall; Anatomist–Douglass; Porter–Tomlinson; Hay-makers–Henry, Malone, Greville, Raworth, Roberts, Miss Hallam, Miss Storer, Miss F. Storer, Miss Wainwright, Mrs. Harman, Mrs. Tomlinson, and Mrs. Wall; Colombine–Miss Cheer.
American Company.
[Source: *New York Journal* (11 February 1768).]

15 February 1768   John St. Theatre, New York
The Recruiting Officer.
The Citizen.
American Company.
[Announced but probably postponed due to the death of Adam Allyn on this day. Source: *New York Gazette & Weekly Post-Boy* (15 February 1768).]

18 February 1768   John St. Theatre, New York
The Recruiting Officer.
   Capt. Plume–Hallam; Capt. Brazen–Henry; Justice Ballance–Morris; Serjeant Kite–Douglass; Worthy–Woolls; Bullock–Tomlinson; Recruits–Tomlinson, Raworth, &c.; Melinda–Miss Storer; Rose–Miss Wainwright; Lucy–Mrs. Harman; Sylvia–Miss Cheer. Singing by Mr. Woolls.
The Citizen.
   The Citizen–Wall; Young Wilding–Henry; Old Philpot–Douglass; Sir Jasper–Tomlinson; Beaufort–Woolls; Quildrive–Malone; Dapper–Greville; Corinna–Mrs. Tomlinson; Maria–Miss Wainwright.
American Company.
[Source: *New York Journal* (18 February 1768).]

22 February 1768   John St. Theatre, New York
Venice Preserved.

Pierre–Hallam; Jaffier–Henry; Priuli–Douglass; Renault–Morris; Bedamar–Wall; Duke–Tomlinson; Conspirators–Woolls, Greville, Malone, Raworth, Roberts, &c.; Attendants–Mrs. Wall and Mrs. Tomlinson; Belvidera–Miss Cheer.

Harlequin Collector: or, the Miller Deceived.
As 11 February 1768, except Miller–Tomlinson; Porter–Roberts.
American Company.
[Source: *New York Gazette & Weekly Post-Boy* (22 February 1768).]

25 February 1768   John St. Theatre, New York
Henry IV, Part 1.
Hotspur–Hallam; King Henry–Morris; Prince of Wales–Wall; Sir Walter Blunt–Henry; Worcester–Tomlinson; Sir Richard Vernon–Greville; Northumberland–Woolls; Westmoreland–Raworth; Prince John–Mrs. Wall; Poins–Malone; Peto–Roberts; Sir John Falstaff–Douglass; Hostess–Mrs. Harman; Lady Percy–Miss Cheer.

The Old Maid.
As 18 December 1767, except Mr. Harlow–Hallam.
American Company.
[Source: *New York Journal* (25 February 1768).]

29 February 1768   John St. Theatre, New York
The Committee.
Teague–Henry; Col. Careless–Douglass; Col. Blunt–Hallam; Mr. Day–Morris; Abel–Woolls; Obadiah–Tomlinson; 1st Committee Man–Wall; 2d Committee-Man–Raworth; 3rd Committee Man–Greville; Mrs. Day–Mrs. Douglass; Arabella–Miss Hallam; Mrs. Chat–Mrs. Tomlinson; Ruth–Miss Cheer.

The Honest Yorkshireman.
Gaylove–Hallam; Sapscull–Wall; Muckworm–Morris; Slango–Tomlinson; Blunder–Raworth; Arabella–Miss Hallam; Combrush–Miss Cheer.
American Company.
[Source: *New York Gazette & Weekly Post-Boy* (29 February 1768).]

3 March 1768   John St. Theatre, New York
Macbeth.
Macbeth–Hallam; Macduff–Douglass; Banquo–Morris; Duncan–Greville; Malcolm–Henry; Donalbain–Malone; Lenox–Wall; Seyton–Tomlinson; Fleance–Miss M. Storer; Hecate–

Woolls; Lady Macduff–Mrs. Douglass; Lady Macbeth–Miss Cheer; Witches–Miss Wainwright, Miss Hallam, Mrs. Harman, Mrs. Tomlinson, Mrs. Wall, Miss Storer, and Miss F. Storer.
American Company.
[Source: *New York Journal* (3 March 1768).

7 March 1768   John St. Theatre, New York
The School for Lovers.
Sir John Dorilant–Douglass; Modely–Hallam; Bellmour–Wall; Steward–Morris; Celia–Miss Hallam; Lady Beverly–Mrs. Harman; Araminta–Miss Cheer.
The Apprentice.
Dick (with the Epilogue)–Wall; Wingate–Morris; Gargle–Henry; President (with a song)–Woolls; Simon–Tomlinson; Spouters–Hallam, Douglass, Malone, Greville, Raworth, Roberts, &c.; Charlotte–Miss Wainwright.
American Company.
[Source: *New York Gazette & Weekly Post-Boy* (7 March 1768); cf. playbill in the Harvard Theatre Collection.]

10 March 1768   John St. Theatre, New York
The Roman Father.
The Roman Father–Hallam; Tullus Hostilius–Douglass; Publius Horatius–Henry; Valerius–Wall; Citizens–Morris, Tomlinson, Malone, Roberts, &c. Valeria–Mrs. Douglass; Horatia–Miss Cheer.
Catherine and Petruchio.
As 8 January 1768, except Musick Master–Raworth; Taylor–Malone.
American Company.
[Source: *New York Journal* (10 March 1768).]

10 March 1768   Bacchus Theatre on the Bay, Charleston, South Carolina colony
Non-theatrical entertainments.
Bayly Company.
[The *South Carolina Gazette* of 8 March 1768 offers the following details of the Bayly Company's activities:

> For the benefit of the poor. On Thursday the tenth of March, at the sign of Bacchus, on the Bay, will be presented the noted Bayly's Medley of Entertainments and Uncommon performances, by Dexterity of hand, [in] a manner different from all other performers of that art. Who has had the honour to perform before most of the nobility and gentry in Europe and America, and gained universal applause: with

several entertainments, drolls, burlettas, dancing, &c. by Mr. Punch, his family, and company of artificial comedians, consisting of thirty figures, near four feet high. By whom will be performed, a farce, called, The Quaker Outwitted, or Punch turned Gaol-keeper; With scenes, decorations, music, &c.

No person will be admitted without tickets, which may be had at any time at the theatre. Boxes, 20sh. Pit, 15sh. Gallery, 10sh. To begin precisely at VII o'clock. N.B. Mr. Bayly continues to perform his entertainments on Monday, Wednesday, and Friday evenings, during his stay.

Any set company of ladies and gentlemen may have a private performance on Tuesdays or Thursdays, giving four hours notice, or be waited on at their own houses. Vivant Rex & Regina.]

14 March 1768   John St. Theatre, New York
The Miser.
  The Miser–Hallam (being his first appearance in that character); Frederic–Douglass; Clermont–Wall; Ramilie–Morris; James–Tomlinson; List–Henry; Decoy–Raworth; Sattin–Greville; Sparkle–Woolls; Furnish–Malone; Charles Bubbleboy–Roberts; Harriet–Miss Hallam; Mrs. Wisely–Mrs. Douglass; Lappet–Mrs. Harman; Wheedle–Mrs. Wall; Mariana–Miss Cheer.
The Chaplet.
  Damon–Wools; Palaemon–Wall; Pastora–Miss Hallam; Laura–Miss F. Storer.
American Company.
  [The afterpiece "never performed here." Source: *New York Gazette & Weekly Post-Boy* (14 March 1768).]

15 March 1768   Charleston
Newspaper notice.
Bayly Company.
  [The *South Carolina Gazette* of this date offers the following information concerning the activities of the Bayly Company (repeated on 22 March):

  Mr. Bayly begs leave to inform the ladies and gentlemen, that he continues his exhibitions on Monday, Wednesday and Friday evenings; and on Thursday the seventh of April, he will perform for the benefit of the debtors in the gaol of this town.
  N.B. The strictest decency and regularity will be observed, as Mr. Bayly has enclosed the boxes, and taken care to remove every obstacle that might tend to interrupt or offend the company, or the performances. Prices as usual. To begin each evening at 7 o'clock.]

17 March 1768   Williamsburg
Newspaper notice.

Virginia Company.

["The Theatre in this City will be opened on Thursday the 31st instant." Source: Rankin 142, following the *Virginia Gazette* (17 March 1768).]

19 March 1768   John St. Theatre, New York
Cato.
    Cato–Douglass; Sempronius–Hallam; Juba–Wall; Portius–Henry; Marcus–Greville; Syphax–Morris; Lucius–Tomlinson; Decius–Woolls; Lucia–Miss Hallam; Marcia–Miss Cheer.
The Witches; or, Harlequin Restored.
    As 15 January 1768, except Petit-Maitre–Wall.
American Company.
    [Source: *New York Journal* (19 March 1768).]

24 March 1768   John St. Theatre, New York
The Fair Penitent.
    Altamont–by a gentleman (being his first appearance on this stage); Lothario–Hallam; Horatio–Douglass; Sciolto–Henry; Rossano–Woolls; Lavinia–Mrs. Douglass; Lucilla–Miss F. Storer; Calista–Miss Cheer.
Neck or Nothing.
    Slip–Hallam; Martin–Morris; Belford–Wall; Stockwell–Tomlinson; Sir Harry Harlow–Henry; Miss Nancy Stockwell–Miss Hallam; Jenny–Miss Storer; Mrs. Stockwell–Mrs. Douglass.
American Company.
    [The afterpiece advertised as "never acted here." Source: *New York Journal* (24 March 1768).]

31 March 1768   The Old Theatre, Williamsburg
Program not identified.
Virginia Company.
    [This evening the company presumably opened its season, but no record exists of the program. Source: *Virginia Gazette* (17 March 1768).]

4 April 1768   John St. Theatre, New York
The Constant Couple.
    Sir Harry Wildair–Hallam; Col. Standard–Douglass; Beaux Clincher–Henry; Young Clincher–Wall; Alderman Smuggler–Morris; Vizard–Tomlinson; Dicky–Woolls; Tom Errand–Greville; Angelica–Miss Cheer; Lady Darling–Mrs. Tomlinson; Parly–Miss F. Storer; Lady Lurewell–Mrs. Douglass.
High Life Below Stairs.

As 8 February 1768, except Sir Harry–Henry; Freeman–Douglass; Lady Bab–Miss Hallam; Lady Charlotte–Miss F. Storer.
American Company.
["By command of His Excellency the General, for the Entertainment of the Cherokee Chiefs and Warriors, lately return'd from the Mohawk Country." Source: *New York Mercury* (4 April 1768).]

4 April 1768   The Old Theatre, Williamsburg
Douglas.
　　Lord Randolph–Bromadge; Glenalvon–Godwin; Norval/Douglas–Verling; Old Norval–Parker; Officer–Walker; Lady Randolph–Mrs. Osborne; Anna–Mrs. Parker.
The Honest Yorkshireman.
　　Sir Penurious Muckworm–Bromadge; Gaylove–Verling; Sapscull–Parker; Slango–Godwin; Blunder–Walker; Arabella–Mrs. Osborne; Combrush–Mrs. Parker.
Virginia Company.
[Rankin (142) claims that the company opened with this bill on 31 March 1768. Thomas Jefferson attended this performance and paid 11s. 6d. for tickets (Jefferson, *Memorandum Books*, 1:73). Prices: boxes 7s. 6d.; pit 5s.; gallery 3s. 9d. Source: *Virginia Gazette* (31 March 1768).]

6 April 1768   John St. Theatre, New York
All in the Wrong* (Arthur Murphy, 1761).
The Mock Doctor.
American Company.
[This performance was presented "by Command of Lady Moore" (i.e., wife of the Lieutenant Governor. Source: *New York Mercury* (4 April 1768).]

6 April 1768   The Old Theatre, Williamsburg
The Drummer.
Miss in Her Teens.
Virginia Company.
[Source: *Virginia Gazette* (31 March 1768).]

7 April 1768   Bacchus Theatre on the Bay, Charleston,
　　　　　　　　South Carolina colony
Non-theatrical entertainments.
Bayly Company.
[For the benefit of the debtors in gaol. The notice provides the following further details of the program:

By whom will be performed, several new entertaining drolls, burlesques, &c. &c. With a court of thirty figures, or Assembly of maids and batchelors. With a pantomime droll; and a curious piece of machinery, representing a view of the sea, in which are seen several ships sailing, fish, sea-monsters, &c. swimming, and the ships of war engaging the castle of Goree. With the curious performances of Punch's son; and sundry exhibitions too tedious to enumerate .... He exhibits this present, and every evening this week.

Source: *South Carolina Gazette* (5 April 1767).]

8 April 1768   John St. Theatre, New York
A Wonder! A Woman Keeps a Secret!
As 18 January 1768, except Lissardo–Greville.
Harlequin Collector.
As 22 February 1768.
American Company.
["The Cherokee Chiefs and Warriors being desirous of making some Return for the friendly reception and civilities they have received in the City, have offered to entertain the public with the WAR DANCE they will exhibit on the stage after the Pantomime." Source: *New York Journal* (7 April 1768).]

8 April 1768   The Old Theatre, Williamsburg
Venice Preserved.
   Duke–Charlton; Priuli–Bromadge; Jaffeir–Godwin; Pierre–Verling; Redamar–Bromadge; Renault–Parker; Eliot–Walker; Belvidera–Mrs. Osborne.
Damon and Phillida.
   Arcas–Bromadge; Corydon–Godwin; Damon–Osborne; Cymon–Parker; Mopsus–Verling; Phillida–Mrs. Parker.
Virginia Company.
[Source: *Virginia Gazette* (7 April 1768).]

11 April 1768   John St. Theatre, New York
Othello.
   Othello–Douglass; Iago–Hallam; Cassio–Henry; Roderigo–Wall; Brabantio–Morris; Duke–Greville; Montano–Malone; Lodovico–Tomlinson; Gratiano–Woolls; Emelia–Mrs. Harman; Desdemona–Miss Cheer.
Damon and Phillida.
   As 28 December 1767, except Arcas–Tomlinson.
American Company.
[Source: *New York Gazette & Weekly Post-Boy* (11 April 1768).]

11 April 1768   The Old Theatre Williamsburg
Program not identified.
Virginia Company.
   [Thomas Jefferson attended this performance and paid 30s. for tickets. Source: Jefferson, *Memorandum Books*, 1:73.]

14 April 1768   John St. Theatre, New York
Romeo and Juliet.
   As 4 January 1768, except Friar Lawrence–Greville; Escalus–Malone; Lady Capulet–Miss Storer.
A Picture of a Playhouse, or, Bucks Have at You All.
Catherine and Petruchio.
   As 10 March 1768, but Music Master not identified.
American Company.
   [Benefit Miss Cheer. Source: *New York Journal* (14 April 1768).]

15 April 1768   The Old Theatre, Williamsburg
The Orphan.
   Acasto–Bromadge; Castalio–Verling; Polydore–Parker; Chamont–Godwin; Chaplain–Charlton; Ernesto–Walker; Page–Miss Dowthwaitte; Monimia–Mrs. Osborne; Serina–Mrs. Parker; Maid–Mrs. Dowthwaitte.
Harlequin Skeleton, or The Burgomaster Tricked*
(Anonymous).
   Harlequin–Godwin; Pantaloon–Verling; Conjurer–Bromadge; Merchant–Walker; Frenchman–Charlton; Clown–Parker; Scaramouch–Walker; Columbine–Mrs. Parker.
Virginia Company.
   [In the pantomime "will be introduced a new scene, not before presented." Source: *Virginia Gazette* (14 April 1768); playbill in the Colonial Williamsburg Foundation.]

18 April 1768   John St. Theatre, New York
The Country Lasses.
   Heartwell–Douglass; Modely–Hallam; Sir John English–Tomlinson; Freehold–Morris; Lurcher–Wall; Carbuncle–Henry; Long Bottom–Woolls; Timothy Shacklefigure–Roberts; Sneak–Raworth; Vulture–Greville; Flora–Miss Wainwright; Aura–Miss Cheer.
The Citizen.
   As 18 February 1768, except Old Philpot–Morris.
American Company.
   [Benefit Miss Wainwright. Source: *New York Gazette & Weekly Post-Boy* (18 April 1768).]

18 April 1768   The Old Theatre Williamsburg
Program not identified.
Virginia Company.
  [Thomas Jefferson attended this performance and paid 5s. for tickets. Source: Jefferson, *Memorandum Books*, 1: 74.]

21 April 1768   John St. Theatre, New York
The Conscious Lovers.
  Young Bevil–Hallam; Sealand–Douglass; Myrtle–Wall; Sir John Bevil–Henry; Cimberton–Greville; Humphrey–Tomlinson; Daniel–Roberts; Tom–Morris; Phillis–Mrs. Harman; Mrs. Sealand–Miss Wainwright; Isabella–Miss Storer; Lucinda–Miss Hallam; Indiana–Miss Cheer. In act Second, singing by Mr. Woolls.
Polly Honeycombe* (George Colman Sr., 1760).
  Mr. Honeycomb–Morris; Scribble (with the Prologue)–Wall; Ledger–Tomlinson; Polly Honeycomb–Miss Wainwright.
American Company.
  [Benefit Morris. Source: *New York Journal* (21 April 1768).]

25 April 1768   John St. Theatre, New York
Cymbeline.
  As 28 December 1768, except Cymbeline–Morris; Queen–Miss Storer; Pisanio–Mrs. Harman.
High Life Below Stairs.
  As 4 April 1768, except Lady Charlotte–Miss Wainwright.
American Company.
  [Benefit announced for Hallam but given to Woolls. The following item relating to this performance appeared in the *New York Gazette & Weekly Post-Boy* of 9 May 1768:

  Mr. Hallam, in the most respectful manner, begs leave to acquaint the public, that his friends and patrons being of opinion, that the failure of the play Cymbeline, acted on Monday, the 25th of April, was entirely owing to a prepossession, which prevail'd, that the house would be crouded, and thereby prevented many from exerting their influence in his favour, have advised him to take another benefit; but as that could not be done without contravening the establish'd rules of the company, and fixing a precedent which might be attended with very troublesome consequences in the future; He, in order to obviate any objections of that nature, but more particularly to convince the town that he has not thoughts of imposing a second benefit upon them, he has relinquish'd the profits of Cymbeline, to Mr. Woolls, and taken his night in return.

Source: *New York Mercury* (25 April 1768).]

27 April 1768   The Old Theatre Williamsburg
Program not identified.
Virginia Company.
[Thomas Jefferson attended this performance and paid 22s. 6d. for tickets. Source: Jefferson, *Memorandum Books*, 1:74.]

27 April 1768   Bacchus Theatre on the Bay, Charleston, South Carolina colony
Lecture on Hearts.
Mr. Bayly.
[The *South Carolina Gazette* of 26 April 1768 provides the following additional details of Mr. Bayly's program:

> By the noted Bayly, with sundry new performances by dexterity of hand, particularly he will eat red hot coals, out of a chaffing-dish, another person blowing them at the same time; With an occasional epilogue, and the facetious humours of Mr. Punch, and his artificial company of comedians, with a court of thirty figures, or, Assembly of Maids and Batchelors; and the performances of Punch's artificial posture-master. With sundry entertainments too tedious to enumerate. To begin exactly at VII o'clock. Boxes, 20s. Pit, 15s. Gallery, 10s.
> Any set company may have a private performance, any other evening in the week, sending only four hours notice. ☞ To be continued on Monday, Wednesday, and Friday evenings.]

28 April 1768   John St. Theatre, New York
All for Love.
    Marc Antony–Hallam; Ventidius–Douglass; Dollabella–Wall; Alexas–Morris; Serapion–Tomlinson; Myris–Woolls; Octavia–Miss Storer; Charmion–Miss Wainwright; Iras–Mrs. Wall; Cleopatra–Miss Cheer; Agrippina, and Antonia (the children of Antony)–Miss M. Storer and Miss Tomlinson.
The Upholsterer.
    The Uphosterer–Douglass; the Barber–Wall; Pamphlet–Hallam; Bellmour–Henry; Rovewell–Woolls; Feeble–Morris; Watchmen–Tomlinson, Malone, Greville, etc.; Harriet–Miss Wainwright; Maid–Mrs. Wall; Termagant–Mrs. Harman.
American Company.
[Benefit Douglass. Source: *New York Journal* (28 April 1768).]

29 April 1768   The Old Theatre Williamsburg
Program not identified.
Virginia Company.
[Thomas Jefferson attended this performance and paid 10s. for tickets. Source: Jefferson, *Memorandum Books*, 1:74.]

29 April 1768   Bacchus Theatre on the Bay, Charleston, South Carolina colony
Lecture on Hearts.
Bayly Company.
   [Source: *South Carolina Gazette* (26 April 1768).]

2 May 1768   John St. Theatre, New York
Richard III.
   King Richard–Hallam; King Henry–Henry; Prince Edward–Miss F. Storer; Duke of York–Miss M. Storer; Tressel–Douglass; Lord Stanley–Morris; Sir Walter Blunt–Wall; Ratcliff–Tomlinson; Catesby–Woolls; Oxford–Greville; Duke of Buckingham–Douglass; Earl of Richmond–Henry; Lady Ann–Miss Storer; Duchess of York–Mrs. Harman; Queen Elizabeth–Miss Cheer.
Taste* (Samuel Foote, 1752).
   Mr. Carmine (the painter)–Wall; Lady Pentweazle (of Blowbladder Street)–Henry,
Miss in Her Teens.
   Captain Loveit–Wall; Puff–Morris; Jasper–Woolls; Capt. Flash–Miss F. Storer; Fribble–Miss M. Storer; Tag–Miss Storer; Miss Biddy–Miss Hallam.
American Company.
   [Benefit Miss Storer, Miss Fanny Storer, and Miss Maria Storer. Source: *New York Mercury* (2 May 1768).]

2 May 1768   The Old Theatre, Williamsburg
Program unidentified.
Virginia Company.
   [George Washington records in his *Diary* that he "went to a Play" on this date. Jefferson also was present and paid 5s for tickets. Source: Jefferson, *Memorandum Books*, 1:74; Washington, *Diaries*, 2:58.]

3 May 1768   Bacchus Theatre on the Bay, Charleston, South Carolina colony
Newspaper notice.
Bayly Company.
   [The *South Carolina Gazette* of this date contains the following notice: "Next Wednesday and Friday evenings, will be the last times of Mr. Bayly's noted performances by dexterity of hand, &c. in this town.–For the particulars, see his hand bills, which are dispersed about town."]

5 May 1768   The Old Theatre, Williamsburg
Program unidentified.
Virginia Company.
   [Though there is no record in his *Diary* of George Washington attending a play on this date, an entry exists in his Cash Account for this date, showing that he bought "Play Tickets 12/6." Source: Washington, *Papers*, 8:82.]

5 May 1768   John St. Theatre, New York
Hamlet.
   As 21 December 1767, except Osric–Roberts; Queen–Mrs. Harman.
The King and the Miller of Mansfield.
   King–Henry; Miller–Hallam; Dick–Morris; Lord Lurewell–Wall; Joe (with a song in character)–Woolls; Courtiers, keepers, etc.–Tomlinson, Greville, Malone, etc.; Peggy–Mrs. Wall; Kate–Mrs. Tomlinson; Margery–Mrs. Harman.
American Company.
   [Benefit Tomlinson. Source: *New York Journal* (5 May 1768).]

6 May 1768   The Old Theatre Williamsburg
Program not identified.
Virginia Company.
   [Thomas Jefferson attended this performance and paid 5s. for tickets. Source: Jefferson, *Memorandum Books*, 1:75.]

9 May 1768   John St. Theatre, New York
The Orphan of China.
   Zamti–Douglass; Zaphimri–Hallam; Timurkan–Henry; Hamet–Wall; Mirvan–Morris; Morat–Tomlinson; Octar–Greville; Orasming–Malone; Zemventi–Woolls; Mandane–Miss Cheer.
The Brave Irishman.
   The Brave Irishman–Henry; Doctor Glyster–Hallam; Doctor Gallipot–Douglass; Cheatwell–Greville; Tradewell–Morris; Serjeant–Tomlinson; Marquis–Roberts; Betty–Miss Wainwright; Lucy (with a song)–Miss Hallam.
American Company.
   [Second benefit for Hallam. Source: *New York Gazette & Weekly Post-Boy* (9 May 1768).]

13 May 1768   John St. Theatre, New York
Venice Preserved.
   As 22 February 1768.
Love a la Mode* (Charles Macklin, 1759).

Sir Callaghan O'Brallaghan (with songs)–Henry; Sir Archy Macsarcasm–Douglass; Squire Groom–Hallam; Beau Mordecai–Morris; Sir Theodore Goodchild–Tomlinson; Charlotte–Miss Hallam.
American Company.
[Benefit Henry. The afterpiece "Being the only time of its being performed this season." Source: *New York Journal* (12 May 1768).]

13 May 1768   The Old Theatre, Williamsburg
Program unidentified.
Virginia Company.
[Benefit Verling. This benefit was announced for 12 May 1768 but was postponed due to heavy rains. Source: Rankin 143.]

16 May 1768   John St. Theatre, New York
Distrest Mother.
Pyrrhus–Douglass; Orestes–Hallam; Pylades–Morris; Phoenix–Tomlinson; Hermione–Miss Cheer; Cephisa–Miss Storer; Cleone–Miss Hallam; Andromache–Mrs. Harman.
A Picture of a Playhouse, or Bucks have at Ye All.
Thomas and Sally.
Squire–Woolls; Sailor–Wall; Dorcas–Mrs. Harman; Sally–Miss Wainwright.
American Company.
[Benefit Mrs. Harman. Source: *New York Gazette & Weekly Post-Boy* (16 May 1768).]

18 May 1768   The Old Theatre, Williamsburg
The Constant Couple.
Sir Harry Wildair–Mrs. Osborne; Col. Standard–Charlton; Vizzard–Bromadge; Alderman Smuggler–Parker; Beau Clincher–Verling; Clincher Jr.–Godwin; Dicky–Farrell; Tom Errand–Walker; Lady Darling–Mrs. Dowthwaitte; Angelica–Miss Dowthwaitte; Parly–Miss Yapp; Lady Lurewell–Mrs. Parker.
The King and the Miller of Mansfield.
King–Verling; Miller–Parker; Lord Lurewell–Godwin; Dick–Bromadge; First Courtier–Mrs. Osborne; Second Courtier–Charlton; Joe–Mrs. Farrell; Madge–Mrs. Dowthwaitte; Kate–Miss Dowthwaitte; Peggy–Mrs. Parker; Keeper–Walker, Farrell, &c.
Virginia Company.

[Benefit for Henrietta Osborne. Source: *Virginia Gazette* (12 May 1768); playbill in the Colonial Williamsburg Foundation.]

19 May 1768   John St. Theatre, New York
Love in a Village.
  Cast as 11 January 1768.
The Lying Valet.
  Lying Valet–Hallam; Beau Trippet–Greville; Gayless–Wall; Drunken Cook–Morris; Justice Guttle–Tomlinson; Melissa–Mrs. Harman; Kitty Pry (for the first time)–Miss Wainwright. The epilogue in character, by Mr. Hallam.
American Company.
  [Benefit Miss Hallam. Source: *New York Journal* (19 May 1768).]

20 May 1768   The Old Theatre, Williamsburg
The Gamester.
Polly Honeycomb.
Virginia Company.
  [Benefit Bromadge. Source: *Virginia Gazette* (19 May 1768).]

23 May 1768   John St. Theatre, New York
Jane Shore.
Miss in Her Teens.
American Company.
  [Announced as a benefit of Mrs. Douglass, but Odell offers grounds for suspicion if indeed this performance occurred: Mrs. Douglass took another benefit with different plays on 2 June 1768, and the play was advertised on 1 May 1769 as "not acted these 7 years." Source: Odell 1: 136.]

25 May 1768   The Old Theatre, Williamsburg
Henry IV, Part 1.
The Old Maid.
Virginia Company.
  [Benefit Parker. The farce "never performed here." Source: *Virginia Gazette* (19 May 1768).]

26 May 1768   John St. Theatre, New York
The Provoked Husband.
  Lord Townly–Hallam; Manly–Douglass; Sir Francis–Morris; Count Basset–Wall; Squire Richard–Woolls; John Moody–Tomlinson; Lady Grace–Mrs. Harman; Lady Wronghead–

Miss Wainwright; Miss Jenny–Miss Hallam; Mrs. Motherly–Mrs. Tomlinson; Myrtilla–Mrs. Wall; Lady Townly–Miss Cheer.
The Honest Yorkshireman.
As 29 February 1768.
American Company.
[Benefit Mr. and Mrs. Wall. Source: *New York Journal* (26 May 1768).]

27 May 1768   The Old Theatre, Williamsburg
The Merchant of Venice.
Shylock–Verling; Portia–Mrs. Osborne.
High Life Below Stairs.
Virginia Company.
[Benefit Miss Yapp. The afterpiece "never performed here." Source: *Virginia Gazette* (19 May 1768).]

30 May 1768   John St. Theatre, New York
The Gamester.
As 8 January 1768, except Dawson–Woolls.
The Devil to Pay.
As 1 February 1768, except Doctor–Robbins (his first appearance on any stage).
American Company.
[Benefit Tomlinson. Source: *New York Gazette & Weekly Post-Boy* (30 May 1768).]

30 May 1768   The Old Theatre Williamsburg
Program not identified.
Virginia Company.
[Thomas Jefferson attended this performance and paid 15s. for tickets. Source: Jefferson, *Memorandum Books*, 1:77.]

2 June 1768   John St. Theatre, New York
The Earl of Essex.
As 15 January 1768, except Queen–Mrs. Harman; Countess of Nottingham–Miss Hallam.
Fanny the Phantom* (Anonymous).
Orator and Peter Paragraph (a noted printer in Dublin)–Wall; Irish Serjeant–Douglass; Counselor Prosequi–Tomlinson; Shadrach Bodkin–Morris; Justice–Woolls.
Catherine and Petruchio.
As 10 March 1768, except Taylor not identified.
American Company.

[Advertised as "Positively the last night," but see 28 June 1768. Benefit Mrs. Douglass. Source: *New York Journal* (2 June 1768).]

3 June 1768   The Old Theatre, Williamsburg
The Beggar's Opera.
   Captain Macheath–Verling (being his first appearance in that character); Matt of the Mint and Diana Trapes–Parker; Filch–Godwin; Mrs. Peachum and Lucky Lockit–Mrs. Osborne; Polly Peachum–Mrs. Parker.
The Anatomist.
Virginia Company.
   ["The musick of the opera to be conducted by Mr. Pelham, and others." Benefit Mrs. Parker. Source: *Virginia Gazette* (26 May 1768); cf. playbill in the Colonial Williamsburg Foundation.]

4 June 1768   The Old Theatre Williamsburg
Program not identified.
Virginia Company.
   [Thomas Jefferson attended this performance and paid 20s. for tickets. Source: Jefferson, *Memorandum Books*, 1:78.]

8 June 1768   The Old Theatre, Williamsburg
The Miser.
   Lovegold–Godwin; Frederick–Charlton; Clerimont–Verling; James and Decoy–Parker; Sparkle and List–Walker; Bubbleboy and Lawyer–Bromadge; Thomas–Leavie; Ramillie–Farrell; Mariana–Mrs. Parker; Harriet–Miss Dowthwaitte; Mrs. Wisely–Mrs. Dowthwaitte; Wheedle–Miss Yapp; Lappet–Mrs. Osborne.
The Brave Irishman.
   O'Blunder–Farell; Tradewell–Walker; Cheatwell–Bromadge; Terence–Parker; Ragout and Dr. Clyster–Godwin; Dr. Gallypot–Charlton; Lucy–Mrs. Parker; Betty–Mrs. Osborne.
A Picture of a Playhouse, or, Bucks have at ye all.
   By Godwin.
Virginia Company.
   [Benefit Charlton. Source: playbill in the Colonial Williamsburg Foundation.]

11 June 1768   Brunswick, North Carolina colony
Correspondence.
Mills Company.
   [On this date Governor William Tryon of North Carolina colony wrote to the Bishop of London, presenting statements

which reveal details concerning the affairs of the company performing in that colony:

> I was solicited a few days ago by Mr. Giffard a young man who is engaged with a company of comedians now in this province to recommend him to your Lordship for ordination orders, he having been invited by some principal gentlemen of the province, to be inducted into a parish, and to set up a school for the education of youth, He assured me it was no sudden caprice that induced him to make this application but the result of very mature deliberation, that he was most wearied of the vague life of his present profession and fully persuaded he could employ his talents to more benefit to society by going into holy orders and superintending the education of the youth in this province. I candidly told Mr. Giffard that his address to me was a matter of some surprise, that as to my own part I could have no reason to obstruct his present intentions, which might if steady and determined, be directed to the benefit of this country, but that I could not flatter him with success of your Lordship, as I was not assured how far your Lordship would choose to take a member of the theatre into the church, I however promised him I would give testimony to your Lordship that during his residence in this province, his behaviour has been decent, regular, and commendable, as such my Lord I beg leave to present him to you leaving the propriety of the ordination to your Lordships wisdom. He takes this letter by way of Providence being under obligation of contract to attend the company there. If your Lordship grants Mr. Giffard his petition you will take off the best player on the American stage. I am, &c. William Tryon.

Source: *The Colonial Records of North Carolina,* 8:786–87.]

15 June 1768   Brunswick, North Carolina
Correspondence.
Mills Company.

[Willard (18) reprints the following letter of this date from North Carolina to Governor Ward of Rhode Island, which is found in the Secretary of State's papers for Rhode Island:

> Sir: Mr. Mills, who is the manager of a company of comedians, intends to solicit your permission to act in some parts of your Government. He has therefore entreated me to mention their behaviour during their stay here of six months, which, as far as I have understood, has been decent, orderly, and proper. I am, sir, your most obedient servant, Wm. Tryon.]

22 June 1768   Mr. Lyon's Long Room, Savannah, Georgia colony
Lethe.
Company unknown.

["By his Excellency's permission, at Mr. Lyon's Long Room, to-morrow evening, will be read, A Farce, called Lethe, or Aesop in the Shades. Among a variety of entertaining characters are the Fine Gentleman and the Fine Lady, with a Song in Character." Source: *Georgia Gazette* (22 June 1768).]

28 June 1768   John St. Theatre, New York
The Distrest Mother.
   As 16 May 1768, except Andromache–Mrs. Douglass; Cephesia–Mrs. Harman.
Damon and Phillida.
   Damon–Woolls; Mopsus–Hallam; Cymon–Mrs. Harman; Arcas–Douglass; Corydon–Morris; Phillida–Miss Wainwright.
American Company.
   [Source: *New York Gazette & Weekly Post-Boy* (27 June 1768).]

30 June 1768   Williamsburg
Newspaper notice.
Virginia Company.
   [The *Virginia Gazette* of this date contains the following notice:

> Run away from the subscriber, on Monday the 27th of June, a Negro woman named Nanny, about 35 years of age, a brisk genteel sensible wench, a little pitted with the smallpox, and had on when she went away a narrow striped Virginia cloth waistcoat and petticoat. It is supposed that she has gone off with some of the comedians who have just left this town, with some of whom, as I have been informed, since she went off, she had connections, and was seen very busy talking privately with some of them .... [terms, 20 shillings, signed] Jane Vobe.]

August 1768   Halifax, Nova Scotia
Correspondence.
Mills Company.
   [A letter of this date refers to the recent arrival of the Mills Company in Halifax:

> To the Printer of the Nova Scotia Gazette.
> Windser, the 11th of August, 1768.
> Sir, I have heard with great pleasure of the Arrival of a Company of Comedians at Halifax. I am very sorry I cannot go down immediately, as our Hay-making is not quite over. Please to let us know what Stay the Players are like to make and what Pieces they propose to Act - I hope the Provok'd Wife is among the Number: Sir John Brute is an

amiable Character. Many of us will be with you when our Harvest is ended ....

Source: *Nova Scotia Gazette* (18 September 1768).]

1 August 1768   Williamsburg
Play unidentified.
Company not known.
   [A benefit for a Christopher Bromadge was performed this evening as implied by the publication of the epilogue spoken by him "last Monday se'nnight, at a benefit acted for him by some young gentlemen, &c. in town." Bromadge left soon after for Great Britain. Source: *Virginia Gazette* of 11 August 1768.]

22 August 1768   John St. Theatre, New York
Lecture on Heads.
Douglass and Hallam.
   [Prices: box, 5s.; pit, 3s.; gallery, 2s. Source: *New York Journal* (18 August 1768).]

26 August 1768   Halifax, Nova Scotia
Douglas.
   Lord Randolph–Platt; Glenalvon and Old Norval–Mills; Officer–Phillips; Servant–Horner; Norval, Douglas–Giffard; Matilda, Lady Randolph–Mrs. Mills; Anna–Mrs. Giffard.
Miss in Her Teens.
   Fribble–Giffard; Flash–Phillips; Capt. Loveit–Platt; Puff–Horner; Jasper–Mills; Miss Biddy–Mrs. Giffard; Tag–Mrs. Mills.
Mills Company.
   [The opening night of the season. Source: *Nova Scotia Gazette* (25 August 1768).]

29 August 1768   John St. Theatre, New York
Lecture on Heads.
Douglass and Hallam.
   [Prices: box, 5s.; pit, 3s.; gallery, 2s. Source: *New York Journal* (25 August 1768).]

2 September 1768   Halifax, Nova Scotia
Jane Shore.
   Duke of Glo'ster–Mills; Lord Hastings and Belmour–Giffard; Ratcliffe–Platt; Catesby–Horner; Attendant–Phillips; Dumont–Mills; Jane Shore–Mrs. Mills; Alicia–Mrs. Giffard.
The Virgin Unmasked.

Goodwill–Platt; Blister–Horner; Coupee–Giffard; Quaver–Mills; Thomas–Phillips; Miss Lucy–Mrs. Giffard.
Mills Company.
[Tickets: Boxes, 5s., Pit, 3s., Gallery, 1s. 6d. "N. B. The Evenings of performing are Mondays and Thursdays. The inclemency of the Weather obliges the Play to be postpon'd till To-morrow." Source: *Nova Scotia Gazette* (1 September 1768).]

5 September 1768   Halifax, Nova Scotia
The Fair Penitent.
Sciolto–Platt; Horatio–Giffard; Altamount–Horner; Ressano–Phillips; Lothario–Mills; Colista–Mrs. Mills; Lavinia and Lucilla–Mrs. Giffard.
The Wonder.
Muckworm–Platt; Gaylove–Mills; Sapsoul–Giffard; Blunder–Horner; Slango–Phillips; Arabella–Mrs. Mills; Combrush–Mrs. Giffard.
Mills Company.
[Source: *Nova Scotia Gazette* (1 September 1768).]

6 September 1768   Grey's Tavern on the Bay, Charleston, South Carolina colony
Non-theatrical performance.
"A person just arrived from the southward."
[The following notice describes the presence of a solo performer in Charleston on this date:

> By permission of his Honour the Lieutenant-Governor. To-morrow evening, at Mr. Grey's Tavern, on the Bay, will be read three books of Milton's Paradise Lost. By a person just arrived from the southward, where he has read with applause, and as he is not unacquainted with accent and emphasis, he flatters himself he shall be able to do his sublime author some tolerable degree of justice, at least his warmest endeavours will not be wanting. If he is so happy as to please, and meet with encouragement, he intends on Friday next, to read a play, and between the acts will be musick, vocal and instrumental. Tickets to be had at the bar of the house at twenty shillings each. To begin precisely at seven o'clock. No person to be admitted without a ticket.

Source: *South Carolina Gazette* (6 September 1768).]

9 September 1768   Halifax, Nova Scotia
The Fair Penitent.
Sciolto–Platt; Horatio–Giffard; Altamount–Horner; Ressano–Phillips; Lothario–Mills; Calista–Mrs. Mills; Lavinia and Lucilla–Mrs. Giffard.
The Wonder.

Muckworm–Platt; Gaylove–Mills; Sapsoul–Giffard; Blunder–Horner; Slango–Phillips; Arabella–Mrs. Mills; Combrush–Mrs. Giffard.
Mills Company
[Source: *Nova Scotia Gazette* (8 September 1768).]

12–19 September 1768   Philadelphia
Newspaper notice.

[The following notice appeared in the *Pennsylvania Chronicle* (12–19 September 1768):

> We hear that the Theatre in Southwark, will be opened, for one month only, on Wednesday the 21st instant, with a comedy. It is said the Right Hon. the Lady Rosehill, (late Miss Cheer) has engaged to perform with Mr. Douglass, in the Theatres of Philadelphia and New-York, for the ensuing winter, at a sum much above ten pounds per week, and a benefit.

In fact, the theatre did not open until 4 October 1768. See entry for that date.]

15 September 1768   Halifax, Nova Scotia
The Revenge.
   Don Alonzo–Mills; Don Carlos–Platt; Don Alavarez–Horner; Manual–Phillips; Zanga–Giffard; Leonora–Mrs. Mills; Isabella–Mrs. Giffard.
The Virgin Unmasked.
Mills Company.

[This program was advertised on 15 September for that evening and for the following Monday and Thursday, suggesting the repertory was quite limited. Source: *Nova Scotia Gazette* (15 September 1768).]

20 September 1768   Alexandria, Virginia
The Inconstant, or the Way to Win Him.
Virginia Company.

[George Washington attended this performance. Source: Washington, *Diaries*, 2:94.]

21 September 1768   Alexandria, Virginia
Douglas.
Virginia Company.

[George Washington attended this performance. For tickets for this date and for 20 September, Washington spent £3.12.6. Source: Washington, *Diaries*, 2:95.]

30 September 1768 Halifax, Nova Scotia
The Beaux' Stratagem.
   Aimwell–Farrell, "being the first time of his appearance here;" Archer–Giffard; Sullen–Horner; Boniface and Foigard–Platt; Sir Charles Freeman–Phillips; Gibbet–Leggett; Scrub–Mills; Mrs Sullen–Mrs. Mills; Dorinda and Cherry–Mrs. Giffard.
The Mock Doctor.
   Sir Jasper–Horner; Leander–Farrell; Doctor Helebore–Platt; James–Mills; Gregory–Giffard; Charlotte–Mrs. Mills; Dorcas–Mrs. Giffard.
Mills Company.
   [Source: *Nova Scotia Gazette* (29 September 1768).]

4 October 1768   Southwark Theatre, Philadelphia
The Provoked Husband.
   Lord Townly–Hallam; Manly–Douglass; Sir Francis Wronghead–Morris; Count Basset–Darby; John Moody–Tomlinson; Squire Richard–Woolls; Lady Wronghead–Mrs. Harman; Lady Grace–Mrs. Douglass; Myrtilla–Miss Storer; Miss Jenny–Miss Hallam; Lady Townly–Miss Cheer; Mrs. Motherly–Mrs. Tomlinson.
Miss in Her Teens.
   Capt. Flash–Hallam; Capt. Loveit–Darby; Puff–Morris; Jasper–Woolls; Mr. Fribble–Miss Maria Storer; Miss Biddy–Miss Hallam.
American Company.
   [The opening night of the season. "For one month only. By authority." Prices: boxes 7s.; pit 5s.; gallery 3s. Source: *Pennsylvania Chronicle* (26 September–3 October 1768).]

6 October 1768   Alexandria, Virginia colony
Program unidentified.
Virginia Company.
   [George Washington purchased a 5s. ticket for another person on this date. Source: Washington, *Diaries*, 2:99.]

6 October 1768   Southwark Theatre, Philadelphia
George Barnwell [i.e., *The London Merchant*].
Catherine and Petruchio.
American Company.
   [Source: *Pennsylvania Journal* (6 October 1768).]

10 October 1768   Halifax, Nova Scotia
A Bold Stroke for a Wife.

Col. Fainwell–Giffard; Sir Philip Modelove–Horner; Tradelove–Leggett; Perriwinkle–Mills; Freeman–Platt;Scabut and Obadiah Prim–Farrell; Simon Pure–Mills; Ann Lovely–Mrs. Mills; Mrs. Prim and Betty–Mrs. Giffard; Quaker Girl–Miss Tunbridge.
The Citizen.
Old Philpot–Mills; Young Philpot–Giffard; Sir Jasper Wilding–Horner; Young Wilding–Farrell; Beaufort and Quildrive–Platt; Dapper–Leggett; Maria–Mrs. Giffard; Corrinna–Mrs. Mills.
Mills Company
["For the Benefit of Mr. and Mrs. Giffard." Source: *Nova Scotia Gazette* (6 October 1768).]

14 October 1768   Southwark Theatre, Philadelphia
Hamlet.
Thomas and Sally.
American Company.
[Source: *Pennsylvania Journal* (13 October 1768).]

14 October 1768   Halifax, Nova Scotia
The Revenge.
As 15 September 1768.
The Reprisal.
Heartly–Mills; Brosh–Horner; Monsieur Champignon–Mills; Lieutenant O'Clabber–Farrell; Ensign Maclaymore–Giffard; Lieutenant Lyon–Leggett; Jack Hanlyard–Phillips; Ben Block–Platt; Harriet (with songs)–Mrs. Giffard.
Mills Company.
["For the benefit of Mr. and Mrs. Mills." Source: *Nova Scotia Gazette* (13 October 1768).]

21 October 1768   Southwark Theatre, Philadelphia
The Spanish Friar.
The Honest Yorkshireman.
American Company.
[Mainpiece advertised as "with alterations by Dr. Johnson." Source: *Pennsylvania Gazette* (20 October 1768).]

21 October 1768   Halifax, Nova Scotia
The London Merchant.
Thorowgood–Mills; Uncle–Farrell; George Barnwell–Giffard; Trueman–Horner; Blunt–Platt; Millwood and Maria–Mrs. Mills; Lucy–Mrs. Giffard.
Catherine and Petruchio.

Petruchio–Giffard; Baptista–Farrell; Hortensio–Platt; Grumio and Music Master–Mills; Biondello and Taylor–Horner; Catherine–Mrs. Giffard; Bianca and Cook–Mrs. Mills.
The Picture of a Playhouse.
  By Platt.
Mills Company.
  ["For the Benefit of Messrs. Platt and Horner ... the last night of playing" Source: *Nova Scotia Gazette* (20 October 1768).]

28 October 1768   Southwark Theatre, Philadelphia
The Mourning Bride.
Miss in Her Teens.
American Company.
  ["The last week but one." Source: *Pennsylvania Gazette* (27 October 1768).]

28 October 1768   Halifax, Nova Scotia
The Recruiting Officer.
  Justice Ballance–Mills; Captain Plume–Giffard; Capt. Brazen–Platt; Mr. Worthy–Horner; Burlock–Leggett; Constable–Phillips; Sergeant Kite–Farrell; 1st and 2nd Recruits–Mills and Horner; Sylvia–Mrs. Giffard; Melinda–Mrs. Mills; Rose and Lucy–"by a person who never appear-ed on this stage."
Catherine and Petruchio.
Harlequin Skeleton.
Mills Company.
  ["Positively the last night of playing." Source: *Nova Scotia Gazette* (27 October 1768).]

4 November 1768   Southwark Theatre, Philadelphia
Cymbeline.
Love a la Mode.
American Company.
  [Source: *Pennsylvania Gazette* (3 November 1768).]

11 November 1768   Southwark Theatre, Philadelphia
The Merchant of Venice.
The Guardian* (David Garrick, 1759).
American Company.
  [Not in Pollock. Source: *Pennsylvania Journal* (10 November 1768).]

18 November 1768   Southwark Theatre, Philadelphia
The Jealous Wife.

An unnamed pantomime.
American Company.
  [Not in Pollock. Source: *Pennsylvania Journal* (17 November 1768).]

25 November 1768   Southwark Theatre, Philadelphia
The Clandestine Marriage.
Lethe.
American Company.
  [Source: *Pennsylvania Journal* (24 November 1768).]

2 December 1768   Southwark Theatre, Philadelphia
Tamerlane.
  Bajazet–Hallam; Moneses–Henry; Axalla–Parker; Omar–Tomlinson; Dervise–Morris; Haly–Wall; Tamerlane–Douglass; Prince of Tanais–Darby; Mirvan–Woolls; Stratocles–Byerley; Zama–Raworth; Selima–Miss Cheer; Arpasia–Miss Hallam.
High Life Below Stairs.
American Company.
  [Source: *Pennsylvania Gazette* (1 December 1768).]

9 December 1768   Southwark Theatre, Philadelphia
The Busy Body.
The Contrivances.
American Company.
  [Prices: boxes 7s. 6d.; pit 5.; gallery 3s.   Source: *Pennsylvania Gazette* (8 December 1768).]

12 December 1768   Southwark Theatre, Philadelphia
King John* (William Shakespeare).
American Company.
  [Source: *Pennsylvania Gazette* (1 December 1768).]

14 December 1768   Southwark Theatre, Philadelphia
Macbeth.
  Macbeth–Hallam; Lady Macbeth–Miss Cheer.
Miss in her Teens.
American Company.
  [Source: *Pennsylvania Chronicle* (5–12 December 1768).]

16 December 1768   Southwark Theatre, Philadelphia
False Delicacy* (Hugh Kelly and David Garrick, 1768).
  Colonel Rivers–Douglass; Cecil–Hallam; Lord Winworth–Henry; Sidney–Byerley; Sir Henry Newburg–Wall; Mrs.

Halley–Mrs. Douglass; Miss Marchmont–Miss Hallam; Miss Rivers–Miss Storer; Lady Betty Lambton–Miss Cheer; Miss Sally–Mrs. Harman.
Catherine and Petruchio.
American Company.
[Source: *Pennsylvania Journal* (15 December 1768).]

23 December 1768   A "commodious room," Broad St., Charleston
Non-theatrical entertainments.
Bayly Company.

[The *South Carolina Gazette* of 20 December 1768 provides the following details of the return of the Bayly Company to Charleston:

> By permission. In a commodious house, now fitted up in theatrical order, for the accommodation of ladies and gentlemen, in Broad-street, near the corner of the Beef-market-square, on Friday evening, the 23d instant, December, will be presented the noted Bayly's Medley of Entertainments, consisting of his uncommon performances, by dexterity of hand, in a manner different from every other pretender to, or performer of that art, without the help or use of pockets, bags, or sleeves. With the tragical, comical, farcical, operatical, whimsical humours of Seignior Punchinello, his wife, son, family, and company of artificial comedians, consisting of thirty-five figures, near four feet high; by whom will be performed a variety of new entertainments, drolls, burlettas, &c.&c.&c.&c. with scenes, decorations, music, &c.
>
> To be continued on Monday, Wednesday, and Friday evenings, during his stay, with different performances each evening. Boxes, 20s. Pit, 15s. Gallery, 10s. Vivant Rex, & Regina.
>
> As the receiving money at the door is attended with difficulties too tedious to particularise, and that gentlemen and ladies may not be detained at the door, Mr. Bayly requests those who will please to honour him with their company, will be provided with tickets, which may be had at any time, at the Bacchus Tavern on the Bay, or at the house of performance. The doors to be opened at half after 4, and the entertainment to begin at 6.
>
> N.B. As my stay in town will be but short, any set company may have a private performance on the evenings of vacation.]

26 December 1768   Southwark Theatre, Philadelphia
Zara* (Aaron Hill, 1736).
An unnamed farce.
Ozman–Hallam; Lusigman–Douglass; Zara–Miss Cheer.
American Company.
[Source: *Pennsylvania Journal* (22 December 1768).]

30 December 1768   Southwark Theatre, Philadelphia
Alexander the Great, or The Rival Queens* (Nathaniel Lee, 1677).
Alexander–Hallam; Clytus–Douglass; Lysimachus–Henry; Hephestion–Wall; Cossander–Morris; Polypherchon–Parker; Philip–Tomlinson; Thestalus–Woolls; Perdiccas–Byerley; Cumenus–Roberts; Meleager–Rawthorn; Aristander–Darby; Sysigambis–Douglass; Statira–Miss Hallam; Paritratis–Miss Storer; Roxana–Miss Cheer.
Fanny the Phantom.
The Orator–Wall; Sergeant Blarney–Douglass; Councellor Prosequi–Tomlinson; Shadrach Bodkin–Morris; Justice–Woolls; Clerk–Raworth; Peter Paragraph–Wall.
The Contrivances (*Pennsylvania Journal*) or
Neck or Nothing (*Pennsylvania Gazette*).
American Company.
[The tragedy advertised as "never acted in America." Source: *Pennsylvania Journal* (29 December 1768).]

1769

The American Company concluded their 1768–69 season in Philadelphia by mid January and returned to New York. Here they enjoyed a solid season until mid June and, after a rocky summer recess, resumed in Southwark, Philadelphia, in the late fall. In February the Virginia Company renamed itself the "New American Company," a direct allusion to their "American Company" rivals under Douglass, the retitling obviously evidencing the growing nationalism, but also the close connection and competition between the two touring companies. Indeed a scroll through the cast list reveals a rather fluid exchange of personnel; e.g., sometime before mid February Mr. Darby and Mr. and Mrs. Parker left the American Company in New York and joined the New American Company in Annapolis. It will be remembered that Mr. Parker (and presumably his wife) had only just left the Verling Company in late 1768 to join Douglass, while on the other side, Patrick Malone left the American Company and joined Verling.

After the New York City season, the American Company separated for the summer. Several members (including Mr. Woolls, Mr. Hallam, Miss Hallam, and Mr. Hulett) remained in New York City, stringing out a short season of musical entertainments at Vauxhall Garden. Part of the company proceeded to Albany, where Dunlap (58) claims the company played 1–30 July 1769, though this assertion is questioned by Seilhamer (1:255–56). That the company was indeed granted permission to play for one month only is noted in the *New York Mercury* (see 10 July). As Albany at the time had no newspapers, very little is known of the brief season beyond one play title, prices, and playing days. Munsell (*Annals of Albany*, 2:294–95) provides the following comment which makes clear that the theatrical community was familiar with the theatrical space in Albany: "After the Revolution, December 1785, when a company returned to Albany, they leased the Old Hospital."

John Henry was not with the company in Albany. He and his wife, Marie (née Storer), were sent to Charleston to solicit subscriptions and to arrange for the construction of a theatre, but encountered insurmountable political difficulties (see 31 July). While in Charleston, Henry presented the *Lecture on Heads*. The whereabouts of the company through August are unknown, though one ex-member, Patrick Malone, Pollock tells us (25), was exhibiting "performances on the slack rope" at the Southwark Theatre in Philadelphia in August. Douglass took his *Lecture on Heads* to Portsmouth, New Hampshire colony, where he played in early September with enough members of his company to perform the first act of Macklin's afterpiece *Love a la Mode*.

By late September the American Company was still unassembled, so Hallam and Henry cobbled together a desperate pre-season in Philadelphia, including six-night-a-week bills, the involvement of amateurs, and radically slashed prices. Pollock (26) reprints an unaddressed letter of petition from David Douglass dated 5 October in which he complains of "a Disappointment at Carolina" and references the severity of the company's situation. He was apparently granted permission to play again in Philadelphia. The "Disappointment at Carolina" no doubt refers to Henry's frustrated visit to Charleston. An 18 January 1770 letter also remarks on the financially disastrous autumn of 1769.

Once the company was fully assembled in Philadelphia, however, the season developed into a particularly strong one, sustaining the company until 1 June 1770. The members of the American Company included the following: Byerley, Miss Cheer (still listed under this name), Mr. Darby, David Douglass, Mrs. Douglass, Lewis Hallam Jr., Nancy Hallam, Mrs. Harman, John Henry, Mrs. Ann Henry, Owen Morris,

Charles Parker, Mr. Raworth, Mr. Roberts, Miss Maria Storer, Mr. Tomlinson, Mrs. Tomlinson, Thomas Wall, Mrs. Wall, Stephen Woolls. Beyond the regulars, Hugdson and Warwell are listed "of the American Company" during the summer entertainments in New York.

The New American Company (formerly Verling's Virginia Company now renamed) opened in Annapolis on 18 February and played there until mid-June, after which they again disappeared from the theatrical, though not the court, calendar. Rankin (151) itemizes a lengthy scroll of legal suits brought against this company, all debt recovery suits, and suggests that the company disbanded soon thereafter. The roster is difficult to establish, as personnel in this company were less stable than those of their more professional counterparts. What notices are preserved reveal fluidity among roles, a steady influx of new faces, and the occasional appearance of amateurs assaying roles for their own gratification. Nonetheless, by the end of the Annapolis engagement, the New American Company had consisted of the following known members: William Burdett, Mrs. Burdett, Mr. Darby, Mrs. Darby, James Godwin, David Jefferson, Mrs. Sarah Jones, Patrick Malone, Mrs. Malone, Henrietta Osborne, Mr. Page, Charles Parker, Mrs. Parker, Frederick Spencer, George Walker, Mrs. Walker, and William Verling. Some, like Mrs. Darby and Mrs. Malone, made only occasional appearances. Mr. and Mrs. Parker (re)joined the company by February, as did Mr. and Mrs. Darby and Mr. and Mrs. Patrick Malone. Mrs. Osborne—in spite of her 12 January 1769 threat to return to England (Rankin 146)—rejoined the company in early April.

A theatre had been constructed in Halifax, North Carolina by June 1769 when the town was surveyed.[15] This venue may be the work of Mr. Mills and his company who played in North Carolina in 1768 and may well have been playing there in 1769, though little corroborating evidence of the company is extant beyond two letters by Governor William Tryon (see entries for 11 and 15 June 1768).

A "person who has read and sung in most of the great towns in America" performed one-man versions of plays and ballad

---

[15] Henderson, "Strolling Players in North Carolina," 25–26; cf., Rankin, 218, note 1.

operas in Philadelphia, Providence, Portsmouth, Boston, and Salem. Until now, the name of this itinerant performer has been a mystery, but the solution is provided in the diary of John Rowe, a Boston resident, who in 1770 identifies him as one "Mr. Joan" (quoted in Bonawitz 18). Joan's presence in Boston during 1770 is established by advertisements in Boston newspapers for various musical concerts for his own benefit (e.g., 19 and 25 February 1770, 21 February 1771). A notice in the *Boston Evening Post* (19 February 1770) records that he is "living at said Concert Hall, where he teaches the violin, German flute, and basse viol." After March 1771 he disappears from the historical record.

Bonawitz (18) also reports that English soldiers residing in Boston mounted plays for their own amusement, but no precise details have survived (see entries for 13 and 20 March 1769).

In New York, an amateur troupe may have presented *The Orphan* in June, as evidenced by an interesting pair of letters in the newspapers on 22 and 26 June 1769. The ladies and gentlemen who proposed to act made clear to the public that "they thought it below their rank and characters to perform for the sake of a little paltry gain." This incident neatly demarcates the dividing line between amateur and professional companies.

✳✳✳

3 January 1769   Southwark Theatre, Philadelphia
A Bold Stroke for a Wife.
American Company.
    [Jacob Hiltzheimer records in his diary for this date, "Tonight went to the play with Israel Waters to see 'A Bold Stroke for a Wife.'" Source: Hiltzheimer 16.]

6 January 1769   Southwark Theatre, Philadelphia
Alexander the Great.
    As 30 December 1768.
Fanny the Phantom.
    As 30 December 1768.
The Contrivances.
American Company.
    ["Benefit of the Debtors." Source: *Pennsylvania Journal* (5 January 1769).]

16 January 1769   John St. Theatre, New York
King John.
   King John–Douglass; Pembroke–Tomlinson; Prince Henry–Mrs. Harman; Melun–Wools; Salisbury–Parker; The Bastard–Hallam; Faulconbridge–Roberts; Austria–Darby; Hubert–Henry; King of France–Byerley; Governor of Angiers–Morris; Chatillion–Raworth; Dauphin–Wall; Pandulph–Morris; Queen Elinor–Mrs. Douglass; Prince Arthur–Miss M. Storer; Lady Blanche–Miss Hallam; Lady Faulconbridge–Miss Storer; Constance–Miss Cheer.
The Old Maid.
   Cleremont–Mrs. Wall; Capt. Cape–Douglass; Harlow–Byerley; Heartwell–Morris; The Old Maid–Mrs. Harman; Trifle–Mrs. Tomlinson; Mrs. Harlow–Miss Cheer.
American Company.
   [This evening is apparently the opening of the new season. Source: *New York Gazette & Weekly Post-Boy* (9 January 1769).]

20 January 1769   John St. Theatre, New York
The Jealous Wife.
Picture of a Playhouse.
Miss in Her Teens.
American Company.
   [Source: *New York Journal* (19 January 1769).]

23 January 1769   John St. Theatre, New York
Hamlet.
The Mayor of Garratt.
American Company.
   [Announced but not performed. "The above play is postponed till Wednesday next." Source: *New York Mercury* (23 January 1769).]

25 January 1769   John St. Theatre, New York
Hamlet.
The Mayor of Garratt.
American Company.
   [Odell (1:147) misdates this performance as 27 January 1769. Source: *New York Gazette & Weekly Post-Boy* (23 January 1769).]

27 January 1769   John St. Theatre, New York
The Beaux' Stratagem.
The Citizen.

American Company.
   [Source: *New York Journal* (26 January 1769).]

30 January 1769   John St. Theatre, New York
Zara.
Love a la Mode.
American Company.
   [Source: *New York Gazette & Weekly Post-Boy* (30 January 1769).]

2 February 1769   John St. Theatre, New York
Romeo and Juliet.
   The funeral procession included Wall, Woolls, Miss Hallam, Miss M. Storer, and Mrs. Harman.
The Guardian.
American Company.
   [Source: *New York Journal* (2 February 1769).]

6 February 1769   John St. Theatre, New York
The English Merchant* (George Colman Sr., 1767).
Catherine and Petruchio.
American Company.
   [Source: *New York Gazette & Weekly Post-Boy* (6 February 1769).]

9 February 1769   John St. Theatre, New York
Cymbeline.
The King and the Miller of Mansfield.
American Company.
   [Source: *New York Journal* (9 February 1769).]

13 February 1769   John St. Theatre, New York
A Bold Stroke for a Wife.
Love a la Mode.
American Company.
   [Source: *New York Mercury* (13 February 1769).]

16 February 1769   The New Theatre, Annapolis
Alteration of theatre.
   [An announcement of plays in the *Maryland Gazette* of this date contains the following item relating to an alteration to the theatre:

   Upper Boxes are now preparing, the passage to which, must be from the Stage; 'tis therefore hoped, such ladies and gentlemen as choose to fix on their seats, will come before the Play, as it is not possible they can be admitted after the curtain is drawn up.]

17 February 1769   John St. Theatre, New York
The Orphan.
Lethe.
American Company.
["The days of Performance for the future, will be Monday, Wednesday, and Friday." Source: *New York Journal* (16 February 1769).]

18 February 1769   The New Theatre, Annapolis
Romeo and Juliet.
The Virgin Unmasked.
New American Company.
[The Virginia Company changed its name to the New American Company as of this date. Source: *Maryland Gazette* (16 February 1769).]

20 February 1769   John St. Theatre, New York
Every Man in His Humour* (Ben Jonson).
The Apprentice.
American Company.
[Source: *New York Gazette & Weekly Post-Boy* (20 February 1769).]

22 February 1769   The New Theatre, Annapolis
Othello.
   Othello–by a Gentleman (for his amusement) being the first time of his ever appearing on any stage.
The Honest Yorkshireman.
New American Company.
[Source: *Maryland Gazette* (16 February 1769).]

24 February 1769   The New Theatre, Annapolis
The Jealous Wife.
The Brave Irishman.
New American Company.
[Source: *Maryland Gazette* (16 February 1769).]

24 February 1769   John St. Theatre, New York
Alexander the Great.
The Contrivances.
American Company.
[Source: *New York Journal* (23 February 1769).]

25 February 1769   The New Theatre, Annapolis
The Beggar's Opera.
   Macheath–Verling; Peachum–Darby; Locket–Parker; Filch–Godwin; Robin of Bagshot, and Drawer–Malone; Jemmy Twitcher–Page; Crook-Finger'd Jack–Walker; Matt of the Mint–Godwin; Ben Budge–Burdett; Nimming Ned–Jefferson; Beggar–Parker; Player–Burdett; Mrs. Peachum and Lucy Locket–Mrs. Walker; Diana Trapes and Mrs. Vixen–Mrs. Jones; Mrs. Slamekin–Mrs. Walker; Mrs. Coaxer–Mrs. Burdett; Jenny Driver–Mrs. Malone; Molly Brazen–Walker; Polly–Mrs. Parker.
The Brave Irishman.
   Captain O'Blunder–Malone.
New American Company.
   [Source: *Maryland Gazette* (23 February 1769).]

27 February 1769   John St. Theatre, New York
The Provoked Husband.
The Mayor of Garratt.
American Company.
   [Source: *New York Mercury* (27 February 1769).]

2 March 1769   The New Theatre, Annapolis
Richard III.
Lethe.
New American Company.
   [Postponed. Source: *Maryland Gazette* (2 March 1769).]

3 March 1769   John St. Theatre, New York
The Beggar's Opera.
   Macheath–Hallam; Polly–Miss Wainwright.
The Witches; or, Harlequin Restored.
American Company.
   [Source: *New York Journal* (2 March 1769).]

4 March 1769   The New Theatre, Annapolis
Douglas.
High Life Below Stairs.
New American Company.
   [Source: *Maryland Gazette* (2 March 1769).]

6 March 1769   The New Theatre, Annapolis
Richard III.
Lethe.

New American Company.
   [Source: *Maryland Gazette* (2 March 1769).]

6 March 1769   John St. Theatre, New York
The Clandestine Marriage.
The Honest Yorkshireman.
American Company.
   [Source: *New York Gazette & Weekly Post Boy* (6 March 1769).]

9 March 1769   The New Theatre, Annapolis
The Jealous Wife.
The Upholsterer.
New American Company.
   [Source: *Maryland Gazette* (2 March 1769).]

10 March 1769   John St. Theatre, New York
Henry IV, Part 1.
The Guardian.
American Company.
   [Source: *New York Journal* (9 March 1769).]

11 March 1769   The New Theatre, Annapolis
Romeo and Juliet.
   Romeo–Verling; Juliet–Mrs. Jones; Mercutio–by a gentleman for his amusement.
The Honest Yorkshireman.
New American Company.
   [Source: *Maryland Gazette* (9 March 1769).]

13 March 1769   Boston
Anti-theatrical commentary.
   [The *Boston Evening Post* of this date contains the following item:

   I am informed that next Tuesday night two plays are to be performed in this town by the soldiers now here. I should be much obliged to any one to inform me what right the commanding officers have to give leave to their men to perform any such entertainments here? Whether we are to be governed by the military law; or the military by the civil I hope the same spirit of piety reigns now as did in former times. Yours, &c.]

14 March 1769   The New Theatre, Annapolis
The Inconstant.
Merlin, or, Harlequin's Delivery* (Anonymous).
   Harlequin–Godwin; Clown–Malone; Columbine–Mrs. Parker.

THE COLONIAL AMERICAN STAGE   329

New American Company.
   [Source: *Maryland Gazette* (9 March 1769).]

15 March 1769   The New Theatre, Annapolis
Douglas.
The Mock Doctor.
New American Company.
   [Source: *Maryland Gazette* (9 March 1769).]

15 March 1769   John St. Theatre, New York
The Wonder!
Harlequin Collector.
American Company.
   [Source: *New York Mercury* (13 March 1769).]

16 March 1769   The New Theatre, Annapolis
The Beaux' Stratagem.
The Devil to Pay.
New American Company.
   [Source: *Maryland Gazette* (9 March 1769).]

17 March 1769   John St. Theatre, New York
The Busy Body.
The Brave Irishman.
American Company.
   [This performance "by particular desire of the Grand Knot, of the Friendly Brothers of St. Patrick." *The New York Mercury* (13 March 1769) advertised *Every Man in His Humor* for this date. Source: *New York Journal* (16 March 1769).]

17 March 1769   The New Theatre, Annapolis
The Miser.
   Lovegold–Godwin; Frederick–Verling; Cleremont–Burdett; List–Malone; Ramillie–Darby; James and Decoy–Parker; Mercer–Page; Lawyer and Sparkle–Walker; Furnish–Jefferson; Mrs. Wisely–Mrs. Burdett; Harriet–Mrs. Jones; Lappet–Mrs. Walker; Wheedle–Mrs. Malone; Mariana–Mrs. Parker.
High Life Below Stairs.
New American Company.
   [Source: *Maryland Gazette* (9 March 1769).]

18 March 1769   The New Theatre, Annapolis
The Revenge.

Don Alonzo–Godwin; Don Carlos–Burdett; Alvarez–Parker; Don Manuel–Malone; Zanga–Verling; Isabella–Mrs. Walker; Leonora–Mrs. Jones.
Damon and Phillida.
Damon–Spencer; Phillida–Mrs. Parker.
New American Company.
[Source: *Maryland Gazette* (9 March 1769).]

20 March 1769   Boston
Pro-theatrical commentary.

[The *Boston Evening Post* of this date prints the following rebuttal to the letter of 13 March 1769:

> A writer in last Thursday's paper says that he is 'credibly informed, and with no small surprize, that a number of the soldiers now here intend shortly to exhibit a play in this town, in open violation of an act of this province for preventing stage plays and other theatrical entertainments.' I would inform this writer and all other intermedlers, that there is an Act of Parliament licensing theatrical performances throughout the King's dominions, which I take upon me to say (and no one can contradict) intirely supercedes the Act of this province, the assembly are restricted to the making laws not contrary to the laws of England, and if so, certainly the act of this province abovementioned can be of no force.–That plays are disagreeable to the inhabitants in general in this town I believe is a mistake: but upon supposition they are disagreeable, as no person is obliged to attend that has not leisure, ability & inclination, there cannot be any reasonable objection in that respect. I am told that a few years ago some bunglers, as the means of making assignations, took upon themselves to exhibit plays at unseasonable hours, which highly incensed the sober part of the town, as well it might; but as the present performers have very different and strictly upright motives, it is to be hoped, and may really be expected, they will meet with the approbation of the public, instead of a prosecution, which this writer's ignorance of the law led him to insinuate would take place—which is the sincere wish of one that purposes in the intended exhibition to be. SPECTATOR.]

27 March 1769   John St. Theatre, New York
The Tender Husband* (Richard Steele, 1705).
The Upholsterer.
American Company.
["For the entertainment of the Right Worshipful the Grand Master, the masters, wardens, and brethren, of the Ancient and Honourable Society of Free and Accepted Masons." Source: *New York Journal* (23 March 1768).]

29 March 1769   John St. Theatre, New York
Love in a Village.

The Old Maid.
American Company.
   [Source: *New York Mercury* (27 March 1769).]

1 April 1769   The New Theatre, Annapolis
The Miser.
The Devil to Pay.
New American Company.
   [Source: *Maryland Gazette* (30 March 1769).]

3 April 1769   John St. Theatre, New York
All in the Wrong.
The Musical Lady* (George Colman Sr., 1762)
American Company.
   ["By particular desire of the Grand Knot of the Friendly Brothers of St. Patrick." *She Would and She Would Not* was originally advertised for this evening in the *New York Mercury* (27 March 1769). Source: *New York Mercury* (3 April 1769).]

3 April 1769   The New Theatre, Annapolis
Hamlet.
The Mayor of Garratt.
New American Company.
   [Source: *Maryland Gazette* (30 March 1769).]

8 April 1769   The New Theatre, Annapolis
Richard III.
Polly Honeycombe.
   Polly Honeycombe–Henrietta Osborne.
New American Company.
   [Benefit Verling. Henrietta Osborne rejoins company. Source: *Maryland Gazette* (30 March 1769).]

10 April 1769   John St. Theatre, New York
Othello.
Flora; or, Hob in the Well.
American Company.
   [The notice for this performance states that

> The part of Othello to be attempted by a Gentleman, assisted by other Gentlemen, in the Characters of the Duke and Senate of Venice. From a benevolent and generous design of encouraging the Theatre, and relieving the performers from some embarrassments in which they are involved .... The boxes and pit will be laid together, at 8s.

Another item in the *Mercury* of 10 April 1769 offers the following remarks:

> We are authoris'd to inform the publick, that the gentleman who is to appear this evening, in the character of Othello, has displayed, at the rehearsals, some very amazing strokes of theatrical genius. We are informed, that the reasons why the pit is made box price, this evening, are first, in compliment to the gentlemen who are to perform; next, on account of a new set of scenes, which were painted at a great expence, for the occasion; and, because the demand for boxes has been so great, that the director of the theatre, could not, otherwise accommodate one half of the ladies and gentlemen who have applied for places.

Odell (following Ireland) suggests that the gentleman performing as Othello was Major James Moncrieff of the British forces. Source: *New York Mercury* (10 April 1769); cf. Odell 1:149.]

14 April 1769　　　John St. Theatre, New York
False Delicacy.
Catherine and Petruchio.
American Company.
　[Source: *New York Journal* (13 April 1769).]

17 April 1769　　　John St. Theatre, New York
Macbeth.
The Musical Lady.
American Company.
　[Source: *New York Mercury* (17 April 1769).]

c. 9–17 April 1769　The New Theatre, Annapolis
Romeo and Juliet.
The Constant Couple.
New American Company.
　[The *Maryland Gazette* of 20 April 1769 prints a letter which mentions performances of two plays sometime during this time frame, as Henrietta Osborne rejoined the company on 8 April:

> I never was in England–nor did I ever see a Play anywhere but in Annapolis, consequently my judgement is formed by such conceptions as nature has pointed out. And, before I mention those things that have shock'd me, I will here acknowledge the great pleasure I felt in Mrs. Osborne's performance of Juliet–Her feeling manner of acting, in my opinion, made amends for a number of incidents that were exceptionable, during the representation of the Play–I staid in town to go to the Constant Couple–and, tho' this lady charmed me by her acting, I own she struck my admiration still more, to find that it was in

the power of the same woman, to express the delicate sensibility of a Juliet–and the levity of a Sir Harry Wildair ....]

18 April 1769   The New Theatre, Annapolis
The Provoked Husband.
The King and the Miller of Mansfield.
New American Company.
   [Benefit Godwin. Source: *Maryland Gazette* (13 April 1769).]

22 April 1769   The New Theatre, Annapolis
The Busy Body.
   Marplot–Spencer; Miranda–Mrs. Parker.
The Genii; or, The Birth of Harlequin* (Henry Woodward, 1752).
   Genii–Master Knapp; Harlequin–Spencer; Columbine–Mrs. Parker.
New American Company.
   [Benefit Spencer.   Source: *Maryland Gazette* (20 April 1769).]

24 April 1769   John St. Theatre, New York
Alexander the Great.
The Citizen.
American Company.
   ["The days of performance, for the remainder of the season, will be Mondays, and Thursdays."   Benefit Miss Cheer. Source: *New York Gazette & Weekly Post-Boy* (24 April 1769).]

25 April 1769   The New Theatre, Annapolis
The Merchant of Venice.
   Shylock–Verling; Portia–Mrs. Osborne.
The Lying Valet.
   Sharp–Verling; Melissa–Mrs. Malone; Kitty Pry–Mrs. Parker.
New American Company.
   [Benefit Patrick Malone. Source: *Maryland Gazette* (20 April 1769).]

27 April 1769   John St. Theatre, New York
King John.
Thomas and Sally.
American Company.
   [Benefit Mr. and Mrs. Tomlinson. Source: *New York Journal* (27 April 1769).]

29 April 1769   The New Theatre, Annapolis
The Mourning Bride.
   Almeria–Mrs. Osborne.
The Honest Yorkshireman.
New American Company.
   [Benefit Jefferson. Source: *Maryland Gazette* (20 April 1769).]

1 May 1769   John St. Theatre, New York
Jane Shore.
The Devil to Pay.
American Company.
   [Benefit Miss Storer and Maria Storer. Source: *New York Gazette & Weekly Post Boy* (1 May 1769).]

1 May 1769   The New Theatre, Annapolis
The Suspicious Husband.
   Ranger–Mrs. Osborne.
The Wrangling Lovers* (William Lyon, 1745).
Lethe.
New American Company.
   [Benefit Burdett. Source: *Maryland Gazette* (20 and 27 April 1769).]

2 May 1769   The New Theatre, Annapolis
Richard III.
High Life Below Stairs.
New American Company.
   [Source: *Maryland Gazette* (27 April 1769).]

May 3 1769   The New Theatre, Annapolis
Douglas.
   Douglas–Verling; Lady Randolph–Mrs. Osborne.
The Mayor of Garratt.
New American Company.
   [Source: *Maryland Gazette* (27 April 1769).]

May 4 1769   The New Theatre, Annapolis
Henry IV, Part 1.
   Falstaff–Verling; Hal–Mrs. Osborne; Poins–Mrs. Parker.
Damon and Phillida.
New American Company.
   [Source: *Maryland Gazette* (27 April 1769).]

4 May 1769   John St. Theatre, New York
Maid of the Mill* (Isaac Bickerstaffe, 1765).
American Company.
   ["Miss Wainwright's performance on Monday se'nnight was advertised for the last, and intended to be so; but at the particular desire of some persons of distinction, she performs in this opera." Source: *New York Journal* (4 May 1769).]

8 May 1769   John St. Theatre, New York
Romeo and Juliet.
   Romeo–Hallam; Juliet–Miss Hallam.
Thomas and Sally.
American Company.
   [Benefit Miss Hallam. Source: *New York Gazette & Weekly Post-Boy* (8 May 1769).]

9 May 1769   The New Theatre, Annapolis
A Bold Stroke for a Wife.
   Feignwell–Verling; Anne Lovely–Mrs. Osborne.
Thomas and Sally.
   Squire–Spencer; Thomas–Verling; Sally–Mrs. Parker; Lorcas–Mrs. Osborne.
New American Company.
   [Benefit Mrs. Malone. *The Farmer's Return from London* (Garrick) was announced as part of the bill in the *Maryland Gazette* of 27 April 1769 but was not performed. Source: *Maryland Gazette* (4 May 1769).]

11 May 1769   John St. Theatre, New York
Jane Shore.
Miss in Her Teens.
The Death of Harlequin* (Anonymous, 1716?).
American Company.
   [Second benefit for Henry and the Storer sisters. Odell remarks that "apparently the first had failed" (1:150). *The Death of Harlequin* is a scene adapted from *Orpheus and Euridyce*. Source: *New York Journal* (11 May 1769).]

13 May 1769   The New Theatre, Annapolis
Othello.
   Othello–"For that night only, will be performed by the same gentleman who played it before"; Desdemona–Mrs. Osborne.
Trick upon Trick* (Joseph Yarrow, 1742).
   Vizard–Verling; Mrs. Mixum–Mrs. Jones.

New American Company.
   [Benefit Mrs. Walker. Source: *Maryland Gazette* (4 May 1769).]

15 May 1769   John St. Theatre, New York
The Spanish Friar.
The Honest Yorkshireman.
American Company.
   [Benefit Wall. Source: *New York Mercury* (15 May 1769).]

16 May 1769   The New Theatre, Annapolis
George Barnwell [i.e., *The London Merchant*].
   Barnwell–Godwin; Maria–Mrs. Walker; Millwood–Mrs. Osborne.
The Brave Irishman.
   O'Blunder–Verling.
New American Company.
   [Source: *Maryland Gazette* (11 May 1769).]

17 May 1769   The New Theatre, Annapolis
The Conscious Lovers.
   Indiana–Mrs. Osborne.
The Citizen.
   Maria–Mrs. Osborne.
New American Company.
   [Benefit Mrs. Osborne. Source: *Maryland Gazette* (4 May 1769).]

18 May 1769   The New Theatre, Annapolis
The Beggar's Opera.
   Macheath–Verling; Lucy–Mrs. Osborne; Polly–Mrs. Parker.
Miss in Her Teens.
New American Company.
   [Source: *Maryland Gazette* (11 May 1769).]

20 May 1769   The New Theatre, Annapolis
The Distrest Mother.
   Pyrrbus–Verling; Orestes–Godwin; Hermione–Mrs. Jones; Andromache–Mrs. Osborne.
Harlequin Skeleton.
   Harlequin–Godwin; Colombine–Mrs. Parker.
New American Company.
   [Source: *Maryland Gazette* (4 May 1769).]

22 May 1769   John St. Theatre, New York
The Maid of the Mill.
The Old Maid.
American Company.
   [Source: *New York Gazette & Weekly Post-Boy* (22 May 1769).]

23 May 1769   The New Theatre, Annapolis
The Way to Keep Him.
   Sir Bashful Constant–Darby; Sir Brilliant Fashion–Spencer; William, Servant to Lovemore–Parker; Sideboard, Servant to Sir Bashful–Burdett; Lovemore–Verling; Mrs. Lovemore–Mrs. Parker; Muslin, Maid to Mrs. Lovemore–Mrs. Walker; Mignionet, Maid to Mrs. Bellmore–Mrs. Jones; Lady Constant–Mrs. Darby (being her first appearance); Widow Bellmore–Mrs. Osborne.
The Mock Doctor.
   Mock Doctor–Darby; Dorcas–Mrs. Parker.
New American Company.
   [Benefit Darby. Source: *Maryland Gazette* (11 May 1769).]

25 May 1769   John St. Theatre, New York
Richard III.
Lecture on Heads.
   Lecture by Douglass.
Love a la Mode.
American Company.
   [Benefit Mrs. Douglass. Source: *New York Mercury* (22 May 1769).]

27 May 1769   The New Theatre, Annapolis
The Earl of Essex.
   Essex–Verling; Southampton–Darby; Lord Burleigh–Burdett; Sir Walter Raleigh–Spencer; Lieutenant–Parker; Queen–Mrs. Jones; Nottingham–Mrs. Parker; Rutland–Mrs. Osborne.
The Chaplet.
   Damon–Mr. Spencer; Palemon–Darby; Laura–Mrs. Osborne; Pastora–Mrs. Parker.
New American Company.
   [Benefit Mrs. Parker. Source: *Maryland Gazette* (18 May 1769).]

29 May 1769   John St. Theatre, New York
The Constant Couple.

The Padlock* (Isaac Bickerstaffe, 1768).
American Company.
   [The afterpiece "never performed in America." Benefit Hallam. Source: *New York Mercury* (29 May 1769).]

30 May 1769   The New Theatre, Annapolis
She Would and She Would Not* (Colley Cibber, 1702).
New American Company.
   [Benefit Mrs. Jones. Source: *Maryland Gazette* (18 May 1769).]

1 June 1769   John St. Theatre, New York
The Earl of Essex.
The Padlock.
American Company.
   [Benefit Woolls. Source: *New York Journal* (1 June 1769).]

3 June 1769   The New Theatre, Annapolis
The Conscious Lovers.
   Young Bevil–Verling; Indiana–Mrs. Osborne.
Catherine and Petruchio.
   Petrucio–Verling; Grumio–Parker; Catharine–Mrs. Walker.
New American Company.
   [Benefit Mrs. Walker. Source: *Maryland Gazette* (25 May 1769).]

5 June 1769   The Academy, Philadelphia
Damon and Phillida.
Mr. Joan?
   [The play read and all the songs sung by a gentleman. Source: Pollock 107, following the *Pennsylvania Chronicle* (5 June 1769).]

6 June 1769   The New Theatre, Annapolis
A Bold Stroke for a Wife.
   Obediah Prim–(for that night only) By a Gentleman, for his amusement; Anne Lovely–Mrs. Osborne.
The Upholsterer.
New American Company.
   [Benefit Page. Source: *Maryland Gazette* (25 May 1769).]

6 June 1769   John St. Theatre, New York
The Revenge.
The Padlock.

American Company.
   [Benefit Morris. Source: *New York Mercury* (5 June 1769).]

8 June 1769   The New Theatre, Annapolis
Play unidentified.
New American Company.
   [A benefit. Source: Rankin 150.]

9 June 1769   John St. Theatre, New York
Love Makes a Man.
The Lying Valet.
American Company.
   [Benefit Mrs. Tomlinson. Source: *New York Journal* (8 June 1769).]

10 June 1769   The New Theatre, Annapolis
Love in a Village.
   Young Meadows–Spencer; Hawthorn–Verling; Rosetta–Mrs. Parker; Lucinda–Mrs. Osborne.
The Anatomist.
   Monsieur le Medecin–Spencer; Crispin–Darby; Beatrice–Mrs. Parker.
New American Company.
   [Benefit Parker. Source: *Maryland Gazette* (25 May 1769).]

13 June 1769   The New Theatre, Annapolis
Theodosius.
The Devil to Pay.
New American Company.
   [Benefit Mrs. Burdett. Source: *Maryland Gazette* (8 June 1769).]

13 June 1769   The Academy, Philadelphia
The Beggar's Opera.
Mr. Joan?
   [The play read and all the songs sung by a gentleman. This performer may possibly be Mr. Joan. Source: Pollock 107, following the *Pennsylvania Chronicle* (12 June 1769).]

13 June 1769   Mr. Burns's Tavern, New York
A concert.
Members of the American Company.
   [While this evening is not a theatrical event, various members of the American Company presented a musical concert for the benefit of fellow actress Mrs. Harman.

Performers included Woolls, Miss Hallam, Miss Wainright, and Miss Maria Storer. Source: *New York Gazette & Weekly Post-Boy* (5 June 1769).]

15 June 1769   John St. Theatre, New York
The Drummer.
The Padlock.
American Company.
[Advertised as the "last of the Season." Benefit Parker and Byerley. Source: *New York Journal* (15 June 1769).]

19 June 1769   The Assembly Room, Lodge Alley, Philadelphia
Love in a Village.
Mr. Joan?
["The play read and all the songs sung by a gentleman." Source: Pollock 107, following the *Pennsylvania Chronicle* (19 June 1769).]

19 June 1769   John St. Theatre, New York
Love for Love.
The Picture of a Playhouse.
Padlock.
American Company.
[The last night of season. Source: *New York Mercury* (19 June 1769).]

22 June 1769   New York
Amateur activity.
[The *New York Chronicle* of 15–22 June 1769 prints the following letter which describes the attempt made by some amateurs to mount Otway's *The Orphan*:

> To the printers of the New-York Chronicle.
> GENTLEMEN,
> On Tuesday evening last, was to have been presented, at the house of J--n Balder D--h, by a number of young gentlemen and ladies, —N.B. I say gentlemen, and ladies!—a tragedy called the ORPHAN or UNHAPPY MARRIAGE; which, from the known abilities of the tragedians, wou'd have been most tragically tragidis'd: This excited the curiosity of a number of young gentlemen, of this city, to draw up nigh the place of execution: But our exhibitors, thought proper not to make their appearance, either in proper person, or by their attorneys, tho' often cited to appear. They remain'd there a full hour, and peaceably withdrew; having had full amends for their disappointment, by said Balder D--h's odd grimaces, crook'd speeches, and uncommon gesticulations of the body; and will do this justice to his merit, by declaring no BUFFOON or MERRY ANDREW in their opinion, can stand

in competition with him! the gentlemen take this opportunity, to return their thanks to the intended performers, for their obliging disappointment: But should be glad to wait of them, any evening they chuse to appoint, if they will engage by their eloquence, to warm the imagination, and move the passions to as great a degree, as the antic tricks of our famous MERRY-ANDREW, rais'd their laughter. Done by order of a Num'rous Society, John Telltruth, speaker.]

23 June 1769   The Assembly Room, Lodge Alley, Philadelphia
The Maid of the Mill.
Mr. Joan?
["The first act of the play read and all the songs sung by a gentleman." Source: Pollock 107, following the *Pennsylvania Gazette* (21 June 1769).]

26 June 1769   The Assembly Room, Lodge Alley, Philadelphia
The Musical Lady.
Mr. Joan?
["The play read and all the songs sung by a gentleman." Source: Pollock 107, following the *Pennsylvania Chronicle* (26 June 1769).]

26 June 1769   New York
Amateur activity.
[The *New York Gazette & Weekly Post-Boy* of this date prints the following letter reacting to the 22 June 1769 letter regarding the aborted performance of *The Orphan*:

22d June, 1769.
My dear Friend, I suppose you have seen the piece in Messr's. Robertson's Chronicle of to-day, wrote by some incendiary, on purpose to blacken the characters of some "young gentlemen," who for their amusement were to have been the "Exhibitors" of a tragedy called, The Orphan, or The Unhappy Marriage, on Tuesday evening last; but on the day of performance, or the day before, the "young gentlemen" were informed by some of their friends, that there were a parcel of counterfeited tickets then selling about the town, (perhaps Mr. Telltruth may assert, that they were not counterfeits, but genuine; if he asserts so, he is mistaken; for there were only 52 genuine tickets struck off, which were given to the "Exhibitor's" particular friends) they immediately on this information, resolved to postpone the performance till some other opportunity, their intention being only amusement, (as may be seen by the tenor of their tickets) they thought it below their rank and characters to perform for the sake of a little paltry gain, which persons unacquainted with their circumstances might, by the instigation of such a person as the author of the 'foremention'd piece (from his manner of writing) might be led to think they did.—The ungenerous, ungentleman-like writer "ought to have thought before he leapt," for though he was put to the expence of buying one of the

counterfeits to satisfy his curiosity, it is to be hoped, that his circumstances are not quite so bad as he need to fear the horrors of a jail on account of the purchase of one of them, and the expence his revenge has put him to. Mr. Telltruth says false in every particular; but especially when he says, "our exhibitors thought proper not to make their appearance either in person or by their attornies," as the major part of the "Exhibitors" which was to have been, were "personally present" at or near the door of the house of exhibition from 5, until near 10 o'clock, that evening. I am, my dear friend, Yours, &c. J. Scan.]

29 June 1769   John St. Theatre, New York
Lecture on Hearts.
Harlequin's Frolick* (Anonymous).
John Henry.
   [Henry presented a lecture

With entertainments, viz. end of the lecture, Hippesly's Drunken Man. Between the different parts of the lecture; The Prince unable, from Alexander's Feast.–Let me Wander, from Handel's Allegro de Penseroso. And, Come ever Smiling Liberty, will be sung by Miss M. Storer. By desire, to conclude with a few pantomime scenes, call'd, Harlequin's Frolick.

Prices: boxes 6s.; pit 4s.; gallery 2s. Source: *New York Journal* (29 June 1769).]

3 July 1769   Vauxhall Garden, New York
A concert of music.
Various members of the American Company.
   [Woolls and Miss Hallam of the American Company presented a concert on this evening. The *New York Mercury* of 10 July 1769 reports that further concerts will be held every Monday and Thursday "during the season." Price: 2s. Source: *New York Mercury* (3 July 1769).]

10 July 1769   The Hospital, Albany, New York colony
Venice Preserved.
An unnamed farce.
"Comedians from the Theatre in New York" (i.e., the American Company).
   ["For one month only. By permission of his Excellency the Governor .... The days of playing will be Mondays, Wednesdays, and Fridays." Prices: boxes, 6s.; pit, 4s.; gallery, 2s. Source: *New York Mercury* (3 July 1769).]

11 July 1769   Mr. Burns's Long Room, New York
"An Attic Evening's Entertainment."

Hugdson and Warwell (of the American Company).
["By permission of his Excellency the Governor." Price: 5s. Source: *New York Mercury* (10 July 1769).]

13 July 1769   Vauxhall Garden, New York
A concert of music.
Various members of the American Company.
[Woolls and Miss Hallam performed various songs this evening. Source: *New York Chronicle* (6–13 July 1769).]

14 July 1769   Mr. Burns's Long Room, New York
"An Attic Evening's Entertainment."
Hugdson and Warwell (of the American Company).
["By permission of his Excellency the Governor." "The last night." Price: 5s. Source: *New York Journal* (13 July 1769).]

17 July 1769   Vauxhall Garden, New York
A concert of music.
Various members of the American Company.
["Mr. Hulet, Mr. and Miss Hallam, having agreed to continue the entertainments there as usual, (Mr. Francis having declined) take this method to inform the ladies and gentlemen, that this evening will be performed a concert of vocal and instrumental music. The vocal parts, by Mr. Woolls, Mr. Hallam, and Miss Hallam. By particular desire, several songs from the Padlock, and the Maid of the Mill." Source: *New York Mercury* (17 July 1769).]

21 July 1769   Mr. Burns's Long Room, New York
"An Attic Evening's Entertainment."
Hugdson and Warwell (of the American Company).
["By permission of his Excellency the Governor." Price: 5s. Source: *New York Journal* (20 July 1769).]

24 July 1769   Boston
Lecture on Heads.
David Douglass.
[Price: one dollar. Source: *Boston Evening Post* (24 July 1769).]

31 July 1769   Boston
Lecture on Heads.
David Douglass.
[Price: one-half dollar. Source: *Boston Evening Post* (31 July 1769).]

31 July 1769   Charleston, South Carolina colony
Notice of intention to build theatre.

[The *South Carolina & American General Gazette* of 24–31 July 1769 contains the following letter from John Henry to the citizens of Charleston:

> To the Publick. The repeated encouragement, countenance, and protection the American theatre has met with here from an audience of one of the most respectable on the continent is deeply known and has deeply imprinted the sentiment of gratitude in the breasts of the American Company of comedians; in consequence of which Mr. Douglass, the manager of that company, has sent me here from New York to build an elegant theatre fit for the accommodation of so numerous and polite an assembly as formerly honored this stage with their patronage. On these principles, with a strict charge to the elegance of the decorations on which neither pains or cost were to have been spared, I set out for this metropolis, but on my arrival was very much disappointed to find the colony involved in the present disagreeable, though glorious struggle. I thought my duty to enquire of our former patrons their opinion with regard to erecting a theatre at this juncture, but found that, until those unhappy differences were subsided, it would be disagreeable to the majority of the inhabitants. Under these circumstances it would be doing the highest injustice to the worthy and respectable public, as well as to our own private principles of gratitude for the innumerable favours received here, to have the most distant thought of what never was meant but as a grateful proof of our constant endeavours to entertain, in the most elegant manner, so generous and judicious an audience; therefore without the least hesitation, in compliance with the general desire, I declined it until a more favourable opportunity. The ladies and gentlemen of this town have always been as particularly conspicuous in their taste for every kind of rational amusement as for their encouragement of the polite arts in general, among which the theatre has always claimed, and as constantly received, their generous protection; and I am fully convinced, did not matters of the utmost importance merit their highest attention at this critical juncture, it would not fail of that patronage it has hitherto been honoured with. I shall beg leave to observe, before I conclude, that from the most sincere gratitude and to endeavour at meriting the favour so generously bestowed on the theatre, the manager has been at a most considerable expence in every decoration belonging to it to render it compleat for the purpose, amounting to some thousand pounds; and it is hoped, as soon as every political affair which concerns the welfare of this valuable colony is settled to general satisfaction, that under such generous and respectable patrons, like every other of the polite arts, the British may not exceed, if equal, the American stage. I have the honour to be, with the utmost respect and deference, the publick's most devoted and very humble servant. July 31, 1769. John Henry.]

2 August 1769   Boston
Lecture on Heads.

David Douglass.
[Price: one-half dollar. Source: *Boston Evening Post* (31 July 1769).]

2 August 1769   Mr. Hawes's Long Room on the Bay, Charleston

Lecture on Heads.
John Henry.
[With singing by Miss Storer. Price: one dollar. Source: *South Carolina & American General Gazette* (24–31 July 1769).

4 August 1769   Bunch of Grapes in King-Street, Boston
Lecture on Heads.
David Douglass.
[Source: *Boston News Letter* (3 August 1769).]

7 August 1769   Bunch of Grapes in King-Street, Boston
Lecture on Heads.
David Douglass.
[Price: one-half dollar. Source: *Boston News Letter* (7 August 1769).]

11 August 1769   Bunch of Grapes in King-Street, Boston
Lecture on Heads.
David Douglass.
[Price: one-half dollar. Source: *Boston Chronicle* (7–10 August 1769).]

14 August 1769   Bunch of Grapes in King-Street, Boston
Lecture on Heads.
David Douglass.
[Price: one-half dollar. Source: *Boston Chronicle* (10–14 August 1769).]

16 August 1769   Bunch of Grapes in King-Street, Boston
Lecture on Heads.
David Douglass.
[Price: one-half dollar. Source: *Boston Chronicle* (10–14 August 1769).]

18 August 1769   Bunch of Grapes in King-Street, Boston
Lecture on Heads.
David Douglass.
[Price: one-half dollar. Source: *Boston Chronicle* (14–17 August 1769).]

7 September 1769 Williamsburg
Newspaper notice.
[The playhouse in Williamsburg was apparently abandoned, as implied by a reference in the *Virginia Gazette* of 7 September 1769:

> Upon being acquainted that a school-master, to teach reading, writing, and arithmetick, was much wanted in this city, and that a proper person for that charge would meet with good encouragement, I was induced to make a trial, and accordingly opened school, about six weeks ago, at the playhouse (the only tolerable convenient place I could procure at that time).]

8 September 1769 Mr. Stavers's Large Room, Portsmouth, New Hampshire colony
Lecture on Heads.
David Douglass.
[Douglass "By Authority" presents a lecture "to conclude with Alexander's Feast, Or the Power of Music, an Ode written by Mr. Dryden, and the first act of Love-a-la Mode." Price: one-half dollar. Source: *New Hampshire Gazette* (8 September 1769).]

14 September 1769 Southwark Theatre, Philadelphia
Lecture on Heads.
American Company.
[The newspaper notice reads as follows:

> Mr. Hallam and Mr. Henry will deliver a Lecture on Heads, with entertainments of singing by Miss Hallam .... To conclude with The Camera Obscura; as introduced with great applause in Harlequin's Invasion, at the Theatre Royal, Drury Lane,–being the first time of its exhibition in America.

Prices: boxes 7s. 6d.; pit 5s.; gallery 3s. Source: *Pennsylvania Journal* (14 September 1769).]

16 September 1769 Mr. Hacker's Assembly Room, Providence, Rhode Island colony
The Beggar's Opera.
Mr. Joan.
[The newspaper notice announces that at

> Mr. Hacker's Assembly-Room, will be read, The Beggar's Opera, by a person who has read and sung in most of the great towns in America. All the songs will be sung. He personates all the characters, and enters

into the different humours or opera. Tickets to be had at the printing office, at half a dollar each.

Source: *Providence Gazette* (16 September 1769).]

25 September 1769   Southwark Theatre, Philadelphia
The Oracle.
A Picture of a Playhouse.
American Company.
   [The following notice appears this day:

> Messrs. Hallam and Henry, finding their expenses so low, have reduced the price as follows.–Boxes 5s. Pit 3s. Gallery 2s. N.B. There will be an entertainment every evening this week, as will be expressed in the bills of the day.

Source: *Pennsylvania Chronicle* (18–25 September 1769).]

28 September 1769   Vauxhall Garden, New York
A concert of music.
Various members of the American Company.
   [Hudgson and Miss M. Storer performed various songs this evening. Source: *New York Chronicle* (21–28 September 1769).]

29 September 1769   formerly Green and Walker's Store (Brattle St.), Boston
The Beggar's Opera.
Mr. Joan.
   [This performance to be presented

> by a person who has read and sung in most of the great towns in America. All the songs will be sung. He personates all the characters, and enters into the different humours, or passions, as they change from one to another throughout the opera.

Price: one-half dollar. Source: *Boston News Letter* (28 September 1769).]

29 September 1769   Southwark Theatre, Philadelphia
The Wrangling Lovers.
The Dwarfs; or, The Cascade Assignation* (Anonymous).
   Harlequin de Bergemasco–Hallam; Venetian pantaloon–Henry; Cooper–Broadbelt; Paiozo Neapolitano–"A Gentleman;" Duenna–Mrs. Douglass; Spaniolo Columbina–Miss Hallam.
American Company.
   [*The Dwarfs* is a pantomime. The notice reads as follows:

N.B. Messrs. Hallam and Henry advertised an entertainment every night this week; but the great trouble they are at in getting the machinery ready for this pantomime, has put it out of their power to fulfill that intention.

Prices: boxes 5s.; pit 3s.; gallery 2s. Source: *Pennsylvania Journal* (28 September 1769).]

30 September 1769   Southwark Theatre, Philadelphia
The Oracle.
   Oberon–Hallam; Fairy Queen–Mrs. Douglass; Cinthia (with a song in character)–Miss Hallam. Other parts by Douglass, Broadbelt, and Henry.
A Picture of a Playhouse.
The Dwarfs.
American Company.
[Source: playbill in the Shaw Theatre Collection; another copy in the Harvard Theatre Collection.]

2 October 1769   Formerly Green and Walker's Store, Boston
Love in a Village.
Mr. Joan.
   [The newspaper notice reads as follows:

This evening, the 2d of October, at a large room in Brattle-Street, formerly Green and Walker's Store, will be read, an opera, called Love in a Village, by a person who has read and sung in most of the great towns in America. All the songs will be sung. He personates all the characters, and enters into the different humours or passions as they change from one to another, throughout the opera.

Price: one-half dollar. Source: *Boston Gazette* (2 October 1769).]

5 October 1769   Philadelphia
Newspaper notice.
   [The following letter from David Douglass to the municipal authorities in Philadelphia does much to indicate the precarious nature of theatrical activities during this season:

Sir:
   The great Indulgence, your Honour has, so often, been good enough to shew me, while it demands every grateful acknowledgment, a Breast, I hope, not insensibly, can possibly entertain, covers me with shame, when the situation of our Affairs, makes so frequent Applications absolutely necessary.

I had flatter'd myself, that I should not, for a year to come, at least, have given your Honour any Trouble, but a Disappointment at Carolina, and the recent loss of a great and honour'd Friend and Patron, whose Memory will be ever dear to our American Theatre, has made such a change in our Circumstances that nothing but an Exertion of that Humanity, which you possess in so eminent a Degree, can save us from Destruction.

Let my Situation speak for me, and, with your usual Goodness, do not think me too importunate, if I sollicite your Honour for Permission to open the Theatre, for a short time, this Winter, previous to my going to Annapolis, where I propose spending the Remainder of it.

The Maid of the Mill, The Padlock, and some other Pieces, not perform'd hitherto, on this Stage, will, I flatter myself, give your Honour some Entertainment.

I shou'd not have made my Application in this Manner, but wou'd have waited on You myself, were not my feelings, upon the Occasion, too great, to permit me to say what I ought.

I shall intrude no farther upon your Time, than to assure you, that it is impossible for any Person, among the Numbers who have been the Objects of your Benevolence, to have a more grateful sense of it, than
    Sir,
        Your Honour's most
          Obedt. and oblig'd hum. Servt.
           David Douglass.

Source: original letter in the Harvard Theatre Collection; reprinted in Odell 1:152.]

5 October 1769   Vauxhall Garden, New York
A concert of music.

[Hudgson and Miss M. Storer performed various songs this evening. Source: *New York Chronicle* (28 September–5 October 1769).]

10 October 1769   Mrs. Jeffrey's, Salem, Massachusetts colony
Damon and Phillida.
Mr. Joan.
[The newspaper notice reads as follows:

This evening, being the 10th instant, at Mrs. Jeffrey's, opposite the Town-House, will be read, a Ballad Opera, call'd Damon & Phillida, by a person who has read and sung in most of the great towns in America. He personates all the characters, and enters into the different humours or passions as they change from one to another, throughout the Opera.

Source: *Essex Gazette* (3–10 October 1769).]

350   THE COLONIAL AMERICAN STAGE

12 October 1769   The New Theatre, Annapolis
Lecture on Heads.
Various professional players.
   [Benefit Mrs. and Miss Dowthwaite (recently of the Virginia Company). Also performing, Wall (American Company). Source: playbill in the Harvard Theatre Collection.]

3 November 1769   Mr. Stavers's Long Room, Portsmouth,
                    New Hampshire colony
Love in a Village.
Mr. Joan.
   [Mr. Joan's advertisement reads as follows:

   By authority, This evening, at Mr. Stavers's Long Room, will be read, an opera, call'd Love in a Village. The songs will be sung, by a person who has read and sung in most of the great towns of America. He personates all the characters, and enters into the different humours or passions, as they change from one to another throughout the opera.

   Source: *New Hampshire Gazette* (3 November 1769).]

8 November 1769   Southwark Theatre, Philadelphia
The Busy Body.
The Padlock (Isaac Bickerstaff, 1768).
American Company.
   [Source: *Pennsylvania Chronicle* (6 November 1769).]

10 November 1769   Southwark Theatre, Philadelphia
Hamlet.
The Musical Lady.
American Company.
   [Source: *Pennsylvania Gazette* (9 November 1769).]

10 November 1769   Mr. Stavers's Long Room, Portsmouth,
                    New Hampshire colony
The Conscious Lovers.
Mr. Joan.
   ["By Authority, This evening, at Mr. Stavers's Long Room, will be read, a comedy, called The Conscious Lovers...." Source: *New Hampshire Gazette* (10 November 1769).]

14 November 1769   Southwark Theatre, Philadelphia
The Gamester.
The Padlock.
American Company.
   [Source: *Pennsylvania Chronicle* (13 November 1769).]

17 November 1769   Southwark Theatre, Philadelphia
The Constant Couple.
The Padlock.
American Company.
   [Source: *Pennsylvania Gazette* (9 November 1769).]

20 November 1769   Southwark Theatre, Philadelphia
Romeo and Juliet.
   Juliet–Miss Hallam.
Love a la mode.
American Company.
   [Source: *Pennsylvania Chronicle* (20 November 1769)].

24 November 1769   Southwark Theatre, Philadelphia
Midas* (Kane O'Hara, 1762).
The Citizen.
American Company.
   [Source: *Pennsylvania Gazette* (23 November 1769).]

1 December 1769   Southwark Theatre, Philadelphia
Douglas.
Midas.
American Company.
   [Source: *Pennsylvania Gazette* (30 November 1769).]

5 December 1769   Southwark Theatre, Philadelphia
Love in a Village.
The Musical Lady.
American Company.
   [Source: *Pennsylvania Chronicle* (4 December 1769).]

8 December 1769   Southwark Theatre, Philadelphia
Cymbeline.
Midas.
American Company.
   [Source: *Pennsylvania Gazette* (7 December 1769).]

12 December 1769   Southwark Theatre, Philadelphia
The Beaux' Stratagem.
   Archer–Hallam; Dorinda–"by a young Gentlewoman, being her first appearance" (i.e., Mrs. Richardson ?); Mrs. Sullen–Mrs. Hallam.
The Padlock.
American Company.
   [Source: *Pennsylvania Chronicle* (11 December 1769).]

15 December 1769   Southwark Theatre, Philadelphia
The Beggar's Opera.
  Macheath–Hallam
Love a la mode.
American Company.
  [Source: *Pennsylvania Gazette* (14 December 1769).]

18 December 1769   Salem, New Hampshire colony
The Beggar's Opera.
Mr. Warwell.
  [A letter dated 2 January 1770 in the *New Hampshire Gazette* of 5 January 1770 reports as follows:

> Generosity and Compassion united. On Monday the 18th [i.e., of December] instant, in the evening, Mr. M. A. Warwell, Gent. read (at the Assembly Room in this Town) the Beggar's Opera, to a Number of Gentlemen and Ladies, and to universal satisfaction. His tickets amounting to £ 7-6-8 lawful Money, the whole of which he generously gave as a charity to the poor and distressed widows & orphans of this place, who are real objects of pity and commiseration.–May the above example excite others, in their several capacities, to go and do likewise.]

19 December 1769   Southwark Theatre, Philadelphia
The Siege of Damascus* (John Hughes, 1720).
Harlequin Collector.
American Company.
  [Source: *Pennsylvania Chronicle* (18 December 1769).]

22 December 1769   Southwark Theatre, Philadelphia
The Suspicious Husband.
Midas.
American Company.
  [Source: *Pennsylvania Gazette* (21 December 1769).]

26 December 1769   Southwark Theatre, Philadelphia
The Clandestine Marriage.
Love a la Mode.
American Company.
  [Source: *Pennsylvania Chronicle* (25 December 1769).]

29 December 1769   Southwark Theatre, Philadelphia
George Barnwell [i.e., *The London Merchant*].
The Witches, or Harlequin Restored.
American Company.
  [Source: *Pennsylvania Gazette* (28 December 1769).]

1770

The American Company continued this year in Philadelphia with an artistically successful, but financially disappointing, season that carried them until June 1. For four consecutive years the company had presented to the Philadelphia audiences a largely predictable rotation of plays. Beginning on 19 January 1770 the repertory suddenly underwent a sea change with the introduction of substantial new material, most notably an emphasis on musical entertainments. A highly spectacular production of *The Tempest* with new decorations and machinery ran for two weeks in late January, after which new titles advertised as "never acted in America" began to appear with some regularity, suggesting that the company was re-supplied with play scripts and machinery.

Less than two weeks after the conclusion of their Philadelphia season, the company arrived in Williamsburg where they played until the middle of August and then arranged to return for the winter season. From Williamsburg they journeyed to Annapolis for the Autumnal Provincial Court and Races, played there from late August to early October, and initiated what proved to be a very encouraging subscription to build a new theatre for the following year. The company then returned to Williamsburg, opening on 23 October playing every evening during the General Assembly.

As no substantive cast lists have survived for the Annapolis or Williamsburg engagements, we have relied upon information from the Philadelphia season to construct the company roster. The American Company is known to have consisted of the following members: Broadbelt, Byerley, David Douglass, Mrs. Douglass, Lewis Hallam, Miss Nancy Hallam, Mrs. Harman, John Henry, Mrs. Henry, Owen Morris, Charles Parker, Miss Mary Richardson, Miss Maria Storer, Mr. Tomlinson, Mrs. Tomlinson, and Thomas Wall. Stephen Woolls is not mentioned in Annapolis, but he is still assumed to be in the company. It will be noted, Charles Parker is once again with the American Company; his appearance may indicate that the New American Company is defunct, or may simply corroborate the fickle allegiances of a temperamental actor. Mary Richardson appeared incognito on 12 December 1769, and joined the company shortly thereafter. Richard Goodman was the name of the young gentleman who appeared on 1 June 1770, the closing day of the Philadelphia season. Wright

(53–54) tells us Goodman was a law student who ran away with the company.

Convention has it that the Verling Company had succumbed to debt and disbanded after the spring of 1769. Surveying the many legal claims for debt recovery against the actors, Rankin (151–54), for example, concludes that the company had cautiously dropped out of sight. This interpretation may well be the case. Nonetheless, two nagging pieces of evidence should be considered before we dismiss Verling's persistent company in Virginia: (1) George Washington purchased four play tickets in Williamsburg on 24 May 1770. Rankin (154) posits that these are advance tickets for the American Company (who arrived in mid June), but he also claims that Washington never used them, instead purchasing additional tickets on four other occasions during the first week of the company's engagement. To be sure, Washington records in his diary for 24 May that he "spent the Evening in my own Room," but this entry does not rule out an afternoon performance. (2) Jefferson's *Memorandum Book* records an entry for 16 April 1770 (1:203): "At Play house 7/6." The corroboration of Jefferson's single entry seems to confirm the presence of commercial entertainment of some nature, and as this cannot be the American Company, the probably surmise is that the Virginia Company reassembled for the spring Court season, though the engagement was short lived. Washington did not return to the theatre until the American Company arrived in mid June, and his diary for late May and early June records a monotonous entry: "Spent the Evening in my own Room" (*Diaries*, 2:238–39, 245–46). Rankin's speculation may still be the most sound conclusion, though what Jefferson saw remains a mystery. As noted below, Verling's Company moved on to St. Croix, Danish West Indies, later in 1770.

Jefferson was again in Williamsburg by 6 October, but, since he leaves no record of theatre attendance before 23 October, and attended extensively thereafter (13 times in 15 playing days), we suggest that the American Company did not open until Tuesday, 23 October. Jefferson's *Memorandum Books*—from which his attendance is extracted—also confirm what the usual schedule of performances during the Court sessions, probably since the Hallams played Williamsburg in 1752: the better companies played six nights a week, Monday through Saturday.[16]

The Theatre in Halifax apparently once again found intermittent use. References to "strollers" and admonitions against encouraging players periodically appear in the pages of the *Nova Scotia Gazette* in 1770, suggesting the possible revisit by a company such as Mills's, but no playbills have survived.

Mr. Joan again performed his solo versions of plays and ballad operas, primarily in Boston (see March entries).

Information about two new companies playing a lower Caribbean touring circuit comes to light this year from the pages of a St. Croix newspaper, serving the Leeward islands of St. Croix, St. Thomas, and St. John. When Daniel Thibou began the *Royal Danish American Gazette* on 7 July 1770, the first theatrical advertisement is for the Leeward Island Company of Comedians. They are playing at the Bass-End Theatre, on Queen street in Christiansted, St. Croix, and apparently performances on the island were already a long established tradition. For example, the Bass-End Theatre is never referred to as the "New Theatre," as is generally the case with subscription seasonal playhouses, nor is the second theatre, "The theatre" in Fredericksted, across the island. With the appearance of the *Gazette* in the summer of 1770 we slice into the story when a large company of familiar names have just opened their fall season.

What a refreshing surprise to discover definitive evidence of the island circuit we had long suspected, sweetened by the bonus of the appearance of so many familiar names playing the islands. It seems all the disgruntled players who dropped out of the American Company found solace in a company of their own. From the preserved newspaper bills the Leeward Islands Company of Comedians contained the following personnel: Mr. Hill, manager; Edward Bullock, Mr. Samuel Darby, Mrs. Darby, John Davies, Mrs. Giffard, Jonathan Godman, John

---

[16] See Johnson, "Thomas Jefferson and the Colonial American Stage." In 1752 George Gilmer wrote in a letter to Walter King that "when Court was in session, they played practically every night ... [while] at other times, they performed three evenings a week" (Gilmer Letter Book, 1752; quoted in Land 48). Cf. "Original Letters," 240–41.

Gray, Miss Guy, Mr. Harris, George Hughes, Thomas Jones, John Kirwan, J. Frederich Linck, Patrick Malone, Mrs. Margaret Malone (non-acting), Charles Parker, Mrs. Parker, Jane Taylor, William Verling, Mr. White. Some of the names (Edward Bullock, John Gray John Kirwan) were likely locals added to the company when dissension split the roster into two competing companies later in the season.

So this is what became of our old friends William Verling and the Virginia Company, last seen strapped for debts in Virginia and Annapolis in 1769: Mr. and Mrs. Parker, Patrick Malone and his wife Margaret, Samuel Darby and his wife, all worked with and left the American Company in 1769 to throw in with Verling. Mrs. Giffard, it will also be remembered, was last seen in Mill's Company in Halifax, Nova Scotia, in December of 1768. No record survives of her husband.

Thus we now can demonstrate that Verling took his company to the islands sometime after the summer of 1769, and for at least the of 1770, merged it with Mr. Hill, who was managing a small company already established at the Bass-End Theatre, St. Croix, Danish West Indies. This joint ensemble opened in perhaps late June or early July 1770 and presented a healthy repertory of Shakespearian titles with a strong—if not contentious—company. They advertised twice a week, but also printed bills of the day, so they were playing perhaps three or four nights in this small island community from July until the end of the year.

Problems however appear with the commencement of the benefit season around the start of October. The first charity evening was announced for September 27, "For the benefit of the Church, the Hospital, and the Poor," and Hill spoke the prologue drafted for the occasion. Then came trouble. George Hughes, as he was the lead actor in Hill's company, received the first actor benefit. No second benefit was announced. Instead, *Romeo and Juliet* was advertised for the next performance on 4 October, with no notice of a benefit accompanying the bill, but the play was never performed. Verling carried off the lion's share of the company—maybe the players with whom he had arrived—and set up production across the island at the theatre in Fredericksted.

Perhaps we could surmise that William Verling took some exception to the ordering of the benefits, as he was accustomed to receiving the first benefit in his own company (see

Williamsburg 1768). Thus piqued at the slight, he carried his actors across the island, titled themselves the West-End Company of Comedians, and immediately began performing at "The Theatre" in Fredericksted.

The personnel of this new company may have been largely the same ensemble Verling had brought to the island: himself, Mr. and Mrs. Darby, Mr. and Mrs. Parker, Miss Guy, Mr. White, Jonathan Godman, Thomas Jones, and Mr. Harris, leaving Mr. Hill with his lead, George Hughes, Patrick Malone and his wife, Mrs. Giffard, John Davies, Jane Taylor, and locals Edward Bullock, John Gray, John Kirwan. Curiously, a dancer and Harlequin, J. Frederich Linck, originally in the Hill Company, quickly broke allegiance and also followed Verling. A rivalry began between the two houses, with Verling clearly dominating the field at the fragile time of benefits. Hill's company was sorely disadvantaged in respect to talent, and created an additional obstacle by offending the printer Daniel Tiboux during the fracas (see entry for 5 October). The Leeward Company struggled through the benefits while Verling's Company offered solid productions (e.g., *The Beggar's Opera*), often on the same nights. Hill's misfortunes were compounded by the lengthy illness ("indisposition") of his new lead performer, Mrs. Giffard, and received the finishing blow with the passing of Patrick Malone in mid November.

In the fashion of *Romeo and Juliet*, the show that split the two houses, it was the death of Malone that brought the feud to an end. A benefit for Mrs. Malone featured actors from both companies, as did a second benefit to defray Malone's funeral costs. Joint performances resumed, sometimes at Bass-End, sometimes in the West-End, until 31 December, when Verling took (a second?) benefit "to defray the expenses of his debts." Sometime after the first of the year (1771) most of the actors left the island, but not all. Mr. Hill remained, as did Mrs. Giffard, Mr. Linck, and enough of a company to continue to perform occasionally into January. Though some of the names associated with the company may have been local—Linck opened a dance school in St. Croix, while Mrs. Giffard and Mrs. Malone certainly remained after Verling's Company departed—Hill's troupe most certainly should be defined as a professional traveling company, even though they worked only a small circuit (for example, leading actor George Hughes is attacked in the paper as a "Stroller"). Whatever their status, this eventful season on the islands featured rival productions from competing companies.

***

2 January 1770   Southwark Theatre, Philadelphia
King John.
The Padlock.
American Company.

[Source: *Pennsylvania Chronicle* (25 December–1 January 1770).]

5 January 1770   Southwark Theatre, Philadelphia
The Maid of the Mill.
The King and the Miller of Mansfield.
American Company.

[Source: *Pennsylvania Gazette* (4 January 1770).]

9 January 1770   Southwark Theatre, Philadelphia
The Orphan.
Flora.
American Company.

[Source: *Pennsylvania Chronicle* (1–8 January 1770).]

12 January 1770   Southwark Theatre, Philadelphia
The Maid of the Mill.
The Witches, or Harlequin Restored.
American Company.

[Source: *Pennsylvania Gazette* (11 January 1770).]

18 January 1770   Southwark Theatre, Philadelphia
Newspaper notice.
American Company.

[The *Pennsylvania Journal* for this date contains the following item suggesting that the season had not been going well:

> Theatrical Intelligence. The Tempest is to be acted to-morrow, written by Shakespeare, and alter'd by Dryden: It is one of those plays, in which the poet of nature has given an unbounded scope to his creative imagination; he has not only form'd beings of a different species to mankind, but endow'd them with faculties adapted to their characters—The scenery, machinery, and decorations for this representation, we are inform'd, have been prepared at a very great expence, and from the general impatience among all ranks of people for its performance, it is imagined there will be a crowded audience: A splendid appearance at the theatre to-morrow, will not only reflect honour on our taste, by patronizing one of the chief d'ouvres of that

immortal genius, but be some compensation to the players, for their bad success this season.]

19 January 1770   Southwark Theatre, Philadelphia
The Tempest* (Shakespeare-Dryden).
Neptune and Amphitrite* (Anonymous).
American Company.
   [Source: *Pennsylvania Gazette* (18 January 1770).]

23 January 1770   Southwark Theatre, Philadelphia
The Tempest.
Neptune and Amphitrite.
The Mayor of Garratt.
American Company.
   [Source: *Pennsylvania Chronicle* (15–22 January 1770).]

29 January 1770   Southwark Theatre, Philadelphia
The Tempest.
Neptune and Amphitrite.
The Mayor of Garratt.
American Company.
   [The mainpiece "with additions and alterations." Source: *Pennsylvania Gazette* (25 January 1770).]

2 February 1770   Southwark Theatre, Philadelphia
The Tempest.
The Padlock.
American Company.
   [Pollock adds *Neptune and Amphitrite.* Source: *Pennsylvania Gazette* (1 February 1770).]

6 February 1770   Southwark Theatre, Philadelphia
Edward the Black Prince* (William Shirley, 1749).
The Citizen.
American Company.
   [Mainpiece advertised as "Never acted in America." Source: *Pennsylvania Chronicle* (5 February 1770).]

9 February 1770   Southwark Theatre, Philadelphia
The Funeral, or Grief a la Mode* (Richard Steele, 1701)
Damon and Phillida.
American Company.
   [Mainpiece advertised as "Never acted in America." Source: *Pennsylvania Journal* (8 February 1770).]

16 February 1770   Southwark Theatre, Philadelphia
The Orphan of China.
The Upholsterer.
American Company.
   [Mainpiece advertised as "not acted these three years." Source: *Pennsylvania Gazette* (15 February 1770).]

19 February 1770   Southwark Theatre, Philadelphia
The Funeral.
The Upholsterer.
American Company.
   ["Mr. Douglass will be extremely obliged to any lady or gentleman who will lend him the burlesque opera of the Dragon of Wantley." Source: *Pennsylvania Chronicle* (12–19 February 1770).]

2 March 1770   Southwark Theatre, Philadelphia
The Merry Wives of Windsor* (William Shakespeare).
High Life Below Stairs.
American Company.
   [Mainpiece advertised as "the second night." Dunlap (29) records that in 1754 when Patrick Malone traveled to Philadelphia to join the Hallam Company, he apparently had a role in *The Merry Wives*, though no record exists of performance of the play from that era. Source: *Pennsylvania Journal* (1 March 1770).]

5 March 1770   Southwark Theatre, Philadelphia
The Tempest.
Neptune and Amphitrite.
The Padlock.
American Company.
   [Source: *Pennsylvania Chronicle* (26 February–5 March 1770).]

9 March 1770   Southwark Theatre, Philadelphia
Comus* (Milton; John Dalton's adaptation, 1738).
Edgar and Emmeline* (John Hawkesworth, 1761).
American Company.
   [Both plays advertised as "never acted in America .... The orchestra to be conducted by Mr. Hallam." Source: *Pennsylvania Journal* (9 March 1770).]

12 March 1770   Southwark Theatre, Philadelphia
Edward, the Black Prince.

Edgar and Emmeline.
American Company.
   [Source: *Pennsylvania Chronicle* (5–12 March 1770).]

16 March 1770   Southwark Theatre, Philadelphia
The Revenge.
The Witches, or Harlequin Restored.
American Company.
   [Source: *Pennsylvania Journal* (15 March 1770).]

20 March 1770   Southwark Theatre, Philadelphia
The Tempest.
Neptune and Amphitrite.
The Devil to Pay.
   Jobson–Hallam; Nell–Miss Hallam.
American Company.
   [*Neptune and Amphitrite* advertised as "the sixth night." Source: *Pennsylvania Chronicle* (12–19 March 1770).]

21 March 1770   Stuart Hall, Boston
The Provoked Husband.
Mr. Joan.
   [Vanbrugh's play is very likely performed by the same person advertised on 23 March 1770 as having "read and sung in most of the great towns in America," who has been identified as one Mr. Joan. Source: *Proceedings of the Massachusetts Historical Society*, 10:28.]

22 March 1770   Southwark Theatre, Philadelphia
The Beaux' Stratagem.
Edgar and Emmeline.
American Company.
   [Source: *Pennsylvania Gazette* (22 March 1770).]

23 March 1770   Concert Hall, Boston
The Beggar's Opera.
Mr. Joan.
   [The play to be performed

   by a person who has read and sung in most of the great towns in America. The songs (of which there are sixty-nine,) will be sung. He personates all the characters, and enters into the different humours, or passions, as they change from one to another throughout the opera.

Price: a half-dollar. Joan's identity is made in the diary of John Rowe, quoted in Bonawitz 18. Rowe also reports "upwards of 100 people there." Source: *Boston News Letter* (23 March 1770); *Proceedings of the Massachusetts Historical Society,* 10:28.]

30 March 1770   Concert Hall, Boston.
The Reprisal.
Damon and Phillida.
Mr. Joan.
   [This performance was advertised as follows:

> To-morrow evening, (being Friday 30th March,) at Concert-Hall, will be read, A Comedy call'd The Reprisal, or the Tars of Old-England: To which will be added, an opera called Damon and Phillida; besides the songs incident to the Opera, will be sung, A Hymn to the Moon, from the opera of Cynthia, and Infancy, from Artaxerxes, accompanied with instrumental musick.

The mainpiece is advertised as "Never Acted there," and the afterpiece as "Not Performed this Season." Source: *Boston News Letter* (29 March 1770).]

30 March 1770   Southwark Theatre, Philadelphia
The Tender Husband.
   Humphrey Gubbin–Hallam; Sir Harry Gubbin–Douglass; Mr. Cleremont–Henry; Capt. Cleremont–Byerley; Mr. Tipkin–Morris; Mr. Pounce–Wall; The Niece–Miss Hallam; Aunt–Mrs. Tomlinson; Fainlove–Mrs. Harman; Jenny–Miss Richardson; Mrs. Cleremont–Mrs. Henry.
Miss in Her Teens.
   Puff–Mr. Morris; Capt. Flash–Henry; Capt. Lovet–Parker; Fribble–Miss Storer; Tag–Mrs. Henry; Jasper–(torn off); Miss Biddy–(torn off).
American Company.
   [Benefit Miss Storer. Source: *Pennsylvania Gazette* (29 March 1770); playbill in the Historical Society of Pennsylvania.]

2 April 1770   Southwark Theatre, Philadelphia
The Fair Penitent.
Harlequin Collector.
American Company.
   [Benefit Mrs. Henry. Announced but not performed. Source: *Pennsylvania Chronicle* (26 March–2 April 1770).]

5 April 1770   Southwark Theatre, Philadelphia
The Fair Penitent.
Harlequin Collector.

Harlequin–Henry, "in which character he will run up a perpendicular scene 20 feet high."
American Company.

[Benefit Mrs. Henry. Afterpiece advertised as "with additions and alterations." Source: *Pennsylvania Journal* (5 April 1770).]

16 April 1770   Southwark Theatre, Philadelphia
Alexander the Great.
Thomas and Sally.
American Company.

[Benefit Mrs. Harman. Source: *Pennsylvania Chronicle* (9–16 April 1770).]

16 April 1770   Williamsburg, Virginia colony
Play not identified.
Virginia Company?

[Thomas Jefferson attended this performance and paid 7s. 6d. for tickets. Source: Jefferson, *Memorandum Books*, 1:203]

20 April 1770   Southwark Theatre, Philadelphia
Jane Shore.
The Padlock.
American Company.

[Benefit Miss Hallam. Afterpiece advertised as "the tenth night." Source: *Pennsylvania Journal* (19 April 1770).]

23 April 1770   Philadelphia
Holiday news.
American Company.

[A letter from Alexander Mackaby to his brother, dated 24 April 1770, details a St. George's Day holiday:

> Would you think that in a city of twenty thousand inhabitants we should find difficulty in collecting twenty native Englishmen to celebrate St. George's Day yesterday? And in that number there were some I had never spoken to before. We should have had the governor at our head, but that the party was only proposed two days before. However, we met at a tavern, stuffed roast beef and plum pudding, and got drunk, *pour l'honneur de St. George*; wore crosses, and finished the evening at the play-house, where we made the people all chorous 'God Save the King', and 'Rule Britannia,' and 'Britains Strike Home' &c., and such like nonsense; and in short, conducted ourselves with all the decency and confusion usual on such occasions.

Source: Mackaby, "Extracts from the letters," 493.]

27 April 1770   Southwark Theatre, Philadelphia
The Good-Natured Man* (Oliver Goldsmith, 1768).
The Devil to Pay.
American Company.

[Benefit Morris. Source: *Pennsylvania Gazette* (26 April 1770).]

3 May 1770   Southwark Theatre, Philadelphia
The Good-Natured Man.
Catherine and Petruchio.
American Company.

[Benefit Tomlinson. Source: *Pennsylvania Gazette* (3 May 1770).]

10 May 1770   Southwark Theatre, Philadelphia
Love for Love.
Wit's Last Stake* (Thomas King, 1768).
American Company.

[Benefit Mrs. Douglass. Afterpiece advertised as "never acted in America." The notice for this evening adds the following caveat:

> The Comedies of Congreve, though replete with wit and humour, have been censured for a levity, incompatible with that purity of manners, which is essentially necessary to render the entertainments of the theatre, subservient to the great and useful purposes, for which it was first instituted; and for which, the drama has been countenanced and protected by the good and wise, in all ages, and in all countries, where the beams of science have dissipated the clouds of ignorance, or where the gloom of superstition and intolerance, has not absorbed every generous sentiment, extinguished every impulse of genuine benevolence—After this remark, it will be, perhaps, superfluous to assure the public, that no line in this play, offensive to delicacy, will appear in the representation—the beauties of the author are preserved, his blemishes expunged.

Source: *Pennsylvania Gazette* (10 May 1770).]

17 May 1770   Southwark Theatre, Philadelphia
Love and a Bottle; The Wild Irishman* (George Farquhar, 1698).
High Life Below Stairs.
American Company.

[Benefit Henry, Mrs. Henry, and Miss [Maria] Storer. Source: *Pennsylvania Journal* (17 May 1770).]

18 May 1770   Concert Hall, Boston
Love in the City* (Isaac Bickerstaffe, 1767).
Mr. Joan?
   [This performance is a "Vocal Entertainment, of three acts. The songs are taken from a celebrated opera, called Love in the City." Source: *Boston News Letter* (17 May 1770).]

24 May 1770   Southwark Theatre, Philadelphia
Cymbeline.
The Guardian.
American Company.
   [Benefit Parker and Broadbelt. Source: *Pennsylvania Journal* (24 May 1770).]

24 May 1770   The Old Theatre, Williamsburg
Journal entry.
Virginia Company?
   [George Washington records in his Cash Accounts that he purchased "By 4 Play Tickets 30/." Rankin (154) assumes that these are advance tickets for the impending American Company visit to Williamsburg, but see an alternative argument for the presence of the Virginia Company in the headnote to this season. Source: Washington, *Papers*, 8:329.]

1 June 1770   Southwark Theatre, Philadelphia
Julius Caesar* (William Shakespeare).
American Company.
   Mark Antony–"by a young gentleman, being his first appearance on any stage."
Harlequin Collector, or, The Miller Deceived.
   Harlequin–Hallam, "being his last appearance in that character in America."
American Company.
   [The "young gentleman" is Goodman. In the afterpiece "will be introduc'd (instead of the skeleton scene) the statue scene from Harlequin Restor'd." This evening advertised as "The last play positively." Source: *Pennsylvania Journal* (31 May 1770).]

2 June 1770   Philadelphia
Correspondence.
American Company.
   [On this date David Douglass wrote to William Bradford, printer, regarding certain financial matters:

   Dear Sir: Mr. Byerley informs me, that you desired Hugh James not to send the money for the sale of last Night's tickets, until you drew out an [account?] against us. You are no Stranger to our very bad success this season, and as I am oblig'd to carry the Company away directly to Williamsburg, that I may not lose the June Court, and am much [streched?] for money, you will very highly oblige me, if you will only deduct the bills [?] for the play out of it, and permit him to send me the Balance. We are getting very [fast?] through our difficulties, and I hope in a short time to settle your whole [account?] By committing to this you'll confer a great favor on , sir, your obliged , D. Douglass

Source: Bradford Correspondence, 1770.]

14 June 1770   The Old Theatre, Williamsburg
Newspaper notice.
American Company.

[The *Virginia Gazette* of this date contains the following notice:

Yesterday Mr. Douglass, with his Company of Comedians, arrived in town from Philadelphia; and, we hear, intend opening the theatre in this city, on Saturday, with the Beggar's Opera, and other entertainments.]

16 June 1770   The Old Theatre, Williamsburg
The Beggar's Opera.
American Company.

[This evening was probably the opening night of the season. George Washington notes in his *Diary* that he attended this performance. Thomas Jefferson also attended and spent 5s. for tickets (*Memorandum Books*, 1:205). Source: Washington, *Diaries*, 2:247; *Virginia Gazette* (14 June 1770).]

18 June 1770   Concert Hall, Boston.
Lionel and Clarissa* (Isaac Bickerstaffe, 1768).
Mr. Joan?

[This performance is "a vocal entertainment, of three acts. The songs (which are numerous) are taken from a new, celebrated opera, call'd Lionel and Clarissa." Source: *Boston Evening Post* (18 June 1770).]

18 June 1770   The Old Theatre, Williamsburg
Play not identified.
American Company.

[George Washington attended this performance, as he records in the following entry in his diary (*Diaries* 2:247): "Came into Williamsburg in the Morning. Dined at the Club and went to the Play in the Afternoon." Thomas Jefferson also attended this performance and paid 5s. for tickets. Source: Jefferson, *Memorandum Books*, 1:205]

19 June 1770   The Old Theatre, Williamsburg
Play not identified.
American Company.
   [George Washington records in his *Diary* that he attended a play on this date. Thomas Jefferson was also present and spent 5s. for tickets (*Memorandum Books*, 1:205). Source: Washington, *Diaries*, 2:247.]

20 June 1770   The Old Theatre, Williamsburg
The Clandestine Marriage.
   Ogleby–Hallam; Melvil–Byerley; Lovewell–Parker; Sterling–Morris; Flower–Douglass; Brush–Henry; Canton–Mrs. Harman; Traverse–Roberts; Truman–Woolls; Mrs. Heidelberg–Mrs. Douglass; Fanny–Miss Richardson; Betty–Mrs. Henry; Chambermaid–Mrs. Hallam; Miss Sterling–Miss Hallam.
Thomas and Sally.
   Squire–Woolls; Sailor–Henry; Dorcas–Mrs. Harman; Sally–Miss Hallam.
American Company.
   [Prices: boxes–7s. 6d.; pit and gallery–5s. Thomas Jefferson attended this performance and paid 5s. for tickets (Jefferson, *Memorandum Books*, 1:205). Also George Washington records in his *Diary* that he attended a play on this date. Source: Washington, *Diaries*, 2:248; playbill in the Colonial Williamsburg Foundation.]

20 June 1770   Philadelphia
American Company.
   [A letter from Alexander Mackaby to his brother, dated 20 June 1770, refers to an incident during the American Company's earlier engagement in Philadelphia:

> I believe I have never told you that we have got Whitefield among us. He preaches like a dragon, curses and blesses us all in a breath, and tells us he hopes to die in the pulpit. He abuses the players, who in turn advertised to perform *The Minor*. The parsons petitioned the Governor against it, and the performance was dropt.

Source: Mackaby, "Extracts from the letters," 494.]

21 June 1770   The Old Theatre, Williamsburg
Play not identified.
American Company.

[Thomas Jefferson attended this performance and paid 27s. 6d. for tickets. Source: Jefferson, *Memorandum Books*, 1:205]

22 June 1770   The Old Theatre, Williamsburg
Play not identified.
American Company.
   [George Washington records in his *Diary* that he attended a play on this date. Source: Washington, *Diaries*, 2:248.]

23 June 1770   The Old Theatre, Williamsburg
Play not identified.
American Company.
   [Thomas Jefferson attended this performance and paid 20s. for tickets. Source: Jefferson, *Memorandum Books*, 1:205]

25 June 1770   The Old Theatre, Williamsburg
Play not identified.
American Company.
   [Thomas Jefferson attended this performance and paid 20s. for tickets. Source: Jefferson, *Memorandum Books*, 1:205]

27 June 1770   The Old Theatre, Williamsburg
Play not identified.
American Company.
   [Thomas Jefferson attended this performance and paid 22s. 6d. for tickets. Source: Jefferson, *Memorandum Books*, 1:205]

28 June 1770   The Old Theatre, Williamsburg
Play not identified.
American Company.
   [Thomas Jefferson attended this performance and paid 5s. 1½d. for tickets. Source: Jefferson, *Memorandum Books*, 1:205]

9 July 1770   Bass-End Theatre, Christiansted, St. Croix
The Beaux' Stratagem.
The Mock Doctor.
Leeward Islands Company.
   ["Tickets (as no cash will be received at the Door) to be had at the Printing-office in Queen Street, at the Taverns, and of Mr. Smith near the Theatre, at Twelve Shillings each." Source: *Royal Danish American Gazette* (7 July 1770).]

12 July 1770   Bass-End Theatre, Christiansted, St. Croix
The Beaux Stratagem.

The Mock Doctor.
Leeward Island company.
   [Source: *Royal Danish American Gazette* (11 July 1770).]

16 July 1770   Bass-End Theatre, Christiansted, St. Croix
The Fair Penitent.
Virgin Unmasked.
Leeward Islands Company.
   [Source: *Royal Danish American Gazette* (14 July 1770).]

18 July 1770   Bass-End Theatre, Christiansted, St. Croix
The Recruiting Officer.
The Wonder, An Honest Yorkshireman!
Leeward Islands Company.
   [Source: *Royal Danish American Gazette* (18 July 1770).]

23 July 1770   Bass-End Theatre, Christiansted, St. Croix
Richard III.
The King and the Miller of Mansfield.
Leeward Islands Company.
   ["N.B. No person can be admitted behind the scenes; nor any Negroe whatever in the House. It has been disagreeable to several Ladies; therefore the manager hopes no person will be offended, as it will render the Theatre more comfortable to the Ladies and Gentlemen who honour it with their appearance. Vivant Rex and Regina." Source: *Royal Danish American Gazette* (21 July 1770).]

26 July 1770   Bass-End Theatre, Christiansted, St. Croix
A Bold Stroke for a Wife.
The Citizen.
Leeward Islands Company.
   [Source: *Royal Danish American Gazette* (25 July 1770).]

30 July 1770   Bass-End Theatre, Christiansted, St. Croix
The London Merchant.
Flora, or Hob in the Well.
Leeward Islands Company.
   [Ticket price: twelve shillings. No boxes. Source: *Royal Danish American Gazette* (28 July 1770).]

2 August 1770   Bass-End Theatre, Christiansted, St. Croix
The Inconstant; or, the Way to Win Him.
The Reprisal; or, Tars of Old England.

Leeward Islands Company.
   [Source: *Royal Danish American Gazette* (1 August 1770).]

6 August 1770   Bass-End Theatre, Christiansted, St. Croix

Romeo and Juliet.
   Romeo–Verling; Juliet–Mrs. Taylor, being her first appearance upon this stage.
Miss in Her Teens.
Leeward Islands Company.
   [The tragedy to be performed "with funeral procession."
Source: *Royal Danish American Gazette* (4 August 1770).]

9 August 1770   Bass-End Theatre, Christiansted, St. Croix

Jane Shore.
The Lying Valet.
   [Source: *Royal Danish American Gazette* [8 August 1770].]

13 August 1770   Bass-End Theatre, Christiansted, St. Croix

The Inconstant.
The Reprisal.
Leeward Island Company.
   [Source: *Royal Danish American Gazette* (11 August 1770).]

16 August 1770   Bass-End Theatre, Christiansted, St. Croix

The Beaux' Strategem.
The Citizen.
Leeward Island Company.
   [Source: *Royal Danish American Gazette* (15 August .]

20 August 1770   Bass-End Theatre, Christiansted, St. Croix

The Beggar's Opera.
   ["A hornpipe in Act 3d, by Mr. Malone." Source: *Royal Danish American Gazette* (18 August 1770).]

23 August 1770   Bass-End Theatre, Christiansted, St. Croix

Hamlet.
Damon and Phillida.
Leeward Islands Company.
   [Source: *Royal Danish American Gazette* (22 August 1770).]

24 August 1770 the House of Peter Pentheny, St. Croix Island
The Lecture on Heads.
 Lecture–Verling; Prologue–Parker; End of Part i, a song–Mrs. Parker; End of Part ii, a hornpipe–Malone.
Miss in her Teens.
Leeward Islands Company.
 ["To conclude with a comic Dance, 'The Drunken Peasant.'"
Source: *Royal Danish American Gazette* (22 August 1770).]

27 August 1770 Bass-End Theatre, Christiansted, St. Croix
Hamlet.
The Virgin Unmasked.
Leeward Islands Company.
 ["N.B. This play was deferred on Thursday last on account of the indisposition of Mr. Hill." Source: *Royal Danish American Gazette* (25 August 1770).]

27 August 1770 The New Theatre, Annapolis
The Suspicious Husband.
Thomas and Sally.
American Company.
 [Source: *Maryland Gazette* (30 August 1770).]

30 August 1770 Bass-End Theatre, Christiansted, St. Croix
The Orphan.
 Castalio–Verling; Chamont–Hill.
Damon and Phillida
Leeward Islands Company.
 [Source: *Royal Danish American Gazette* (29 August 1770).]

30 August 1770 The New Theatre, Annapolis
Cymbeline.
 Imogen–Miss Hallam; other parts by Mrs. Harman, Mrs. Douglass, and Miss Storer.
The King and the Miller of Mansfield.
American Company.
 ["The company's engagement in Virginia will prevent them from performing here any longer than the end of next month." Source: *Maryland Gazette* (30 August 1770).
 A lengthy review of this performance appears in the *Maryland Gazette* of 6 September 1770:

I shall not, at present, expatiate on the merits of the whole performance, but confine myself principally to one object. The actors are, indubitably, intitled to a very considerable portion of praise. But, by your leave, gentlemen (to speak the language of Hamlet), here's metal more attractive. On finding that the part of Imogen was to be played by Miss Hallam, I instantly formed to myself, from my predilection for her, the most sanguine hope of entertainment. But how was I ravished on experiment! She exceeded my utmost idea. Such delicacy of manner! Such classical strictness of expression! The musick of her tongue! The Vox Liquida, how melting! Notwithstanding the injuries it received from the horrid ruggedness of the roof, and the untoward construction of the whole house; methought I heard once more the warbling of Cibber in my ear. How true and thorough her knowledge of the character she personated! Her whole form and dimensions how happily convertible, and universally adapted to the variety of her part. A friend of mine, who was present, was so deeply impressed by the bewitching grace and justness with which the actress filled the whole character, that, immediately on going home, he threw out warm from the heart, as well as brain, the verses which I inclose you.

The house, however, was thin, I suppose for want of a sufficient acquaintance with the general, as well as particular merits of the performers. The characteristical propriety of Mrs. Douglass cannot but be too striking to pass unnoticed. The fine genius of that young creature, Miss Storer unquestionably affords the most pleasing prospect of an accomplished actress. The discerning part of an audience must cheerfully pay the tribute of applause due to the solid sense which is conspicuous in Mrs. Harman, as well as to her perspicuity and strength of memory.

The sums lavished on a late set, whose merits were not of the transcendent kind, in whatever point of light they are viewed, are still fresh in our memories. And should these, their successors, whose deportment, decency, and an unremitting study to please, have ever confessedly marked, meet with discountenance, methinks such a conduct would not reflect the highest honour either on our taste or spirit. The merit of Mr. Douglass's company is, notoriously, in the opinion of every man of sense in America, whose opportunities give him a title to judge–take them for all in all–superior to that of any company in England, except those of the Metropolis. The dresses are remarkably elegant; the dispatch of the business of the theatre uncommonly quick; and the stillness and good order preserved behind the scenes, are proofs of the greatest attention and respect paid to the audience. Y.Z.]

1 September 1770   The New Theatre, Annapolis
Love in a Village.
American Company.
   [Source: *Maryland Gazette* (30 August 1770).]

3 September 1770   Bass-End Theatre, Christiansted, St. Croix
Douglas.

The Old Maid.
Leeward Islands Company.
   [Source: *Royal Danish American Gazette* (1 September 1770).]

8 September 1770   Bass-End Theatre, Christiansted, St. Croix

1 Henry IV.
   Falstaff–Verling; Comic Dance–Malone.
The Mock Doctor.
Leeward Islands Company.
   [Source: *Royal Danish American Gazette* (5 September 1770).]

10 September 1770   Bass-End Theatre, Christiansted, St. Croix

Richard III.
Leeward Island Company.
   ["With amusements, as will be expres'd in the Bills of the Day." Source: *Royal Danish American Gazette* (8 September 1770).]

13 September 1770   Bass-End Theatre, Christiansted, St. Croix

The Revenge.
Harlequin Triumphant; or, The Burgomaster Trick'd.
Leeward Islands Company.
   ["With machinery, dresses, and Dances, incident to the Piece." Source: *Royal Danish American Gazette* (12 September 1770).]

17 September 1770   Bass-End Theatre, Christiansted, St. Croix

King Lear.
   End of 3d Act, a Comick Dance called "The School-Master's Ballet"–Linck, Malone, and others.
Harlequin Triumphant.
Leeward Islands Company.
   [Source: *Royal Danish American Gazette* (15 September 1770).]

24 September 1770   Bass-End Theatre, Christiansted, St. Croix

Romeo and Juliet.
The Cheats of Scapin* (anonymous).

Leeward Islands Company.

["Ladies and Gentlemen having any Tickets by them, are requested to make use of them at this Play, as they cannot be received at the Benefits." Source: *Royal Danish American Gazette* (22 September 1770).]

27 September 1770   Bass-End Theatre, Christiansted, St. Croix

The Orphan.
   Occasional prologue–Hill.
The Mock Doctor.
Leeward Islands Company.

["For the benefit of the Church, the Hospital, and the Poor." Source: *Royal Danish American Gazette* (26 September 1770).]

late September 1770   The New Theatre, Annapolis
Newspaper notice.
American Company.

[That plays were being presented during the latter part of this month is suggested by the following item in the *Maryland Gazette* of 4 October 1770: "Left at the Play-House last week, or taken from Mr. Joshua Frazer's by mistake, a new frize drab great coat."]

1 October 1770   Bass-End Theatre, Christiansted, St. Croix

The Gamester.
The Brave Irishman.
Leeward Islands Company.

[Benefit for Hughes. Source: *Royal Danish American Gazette* (29 September 1770).]

4 October 1770   Bass-End Theatre, Christiansted, St. Croix

Romeo and Juliet.
Flora; or, Hob in the Well.
Leeward Islands Company.

[Source: *Royal Danish American Gazette* (3 October 1770).]

4 October 1770   Annapolis
Proposal to erect theatre.
American Company.

[A lengthy notice of a proposal by Douglass to erect a theatre in Annapolis is published in the *Maryland Gazette* of this date:

Annapolis, October 1, 1770. A well regulated Theatre has been allowed by men of liberal sentiments, in all ages, and in all countries, where the polite arts have been cherished, to be a noble institution; calculated, according to Addison, for the improvement and refinement of human society; to be the most rational entertainment an enlarged mind can enjoy; and of the utmost utility to the Commonwealth, by polishing the manners, and forming the taste of the people.

The encouragement that the ladies and gentlemen of Maryland have always given to theatrical representations, and the approbation that has attended the performances of the American Company, though under every disadvantage from the situation, size, and aukward construction of the House, induce Mr. Douglass to imagine, that if a commodious theatre was erected in a convenient part of the city of Annapolis, a decent company, and he flatters himself his friends are not too partial when they pronounce the present to be such, might, for about six weeks every year, including the Autumnal Provincial Court and Races, be resorted to by sufficient audiences, to stimulate them to a grateful exertion of their faculties for the entertainment of the publick, whose favours this season they acknowledge to have been infinitely superior to their expectations.

But as the expenses of building a Theatre would be more than the company could possibly pay out of the receipts of one season, after deducting the incidental nightly charge, and allowing the performers a moderate support; Mr. Douglass, urged by a number of his friends, begs leave to solicit the assistance of the publick to a scheme, which will enable him effectually to carry the design into execution, and at the same time will not be disadvantageous to the ladies and gentlemen, whose publick spirit, and taste for the rational entertainments of the stage, may lead them to patronise the undertaking. It is proposed, then, to deliver to any lady or gentleman, subscribing five pounds or upwards, the value of their respective sums in tickets; one half of which will be admitted the first season, and the remainder the season following; the money to be deposited with William Paca and Samuel Chase, Esqrs; of the city of Annapolis, and the land conveyed to them in trust to the subscribers, until the House is built, and this proposal be fully complied with on the part of the company.

Copies of this address will be circulated in the different counties, and as soon as a sufficient sum, not exceeding £600, is subscribed, the tickets will be made out, signed by Mr. Douglass, and delivered; when it is hoped the money will be paid, that materials may be collected in time, and an engagement entered into with a builder, to complete the theatre for the next season.

Subscriptions are taken in at Mr. Colin Campbell's store, at the Printing-Office, at Mr. Cornelius Garrestson's, and at Mr. Whetcroft's.]

c. 5 October 1770   St. Croix
Newspaper notice.

[The *Royal Danish American Gazette* of 3 October 1770 contains the following theatrical items:

Sir: please inform the Publick what was the reason of Romeo and Juliet not being performed last night, agreeable to the advertisement published in your Wednesday's paper: as you ought to be an intelligent person, your compliance with the above request (if possible) will not only oblige your constant reader, but the Publick in gereral, who have been shamefully abused.

Your's, etc, C. D.

The author of the above, we expect, will be informed by Mr. Hill, the manager of the theatre, as we are entirely ignorant of the cause that prevented the play being performed according the advertisement.

We hear from Fredericksted, that the company of Comedians there meet with uncommon success; that last week they performed thrice, to polite and crowded audiences; and that they received universal approbation.

The paper, not being published in due time, the Publick are desired to charge to account of one Hill, who endeavored by artful insinuations to obstruct the usual intelligence.]

8 October 1770　　　　　　　Bass-End Theatre, Christiansted, St. Croix

Tamerlane the Great.
Lethe.
Leeward Islands Company.
　　[Benefit for Davies. "At the end of the play, a dance, call'd 'The Merry Millers,' by Messrs. Malone, Linck, and others." Source: *Royal Danish American Gazette* (6 October 1770).]

11 October 1770　　　　　　Bass-End Theatre, Christiansted, St. Croix

The Recruiting Officer.
Wonder, an Honest Yorkshireman.
Leeward Islands Company.
　　[Source: *Royal Danish American Gazette* (10 Oct 1770).]

18 October 1770　　　　　　The Theatre, Fredericksted, St. Croix

The Beaux' Stratagem .
　　　Aimwell–Darby; Archer–Verling; Sullen–Jones; Bonniface,–Harris; Sir Charles Freeman–White; Foigard–Godman; Scrub–"Scrub"; Mrs. Sullen–Mrs. Parker; Dorinda–Miss Guy; Cherry–Mrs. Darby. Singing between the Acts by Mrs. Parker and Mr. Jones.
The Mock Doctor.
　　　Sir Jasper–Harris; Leander–Jones; Gregory the Doctor–Darby; James–White; Harry–Godman; Welch Davie–Verling; Dorcas–Mrs. Parker; Charlotte–Miss Guy.

West-End Company.

[A brief notice of "Scrub's" performance appears in the *Royal Danish American Gazette* of 24 October 1770: "We hear from the West-End that Scrub, mentioned in last paper, played his part in status quo (as he had in many other places) before a very judicious audience." This person apparently was an amateur playing for his own diversion. Source: *Royal Danish American Gazette* (17 October 1770).]

20 October 1770   The Theatre, Fredericksted, St. Croix

The Gamester.
The Virgin Unmasked.
West-End Company.

[Source: *Royal Danish American Gazette* (17 October 1770).]

22 October 1770   Bass-End Theatre, Christiansted, St. Croix

The Provoked Husband.
High Life Below Stairs.
Leeward Islands Company

[Benefit for Mrs. Giffard. Announced, but postponed "on account of indisposition." Source: *Royal Danish American Gazette* (17 October 1770); notice of postponement: *Royal Danish American Gazette* (20 October 1770).]

23 October 1770   The Old Theatre, Williamsburg
Play not identified.
American Company.

[Thomas Jefferson attended on this date and paid 10s. for tickets. Source: Jefferson, *Memorandum Books*, 1:210.]

26 October 1770   The Theatre, Frederickstead, St. Croix

The Orphan.
    Acastro–Harris; Castalio–Verling; Polydore–Mr. Parker; Chamont–Darby; Chaplain–Jones; Ernesto–Godman; Servant–White; Page–Miss Guy; Monimia–Mrs. Parker; Serina–Mrs. Darby.

Hob in the Well.
    Sir Thomas Testy–Harris; Friendly–Jones; Dick–White; Old Hob–Darby; Master Puzzle–Verling; Master Thickskull–Godman; Young Hob–Parker; Flora–Mrs. Parker; Betty–Miss Guy; Old Hob's Wife–Mrs. Darby.

West End company.
[For the Benefit of the Danish Church and Hospital. Source: *Royal Danish American Gazette* (17 October 1770).]

26 October 1770   The Old Theatre, Williamsburg
Play not identified.
American Company.
[Thomas Jefferson attended on this date and paid 5s. for tickets. Source: Jefferson, *Memorandum Books*, 1:210.]

27 October 1770   The Old Theatre, Williamsburg
Play not identified.
American Company.
[Thomas Jefferson attended on this date: "Pd. for play ticket 7/6." Source: Jefferson, *Memorandum Books*, 1:210.]

29 October 1770   Bass-End Theatre, Christiansted, St. Croix
The Provoked Husband.
High Life Below Stairs.
Leeward Islands Company.
[Benefit for Mrs. Giffard. Source: *Royal Danish American Gazette* (20 October 1770).]

29 October 1770   The Old Theatre, Williamsburg
Play not identified.
American Company.
[Thomas Jefferson attended on this date: "Pd. for play ticket 7/6." Source: Jefferson, *Memorandum Books*, 1:210.]

30 October 1770   The Old Theatre, Williamsburg
Play not identified.
American Company.
[Thomas Jefferson attended on this date: "Pd. for play ticket 5/." Source: Jefferson, *Memorandum Books*, 1:210.]

31 October 1770   The Old Theatre, Williamsburg
Play not identified.
American Company.
[Thomas Jefferson attended on this date: "Pd. for play ticket 7/6." Source: Jefferson, *Memorandum Books*, 1:210.]

1 November 1770   The Theatre, Fredericksted, St. Croix
The Gamester.

Miss in her Teens.
West-End Company.
 [Benefit for Miss Guy. Postponed; see entry for 2 November 1770. Source: *Royal Danish American Gazette* (24 October 1770).]

1 November 1770   The Old Theatre, Williamsburg
Play not identified.
American Company.
 [Thomas Jefferson attended on this date: "Pd. for play ticket 7/6." Source: Jefferson, *Memorandum Books*, 1:210.]

2 November 1770   The Theatre, Fredericksted, St. Croix
The Gamester.
Miss in her Teens.
West-End Company.
 [Benefit for Miss Guy. Source: *Royal Danish American Gazette* (31 October 1770).]

2 November 1770   The Old Theatre, Williamsburg
Play not identified.
American Company.
 [Thomas Jefferson attended on this date: "Pd. for d[itt]o 7/6." Source: Jefferson, *Memorandum Books*, 1:210.]

3 November 1770   The Theatre, Fredericksted, St. Croix
Othello.
> Othello–Verling; Barbatino–Harris; Lodovico–Jones; Cassio–White; Rodorigo–Parker; Montano–Godman; Iago–Darby; Desdemona–Mrs. Parker; Amilia–Miss Guy; Attendant–Mrs. Darby.

The Lying Valet.
> Gayless–Jones; Justice Guttle–Harris; Beau Tippet–Godman; Drunken Cook–Parker; Sharp–Darby; Melissa–Miss Guy; Kitty Pry–Mrs. Parker; Mrs. Gadabout–Mrs. Darby.

West-End Company.
 [Benefit for Darby. Source: *Royal Danish American Gazette* (27 October 1770).]

3 November 1770   The Old Theatre, Williamsburg
Play not identified.
American Company.
 [Thomas Jefferson attended on this date: "Pd. for play ticket 7/6." Source: Jefferson, *Memorandum Books*, 1:210.]

5 November 1770   The Old Theatre, Williamsburg
Play not identified.
American Company.

[Thomas Jefferson attended on this date: "Pd. for play ticket 2/6." Source: Jefferson, *Memorandum Books*, 1:211.]

5 November 1770   Bass-End Theatre, Christiansted, St. Croix
The Minor.
The Apprentice; or, the Humors of a Spouting Club.
Leeward Islands Company.

[Benefit for Brother Kirwan. Prologue spoken by Hill. Source: *Royal Danish American Gazette* (31 October 1770).]

6 November 1770   The Old Theatre, Williamsburg
Play not identified.
American Company.

[Thomas Jefferson attended on this date: "Pd. for play ticket 7/6." Source: Jefferson, *Memorandum Books*, 1:211.]

7 November 1770   The Old Theatre, Williamsburg
Play not identified.
American Company.

[Thomas Jefferson attended on this date: "Pd. for play ticket 7/6." Source: Jefferson, *Memorandum Books*, 1:211.]

8 November 1770   The Theatre, Fredericksted, St. Croix
The Merchant of Venice.
> Bassanio and Gratiano–to be performed by two Gentlemen for their Amusement; Portia–by a Lady for her Amusement. Between the Acts of the Play will be performed a Comick Dance, called "The Wapping Landlady." The Principal parts to be performed by Malone, &c. Wapping Landlady–Mrs. Parker.

The Apprentice; or, the Spouting Club.
West-End Company.

[Benefit for Mrs. Parker. Prices: still twelve shillings. Source: *Royal Danish American Gazette* (3 November 1770).]

8 November 1770   The Old Theatre, Williamsburg
Play not identified.
American Company.

[Thomas Jefferson attended on this date: "Pd. for play ticket 7/6." Source: Jefferson, *Memorandum Books*, 1:211.]

12 November 1770   Bass-End Theatre, Christiansted, St. Croix
The Provoked Husband.
    With comic dances by Malone and Linck.
High Life Below Stairs.
Leeward Islands Company.
    [Benefit of Mrs. Giffard, who had apparently been ill for some time. Source: *Royal Danish American Gazette* (7 November 1770).]

15 November 1770   The Theatre, Fredericksted, St. Croix
Venice Preserved.
    Jaffier and Pierre–to be performed by Gentlemen for their Amusement; Belvidera–by a Lady for her Amusement.
Harlequin Skeleton; or the Burgomaster Tricked ("never performed here").
    Harlequin–by a Gentleman for his own amusement; Clown–Parker; Columbine–Mrs. Parker.
West-End Company.
    [Benefit for Parker. Subsequent advertisements reveal that this program was postponed until 1 December 1770 and altered. From the *Royal Danish American Gazette* (10 November 1770) we learn that the gentleman disinclined to undertake Harlequin so Linck from the Leeward Islands Company took on the role. Source: *Royal Danish American Gazette* (3 November 1770).]

17 November 1770   The Theatre, Fredericksted, St. Croix
1 Henry IV.
    Falstaff–Verling.
The Devil to Pay.
    Sir John Loverule–Jones; Nell–Mrs. Parker;
West-End Company.
    [Benefit for Verling. "After the play, an Epilogue in praise of Masonry, written and to be spoke by Mr. Verling, in Character of a Master Mason. Between the Acts will be introduced several Mason Songs, with a proper Chorus, &c. With entertainments of Dancing by Messers. Linck and Harris." Source: *Royal Danish American Gazette* (14 November 1770).]

17 November 1770   St. Croix
Announcement.
    The *Royal Danish American Gazette* of this date contains the following notice: "All persons whom John Gray is indebted

to, are desired to render him their accounts, as he intends leaving the island immediately." Cf., Gray's benefit on 26 November 1770.]

19 November 1770   Bass-End Theatre, Christiansted, St. Croix

Hamlet.
The Mayor of Garratt.
Leeward Island Company.
    [Benefit for Gray. Dancing by Mr. Linck. Postponed; see 26 November 1770. Apparently Malone died on this day. Source: *Royal Danish American Gazette* (14 November 1770).]

20 November 1770   The Theatre, Fredericksted, St. Croix
The Suspicious Husband.
    Ranger–Verling; Strickland–Darby; Frankly–Jones; Bellamy–White; Jack Maggot–Harris; Tester–Parker; Simon–Godman; Clarinda–Mrs. Parker; Jacintha–Miss Guy; Mrs. Strickland–Mrs. Darby.
Lethe.
    Aesop–Godman; Charon–Harris; Fine Gentleman–Verling; Drunken Man–Darby; French Man–White; Old Man–Parker; Snip–Harris; Mercury–Jones; Fine Lady–Mrs. Parker.
West-End Company
    [Benefit for Harris. Source: *Royal Danish American Gazette* (10 November 1770).]

23 November 1770   The Theatre, Fredericksted, St. Croix
Richard III.
    Epilogue in the Character of a Master Mason by White.
The Brave Irishman.
    Captain O'Blunder–Verling; Comic dancing–Linck.
West-End Company.
    [Benefit for White. Announced but rescheduled; see 29 November 1770. Source: *Royal Danish American Gazette* (17 November 1770).]

24 November 1770   St. Croix
Newspaper notice.
    [The *Royal Danish American Gazette* of this date contains the following item: "All persons who have any demands against Mrs. Giffard, are desired to send them to her, as she intends leaving the island immediately."]

26 November 1770 Bass-End Theatre, Christiansted, St. Croix

Hamlet.
The Mayor of Garratt.
"To conclude with an epilogue in the character of a country boy, by Mr. Darby."
Leeward Islands Company.
[Benefit for Gray. Dancing by Linck. "The unfortunate demise of Mr. Malone is the occasion of this Benefit being postponed until the 26th inst." Source: *Royal Danish American Gazette* (24 November 1770).]

27 November 1770 The Theatre, Fredericksted, St. Croix
The Fair Penitent.
The Lying Valet.
West-End Company
["For the Benefit of Miss Guy and to her relief under a burthensome expense of a lawsuit." Source: *Royal Danish American Gazette* (24 November 1770).]

29 November 1770 The Theatre, Fredericksted, St. Croix
The Revenge.
The Brave Irishman.
Harlequin Skeleton.
West-End Company.
[Benefit for White, rescheduled from 23 November 1770 "Mr White begs leave to inform the Publick, that the reason of his changing the Play of Richard: is by the advice of his Friends, some of whom being resolved to assist him, by performing a part in the Revenge." Source: *Royal Danish American Gazette* (24 November 1770).]

1 December 1770 The Theatre, Fredericksted, St. Croix
Venice Preserved.
Jaffeir and Pierre–by two gentlemen for their own amusement (see above)
A Harlequin Entertainment.
Harlequin–Linck.
West-End Company.
[Benefit for Parker; rescheduled from 15 November 1770. Source: *Royal Danish American Gazette* (28 November 1770).]

5 December 1770   The Bass-End Theatre, Christiansted, St. Croix
The Mourning Bride.
   King–Hughes; Osmyn–Hill; Almeria–Mrs. Parker; Zara–Mrs. Giffard.
The Devil to Pay.
Leeward Islands Company.
   [Benefit for Widow Malone. Members of the West-End company lent their talent to the evening. Source: *Royal Danish American Gazette* (5 December 1770).]

5 December 1770   St. Croix
Newspaper notice.
   [From the *Royal Danish American Gazette* of this date we learn that several members of both companies announced their imminent departure: Charles Parker, John Davies, Thomas Jones, Jonathan Godman.]

11 December 1770   Bass-End Theatre, Christiansted, St. Croix
The Beggar's Opera.
   Macheath—Hill; Peachum—Verling; Locki—Parker; Polly—Mrs. Giffard. Mrs. Peachum and Lucy—Mrs. Parker.
Chrononhotonothologos* (Henry Carey, 1734).
Leeward Islands Company.
   [Benefit for Bullock. "The songs of the Opera to be accompanied with Musick, by Gentlemen for their own Amusement." Source: *Royal Danish American Gazette* (8 December 1770).]

12 December 1770   Bass-End Theatre, Christiansted, St. Croix
Newspaper notice.
   [A notice in the *Royal Danish American Gazette* of this date remarks that Edward Bullock added his name to those leaving the island of St. Croix.]

13 December 1770   The Theatre, Fredericksted, St. Croix
Richard III.
   Richard, Mr. Hill; King Henry, Mr. Verling;
The Old Maid.
West-End Company.

[Afterpiece "never performed here. For the Benefit of the wardrobe for Mrs. Parker." Source: *Royal Danish American Gazette* (12 December 1770).]

17 December 1770   Bass-End Theatre, Christiansted, St. Croix

Douglas.
Damon and Phillida.
Leeward Islands Company.
    ["For the defraying the Funeral Charges and Debts of the deceast Mr. Malone." Parker spoke the epilogue and Linck danced. Source: *Royal Danish American Gazette* (15 December 1770).]

21 December 1770   The Theatre, Fredericksted, St. Croix

The Lecture on Heads.
Fanny the Phantom.
West-End Company.
    [Source: *Royal Danish American Gazette* (19 December 1770).]

22 December 1770   Bass-End Theatre, Christiansted, St. Croix

The London Merchant.
A Wonder, an Honest Yorkshireman.
Leeward Islands Company
    [Benefit for Linck. To begin at half past six. Source: *Royal Danish American Gazette* (19 December 1770).]

22 December 1770   The Theatre, Fredericksted, St. Croix

The Beggar's Opera.
    Macheath—Jones; Polly—Mrs. Parker; Mrs. Peachum—"by a Lady who never appeared on this Stage" [Mrs. Taylor?].
What we must all Come to* (Arthur Murphy, 1764).
    Sir Charles Racket—Darby; Mr. Drugget—Parker; Lady Racket—Mrs. Parker; Mrs. Drugget—Mrs. Taylor.
West-End Company.
    ["N.B. The Ladies and Gentlemen who please to favour us with their Company at the above entertainments may assure themselves they will not be altered by performed to whatever audience shall appear at the Theatre. To begin at

half past six." Source: *Royal Danish American Gazette* (19 December 1770).]

22 December 1770 St. Croix
Newspaper notice.
    [Jane Taylor, Samuel Darby, and John Kirwan had added their names to those performers soon to be departing the island. Source: *Royal Danish American Gazette* (22 December 1770).]

31 December 1770 The Bass-End Theatre, Christiansted, St. Croix
The Earl of Essex.
A farce, expressed in the Bills.
Joint company.
    ["For the Benefit of Mr. Verling, and in order to pay his Debts." Source: *Royal Danish-American Gazette* (19 December 1770).]

1771

What few records exist for the spring of this year we owe to Washington and Jefferson. George Washington attended performances in several Virginia cities and recorded his presence in his *Diary*. That Jefferson was in Williamsburg from 8 April 1771 but did not record theatrical attendance until 26 April implies that the American Company did not perform at the capitol during 8–25 April, but some evidence exists to suggest they were in residence somewhat before 8 April: a letter from Hudson Muse (see 19 April 1771) remarks that the players performed in Williamsburg for at least an eleven-day period, which we suggest would have been prior to 8 April.

We also know that the American Company toured Virginia—Dumfries, Williamsburg, Fredericksburg and Alexandria—during July 1771. Rankin (160–61) suggests the company played short engagements from Fredericksburg northward to Annapolis. The company in May is known to have included the following members: David Douglass, Mrs. Douglass, Lewis Hallam, Jr., Miss Hallam, Mrs. Henry, Owen Morris, Mrs. Morris, Miss Richardson, Miss Storer, Mr. Tomlinson, Mrs. Tomlinson, Thomas Wall, and Stephen Woolls.

By 9 September, full cast lists are again available when the company opened their new West Street Theatre in Annapolis. The American Company then consisted of the following known members: Byerley, David Douglass, Mrs. Douglass, Richard Goodman, Lewis Hallam Jr., Miss Nancy Hallam, John Henry, Mrs. Henry, Owen Morris, Charles Parker, Mr. Roberts, Mr. Tomlinson, Thomas Wall, and Stephen Woolls. One Mrs. Stamper also appeared briefly with the company while in Williamsburg (cf. Rankin 166) but did not continue with them in their travels.

Sometime in the summer, John Henry was sent to England to recruit personnel and to purchase scenery. He returned with new scenes and plays, but no new actors, shortly after the new theatre opened in Annapolis in early September. The Annapolis season extended once again through the Autumn Court sessions and October Races. Sometime in mid-October, the company journeyed back to Williamsburg where they opened their new theatre on 23 October with the latest hit of the London season, Cumberland's *The West Indian*, and remained until the end of the year.

On St. Croix, after the departure of Verling's Company (see Header 1770), Mr. Hill tarried awhile on the island and offered an occasional production into January, but his available roster must not have been large. Only two productions are advertised, both supplemented with amateurs, after which the season shortly sputtered to a close, and no more is heard of Mr. Hill, the manager of the Leeward Islands Company of Comedians. A few actors remained. Mr. Linck, the dancer, took up residence in Christianstead and opened a dance Academy. Mrs. Giffard was also available, as we shall see, as well as several locals, such as John Gray who had stage experience.

In March of the year a stranger appeared on St. Croix, a man who advertised himself as having sung in most of the major American cities. This was Mr. Warwell, touring his one-person version of operas. Here he alighted and hired a hall, performed initially solo, and then partnered with Mrs. Giffard and together they presented scenes from several plays. The performances soon attracted other part-time actors, and together they ambitiously mounted *The Beggar's Opera*. "The rest of the characters will be disposed of to the best advantage" is how Warwell described his casting options. His season is short, and by mid-April he moved on.

388   THE COLONIAL AMERICAN STAGE

There is a large gap in the run of the *Royal Danish-American Gazette* with no preserved issues between May 1771 and July 1772. We suspect a company of players returned in the fall of 1771, as they did the following year, and perhaps had done prior to the establishment of the press, making the Bass-End Theatre an annual stop, but there is no direct evidence upon which to support this claim.

✳✳✳

2 January 1771   venue unknown, vicinity of New Haven, Connecticut colony
The Conscious Lovers.
The Toy Shop.
Students of Yale College.
   [Bloom (44) documents theatrical activity by the young Nathan Hale and other student members of the Linonian Club of Yale College.]

15 January 1771   Bass-End Theatre, Christiansted, St. Croix
The Spanish Fryar.
   Don Gomez—Hill.
An Old Man Taught Wisdom.
   [Source: *Royal Danish American Gazette* (12 January 1771).]

18 January 1771   Annapolis
Correspondence.
American Company.
   [Rankin (158) records a portion of a letter by William Eddis, a surveyor, regarding the American company:

> My pleasure and my surprise were therefore excited in proportion, on finding performers in this country equal, at least, to those who sustain the best of the first characters in your more celebrated provincial theatres. Our governor ... patronizes the American Company; and as their present place of exhibition is in a small scale, and inconveniently situated, a subscription, by his example, has been rapidly completed to erect a new theatre, on a commodious, if not an elegant plan. The manager is to deliver tickets for two seasons, to the amount of the respective subscriptions, and it is imagined, that the money received at the doors, from non-subscribers, will enable him to conduct the business without difficulty; and when the limited number of performances is completed, the entire property is to be vested in him. This will be a valuable addition to our catalogue of

amusements. The building is already in a state of forwardness, and the day of opening is anxiously awaited.]

23 January 1771　　　The Assembly Room, Dumfries, Virginia colony

The Recruiting Officer.
American Company.
　[George Washington attended this performance. Source: Washington, *Diaries*, 3:3.]

28 January 1771　　　Bass-End Theatre, Christiansted, St. Croix

The Revenge.
　Zanga—Hill; Don Manuel—a gentleman for his amusement.
Aesop in the Shades.
　Lord Chalkstone—Hill.
　[Tickets: 12 shillings. Source: *Royal Danish American Gazette* (23 January 1771).]

29 January 1771　　　The Assembly Room, Dumfries, Virginia colony

Play not identified.
American Company.
　[George Washington records in his *Diary* that he attended a performance on this date, and his Cash Accounts show that he spent "10/" for tickets and 6s. 3d. for "Exps. at the Play." Source: Washington, *Diaries*, 3:4; *Papers*, 8:424.]

18 March 1771　　　Mr. Williams' Tavern, St. Croix
The Provoked Husband.
Thomas Warwell.
　["Read ... by a Person who has read and sung in all the great towns in North America: He personates all the characters, and enters into the different humours, or passions, as they change alternately, throughout the Comedy. Between the Acts will be sung some of the most celebrated songs, accompanied by different instruments." This is Warwell; see entry for 9 April 1771. Source: *Royal Danish American Gazette* (13 March 1771).]

20 March, 1771　　　Mr. Williams' Tavern, St. Croix
The Beggar's Opera.
Thomas Warwell.
　[Tickets: 12 shillings. "N.B. To prevent disappointment, those Ladies and Gentlemen who may incline to favour the

Performer with their company, are informed, that he does not read the Opera, unless thirty tickets are sold." Source: *Royal Danish American Gazette* (20 March 1771).]

9 April 1771   The Heyliger House, St. Croix
The Provoked Husband (selected scenes).
        Lord Townley—Warwell; Lady Townley— Mrs. Giffard.
Damon and Phillida.
        Damon—Warwell; Phillida—Mrs. Giffard.
[Source: *Royal Danish American Gazette* (6 April 1771).]

10 April 1771   The Heyliger House, St. Croix
The Beggar's Opera.
        Macheath—Warwell; Polly—Mrs. Giffard.
["The rest of the characters to be disposed of to the best advantage." Source: *Royal Danish American Gazette* (10 April 1771).]

13 April 1771   The Heyliger House, St. Croix
The Beggar's Opera.
        Cast as 10 April.
        [Source: *Royal Danish American Gazette* (13 April 1771).]

19 April 1771   Williamsburg
Correspondence.
    [A letter from Hudson Muse to his brother Thomas on this date offers a firsthand account of theatrical affairs and the social possibilities of Williamsburg at Court season:

> In a few days after I got to Virginia, I set out to Wmsburg, where I was detained for 11 days, tho' I spent the time very agreeably, at the plays every night, and realy must join Mr. Ennalls and Mr. Basset in thinking Miss Hallam super fine. But must confess her luster was much sullied by the number of Beauties that appeared at that court. The house was crowded every night, and the gentlemen who have generally attended that place agree there was treble the number of fine Ladies that was ever seen in town before—for my part I think it would be impossible for a man to have fixed upon a partner for life, the choice was too general to have fixed on one.
>
> About the latter end of this month, I intend down again, and perhaps shall make out such another trip, as the players are to be there again, and its an amusement I am so very fond of.

Source: "Original Letters," 240–41.]

26 April 1771   The Old Theatre, Williamsburg
The Tender Husband.
The Honest Yorkshireman.
American Company.
    [Opening night? Thomas Jefferson attended this performance: "Pd. for play ticket 7/6" (*Memorandum Books*, 1:254). Source: *Virginia Gazette* (25 April 1771).]

1 May 1771   The Old Theatre, Williamsburg
Love in a Village.
    Woodcock–Douglass; Hawthorn–Woolls; Young Meadow–Wall; Eustace–Byerley; Sir William Mead–Morris; Hodge–Parker; Lucinda–Miss Storer; Mrs. Woodcock–Mrs. Douglass; Margery–Mrs. Morris; Rosetta–Miss Hallam; Servants at the Statue–Goodman, Tomlinson, Roberts, Mrs. Henry, Mrs. Hallam, Mrs. Wall, Mrs. Tomlinson, and Miss Richardson.
The Buck; or, The Englishman in Paris* (Samuel Foote, 1753).
    Buck–Hallam; Subtle–Douglass; Classick–Parker; Solitaire–Wall; Marquis–Byerley; Sir John Buck–Morris; Dauphine–Roberts; Mrs. Subtle–Miss Richardson; Lucinda (with a song)–Miss Hallam.
American Company.
    [Prices: box–7s. 6d.; pit–5s. Source: playbill in the Colonial Williamsburg Foundation.]

2 May 1771   The Old Theatre, Williamsburg
The Clandestine Marriage.
The Padlock.
American Company.
    ["By command." Thomas Jefferson attended this performance: "Pd. for play ticket 5/" (*Memorandum Books*, 1:254). George Washington records in his *Diary* that he also attended on this date (*Diaries*, 3:25). Source: playbill of 1 May 1771 in the Colonial Williamsburg Foundation.]

3 May 1771   The Old Theatre, Williamsburg
Play not identified.
American Company.
    [Thomas Jefferson attended this performance: "Pd. for play ticket 7/6" (*Memorandum Books*, 1:254). George Washington records in his *Diary* that he also was present. Source: Washington, *Diaries*, 3:25.]

6 May 1771   The Old Theatre, Williamsburg
Play not identified.
American Company.
   [Thomas Jefferson attended this performance: "Pd. for play ticket 7/6." Source: Jefferson, *Memorandum Books*, 1:254.]

8 May 1771   The Old Theatre, Williamsburg
Play not identified.
American Company.
   [George Washington records in his *Diary* that he attended a performance on this date. For tickets for this performance and for those of 2 and 3 May, Washington spent "52/6." Source: Washington, *Diaries*, 3:25.]

16 May 1771   Fredericksburg, Virginia colony
Newspaper notice.
American Company.
   [The *Virginia Gazette* of this date prints the following notice: "The American Company of Comedians will open the theatre in Fredericksburg the latter end of this month, and perform every Tuesday, Wednesday, and Thursday, during their residence there."]

28 May 1771   Fredericksburg, Virginia colony
The Provoked Husband.
        Townly–Hallam; Manly–Douglass; Sir Francis–Morris; Richard–Woolls; Basset–Wall; Moody–Tomlinson; Lady Grace–Mrs. Henry; Lady Wronghead–Mrs. Douglass; Jenny–Miss Storer; Myrtilla–Miss Richardson; Mrs. Motherly–Mrs. Tomlinson; Trusty–Mrs. Morris; Lady Townly–Miss Hallam.
Love a la mode.
American Company.
   [Tickets: 6s. Source: playbill in the Colonial Williamsburg Foundation.]

29 May 1771   Fredericksburg, Virginia colony
Hamlet.
American Company.
   [Source: playbill of 28 May 1771 in the Colonial Williams-burg Foundation.]

31 May 1771   Fredericksburg, Virginia colony
All in the Wrong.
American Company.

[Source: playbill of 28 May 1771 in the Colonial Williams-burg Foundation.]

6 June 1771   Annapolis
Construction of theatre.
American Company.

[The *Maryland Gazette* of 13 June 1771 contains the following notice:

> Mr. Douglass begs leave to acquaint the gentlemen, who have subscribed to the new Theatre in Annapolis, that all the materials for the building are now purchased, and workmen engaged to complete it by the First of September: He assures them, that nothing will be wanting on his part, nor on the parts of the gentlemen who have undertaken to superintend the work, to render it as commodious and elegant as any theatre in America. He has sent to London to engage some performers, and expects them, and a new set of scenes, painted by Mr. Doll, in a few weeks. In short, the publick, whose favours he most gratefully acknowledges, will, he flatters himself, be convinced, by the efforts he makes to entertain them, that he has a proper sense of their goodness, and an unremitting desire to make every return in his power, for the obligations he is under to them. He would esteem it as a very great favour, if the gentlemen who have neglected to pay their subscription money, will be good enough to send it as soon as possible, as the sum collected, is by no means sufficient to answer the necessary demands that will very soon be made. Annapolis, June 6, 1771.]

25 July 1771   Fredericksburg, Virginia colony
Play not identified.
American Company.

[Though Ford (21) presumes that George Washington attended a performance in Alexandria on 23 July, Rankin (160) states that Washington saw a play in Fredericksburg on 24 July 1771. In point of fact, Washington (*Diaries*, 3:43) attended in Fredericksburg on 25 July 1771.]

9 September 1771   West Street Theatre, Annapolis
The Roman Father.
> The Roman Father–Hallam; Tullus Hostilius–Douglass; Publius–Goodman; Valerius–Wall; First Citizen–Morris; Second Citizen–Woolls; Third Citizen–Parker; Fourth Citizen–Roberts; Soldier–Tomlinson; Valeria–Mrs. Henry; Horatia–Miss Hallam.

The Mayor of Garratt.
American Company.

[On this evening the company opened its new theatre in Annapolis, which is described in the *Maryland Gazette* of 12 September 1771:

> On Monday last, the new Theatre in West-Street was opened with the Roman Father and Mayor of Garrat, to a numerous and brilliant audience, who expressed the greatest satisfaction not only at the performance, but with the House, which is thought to be as elegant and commodious, for its size, as any theatre in America.

Another account of the theatre appears in a letter of William Eddis, dated 2 November 1771 (Eddis 108):

> Our new theatre, of which I gave you an account in a former letter, was opened to a numerous audience the week preceding the races. The structure is not inelegant, but, in my opinion, on too narrow a scale for its length; the boxes are commodious, and neatly decorated; the pit and the gallery are calculated to hold a number of people without incommoding each other; the stage is well adapted for dramatic and pantomimical exhibitions; and several of the scenes reflect great credit on the ability of the painter. I have before observed that the performers are considerably above mediocrity; therefore little doubt can be entertained of their preserving the public favour, and reaping a plenteous harvest.

The prologue spoken by Douglass and the epilogue spoken by Mrs. Henry also appear in the *Maryland Gazette* of 12 September 1771. Source: *Maryland Gazette* (5 September 1771).]

11 September 1771   Norfolk, Virginia colony
Newspaper notice.
American Company.
   [The *Maryland Gazette* of 19 September 1771 contains the following item: "On Tuesday September the 11th arrived at Norfolk, the Brigantine Jenny, Isaac Mitchinson, Master, from Whitehaven; in whom came passenger, Mr. Henry of the American Company of Comedians."]

20 September 1771   West Street Theatre, Annapolis
The Maid of the Mill.
The Old Maid.
American Company.
   [Source: *Maryland Gazette* (19 September 1771).]

24 September 1771   West Street Theatre, Annapolis
Play not identified.
American Company.

THE COLONIAL AMERICAN STAGE 395

[George Washington records in his *Diary* that he attended a performance on this date. Source: Washington, *Diaries*, 3: 56.]

25 September 1771   West Street Theatre, Annapolis
Play not identified.
American Company.
   [George Washington records in his *Diary* that he attended a performance on this date. Source: Washington, *Diaries*, 3:56.]

26 September 1771   West Street Theatre, Annapolis
Play not identified.
American Company.
   [George Washington records in his *Diary* that he attended a performance on this date. Source: Washington, *Diaries*, 3:56.]

28 September 1771   West Street Theatre, Annapolis
Play not identified.
American company.
   [George Washington records in his *Diary* that he attended a performance on this date. Source: Washington, *Diaries*, 3: 56.]

5 October 1771   West Street Theatre, Annapolis
The Jealous Wife.
Midas.
American Company.
   [Source: *Maryland Gazette* (3 October 1771).]

7 October 1771   West Street Theatre, Annapolis
Cymbeline.
   Imogen–Miss Hallam.
American Company.
   [Source: *Maryland Gazette* (10 October 1771).

23 October 1771   The Old Theatre, Williamsburg
The West Indian* (Richard Cumberland, 1771).
The Musical Lady.
American Company.
   [This performance, though announced as the opening of the season, may not have transpired. The same bill is repeated on 26 October 1771, and Thomas Jefferson, who was an avid

theatrical patron, does not record his first ticket purchase until that date. Source: *Virginia Gazette* (17 October 1771).]

26 October 1771   The Old Theatre, Williamsburg
The West Indian.
The Musical Lady.
American Company.
    [Opening of the season? Thomas Jefferson attended this performance: "Pd. for play ticket 5/" (*Memorandum Books*, 1:262). Source: *Virginia Gazette* (24 October 1771).]

28 October 1771   The Old Theatre, Williamsburg
Play not identified.
American Company.
    [Thomas Jefferson attended this performance: "Pd. for play ticket 5/." Source: Jefferson, *Memorandum Books*, 1: 262.]

29 October 1771   The Old Theatre, Williamsburg
Play not identified.
American Company.
    [George Washington records in his *Diary* that he attended a performance on this date: "Reached Williamsburg before Dinner. And went to the Play in the Afternoon." Source: Washington, *Diaries*, 3:63.]

30 October 1771   The Old Theatre, Williamsburg
Play not identified.
American Company.
    [Thomas Jefferson attended this performance: "Pd. for play tickets 10/" (*Memorandum Books*, 1:263). George Washington records in his *Diary* that he also was present. Source: Washington, *Diaries*, 3:65.]

31 October 1771   The Old Theatre, Williamsburg
Play not identified.
American Company.
    [George Washington records in his *Diary* that he attended a performance on this date: "Dined at the Governors and went to the Play." Source: Washington, *Diaries*, 3:65.]

1 November 1771   The Old Theatre, Williamsburg
Play not identified.
American Company.

[George Washington records in his *Diary* that he attended a performance on this date: "Went to the Fireworks in the Afternoon and to the Play at Night." Source: Washington, *Diaries*, 3:67.]

4 November 1771   The Old Theatre, Williamsburg
Play not identified.
American Company.
[George Washington records in his *Diary* that he attended a performance on this date. Source: Washington, *Diaries*, 3:68.]

12 November 1771 The Old Theatre, Williamsburg
King Lear.
An unnamed farce.
American Company.
[Source: *Virginia Gazette* (7 November 1771).]

23 November 1771 The Old Theatre, Williamsburg
Every Man in his Humor.
Damon and Phillida.
American Company.
[Source: Seilhamer 1:282]

21 December 1771 The Old Theatre, Williamsburg
The Jealous Wife.
The Padlock.
American Company.
[Source: *Virginia Gazette* (19 December 1771).]

1772

At the start of the year the American Company traveled to Norfolk for a short season before returning to Williamsburg (see 2 January). A 14 April 1772 newspaper notice announces that they intended to play "until the end of the April court," but they actually performed into May, after which the company temporarily drops from the record. Rankin (166) suggests a short engagement in Richmond, which he notes, "boasted a theatre at that date." The summer of 1772 saw new territory for the company, Baltimore, where they played sometime in August "notwithstanding the disadvantages of an inconvenient playhouse, and hot nights" (see August 1772). By the first of September the company had returned to their new theatre in

Annapolis where they played the Court and Race season to mid October, after which the company repaired to Philadelphia where they opened by late October and remained until the close of the year. From the Philadelphia cast lists we have derived the following known personnel for the American Company: Byerley, David Douglass, Richard Goodman, Lewis Hallam, Miss Hallam, John Henry, Mrs. Henry, Mr. Johnson, Owen Morris, Mrs. Morris, Charles Parker, Miss Mary Richardson, Mr. Roberts, Miss Storer, Thomas Wall, Mrs. Wall, and Stephen Woolls. In addition, Henrietta Osborne appeared with the company on 28 September for a one-time final benefit. Owen Morris, by this time, had remarried to Elizabeth Walker (his first wife, Mary Morris, had drowned crossing to New York in December 1767).

Another company breaks into visibility during this year. A Mr. Morgan, after having performed a series of comic lectures, was encouraged to open a theatre in Portsmouth, New Hampshire, in May of this year, for the display of entertainments "after the manner of Saddler's Wells." Morgan solicited subscriptions in June (see 19 June), and by early October the company apparently was playing three nights a week. The names of the of the following personnel are recorded for the Morgan Company: Mr. Deacon, "Mr. Deacon the minor," Mr. Foster, Mrs. Foster, and Mr. Morgan. Undoubtedly additional members performed at this time, but their names are not recorded until the following year.

A gentleman who announced himself as "lately arrived from London" toured Stevens's *Lecture on Heads* between Philadelphia and New York during the summer of this year. Kahan (132) identifies this person as Mr. Martin Foy, a former student of Mr. Garner's.

In Boston some evidence implies that Mercy Otis Warren's *The Adulateur* may have been performed during late March or early April 1772 (see 26 March 1772). The advertisement, though seeming to be plausible, however, conforms to the rhetoric of the era by which a "performance," in fact, meant the transpiring of actual historical events, and so must be interpreted with caution. Another instance of this type of advertisement involving a Warren play occurred during May 1773 (see headnote for that year). If this entry is bonafide, then we have here the first recorded performance of a play by an American female playwright.

Two sources of information reveal the presence of two independent companies playing in the islands beyond Jamaica. The Leeward Islands Company is playing in St. Croix, and a second, unidentified company, who suffer great loss due to a Hurricane, were working in Antigua.

In St. Croix, a large gap in the *Royal Danish American Gazette* from May 1771 to July 1772 leaves us uninformed about the activities of the players. The first extant issue is for 8 July 1772 (issue 200), with no theatrical notices, but by the next preserved issue, 3 August 1772 (issue 217), we learn that the Leeward Islands Company has returned to St. Croix. Three published play advertisements allow us to deduce that this is the same company who had played the island two years earlier, and perhaps during 1771, as well. New personnel include Mr. Spencer, and James Verling Godwin, whom we recall from Verling's Virginia Company, and a man whom Rankin (141) assumed to be related to William Verling. Their season was hardly opened before the island was devastated by a powerful hurricane on 31 August 1772. This hurricane caused loss of life and great damage, completely disrupting affairs in the area, including the destruction of both theatres. If the players survived, the playhouses were not rebuilt during our period, and no further reference to the Bass-End Theatre or the Theatre in Frederickstead is recorded through 1775. Professional theatrical activity of any sort ceases as well.

This same hurricane of 31 August 1772 also destroyed the playhouse of a second, unidentified, company playing in Antigua (see entry for that date). Of that company, unfortunately, nothing else in known.

***

2 January 1772   Norfolk, Virginia colony
Newspaper notice.
American Company.
 [The *Virginia Gazette* of this date contains the following notice of the American Company's activities:

> Next week the theatre in Norfolk will be opened by the American Company of Comedians, where they are to remain but a short while, as they intend for this place [i.e., Williamsburg] again by the meeting of the General Assembly, and to perform till the end of the April court. They then proceed to the northward, by engagement, where it is probable they will continue some years.]

23 January 1772   Williamsburg
Newspaper notice.
American Company.
    [The *Virginia Gazette* of this date contains the following notice: "The American Company of Comedians intend for this place by the meeting of the General Assembly, and to perform till the end of the April Court. They then proceed to the Northward by engagement, where it is probable they will continue some years."]

11 March 1772   The Old Theatre, Williamsburg
American Company.
    [George Washington records in his *Diary* that he attended a performance on this date. Source: Washington, *Diaries*, 3:95.]

12 March 1772   Williamsburg
Newspaper notice.
American Company.
    [The *Virginia Gazette* of this date records the following puff:

> We hear that a new comedy, called The Brothers, written by Mr. Cumberland, author of the much approved West Indian, is now in rehearsal, and will soon make its appearance on our theatre; also that False Delicacy, and A Word to the Wise, the productions of the ingenious Mr. Hugh Kelly, whose spirited letter to the Lord Mayor has been read by most people, are in great forewardness.

The Lord Mayor was Mr. Beckford.]

13 March 1772   The Old Theatre, Williamsburg
The Tender Husband.
American Company.
    [Source: copy of a playbill in the Colonial Williamsburg Foundation.]

17 March 1772   The Old Theatre, Williamsburg
Play not identified.
American Company.
    [George Washington records in his *Diary* that he attended a performance on this date. Source: Washington, *Diaries*, 3:96.]

19 March 1772   The Old Theatre, Williamsburg
Play not identified.

American Company.

[George Washington records in his *Diary* that he attended a performance on this date. Source: Washington, *Diaries*, 3:96; cf. *Virginia Gazette* (19 March 1772).]

25 March 1772   The Old Theatre, Williamsburg
Play not identified.
American Company.

[George Washington records in his *Diary* that he attended a performance on this date. Source: Washington, *Diaries*, 3:97.]

26 March 1772   The Old Theatre, Williamsburg
A School for Libertines, or A Word to the Wise * (Hugh Kelly, 1770).
American Company.

[George Washington records in his *Diary* that he attended this performance, a review of which appears in the *Virginia Gazette* of 2 April 1772:

> Mr. Kelly's new comedy of A Word to the Wise was performed at our theatre last Thursday, for the first time, and repeated on Tuesday to a very crowded and splendid audience. It was received both nights with the warmest marks of approbation; the sentiments with which this excellent piece is replete were greatly, and deservedly applauded; and the audience, while they did justice to the merit of the author, did no less honour to their own refined taste. If the comick writers would pursue Mr. Kelly's plan, and present us only with moral plays, the stage would become (what it ought to be) a school of politeness and virtue. Truth, indeed, obliges us to confess, that, for several years past, most of the new plays that have come under our observation have had a moral tendency, but there is not enough of them to supply the theatre with a variety of exhibitions sufficient to engage the attention of the publick; and the most desirable entertainments, by too frequent a repetition, become insipid.

Source: Washington, *Diaries*, 3:97; *The Virginia Gazette* (2 April 1772).]

26 March 1772   Boston
The Adulateur* (by Mercy Otis Warren).
Company not identified.

[Warren's play may have received performance around this date, as suggested in the following advertisement:

> To be exhibited for the entertainment of the public, at the grand parade in Upper Servia. The Adulateur, a dramatic performance,

consisting of three acts. As a specimen of the work, we have extracted the following passages ...constructed from political events in Boston, with a soliloquy by Cassius mourning the fate of his country at the end.

Source: *Massachusetts Spy* (26 March 1772).]

31 March 1772   The Old Theatre, Williamsburg
A School for Libertines, or A Word to the Wise.
American Company.
 [Source: A review in the *Virginia Gazette* of 2 April 1772 establishes this performance.]

3 April 1772   The Old Theatre, Williamsburg
Play not identified.
American Company.
 [George Washington records in his *Diary* that he attended a performance on this date. Source: Washington, *Diaries*, 3:99.]

7 April 1772   The Old Theatre, Williamsburg
Play not identified.
American Company.
 [George Washington records in his *Diary* that he attended a performance on this date. Source: Washington, *Diaries*, 3: 100.]

14 April 1772   The Old Theatre, Williamsburg
False Delicacy.
American Company.
 ["It may not be improper to give notice that the theatre in Williamsburg will be closed at the end of the April Court, the American Company's engagements calling them to the northward, from whence, it is probable, they will not return for several years." Source: *Virginia Gazette* (9 April 1772).]

15 April 1772   venue unknown, Connecticut colony
The Beaux' Stratagem.
Students of Yale College.
 [Bloom (48) documents theatrical activity by students in the Linonian Club of Yale College.]

21 April 1772   The Old Theatre, Williamsburg
The Provoked Husband.
Thomas and Sally.
    Dorcas–Mrs. Stamper.

American Company.
[Thomas Jefferson attended this perfomance: "Pd. for play ticket 5/" (*Memorandum Books*, 1:228). Source: *Virginia Gazette* (16 April 1772).]

28 April 1772   The Old Theatre, Williamsburg
The Way to Keep Him.
The Oracle.
American Company.
[Source: *Virginia Gazette* (23 April 1772).]

4 May 1772   The Old Theatre, Williamsburg
Play not identified.
American Company.
[Thomas Jefferson attended on this date: "Pd. for play ticket 5/." Source: Jefferson, *Memorandum Books*, 1:289.]

7 May 1772   The Old Theatre, Williamsburg
Newspaper notice.
American Company.
[The *Virginia Gazette* of this date contains the following notice:

> We are authorized to inform the public that the new comedy of the *Fashionable Lover*, now acting at the Theatres Royal, Drury Lane and Edinburgh with the utmost applause, will shortly appear on our theatre. Such is the industry of the American Company, that, though the piece has not been above ten days in the country, it has been rehearsed more than once, and is already, we hear, for representation.

This play, by Richard Cumberland, had premiered in London on 20 January 1772.]

14 May 1772   The Old Theatre, Williamsburg
Play not identified.
American Company.
[Thomas Jefferson attended on this date: "Pd. for play ticket 5/." Source: Jefferson, *Memorandum Books*, 1:289.]

16 May 1772   The Old Theatre, Williamsburg
Play not identified.
American Company.
[Thomas Jefferson attended on this date: "Pd. for play ticket 5/." Source: Jefferson, *Memorandum Books*, 1:290.]

12 June 1772   Assembly Room, Portsmouth, New Hampshire colony

Program not identified.
Mr. Morgan.

[The following notice announces an evening of entertainment:

> By Permission of His Excellency the Governor, this evening at the new Assembly room will be exhibited several serious and comic pieces of Oratory, interspersed with Music and singing... N. B. The public may be assured that nothing will be delivered in the above Exhibition but what is condusive and consistant with politeness and morality.

Source: *New Hampshire Gazette* (12 June 1772).]

19 June 1772   Assembly Room, Portsmouth, New Hampshire colony

Program not identified.
Mr. Morgan.

[The following notice announces an evening of entertainment:

> By Permission of His Excellency the Governor, this evening at the new Assembly room will be exhibited several serious and comic pieces of Oratory, interspersed with Music and singing... N. B. The public may be assured that nothing will be delivered in the above Exhibition but what is conducive and consistent with politeness and morality.

Source: *New Hampshire Gazette* (19 June 1772).]

19 June 1772   Portsmouth, New Hampshire colony
Subscription proposal.
Morgan Company.

[The *New Hampshire Gazette* of this date (and repeated on 26 June 1772) contains the following proposal by Mr. Morgan for a subscription series of performances:

> The great encouragement received by the exhibitor, of the serious & comic lectures, and the natural propensity the ladies and gentlemen seem to have to dramatic entertainment, has embolden'd him to publish, the following proposals for a subscription, to enable him to follow a more enlarg'd plan for the amusement of the public, he having engag'd considerable additional help, and purposes to exhibit a variety of new and surprising performances never seen in this country, consisting of Italian dances, and pantomimical interludes in grotesque characters, with elegant scenes and machinery and every other

decoration after the manner of the entertainments at Sadler's Wells. Subscribers to pay eight dollars, and to have two tickets each, for twelve nights, one for the front seats, and one for the second seats. Non-subscribers to pay, front seats, three pistereens, second seats, two pistereens. And back seats, one pistereen, each night. And as the tickets will be transferable, the public will find that subscribing is only fixing the same price as the projector first exhibited at, and to ascertain a certain number to put the design in execution. The public may be assured that no expence will be spared to have every decoration the country can afford, and as the projector cannot proceed till a sufficient number is subscribed, it is hoped that those ladies and gentlemen who are inclined to favour the above scheme will be expeditious in signing, as the season advances, and he is obliged to go to the southward in October next. Subscriptions taken in at the Printing-Office, and by Mr. Morgan.]

26 June 1772   Assembly Room, Portsmouth, New Hampshire colony

Program not identified.
Mr. Morgan.
[The following notice announces an evening of entertainment:

By Permission of His Excellency the Governor, this evening at the new Assembly room will be exhibited several serious and comic pieces of Oratory, interspersed with Music and singing ... N. B. The public may be assured that nothing will be delivered in the above Exhibition but what is conducive and consistent with politeness and morality.

Source: *New Hampshire Gazette* (26 June 1772).]

10 July 1772   New Theatre, Baltimore
Masque of Comus.
Comus–Henry; First Spirit–Byerley; Second Spirit–Morris; Third Spirit–Woolls; Elder Brother–Parker; Second Brother– Goodman; Euphrosine–Miss Storer; The Lady–Mrs. Henry; Bacchanals–Woolls, Douglass, Wall, Johnson, and Roberts; Bacchants–Miss Storer, Mrs. Morris, Mrs. Harman, Miss Richardson, and Mrs. Wall.
High Life Below Stairs.
Lovel–Hallam; Freeman–Parker; Lord Duke's Servant–Wall; Sir Harry's Servant–Henry; Philip–Morris; Coachman–Woolls; Kingston–Byerley; Tom–Johnson; Lady Bab's Servant–Miss Storer; Lady Charlotte's

Servant–Miss Richardson; Cook–Mrs. Harman; Cloe–Roberts; Kitty–Mrs. Henry.
American Company.
[Prices: boxes 7s. 6d.; pit 5s. Written on the playbill are the words "in an Old Stable belonging to Mr. Little." Source: playbill in the New York Historical Society, reproduced in Ritchey, "A History of the Baltimore Stage," iii.]

27 July 1772 Long Room, Videll's Alley, Philadelphia
Lecture on Heads.
Martin Foy.
["By Permission, the Ladies and Gentlemen, who intend to honour the Exhibition of the Lecture on Heads, with their presence, are requested to take notice, that the first time of performing will be this evening, the 27th instant, at the Long-Room in Videll's Alley, between Chestnut and Walnut Streets, in Second-Street." Price: one dollar. Source: *Pennsylvania Packet* (27 July 1772).]

August 1772 New Theatre, Baltimore
various plays: *The Gamester; The Provoked Husband; Love in a Village; The Padlock.*
American company.
[The *Maryland Gazette* of 20 August 1772 prints a letter dated 5 August 1772 from Baltimore Town:

> Before I close my letter, I must desire you till tell B– and W– that (contrary to their prognostications) I have spent my time here most agreeably ... from an entertainment I received here as agreeable as it was unexpected; I mean the Theatre. The American Company have performed here the greater part of the summer, and notwithstanding the disadvantages of an inconvenient playhouse, and hot nights, have been universally well received and encouraged. They really have much merit. You know I was always of opinion, that I could never sit out a play represented by American actors–but I must acknowledge my error; and it is with gratitude I confess I know not which to thank them for most, the pleasure they actually gave me–or the endeavours they used, to do so, even when it was not crowned with success. To find on this continent a stage conducted with decorum, to find a self instructed actor whose conceptions could imbibe the various characters of a Beverley, a Lord Townley, and a Mungo, and display them with propriety–To see two little engaging girls, whose manner of acting and sweetness of voice were (not to take from the merit of others in the piece) in a manner the support of the opera of Love in a Village, was what I own surprised me.]

1 August 1772   Long Room, Videll's Alley, Philadelphia
Lecture on Heads.
Martin Foy.
   [Source: Kahan 132.]

3 August 1772   Bass-End Theatre, Christiansted, St. Croix
Venice Preserved.
The Lying Valet.
Leeward Islands Company.
   [Source: *Royal Danish American Gazette* (1 August 1772).]

4 August 1772   Long Room, Videll's Alley, Philadelphia
Lecture on Heads.
Martin Foy.
   [The 3rd night. Source: *Pennsylvania Packet* (3 August 1772).]

6 August 1772   Long Room, Videll's Alley, Philadelphia
Lecture on Heads.
Martin Foy.
   [Source: Kahan 132.]

8? August 1772   Long Room, Videll's Alley, Philadelphia
Lecture on Heads.
Martin Foy.
   [Source: Kahan 132.]

10 August 1772   Bass-End Theatre, Christiansted, St. Croix
Venice Preserved.
The Lying Valet.
Leeward Islands Company
   [Source: *Royal Danish American Gazette* (8 August 1772).]

18 August 1772   Long Room, Videll's Alley, Philadelphia
Lecture on Heads.
Martin Foy.
   [The 6th night. Price: one-half dollar. "For the benefit of the Hospital." Source: *Pennsylvania Chronicle* (8–15 August 1772); cf. Pollock 29 n. 74.]

21 August 1772   Portsmouth, New Hampshire colony
Newspaper notice.
Morgan Company.

[The *New Hampshire Gazette* of this date contains the following notice: "Mr. Morgan begs leave to inform his subscribers, and the public in general, that the 2d week in September his exhibition will begin with a benefit night for the poor of the town.–and the subscribers nights will commence the ensuing evening." In fact, the theatre did not open until very late September or early October; see 25 September 1772.]

27 August 1772   New York
Newspaper notice.

[The *New York Journal* of this date contains the following notice:

> By permission: The gentleman who lately arrived from London, and has had the honour of exhibiting (by permission) in Philadelphia, Mr. George Alexander Steavens's celebrated Lecture on Heads; presents his most humble and respectful compliments to the ladies and gentlemen of this city, and acquaints them, that he intends (under their patronage) to exhibit for three nights, in the Assembly room, in the Broad-Way ...with a concert of vocal and instrumental musick .... [The performer] flatters himself with being able to produce a musical genius, who, for his vocal abilities, is not inferior, (if equalled,) to any publick performer on this side the Atlantic .... Monday evening the 31st inst. is fixed for the first night.]

29 August 1772   Philadelphia
Newspaper notice.

[The *Pennsylvania Chronicle* of 22–29 August 1772 contains the following notice:

> The exhibitor of the Lectures on Heads, returns his most grateful thanks to the ladies and gentlemen who have honoured his exhibition with their presence, and takes this opportunity of acquainting them, and the public in general, that he intends to open his dancing school on the first of October next, with a Ball, at which time some of the scholars, whom he has already taught since his residence in this city, will perform some new dances .... N. B. He also teacheth fencing.]

31 August 1772   Assembly Room, Broadway, New York
Lecture on Heads.
Martin Foy.

[Price: one dollar. "By permission. The gentleman who lately arrived from London, and has had the honour of exhibiting (by permission) in Philadelphia, Mr. George Alexander Steavens's celebrated Lecture on Heads; presents his most humble and respectful compliments to the ladies and gentlemen of this city, and acquaints them, that he intends (under their patronage) to exhibit for three nights, in the Assembly Room, in the Broadway." Source: *New York Mercury* (31 August 1772).]

31 August 1772   Bass-End Theatre, Christiansted, St. Croix

Douglas.
  Douglas—Spencer ("who never yet appeared on this stage");
Catherine and Petruchio.
Leeward Islands Company.
  [This performance may have been canceled due to the hurricane of this evening. See following entries for details concerning the storm and its effects. Tickets: 2 pistoles. Comic dance—Spencer and Godwin. Source: *Royal Danish American Gazette* (29 August 1772).]

31 August 1772   St. Croix
Notice of hurricane.
  [One account of this violent storm was published some time afterwards in the *Royal Danish American Gazette* of 7 October 1772, written by the young Alexander Hamilton:

> I take up my pen just to give you an imperfect account of one of the most dreadful Hurricanes that memory or any records whatever can trace, which happened here on the 31st ultimo at night. It began about dusk, at North, and raged very violently till ten o'clock. Then ensued a sudden and unexpected interval, which lasted about an hour. Meanwhile the wind was shifting round to the South West point, from whence it returned with redoubled fury and continued so till near three o'clock in the morning. Good God! What horror and destruction—it is impossible for me to describe—or you to form any idea of it. It seemed as if a total dissolution of nature was taking place. The roaring of the sea and wind—fiery meteors flying about in the air—the portentous glare of almost perpetual lighting—the crash of the falling houses—and the ear-piercing shrieks of the distressed, were sufficient to strike astonishment into Angels. A great part of the buildings throughout the island are leveled to the ground—almost all the rest very much shattered—several persons killed and numbers utterly ruined—whole familes running about the streets, unknowing where to find a place of shelter....]

31 August 1772   St. John's, Antigua
Newspaper account.
[Additional details are here reported concerning the hurricane that ravaged the island and which destroyed or badly damaged theatrical facilities:

> The wind found entrance into the Free Mason's lodge, which is lett to a company of Comedians, who had obtained his Excellency's permission to play here, and destroyed all their scenery &c. so that it will take them up a fortnight before they can put it in status quo and open it ....

Source: *Pennsylvania Gazette* (14 October 1772).]

1 September 1772   Assembly Room, Broadway, New York
Lecture on Heads.
Martin Foy.
[Source: *New York Journal* (27 August 1772).]

1 September 1772   West St. Theater, Annapolis
A Word to the Wise.
Captain Dormer–Hallam; Sir George Hastings–Henry; Sir John Dormer–Douglass; Willoughby–Morris; Villars–Goodman; Miss Dormer–Mrs. Henry; Mrs. Willoughby–Mrs. Morris; Miss Willoughby–Miss Storer; Jenny–Mrs. Wall; Lucy–Miss Richardson; Miss Montagu–Miss Hallam.
Lethe.
Frenchman and Drunkenman–Hallam; Aesop–Douglass; Mercury–Woolls; Old Man–Morris; Mr. Tattoo–Goodman; Charon–Johnson; Mrs. Riot–Miss Storer; Mrs. Tattoo–Miss Hallam.
American Company.
[Opening night of the autumn season. Prices: boxes 7s. 6d.; pit 5s. "Places in the boxes to be had at the Theatre, where a book is kept for that purpose. Ladies and gentlemen who take places will please to send their servants at five o'clock, and they shall be put in possession of them. (To begin exactly at six o'clock.)"   Source: *Maryland Gazette* (27 August–2 September 1772).

A review of the opening evening, along with the text of the Prologue as spoken by Hallam appears in the *Maryland Gazette* of 3–10 September 1772:

> On Tuesday last the theatre in this city was opened, to a brilliant and judicious assembly, with Kelly's Word to the Wise, which was received with the greatest marks of approbation.

> The alterations and improvements since last season, have made this theatre the most commodious and elegant of any, that we know of, in America. When the curtain drew up, the new scenes painted by Mr. Richards [of London], presented themselves to us, and exhibited a view of a superb apartment, at the end of a fine colonnade of pillars of the Ionic order, which, by a happy disposition of the lights, had a most pleasing effect.]

3 September 1772   Assembly Room, Broadway, New York
Lecture on Heads.
Martin Foy.

["The concert, and exhibition of the Lecture on Heads, was by desire postponed on account of the badness of the weather (yesterday) until this evening." Source: *New York Journal* (3 September 1772).]

4 September 1772   Portsmouth, New Hampshire colony
Newspaper notice.
Morgan Company.

[The *New Hampshire Gazette* of this date contains the following item:

> Mr. Morgan informs his subscribers and the public in general, that he is preparing a large room, opposite to Doctor Hall Jackson's in Pitt-Street, for his intended Exhibitions, which will be finished with all expedition.—It is humbly requested, those gentlemen who purpose honouring the subscription with their names will be so kind as to send them either to the Printing-Office, or to Mr. Morgan, the book being intended to be closed after the first night's performance.]

7 September 1772   Assembly Room, Broadway, New York
Lecture on Heads.
Martin Foy.

[Source: *New York Mercury* (7 September 1772).]

10 September 1772   New York
Newspaper notice.

[The *New York Journal* of this date contains the following item:

> The exhibiter of the Lecture on Heads, begs leave to acquaint the ladies and gentlemen, that he is making preparations for a concert and ball (before his departure from this city for Philadelphia) which he proposes to be on the beginning of the ensuing week, at Mr. Hull's Assembly Room in the Broad-Way.]

25 September 1772   Portsmouth, New Hampshire
Newspaper notice.
Morgan Company.

[The *New Hampshire Gazette* of this date prints the following item:

> The Oratorical Academy Room in Pitt-Street is nearly finish'd, and will be open'd very soon, with a Charity Night for the benefit of the poor of the town, when the following exhibitions will be performed, viz.
> 1. A Prologue in praise of charity.
> 2. The Politicians, or what News, a dramatic satire.
> 3. A comic dance, called the Irish Lilt.
> 4. A pantomimical entertainment in grotesque characters call'd the Escape or Harlequin turn'd Doctor.
>
> To conclude with an Address.]

27 September 1772   Annapolis
Correspondence.

[A letter from Alice Lee comments on her anticipation of the impending theatrical season in Annapolis:

> The Annapolis races commence the sixth of October. The company is expected to be numerous [and] The American Company of players are here and are said to be amazingly improved. I should like to see them as I think Theatrical entertainments [a rational?] amusement— but I shall not be there.

Source: Alice Lee, correspondence; Virginia Historical Society.]

28 September 1772   West St. Theater, Annapolis
The Constant Couple.
   Sir Harry Wildair–Mrs. Osborne; Colonel Standard–Douglass; Beau Clincher–Goodman; Alderman Smuggler–Morris; Vizard–Byerley; Young Clincher–Wall; Dickey–Woolls; Tom Errand–Parker; Angelica–Miss Hallam; Lady Darling–Mrs. Harman; Parley–Miss Richardson; Mob's Wife–Mrs. Wall; Lady Lurewell–Mrs. Morris.
American Company.
   [Benefit Henrietta Osborne. Source: *Maryland Gazette* (24 September 1772).]

1 October 1772   West St. Theater, Annapolis
Newspaper notice.
American Company.

[A publications notice appears in the *Maryland Gazette* of this date for the songs in *Lionel and Clarissa*, a comic opera "shortly to be performed at the theatre in Annapolis; by the American Company."]

3 October 1772   West St. Theater, Annapolis
Play not identified.
American Company.
    [A performance was held this evening, as implied by the following notice in the *Maryland Gazette* for 29 October 1772: "Lost at the play-house door on Saturday the third inst. a green leather pocket book."]

5 October 1772   West St. Theater, Annapolis
Play not identified.
American Company.
    [George Washington records in his *Diary* that he attended a performance on this date. Source: Washington, *Diaries*, 3:136.]

7 October 1772   Academy House, Portsmouth, New Hampshire
The Politicians; or, What News? A Dramatic Satire* (Anonymous).
The Escape; or, Harlequin Turned Doctor* (Anonymous).
Morgan Company.
    [Announced but postponed due to bad weather. Source: *New Hampshire Gazette* (2 and 9 October 1772).]

7 October 1772   West St. Theater, Annapolis
Play not identified.
American Company.
    [George Washington records in his *Diary* that he attended a performance on this date and spent "6 [s.]" for a ticket. Source: Washington, *Diaries*, 3:137.]

8 October 1772   West St. Theater, Annapolis
Play not identified.
American Company.
    [George Washington records in his *Diary* that he attended a performance on this date and spent "6 " for a ticket. Source: Washington, *Diaries*, 3:137; *Maryland Gazette* (8 October 1772).]

9 October 1772   West St. Theater, Annapolis
The West Indian.
The Padlock.

Mungo–Hallam.
American Company.
[George Washington records in his *Diary* that he attended a performance on this date. Source: Washington, *Diaries*, 3:137; *Maryland Gazette* (8 October 1772).]

10 October 1772   West St. Theater, Annapolis
The Maid of the Mill.
American Company.
[George Washington attended this performance and spent "12 [s.]" for tickets. Source: *Maryland Gazette* (8 October 1772); Ford (23).]

12 October 1772   Academy House, Portsmouth, New Hampshire colony
The Politicians; or, What News? A dramatic satire.
The Escape; or, Harlequin turned Doctor.
Morgan Company.
[Tickets at 3 pistereens, 2 pistereens and 1 pistereen each. Source: *New Hampshire Gazette* (9 October 1772).]

16 October 1772   Academy House, Portsmouth, New Hampshire colony
The Politicians; or, What News? A dramatic satire.
The Escape; or, Harlequin turned Doctor.
Morgan Company.
[Source: *New Hampshire Gazette* (16 October 1772).]

27 October 1772   Academy House, Portsmouth, New Hampshire colony
The Devil and the Doctor, or a Hint to the College of Physicians; A Dramatic Satire* (Anonymous).
Win Her, and Wear Her; or Harlequin Skeleton*
(Anonymous).
Morgan Company.
["Complaints having been made that the first gallery was very incommodious, Mr. Morgan takes this opportunity of informing the town, that he has alter'd it as much for the better as the house will allow, in order to do which he has been oblig'd to take away the upper gallery intirely." Source: *New Hampshire Gazette* (23 October 1772).]

28 October 1772   Southwark Theater, Philadelphia
A Word to the Wise.

Capt. Dormer–Hallam; Sir George Hastings–Henry; Sir John Dormer–Douglass; Villars–Goodman; Willoughby–Morris; Miss Dormer–Mrs. Henry; Mrs. Willoughby–Mrs. Morris; Miss Willoughby–Miss Storer; Miss Montagu–Miss Hallam; Lucy–Miss Richardson.
The Padlock.
Mungo–Hallam; Don Diego–Woolls; Leander–Wall; Ursula–Mrs. Morris; Leonora–Miss Hallam.
American Company.

[The opening of the season. Prices: boxes 7s. 6d.; pit 5s.; gallery 3s. Source: *Pennsylvania Journal* (28 October 1772).

A lengthy review of this performance appears in the *Pennsylvania Chronicle* of 24–31 October 1772, a portion of which we present here:

> On Wednesday last the theatre in Southwark was opened, by the American Company, with Kelly's Word to the Wise, and the Padlock; to a most crouded and brilliant audience–The Padlock we have, with pleasure, seen many repetitions of the last season, and Mr. Hallam, in Mungo, was, then, supposed excellent, but we, now, upon the judgement of gentlemen of undoubted knowledge and taste in theatrical performances, pronounce him to be the best Mungo upon the British stage; the other characters, except Leander, which we verily believe Mr. Wall does as well as he can, and therefore we must by no means censure him, are well supported . . . The performers in the Word to the Wise are entitled to much praise, for being so correct, spirited, and characteristic–The ladies, besides their pleasing figures, were genteel, elegant, and fashionable, in their deportment–Miss Hallam, in the sprightly Miss Montagu, was as much a woman of fashion as we have seen on the stage–But there is one grievance loudly to be complained of, and which must be remedied–Some ruffians in the gallery, who so frequently interrupted the performance, and in the most interesting scenes, deserve the severest reprehension–they are too despicable to argue with, otherwise they might be told, that, because they pay three shillings for their admittance into a public assembly, they are not, therefore, warranted to commit repeated outrages, upon that part of the audience who go there really to see the play, and be instructed and entertained; or to interrupt the actors who are doing their best to please them–They might be informed, that, tho' they have an undoubted right to every species of entertainment, promised them in the bills, they have not the smallest title to any thing else, and that if they call for a song, or a prologue, of which no notice is given in the bills, the actors have an equal demand upon them for an extraordinary price for a compliance with their request–which of those vociferous gentlemen, if a carpenter, mason, or taylor, will do more work than he bargains for without an adequate compensation? Are not the players in the same predicament.–But

416   THE COLONIAL AMERICAN STAGE

>to dismiss the subject, the directors of the theatre are thus publicly desired to engage a number of constables, and dispose them in different parts of the gallery, who upon the smallest disturbance, for the future, may be authorized, by any magistrate, and there are always enough in the house, to apprehend, and carry to the Work-house, such rioters, by which means, peace will be restored, and a few examples deter others from the like outrages. I am, Sir, your humble servant, Philo-theatricus. Oct. 30, 1772.]

30 October 1772   Academy House, Portsmouth, New Hampshire colony
The Devil and the Doctor, or a Hint to the College of Physicians; A Dramatic Satire.
Win Her, and Wear Her; or Harlequin Skeleton.
Morgan Company.
>[Source: *New Hampshire Gazette* (30 October 1772).]

2 November 1772   Southwark Theater, Philadelphia
The Roman Father.
>The Roman Father–Hallam; Tullus Hostilius–Douglass; Publius–Goodman; Valerius; Wall; 1st Citizen–Morris; 2nd Citizen–Byerley; 3rd Citizen–Woolls; 4th Citizen–Johnson; Soldier–Parker; Valeria–Mrs. Henry; Horatia–Miss Hallam.

Midas.
>Midas–Goodman; Apollo–Woolls; Jupiter–Morris; Sileno–Parker; Damaetas–Wall; Pan–Byerley; Juno–Mrs. Henry; Mysis–Mrs. Harman; Daphne–Mrs. Morris; Myra–Miss Storer.

American Company.
>[Source: *Pennsylvania Chronicle* (24–31 October 1772).]

3 November 1772   Academy House, Portsmouth, New Hampshire colony
The Devil and the Doctor, or a Hint to the College of Physicians; A Dramatic Satire.
Win Her, and Wear Her; or Harlequin Skeleton.
Morgan Company.
>[Source: *New Hampshire Gazette* (3 November 1772).]

4 November 1772   Southwark Theater, Philadelphia
Love in a Village.
>Justice Woodcock–Douglass; Young Meadows–Morris; Hawthorn–Woolls; Eustace–Byerley; Hodge–Parker; Rosetta–Miss Hallam; Lucinda–Miss Storer; Mrs. Debra Woodcock–Mrs. Douglass; Margery–Mrs. Morris;

Servants at the Statue–Goodman, Wall, Johnson, Roberts, Mrs. Harman, Miss Richardson, etc., etc.
The Old Maid.
Capt. Cape–Morris; Cleremont–Wall; Mr. Harlow– Byerley; Mr. Heartly–Parker; The Old Maid–Mrs. Harman; Mrs. Harlow–Mrs. Henry.
American Company.
[Source: *Pennsylvania Journal* (4 November 1772).]

5 November 1772   Portsmouth, New Hampshire colony
Opening of theatre.
Morgan Company.
[The *Massachusetts Spy* of this date records the following item establishing the Morgan Company's activities: "Mr. Morgan has opened a theatre at Portsmouth, New-Hampshire. The exhibitions are on Tuesday and Friday evenings."]

6 November 1772   Academy House, Portsmouth, New Hampshire colony
The Devil and the Doctor, or a Hint to the College of Physicians; A Dramatic Satire.
Win Her, and Wear Her; or Harlequin Skeleton.
Morgan Company.
[Source: *New Hampshire Gazette* (6 November 1772).]

9 November 1772   Southwark Theater, Philadelphia
The West Indian.
Belcour–Henry; Major O'Flaherty–Goodman; Mr. Stockwell– Morris; Captain Dudley–Douglass; Charles Dudley–Wall; Fulmer–Byerley; Varland–Parker; Stukely–Johnson; Sailor– Woolls; Lady Rusport–Mrs. Douglass; Louisa Dudley–Miss Storer; Lucy–Miss Richardson; Mrs. Fulmer–Mrs. Henry; Charlotte Rusport–Miss Hallam.
Miss in her Teens.
Captain Flash–Henry; Mr. Fribble–Wall; Capt. Loveit–Johnson; Puff–Morris; Jasper–Woolls; Tag–Mrs. Henry; Miss Biddy–Miss Storer.
American Company.
[Source: *Pennsylvania Chronicle* (31 October–7 November 1772).]

11 November 1772   Southwark Theater, Philadelphia
The Mourning Bride.

Osmyn–Hallam; King–Douglass; Garcia–Henry; Gonsalez–Morris; Heli–Parker; Selim–Wall; Alonzo–Byerley; Perez–Woolls; Zara–Mrs. Morris; Leonora–Miss Storer; Almeria–Miss Hallam.

The Mayor of Garratt.
Major Sturgeon–Goodman; Sir Jacob Jollup–Douglass; Sneak–Morris; Lint–Wall; Bruin–Byerley; Roger–Parker; Mrs. Bruin–Mrs. Hallam; Mrs. Sneak–Mrs. Henry.

American Company.

[The afterpiece "with alterations." Source: *Pennsylvania Journal* (11 November 1772).]

13 November 1772 Academy House, Portsmouth, New Hampshire colony
The Escape; or, Harlequin Turned Doctor.
The Politician; or, What News?
Morgan Company.

["By Desire Of the Right Worshipful the Master, and Brethren of the New-Hampshire Lodge of Free and Accepted Masons." The afterpiece is being presented for the last time. Tickets at 3 pistereens and 2 pistereens. Source: *New Hampshire Gazette* (13 November 1772).]

16 November 1772 Southwark Theater, Philadelphia
Hamlet.
Hamlet–Hallam; King–Douglass; Polonius–Morris; Laertes–Henry; Ghost–Goodman; Horatio–Parker; Marcellus–Woolls; Bernardo–Byerley; Player King–Wall; Lucianus–Roberts; Francisco–Johnson; Guildenstern–Woolls; Rosencrantz– Byerley; Player Queen–Miss Richardson; Queen–Mrs. Douglass; Ophelia–Miss Hallam; Grave-Diggers–Morris and Byerley.

The King and the Miller of Mansfield.
King–Henry; Miller–Morris; Richard–Byerley; Lord Lovewell–Wall; Joe–Woolls· Peggy–Miss Richardson; Kate–Miss Storer; Margery–Mrs. Harman.

American Company.

[Source: *Pennsylvania Chronicle* (7–14 November 1772).]

18 November 1772 Southwark Theater, Philadelphia
The Shipwreck; or, The Brothers* (Richard Cumberland, 1769).
Young Belfield–Hallam; Belfield–Henry; Capt. Ironsides–Goodman; Sir Benjamin Dove–Morris; Pater-

son–Byerley; Skiff–Woolls; Old Goodwin–Douglass; Philip–Wall; Jonathan–Parker; Francis–Johnson; Sailors–Parker, Roberts, etc.; Violetta–Mrs. Henry; Lady Dove–Mrs. Morris; Sophia– Miss Hallam; Lucy Waters–Miss Storer; Fanny–Miss Richardson.

Lethe.
Frenchman and Drunken man–Hallam; Mercury–Woolls; Old Man–Morris; Fine Gentleman–Byerley; Charon–Johnson; Tattoo–Goodman; Mrs. Riot–Miss Storer; Aesop– Douglass; Mrs. Tattoo–Miss Hallam.

American Company.

[While this is the first known performance of Cumberland's play, the piece is mentioned as in rehearsal at Williamsburg in the *Virginia Gazette* of 12 March 1772. Source: *Pennsylvania Journal* (18 November 1772).]

23 November 1772   Southwark Theater, Philadelphia
The Way to Keep Him.
Lovemore–Mr. Hallam; Sir Brilliant Fashion–Henry; Sir Bashful Constant–Douglass; Sideboard–Morris; William–Goodman; Thomas–Roberts: Richard–Parker; Widow Belmour–Miss Hallam; Lady Constant–Miss Storer; Mrs. Lovemore–Mrs. Henry; Mignionet–Miss Richardson; Furnish–Mrs. Harman.

An Honest Yorkshireman.
Gaylove–Woolls; Sapscul–Wall; Muckworm–Morris; Blunder–Parker; Slango–Byerley; Combrush–Mrs. Morris; Arabella–Miss Storer.

American Company.

[Source: *Pennsylvania Chronicle* (14–21 November 1772).]

25 November 1772   Southwark Theater, Philadelphia
The Maid of the Mill.
Lord Aimworth–Hallam; Fairfield–Douglass; Sir Harry Sycamore–Goodman; Farmer Giles–Woolls; Ralph–Wall; Merwin–Parker; Lady Sycamore–Mrs. Douglass; Theodosia–Miss Richardson; Patty–Miss Hallam; Fanny–Miss Storer; Gipsies–Morris, Byerley, Roberts, Mrs. Henry, Mrs. Morris, Mrs. Harman, etc.

The Lying Valet.
Sharp–Morris; Gayless–Wall; Justice Guttle–Goodman; Beau Trippet–Byerley; Drunken Cook–Parker; Mrs. Gadabout–Mrs. Harman; Mrs. Trippet–Miss Richardson; Melissa–Mrs. Morris; Kitty Pry–Mrs. Henry.

American Company.
>   [Source: *Pennsylvania Journal* (25 November 1772).]

27 November 1772 Academy House, Portsmouth, New Hampshire colony
Lethe.
>   Aesop–Foster; Mercury (with a song), Frenchman, and Snip the Taylor–Deacon; Old Man and Drunken Man–Morgan.

The Witches; or, Harlequin Mercury* (Anonymous).
>   Harlequin–Morgan; Don Choleric Chap Shorto de Testy–Deacon; Lumberhead–Foster; Columbine–Mrs. Foster

Morgan Company.
>   [The following item appeared in the local newspaper:

>> As many complaints have been made by persons from the country, being disappointed at there being no performance, on account of extremity of weather, Mr. Morgan gives this public assurance that nothing of that nature shall happen again, but will positively exhibit on Mondays, Wednesdays, and Fridays, 'till notice is given in this paper, for a stop to prepare something new.

Source: *New Hampshire Gazette* (27 November 1772).]

30 November 1772   Southwark Theater, Philadelphia
The Fashionable Lover* (Richard Cumberland, 1772).
>   Mortimer–Hallam; Tyrrel–Goodman; Lord Abberville–Byerley; Dr. Druid–Morris; Bridgemore–Parker; Napthali–Wall; Jarvis–Woolls; La Jeunesse–Roberts; Colin Macloid–Douglass; Aubrey–Henry; Lucinda–Mrs. Henry; Mrs. Bridgemore–Mrs. Douglass; Betty–Miss Storer; Mrs. Macintosh–Miss Richardson; Augusta Aubrey–Miss Hallam.

The Guardian.
>   The Guardian–Hallam; Lucy–Henry; Sir Charles Clochit–Morris; Young Clochit–Wall; Miss Harriet–Miss Hallam.

American Company.
>   [While this is the first known performance of Cumberland's play, the piece is mentioned as in rehearsal at Williamsburg in the *Virginia Gazette* of 7 May 1772. Source: *Pennsylvania Chronicle* (21–28 November 1772).

2 December 1772   Southwark Theater, Philadelphia
George Barnwell [i.e., *The London Merchant*].

George Barnwell–Hallam; Thorowgood–Douglass; Truman–Parker; Uncle–Henry; Blunt–Morris; Maria–Miss Storer; Lucy–Mrs. Harman; Millwood–Mrs. Morris.
Love a la Mode.
Sir Callaghan O'Brallaghan–Henry; Sir Theodore–Mr. Parker; Sir Archy Macsarcasm–Douglass; Squire Groom–Wall; Beau Mordecai–Morris; The Lady–Miss Richardson.
American Company.
[Source: *Pennsylvania Journal* (2 December 1772).]

4 December 1772   Academy House, Portsmouth, New Hampshire colony
Lethe.
The Witches; or, Harlequin Mercury.
Morgan Company.
[Source: *New Hampshire Gazette* (4 December 1772).]

7 December 1772   Southwark Theater, Philadelphia
Cymbeline.
Posthumous–Hallam; Cymbeline–Douglass; Jachimo–Henry; Bellarius–Goodman; Guiderius–Parker; Cloten–Wall; Arviragus–Woolls; Caius Lucius–Byerley; Pisanio–Morris; Philario–Parker; Cornelius–Roberts; Frenchman–Woolls; Captain–Johnson; Queen–Mrs. Douglass; Imogen–Miss Hallam; Helen–Miss Richardson.
The Upholsterer.
Barker–Wall; Quidnunc–Byerley; Feeble–Morris; Rovewell–Woolls; Bellmore–Mrs. Parker; Harriet–Miss Richardson; Termagant–Mrs. Henry.
American Company..
[Source: *Pennsylvania Chronicle* (28 November–5 December 1772).]

9 December 1772   Southwark Theater, Philadelphia
The West Indian.
As for 9 November 1772, except Charles Dudley–Hallam; Stuckley–Wall.
The Devil to Pay.
Sir John Loverule–Woolls; Jobson–Henry; Butler–Mr. Morris; Doctor–Byerley; Coachman–Johnson; Cook–Parker; Footman–Wall; Blind Fiddler–Roberts; Lady Loverule–Mrs. Harman; Lettice–Mrs. Wall; Lucy– Miss Richardson; Nell–Miss Storer.

American Company.

[A disturbance at the door took place this evening, and after the performance the theatre was vandalized. See the *Pennsylvania Packet* of 14 December 1772. Source: *Pennsylvania Journal* (9 December 1772).]

10 December 1772   Southwark Theater, Philadelphia
Theatre vandalized.

[The following notice appeared in the *Pennsylvania Chronicle* (5–12 December 1772):

> December 10, 1772. Ten Pounds Reward. A Burglary. Whereas a number of evil disposed persons, in the night between the ninth and tenth instant, burglariously and feloniously, broke open the gallery door of the theatre, tore off and carried away the iron spikes, which divide the galleries from the upper boxes; and had they not been detected, and put to flight by the servants of the theatre, who dwell in the house, would, there is reason to imagine, have compleated their malicious designs. In order, therefore, that the perpetrators may be brought to justice, the above reward is offered, to whoever will discover any of the persons concerned in the said burglary, to be paid on their conviction. David Douglass.]

14 December 1772   Southwark Theater, Philadelphia
Lionel and Clarissa; or, The School for Fathers.
  Col. Oldboy–Goodman; Lionel–Woolls; Sir John Flowerdale–Douglass; Mr. Jessamy–Wall; Jenkins–Parker; Harman–Henry; Lady Mary Oldbody–Mrs. Harman; Clarissa–Miss Storer; Diana Oldboy–Miss Hallam; Jenny–Mrs. Henry.
High Life Below Stairs.
  Lovell–Hallam; Freeman–Parker; Lord Duke–Wall; Sir Harry–Henry; Philip–Morris; Coachman–Woolls; Kinaston–Byerley; Chloe–Roberts; Lady Bab–Miss Storer; Lady Charlotte–Miss Richardson; Cook–Mrs. Harman; Kitty–Mrs. Henry.
American Company.
  [Source: *Pennsylvania Chronicle* (5–12 December 1772).]

16 December 1772   Southwark Theater, Philadelphia
Romeo and Juliet.
  Romeo–Hallam; Mercutio–Douglass; Capulet–Henry; Fryer Lawrence–Morris; Escalus–Goodman; Paris–Woolls; Benvolio–Wall; Tibalt–Parker; Montague–Byerley; Apothecary–Roberts; Lady Capulet–Mrs. Douglass; Nurse–Mrs. Harman; Juliet–Miss Hallam.

The Old Maid.
    As 4 November 1772.
American Company.
    [Source: *Pennsylvania Chronicle* (12–19 December 1772); playbill held by the Library Company of Philadelphia.]

18 December 1772   Academy House, Portsmouth, New Hampshire colony
Lethe.
The Witches; or, Harlequin Mercury.
Morgan Company.
    [Source: *New Hampshire Gazette* (18 December 1772).]

21 December 1772   Southwark Theater, Philadelphia
Romeo and Juliet.
    As 16 December 1772.
The Old Maid.
    As 16 December 1772.
American Company.
    [Source: *Pennsylvania Packet* (21 December 1772).]

22 December 1772   Academy House, Portsmouth, New Hampshire colony
A new pantomime entertainment.
Morgan Company.
    [Benefit "Mr. Deacon the minor." Source: *New Hampshire Gazette* (18 December 1772).]

23 December 1772   Southwark Theater, Philadelphia
The Suspicious Husband.
    Ranger–Hallam; Strictland–Douglass; Frankly–Henry; Jack Meggot–Wall; Tester–Morris; Buckel–Woolls; Simon–Johnson; Mrs. Strictland–Mrs. Henry; Jacintha–Mrs. Morris; Lucetta–Miss Richardson; Milliner–Miss Storer; Landlady–Mrs. Harman; Maid–Mrs. Wall; Clarinda–Miss Hallam.
Thomas and Sally.
    The Squire–Woolls; Sailor–Henry; Dorcas–Mrs. Harman; Sally–Miss Hallam.
American Company.
    [Source: *Pennsylvania Journal* (23 December 1772).]

28 December 1772   Southwark Theater, Philadelphia
Richard III.

King Richard–Hallam; Edward IV–Wall; Earl of Richmond–Henry; Henry VI–Morris; Duke of Buckingham–Douglass; Duke of York–Richardson; Tressel–Henry; Catesby–Parker; Ratcliff–Woolls; Oxford– Johnson; Tyrrell–Roberts; Lady Ann–Mrs. Henry; Duchess of York–Mrs. Harman; Queen Elizabeth–Mrs. Morris.
The Musical Lady.
Old Mash–Morris; Mash–Wall; Freeman–Parker; Rosini–Roberts; Lady Scrape–Miss Storer; Laundress–Mrs. Harman; Sophy–Miss Hallam.
American Company.
[Source: *Pennsylvania Chronicle* (19–26 December 1772).]

30 December 1772   Southwark Theater, Philadelphia
The School for Lovers.
Modley–Hallam; Sir John Dorilant–Douglass; Bellmour–Wall; Lady Beverly–Mrs. Morris; Steward–Morris; Aramita–Mrs. Henry; Celia–Miss Hallam.
The Padlock.
As 28 October 1772.
American Company.
["Not acted these five years." Source: *Pennsylvania Journal* (30 December 1772).]

30 December 1772   Academy Room in Pitt St., Portsmouth, New Hampshire colony
The Register Office* (James Reed, 1761).
The Elopement; or, Harlequin's Court* (Anonymous, 1767).
Morgan Company.
[The afterpiece is advertised as "a new pantomime entertainment .... The Scenes and Machinery entirely new." Source: *New Hampshire Gazette* (25 December 1772).]

1773

The American Company continued their season in Philadelphia. After 2 April, the company—perhaps availing themselves of Passion Week—traveled to New York where they opened on 16 April. In spite of their announcement of a brief season, they played through the first of August. Sometime after this New York season, Henry adjourned to Annapolis to prepare the theatre for the company's fall arrival. Douglass dropped from the cast lists after 1 July and commuted to

Charleston to make preparations for the company after their engagement at Annapolis. Willis (61) informs us that "during the spring and summer of 1773 a large subscription was raised" to build a fine new playhouse in Charleston. Several letters testify to the progress of the theatre during the summer (see 5, 9, and 14 August, and 6 September).

Douglass rejoined the company when they traveled from New York to Annapolis. Here they began by late September and played through the October Races. As the new theatre in Charleston was apparently not yet ready to accommodate the company, they traveled to Philadelphia for an abbreviated season (a fortnight) beginning 1 November, with a possible engagement in Baltimore along the way. Colonel J. Thomas Scharf records in his *Chronicles of Baltimore* (112–13) concerning theatrical activities in that city, that "In the year 1773 a large warehouse, which stood at the corner of Baltimore and Frederick Streets, was occasionally converted into a theatre, on the boards of which the company of Messrs. Douglass and Hallam performed plays from time to time for the edification of the colonists." From Philadelphia the American company sailed to Charleston by the end of November. Here they readied their new theatre and opened it on 22 December 1773. The repertory of the company is largely known from an important list of performances published in the *South Carolina Gazette* of 30 May 1774. This issue bears an unusual date, reading "13 December 1773–30 May 1774," as the paper was not issued during the intervening months.

The company during this year consisted of the following known personnel: Mr. Byerley, Mr. Dermont, David Douglass, Richard Goodman, Lewis Hallam Jr., Miss Nancy Hallam, Mrs. Harman, John Henry, Mrs. Henry, Mr. Johnson, Owen Morris, Mrs. Morris, Charles Parker, Miss Mary Richardson, Mr. Roberts, Miss Storer, Thomas Wall, Mrs. Wall, and Stephen Woolls. Though perhaps not a member per se, a Mr. Blackler also performs in New York with the American Company briefly in June.

The usual flux of personnel continued. Mrs. Harman (the granddaughter of Poet Laureate Colley Cibber) died in May; Mrs. Douglass was reported dead in Philadelphia in September (see 21 September), but the reports were, as they say, exaggerated, and quickly retracted. She was, as Pollock remarks (32), "demonstrably still alive" and appeared with the company in Annapolis and Philadelphia, and traveled with them to Charleston. Mr. George Hughes joined the company quite late in their New York engagement, making his debut 26 July. Miss Wainwright rejoined the company in Philadelphia, after an absence of six years. Two members left the company in Philadelphia as well: Thomas Wall remained behind to teach music; and Mary Richardson married and retired from the stage.

Mr. Morgan's company continued to strut and fret in Portsmouth, New Hampshire colony, for another half month in January, and then were heard no more. The following names of personnel are recorded in the newspaper notices: Mr. Deacon, "Mr. Deacon the minor," Mr. Foster, Mrs. Foster, Mr. Morgan, Madame Philibert, and Mr. Phipps. After a January 15 performance, the company drops from the record.

Also appearing in the colonies this year is Mr. Martin Foy presenting the *Lecture on Heads* in New York and elsewhere. the same gentleman "lately from London" who appeared during the 1772 season (Kahan 134–35); Foy can also be placed on St. Croix (see below). Likewise a "Mr. Hoar" presents the "Lecture" on 16 February 1773 in New York, but we do not know if he is responsible for the later presentations.

In Boston, Mercy Otis Warren's *The Defeat* was advertised as "lately exhibited" in late May 1773. As discussed in the headnote for the 1772 season regarding her play *The Adulateur*, however, the possibility of performance must be treated with great caution (see 24 May 1773).

In Providence, Rhode Island colony, amateur activity appeared this year. "Young Gentlemen of the town" mounted two plays on successive nights in May 1773.

In Halifax, Nova Scotia, "Gentlemen of the Army and Navy" performed during the spring on multiple occasions, beginning in April of this year, and the following winter of 1773–74 another round of plays was mounted. Very few particulars have survived.

The Playhouse on St. Croix, destroyed in the hurricane of 31 August 1772, was not rebuilt, and no record of theatrical activity on this island exists for this year. One sign of emerging possibilities, however, appears in the arrival of Martin Foy, who arrived on the island in the early summer of this year and opened a dancing school in Christianstead.

1 January 1773   Academy Room in Pitt St., Portsmouth, New Hampshire colony
The Register Office.
   Gulwell–Foster; Capt. LeBrush and Mons. Frisseron–Deacon; Williams–Phipps; Donald Macintosh and Patrick O'Carrol–Morgan.
The Elopment; or, Harlequin's Court.
   Harlequin–Morgan; Squire Gawkey–Deacon; Nincompoop–Foster; Magus–Phipps; Colombine–Madame Philibert.
Morgan Company.
   [Source: *New Hampshire Gazette* (1 January 1773).]

4 January 1773   Southwark Theater, Philadelphia
Lionel and Clarissa.
   As 14 December 1772.
Love a la mode.
   As 2 December 1772.
American Company.
   [Source: *Pennsylvania Chronicle* (2 January 1772).]

6 January 1773   Southwark Theater, Philadelphia
Tamerlane.
   Bajazet–Hallam; Tamerlane–Douglass; Moneses–Goodman; Axalla–Wall; Omar–Henry; Dervise–Morris; Haly–Parker; Prince of Tanais–Woolls; Zama–Johnson; Mirvan–Roberts; Selima–Mrs. Henry; Arpasia–Mrs. Morris.
Catherine and Petruchio.
   Petruchio–Goodman; Grumio–Morris; Biondello–Wall; Hertensio–Parker; Baptisa–Byerley; Taylor–Roberts; Curtis–Mrs. Harman; Bianca–Miss Richardson; Catherine–Mrs. Morris.
American Company.
   [Source: *Pennsylvania Journal* (6 January 1773).]

11 January 1773   Southwark Theater, Philadelphia
Henry IV, Part 1.
   Hotspur–Hallam; King Henry–Morris; Prince of Wales–Henry; Sir Walter Blunt–Goodman; Worcester–Byerley; Vernon–Parker; Westmoreland–Wall; Northumberland–Woolls; Bardolph–Johnson; Francis–Roberts; Sir John Falstaff–Douglass; 1st Carrier–Goodman; Poins–Byerley; Douglass–Woolls; 2nd Carrier–Parker; Peto–Wall; Prince

428   THE COLONIAL AMERICAN STAGE

    John–Roberts; Hostess Quickly–Mrs. Harman; Lady Percy– Mrs. Morris.
The Devil to Pay.
  As 14 December 1772.
American Company.
  [Source: *Pennsylvania Packet* (11 January 1773).]

13 January 1773 Southwark Theater, Philadelphia
Love for Love.
    Valentine–Hallam; Sir Sampson Legen–Henry; Scandal–Douglass; Tattle–Wall; Foresight–Morris; Jeremy–Byerley; Trapland–Parker; Buckram–Woolls; Ben–Goodman; Miss Prue–Miss Storer; Angelica–Mrs. Henry; Nurse–Mrs. Harman; Mrs. Foresight–Miss Richardson; Mrs. Frail–Mrs. Morris.
High Life Below Stairs.
  As 14 December 1772.
American Company.
  [Source: *Pennsylvania Journal* (13 January 1773).]

15 January 1773 Academy Room in Pitt St., Portsmouth,
          New Hampshire colony
Play not identified.
Morgan Company.
  [Benefit Mrs. Foster. Source: *New Hampshire Gazette* (15 January 1773).]

18 January 1773 Southwark Theater, Philadelphia
The Conscious Lovers.
    Young Bevil–Hallam; Mr. Sealand–Douglass; Sir John Bevil–Goodman; Cimberton–Byerley; Humphry–Parker; Daniel–Roberts; Tom–Morris; Myrtle–Mrs. Wall; Mrs. Sealand–Mrs. Harman; Phillis–Miss Storer; Isabella–Mrs. Douglass; Lucinda–Miss Richardson; Indiana–Mrs. Morris.
Love a la Mode.
  As 2 December 1772.
American Company.
  [Source: *Pennsylvania Packet* (18 January 1773).]

19 January 1773 Cox's Long Room, New York
Lecture on Heads.
Martin Foy.

[Price: 5s. Source: *New York Mercury* (18 January 1773).]

20 January 1773   Southwark Theater, Philadelphia
The Shipwreck [i.e., *The Brothers*].
    As 18 November 1772, except Sophia–Miss Storer; Fanny–Mrs. Wall; Lucy Waters–Miss Richardson.
The Buck; or, the Englishman in Paris.
    Buck–Goodman; Sir John Buck–Morris; Mr. Subtle–Henry; Classic–Parker; Dauphine–Roberts; Solitaire–Wall; Gamut–Woolls; Roger–Johnson; Marquis–Byerley; Mrs. Subtle–Miss Richardson; Lucinda–Miss Storer.
American Company.
    [Source: *Pennsylvania Gazette* (20 January 1773).]

25 January 1773   Southwark Theater, Philadelphia
False Delicacy.
    Cecil–Hallam; Col. Rivers–Douglass; Lord Winworth–Henry; Sir Harry Newburg–Wall; Sidney–Byerley; Miss Betty Lambton–Mrs. Morris; Miss Marchmont–Miss Storer; Miss Rivers–Mrs. Henry; Sally–Miss Richardson; Mrs. Harly–Mrs. Douglass.
Lethe.
    As 18 November 1772, except Mrs. Tattoo–Mrs. Henry.
American Company.
    [Source: *Pennsylvania Chronicle* (25 January 1773).]

26 January 1773   De La Montagne's Long Room, New York
Lecture on Heads.
Martin Foy.
    [Price: 5s. Source: *New York Journal* (28 January 1773).]

27 January 1773   Southwark Theater, Philadelphia
Othello.
    Othello–Hallam; Iago–Douglass; Cassio–Goodman; Roderigo–Wall; Lodorico–Henry; Brabantio–Morris; Duke–Byerley; Montano–Parker; Officer–Johnson; Gratiano–Woolls; Messenger–Roberts; Desdemona–Mrs. Henry; Emilia–Mrs. Douglass.
Midas.
    As 2 November 1772, except Juno–Wall; Mysis–Miss Richardson.
American Company.
    [Source: *Pennsylvania Journal* (27 January 1773).]

29 January 1773   De La Montagne's Long Room, New York
Lecture on Heads.
Martin Foy.
    ["(By permission.) At Mr. De La Montagne's Long Room, at the King's Arms, near the Liberty Pole. The exhibiter of the Lecture on Heads, returns his most sincere thanks to the ladies and gentlemen, who honoured him with their presence."
Source: *New York Journal* (28 January 1773).]

1 February 1773   Southwark Theater, Philadelphia
The Tempest.
    Prospero–Douglass; Ferdinand–Hallam; Alonzo–Byerley; Antonio–Parker; Hypolito–Wall; Gonzalo–Johnson; Stephano–Morris; Trinculo–Henry; Ventoso–Johnson; Mustachio–Woolls; Ariel–Miss Storer; Miranda and Dorinda–Mrs. Henry and Miss Hallam; Caliban and Sycano–Goodman and Roberts.
Neptune and Amphitrite.
    Neptune–Woolls; Amphitrite–Miss Storer.
Miss in her Teens.
    As 9 November 1772, except Captain Loveit is not named.
American Company.
    [Source: *Pennsylvania Chronicle* (25 January–1 February 1773).]

3 February 1773   Southwark Theater, Philadelphia
The Tempest.
Neptune and Amphitrite.
    As 1 February 1773.
High Life Below Stairs.
    As 14 December 1772, except Freeman–Byerley; Kingston–Parker; Cook–Mrs. Wall.
American Company.
    [Source: *Pennsylvania Journal* (3 February 1773).]

8 February 1773   Southwark Theater, Philadelphia
The Beggar's Opera.
    Capt. Macheath–Hallam; Peachum–Douglass; Mat o'th' Mint–Goodman; Lockit–Morris; Nimming Ned–Byerley; Filch–Wall; Jerry Twitcher–Johnson; Ben Budge–Parker; Moll Brazen–Roberts; Mrs. Peachum–Mrs. Morris; Lucy–Miss Storer; Mrs. Coaxer–Mrs. Henry; Jenny Diver–Miss Richardson; Mrs. Slammekin–Mrs. Wall; Diana Trapes–Miss Richardson; Polly–Miss Hallam.

The Mayor of Garratt.
>As 11 November 1772.
>American Company.
>>[Source: *Pennsylvania Chronicle* (1-8 February 1773).]

10 February 1773   Southwark Theater, Philadelphia
Theodosius.
>Varanes-Hallam; Theodosius-Henry; Marcian-Douglass; Leontine-Goodman; Cetticus-Woolls; Lucius-Parker; Aranthes-Wall; Priests-Morris & Byerley; Pulcheria-Morris; Marina-Miss Storer; Julia-Mrs. Wall; Flavilla-Miss Richardson; Anthenais-Miss Hallam.

The Honest Yorkshireman.
>As 23 November 1772.
>American Company.
>>[Source: *Pennsylvania Journal* (10 February 1773).]

15 February 1773   Southwark Theater, Philadelphia
Lionel and Clarissa.
>As 4 January 1773, except Lady Mary Oldboy-Mrs. Douglass.

Edgar and Emmeline.
>Edgar-Hallam; Florimond-Wall; First Aerial Spirit-Miss Storer; Second Aerial Spirit-Mrs. Henry; Woman to Elfida- Miss Richardson; Emmeline-Miss Hallam; Other Spirits- Goodman, Woolls, Byerley, Parker, Mrs. Morris, Mrs. Wall, &c.

American Company.
>>[Source: *Pennsylvania Chronicle* (8-15 February 1773).]

16 February 1773   Hull's Tavern, New York
Lecture on Heads.
Mr. Hoar.
>[To conclude with a ball. Price: one dollar. The complete notice provides further details:

>>Mr. Hoar, begs leave to acquaint the ladies and gentlemen of this city, that he has just received a copy of Mr. George Alexander Stevens's new lectures (with charatura heads and dresses) as they are now delivered in London, by that celebrated genius; which Mr. Hoar proposes (under their patronage) exhibiting on Tuesday the 16th inst. in the ball room, at Mr. Hull's Tavern, in the Broad Way, with a humorous epilogue, and a real representation of a married blood of the first rate, after he has been keeping it up. Between the acts, the young lad will sing a number of favourite songs, with proper accompaniments.–The whole to conclude with a ball, under

the same restrictions of the concert and ball which he had the honour of conducting on the 5th of October last.

Source: *New York Journal* (4 February 1773).]

17 February 1773   Southwark Theater, Philadelphia
The Conquest of Canada* (George Cockings, 1766).
General Wolfe–Hallam; Leonatus–Douglass; Britannicus–Henry; Montcalm–Goodman; Bougainville–Wall; Levi–Morris; Peryton–Byerley; First Caledonian Chief–A Gentleman (being his first appearance on any stage); Second Caledonian Chief–Woolls; Jemmy Chaunter–Woolls; Sailors–Johnson, Roberts, etc.; Sophia–Miss Hallam; Abers–Mrs. Morris; First Nun–Mrs. Henry; Second Nun–Miss Storer; Maid–Miss Richardson; Sophronia–Mrs. Douglass; Sea and Land Officers–Byerley, Johnson, Parker, Woolls, Roberts, and a young gentleman (who never appeared on any stage before).
American Company.
[Premiere of the mainpiece:

It will be taken as a favor if the town, for this night, will dispense with a farce, as the stage will be much crowded with the artillery, boats, &c. necessary for the representation of the piece, and with the men from both corps, which assistance the commanding officers are good enough to indulge us with.

Source: *Pennsylvania Journal* (17 February 1773).]

22 February 1773   Southwark Theater, Philadelphia
The Conquest of Canada.
As 17 February 1773.
Love a la mode.
As 4 January 1773, except Sir Theodore–Byerley.
American Company.
[This is the third performance of the mainpiece. Source: *Pennsylvania Chronicle* (15–22 February 1773).]

26 February 1773   Southwark Theater, Philadelphia
A Word to the Wise.
As 28 October 1772.
Catherine and Petruchio.
As 6 January 1773, except Curtis–Mrs. Wall.
American Company.
[Source: *Pennsylvania Journal* (24 February 1773).]

3 March 1773   Southwark Theater, Philadelphia
Cymon* (David Garrick and Thomas Arne, 1766).
   Cymon–Hallam; Merlin–Goodman; Linco–Woolls; Dorus–Morris; Damon–Wall; Dorillas–Byerley; First Demon of Revenge–Woolls; Cupid–Miss Storer; Urganda–Mrs. Morris; Fatima–Mrs. Henry; Dorcas–Miss Richardson; First Shepherdess–Miss Storer; Second Shepherdess–Miss Richardson; Sylvia–Miss Hallam.
American Company.
   [Source: *Pennsylvania Chronicle* (22 February–1 March 1773).]

5 March 1773   Hull's Tavern, New York
Lecture on Heads.
Mr. Hoar.
   [To conclude with a ball. Price: one dollar. Source: *New York Journal* (4 March 1773).]

8 March 1773   Southwark Theater, Philadelphia
The Fashionable Lover.
   As 30 November 1772 except Lord Abberville–Wall; Bridgemore–Byerley; Napthali–Roberts; Mrs. Bridgemore–Mrs. Morris.
Edgar and Emmeline.
   As 15 February 1773, except Another Spirit–Roberts and "Woman to Elfrida" not mentioned.
American Company.
   [Benefit Mr. and Mrs. Douglass. Source: *Pennsylvania Chronicle* (1–8 March 1773).]

10 March 1773   Southwark Theater, Philadelphia
The Merchant of Venice.
   Antonio–Hallam; Bassanio–Douglass; Shylock–Henry; Gratiano–Goodman; Lorenzo–Woolls; Duke–Byerley; Salanio–Wall; Solarino–Dermont; Tubal–Roberts; Gobbo–Byerley; Lancelot–Morris; Jessica–Miss Hallam; Nerissa–Miss Richardson; Portia–Mrs. Morris.
Flora; or, Hob in the Well.
   Hob–Hallam; Old Hob–Byerley; Sir Thomas Tasty–Morris; Countrymen–Wall, Roberts, and Dermont; Dick–Johnson; Friendly–Woolls; Hob's Mother–Miss Richardson; Betty–Mrs. Henry; Flora–Miss Storer.
American Company.
   [Benefit Mr. and Mrs. Henry. Source: *Pennsylvania Journal* (10 March 1773).]

15 March 1773   Southwark Theater, Philadelphia
The West Indian.
    As 9 November 1772, except Belcour–Hallam; Charles Dudley–Henry; Varland–Woolls; The Sailor–Roberts; Stukely–Wall; Lady Rusport–Mrs. Morris.
The Padlock.
    As 28 October 1772.
The Picture of a Playhouse; or, Bucks Have at Ye All.
American Company.
    [Benefit Hallam. Source: *Pennsylvania Chronicle* (8–15 March 1773).]

17 March 1773   Southwark Theater, Philadelphia
The Beaux' Stratagem.
    Archer–Hallam; Aimwell–Douglass; Sullen–Henry; Forgard–Goodman; Freeman–Wall; Gibbet–Woolls; Boniface–Byerley; Bagshot–Dermont; Hounslow–Roberts; Scrub–Morris; Dorinda–Miss Richardson; Cherry–Mrs. Henry; Lady Bountiful–Mrs. Wall; Gipsy–Miss Storer; Mrs. Sullen–Mrs. Morris.
Catherine and Petruchio.
    As 6 January 1773, except Hortentio–Dermont; Curtis–Mrs. Wall.
American Company.
    [Benefit Mr. and Mrs. Morris. Source: *Pennsylvania Journal* (17 March 1773).]

22 March 1773   Southwark Theater, Philadelphia
The Earl of Essex.
    Essex–Hallam; Southampton–Henry; Burleigh–Morris; Lieutenant–Woolls; Raleigh–Byerley; Queen Elizabeth–Mrs. Morris; Countess of Rutland–Miss Hallam; Countess of Nottingham–Mrs. Henry.
The Citizen.
    Young Wilding–Hallam; Young Philpot–Wall; Old Philpot–Morris; Beaufort–Woolls; Sir Jasper–Byerley; Quildrive–Roberts; Corinna–Miss Richardson; Maria–Miss Hallam.
American Company.
    [Announced but probably not performed. See 27 March 1773. Benefit Woolls and Wall. Source: *Pennsylvania Chronicle* (15–22 March 1773).]

24 March 1773   Southwark Theater, Philadelphia
The Recruiting Officer.

Capt. Plume–Hallam; Sergeant Kite–Douglass; Capt. Brayers–Byerley; Mr. Worthy–Woolls; Justice Balance–Morris; Bullock–Goodman; Justice Scale–Dermont; 1st Recruit–Wall; 2nd Recruit–Roberts; Rose–Miss Hallam; Melinda–Mrs. Henry; Lucy–Miss Richardson; Sylvia (by particular desire)–Mrs. Morris.
Edgar and Emmeline.
Edgar–Hallam; Florimond–Wall; Emmeline–Miss Hallam.
American Company.
[Benefit Byerley, Parker, and Johnson. Source: *Pennsyl-vania Journal* (24 March 1773).]

25 March 1773 New York
Newspaper notice.
Mr. Hoar.
[The *New York Journal* of this date contains the following notice regarding the activities of Mr. Hoar:
> Mr. Hoar returns his most grateful acknowledgments to the ladies and gentlemen, as well as the public in general, for the many favours he has received at their hands since his residence in this city, and with the greatest concern finds that the public character he has appeared in, has laid him open to the malevolence and dark assassinations of a few enemies, who have with some degree of success propagated many (equally base as false) reports to his disadvantage, he being conscious of his own innocence; takes this public method of daring his greatest foes to step forth, and if in their power, make good their assertions, which, if true, will be doing an act of justice, that the impartial public is intitled to. N.B. He likewise humbly requests, (thro' humanity, as well as for justice sake) that any gentleman who can give him the author of any of the base reports, which have been propagated injurious to his character, will not conceal the assassin.]

27 March 1773 Southwark Theater, Philadelphia
The Earl of Essex.
As 22 March 1773.
The Citizen.
As 22 March 1773.
A Picture of a Playhouse.
By Hallam.
American Company.
[Benefit Woolls and Wall. Source: playbill in the Harvard Theatre Collection.]

29 March 1773 Southwark Theater, Philadelphia
A Wonder! A Woman Keeps a Secret!

Don Felix–Hallam; Colonel Briton–Henry; Don Pedro–Goodman; Don Lopez–Byerley; Frederick–Woolls; Lissando–Morris; Vasquez–Roberts; Gibby–Douglass; Donna Isabella–Miss Storer; Flora–Mrs. Henry; Inis–Miss Richardson; Donna Violante–Miss Hallam.
The Register Office.
Capt. LeBrush–Hallam; Lord Brilliant–Goodman; Scotchman–Douglass; Irishman–Henry; Frenchman–Roberts; Harwood–Wall; Tricket–Morris; Gulwell–Byerley; Frankly–Woolls; Williams–Johnson; Maria–Miss Storer; Margery Moorpont–Mrs. Henry.
American Company.
[Second benefit for Mr. and Mrs. Henry. The afterpiece advertised as "never performed in America," but see 30 December 1772. Source: *Pennsylvania Chronicle* (22–29 March 1773).]

31 March 1773   Southwark Theater, Philadelphia
The Tempest.
As 3 February 1773, except Antonio–Dermont.
Neptune and Amphitrite.
The Guardian.
As 30 November 1772.
American Company.
["The last night but one." Pollock comments that "Probably the last night came on Friday, April 2, but we have no record" (127). The American Company then traveled to New York. Source: *Pennsylvania Journal* (31 March 1773).]

31 March 1773   Southwark Theater, Philadelphia
Newspaper notice.
[The *Pennsylvania Journal* of this date contains the following item:
"All person having any demands on the American Theatre are requested to send in their accounts to the subscriber, that they may be paid. John Henry."]

13 April 1773   Atwater's Tavern, New Haven, Connecticut colony
The West Indian.
Students of Yale College.
[Bloom (53–4) records that the student members of the Linonian Club of Yale College performed this play.]

14 April 1773   John St. Theater, New York
The Way to Keep Him.

Catherine and Petruchio.
American Company.
[The company's opening night in New York. The play titles, which are not given in the newspaper notice, are from Seilhamer (1:317), who does not provide a reference. Source: *New York Gazette & Weekly Post-Boy* (12 April 1773).]

16 April 1773   John St. Theater, New York
The West Indian.
    Belcour–Hallam; Major O'Flaherty–Henry; Capt. Dudley–Douglass; Stockwell–Morris; Charles Dudley–Wall; Fulmer–Byerley; Varland–Woolls; Lady Rusport–Mrs. Morris; Lady Dudley–Miss Storer; Mrs. Fulmer–Mrs. Henry; Lucy–Miss Richardson; Charlotte–Miss Hallam.
Miss In Her Teens.
    Flash–Henry; Fribble–Wall; Loveit–Byerley; Puff–Morris; Tag–Mrs. Henry; Miss Biddy–Miss Storer.
American Company.
[Source: *New York Journal* (15 April 1773); cast from a playbill in the Harvard Theatre Collection.]

19 April 1773   John St. Theater, New York
The Clandestine Marriage.
    Lord Ogleby–Hallam; Sir John Melvill–Douglass; Lovewell–Henry; Sterling–Morris; Serjeant Flower–Goodman; Traverse–Byerley; Truman–Woolls; Canton–Roberts; Brush–Wall; Miss Sterling–Miss Hallam; Miss Fanny–Miss Storer; Betty–Mrs. Henry; Chambermaid–Miss Richardson; Mrs. Heidelberg–Mrs. Morris.
The Padlock.
    Mungo–Hallam; Don Diego–Woolls; Leander–Wall; Ursula–Mrs. Morris; Leonora–Miss Hallam.
American Company.
[Source: *New York Mercury* (19 April 1773).]

23 April 1773   John St. Theater, New York
The Way to Keep Him.
    Lovemore–Hallam; Sir Bashful Constant–Douglass; Sir Brilliant Fashion–Henry; William–Goodman; Sideboard–Morris; Mrs. Lovemore–Mrs. Henry; Lady Constant–Mrs. Morris; Muslin–Miss Storer; Mignionet–Miss Richardson; Furnish–Mrs. Wall; Widow Belmore (with a song)–Miss Hallam.
Catherine and Petruchio.

Petruchio–Goodman; Grumio–Morris; Baptista–Byerley; Biondello–Wall; Hortentio–Parker; Taylor–Roberts; Bianca–Miss Richardson; Curtis–Mrs. Wall; Catharine–Mrs. Morris.
American Company.
[Source: *Rivington's New York Gazette* (22 April 1773).]

23 April 1773   Halifax, Nova Scotia
The Suspicious Husband.
The Citizen.
Gentlemen of the Army and Navy.
[Source: Ferguson 424.]

26 April 1773   John St. Theater, New York
King Lear.
King Lear–Hallam; Edgar–Henry; Bastard–Douglass; Kent–Goodman; Gloster–Morris; Albany–Parker; Cornwall–Byerley; Gentleman Usher–Wall; Burgundy–Woolls; Goneril–Mrs. Morris; Regan–Mrs. Henry; Arante–Miss Richardson; Cordelia–Miss Hallam.
The Citizen.
The Citizen–Wall; Old Philpot–Morris; Young Wilding–Parker; Sir Jasper–Byerley; Beaufort–Woolls; Corinna–Miss Richardson; Maria–Miss Hallam.
American Company.
[Source: *New York Mercury* (26 April 1773).]

30 April 1773   John St. Theater, New York
The Earl of Essex.
Earl of Essex–Hallam; Earl of Southampton–Henry; Lord Burleigh–Morris; Sir Walter Raleigh–Byerley; Lieutenant of the Tower–Woolls; Queen Elizabeth–Mrs. Morris; Countess of Nottingham–Mrs. Henry.
The Englishman in Paris.
Buck–Goodman; Mr. Subtle–Henry; Sir John Buck–Morris; Classic–Parker; Marquis–Byerley; Dauphine–Roberts; Solitaire–Wall; Gamut–Woolls; Roger–Dermont; Mrs. Subtle– Miss Richardson; Lucinda (with a song)–Miss Storer.
American Company.
[Source: *Rivington's New York Gazette* (29 April 1773).]

3 May 1773   John St. Theater, New York
The Beaux' Stratagem.

Archer–Hallam; Aimwell–Douglass; Sullen–Henry; Foigard–Goodman; Freeman–Wall; Gibbet–Woolls; Boniface–Byerley; Scrub–Morris; Dorinda–Miss Richardson; Cherry–Mrs. Henry; Gipsey–Miss Storer; Lady Bountiful–Mrs. Wall; Mrs. Sullen–Miss Hallam.

Midas.
Apollo–Woolls; Jupiter–Morris; Mars–Douglass; Neptune–Dermont; Mercury–Roberts; Pan–Byerley; Midas–Goodman; Sileno–Parker; Damaetas–Wall. Daphne–Mrs. Morris; Mysis–Miss Richardson; Nysa–Miss Storer; Juno–Mrs. Wall; Venus–Mrs. Henry; Diana–Miss Hallam.
American Company.

[Afterpiece advertised as "performed but once." The company was being plagued by disruptive gallery clientele, as evidenced by the following paragraph appended to this day's program:

> The repeated insults, which some mischievous persons in the gallery have given, not only to the stage and orchestra, but to the other parts of the audience, call loudly for reprehension; and since they have been, more than once, ineffectually admonish'd of the impropriety of such a conduct in a public assembly, they are now (for the last time) inform'd, that unless the more regular and better dispos'd people, who frequent that part of the theatre, will interfere, either by turning out the offenders, or pointing them out to the constables, who attend there on purpose, that they may be brought to justice, the gallery for the future must be shut up.

Source: *New York Mercury* (3 May 1773).]

5 May 1773　　　　　John St. Theater, New York
The Tempest.
American Company.

[The following critical remarks appeared in the *New York Mercury* (10 May 1773), which provides the evidence for this performance:

> Last Wednesday the play of the Tempest, or the Inchanted Island, written by Shakespear, and altered by Dryden, was perform'd at the Theatre in this city, to a numerous and brilliant audience with universal applause; the machinery is elegant, and the whole is allowed to be one of the most pleasing pieces that has made its appearance on the American Theatre.]

7 May 1773   John St. Theater, New York
Love in a Village.
The Mayor of Garratt.
American Company.
   [Afterpiece advertised as "with alterations." Source: *Rivington's New York Gazette* (6 May 1773).]

10 May 1773   John St. Theater, New York
The Gamester.
   Beverley–Hallam; Stukely–Douglass; Lewson–Goodman; Jarvis–Morris; Dawson–Woolls; Bates–Byerley; Charlotte–Miss Storer; Lucy–Miss Richardson; Mrs. Beverley–Miss Hallam.
The Padlock.
   Mungo–Hallam; Don Diego–Woolls; Leander–Wall; Ursula–Mrs. Morris; Leonora–Miss Hallam.
American Company.
   [This performance may have been postponed. As noted by Odell (1: 163), one Josia Quincy, a visitor from Massachusetts, records in his journal that he saw this program on 11 May 1773. Dunlap (122) reprints Quincy's remarks on this evening's program:

> Went to the playhouse in the evening, saw The Gamester and Padlock performed. The players made an indifferent figure in tragedy. They make a much better in comedy. Hallam has merit in every character he acts. Mr. Wools, in the character of Don Diego, and Mrs. Morris in that of Ursula, I thought, acted superlatively. I was however much gratified upon the whole, and I believe if I had staid in town [i.e., New York] a month, I should go to the theatre every acting night. But, as a citizen and friend to the morals and happiness of society, I should strive hard against the admission, and much more the establishment, of a play-house in any state of which I was a member.

Source: *New York Mercury* (10 May 1773).]

11 May 1773   Hull's Assembly Room, New York
Musical concert.
Members of the American Company.
   [While not a theatrical performance, a number of the American Company personnel performed for the benefit of Mr. Zedwitz, a musician, and possibly a composer for the American Company. Entertainers included Hulett, Miss Hallam, and Miss Storer. Source: *New York Mercury* (10 May 1773).]

THE COLONIAL AMERICAN STAGE 441

13 May 1773   John St. Theatre, New York
The Tempest.
The Honest Yorkshireman.
Neptune and Amphitrite.
American Company.
[Josiah Quincy recorded the following account of this program:

> Spent the day in riding and rambling, and the evening at the playhouse. The Tempest of Shakespear, the Masque of Neptune and Amphitrite, and the Honest Yorkshireman was performed. The scenery of The Tempest was far beyond what I thought practicable. The players excell in comedy; are but indifferent in tragedy.

Source: Quincy, *Journal,* 479–80.]

14 May 1773   John St. Theater, New York
The Mourning Bride.
    Osmin–Hallam; The King–Douglass; Garcia–Henry; Gonsalez–Morris; Selim–Wall; Alonzo–Byerley; Perez–Woolls; Heli–Parker; Zara–Mrs. Morris; Leonora–Miss Storer; Almeria–Miss Hallam.
Midas.
    As 3 May 1773, except Minerva–M. Hallam.
American Company.
[Afterpiece "by desire." Source: *Rivington's New York Gazette* (13 May 1773).]

17 May 1773   John St. Theater, New York
The Maid of the Mill.
    Lord Ainsworth–Hallam; Sir Harry Sycamore–Goodman; Miller Fairfield–Douglass; Farmer Giles–Woolls; Mervin–Parker; Ralph–Wall; Lady Sycamore–Mrs. Morris; Fanny–Miss Storer; Theodosia–Miss Richardson; Patty–Miss Hallam; Gipsies–Morris, Byerley, Dermont, Mrs. Henry, Mrs. Wall, &c.
High Life Below Stairs.
    Lovel–Hallam; Freeman–Byerley; Lord Duke–Wall; Sir Harry–Henry; Coachman–Woolls; Tom–Dermont; Lady Bab (with a song)–Miss Storer; Lady Charlotte–Miss Richardson; Cook–Mrs. Wall; Chloe–Roberts; Kitty–Mrs. Henry,
American Company.
[Source: *New York Mercury* (17 May 1773).]

21 May 1773   John St. Theater, New York
The Beggar's Opera.
    Capt. Macheath–Hallam; Peachum–Douglass; Lockit–Morris; Matt o' th' Mint–Wall; Ben Budge–Parker; Jemmy Twitcher–Byerley; Nimming Ned–Dermont; Lucy–Miss Storer; Mrs. Peachum–Mrs. Morris; Jenny Diver–Miss Richardson; Mrs. Coaxer–Mrs. Henry; Mrs. Slammakin–Mrs. Wall; Polly–Miss Hallam.
Catherine and Petruchio.
    Petruchio–Goodman; Grumio–Morris; Baptista–Byerley; Biondello–Wall; Hortentio–Parker; Taylor–Roberts; Bianca–Miss Richardson; Curtis–Mrs. Wall; Catherine–Mrs. Morris.
American Company.
    [Source: *Rivington's New York Gazette* (20 May 1773).]

24 May 1773   John St. Theater, New York
Theodosius.
    Varanes–Hallam; Theodosius–Henry; Marcian–Douglass; Leontine–Goodman; Atticus–Woolls; Lucius–Parker; Aranthes–Wall; Pulcheria–Mrs. Morris; Flavilla–Miss Storer; Marina–Miss Richardson; Julia–Mrs. Wall; Athenais–Miss Hallam.
The Lying Valet.
    Sharp–Morris; Gayless–Wall; Justice Guttle–Goodman; Beau Trippet–Byerley; Drunken Cook–Parker; Melissa–Mrs. Morris; Mrs. Gadabout–Miss Richardson; Mrs. Trippet–Mrs. Wall; Kitty Pry–Mrs. Henry.
American Company.
    [Source: *New York Mercury* (24 May 1773).]

24 May 1773   Boston
The Defeat* (Mercy Otis Warren).
    [The following notice suggests the possibility that Warren's play may have been performed sometime prior to this date:

> Messrs Edes and Gill, As many of your country readers have been out of the way of the theatrical amusements of the last season, it may perhaps be some entertainment to them to see a few extracts from The Defeat, a dramatic performance lately exhibited. The author has thought proper to give as a prologue, the following lines of a celebrated writer.
>
>   O how I laugh when I a Blockhead see
>   Thanking a villain for his probity,
>   Who stretches out a most respectful ear
>   With snares for wood-cocks in his holy leer,

> It tickles tho' my soul to hear the Cock's,
> Sincere encomium on his friend the fox,
> Sole patron of his liberties and rights,
> While graceless reynard listens — till he bites.

Source: *Boston Gazette* (26 May 1773).]

24 May 1773 Mr. Hacker's Hall, Providence, Rhode Island colony

The Orphan.
  Polidore–[Thomas] Halsey; Castilo–Harris; Thamont–[William] Bloget; Monimia–Joseph Rus[s]el.
Miss in Her Teens.
Acted by "Young Gentlemen of the town."
  [See the contemporary account in the entry for 30 May 1773. Source: *Providence Gazette* (29 May 1773).]

25 May 1773 Mr. Hacker's Hall, Providence, Rhode Island colony

The Orphan.
  Presumably as 24 May 1773.
Miss in Her Teens.
Acted by "Young Gentlemen of the town."
  [Source: *Providence Gazette* (29 May 1773).]

27 May 1773 New York
Death of performer.
  [The *New York Mercury* of 7 June 1773 contains the following notice of the death of Mrs. Harman:

> [On 27 May] "departed this life in her 43d year, Mrs. Catharine Maria Harman, grand daughter to the celebrated Colley Cibber, Esq; and one of the American Company of Comedians, by all of whom she was much esteemed: The Saturday following her remains were decently interred in Trinity Church Yard.

A similar notice in the *Pennsylvania Chronicle* of 31 May–7 June 1773 adds the following remarks:

> she was a just actress, possessed much merit in low comedy, and dressed all her characters with infinite propriety, but her figure prevented her from succeeding in tragedy, and in genteel comedy. In private life, she was sensible, humane and benevolent, her little fortune she has left to Miss Cheer, and her obsequies were on Saturday night attended by a very genteel procession to the cemetery of the Old English Church.]

28 May 1773   John St. Theater, New York
Hamlet.
      Hamlet–Hallam; Claudius–Douglass; Laertes–Henry; Polonius–Morris; Horatio–Parker; Player King–Wall; Guildenstern–Woolls; Rosencrantz–Byerley; Grave diggers–Morris and Wall; Ghost–Goodman; Gertrude–Mrs. Douglass; Player Queen–Miss Richardson; Ophelia–Miss Hallam.
Cross Purposes* (William O'Brien, 1772).
      Grub–Goodman; Francis Bevil–Douglass; Harry Bevil–Henry; George Bevil–Hallam; Chapeau–Wall; Robin–Morris; Consol–Byerley; Emily–Miss Storer; Maid–Miss Richardson; Mrs. Grub–Mrs. Morris.
American Company.
      [O'Brien's farce had premiered in London on 5 December 1772 (Covent Garden). George Washington records in his *Diary* that he attended this performance. Source: *Rivington's New York Gazette* (27 May 1773); Washington, *Diaries*, 3: 182.]

30 May 1773   Providence, Rhode Island colony
Review of performance.
      [Referring to the 24 and 25 May 1773 amateur productions in Providence, Nathanael Greene wrote to Samuel Ward, Jr. on 30 May 1773 the following sarcastic account of the productions:

> Ring the Bells backward. Cry fire, the church is in danger. There has been a play acted in Providence known by the Name of the Unhappy Orphan. Joseph Rus[s]el acted Monemia; Mr. Halsey, Polid; Mr. Harris, Castalis; Mr. Bloget, Thamont. I have forgot the under characters, but it is said they performd inimitably well, and to the satisfaction of all the spectators. They had Hackers Hall with regular Scenes formd for that purpose, all tastely and in good order. You say there's nothing new under the Sun. This is new, for it's the first attempt ever made in this Colony by its inhabitants. Various are the Sentiments with regard to its Consequences, but the Priests and Levites of every Order cries out against it as subversion of Morallity and dangerous to the Church.

Source: Greene, *Papers*, 1: 57–58.]

31 May 1773   John St. Theater, New York
Cymon.
      Cymon–Hallam; Merlin–Goodman; Linco–Woolls; Dorus–Morris; Dorilas–Wall; Damon–Byerley; Cupid–Miss

THE COLONIAL AMERICAN STAGE 445

Storer; Urganda–Mrs. Morris; Fatima–Mrs. Henry; Dorcas–Miss Richardson; Sylvia–Miss Hallam.
American Company.
[Source: *New York Mercury* (31 May 1773).
The following item apropos to *Cymon* also appeared in the *New York Mercury* of 31 May 1773:

> The scenery, decorations, dresses and machinery of the opera of Cymon, to be performed this evening, are allowed by the most critical judges of theatrical splendor, to be more magnificent than cou'd be expected at so early a period, on the American stage. During its run at Philadelphia, several gentlemen from London, attended the representation, and made comparisons much to the honour of our infant Western theatre. We are informed that as it is so very late in the season, it can only be performed one night.]

3 June 1773   John St. Theater, New York
The Tempest.
Prospero–Douglass; Ferdinand–Hallam; Alonzo–Byerley; Hippolito, Duke of Mantua (a man who never saw a woman)–Wall; Stephano–Morris; Trincalo–Henry; Mustachio–Woolls; Ventoso–Parker; Ariel–Miss Storer; Antonio–Parker; Caliban–Goodman; Sycorax–Roberts; Miranda–Mrs. Henry; Dorinda (who never saw men)–Miss Hallam.
Neptune and Amphitrite.
Neptune–Woolls; Amphitrite–Miss Storer.
Damon and Phillida.
Damon–Woolls; Arcas–Byerley; Corydon–Morris; Mopsus–Parker; Cymon–Wall; Philida–Miss Storer.
American Company.
[Source: *Rivington's New York Gazette* (3 June 1773).]

7 June 1773   John St. Theater, New York
Cymon.
As 31 May 1773.
Cross Purposes.
As 28 May 1773.
American Company.
[Source: *New York Mercury* (7 June 1773).]

11 June 1773   John St. Theater, New York
School for Lovers.
Modely–Hallam; Araminta–Miss Cheer.
Lethe.

Frenchman and drunken man–Hallam; Mrs. Tattoo–Miss Hallam.
American Company.
[Source: *Rivington's New York Gazette* (10 June 1773).]

14 June 1773   John St. Theater, New York
Richard III.
King Richard–Hallam; King Henry–Morris; Prince Edward–Wall; Duke of York–Miss Richardson; Buckingham–Douglass; Tressel–Henry; Norfolk–Goodman; Lord Stanley–Byerley; Ratcliff–Woolls; Richmond–a gentleman (being his first appearance); Lady Anne–Miss Hallam; Duchess of York–Mrs. Douglass; Queen Elizabeth–Miss Cheer.
Midas.
As 3 May 1773.
American Company.
[Benefit Mr. and Mrs. Douglass. Source: *New York Mercury* (14 June 1773).]

17 June 1773   John St. Theater, New York
Play not identified.
American Company.
[Announced but not performed "on account of Mr. Hallam's indisposition." Source: *New York Journal* (17 June 1773).]

21 June 1773   John St. Theater, New York
Newspaper notice.
[The *New York Mercury* of this date contains the following notice: "All persons having any demands on the American Theatre, are requested to render in their accounts to the subscriber, that they may be paid. John Henry."]

21 June 1773   John St. Theater, New York
Comus.
Comus–Henry; First Spirit–Byerley; Second Spirit–Morris; Third Spirit–Woolls; Elder Brother–Parker; Youngest Brother–Goodman; Bacchanals–Woolls, Douglass, Wall, Dermont, Roberts; Bacchants–Miss Hallam, Miss Storer, Mrs. Morris, Miss Richardson, and Mrs. Wall; Euphrosyne–Miss Storer; Sabrina (and the song of Sweet Eccho)–Miss Hallam; The Lady–Miss Cheer.
High Life Below Stairs.
Lovel–Hallam; Freeman–Byerley; Lord Duke–Wall; Sir Harry–Henry; Philip–Morris; Kingston–Parker; Coach-

man–Woolls; Tom–Dermont; Lady Bab (with a song)–
Miss Storer; Lady Charlotte–Miss Richardson; Cook–
Mrs. Wall; Chloe–Roberts; Kitty–Miss Cheer.
American Company.
[Benefit Woolls and Miss Cheer. Prices: boxes 8s.; pit 5s.; gallery 3s. Source: *New York Gazette & Weekly Post-Boy* (21 June 1773).]

24 June 1773   John St. Theater, New York
The West Indian.
As 16 April 1773, except Lady Rusport–Mrs. Douglass; Mrs. Fulmer–Miss Richardson; Lucy–Mrs. Wall.
Love a la Mode.
Sir Callaghan O'Brallaghan (with songs)–Henry; Sir Archy Macsarcasm–Douglass; Squire Groom–Wall; Sir Theodore–Morris; The Lady–Miss Richardson.
American Company.
["By order of the Right Worshipful the Provincial Grand Master, the Worshipful the Deputy Grand Master, and the Masters of the Lodges in this City." Benefit Henry and Wall. Source: *Rivington's New York Gazette* (24 June 1773).]

8 June 1773   John St. Theater, New York
Tamerlane.
Bajazet–Hallam; Tamerlane–Douglass; Moneses–Goodman; Axalla–Wall; Omar–Henry; Dervise–Morris; Haly–Byerley; Prince of Tenais–a gentleman (being his first appearance); Mirvan–Blackler; Zama–Parker; Selima–Miss Hallam; Arpasia–Mrs. Morris.
The Irish Widow* (David Garrick, 1772).
Sir Patrick O'Neal–Goodman; Kecksey–Morris; Whistle–Byerley; Nephew–Wall; Bates–Blackler; Thomas–Parker; Pompey–Dermont; The Irish Widow (with a song in character)–Mrs. Morris.
American Company.
[Benefit Mr. and Mrs. Morris. Afterpiece advertised as "never performed in America." Source: *New York Mercury* (28 June 1773).]

1 July 1773   John St. Theater, New York
The Constant Couple.
Sir Henry Wildair–Hallam; Colonel Standard–Douglass; Beau Clincher–Goodman; Alderman Smuggler–Morris; Young Clincher–Wall; Vizard–Byerley; Dickey–Woolls; Angelica–Miss Hallam; Lady Darling–Mrs. Douglass; Parley–Miss Richardson; Lady Lurewell–Mrs. Morris.

A Picture of a Playhouse; or, Bucks Have at Ye All.
Harlequin Collector; or, The Miller Deceived.
    First Harlequin–Hallam; Second Harlequin–Wall; Miller–Goodman; Clown–Morris; Magician–Woolls; Anatomist–Beyerley; Statuary–Douglass; Colombine–Miss Hallam.
American Company.
    [Benefit Hallam and Goodman. Source: *New York Journal* (1 July 1773).]

5 July 1773   John St. Theater, New York
Romeo and Juliet.
    Romeo–Hallam; Mercutio–Goodman; Capulet–Henry; Fryar Lawrence–Morris; Paris–Woolls; Benvolio–Wall; Tibalt–Parker; Mountague–Byerley; Fryar John–Dermont; Apothecary–Roberts; Lady Capulet–Miss Richardson; Nurse–Mrs. Morris; Juliet–Miss Hallam.
The Irish Widow.
    As 8 June 1773, except Bates–Hughes; Thomas–Woolls.
American Company.
    [Benefit Miss Hallam and Miss Storer. "After the play, by particular desire, The Soldier Tired of War's Alarms, by Miss Hallam, accompanied by the band of his Majesty's 23rd Regiment." Source: *New York Mercury* (5 July 1773).]

5 July 1773   Charleston
Subscription to erect theatre.
    [The *Maryland Journal* of 20–28 August 1773 prints a letter from Charleston, dated 5 July 1773, which reports the following news: "A large subscription has been solicited and is raising, for building an elegant Theatre in this town, in which Mr. Douglass's American Company will perform during the winter."]

8 July 1773   John St. Theater, New York
The Recruiting Officer.
    Capt. Plume–Hallam; Justice Ballance–Morris; Worthy–Woolls; Capt. Brazen–Byerley; Serjeant Kitt–Henry; Bullock–Goodman; First Recruit–Parker; Welch Collier–Roberts; Servant–Dermont; Melinda–Miss Storer; Rose–Miss Hallam; Lucy–Miss Richardson; Collier's Wife–Mrs. Wall; Sylvia–Mrs. Morris.
The Picture of a Playhouse: Or Bucks Have at Ye All!
    By Hallam.
The Guardian.

The Guardian–Hallam; Sir Charles Clackit–Wall; Lucy–Miss Richardson; Miss Harriet–Miss Hallam.
American Company.
[Benefit Byerley and Parker. Source: *Rivington's New York Gazette* (8 July 1773).]

12 July 1773   John St. Theater, New York
Jane Shore.
Lord Hastings–Hallam; Duke of Gloster–Morris; Belmour–a gentleman (for his amusement); Ratcliff–Woolls; Catesby–Byerley; Earl of Derby–Goodman; Lords of the Council–Wall, Hughes, Roberts, Dermont, &c.; Dumont–Henry; Alicia–Miss Hallam; Jane Shore (first time)–Mrs. Morris.
Flora; or, Hob in the Well.
Hob–Henry; Friendly–Woolls; Sir Thomas Testy–Morris; Old Hob–Byerley; Dick–Parker; Roger–Wall; Hob's Mother–Miss Richardson; Betty–Mrs. Wall; Flora–Miss Storer.
American Company.
[Benefit Roberts and Miss Richardson. Source: *New York Mercury* (12 July 1773).]

15 July 1773   John St. Theater, New York
The Merchant of Venice.
Catherine and Petruchio.
American Company.
[Announced but probably not performed. Benefit Dermont and Francis. Source: *New York Journal* (15 July 1773).]

19 July 1773   John St. Theater, New York
The Merchant of Venice.
Shylock–Hallam; Bassanio–Byerley; Antonio–Henry; Gratiano–Hughes; Lorenzo (with a song)–Woolls; Duke and Launcelot–Morris; Solarino–Roberts; Salanio–Wall; Tubal–Dermont; Jessica–Miss Storer; Nerissa–Miss Richardson; Portia–Mrs. Morris.
The King and the Miller of Mansfield.
King–Henry; Miller–Morris; Lord Lurewell–Wall; Richard–Byerley; Joe (with a song)–Woolls; Peggy–Miss Richardson; Kate–Miss Storer; Madge–Mrs. Wall.
American Company.
[Benefit Dermont and Francis. Source: *New York Mercury* (19 July 1773).]

21 July 1773   Hull's Great Room, New York
Lecture on Heads.
Mr. Wall.
    ["By permission of his Excellency the Governor. Mr. Wall, comedian, will exhibit, at Mr. Hull's great room, on Wednesday evening, the 21st of July, 1773. A new lecture, written by the author of the much admired Lecture on Heads, The paintings, &c. are entirely new, and never before exhibited in America." Source: *New York Gazette* (19 July 1773).]

26 July 1773   John St. Theater, New York
The London Merchant.
    George Barnwell–Hallam; Thorowgood–Morris; Truman–Goodman; Uncle–Henry; Blunt–Byerley; Maria–Miss Storer; Lucy–Miss Richardson; Millwood–Mrs. Morris.
Edgar and Emmeline.
    Edgar–Hallam; Florimond–Wall; First Aerial Spirit–Miss Storer; Second Aerial Spirit–Mrs. Morris; Other Spirits–Woolls, Goodman, Hughes, Byerley, Mrs. Morris, Mrs. Wall, &c.; Attendant–Miss Richardson; Emmeline–Miss Hallam.
American Company.
    ["For the benefit of the hospital to be erected in New York." Source: *New York Journal* (22 July 1773). The *New York Journal* of 5 August 1773 reports that "a very numerous and polite audience" attended this benefit, and prints a prologue written especially for the occasion.]

27 July 1773   Charleston
Newspaper notice.
    [The *South Carolina Gazette* of this date contains the following notice: "On Friday last arrived the Brig Betsey, Captain Schermerhorn, from New-York, in whom came ... Mr. Douglass, Manager of the American Company of Comedians, who we hear, proposes to erect a theatre here."]

28? July 1773   Hull's Great Room, New York
A New Lecture* (George Alexander Stevens).
Mr. Wall.
    ["By permission of his Excellency the Governor. Mr. Wall, comedian, will exhibit, at Mr. Hull's great room, on Wednesday evening, the 21st [sic] of July, 1773. A new lecture, written by the author of the much admired Lecture on Heads. The paintings, &c. are entirely new, and never before

exhibited in America." Source: *New York Mercury* (26 July 1773).]

2 August 1773   John St. Theater, New York
She Stoops to Conquer* (Oliver Goldsmith, 1773).
　　　Tony Lumpkin–Hallam; Hardcastle–Goodman; Young Marlow–Henry; Hastings–Byerley; Sir Charles Marlow–Morris; Diggory–Hughes; Landlord–Woolls; Mrs. Hardcastle–Mrs. Morris; Miss Neville–Miss Storer; Maid–Miss Richardson; Miss Hardcastle–Miss Hallam.
The Musical Lady.
　　　Mask–Byerley; Old Mask–Morris; Freeman–Hughes; Rosini– Roberts; Lady Scrape–Miss Storer; Laundress–Miss Richardson; Sophy (with a song in character)–Miss Hallam.
American Company.
　　　[Goldsmith's play had premiered in London on 15 March 1773. See review in 5 August 1773. Source: *New York Journal* (29 July 1773).]

5 August 1773   John St. Theater, New York
She Stoops to Conquer.
　　　As 2 August 1773.
The Padlock.
　　　As 10 May 1773, except Leander–Henry.
American Company.
　　　[Source: *Rivington's New York Gazette* (5 August 1773).]

5 August 1773   New York
Review of performance.
American Company.
　　　[*Rivington's New York Gazette* of this date contains the following review of *She Stoops to Conquer,* which also includes information concerning the company's intentions :

> On Monday evening [i.e., 2 August] the new play called She Stoops to Conquer, was acted at this Theatre in this City to a judicious and polite audience; its success in England was unprecedented and on our stage unexampled. Mr. Hallam and every other actor exerted all their comic powers, and appeared thrice themselves on this occasion. The excessive mirth produced by these scenes of genuine wit, fun, and comicality presage a very numerous resort to the last performance of them, with the facetious distresses of that jetty varlet Mungo in the Padlock this evening, [after] which the Company will take leave of the town, and in a day or two Mr. Henry, their treasurer, will set out for Annapolis to prepare for opening the Theatre in that City, at the ensuing races. Mr.

Douglass, Manager of the American Company of Comedians, is gone to Charles-Town, South-Carolina, to arrange matters against the arrival of the actors, after they have performed a month at Annapolis.]

9 August 1773   Charleston
Newspaper notice.
American Company.

[The *South Carolina Gazette* of this date prints a long letter from "Benevolus" which mentions that

Within a few days past, there has been a numerous distribution amongst us, of printed copies of 'An Address to the Public by D. Douglass,' wherein "he offers an exertion of the abilities of a Company of Comedians, under his direction, the ensuing winter, to the favour and patronage of the ladies and gentlemen of South-Carolina.]

17 August 1773   Charleston
Newspaper notice.
American Company.

[The *South Carolina Gazette* of this date contains the following notice from Douglass to the citizens of Charleston:

Mr. Douglass returns his most grateful thanks to the public, for the very generous countenance they have given to his Address. He begs leave to inform them, that the subscription is in great forewardness, and a considerable part of the money already collected, and deposited in the proper hands for carrying the design into execution; the receipts for which are lodged at Mr. Wells's, on the Bay, for the inspection of the subscribers.–Materials are collecting, builders engaged, and every possible step taken to compleat the undertaking, early in November. Those gentlemen who have not yet subscribed, and would choose to add their names to a catalogue, already honoured with the notice of a number of most respectable characters, will be obliging enough to signify their intentions as soon as possible, at the places mentioned in the Address.]

28 August 1773   Charleston
Lease of ground to erect a playhouse.

[David Douglass entered into the following agreement for a theatre in Charleston:

Lease by Robert Wells, Robert Rowand, John Deas and Alexander Michie, gentlemen of Charles Town to David Douglass gentleman for £5 current money of S.C. and a yearly rent of £100 current money of S.C. The property leased for a term of fifteen years is lot #40 on the West side of Church Street, Charlestown. Douglass agrees "within three months ... at his own proper costs ... to be Erected and built ... A Building suitable for the exhibition of dramatical Entertainments of the construction and materials following ... a Brick foundation at least ten feet in height above the surface of the ground and thereupon a wooden frame of good and Substantial materials to be filled up with Bricks and also covered with brick on the outside with proper Necessary and convenient windows locks hinges bolts and other materials ...". The building will be available for other purposes when the Company of Comedians are not in the Province. Douglass also agrees that the Company will in every season present a Benefit dramatical play or entertainment together with a farce provided that they are in the Catalogue of the Company. Douglass shall "find supply and provide the Necessary and usual scenes decorations and other Necessary Articles" with an allowance from the Lessors of £200. The Lessors will receive the profits from the sale of the tickets to the Benefit. Ten days previous notice is required for this performance. To guarantee terms of the lease, each of the parties binds himself to the others in the penal sum of £7,000 current money of S.C.

Source: Charleston Country Lands Records, Misc., 1779–1781, 47.]

30 August 1773   Long Room, Videll's Alley, Philadelphia
A New Lecture.
Mr. Wall.
[Price: one-half dollar. "By Authority." Source: *Pennsylvania Packet* (30 August 1773).]

31 August 1773   Long Room, Videll's Alley, Philadelphia
A New Lecture.
Mr. Wall.
["By Authority." The last evening. Source: *Pennsylvania Packet* (30 August 1773).]

6 September 1773   Charleston
Newspaper notice.
American Company.
[The *South Carolina Gazette* of this date offers the following item:

Last Tuesday [i.e., 2 September] embarked in the Brigt. Sea-Nymph, Captain Blewer, for Philadelphia, ... Mr. Bellamy, Mr. Douglass, Manager of a Company of Comedians, whose Theatre (erecting by subscription) is going on with rapid progress, and several other passengers.]

c. 21 September 1773   Philadelphia
False obituary of performer.

[The following false notice appeared in the *New York Mercury* (27 September 1773):

> Last week died at Philadelphia, Mrs. Douglass, wife of Mr. Douglass, manager of the American Company of Comedians, mother of Mr. Lewis Hallam, and of Mrs. Mattocks, of Covent Garden theatre, and aunt of Miss Hallam, a lady who by her excellent performances upon the stage, and her irreproachable manners in private life, had recommended herself to the friendship and affection of many of the principal families on the continent and in the West Indies.

Mrs. Douglass had not died. See 1773 headnote for commentary.]

27 September 1773   West St. Theater, Annapolis
Play not identified.
American Company.
    [George Washington records in his *Diary* that he attended a performance on this date. Source: Washington, *Diaries*, 3:205.]

28 September 1773   West St. Theater, Annapolis
Play not identified.
American Company.
    [George Washington records in his *Diary* that he attended a performance on this date. Source: Washington, *Diaries*, 3:205.]

29 September 1773   West St. Theater, Annapolis
Play not identified.
American Company.
    [George Washington records in his *Diary* that he attended a performance on this date. Source: Washington, *Diaries*, 3:205.]

early October 1773   Annapolis
Company activity.
American Company.
    [During late September and early October, the Annapolis Races took place, which attracted people from throughout the colonies. The "Theatrical Purse" of £50, which was awarded in early October, was sponsored during several years by the American Company, e.g., 6 October 1772. Source: *Maryland Gazette* (5 August and 23 September 1773).]

7 October 1773   Annapolis
Newspaper notice.
[The *Maryland Gazette* of this date contains the following notice:

> By Authority. Mr. Wall, Comedian, on the evening after the last play, will present, at the Theatre, a New Lecture performed with great applause to a very polite and judicious audience at New-York, and likewise at Philadelphia: written by the author of the much admired Lecture on Heads. The paintings, &c. are entirely new, and never before exhibited in Annapolis.]

9 October 1773   West St. Theater, Annapolis.
Jane Shore.
   Lord Hastings–Hallam; Dumont–Henry; Gloster–Morris; Derby–Goodman; Belmour–Hughes; Ratcliff–Woolls; Catesby–Dermont; Alicia–Miss Hallam; Jane Shore–Mrs. Morris.
The Irish Widow.
   Sir Patrick–Goodman; Whittle–Morris; Bates–Henry; Nephew–Wall; Kecksy–Hughes; Thomas–Woolls; Pompey–Dermont; Irish Widow–Mrs. Morris.
American Company.
   [Prices: Boxes, 7s. 6d.; pit, 5s. Source: playbill in the Historical Society of Pennsylvania.]

14 October 1773   West St. Theater, Annapolis.
Play not identified.
American Company.
   [Performance on this evening is implied by an advertisement by Thomas Wall for his 15 October *New Lecture*, to be performed "on the evening after the last play." Source: *Maryland Gazette* (7 October 1773).]

14 October 1773   New York
False obituary of performer.
   [The *Virginia Gazette* of this date prints the following letter reporting the "death" of Mrs. David Douglass:

> New York, September 23. Last week died, at Philadelphia, Mrs. Douglas, wife of Mr. Douglas, Manager of the American Company of Comedians, mother of Mr. Lewis Hallam, and of Mrs. Mattocks of Covent Garden Theatre, and aunt of Miss Hallam; a lady who by her excellent performances upon the stage, and her irreproachable manners in private life, had recommended herself to the friendship and affection of many of the principal families on the Continent and in the West Indies.

A correction in the 14 October 1773 Supplement discredits this report.]

15 October 1773   West St. Theater, Annapolis
A New Lecture.
Thomas Wall.
    [Prices: boxes, 5s.; pit, 3s. 9d. Source: *Maryland Gazette* (14 October 1773).]

1 November 1773   Southwark Theater, Philadelphia
Lionel and Clarissa.
    Col. Oldboy–Goodman; Lionel–Woolls; Sir John Flowerdale–Douglass; Mr. Jessamy–Henry; Jenkins–Parker; Clarissa–Miss Storer; Jenny–Mrs. Henry; Diane Oldboy–Miss Hallam.
Love a la Mode.
    Archy Macsarcasm–Douglass; Squire Groom–Wall; Beau Mordecai–Morris; Sir Theodore–Parker; Lady–Miss Richardson.
American Company.
    [Prices: boxes, 7s. 6d.; pit, 5s; gallery, 3s. Throughout November 1773 and in the weeks following, a controversy raged in the Philadelphia papers as to whether theatrical companies ("strollers") should be allowed to perform in Pennsylvania. Source: *Pennsylvania Packet* (1 November 1773).]

3 November 1773   Southwark Theater, Philadelphia
The Earl of Essex.
    As 22 March 1773, except Sir Walter Raleigh–Mr. Hughes; Countess of Nottingham–Miss Storer.
The Citizen.
    The Citizen–Wall; Beaufort–Woolls; Young Wilding–Hallam; Dapper–Douglass; Sir Jasper Wilding–Hughes; Old Philpot–Morris; Corinna–Miss Richardson; Maria–Miss Wainwright, being her first appearance these six years.
American Company.
    ["Mr. Douglass assures the public, that the house will be open for a fortnight only, as the company propose, about that time, embarking for South-Carolina." Cf. Rankin 181. Source: *Pennsylvania Journal* (3 November 1773).]

8 November 1773   Southwark Theater, Philadelphia
Hamlet.
The Irish Widow.
American Company.
   [Source: *Pennsylvania Packet* (8 November 1773).]

10 November 1773   Southwark Theater, Philadelphia
The Clandestine Marriage.
   Lord Ogleby–Hallam; Sir John Melville–Douglass; Lovewell– Henry; Sergeant Flower–Goodman; Sterling–Morris; Canton–Hughes; Traverse–Dermont; Truman–Woolls; Miss Sterling–Miss Hallam; Betty–Miss Richardson; Miss Fanny–Miss Storer; Chambermaid–Miss Wainwright; Housekeeper–Mrs. Wall; Mrs. Heidelberg–Mrs. Douglass.
The Padlock.
   As 28 October 1772.
American Company.
   [Source: *Pennsylvania Journal* (10 November 1773).]

15 November 1773   Southwark Theater, Philadelphia
The West Indian.
   The West Indian–Hallam; Major O'Flaherty–Mr. Henry; Capt. Dudley–Douglass; Mr. Stockwell–Morris; Varland–Woolls; Fulmer–Hughes; Lady Rusport–Mrs. Douglass; Mrs. Fulmer–Miss Richardson; Louisa Dudley–Miss Storer; Charlotte Rusport–Miss Hallam; Lucy–Miss Wainwright; Charles Dudley–a "young gentleman who never appeared on any stage before."
Cross Purposes.
   Mr. Grub–Morris; The Bevils–Hallam, Douglass, and Henry; Chapeau–Wall; Consol–Dermont; Robin–Hughes; Mrs. Grub–Morris; Emily–Miss Storer.
American Company.
   [Prologue by the "Young Gentleman"; a "farewell epilogue" by Hallam. An alternative epilogue, "Intended to be spoken by Mr. Goodman the last night," appeared in the *Pennsylvania Packet* of 22 November 1773.   Source: *Pennsylvania Packet* (15 November 1773).]

22 November 1773   Philadelphia
A New Lecture.
Mr. Wall.
   ["By permission of his Excellency the Governor. Mr. Wall, comedian, will exhibit, at Mr. Hull's great room, on

Wednesday evening, the 21st [sic] of July, 1773. A new lecture, written by the author of the much admired Lecture on Heads, The paintings, &c. are entirely new, and never before exhibited in America." Source: *Pennsylvania Journal* (17 November 1773).]

30 November 1773   Charleston
Newspaper notice.
American Company.

[The *South Carolina Gazette* of this date contains the following notice:

> On Thursday last ... returned from Philadelphia, in the Brigt. Sea Nymph ... many other passengers: amongst the latter, Mr. David Douglass, Manager of the American Company of Comedians, together with Mrs. Douglass, Mrs. Morris, Mr. Lewis Hallam, Miss Hallam, Miss Storer, Mr. Henry, Mr. Woolls, Miss Wainwright; the remainder of this Company may be hourly expected in a sloop. The Theatre is [in] such forwardness, that we are told, it may be finished before Christmas.]

21 December 1773   Halifax, Nova Scotia
Prologue.

[The *Nova Scotia Gazette* of this date published a prologue "for the opening of the Theatre at Halifax" which laments the loss of their "veteran" actors, as indicated in the following couplet: "Some new recruits indeed our stage may boast, / Yet still we must lament the vet'rans lost." These lines suggest that a company of some nature, perhaps Mr. Mills's, revisited the outpost on more occasions than their inaugural 1768 summer season. Source: *Nova Scotia Gazette* (21 December 1773).]

22 December 1773   Church St. Theater, Charleston
A Word to the Wise.
High Life Below Stairs.
American Company.

[The theatre opened this evening. *Rivington's New York Gazette* of 24 February 1774 prints the following account:

> On Wednesday last, the new theatre in this town was opened with Mr. Kelly's Word to the Wise, and High Life below Stairs, with an occasional prologue and epilogue spoken by Mr. Hallam and Mrs. Douglass. The performance gave universal satisfaction; Mr. Hallam in particular, in Captain Dormer, displayed his extraordinary theatrical talents, in a most spirited manner. Indeed all the performers did great justice to their characters; but that

gentleman's superior abilities were so remarkably striking, that we could not pass them over unnoticed. The House is elegantly finished, and supposed, for the size, to be the most commodious on the continent. The scenes, which are new and well designed, the dresses, the music, and what had a very pleasing effect, the disposition of the lights, all contributed to the satisfaction of the audience, who expressed the highest approbation of their entertainment.

Source: *South Carolina Gazette* (13 December 1773–30 May 1774). Note: for an explanation of the unusual date of this newspaper, see the headnote for 1773.]

24 December 1773   Church St. Theater, Charleston
Hamlet.
Cross Purposes.
American Company.
   [Source: *South Carolina Gazette* (30 May 1774).]

27 December 1773   Church St. Theater, Charleston
The Suspicious Husband.
Catherine and Petruchio.
American Company.
   [Prices: boxes 35s.; pit 25s. Source: *South Carolina & American General Gazette* (17–24 December 1773).]

30 December 1773   Church St. Theater, Charleston
The Clandestine Marriage.
The Mayor of Garratt.
American Company.
   [Source: *South Carolina Gazette* (30 May 1774).]

1774

After a successful season in Charleston that lasted until 19 May, the American Company broke up for the summer. Richard Goodman remained in Charleston performing *A Lecture on Heads* with Mr. Allyn, late of the Theatre Royal in Edinburgh. The pair of them worked their way up to Philadelphia, where they performed variety entertainments throughout the summer. At the close of the Charleston season, Lewis Hallam, Jr. returned to England to gather new recruits. Willis (75) provides the shipping calendar that indicate Mr. and Mrs. Douglass sailed to New York with the scenes and machines and several other members of the company to make preparations for a winter season in that city. Mr. Henry and the Storers boarded for England, while the Morrises repaired first to Philadelphia and then on to New York. The company planned to rendezvous in New York at the start of the fall season "with a theatrical force hitherto unknown in America" (see 27 May). Unfortunately, hostilities between the colonies and England escalated, and the Continental Congress thought it prudent to curtail all extravagance, thereupon prohibiting plays.[17] This injunction initiated a decade's lacuna in the narrative of colonial theatre. The American Company remained in New York, awaiting congressional dispensation until early 1775, when, finally acknowledging the severity of the political situation, the company embarked for Jamaica to sit out the Revolutionary War and to play the West Indies.

The American Company in Charleston consisted of the following known members: Mr. Davies, Mrs. Davies, Mr. Dermont, David Douglass, Mrs. Douglass, Richard Goodman, Lewis Hallam Jr., Miss Hallam, John Henry, George Hughes, Owen Morris, Mrs. Morris, Mr. Roberts, Miss Storer, Miss Wainwright, and Stephen Woolls. Sometime in the late summer, Mrs. Douglass died. It will be noticed that after eight seasons with the American company, Mr. and Mrs. Thomas Wall no longer appear in the cast lists. Their last recorded performance was at the conclusion of the Philadelphia season, 15 November 1773.

Ironically, several new professionals entered the colonial circuit this year. Mr. Allen (or Allyn) from Edinburgh (mentioned above) and, quite late in the year, a number of players, including Thomas Wignell, directly from London, arrived in New York only to find the city shut to performers. These were, in all probability, the recruits gathered by Lewis Hallam, Jr. in London and directed to New York.

One curious entry for 4 June 1774 suggests a company of some stature played in Richmond after the American Company is presumed to have broken up. This company apparently had the authority of the governor, but nothing else is known beyond a broadside which was posted near a playbill.

---

[17] For a more thorough discussion on the moratorium, see Withington, *Toward a More Perfect Union*, pp. 20–47.

A troupe of "Gentlemen of the Army and the Navy" continued performances early in this year in Halifax, Nova Scotia. Of note was the announcement of the impending premiere of a "native work," *Arcadius; or, Love in a Calm*. Though no exact date of performance is known, Fergussan (425) tells us the author intended the piece to be acted twice "for the benefit of poor Housekeepers or the late sufferers of Fire."

Amateur performances took place in New York and Charleston. In New York, "a select party of little masters and misses" presented plays on two occasions in early January, while in Charleston, after the departure of the American Company, on 29 June 1774 pupils of James Thomson, late tutor of New Jersey College, performed *Cato*. Six weeks later pupils of Oliver Dale, presented the same play.

※※※

1 January 1774   Church St. Theater, Charleston
The Earl of Essex.
The Irish Widow.
American Company.
    [Source: *South Carolina Gazette* (30 May 1774).]

3 January 1774   Church St. Theater, Charleston
Love in a Village.
Lethe.
American Company.
    [Source: *South Carolina Gazette* (30 May 1774).]

5 January 1774   Church St. Theater, Charleston
The Gamester.
High Life Below Stairs.
American Company.
    [Source: *South Carolina Gazette* (30 May 1774).]

7 January 1774   Hull's Long Room, New York
The Tragedy of King Bassias* (Anonymous).
Cymon.
The Padlock.
Local children.
    [These plays "acted by a select party of little masters and misses." The authorship of *King Bassias* has not been identified. Source: *New York Mercury* (3 January 1774).]

8 January 1774   Church St. Theater, Charleston
The Beaux' Stratagem.
The King and the Miller of Mansfield.
American Company.
    [Source: *South Carolina Gazette* (30 May 1774).]

10 January 1774   Church St. Theater, Charleston
The Constant Couple.
Catherine and Petruchio.
American Company.
    [Source: *South Carolina Gazette* (30 May 1774).]

13 January 1774   Church St. Theater, Charleston
The Mourning Bride.
The Lying Valet.
American Company.
    [Source: *South Carolina Gazette* (30 May 1774).]

15 January 1774   Church St. Theater, Charleston
She Stoops to Conquer.
The Irish Widow.
American Company.
    [Source: *South Carolina Gazette* (30 May 1774).]

17 January 1774   Church St. Theater, Charleston
Jane Shore.
Cross Purposes.
American Company.
    [Source: *South Carolina Gazette* (30 May 1774).]

19 January 1774   Church St. Theater, Charleston
The Busy Body.
Love a la Mode.
American Company.
    [Source: *South Carolina Gazette* (30 May 1774).]

21 January 1774   Church St. Theater, Charleston
Cymbeline.
The Honest Yorkshireman.
American Company.
    [Source: *South Carolina Gazette* (30 May 1774).]

25 January 1774   Church St. Theater, Charleston
The Beggar's Opera.
Love a la Mode.

American Company.
> [Source: *South Carolina Gazette* (30 May 1774).]

27 January 1774   Church St. Theater, Charleston
Romeo and Juliet.
Miss in Her Teens.
American Company.
> [Source: *South Carolina Gazette* (30 May 1774).]

29 January 1774   Church St. Theater, Charleston
The Merchant of Venice.
The Devil to Pay.
American Company.
> [Source: *South Carolina Gazette* (30 May 1774).]

31 January 1774   Church St. Theater, Charleston
Richard III.
> Queen Elizabeth–Mrs. Morris.

Thomas and Sally.
> The Squire–Woolls; The Sailor–Henry; Dorcas–Miss Storer; Sally–Miss Hallam.

American Company.
> [Source: *South Carolina & American General Gazette* (21–28 January 1774).]

2 February 1774   Church St. Theater, Charleston
The Tempest.
American Company.
> [*Rivington's New York Gazette* of 24 February 1774 prints the following account of this evening's performance:
>
>> 4 February. On Wednesday last The Tempest was performed at the theatre in this town, to a crouded and brilliant audience, who expressed the highest satisfaction at their entertainment. The characters were, in general, well supported; but the deceptions, machinery, and decorations, surpassed every body's expectation; and the public appear impatient for a second representation of that excellent comedy. We hear that The Rival Queen, or Alexander the Great, will shortly be presented, and that the play will be entirely new dressed; a set of most superb habits having been just imported from London for that piece, at an immense expence.
>
> Source: *South Carolina Gazette* (30 May 1774).]

4 February 1774   Church St. Theater, Charleston
Love in a Village.

Love a la Mode.
American Company.
    [Source: *South Carolina Gazette* (30 May 1774).]

7 February 1774   Church St. Theater, Charleston
The Wonder!
Midas.
American Company.
    [Source: *South Carolina Gazette* (30 May 1774).]

10 February 1774   Church St. Theater, Charleston
Alexander the Great.
The King and the Miller of Mansfield.
American Company.
    [Source: *South Carolina Gazette* (30 May 1774).]

12 February 1774   Church St. Theater, Charleston
The Tempest.
The Guardian.
American Company.
    [Source: *South Carolina Gazette* (30 May 1774).]

14 February 1774   Church St. Theater, Charleston
The London Merchant.
Edgar and Emmeline.
American Company.
    [Source: *South Carolina Gazette* (30 May 1774).]

15 February 1774   Mr. Pike's New Assembly Room,
                             Charleston
Musical entertainments.
Members of the American Company.
    [Miss Hallam, Miss Storer, Miss Wainright, and Woolls performed this evening. Source: *South Carolina Gazette* (31 January 1774).]

17 February 1774   Church St. Theater, Charleston
Henry IV, Part 1.
Thomas and Sally.
American Company.
    [Source: *South Carolina Gazette* (30 May 1774).]

19 February 1774   Church St. Theater, Charleston
Theodosius.
The Citizen.

American Company.
[Source: *South Carolina Gazette* (30 May 1774).]

21 February 1774   Church St. Theater, Charleston
A Bold Stroke for a Wife.
The Mayor of Garratt.
American Company.
[Source: *South Carolina Gazette* (30 May 1774).]

24 February 1774   Church St. Theater, Charleston
Othello.
Damon and Phillida.
American Company.
[Source: *South Carolina Gazette* (30 May 1774).]

26 February 1774   Church St. Theater, Charleston
She Stoops to Conquer.
Edgar and Emmeline.
American Company.
[Source: *South Carolina Gazette* (30 May 1774).]

28 February 1774   Church St. Theater, Charleston
The Jealous Wife.
The Citizen.
American Company.
[Source: *South Carolina Gazette* (30 May 1774).]

28 February 1774   Charleston
Legislative activity.
[The *South Carolina Gazette* of this date prints the following item which reports a "Presentment to the Grand Jury" which was "Quashed":

> IX. We present as a grievance, the Company of Players, A Play-House in Charles-Town, being unfit for the present low estate of the Province; for, although there is great want of money to procure the conveniencies, and even the necessaries of life, yet large sums are weekly laid out for amusements there, by persons who cannot afford it; and is a means of promoting the frequent robberies that are committed, and of vice and obscenity. We recommend, that the Legislature may suppress the same, tending to the corruption of youth, and the injury of many families.]

2 March 1774   Church St. Theater, Charleston
The Shipwreck [i.e., *The Brothers*].
Catherine and Petruchio.

American Company.
[Source: *South Carolina Gazette* (30 May 1774).]

4 March 1774   Church St. Theater, Charleston
The School for Fathers* (Isaac Bickerstaffe, 1770).
Lethe [or *Lionel and Clarissa*; see below].
American Company.
[The *South Carolina Gazette* ambiguously offers both *Lethe* and *Lionel and Clarissa* for this date. Source: *South Carolina Gazette* (30 May 1774).]

7 March 1774   Church St. Theater, Charleston
The Fashionable Lover.
The Padlock.
American Company.
[Source: *South Carolina Gazette* (30 May 1774).]

10 March 1774   Church St. Theater, Charleston
The Maid of the Mill.
High Life Below Stairs.
American Company.
[Source: *South Carolina Gazette* (30 May 1774).]

12 March 1774   Church St. Theater, Charleston
King Lear.
The Irish Widow.
American Company.
[Source: *South Carolina Gazette* (30 May 1774).]

14 March 1774   Church St. Theater, Charleston
The Tempest.
The Padlock.
American Company.
[Source: *South Carolina Gazette* (30 May 1774).]
]
16 March 1774   Church St. Theater, Charleston
Cymon.
Miss in her Teens.
American Company.
[Source: *South Carolina Gazette* (30 May 1774).]

18 March 1774   Church St. Theater, Charleston
The Recruiting Officer.
The Oracle.

American Company.
   [Source: *South Carolina Gazette* (30 May 1774).]

21 March 1774   Church St. Theater, Charleston
The West Indian.
The Devil to Pay.
American Company.
   [Source: *South Carolina Gazette* (30 May 1774).]

25 March 1774   Church St. Theater, Charleston
The Provoked Husband.
The Lying Valet.
American Company.
   [Source: *South Carolina Gazette* (30 May 1774).]

26 March 1774   Church St. Theater, Charleston
Romeo and Juliet.
Flora.
American Company.
   [Source: *South Carolina Gazette* (30 May 1774).]

4 April 1774   Church St. Theater, Charleston
School for Fathers.
[*A Picture of a Playhouse; or,*] *Bucks Have at Ye All.*
Lionel and Clarissa.
American Company.
   [Source: *South Carolina Gazette* (30 May 1774).]

6 April 1774   Church St. Theater, Charleston
The English Merchant.
The Contrivances.
American Company.
   [Source: *South Carolina Gazette* (30 May 1774).]

8 April 1774   Church St. Theater, Charleston
The Fair Penitent.
Cross Purposes.
American Company.
   [Source: *South Carolina Gazette* (30 May 1774).]

11 April 1774   Church St. Theater, Charleston
The Roman Father.
The Irish Widow.
American Company.
   [Source: *South Carolina Gazette* (30 May 1774).]

12 April 1774   venue unknown, Connecticut colony
Play unidentified.
Students of Yale College.
    [Bloom (66-7) records that the student members of Yale College's Linonian Club performed a play on this date.]

13 April 1774   Church St. Theater, Charleston
The Way to Keep Him.
The Contrivances.
American Company.
    [Source: *South Carolina Gazette* (30 May 1774).]

15 April 1774   Church St. Theater, Charleston
The Constant Couple.
The Lying Valet.
American Company.
    [Source: *South Carolina Gazette* (30 May 1774).]

18 April 1774   Church St. Theater, Charleston
False Delicacy.
The Witches.
American Company.
    [Source: *South Carolina Gazette* (30 May 1774).]

20 April 1774   Church St. Theater, Charleston
Julius Caesar.
The Register Office.
American Company.
    [Source: *South Carolina Gazette* (30 May 1774).]

22 April 1774   Church St. Theater, Charleston
Macbeth.
The Young American in London* (Anonymous).
American Company.
    [Presumably the afterpiece is lost; Davis (1301) claims this play was "possibly by a South Carolina author." Source: *South Carolina Gazette* (30 May 1774).]

25 April 1774   Church St. Theater, Charleston
The West Indian.
        Belcour–a gentleman for his amusement, who never appeared on any stage; Major O'Flaherty–Goodman; Captain Dudley–Douglass; Stockwell–Morris; Charles Dudley–Hughes; Varland–Woolls; Fulmer–Dermont;

Stukley–Davies; Lucy–Miss Wainwright; Charlotte Rusport–Miss Hallam.

A Picture of a Playhouse.
By Hallam.

Midas.
Fabulous Deities. Apollo–Hallam; Jupiter–Morris; Mars–Douglass; Pan–Dermont; Juno–Mrs. Davies; Minerva–Miss Hallam; Mercury–Roberts. Mortals–[not listed]; Midas–Goodman; Sileno–Woolls; Dametas–Henry; Daphne–Morris; Mysis–Miss Wainwright; Mysa–Miss Storer.
American Company.

[Benefit Goodman. Source: *South Carolina & American General Gazette* (15–22 April 1774).]

27 April 1774   Church St. Theater, Charleston
Tamerlane.
Catherine and Petruchio.
American Company.

[Source: *South Carolina & American General Gazette* (22–26 April 1774).]

29 April 1774   Church St. Theater, Charleston
Cymbeline.
Love a la Mode.
American Company.

[Source: *South Carolina Gazette* (30 May 1774).]

2 May 1774   Church St. Theater, Charleston
A Bold Stroke for a Wife.
Colonel Fainwell–Hallam; Obadiah Prim–Henry; Tradelove–Douglass; Periwinkle–Morris; Simon Pure–Woolls; Sir Philip Modelove–Hughes; Freeman–Davies; Sackbut–Woolls; Mrs. Prim–Mrs. Douglass; Betty–Miss Wainwright; Ann Lovely–Miss Storer.

Neck or Nothing.
Sir Harry Harlow–Henry; Slip–Hughes; Martin–Morris; Stockwell–Dermont; Belford–Davies; Mrs. Stockwell–Mrs. Douglass; Jenny–Miss Wainwright; Miss Nancy–Miss Storer.
American Company.

[Source: *South Carolina & American General Gazette* (26–29 April 1774).]

4 May 1774   Church St. Theater, Charleston
The Orphan.

Miss in Her Teens.
American Company.
> [Source: *South Carolina Gazette* (30 May 1774).]

7 May 1774   Church St. Theater, Charleston
The Clandestine Marriage.
The Apprentice.
American Company.
> [Source: *South Carolina Gazette* (30 May 1774).]

11 May 1774   Church St. Theater, Charleston
Cato.
> Cato–Douglass; Sempronius–Hallam; Portius–Henry; Marcus–Goodman; Juba–Hughes; Syphax–Morris; Lucius–Dermont; Decius–Woolls; Lucia–Miss Storer; Marcia–Mrs. Morris.

The Reprisal, or the Tars of Old England.
> Lt. O'Clabber (with a song)–Henry; Ensign Maclaymore–Douglass; Lt. Lyon–Goodman; Capt. Champignon–Roberts; Block–Hallam; Heartly–Davies; Brush–Hughes; Hallyard (with "Hearts of Oak")–Woolls; Harriet (with a song in character)–Miss Storer.

American Company.
["For the benefit of the charity fund of the Union-Kilwinning Lodge, appropriated to the relief of the members of the Society of Free Masons, their wives, widows, children, and orphans, when in distress." Prices: boxes 35s.; pit, 25s.; gallery, 25s. Source: *South Carolina & American General Gazette* (15–22 April 1774).

16 May 1774   Church St. Theater, Charleston
Douglas.
> Douglas–Hallam; Lord Randolph–Douglass; Glenalvon–Henry; Old Nerval–Morris; Officer–Hughes; Anna–Miss Storer; Lady Randolph–Mrs. Douglass.

The Devil to Pay.
> Sir John Loverule–Woolls; Jobson–Henry; Butler–Morris; Lettice–Mrs. Davies; Nell–Miss Storer.

American Company.
["The last play for these three years." Prices: boxes, 35s; pit, 25s; gallery, 20s. Source: *South Carolina & American General Gazette* (6–13 May 1774). The following information is appended to the advertisement for this evening:

> As it is almost impossible that the performers can do their characters that justice their duty to the publick requires, when the

THE COLONIAL AMERICAN STAGE 471

stage is crowded, as it has been for several nights past: Mr. Douglass, at the earnest desire, not only of the performers, but of a very numerous and respectable part of the audience, begs leave to inform the town that no person, on any account whatsoever will be admitted at the stage door; and he is well assured that, after this representation, no gentlemen will insist upon it.]

19 May 1774 Church St. Theater, Charleston
King John.
The Guardian.
American Company.

[The last performance of the season. Source: *South Carolina Gazette* (30 May 1774).]

19 May 1774 Charleston
Newspaper notice.
American Company.

[The *Virginia Gazette* of 16 June 1774 prints the following account of the Charleston season and the company's plans:

> On Friday last [i.e., 19 May] the Theatre, which opened here the 22d of December, was closed. Warmly countenanced and supported by the publick, the Manager and his Company were excited to the most strenuous efforts to render their entertainments worthy of so respectable a patronage. If it is considered how late it was in the season before the house could be opened, the variety of scenery and decorations necessary to a regular theatre, the number of plays represented (fifty-eight) and that almost every piece required particular preparations, it must be confessed that the exertions of the American Company have been uncommon, and justly entitle them to those marks of publick favour that have, for so many years, stamped a merit on their performances. The choice of plays hath been allowed to be very judicious, the director having selected from the most approved English poets such pieces as possess, in the highest degree, the Utile Dulci, and while they entertain improve the mind, by conveying the most useful lessons of morality and virtue. The Company have separated until the winter, when the New York Theatre will be opened, Mr. Hallam being embarked for England to engage some recruits for that service. The year after they will perform at Philadelphia, and in the winter following we may expect them here with a theatrical force hitherto unknown in America.]

4 June 1774 Richmond, Virginia colony
Play not identified.
Performers unknown.

[A broadside attacking the theatre on moral grounds is identified as having been "stuck up at Richmond ...close to the playbill for that day." The identity of the company and the venue remain a mystery. Source: satirical handbill assigned to Rowland Hill in the American Antiquarian Society; Early American Imprints.]

21 June 1774   Charleston
Newspaper notice.
 [The *Carolina Gazette* for this date contains the following item: "Mr. David Douglass, manager of the American Company of Comedians, and Mrs. Douglass, sailed in the Schooner Rose, Captain Ogilvie, for New-York."]

27 June 1774   Charleston
Newspaper notice.
 [The *South Carolina Gazette* for this date contains the following item: "The whole Company of American Comedians, are now gone, different ways; except Mr. Goodman, who remains to deliver Mr. Steven's Lectures upon Heads." For a complete list of departures, see Willis 75. This announcement notwithstanding, apparently not all of the company had departed; see 14 August 1774.]

29 June 1774   Charleston
Cato.
Local students.
 ["On Wednesday evening last a number of young gentlemen, pupils of James Thomson, A. M. late tutor of New-Jersey College, performed the Tragedy of Cato in the presence of several hundreds. Their performance did great honour both to the pupils and preceptor, and exhibited fair promises of superior eminence in their future professions." Source: *South Carolina Gazette* (4 July 1774).]

4 July 1774   Church St. Theater, Charleston
Lecture on Heads.
[A Picture of a Playhouse; or] Bucks Have at Ye All.
Goodman and Allen.
 [By Goodman of the American Company and Allen of the Theatre Royal, Edinburgh. Source: Willis 75.]

6 July 1774   Church St. Theater, Charleston
Lecture on Heads.
[A Picture of a Playhouse; or] Bucks Have at Ye All.
Goodman and Allen.

THE COLONIAL AMERICAN STAGE 473

[By Goodman of the American Company and Allen of the Theatre Royal, Edinburgh. Source: *South Carolina & American General Gazette* (24 June–1 July 1774).

7 July 1774   Williamsburg, Virginia colony
Newspaper notice.
American Company.
    [The *Virginia Gazette* of this date prints the following item:

> By letters from Charlestown we are informed that the governments of South Carolina and Georgia had prohibited all trade and intercourse with the Creek Indians; the theatre in that city was closed after performing 51 plays, and that Lewis Hallam, Miss Hallam, and Mr. Woolls, were embarked for England; the rest of the company are expected very soon in this city.]

July 1774   Church St. Theater, Charleston
Theatre for rent.
    [The *South Carolina & American General Gazette* of 8–15 July 1774 contains the following notice:

> The new Play-House in Church Street, during the absence of the American Company from this province, is to be let for the benefit of the charity fund of the Union-Kilwinning Lodge; and as it is now entirely vacant, any person desiring to rent the same for one or two years may apply for further particulars to Robert Wells.]

15 July 1774   New York
Newspaper notice.
American Company.
    [The *Massachusetts Spy* of this date contains the following item:

> New-York ... last Wednesday afternoon Capt. Ogilvie, arrived here in a schooner from West-Florida, but last from Charlestown, in South-Carolina, in whom came David Douglass, Esq; Manager of the American Comedians, and Mrs. Douglas; with all the necessary apparatus for performing here this winter.]

11 August 1774   Charleston
Cato.
Local students.
    ["Charles-Town, August 22. On Saturday last died, much regretted, Mr. Oliver Dale; some of whose pupils had, no longer than the Thursday se'nnight before, presented the

Tragedy of Cato, with applause, at the Theatre in this town."
Source: *South Carolina Gazette* (19 September 1774).]

14 August 1774   Charleston
Newspaper notice.
American Company.
 [The *South Carolina Gazette* of 19 September 1774 reports that on this date four members of the American Company set sail for Philadelphia.]

19 September 1774   Southwark Theatre, Philadelphia
Lecture on Heads.
A Picture of a Playhouse.
Lectures on a variety of subjects.
Goodman and Allen.
 [By Goodman of the American Company and Allen of the Theatre Royal, Edinburgh. Source: *Pennsylvania Packet* (19 September 1774).]

23 September 1774   Southwark Theatre, Philadelphia
Lecture on Heads.
A Picture of a Playhouse.
Lectures on a variety of subjects.
Goodman and Allen.
 [By Goodman of the American Company and Allen of the Theatre Royal, Edinburgh. Source: *Pennsylvania Journal* (21 September 1774).]

20 October 1774
Congressional resolution.
 [The Continental Congress passed a resolution to encourage the "discontenuance and discourage every species of extravagance and dissipation, especially all horse-racing, and all kinds of gaming, cock-fighting, exhibitions of shews, plays, and other expensive diversions and entertainments." This resolution marked the closure of all theatrical activities throughout the colonies. Source: Quinn 32.]

15 December 1774   New York
Newspaper notice.
 [The *New York Journal* of this date prints a letter which alludes to the presence of a new company:

> As a number of players have arrived in the Lady Gage, from London, and it is reported that they are to act among us this winter, I beg leave through the channel of your paper, to invite the

attention of the public to the eighth article of the association, agreed upon by the Continental Congress.

The author, "Pro Patria," goes on to accord Mr. Douglass the following respects:

> From my knowledge of Mr. Douglass's urbanity, I am persuaded he would not wish to give any offence to the good people of this city, whose favour he has formerly experienced, and who may hereafter render him more essential service, and I doubt not such an application, as I have mentioned above, will have a proper effect.]

Coda

2 January 1775   New York
Newspaper notice.
American Company.

["New York, January 2. The Company of Comedians, with Mr. Douglass, the manager, are preparing to embark for the island of Jamaica, and they will not return to the continent, until its tranquility is restored." Source: *Virginia Gazette* (28 January 1775).]

January 1775   New York
Newspaper notice.
American Company.

[The *New York Mercury* of this date contains the following item: "The intelligence in Mr. Rivington's last Gazetteer, of the American Company of Comedians preparing to embark for the island of Jamaica, we are informed, is rather premature."]

6 February 1775   New York
Departure of company.
American Company.

[The *New York Mercury* of this date contains the following item:
> On Thursday last [i.e., 2 February] embarked in the ship Sally, Capt. Bruce, for Jamaica, the American Company of Comedians, under the direction of David Douglass, Esq; where they intend exerting their justly applauded talents for the entertainment of the ladies and gentlemen of that polite and opulent island, until the unhappy differences that subsist between the mother country and her colonies in America subside.]

476   THE COLONIAL AMERICAN STAGE

12 March 1775   Jamaica
Correspondence.
American Company.
   [The following excerpt of a letter from Sir Basil Keith, Governor of Jamaica, to Cadwallader Colden sheds light on the American Company's activities during this period:

                              Jamaica, 12 March 1775.
       Sir
       A few days ago I received your favour of the 28th of January. I am at present at a considerable distance from the Towns; but on my return which will be in five or six weeks hence; I will with pleasure give all my countenence and protection to Mr. Douglass and his Company.

Source: Colden, *Letters and Papers*, 9:236–37.]

27 April 1775   Kingston, Jamaica
The West Indian.
Miss in Her Teens.
American Company.
   [A letter reprinted in the *Pennsylvania Evening Post* (13 July 1775) describes the arrival and activities of the American Company in Jamaica and establishes details pertaining to a new venue:

       6 May. On Thursday the 27th ult. the new theatre, on the parade in this town, was opened by the American Company of Comedians, under the direction of Mr. Douglass.... The applause which attended the whole of the performance, as it stamped the mark of approbation on the merit of the performers, who did all imaginable justice to their several characters, so it reflected honour upon the taste and judgement of their auditors.

The context further suggests that the company performed in a different venue prior to this opening night. Cf., Hill (25–29).]

6 June 1775   Annapolis
Building notice.
   [At a meeting of the vestry of St. Anne's Parish, Annapolis, "the Vestry agreed that the Playhouse be fitted up for a place of divine worship." Source: "Vestry Proceedings, St. Anne's Parish," 140.]

17 May 1777   Montego Bay, Jamaica
Tamerlane.

Edgar and Emmeline.
American Company.
[This was the company's last night in Jamaica, by which time Henry had become the manager, as reported in the *New York Mercury* of 16 June 1777:

> Montego-Bay, in Jamaica, May 17. On Tuesday night the Theatre in this town was closed, with the tragedy of Tamerlane, and the farce of Edgar and Emmeline, to a crouded audience. It must be acknowledged, that the company in general, have been studious in their endeavours to please; and upon the whole, this town and the neighbouring parishes, have been agreeably entertained by their performances–As soon as the farce was ended, Mr. Henry, the manager, in a polite and becoming manner, addressed the audience, in words ... which were received throughout the whole house with the highest approbation.]

July 1781   Charleston
Possible return of company to the mainland.
American Company.
[The *Charleston Royal Gazette* offered the following item concerning the affairs of the American Company: "The lovers of theatrical entertainments will doubtless be happy to learn, that there is some probability of the American Company, under the direction of Mr. Hallam, being here next winter."]

24 April 1783   New York
Return of company to the mainland.
American Company.
[The *Continental Journal* of this date reprints the following letter from London which describes American Company affairs:

> London. Feb. 8. Mr. Hallam, brother to Mrs. Mattocks, has lately had a letter from America, inviting him to the direction of three theatres in the principle cities in America, viz, New-York, Boston, and Philadelphia. Mr. Henry, joint manager with Mr. Hallam, is now in town raising some theatrical troops for the company, at handsome salaries. –Mr. Hallam, at the beginning of the war, having an intimation from Congress, that he and his company would be dispensed with in America, went to the West Indies, where he has since mostly remained; but the war being now over, he has received a genteel invitation, to recompence him, in some measure, for his honorary banishment.]

18 October 1783   Kingston, Jamaica
Return of company to the mainland.
American Company.

[The activities of Lewis Hallam are clarified by the following letter, reprinted in the *Pennsylvania Evening Post* of 13 December 1783:

> Kingston (Jamaica) October 18. We hear his excellency the governor has been pleased to appoint William Smith, Esq; master of the revels, in the room of Lewis Hallam, Esq; who sails for America in a day or two, with the proviso, that should Mr. Hallam return here in the course of six months, he is to be restored to that place; Mr. Smith will be superceded.]

Bibliography

PRIMARY SOURCES

Playbills
    Colonial Williamsburg Foundation; Harvard Theatre Collection; Historical Society of Pennsylvania; Library Company of Philadelphia; Maryland Historical Society; New York Public Library

Manuscripts
    Bradford, William. Correspondence, 1770. MS. collection, Historical Society of Pennsylvania.
    Charlton, Edward. Account book. Colonial Williamsburg Foundation.
    Gilmer, George. Letter book. Colonial Williamsburg Foundation.
    Hunter, William. Daybook. Colonial Williamsburg Foundation.
    Jones, Joseph. Papers. Manuscript Division. Library of Congress.
    Lee, Alice. Correspondence. Virginia Historical Society.
    Rose, Duncan. Account Book. Virginia Historical Society.
    Smith, John. Manuscript diary. Ridgeway Branch of the Free Library of Philadelphia.

Legal Records
    Accomac County Records, vol. 1663–66.
    Charleston Country Land Records, Misc. Pt. 64, Book C5, 1779–1781, 47.
    Charter to William Penn and the Laws of the Province of Pennsylvania Passed between the Years 1682-1700. Edited by John Blair Linn. Harrisburg, 1879.
    The Colonial Records of North Carolina. Vol. 7. Edited by William L. Saunders. Raleigh: Josephus Daniels, 1890.
    The Statutes at Large of Pennsylvania. Vol. II.
    The Colonial Records of North Carolina. Edited by William L. Saunders. Raleigh: Joseph Daniels, 1890.
    Pennsylvania Archives. 2nd Series. VII. Harrisburg, 1878.
    Proceedings of the Massachusetts Historical Society.
    Provincial Papers–New Hampshire. Edited by Nathaniel Bouton. Manchester, NH: New Hampshire Historical Society, 1877. Vol. 6 (1747–1763).
    Public Records of the Colony of Connecticut from May 1717 to

October 1725. Edited by Charles J. Hoadly. Hartford: Lockwood and Brainard, 1890.
Records of the Massachusetts Colonial Society.
Rhode Island Colonial Records, 1757–1769. Providence, 1861.
Statutes at Large of South Carolina. Columbia, SC, 1836-41.
York County [Virginia]. *Records, Orders, Wills, etc.* Book XV.
———. *Judgements and Orders,* Book II.

SECONDARY SOURCES

Ames, Susie M. *"The Bear and the Cub." Eastern Shore News* [Onancock, VA]. October, 1965.
Andrews, William L., ed. *Journeys in New Worlds: Early American Women's Narratives.* Madison, WI: University of Wisconsin Press, 1990.
Armstrong, Susan S. *A Repertoire of the Colonial American Theatre Compiled from Material Gathered for The Colonial Stage by Hugh Rankin.* Colonial Williamsburg Foundation Library. Research Report Series, 1955.
Arnold, Samuel Greene. *History of the State of Rhode Island.* Vol 2. New York: D. Appleton and Co., 1878.
Aston, Anthony. *The Fool's Opera; or, Taste of the Town.* London, 1731.
"Attempt to Establish a Play-House in New Hampshire, 1762." *Collections of the New Hampshire Historical Society* 5 (1937): 247–50.
Bains, Y. S. "The American Company of Comedians in Halifax in 1768." *The Dalhousie Review* 56: 2 (Summer 1976): 240–46.
———. *English Canadian Theatre: 1765–1826.* New York: Peter Lang, 1998.
Black, Mary Childs. "The Theatre in Colonial Annapolis." M.A. thesis, George Washington University, 1952.
Blair, John. "The Diary of John Blair." *William and Mary College Quarterly* 7.3 (1899): 133–53.
Blake, Charles. *An Historical Account of the Providence Stage.* 1868. Reprint, New York: Blom, 1971.
Bloom, Arthur W. "A History of the Theatre in New Haven, Connecticut before 1860." Ph.D. diss., Yale, 1966.
Bonawitz, Dorothy M. "The History of the Boston Stage from the Beginning to 1810." Ph.D. diss., The Pennsylvania State University, 1936.
Borgers, Edward William. "A History of Dramatic Production in Princeton, New Jersey." Ph.D. diss., New York University, 1950.
Brown, B. W. "The Colonial Theatre in New England". *Special Bulletin of the Newport Historical Society* 76 (July 1930).
Brown, T. Allston. *History of the New York Stage.* 1903. Reprint, New York: Blom, 1964.
Brown, B. W. "The Colonial Theatre in New England." *Special Bulletin of the Newport Historical Society* 76 (July 1930).
Burling, William. *A Checklist of New Plays and Entertainments on the London Stage, 1700–1737.* Madison, NJ: Fairleigh Dickinson University Press, 1993.
———. "New Light on the Colley Cibber Canon: *The Bulls and Bears* and *Damon and Phillida.*" *Philological Quarterly* 68 (1988): 117–23.

THE COLONIAL AMERICAN STAGE 481

———. *Summer Theatre in London, 1661–1820, and the Rise of the Haymarket Theatre.* Madison, NJ: Fairleigh Dickinson University Press, 2000.

Burling, William J. and Timothy J. Viator. *The Plays of Colley Cibber.* Vol. 1. Madison, NJ: Fairleigh Dickinson University Press, 2000.

Byrd, William. *William Byrd of Virginia, The London Diary and Other Writings.* Edited by Marion Tinling and Louis B. Wright. New York: Oxford University Press, 1958.

Cambridge Guide to African and Caribbean Theatre. Edited by Marin Bahman, Errol Hill, George Woodyard, and Olu Obafemi. New York: Cambridge University Press, 1994.

Caribianna. London, 1741.

Carter, Col. Landon. *The Diary of Colonel Landon Carter of Sabine Hall, 1752-1778.* Edited by Jack P. Greene. Charlottesville: University Press of Virginia, 1965.

Clapp, William W. *A Record of the Boston Stage.* Boston and Cambridge: James Munroe and Co., 1853.

Clark, William Smith. *The Irish Stage in the County Towns, 1720–1800.* Oxford: Clarendon Press, 1965.

Cohen, Hennig. *The South Carolina Gazette: 1732–1775.* Columbia: University of South Carolina Press, 1953.

Colden, Cadwallader. *The Letters and Papers of Cadwallader Colden.* Vol. 9. New York: New York Historical Society, 1937.

The Correspondence of the Three William Byrds of Westover, Virginia, 1684–1776. Volume 1. Edited by Marion Tinling. Virginia Historical Society. Charlottesville: University Press of Virginia, 1977.

Corry, Mary Jane, Kate Van Winkle Keller, and Robert M. Keller. *The Performing Arts in Colonial American Newspapers, 1690–1783.* Text, Database, and Index. CD-rom. New York: Univesity Music Editions, 1997.

Curtis, Mary Julia. "The Early Charleston Stage: 1703–1798." Ph. D. diss., Indiana University, 1968.

———. "A Note on Henry Holt." *South Carolina Historical Magazine* 79:1 (1978): 5.

Daly, Charles P. *First Theatre in America.* New York: Burt Franklin, 1896.

Davis, Richard Beale. *Intellectual Life in the Colonial South, 1685–1763.* Knoxville: University of Tennessee Press, 1978.

Dormon, James H. *Theater in the Antebellum South 1815–1861.* Chapel Hill: University of North Carolina Press, 1967.

Douglass, David. "To the Public." Broadside. Charleston, SC. 4 November 1765. Evan's Early American Imprints, First Series, 41534.

———. "Proposal to open the theatre." Broaside in the South Carolina Historical Society, ms. collection. Early November 1765.

Duerr, Edwin. "Charles Ciceri and the Background of American Stage Design." *Theatre Arts Monthly* 16 (Dec. 1932): 983–90.

Dunlap, William. *History of the American Theatre.* 2$^{d.}$ ed., 1797. Reprint, New York: Franklin, 1963.

Durang, Charles. "The Philadelphia Stage from 1749 to 1821." Series published in *Philadelphia Sunday Dispatch*, vol. 3, 1854.

Durnam, Weldon. *American Theatre Companies, 1749–1887.* New York: Greenwood, 1986.

Dye, William S., Jr. "Pennsylvania vs. the Theatre." *Pennsylvania Magazine of History and Biography* 55 (1931): 333-371.

Eddis William. *Letters from America, Historical and Descriptive: Comprising Occurences from 1769 to 1777, Inclusive.* London, 1792.

———. *Letters from America.* Edited by Aubrey C. Land. Cambridge: Harvard University Press, 1969.

Engle, Ron and Tice L. Miller, eds. *The American Stage: Social and Economic Issues from the Colonial Period to the Present.* New York: Cambridge University Press, 1993.

Fergussan, C. B. "The Rise of the Theatre in Halifax." *The Dalhousie Review* 24.4 (January 1950): 419-27.

Fitzgerald, Percy. *The Book of Theatrical Anecdotes.* London, 1874.

Ford, Paul Leicester. *Washington and the Theatre.* 1899. Reprint, New York: Blom, 1967.

Fowler, Henry. "A History of the Theatre in Jamaica." *The Jamaican Journal* 2.1 (1968): 55.

Gardner, David. "Early performances in Canada." In *Oxford Companion to Canadian Theatre.* Edited by Eugene Benson and L. W. Conolly. Toronto: Oxford University Press, 1989.

Grayton, Alexander. *Memoirs of his own Time, with Reminiscences of the Men and Events of the Revolution.* Edited by John Stockton Littell. Philadelphia: Lindsay and Blakiston, 1846.

Greene, Nathanael. *The Papers of General Nathanael Greene.* Edited by Richard K. Showman. Chapel Hill: University of North Carolina, 1976.

Haims, Lynn. "First American Theatre Contracts: Wall and Lindsay's Maryland Company of Comedians, and the Annapolis, Fell's Pond, and Baltimore Theatres, 1781-1783." *Theatre Survey* 17 (November 1976): 179-94.

Hall, Wilmer L., ed. *Executive Journal, Council of Colonial Virginia.* Vol. 5. Richmond, VA: State Library Press, 1945.

Harrison, Fairfax. "Stage Plays Prohibited." *Virginia Historical Magazine* 31 (July 1923): 270.

Henderson, Archibald. "Strolling Players in North Carolina." *The Carolina Play-Book* 15 (March, 1942): 24-26.

Henderson, Mary. *The City and the Theatre.* Clifton, NJ: James T. White, 1973.

———. "Scenography, Stagecraft, and Architecture in the American Theatre. Beginnings to 1870." In *The Cambridge History of American Theatre*, edited by Wilmeth and Bigsby, 373-423.

Highfill, Philip H. Jr. "The British Background of the American Hallams." *Theatre Survey* 11 (May 1970): 1-35.

Highfill, Philip H. Jr., Kalman A. Burnim, and Edward A. Langhans. *A Biographical Dictionary of Actors, Actresses, Musicians, Dancers, Managers, and Other Stage Personnel in London, 1660-1800.* 16 vols. Carbondale: Southern Illinois University Press, 1973-95.

Hill, Errol. *The Jamaican Stage 1655 to 1900: Profile of a Colonial Theatre.* Amherst, MA: University of Massachusetts Press, 1992.

Hill, Frank Pierce. *American Plays Printed 1714-1830.* Stanford: Stanford University Press: 1900.

Hiltzheimer, Jacob. *Extracts from the Diary of Jacob Hiltzheimer.* Edited by Jacob Cox Parson. Philadelphia: Wm. F. Fell, 1893.

Hornblow, Arthur. *A History of the Theatre in America.* New York: Blom, 1965.
Hughes, Glen. *A History of the American Theatre: 1700–1950.* New York: Samuel French, 1951.
Ireland, J. N. *Records of the New York Stage from 1750 to 1860.* Vol 1. Reprint, New York: Blom, 1966.
Jefferson, Thomas. *Jefferson's Memorandum Books, Accounts, with Legal Records and Miscellany, 1767-1826.* Vol 1. Edited by James A. Bear, Jr. and Lucia C. Stanton. Princeton: Princeton University Press, 1997.
———. *The Papers of Thomas Jefferson.* Edited by Julian Boyd. Princeton: Princeton University Press, 1950.
Johnson, Odai. "Thomas Jefferson and the Colonial American Stage." *Virginia Magazine of History and Biography* 108 (2000): 139–54.
Johnson, Robert Charles. "The Struggle Over the Theatre in Colonial Pennsylvania (1723–1773)." M.A. thesis, University of Washington, 1950.
Jones, Hugh. *The Present State of Virginia.* London, 1724. Reprint, New York, 1865.
Jones, Vernon. "The Theatre in Colonial Virginia." *Reviewer* 5 (January 1925): 81–88.
Kahan, Gerald. *George Alexander Stevens and The Lecture on Heads.* Athens: University of Georgia Press, 1984.
Kollatz, Harry E. *Walking Shadow: a general history of the colonial theatre in Williamsburg, Virginia.* "A Fair Booth Theatre Project." N.p.: n.p., 1988.
Leslie, Charles. *A New History of Jamaica in 13 Letters from a Gentleman to his Friend.* Dublin, 1741.
Land, Robert Hunt. "The First Williamsburg Theatre." *William and Mary Quarterly* 3rd. ser., 5 (1948): 359–74.
———. "Theatre in Colonial Virginia." M.A. thesis, University of Virginia, 1936.
Larson, Carl F. W. *American Regional Theatre History to 1900: A Bibliography.* Metuchen, NJ: Scarecrow, 1979.
Lewis, Lawrence Jr. "Edward Shippen, Chief-Justice of Pennsylvania." *Pennsylvania Magazine of History and Biography* 7 (1883): 11–34.
Long, Edward. *The History of Jamaica.* London, 1774.
The Lower Norfolk County Virginia Antiquary. Edited by Edward W. James. New York: Peter Hill, 1951.
Mackaby, Alexander. "Extracts from the letters of Alexander Mackaby to Sir Philip Francis." *The Pennsylvania Magazine of History and Biography* 11.2 (1887): 276–87, 491–95.
Malone, Diane B. "A Survey of Early Military Theatre in America." *Theatre Survey* 16.1 (May 1975): 56–64.
Manigault, Mrs. Ann. "Extracts of the Journal of Mrs. Ann Manigault." *South Carolina Historical and Genealogical Society* 20.3 (1919): 52–63, 204–212.
Mather, Increase. *Testimony Against Several Profane and Superstitious Customs.* London, 1687.
Mays, David D. "The Achievements of the Douglass Company in North America: 1758-1774." *Theatre Survey* 23.2 (November 1982): 141–50.

McCusker, John J. *Money and Exchange in Europe and America, 1600–1775. A Handbook.* Institute of Early American History and Culture. Chapel Hill: University of North Carolina Press, 1978.

McDermott, Douglas. "Structure and Management in the American theatre from the Beginnings to 1870." In *The Cambridge History of American Theatre,* 182–215. Edited by Don B. Wilmeth and Christopher Bigsby.

Myers, Robert J. and Brodowski, Joyce. "Rewriting the Hallams: Research in 18th Century British and American Theatre." *Theatre Survey* 41:1 (May 2000): 1–22.

Montressor, Capt. *The Journals of Capt. Montressor. Collections of the New York Historical Society for 1881.* Edited by G. D. Scull. New York, 1882.

Munsell, Joel. *Annals of Albany.* 2 vols. Albany, 1870.

Nixon, Lily Lee. *James Burd, Frontier Defender 1726–1793.* Philadelphia: University of Pennsylvania Press, 1941.

"Notes and Queries." *Historical Magazine and Notes and Queries Concerning Antiquities, History, and Biography of America* 9.3 (9 April 1865): 118.

Odell, George C. D. *Annals of the New York Stage.* Vol 1. New York: Columbia University Press, 1927.

Oldmixon, John. *The British Empire in America,* 2d. ed. [1741].

O'Neill, Patrick B. "Theatre in Nova Scotia." In *Oxford Companion to Canadian Theatre.* Edited by Eugene Benson and L. W. Conolly. Toronto: Oxford University Press, 1989.

"Original Letters." *William and Mary Quarterly* 2 (1893): 240–41.

Pedicord, Harry W. *The Theatrical Public in the Time of Garrick.* Carbondale, IL: Southern Illinois University Press, 1954.

Phèlps, H. P. *Players of a Century: A Record of the Albany Stage.* Reprint, New York: Blom, 1972.

Pollock, Thomas Clark. *The Philadelphia Theatre in the Eighteenth Century.* New York: Greenwood, 1968.

Quincy, Josiah. *The Journal of Josiah Quincy.* Boston: Cummings, Hilliard, and Co., 1825.

Quinn, Arthur Hobson. *A History of the American Drama. From the Beginning to the Civil War.* 2d. ed. New York: F. S. Crofts, 1943.

Rankin, Hugh F. *The Theatre in Colonial America.* Chapel Hill: University of North Carolina Press, 1960.

Ritchey, Robert D. "A History of the Baltimore Stage in the Eighteenth Century." Ph.D. diss., Louisiana State University, 1971.

Rosenfeld, Sybil. *Strolling Players and Drama in the Provinces, 1660-1765.* London: Cambridge University Press, 1939.

Rowe, John. *The Letters and Diary of John Rowe, Boston Merchant.* Boston: W. B. Clarke, 1903.

Scharf, Col. J. Thomas. *The Chronicles of Baltimore.* Baltimore, 1874.

Scott, James G. and Edward A. Wyatt IV. *Petersburg's Story, A History.* Petersburg, VA: Titmus Optical Co., 1960.

Scouten, Arthur H. and Robert D. Hume. "'Restoration Comedy' and its Audiences, 1660–1776." In Robert D. Hume, *The Rakish Stage: Studies in English Drama, 1660–1800.* Carbondale, IL: Southern Illinois University Press, 1983. Chapter 2.

Seilhamer, George O. *History of the American Theatre*. 3 vols. 1888–91. Reprint, New York: Blom, 1968.
Sewall, Samuel. *The Letter Book of Samuel Sewall*. In *Collections of the Massachusetts Historical Society*, 6th ser., vol. 2. Boston, 1888.
Sherman, Susanne M. *Comedies Useful: Southern Theatre History 1775-1812*. Williamsburg: Celest Press, 1998.
Sonneck, O. G. *Early Opera in America*. 1943. Reprint, New York: Blom, 1963.
Stiles, Ezra. "Extracts from the Travel Diary of Ezra Stiles." *Proceedings of the Massachusetts Historical Society*. 2d ser., vol. 7 (1801–1892): 340.
Stone, George Winchester. *The London Stage, 1660–1880*. Part 4: 1747–1776. 3 vols. Carbondale, IL: Southern Illinois University Press, 1962.
Thomas, Isaiah. *The History of Printing in America*. New York: Weathervane Books, 1970.
Toner, Joseph M. *Washington's Barbados Journal*. Albany. 1892.
Tyler, Lyon G. *Williamsburg, the Old Colonial Capital*. Richmond: Whittet and Shepperson, 1907.
"Vestry Proceedings, St. Anne's Parish." *Maryland Historical Magazine* 10.1 (1915): 140.
Walker, Lewis Burd. "The Life of Margaret Shippen, wife of Benedict Arnold." *Pennsylvania Magazine of History and Biography* 24.4 (1900): 401–29.
Washington, George. *The daily journal of Major George Washington, in 1751-2 kept while on a tour from Virginia to the island of Barbados, with his invalid brother, Maj. Lawrence*. Ed. Joseph M. Toner. Albany, New York: J. Munsell's Sons, 1892.
———. *The Diaries of George Washington*. Edited by Donald Jackson and Dorothy Twohig. Charlottesville: University Press of Virginia. Vol. 2: 1766–1770 (1976); Vol. 3: 1771–1775, 1780–1781 (1978).
———. *The Papers of George Washington: Colonial Series*. Edited by Abbot, W.W. and Dorothy Twohig. 10 vols. Charlottesville: University Press of Virginia, 1993.
Wegelin, Oscar. *Early American Plays 1714–1830*. New York: The Dunlap Society, 1900.
Wemyss, Francis. *Chronology of the American Stage, from 1752-1852*. New York: O. A. Roorbach, 1852.
Whitelaw, Ralph T. *Virginia's Eastern Shore, A History of Northampton and Accomack Counties*. Richmond: Virginia Historical Society, 1951. 1: 712–13.
Wilkinson, Tate. *Memoirs of His Own Life*. 4 vols. York, 1790.
Willard, George Owen. *The Providence Stage: 1762–1891*. Providence: Providence News Company, 1891.
Willis, Eola. *The Charleston Stage in the XVIII Century*. 1924. Reprint, New York: Blom, 1968.
Wilmeth, Don B. and Christopher Bigsby, eds. *The Cambridge History of American Theatre. Volume One: Beginnings to 1870*. Cambridge: Cambridge University Press, 1998.
Wise, Henry Alexander. *Ye Kingdome of Accawmacke or the Eastern Shore of Virginia in the Seventeenth Century*. 1911. Reprint, Baltimore: Regional Press, 1967.

Witham, Barry. *The Theatre in the United States: A Documentary History.* Vol. 1. Cambridge: Cambridge University Press, 1996.
Withington, Ann Fairfax. *Toward a More Perfect Union: Virtue and the Formation of American Republic.* New York: Oxford University Press, 1991.
Wolcott, John R. "Scene Painters and Their Work in America Before 1800." *Theatre Survey* 18.1 (May 1977): 57–85.
Wolf, Edwin II. "Colonial American Playbills." *Pennsylvania Magazine of History and Biography* 97 (1973): 99–106.
Wright, Richardson. *Revels in Jamaica 1682–1838.* 1937. Reprint, New York: Blom, 1969.
——. *Hawkers and Walkers in Early America.* 1927. Reprint, New York: Ungar, 1965.
Wyatt, Edward A., IV. "Three Petersburg Theatres." *William and Mary College Quarterly* 2d. ser. 21 (April 1941): 83–110.
Young, William. *Documents of American Theatre History.* Vol. 1. Chicago: American Library Association, 1993.
——. *Famous American Playhouses, 1716-1899.* Chicago: American Library Association, 1973.

Contemporary Periodicals

American Chronicle
American Weekly Mercury
Barbados Gazette
Boston Chronicle
Boston Gazette
Boston News Letter
Boston Post-Boy
Boston Evening Post
Connecticut Gazette
Gaine's Mercury
Gentleman's Magazine
The Independent Journal
Jamaica Gazette
Maryland Gazette
Maryland Journal
Massachusetts Spy
New England & Boston Gazette
New Hampshire Gazette
Newport Mercury
New York Gazette (Bradford's)
New York Gazette & Weekly Post-Boy
New York Mercury
New York Weekly Post-Boy
Norfolk Virginia Gazette
Nova Scotia Gazette
Pennsylvania Chronicle
Pennsylvania Gazette
Pennsylvania Journal
Pennsylvania Ledger

Providence Gazette
Rivington's Gazette
Royal Danish American Gazette
South Carolina & American General Gazette
South Carolina Gazette
South Carolina Star & Public Advertiser
Williamsburg Virginia Gazette
Zenger's Journal

Person Index

Abington, George, 189
Adcock, William, 32, 151, 165–77
Adcock, Mrs. (1st), 32, 151, 165–77
Adcock, Mrs. (2nd). *See* Miss Palmer
Allen, Mr. (also Allyn), 87, 459–60, 472–74
Allman, Thomas. *See* Thomas Vernon
Allyn, Adam, 35, 189–98, 200, 209–10, 215–16, 218, 221–25, 227–30, 233, 235–36, 243, 253–76, 281–85, 287, 289–94
Allyn, Mrs., 209, 218, 233, 235, 243
American Company, The: 23–25, 28; actor recruitment, 31–34; audiences, 88–90; building theatres, 45–58; finances of, 81–83; in Albany (1769), 321, 342; in Annapolis (1770), 353, 371–72, 374–75; (1771), 386–88, 393–95; (1772), 398, 410–14; (1773), 425, 454–56; in Baltimore (1772), 397, 405–6; in Barbados (1765–66), 238–41, 243; in Charleston (1763–64), 230–37; (1765–66), 239–47; (1773–74), 425, 458–71; in Dumfries, Virginia colony (1771), 386, 389; in Fredericksburg, Virginia colony (1771), 392–93; in Jamaica, 475–77; in Maryland (1760), 200–209; in Newport, Rhode Island colony (1761), 210–15; (1762), 219, 227; in New York (1758–59), 185, 187–92; (1761), 210, 212, 215–18, 220–26; (1767–68), 283–87, 289–309, 311; (1769), 320, 324–40; (1773), 424–25, 436–52; in Philadelphia (1759), 192–200; (1766–67), 252–77, 280–83; (1768–69), 315–20, 323; (1769–70), 321, 347–53, 358–66; (1772–73), 398, 414–24, 427–36; (1773), 425, 456–57; in Portsmouth, New Hampshire colony (1762), 218–19, 226–27; in Providence, Rhode Island colony (1762), 219, 227–29; in Williamsburg (1760–61), 209–211; (1762–63), 220, 229–31; (1770), 353, 366–68, 377–80; (1771), 386, 390–92, 395–97; (1772), 397, 400–3; music 42–43; opposition to, 72–73; scenery, 40–41; subscription strategies, 85–86. *See also* David Douglass
Annapolis Company, The. *See* Murray-Kean Company
Ansel, Mary, 102–3
Antigua Company, The, 23, 29, 399, 410
Arne, Thomas, 33
Ashbridge, Elizabeth, 110–11
Aston, Anthony, 23, 29, 97

Barry, Mr., 43, 233, 235–36
Bayly, Mr.: Bayly's Company, 22–23, 28–29; in Charles-

ton, 51, 286, 289, 296–7, 299–300, 303–4, 319; in New York, 62, 256, 270–72, 274
Becceley, Mrs., 151, 155, 165–77
Bell, Charles, 165–75
Bertrand, Dr. Joachimus, 106–7
Bessel, Mr. R., 107
Blackler, Mr., 425, 447
Blair, Alexander, 113
Blair, Archibald, 103–4
Blair, John, 113
Brenan, Miss, 107
Broadbelt, Mr., 255–77, 347–48, 353, 365
Bromadge, Christopher, 286–87, 299–309, 312
Bullock, Edward, 355, 384
Burrows, Thomas, 38
Burd, James, 130–32
Burdett, William, 322, 327, 329, 339
Burdett, Mrs., 322, 327, 329, 339
Byerley, Thomas, 287, 318–21, 324, 340, 353, 362, 365, 367, 391, 398, 405, 412, 416–22, 425, 427–42, 444–51
Byrd, Maria Taylor, 209
Byrd, William, 103
Byrd, William II, 106, 116

Centour, Mr., 107
Centour, Mrs., 107
Charlton, Jack, 30
Charlton, Thomas, 286–87, 301–9
Chase, Mr., 107
Chase, Mrs., 107
Cheer, Margaret: 34–35, 42–43, 233–43, 252–76, 280–85, 289–308, 314, 318–22, 324, 333; as Lady Rosehill, 287, 314; beneficiary of Mrs. Harman, 443; return to stage, 445–47
Cherokees, 160, 284, 299, 300
Clarkson, Thomas, 151, 159, 165–77
Clarkson, Mrs., 151, 165–77
Colden, Cadwallader, 234, 244, 476
Cone, Mr., 107,
Conner, Elizabeth, 286
Crane, Mrs. (Miss), 200, 204–9, 218, 221–25, 228, 230, 233, 235–36

Dale, Oliver, 24, 26, 461, 473–74
Daniels, William, 140, 180, 181
Daniels, Mary, 140
Darby, Samuel, 287, 315, 318–22, 324, 327–29, 337, 339, 355–57, 376–79, 382–83, 385–86
Darby, Mrs., 322, 337, 355–57, 376–79, 382
Darby, William, 23, 92–94
Davies, John, 355, 376, 384
Davies, Mr. (John?), 460, 469–70
Davies, Mrs., 460, 469–70
Davis, Mrs., 140, 147
Deacon, Mr., 398, 420, 426–27
Deacon, Mr. Jr., 398, 423, 426
Denny, William, 190
Dermont, Mr., 441, 447–49 455, 457, 460, 468–69
Doll, Nicholas, 38, 47, 238–39, 393

Donald, Mr., 140
Douglass, David, (Manager of the American Company): 26, 28, 31–33, 35, 38, 41; as actor (ensemble), 128, 151, 189, 192–98, 200–209, 215–16, 218, 220–25, 227–30, 233, 235, 242–43, 245, 252–53, 255, 257, 259–60, 262–69, 271, 273–76, 280, 282–87, 289–308, 315, 318–21, 324, 353, 362, 386–87, 391–94, 398, 405, 410, 412, 415–25, 427–42, 444–47, 456–60, 468–70; (solo), 61, 86, 247–48, 250, 254, 277–80, 312, 345–46; audience relations, 89, 226, 422, 439, 470–471; building theatres, 46–47, 49–50, 53–54, 57, 61; character letters, 180, 212, 215, 217–18, 234–35, 475–76; finances, 78, 81–85, 221, 365–66; in Jamaica (1756–58), 180, 184–85; in London (1765), 237–39; leasing playhouse, 452–53; securing permission to play, 72–74, 79–80, 187–88, 210–12, 226–27, 348–49; subscriptions, 374–75, 388–89, 393, 450, 452–53
Mrs. Douglass (Sarah Smythies Hallam Douglass) 35, 184, 191–98, 200, 209, 215–18, 220–25, 227, 230, 232–36, 242–43, 245, 253–76, 279, 280–85, 287, 290–309, 311, 315, 319–22, 324, 347–48, 353, 364, 367, 371–72, 386–87, 391–93, 416–23, 425, 444, 446–47, 457–60, 469–70; false report of death, 425, 454–55. *See also* Mrs. Hallam
Dowthaite, Miss S., 200, 203–9, 243, 253–54, 286–87, 306, 309, 350
Dowthaite, Mrs., 200, 203–9, 286–87, 306, 309, 350
Drown, Mr., 107
Drown, Mrs., 107

Eastlake, Mr., 107
Emmet, Mr., 233, 235–36, 242–43, 245
Eyanson, Mr., 151

Farrell, Thomas (O'Farrell; Furrell, Furrel), 43, 233, 235–36, 286–89, 306, 309, 315–17
Farrell, Mrs., 286, 288, 306
Finny, Alexander, 55
Fitzgerald, Mr., 150
Foster, Mr., 398, 420, 426–27
Foster, Mrs., 398, 420, 426, 428
Foy, Martin, 23, 35–36, 398, 406–11, 426, 428–30
Francis, William, 449
Furrell, Mr. *See* Thomas Farrell

Garner, Joseph, 23, 35–36, 242, 244, 246–48, 250–51, 256, 258–63, 398
George, Nancy, 133, 140, 144–45
Giffard, Henry, Jr., 22, 34–35, 288, 310, 312–17
Giffard, Mrs., 288, 312–17, 355–57, 377–78, 381–82, 384, 387, 390

Gilmer, George, Dr., 113, 116, 119, 127, 152, 157, 355n 16
Godwin, James Verling: with Leeward Islands Company, 399, 409; with Verling's Virginia Company, 243, 255, 258–68, 286–87, 299–305, 322, 327–30, 336
Goodman, Richard, 33, 87, 353, 365, 387, 391, 393–94, 398, 405, 410, 412, 415, 416–22, 425, 427–42, 444–51, 455–56, 459–60, 468–70, 472–74
Graffenriedt, Madame La Baronne de, 117
Gray, John, 356, 381–82, 387
Greville, Samuel, 255–77, 282, 287, 289
Guy, Miss, 356–57, 376–79, 382–83

Hallam Company: mentioned, 22, 23, 27–28, 32–34, 37–38, 52, 56–57, 71–72; arrival in America, 151–52, 156–57; finances, 80–81, 83–84; in Charleston (1754–55), 172, 178–181; in Jamaica, 180; in New York (1753), 162–76; in Philadelphia (1754), 172, 176–78; in Williamsburg (1752), 159–61
Hallam, Adam, 185, 189–90, 192–98, 200, 202–9, 215–16, 218, 220–25, 228–36, 243
Hallam, Ann (wife of William), 187
Hallam, Ann (daughter of William and Ann), 187
Hallam, Helen, 151, 159, 165–73, 177, 185
Hallam, Lewis Sr., 24, 31–32, 34, 80–81, 140, 151, 159–60, 163–64, 166–77, 180, 184, 232
Hallam, Lewis Jr. 35–36, 39, 42, 87–88, 151, 159, 165–77, 185–89, 192–98, 200, 202–9, 215–16, 218, 220–25, 227–36, 243, 253–76, 280–85, 287, 289–307, 311–12, 315, 318–22, 324, 327, 335, 338, 343, 346–48, 351–55, 360–67, 386–87, 391–93, 398, 405, 410, 415, 416–25, 427–42, 444–51, 455–60, 468–69, 470, 473, 477–78. *See also* Hallam Company; American Company
Hallam, Mary (daughter of William and Ann), 187
Hallam, M. (Mirvan, son of Lewis Jr. and Sarah Perry), 441
Hallam, Nancy (Miss), 39, 42, 189, 193, 196, 200, 242, 245–46, 253–55, 260, 263–67, 273, 276–77, 280, 282–85, 289–99, 302, 304–8, 315, 318–21, 324–25, 335, 340, 342–43, 347–48, 351, 353, 361–63, 367, 371–72, 386–87, 390–93, 395, 398, 410, 412, 415, 416–25, 444–51, 454–60, 463–64, 469, 473
Hallam, Sarah Smythies (Mrs. Hallam; later Mrs. Douglass), 151, 159, 165–77, 184. *See also* Mrs. Douglass

Hallam, Sarah Perry (wife of Lewis Hallam Jr.), 87, 197, 210, 215–16, 218, 220, 222, 224–25, 228–29, 367
Hallam, William: co-manager of Hallam Company, 184–85; death in Tortola, 185–87; visits America, 164–65, 172
H., Mr. C., 35, 107
Hamilton, Alexander, 409
Hamilton, Governor, 176–77
Hamilton, Miss, 140, 180
Harman, Catherine, 61, 185, 192–98, 200, 232–33, 243, 252–75, 287, 289–307, 311, 315, 319–21, 324–25, 339, 353, 362–63, 367, 371–72, 405, 412, 416–25, 427–28; death of, 425, 443
Harman, John, 185, 189, 192–98, 200
Harris, Mr., 356–57, 376–79, 381–82
Heady, Thomas, 22, 107, 109
Henry, John: as actor, 31, 33, 35–36, 49–50, 85, 255, ·287, 289–98, 300–306, 318–22, 324, 335, 342, 344–48, 353, 362–64, 367, 387, 394, 398, 405, 410, 415, 416–25, 427–42, 444–51, 455–60, 463, 469–70; as manager, 477
Henry, Mrs. (2nd wife, Ann Storer), 321, 362–64, 367, 386–87, 391, 394, 398, 405, 410, 415, 416–25, 427–42. *See also* Ann Storer
Herbert, Mr., 32, 151, 159, 161–62
Hill, Mr., 355–57, 371, 374, 376, 380, 384, 387–89.

See also Leeward Islands Company
Hoar, Mr., 23, 35, 426, 431–33, 435
Holt, Henry: Holt's Company, 22, 29, 48, 85, 87; in Charleston, 112–15, 117–123; in New York, 123–24
Horne, Mr., 185, 189, 192–98, 200
Horner, Mr., 288, 312–17
Howard, Philip, 23, 92–94
Hugdson, Mr., 322, 343, 347, 349
Hughes, George: with Leeward Islands Company, 356–57, 374, 384; with American Company, 426, 455–57, 460, 468–70
Hulett, William, 32, 42, 87, 166, 320, 343, 440
Hunter, Richard, 23, 29, 96
Hunter, Robert, 71, 98
Hurleston, Nicholas, 102
Hymes, Mr., 256

Ives, Alice, 102, 104
Ives, Elizabeth, 102–4

Jago, Mr., 133, 140, 147
James, Mr., 150
Jefferson, David, 322, 327, 329, 334
Jefferson, Thomas: letter, 230–31; attends plays, 299, 301–9, 354, 363, 366–68, 377–80, 386, 391–92, 395–96, 403
Joan, Mr., 23, 35–36, 62, 322–323, 338–41, 346, 348–50, 355, 361, 365–66
Johnson, Mr., 398, 405, 410, 416–18, 421–25, 427–30, 432–33, 436

Jones, John Paul, 289
Jones, Sarah, 286, 322, 327–30, 335–38
Jones, Thomas, 356, 376–79, 382, 384–85
Jones, William, 102

Kean, Thomas. *See* Murray-Kean Company
Keith, Sir Basil, governor of Jamaica, 476
Keith, Sir William, 30, 104
Kershaw, Mr., 140, 180
Kershaw, Mrs., 140
Kirwan, John, 356–57, 380, 386

Leggitt, Mr., 288, 315–17
Leigh, Mr., 32, 133, 140, 150, 154
Leigh, Mrs., 32, 133, 140, 148, 150
Leavie, Mr., 286–87, 309
Leeward Islands Company, 23, 29, 355–57, 368–87, 399, 407, 409
Levingston, William, 22, 36–37, 55, 99–104
Linck, J. Frederick, 356–57, 373, 376, 381–83, 385, 387
Logan, James, 30, 104–5
Love, Charles, 32, 35, 42, 171–72, 175, 189
Love, Mrs., 169, 171–72, 174–75, 185, 189, 193–98, 200

Malone, Patrick: 32, 35–36; death, 382–83; funeral, 385; with American Company, 255, 282, 287, 290–97, 300, 303; with Hallam Company, 151, 159, 161, 165–73; with Leeward Islands Company, 356–57, 360, 370–71, 373, 380–82; with Verling's Company: 320–22, 327, 330, 333
Malone, Mrs.: 31; with Hallam Company, 171; with the Leeward Islands Company, 356–57, 384; with Verling's Company, 320–22, 327, 329, 333, 335
Mallory, Mr., 286
Marks, Mr., 133, 140, 147
Martin, Edward, 92–94
Martin, Mr., 256, 274
Mather, Increase, 95
Mathews, Mr., 243, 253–54, 268
McFarlin, George, 102
Mentges, Francis. *See* William Francis.
Miller, Mr., 165–77
Mills, Mr.: Mill's Company, 22–23, 28–29, 58, 71; in Halifax, Nova Scotia, 311–17, 355, 458; in North Carolina, 286, 288–89, 309–10, 322
Mills, Mrs., 312–17
Moncrieff, Major James, 331–32
Moody, John, 23, 31, 42, 127–28, 133, 140, 242–43
Moore, John, 133, 140, 147
Morgan, Mr., 22–23, 35, 39, 60, 62, 86, 219, 398, 404–5, 408, 411–14, 416–18, 420, 426–28
Morris, Mary, 35, 43, 128, 140, 180, 185, 200, 202–9, 215–16, 218, 220–25, 227–30, 233, 235–36, 243, 253–75, 282–83

Morris, Owen, 128, 140, 180, 185, 189, 192–98, 200, 202–9, 215–16, 218, 221–25, 227–30, 233, 235–36, 243, 252–76, 280–85, 287, 289–308, 311, 315, 318–21, 324, 339, 353, 362, 364, 367, 386–87, 391–93, 398, 405, 410, 412, 415–25, 427–42, 444–51, 455–60, 468–70

Morris, Mrs. (2nd). *See* Elizabeth Walker

Murray, Dick, 133, 146

Murray-Kean Company: 22–23, 27–28, 32, 34, 37, 52, 55–56, 59, 85; in Maryland (1752), 157–62; in New York (1750–51), 133–48; in Philadelphia (1749), 129–32; in Virginia (1752), 148–56; referenced in Hallam letter, 164

Murray, Walter, 33, 133, 140–42, 149, 151, 155, 200, 203–9. *See also* Murray-Kean Company

Nanfran, John, 30, 71, 96

New American Company. *See* William Verling

Nichols, Abraham, 37, 116, 119

Ogle, Cuthbert, 42

Osborne, Mrs. Henrietta: final benefit with American Company, 398, 412; with Murray-Kean Company, 133, 140, 147–48, 150, 154; with American Company, 242, 245; with Verling's Virginia Company, 286–87, 291, 299–301, 306–9, 322, 331–39

Osborne, Miss Jane, 32, 133, 140, 144, 147, 151, 154, 162

Page, Mr., 322, 327, 329, 338

Palmer, John, 189, 197–200, 202–5

Palmer, Miss (later the 2nd Mrs. Adcock), 151, 159

Parker, Charles: first return to American Company, 353, 362, 365, 367; in American Company, 287, 318–322, 324; in Leeward Islands Company, 356–57, 371, 377–379, 381–85; in Verling's Virginia Company, 286–87, 299–301, 306–7, 309; returns to Verling's Company, 327–30, 333–40; second return to American Company, 387, 391, 393, 398, 405, 412, 416–25, 427–32, 435, 441–42, 444–49, 456

Parker, Mrs.: in American Company, 322, 421; in Leeward Islands Company, 356–57, 371, 376–82, 384–85; in Verling's Company, 286–88, 299–301, 306–7, 309; returns to Verling's Company, 327–30, 333–40

Peel, Mary, 103, 103

Pelham, Peter, 42, 309

Petty, Mr., 150

Philibert, Madam, 426–27

Phillips, Mr., 288, 312–17

Phillips, Constantina, 182–83

Philo-Theatricus, 415–16

Phipps, Mr., 426–27

Pickle Herring, 105
Platt, Mr., 255–76, 288–89, 312–17
Potter, Henry, Dr., 27, 37, 116, 119

Quakers, 76, 98, 250–51,
Quelch, Mr., 209, 215–16, 218, 220–25, 227–30, 232–36

Rayworth, Mr. (also Raworth), 287, 318–22, 324
Rayworth, Mrs. *See* Miss Garvey.
Reed, Mr., 185, 189, 192–98, 209, 215–16, 218, 221–25
Rice, Mr., 106
Richards, Mr., 38–39, 411
Richardson, Miss Mary, 33, 351, 353, 362, 367, 386–87, 391, 398, 405, 410, 412, 415, 417–442, 444–451
Rigby, William, 151, 159–60, 165–77
Rigby, Mrs., 151, 165–74
Robbins, Mr., 308
Roberts, Mr., 255, 280, 282, 287, 290–97, 301–2, 305, 324, 367, 391, 398, 405, 417–25, 427–39, 441–42, 469–70
Rosehill, Lady. *See* Margaret Cheer.

Scott, Mr., 133, 140, 146, 189, 195–98, 200, 202–8
Sellers, Little Thomas, 102
Sewall, Samuel, 98–99
Shaw, Mr., 256
Shepherd, Charles, 48, 110, 112, 115. *See also* Henry Holt

Singleton, John, 42, 151, 159, 165–77
Smith, Mr., 140, 148, 180
Smith, Mrs., 140, 180
Snow, John, 108
Snyder, Jacob, 38, 189
Spencer, Frederick: with Leeward Islands Company, 399, 409; with Verling's Virginia Company, 322, 330, 333, 335, 337, 339
Stagg, Charles, 37, 42, 55, 99–102, 113, 117
Stagg, Mary, 37, 55, 99–102
Stamper, Mrs., 387
Stoaks, Mr., 23, 35–36, 131–32

Storer, Ann (Miss), 255–56, 281, 283, 285, 287, 290, 292–94, 296, 298, 302, 304, 315, 319–22, 324, 334–35, 345; as (2nd) Mrs. Henry: 353, 362–64, 367, 387, 391–94, 398, 405–6, 410, 415–25, 427–42, 444–51, 456–58, 460, 463–64, 469–70
Storer, Fanny, 255–56, 287, 294, 296–99, 304, 335
Storer, Jane (Helen; 1st Mrs. Henry): 255; death of, 256–57, 279
Storer, Mary (Maria; 3rd Mrs. Henry), 255–65, 287, 294–95, 303–4, 315, 322, 324–25, 334–35, 340, 347, 353; ("Miss" after Ann marries John Henry), 362, 364, 371–72, 391–92, 398, 405, 410, 415–25, 428–34, 436–42, 444–51, 456–58, 460, 463–64, 469–70

Sturt, Mr., 209, 215-16, 218, 221-25, 228

Taylor, Miss, 140
Taylor, Jane (Mrs.): with Leeward Islands Company, 356-57, 370-71, 385-86 ; with Murray-Kean Company, 133, 140, 143
Taylor, Mr., 133, 140
Tea, Mr., 256, 271-72, 274
Tinker, John, governor, 128
Tomlinson, Anna (Mrs.), 32, 185, 189, 192-98, 254-76, 282, 287, 290-308, 315, 322, 324, 333, 339, 353, 362, 386-87, 391
Tomlinson, Jane, 266, 303
Tomlinson, Mr.: as actor, 32, 185, 189, 192-98, 209, 215-16, 218, 221-25, 237, 252-76, 280-85, 287, 289-99, 301-8, 315, 318-22, 333, 353, 362, 364, 386-87, 391; as manager of Company, 23, 72, 243-44, 246-48;. *See also* New York (Chapel Street Riot)
Tremaine, John, 32, 34-35, 133, 240, 146, 150, 154, 209, 215-16, 218, 224-25
Tremaine, Mrs., 150
Tryon, William, 22, 34, 309-310

Upton, Robert: as advance agent for the Hallam Company, 36, 52, 140-41; as manager of Company, 23, 32, 34, 71-72, 141, 150, 153-55
Upton, Mrs., 150, 154

Valton, Peter, 142

Van Dam, Rip, 51, 108, 109, 134
Vaughan, Mr., 106
Verling, William: 22, 23, 28-29, 31, 32, 35-36, 57; in Annapolis, 322, 326-39; in St. Croix, 354-57, 368-86, 387-88, 399 solo, 256-58; with American Company, 243, 245-46; with Virginia Company and New American Company in Virginia, 286-88, 291, 299-309, 311, 314-15, 363, 365
Vernon, Thomas, 126
Virginia Company. *See* William Verling.
Vobe, Jane, 311

Wainwright, Sarah, 23, 42, 86, 238, 241-43, 245, 253-75, 280, 287, 289-308, 311, 327, 335, 340; return to stage, 426, 456-57, 460, 464, 469
Walker, Elizabeth: 322, 327-30, 336-38; after 1771 as Mrs. Morris (2nd), 398, 405, 410, 412, 415-16, 419, 421, 423-25, 427-42, 444-51, 455, 457, 460, 463, 470
Walker, George, 286-87, 299, 301, 306, 309, 322, 327, 329, 336
Wall, Mary (Mrs.), 255, 277, 287, 291, 293-94, 297, 303, 305, 308, 324, 391, 398, 405, 410, 412, 425, 430-32, 434, 437-39, 441-42
Wall, Thomas Llewellyn Lechmere: as actor, 42, 238, 242-43, 245, 252-76,

280–85, 287, 289–98, 300–308, 318–22, 324–25, 336, 350, 353, 362, 386–87, 391–93, 398, 405, 412, 415–25, 427–42, 444–50; as manager of Company, 58; as music teacher, 87, 426; as solo performer, 36, 39, 87, 450–51, 453, 455–58
Ward, Samuel, Governor of Rhode Island colony, 310, 444
Warwell, M. A. (Thomas), 23, 35, 62, 322, 343, 352, 387, 389–90
Washington, George: in attendance at theatres, 42, 44, 60, 149, 186, 209, 211, 229–31, 304–5, 314–15, 354, 365–68, 386, 389, 391–93, 395–97, 400–402, 413–14, 444, 454
Watkinson, Cornelius, 23, 92–94
Wells, Robert, 50, 452–53, 473
West End Company, 23, 29, 357, 376–86
White, Mr., 356–57, 379, 382–83
Whitefield, George, 76, 125, 367
Whiten, Miss, 108
Wignell, Thomas, 460
Williams, William, 38, 189–90
Woodham, Charles Somerset: with Murray-Kean Company, 133, 140–41, 144, 147, 149, 151; in Jamaica, 32, 181
Woolls, Stephen, 33, 42, 86, 243, 253–77, 280–85, 287, 290–98, 300–308, 311, 315, 318, 320–22, 324–25,

340, 342–43, 353, 367, 386–87, 391–93, 398, 405, 410, 412, 415–25, 427–42, 444–49, 455–56, 458, 460, 463–64, 468–70, 473
Wynell, Mr., 32, 151, 159, 161–62

Yapp, Miss, 286–287, 308–9

Zedwitz, Mr., 440

Subject and Place Index

Academy House, Portsmouth, New Hampshire colony, 60
Albany, New York colony, 10–11, 27, 182–83, 321, 342
Alexandria, Virginia colony, 10, 287, 315, 386
Amateur productions, 21–27, 106–7, 113, 116–17, 119–20, 128, 133–34, 200–201, 232, 238, 256, 265–66, 312, 323, 340–42, 426, 443, 461. *See also* student productions; military productions
Annapolis, Maryland colony: 9, 11, 22, 25, 33, 38–39, 44–47, 151; American Company present, 200–207, 353, 371–72, 374–75, 386–88, 393–95, 398, 410–14, 425, 454–56; Murray-Kean Company present, 157–58, 160–62; New Theatre, 45, 157–58, 160–62, 200–207, 325–40, 371–72, 374; Verling's Company present, 322, 325–40; West Street Theatre, 46–47, 374–75, 387, 393–95, 398, 410–14, 454–56, 476
Antigua, 29, 47, 399, 409
Anti-theatrical legislation, 25, 71–72, 76–77, 95–98, 102, 131, 133–36, 156–57, 190, 192, 199, 465, 474
Anti-theatrical letters, 98–99, 214, 226–27, 250–52, 270, 279–80, 330, 456
Assembly Room, Broadway, New York. *See* New York (Hull's Assembly Room)
Assembly Room, Dumfries, Virginia colony, 60,
Assembly Room. *See* Philadelphia

Bacchus on the Bay Theatre. *See* Mr. Bayly; Charleston
Bahamas, 9, 127–28
Baltimore, 9, 44, 57–58, 397, 405–6, 425
Barbados, 9, 24, 31, 42, 47, 106, 108, 140, 149, 152, 163, 180, 234, 238–40, 243
Bass-End Theatre, Danish West Indies. *See* St. Croix
Beekman Street Theatre. *See* New York (Chapel Street Theatre)
Benefits: for actors (passim); for churches, 356, 374, 378; for colleges and schools, 79, 135, 162, 177, 199, 225; for hospitals, 79, 199, 356, 374, 378, 407, 450; for the poor (also debtors), 81, 213, 215, 242, 247, 258, 262–63, 267, 296–97, 323, 352, 356, 374, 412; for the prisoners, 43, 239, 269–70, 299
Boston, 27, 35–36; anti-theatrical legislation, 135–36, 190, 199, 200–201; opposition to theatre, 73–77, 98–99, 214, 268–269; Bunch of Grapes, (Long Room), 61, 345; Douglass present, 345; Mr. Joan present, 323,

347–48, 355, 361–62, 365–66; theatricals in, 98–99, 200–201, 232, 238, 265, 270, 328, 330, 343–44
Bunch of Grapes (Longroom). *See* Boston
Burglaries: at the playhouse, 422; of actor's costumes, 258
Burn's Long Room. *See* New York

Cambridge, Massachusetts colony, 25–26, 95. *See also* Harvard
Camera Obscura, 346
Chapel Street Theatre. *See* New York
Charleston, South Carolina colony: 29, 31, 33, 35, 37, 39, 42–44, 47–51, 83; American Company present, 230–37, 239–48, 425, 458–73; Bacchus on the Bay, 51, 62, 289, 296–300, 304, 319. Church Street Theatre, 452–53, 458–59, 461–73; Court Room, 110, 112–15; Douglass present 450, 452–53; Grey's Tavern on the Bay, 313; Hallam Company present, 178–81; Hawes's Long Room on the Bay, 345; Holt Company present, 112–23; John Henry present, 321, 344–45; Mr. Stoaks present, 131–132; New Theatre, 178–181; Pike's Assembly Room, 464; Queen Street Theatre, 115, 117, 120–23, 178, 230–37, 241, 244–48, 250

Chestertown, Maryland colony, 160, 200–201
Church Street Theatre. *See* Charleston
College of Philadelphia, 183–84
Continental Congress, 460, 474
Courts: actors in court, 92–94, 103, 129, 131, 354; autumnal court (Annapolis), 45, 353, 375, 387, 397–98, 424–25; spring court (Williamsburg), 354–55, 366, 390, 397, 399–400, 402
Cowle's Tavern, Accomac County, Virginia colony, 92–93
Cox's Long Room. *See* New York
Cruger's Wharf Theatre. *See* New York
Cuba, 9, 47, 220, 229–30

Danish West Indies. *See* St. Croix, Tortola, Monserrat
De La Montagne's Long Room. *See* New York
Dumfries, Virginia colony, 60, 386, 389

Fireworks, 160, 397
Fort Anne, Nova Scotia, 126
Fort Cumberland, the frontier, 27, 185–86
Fredericksburg, Virginia colony, 10–11, 85, 151, 156, 386, 392–93
Freemasons, 43, 123, 171, 186, 217, 246, 285, 330, 381, 410, 418, 470

Grey's Tavern on the Bay. *See* Charleston

Hacker's Assembly Room. *See* Providence, Rhode Island colony
Halifax, North Carolina colony, 44, 57–58, 288, 322
Halifax, Nova Scotia, 9–11, 27, 29, 59, 126–27, 288–89, 311–17, 355, 426, 438, 461
Hartford, Connecticut colony, 87
Harvard College, 25, 95, 185–86, 190, 192, 241
Hawes's Long Room on the Bay. *See* Charleston
Histrionic Academy. *See* New York
Hobb's Hole, Virginia colony, 151, 156
Holt's Long Room. *See* New York
Horse Racing: October Races at Annapolis, 45, 387, 425, 454
Hull's Assembly Room. *See* New York
Hurricanes: (1752), 48, 178; (1757), 74; (1772), 399, 409–10, 426

Jamaica: 9–10, 47, 94, 124, 126–28, 130, 133, 180–84, 255, 279, 286, 289, 475–78
John Street Theatre. *See* New York

King's Arms Tavern, Newport, Rhode Island colony, 59, 219, 227

Kingston, Jamaica, 110, 140, 171, 178, 186

Lancaster, Pennsylvania colony, 106
Leeward Islands Company of Comedians, 23, 29
Linonian Club, 388, 402, 436, 468. *See also* Yale
Louisburg, Nova Scotia, 190, 192
Lyon's Long Room, Savannah, Georgia colony, 60, 310–11

Masons. *See* Freemasons
Military performances, 23–24, 27, 126–27, 182–83, 185–86, 229–230, 237, 239, 323, 328, 330, 426, 438, 461
Montserrat, 9, 31, 47, 110
Musical concerts, 43, 86, 263, 339–40, 342–43, 347, 464

Nassau Street Theatre. *See* New York
New Bern, North Carolina colony, 288
New Booth on Society Hill. *See* Philadelphia (Society Hill Theatre)
Newport, Rhode Island colony, 11–12, 57–58; bans theatre, 77–78; finances 81–82; theatricals, 189, 210–15, 219, 227
Newton's Great Room, Captain, Norfolk, Virginia colony, 149
New York: 10–11, 34, 37, 40, 44; American Company, 185, 187–192, 211–12, 215–18, 220–26, 283–86, 287, 289–309, 311–12,

320, 324–40, 424–25, 436–52, 459–60, 473, 475, 477; amateur productions, 106–7, 340–41, 462; Bayly's Company, 256, 267, 269–72, 274; Burn's Long Room, 43, 61–62, 86, 277–79, 291, 339–40, 342–43; Chapel Street Theatre (Beekman Street Theatre), 53, 211–12, 215–18, 220–26, 236, 238–39, 244; Chapel Street Theatre finances, 82–83; Chapel Street Theatre riot, 248–50; Cox's Long Room, 428–29; Cruger's Wharf Theatre 52, 188, 190–92; De La Montagne's Long Room, 429–30; First Nassau Street Theatre, 51–52, 107–9, 134–39, 142–48, 150, 153–55; Hallam Company, 163–76; Heady Company, 107–111; Histri-onic Academy, 79, 87, 185, 187–88; Holt's Company, 122–124; Holt's Long Room, 123–24; Hull's Assembly Room, 60, 408–11, 431–33, 440, 450–51, 461; John Street Theatre, 53, 255–56, 283–85, 289–309, 311–12, 324–40, 436–52; Murray-Kean Com-pany, 133–48; New Theatre, 52, 125; The Orange Tree, 62, 256, 267, 269–72, 274; prohibits theatre, 98; Revenge Meet-ing House, 106–7 Second Nassau Street Theatre, 52, 165–176; theatre survey, 51–53; Tomlinson's Com-pany, 237–39, 244, 246–50; Upton's Company, 150–55; Vaux-Hall Garden, 62, 86, 237, 320, 342–43, 347, 349

Norfolk, Virginia colony, 10, 57, 141, 149–50, 286–87, 291, 293, 397, 399

Orange Tree, The. *See* New York

Pamphret, Connecticut colony, 26

Pennsylvania: allows plays, 192; prohibits plays, 95–98,192. *See also* Philadelphia

Perth Amboy, New Jersey colony, 63n. 11, 189

Petersburg, Virginia colony, 57, 59, 141, 150–51, 230–31,

Philadelphia: 10, 30, 33, 40, 44, 84; allows theatre, 104–5; American Company present, 189–90, 193–99, 242, 252–55, 257–77, 280–83, 314–20, 346–48, 350–53, 358–67, 398, 414–25, 427–36, 456–57; Assembly Room, 248, 250–51, 258–62, 340–41; Hallam Company present, 172, 176–78; Murray-Kean Company present, 129–34; New Theatre (Plumsteads), 172, 176–78; petitions against players, 250–52; Society Hill Theatre, 54, 189, 193–99; Society Hill Theatre (New Booth), 38, 54; Southwark Theatre, 54, 242, 252–54, 257–77, 280–83, 314–20, 346–48, 350–53, 358–66, 414–24, 427–36, 456–57, 474; tav-

ern performances, 406–7, 453; Water Street Theatre (Plumsteads), 54, 130–31
Piscataway, Maryland colony, 10, 151, 162
Plumstead's Warehouse. See Philadelphia
Portsmouth, New Hampshire colony, 36, 39, 60, 84–85; Assembly Room, 404–5; bans theatre, 77; Douglass denied permission, 218, 226–27; Douglass Company, 321; Mr. Joan, 346, 350; Morgan Company, 219, 398, 404–5, 408, 411–14, 416–21, 423–24, 426–28; Oratorical Academy House, 412–14, 416–18, 420–21, 423–24, 427–28
Port Tobacco, Maryland colony, 151, 162
Princeton, New Jersey colony (Princeton College), 178, 461, 472
Providence, Bahamas, 84–85
Providence, Rhode Island colony, 11, 29, 36, 38, 44, 189, 219, 227–29, 288, 310; Hacker's Assembly Room, 346–47, 426, 443–44

Queen Street Theatre. See Charleston

Revenge Meeting House, The. See New York
Richmond, Virginia colony, 31, 44, 78, 460, 471–72
Riots: at Chapel Street theatre, 53, 72, 78, 87–88, 89–90, 244, 247–50

Runaways, 126, 311

Sadler's Wells (England), 39, 60, 256, 398
Salem, Massachusetts colony, 36, 323, 349, 352
Savannah, Georgia colony, 9, 141. See also Lyon's Long Room
Scenes and Machines, 36–41, 47, 353, 358–59, 373, 404, 424, 439, 445, 459
Society Hill Theatre. See Philadelphia
Southwark Theatre. See Philadelphia
Spanish Town, Jamaica, 94, 124–25
St. Croix: 29, 47, 387, 399, 426; Bass-End Theatre (Christiansted), 354–57, 368–78, 380–86, 387–89, 399, 407, 409; Heyliger House, 390; hurricane damages, 399, 409, 426; The Theatre (Fredericksted), 356–57, 376–86, 399; William's Tavern, 389–90
Stamp Act, 90, 244, 246
Staver's Long Room, Portsmouth, New Hampshire colony, 61, 346, 350
Student performances, 23–26, 95, 96–97, 116, 119–20 142, 149, 172, 178, 179–86, 190, 388, 402, 461, 468, 472, 473–74. See also Linonian Club
Subscription series: overview, 85–86; Annapolis (1770–71), 45–47, 375, 388–89, 393; Bahamas (1746),

127–28; Charleston (1735), 115; (1769), 49–50, 321, 344; (1773), 50–51, 425, 448, 452–53; for Lecture Series (1766), 247; Ja-maica (1745), 127; Portsmouth, New Hampshire colony (1772), 404–5, 408, 411; Williamsburg (1751), 55–56, 141, 148–49

Tappahannock, Virginia colony, 151n 7
Theatrical Purse, The, 454
Tortola, 185–87

Upper Marlborough, Maryland colony , 10, 39, 151, 158–59, 162, 200, 207–9

Vaux-Hall Garden. *See* New York

Water Street Theatre (Plumsteads). *See* Philadelphia
West Indies. *See* individual island entries
West Street Theatre. *See* Annapolis

Williamsburg, Virginia colony: 10, 27, 34, 36–37, 42, 44; American Company present, 200, 209–11 220, 229–31, 353–54, 366–68, 377–80, 386, 390–92, 395–97, 400–3; first theatre, 99–104, 119–20, 127; Hallam Company present, 151–52, 156–57, 159–62; Hallam's dancing school, 87; Murray-Kean Company present, 148–50, 155–56; New Theatre, 200, 200n11, 209–211, 229, 231; "Old Theatre", 298–309, 366–68, 377–80, 391– 92, 395–97, 400–3; second theatre, 141–50, 159–61; theatre survey, 55–57; ticket pricing, 83–84; Verling (Virginia) Company present, 256–58, 287, 298–309, 311, 354, 363, 365

William and Mary College, 26–27, 96–97, 116, 149
Wilmington, North Carolina colony, 29, 288

Yale, 25, 172, 179–82, 225, 388, 402, 436, 468. *See also* Linonian Club

Title and Author Index

Addison, Joseph: *Cato*, 24, 26, 65–66, 79, 109, 113, 116, 119–21, 129–132, 137–38, 143, 149, 160, 179, 186, 201, 220, 228, 247, 256, 262, 298, 461, 470, 472–73; The *Drummer*, 26, 120, 158, 172, 191–92, 194, 273, 299, 340.

Adulateur, The (Warren), 398, 401–2, 426

Adventures of Half an Hour, The (Bullock), 193, 195

Adventures of Harlequin and Scaramouche, The (anon.), 113

Aesop in the Shades. See *Lethe*

Albion Queens, The (Banks), 175

Alexander the Great, or the Rival Queens (Lee), 42, 320, 323, 326, 333, 363

Alfred. See *The Masque of Alfred the Great*

All for Love (Dryden), 266, 272, 303

All in the Wrong (Murphy), 299, 331, 392

Amphitryon; or, The Two Sosias (Dryden), 138

Anatomist, The; or Sham Doctor (Ravenscroft), 152, 159, 162, 167, 269, 273, 294, 203, 235, 309, 339

Androboros (Hunter), 71, 98

Apprentice, The (Murphy), 272, 277, 296, 326, 380, 470

Arcadius; or Love in a Calm (anon.), 461

Arne, Thomas: *Cymon* (with Garrick), 40, 433, 444–45, 461, 466

Banks, John: *The Albion Queens*, 175

Baker, Thomas: *Tunbridge Walks*, 153, 166, 176

Barnwell, George. See *The London Merchant*

Barton, Andrew (pseudonym). See Thomas Forrest

Bayly, Mr.: *The Quaker Outwitted*, 297

Bear and the Cub, The (anonymous), 24, 70, 92–94

Beggar's Opera, The (Gay), 36, 42, 63–64, 68, 70, 84, 128, 139, 142, 146, 157–60, 169, 175, 194, 197, 220, 253, 309, 327, 336, 339, 346–47, 352, 361, 366, 370, 384–85, 387, 389–90, 430, 442, 462

Beau in the Suds, The (Coffey), 69, 134, 139, 147–48, 158

Beaux' Stratagem, The (Farquhar), 24, 26, 63–64, 109, 119–20, 125, 136, 138, 143–44, 152, 157, 170, 183, 191, 203, 206–7, 224, 233, 260, 274, 281, 283, 315, 324, 329, 351, 361, 368, 370, 376, 402, 434, 438, 462

Bickerstaffe, Isaac: *Lionel and Clarissa*, 366, 412, 422, 427, 431, 456, 466–67; *Love in a Village*, 42, 69, 244, 259, 266, 275, 281, 290, 293, 307, 330, 339–

505

40, 348, 350–51, 372, 391, 406, 416, 440, 461, 463; *Love in the City*, 365; *The Maid of the Mill*, 69, 335, 337, 341, 343, 349, 358, 394, 414, 419, 441, 466; *The Padlock*, 63n22, 68–69, 338, 340, 343, 349–51, 358–60, 363, 391, 397, 406, 413, 415, 424, 434, 437, 440, 451, 457, 461, 466; *The School for Fathers*, 466–67; *Thomas and Sally*, 69, 252, 264, 285, 306, 316, 333, 335, 363, 367, 371, 402, 423, 463–64

Bold Stoke for a Wife, A (Centlivre), 139, 142, 154, 158, 178, 203, 223, 271–72, 292, 315, 323, 325, 335, 338, 369, 465, 469

Brave Irishman, The (T. Sheridan), 239, 245, 266, 283, 305, 309, 326–27, 329, 336, 374, 382–83

Brothers, The (Cumberland), 400, 418, 429, 465

Buck, The. See The Englishman in Paris

Bullock, Christopher: *The Adventures of Half an Hour*, 193, 195; *Woman's A Riddle*, 173

Busy Body, The (Centlivre), 26, 109, 116, 119, 145–46, 157, 203, 289, 318, 329, 333, 350, 462

Captain O'Blunder. See The Brave Irishman

Careless Husband, The (Cibber), 152, 169, 177

Carey, Henry: *Chrononhotonthologos*, 384; *The Contrivances*, 69, 271, 290, 318, 320, 323, 326, 467, 468; *Damon and Phillida*, 68, 144–46, 148, 152, 158, 166, 171, 173, 191–92, 203, 216, 222–23, 228, 233, 264–65, 285, 300, 311, 330, 334, 338, 349, 359, 362, 370, 371, 385, 390, 397, 445, 465; *The Honest Yorkshireman*, 68–69, 154, 155, 193, 204–6, 215, 220, 225, 295, 299, 308, 316, 326, 328, 334, 336, 376, 385, 391, 419, 431, 441, 462

Cato (Addison), 24, 26, 65–66, 79, 109, 113, 116, 119–21, 129–132, 137–38, 143, 149, 160, 179, 186, 201, 220, 228, 247, 256, 262, 298, 461, 470, 472–73

Catherine and Petruchio (Garrick), 67–68, 252, 263, 274, 290, 293, 296, 301, 315–17, 319, 325, 332, 338, 364, 409, 427, 432, 434, 437, 442, 449, 459, 462, 465, 469

Centlivre, Susanna: *A Bold Stoke for a Wife*, 139, 142, 154, 158, 178, 203, 223, 271–72, 292, 315, 323, 325, 335, 338, 369, 465, 469; *The Busy Body*, 26, 109, 116, 119, 145–46, 157, 203, 289, 318, 329, 333, 350, 462; *A Wife Well Managed*, 177; *The Wonder*, 236, 252, 277, 282, 291, 300, 313, 329, 369, 435, 464

Chaplet, The (Mendez), 69, 275, 282, 297, 337
Cheats of Scapin, The (anon.), 373
Chrononhotonothologos (Carey), 384
Cibber, Colley: *The Careless Husband*, 152, 169, 177; *Love Makes a Man*, 266, 339; *The Provoked Husband*, (with Vanbrugh), 63–64, 152–53, 177, 193, 196–97, 202, 204–5, 207, 213, 215, 233, 245, 252, 265, 307, 315, 327, 333, 361, 377–78, 381, 389–90, 392, 402, 406, 467; *Richard III*, 63, 67, 70, 134, 136, 144, 148, 152–54, 161–62, 168, 192–93, 202, 205, 208, 221, 253, 266, 284, 304, 327, 331, 334, 337, 369, 373, 382–84, 423–24, 446, 463; *The School Boy*, 195, 198; *She Would and She Would Not*, 338
Cibber, Susannah: *The Oracle*, 245–46, 253, 257, 268, 281, 284, 347–48, 403, 466
Citizen, The (Murphy), 252, 262, 277, 281, 294, 301, 316, 324, 333, 336, 351, 359, 369–70, 434, 435, 438, 456, 464–65
Clandestine Marriage, The (with Colman Sr.), 283–84, 318, 328, 352, 367, 391, 437, 457, 459, 470
Cockings, George: *The Conquest of Canada*, 41, 432
Coffey, Charles : *The Beau in the Suds*, 69, 134, 139, 147–48, 158; *The Devil to Pay*, 69, 118, 142–43, 152, 158, 168, 173, 175, 204–5, 208, 217, 225, 232–33, 254, 259, 272, 282, 293, 308, 329, 331, 334, 339, 361, 364, 381, 384, 421, 428, 463, 467, 470
Colin and Phebe (anon.), 137
Colman, Benjamin: *Gustavus Vasa*, 26, 95
Colman, George Sr.: *The Clandestine Marriage*, (with Garrick.), 283–84, 318, 328, 352, 367, 391, 437, 457, 459, 470; *The Deuce is in Him*, 266, 289; *The English Merchant*, 325, 467; *The Jealous Wife*, 235, 273, 281, 317, 324, 326, 328, 395, 397, 465; *The Musical Lady*, 331–32, 341, 350–51, 395–96, 424, 451; *Polly Honeycomb*, 302, 307, 331
Committee, The (Howard), 145, 152, 169, 222–23, 225, 273, 295
Comus (Dalton and Milton), 40, 42, 360, 405, 446
Congreve, William: *Love for Love*, 76, 137, 143, 167, 170, 224, 235, 264, 340, 364, 428; *The Mourning Bride*, 232–33, 235, 260, 271, 286, 317, 334, 384, 417, 441
Conquest of Canada, The (Cockings), 41, 432
Conscious Lovers, The (Steele), 152, 165–67, 171, 216, 235, 263, 302, 336, 338, 350, 388, 428

Constant Couple, The (Farquhar), 64–65, 136, 152, 155, 160–61, 167, 186, 204, 206, 216, 245, 254, 277, 298, 306, 332, 337, 351, 412, 447, 462, 468

Contrivances, The (Carey), 69, 271, 290, 318, 320, 323, 326, 467, 468

Coriolanus (Thomson), 276

Country Lasses, The (Johnson), 275, 301

Country Wake, The; or, Hob in the Well (Hippisley), 176. See also *Flora, or Hob in the Well.*

Cross Purposes (O'Brien), 69, 444–45, 457, 459, 462, 467

Crowne, John: *Sir Courtly Nice,* 106

Cumberland, Richard: *The Brothers,* 400, 418, 429, 465; *The Fashionable Lover,* 403, 420, 433, 466; *The West Indian,* 65, 387, 395–96, 400, 413, 417, 421, 434, 436–37, 447, 457, 467–68, 476

Cymbeline (Shakespeare), 39, 67, 275, 277, 285, 302, 317, 325, 351, 365, 371, 395, 421, 462, 469

Cymon (Garrick and Arne), 40, 433, 444–45, 461, 466

Dalton, John: *Comus* (adap. from Milton), 40, 42, 360, 405, 446

Damon and Phillida (Carey), 68, 144–46, 148, 152, 158, 166, 171, 173, 191–92, 203, 216, 222, 223, 228, 233, 264–65, 285, 300, 311, 330, 334, 338, 349, 359, 362, 370–71, 385, 390, 397, 445, 465

Davenant, William: *Macbeth,* 67, 196–97, 267–68, 295, 318, 332, 468; *The Tempest* (with Dryden), 40, 65, 353, 358–61, 430, 436, 439, 441, 445, 463, 466

Death of Harlequin, The (anon.), 335

Decoy, The (Potter), 27

Defeat, The (Warren), 426, 442–43

Deuce is in Him, The (Colman Sr.), 266, 289

Devil and the Doctors, The; or, a Hint to the College of Physicians (Morgan?), 414, 416–17

Devil in the Wine Cellar, The. See *The Walking Statue*

Devil to Pay, The (Coffey), 69, 118, 142–43, 152, 158, 168, 173, 175, 204–5, 208, 217, 225, 232–33, 254, 259, 272, 282, 293, 308, 329, 331, 334, 339, 361, 364, 381, 384, 421, 428, 463, 467, 470

Devil Upon Two Sticks, The (Foote), 147

Disappointment, The (Forrest), 271

Distrest Mother, The (Philips), 147–48, 168, 179, 225, 229, 244, 252, 306, 311, 336

Dodsley, Robert: *The King and the Miller of Mansfield,* 68, 153, 154, 174, 179, 202, 204, 208–9, 213, 215, 223, 248, 253, 282, 305–6, 325,

333, 358, 369, 371, 418, 449, 462, 464; *Sir John Cockle at Court,* 154; *The Toy Shop,* 196, 207, 213, 216, 388
Don Quixote in England (Fielding), 274
Double Disappointment, The (Mendez), 276
Douglas (Home), 65–66, 191, 193, 195, 206–7, 214, 217, 223, 234, 244, 252, 299, 312, 314, 327, 329, 334, 351, 372, 385, 409, 470
Dr. Faustus (Marlowe), 75
Drummer, The; or the Haunted House (Addison), 26, 120, 158, 172, 191–92, 194, 273, 299, 340
Dryden, John: *All for Love,* 266, 272, 303; *Amphitryon,* 138; *The Spanish Friar,* 114, 134, 138, 145, 169, 190, 316, 336, 388; *The Tempest* (with Davenant), 40, 65, 353, 358–61, 430, 436, 439, 441, 445, 463, 466
Dwarfs, The; or, The Cascade Assignation (anon.), 347–48

Earl of Essex, The (Jones), 174, 267, 291, 308, 337–38, 386, 434–35, 438, 456, 461
Edgar and Emmeline (Hawkesworth), 360–61, 431, 435, 438, 450, 464–65, 477
Edward the Black Prince (Shirley), 359–60
Elopement, The; or Harlequin's Court (anon.), 424, 427
Enchanted Lady of the Grove, The (anon.), 270, 272

Englishman in Paris, The (Foote), 391, 429, 438
English Merchant, The (Colman Sr.) 325, 467
Escape, The; or Harlequin Turned Doctor (anon.), 413–14, 418
Every Man in His Humour (Jonson), 326, 397

Fair Penitent, The (Rowe), 63, 65, 139, 144–45, 152–55, 170, 176, 178, 195, 202, 205, 212, 215, 228–29, 238, 268, 298, 313, 362, 368, 383, 467
False Delicacy (Kelly and Garrick), 318, 332, 400, 402, 429, 468
Fanny the Phantom (anon.), 308, 320, 323, 385
Farmer's Return from London, The (Garrick), 335
Farquhar, George: *The Beaux' Stratagem,* 24, 26, 63–64, 109, 119, 120, 125, 136, 138, 143–44, 152, 157, 170, 183, 191, 203, 206–7, 224, 233, 260, 274, 281, 283, 315, 324, 329, 351, 361, 368, 370, 376, 402, 434, 438, 462; *The Constant Couple,* 64–65, 136, 152, 155, 160, 161, 167, 186, 204, 206, 216, 245, 254, 277, 298, 306, 332, 337, 351, 412, 447, 462, 468; *The Inconstant,* 190, 224, 264, 314, 328, 369–70; *Love and a Bottle,* 364; *The Recruiting Officer,* 26, 64, 74, 109, 117, 119, 121–23, 137, 142, 147–48, 150, 152, 158, 179, 183,

191, 193, 195, 202, 220, 294, 317, 369, 376, 389, 434, 448, 466; *Sir Harry Wildair*, 138, 146–47; *The Stage Coach*, 137, 169, 175, 191, 194–95, 197, 202, 204; *The Twin Rivals*, 137, 152, 171, 247–49
Fashionable Lover, The (Cumberland), 403, 420, 433, 466
Female Parson, The. See The Beau in the Suds.
Fielding, Henry: *Don Quixote in England*, 274; *The Miser*, 263, 265, 276, 297, 309, 329, 331; *The Mock Doctor*, 69, 136, 145, 152, 158, 178, 188, 190, 193, 202, 205, 213, 216, 225, 245, 257, 299, 315, 329, 368–69, 373–74, 376; *Tom Thumb*, 167, 178, 275; *The Virgin Unmasked*, 69, 145–46, 158, 167, 175, 192, 198, 206–7, 216, 222, 312, 314, 326, 369, 371, 377, 388
Flora, or Hob in the Well (Hippisley), 69, 114, 121, 146–47, 152, 168, 170, 216, 224, 272, 292, 331, 358, 369, 374, 377, 433, 449, 467
Foote, Samuel: *The Devil Upon Two Sticks*, 147; *The Englishman in Paris*, 391, 429, 438; *The Mayor of Garratt*, 47, 264, 267, 275, 281, 284, 324, 327, 334, 359, 382–83, 393–94, 418, 431, 440, 459, 465; *The Minor*, 367, 380; *Taste*, 304
Forrest, Thomas: *Disappointment The*, 271

Funeral, The; or, Grief a la Mode (Steele), 359–60

Gamester, The (Moore and Garrick), 65–66, 174–75, 177, 198, 207–8, 217, 232–33, 245, 269, 277, 281, 290, 307, 308, 350, 374, 377–78, 379, 406, 440, 461
Garrick, David: *Catherine and Petruchio*, 67–68, 252, 263, 274, 290, 293, 296, 301, 315–17, 319, 325, 332, 338, 364, 409, 427, 432, 434, 437, 442, 449, 459, 462, 465, 469; *The Clandestine Marriage* (with Colman Sr.), 283–84, 318, 328, 352, 367, 391, 437, 457, 459, 470; *Cymon* (with Arne), 40, 433, 444–45, 461, 466; *False Delicacy* (with Kelly), 318, 332, 400, 402, 429, 468; *The Farmer's Return from London*, 335; *The Gamester* (with Moore), 65–66, 174–75, 177, 198, 207–8, 217, 232–33, 245, 269, 277, 281, 290, 307, 308, 350, 374, 377–78, 379, 406, 440, 461; *The Guardian*, 67–68, 317, 325, 328, 365, 420, 436, 448, 464, 471; *Lethe*, 67–68, 150, 152–53, 170, 173, 174, 191, 193–95, 201–3, 206–8, 212, 215, 217, 221, 232–33, 254, 270, 283, 310, 318, 326–27, 334, 376, 382, 389, 410, 419–21, 423, 429, 445, 461, 466; *The Irish Widow*, 68, 447–48,

455, 457, 461–62, 467; *The Lying Valet,* 67–68, 82, 136–39, 144–45, 152–53, 157–60, 162, 168–69, 196, 203, 205–6, 220–21, 228, 238, 245, 252, 268, 273, 276, 283, 307, 333, 339, 370, 379, 383, 407, 419, 442, 462, 467–68; *Miss in her Teens,* 67–68, 142–43, 152, 154, 160–61, 176–77, 197, 202, 205, 208, 224, 247, 281, 290, 299, 304, 307, 312, 315, 317–18, 324, 335–36, 362, 370–71, 379, 417, 430, 437, 443, 463, 466, 470, 476; *Neck or Nothing,* 276, 282, 298, 320, 469

Gay, John: *The Beggar's Opera,* 36, 42, 63–64, 68, 70, 84, 128, 139, 142, 146, 157–58, 159, 160, 169, 175, 194, 197, 220, 253, 309, 327, 336, 339, 346–47, 352, 361, 366, 370, 384–85, 387, 389–90, 430, 442, 462

Genii, The; or, the Birth of Harlequin (Woodward), 333

George Barnwell. See *The London Merchant*

Godfrey, Thomas: *Prince of Parthia, The,* 271

Goldsmith, Oliver: *The Good Natured Man,* 364; *She Stoops to Conquer,* 69, 451, 462, 465

Good Natured Man, The (Goldsmith), 364

Guardian, The (Garrick), 67–68, 317, 325, 328, 365, 420, 436, 448, 464, 471

Gustavus Vasa (B. Colman), 26, 95

Hamlet (Shakespeare), 67, 69, 152, 194–95, 199, 215, 225, 257, 270, 281, 285, 305, 316, 324, 331, 350, 370–71, 382–83, 392, 418, 444, 457, 459

Harlequin Collector; or, the Miller Deceived (anon.), 69, 160, 170, 177, 194, 197–98, 220, 223, 224, 229, 265–67, 270, 272, 281, 294–95, 300, 329, 352, 362, 365, 448

Harlequin and the Miller. See *Harlequin Collector*

Harlequin's Escape (anon.), 272

Harlequin's Frolick (anon.), 342

Harlequin Restored; or, the Miller Deceived. See *Harlequin Collector*

Harlequin Skeleton; or, the Miller Deceived, (anon., same as *Harlequin Collector*?), 174–75, 317, 336

Harlequin Skeleton; or, the Burgomaster Trick'd (anon., same as *Harlequin Collector*?), 301, 381, 383

Harlequin and Scaramouche, or the Spaniard Trick'd (anon.), 124

Harlequin Statue (anon.), 274

Harlequin's Vagaries (anon.), 284

Harlequin Triumphant; or, the Burgomaster Trick'd (anon.; same as *Harlequin Collector*?), 373

Hawkesworth, John: *Edgar and Emmeline,* 360–61,

431, 435, 438, 450, 464–65, 477
Henry IV, Part I (Shakespeare), 66–67, 216, 295, 307, 328, 334, 373, 381, 427, 464
Henry VIII (Shakespeare), 66
High Life Below Stairs (Townley), 68–69, 260, 263, 275, 281, 293, 298, 302, 308, 318, 327, 329, 334, 460, 364, 377–78, 381, 405, 422, 428, 430, 441, 446, 458, 461, 466
Hill, Aaron: *The Walking Statue*, 74, 147, 155; *Zara*, 319, 325
Hippisley, James: *The Country Wake*, 176; *Flora*, 69, 114, 121, 146–47, 152, 168, 170, 216, 224, 272, 292, 331, 358, 369, 374, 377, 433, 449, 467
Hoadly, Benjamin: *The Suspicious Husband*, 65, 69, 152, 174, 198, 205, 216, 232–33, 293, 334, 352, 371, 382, 423, 438, 459
Home, John: *Douglas*, 65–66, 191, 193, 195, 206–7, 214, 217, 223, 234, 244, 252, 299, 312, 314, 327, 329, 334, 351, 372, 385, 409, 470
Honest Yorkshireman, The (Carey), 68–69, 154–55, 193, 204–6, 215, 220, 225, 295, 299, 308, 316, 326, 328, 334, 336, 376, 385, 391, 419, 431, 441, 462
Howard, Sir Robert: *The Committee*, 145, 152, 169, 222–23, 225, 273, 295

Hughes, John: *The Siege of Damascus*, 352
Hunter, Robert:: *Androboros*, 71, 98

Inconstant, The (Farquhar), 190, 224, 264, 314, 328, 369–70
Irish Widow, The (Garrick), 68, 447–48, 455, 457, 461–62, 467
Jane Shore (Rowe), 63n. 22, 152, 175, 188, 213, 235, 253, 307, 312, 334–35, 363, 370, 449, 455, 462
Jealous Wife, The (Colman Sr.), 235, 273, 281, 317, 324, 326, 328, 395, 397, 465
Jew of Venice, The; or, the Female Lawyer (Landsdowne), 207
Johnson, Charles: *The Country Lasses*, 275, 301
Jones, Henry: *The Earl of Essex*, 174, 267, 291, 308, 337–38, 386, 434–35, 438, 456, 461
Jonson, Ben: *Every Man in His Humour*, 326, 397
Julius Caesar (Shakespeare), 66–67, 365, 468

Kelly, Hugh: *False Delicacy* (with Garrick), 318, 332, 400, 402, 429, 468; *A Word to the Wise*, 39, 400–402, 410, 414, 432, 458
King and the Miller of Mansfield, The (Dodsley), 68, 153–54, 174, 179, 202, 204, 208–9, 213, 215, 223, 248, 253, 282, 305–6, 325,

333, 358, 369, 371, 418, 449, 462, 464
King John (Shakespeare), 66–67, 318, 324, 333, 358, 471
King Lear (Tate), 67, 173, 195, 236, 262, 282, 292, 373, 397, 438, 466
King, Thomas: *Picture of a Playhouse*, 273, 301, 306, 309, 317, 324, 340, 347–48, 434–35, 448, 467, 469, 472, 474; *Wit's Last Stake*, 364

Landsdowne, George Granville, earl of: *The Jew of Venice*, 207
Lecture on Heads (Stevens), 22, 36, 39, 60–61, 84, 86, 242, 244, 246–48, 250–51, 254, 256–261, 277–80, 312, 321, 337, 343–46, 350, 371, 385, 398, 406–11, 426, 428–31, 433, 450, 458, 459, 472, 474
Lecture on Hearts (anon.), 303, 304, 342
Lee, Nathaniel: *Alexander the Great, or the Rival Queens*, 42, 320, 323, 326, 333, 363; *Theodosius, or The Force of Love*, 38, 152, 194, 197, 222, 236, 254, 282, 339, 431, 442, 464
Lethe (Garrick), 67–68, 150, 152–53, 170, 173–74, 191, 193–95, 201–3, 206–8, 212, 215, 217, 221, 232–33, 254, 270, 283, 310, 318, 326–27, 334, 376, 382, 389, 410, 419–21, 423, 429, 445, 461, 466

Lillo, George: *The London Merchant*, 64–66, 117–18, 136, 138, 147, 149, 152, 158, 168, 179, 194, 198, 203, 213, 217, 235, 238, 264, 293, 315–16, 336, 352, 369, 385, 420, 450, 464
Lionel and Clarissa (Bickerstaffe), 366, 412, 422, 427, 431, 456, 466–67
London Merchant, The (Lillo), 64–66, 117–18, 136, 138, 147, 149, 152, 158, 168, 179, 194, 198, 203, 213, 217, 235, 238, 264, 293, 315–16, 336, 352, 369, 385, 420, 450, 464
Love a la Mode (Macklin), 305, 317, 321, 325, 337, 346, 351–52, 392, 421, 427–28, 432, 447, 456, 462, 464, 469
Love and a Bottle; or, the Wild Irishman (Farquhar), 364
Love for Love (Congreve), 76, 137, 143, 167, 170, 224, 235, 264, 340, 364, 428
Love in a Village (Bickerstaffe), 42, 69, 244, 259, 266, 275, 281, 290, 293, 307, 330, 339–40, 348, 350–51, 372, 391, 406, 416, 440, 461, 463
Love in the City (Bickerstaffe), 365
Love, James: *The Witches*, 269–70, 281, 291–92, 298, 327, 352, 358, 361, 468
Love Makes a Man (Cibber), 266, 339
Lover's Quarrel (anon.), 170, 191

Lying Valet, The (Garrick), 67–68, 82, 136–39, 144–45, 152–53, 157–60, 162, 168–69, 196, 203, 205–6, 220–21, 228, 238, 245, 252, 268, 273, 276, 283, 307, 333, 339, 370, 379, 383, 407, 419, 442, 462, 467–68

Lyon, William: *Wrangling Lovers, The*, 334, 347

Macbeth (Davenant), 67, 196–97, 267–68, 295, 318, 332, 468

Macklin, Charles: *Love a la Mode*, 305, 317, 321, 325, 337, 346, 351–52, 392, 421, 427–28, 432, 447, 456, 462, 464, 469

Maid of the Mill, The (Bickerstaffe), 69, 335, 337, 341, 343, 349, 358, 394, 414, 419, 441, 466

Mallet, David: *The Masque of Alfred the Great* (with Thomson), 25, 182–84

Marlowe, Christopher: *Dr. Faustus*, 75

Masque of Alfred the Great, The (Mallet and Thomson), 25, 182–84

Mayor of Garratt, The (Foote), 47, 264, 267, 275, 281, 284, 324, 327, 334, 359, 382–83, 393–394, 418, 431, 440, 459, 465

Mendez, Moses: *The Chaplet*, 69, 275, 282, 297, 337; *The Double Disappointment*, 276

Merchant of Venice, The (Shakespeare), 67, 159, 253, 276, 292, 308, 317, 333, 380, 433, 449, 463

Merlin; or, Harlequin's Delivery (anon.), 328

Merry Wives of Windsor, The (Shakespeare), 67, 360

Midas (O'Hare), 69, 351–52, 395, 416, 429, 439, 441, 446, 464, 469

Milton, John: *Comus* (adap. Dalton), 40, 42, 360, 405, 446

Minor, The (Foote), 367, 380

Misanthrope, The (Moliere), 126

Miser, The (Fielding), 263, 265, 276, 297, 309, 329, 331

Miss in her Teens (Garrick), 67–68, 142–43, 152, 154, 160–61, 176–77, 197, 202, 205, 208, 224, 247, 281, 290, 299, 304, 307, 312, 315, 317–18, 324, 335–36, 362, 370–71, 379, 417, 430, 437, 443, 463, 466, 470, 476

Mock Doctor, The (Fielding), 69, 136, 145, 152, 158, 178, 188, 190, 193, 202, 205, 213, 216, 225, 245, 257, 299, 315, 329, 368–69, 373–74, 376

Moliere: *Misanthrope, The*, 126; *Tartuffe*, 75

Moore, Edward: *The Gamester* (with Garrick), 65–66, 174–75, 177, 198, 207–8, 217, 232–33, 245, 269, 277, 281, 290, 307–8, 350, 374, 377–79, 406, 440, 461

Moral Dialogues (anon.; alteration of *Othello*), 79, 210–11, 219, 227

Morgan, Mr.: *The Devil and the Doctors*, 414, 416–17; *The Politicians*, 412–14, 418

Mourning Bride, The (Congreve), 232–33, 235, 260, 271, 286, 317, 334, 384, 417, 441

Much Ado About Nothing (Shakespeare), 66

Murphy, Arthur: *All in the Wrong*, 299, 331, 392; *The Apprentice*, 272, 277, 296, 326, 380, 470; *The Citizen*, 252, 262, 277, 281, 294, 301, 316, 324, 333, 336, 351, 359, 369–70, 434–35, 438, 456, 464–65; *The Old Maid*, 253, 285, 295, 307, 324, 331, 337, 373, 384, 394, 423; *The Orphan of China*, 235, 258, 263, 305, 360; *The Upholsterer*, 260, 286, 303, 328, 330, 338, 360, 421; *The Way to Keep Him*, 245, 403, 419, 436–37, 468; *What We Must All Come To*, 385

Musical Lady, The (Colman Sr.), 331–32, 341, 350–51, 395–96, 424, 451

Neck or Nothing (Garrick), 276, 282, 298, 320, 469

Neptune and Amphitrite (anon.), 40, 359–61, 430, 436, 441, 445

New Lecture, A (Stevens), 450, 453, 456–57

O'Brien, William: *Cross Purposes*, 69, 444–45, 457, 459, 462, 467

O'Hare, Kane: *Midas*, 69, 351–52, 395, 416, 429, 439, 441, 446, 464, 469

Old Maid, The (Murphy), 253, 285, 295, 307, 324, 331, 337, 373, 384, 394, 423

Old Man Taught Wisdom, An. See *The Virgin Unmask'd.*

Oracle, The (S. Cibber), 245–46, 253, 257, 268, 281, 284, 347–48, 403, 466

Orphan, The (Otway), 25, 63, 65, 112–13, 117–18, 134–35, 144, 178, 190, 201–2, 206, 232, 238, 274, 294, 301, 323, 326, 340–41, 358, 370, 374, 377, 443, 469

Orphan of China, The (Murphy), 235, 258, 263, 305, 360

Othello (Shakespeare), 63n 22, 67, 82, 150, 152, 154, 160, 191, 204, 221, 300, 326, 332, 379, 429, 465. See also *Moral Dialogues*

Otway, Thomas: *The Orphan*, 25, 63, 65, 112–13, 117–18, 134–35, 144, 178, 190, 201–2, 206, 232, 238, 274, 294, 301, 323, 326, 340–41, 358, 370, 374, 377, 443, 469; *Venice Preserved*, 63n 11, 154, 191, 202, 205, 220, 282, 294, 300, 305, 342, 381, 383, 407

Padlock, The (Bickerstaffe), 63n22, 68–69, 338, 340, 343, 349–51, 358–60, 363, 391, 397, 406, 413, 415,

424, 434, 437, 440, 451, 457, 461, 466
Pastoral Colloquy, A (anon.), 26, 96
Philips, Ambrose: *The Distrest Mother*, 147–48, 168, 179, 225, 229, 244, 252, 306, 311, 336
Picture of a Playhouse; or, Bucks Have at ye all (King), 273, 301, 306, 309, 317, 324, 340, 347–48, 434–35, 448, 467, 469, 472, 474
Politicians, The; or, What News? (Morgan?), 412–14, 418
Polly Honeycomb (Colman Sr.), 302, 307, 331
Potter, Henry: *Decoy, The*, 27
Prince of Parthia, The (Godfrey), 271
Provoked Husband, The (Vanbrugh and Cibber), 63–64, 152–53, 177, 193, 196–97, 202, 204–5, 207, 213, 215, 233, 245, 252, 265, 307, 315, 327, 333, 361, 377–78, 381, 389–90, 392, 402, 406, 467

Quaker Outwitted, The (Bayly?), 297

Ravenscroft, Edward: *The Anatomist*, 152, 159, 162, 167, 269, 273, 294, 203, 235, 309, 339
Recruiting Officer, The (Farquhar), 26, 64, 74, 109, 117, 119, 121–23, 137, 142, 147–48, 150, 152, 158, 179, 183, 191, 193, 195, 202, 220, 294, 317, 369, 376, 389, 434, 448, 466
Reed, Joseph: *The Register Office*, 424, 427, 436, 468
Register Office, The (Reed), 424, 427, 436, 468
Reprisal, The; or, the Tars of Old England (Smollett), 262–63, 273, 277, 292, 316, 362, 369–70, 470
Revenge, The (Young), 203, 206, 275, 314, 316, 329, 338, 361, 373, 383, 389
Rich, John: *The Spirit of Contradiction*, 273
Richard III (Cibber), 63, 67, 70, 134, 136, 144, 148, 152–54, 161–62, 168, 192–93, 202, 205, 208, 221, 253, 266, 284, 304, 327, 331, 334, 337, 369, 373, 382–84, 423–24, 446, 463
Roman Father, The (Whitehead), 26, 40, 47, 186, 276, 280, 296, 393–94, 416, 467
Romeo and Juliet (Shakespeare), 25, 39, 63–66, 70, 107, 173, 175, 196, 198, 204–5, 208–9, 220, 223, 236, 263, 270, 273, 281, 290, 301, 325–26, 328, 332, 335, 351, 356–57, 370, 373, 374–76, 422–23, 448, 463, 467
Rowe, Nicholas: *The Fair Penitent*, 63, 65, 139, 144–45, 152–55, 170, 176, 178, 195, 202, 205, 212, 215, 228–29, 238, 268, 298, 313, 362, 368, 383, 467; *Jane Shore*, 63n. 22, 152, 175, 188, 213, 235, 253, 307, 312, 334–35, 363,

370, 449, 455, 462; *The Royal Convert*, 106, 108; *Tamerlane*, 152, 177–78, 191–92, 216, 257, 318, 376, 427, 447, 469, 476

Royal Convert, The (Rowe), 106, 108

School Boy, The (Cibber), 195, 198
School for Fathers, The (Bickerstaffe), 466–67
School for Libertines, The. See *A Word to the Wise*
School for Lovers, The (Whitehead), 246, 253, 276, 284, 296, 424, 445
Shakespeare, William: *Cymbeline*, 39, 67, 275, 277, 285, 302, 317, 325, 351, 365, 371, 395, 421, 462, 469; *Hamlet*, 67, 69, 152, 194, 195, 199, 215, 225, 257, 270, 281, 285, 305, 316, 324, 331, 350, 370–71, 382–83, 392, 418, 444, 457; 459; *Henry IV, Part I*, 66–67, 216, 295, 307, 328, 334, 373, 381, 427, 464; *Henry VIII*, 66; *Julius Caesar*, 66–67, 365, 468; *King John*, 66–67, 318, 324, 333, 358, 471; *The Merchant of Venice*, 67, 159, 253, 276, 292, 308, 317, 333, 380, 433, 449, 463; *The Merry Wives of Windsor*, 67, 360; *Much Ado About Nothing*, 66; *Othello*, 63n 22, 67, 82, 150, 152, 154, 160, 191, 204, 221, 300, 326, 332, 379, 429, 465; *Romeo and Juliet*, 25, 39, 63–66, 70, 107, 173, 175, 196, 198, 204–5, 208–9, 220, 223, 236, 263, 270, 273, 281, 290, 301, 325–26, 328, 332, 335, 351, 356–57, 370, 373, 374–76, 422–23, 448, 463, 467. See also *King Lear*, *Macbeth*, *Moral Dialogues*, *Richard III*, and *The Tempest*
Sheridan, Thomas: *The Brave Irishman* (T. Sheridan), 239, 245, 266, 283, 305, 309, 326–27, 329, 336, 374, 382–83
She Stoops to Conquer (Goldsmith), 69, 451, 462, 465
She Would and She Would Not (Cibber), 338
Shipwreck, The. See *The Brothers*
Shirley, James: *Edward the Black Prince*, 359–60
Siege of Damascus, The (Hughes), 352
Sir Courtly Nice (Crowne), 106
Sir Harry Wildair (Farquhar), 138, 146–47
Sir John Cockle at Court (Dodsley), 154
Smollett, Tobias: *Reprisal, The*, 262–63, 273, 277, 292, 316, 362, 369–70, 470
Spanish Friar, The (Dryden), 114, 134, 138, 145, 169, 190, 316, 336, 388
Spirit of Contradiction, The (Rich), 273
Stage Coach, The (Farquhar), 137, 169, 175, 191, 194–95, 197, 202, 204
Steele, Sir Richard: *The Conscious Lovers*, 152,

165–67, 171, 216, 235, 263, 302, 336, 338, 350, 388, 428; *The Funeral*, 359–60; *The Tender Hus-band*, 330, 362, 391, 400
Stevens, George Alexander: *Lecture on Heads*, 22, 36, 39, 60–61, 84, 86, 242, 244, 246–48, 250–51, 254, 256–61, 277–80, 312, 321, 337, 343–46, 350, 371, 385, 398, 406–11, 426, 428–31, 433, 450, 458–59, 472, 474; *A New Lecture*, 450, 453, 456–57
Suspicious Daughter, The (T. T. Jr.), 133
Suspicious Husband, The (Hoadly), 65, 69, 152, 174, 198, 205, 216, 232–33, 293, 334, 352, 371, 382, 423, 438, 459

Tamerlane (Rowe), 152, 177–78, 191–92, 216, 257, 318, 376, 427, 447, 469, 476
Tartuffe (Moliere), 75
Taste (Foote), 304
Tate, Nahum: *King Lear*, 67, 173, 195, 236, 262, 282, 292, 373, 397, 438, 466
Tempest, The (Dryden and Davenant), 40, 65, 353, 358–61, 430, 436, 439, 441, 445, 463, 466
Tender Husband, The (Steele), 330, 362, 391, 400
Theodosius, or The Force of Love (Lee), 38, 152, 194, 197, 222, 236, 254, 282, 339, 431, 442, 464
Thomas and Sally (Bickerstaffe), 69, 252,
264, 285, 306, 316, 333, 335, 363, 367, 371, 402, 423, 463–64
Thomson, James: *Coriolanus*, 276; *The Masque of Alfred the Great* (with Mallet), 25, 182–84
T. , T. Jr.: *Suspicious Daughter, The*, 133
Tom Thumb (Fielding), 167, 178, 275
Townley, James: *High Life Below Stairs*, 68–69, 260, 263, 275, 281, 293, 298, 302, 308, 318, 327, 329, 334, 460, 364, 377–78, 381, 405, 422, 428, 430, 441, 446, 458, 461, 466
Toy Shop, The (Dodsley), 196, 207, 213, 216, 388
Tragedy of King Bassias, The (anon.), 461
Trick Upon Trick (Yarrow), 335
Tunbridge Walks (Baker), 153, 166, 176
Twin Rivals, The (Farquhar), 137, 152, 171, 247–49

Upholsterer, The (Murphy), 260, 286, 303, 328, 330, 338, 360, 421

Vanbrugh, Sir John: *The Provoked Husband* (with Cibber), 63–64, 152–53, 177, 193, 196–97, 202, 204–5, 207, 213, 215, 233, 245, 252, 265, 307, 315, 327, 333, 361, 377–78, 381, 389–90, 392, 402, 406, 467
Venice Preserved (Otway), 63n 11, 154, 191, 202, 205,

220, 282, 294, 300, 305, 342, 381, 383, 407
Virgin Unmasked, The (Fielding), 69, 145–46, 158, 167, 175, 192, 198, 206–7, 216, 222, 312, 314, 326, 369, 371, 377, 388

Walking Statue, The (Hill), 74, 147, 155
Warren, Mercy: *The Adulateur*, 398, 401–2, 426; *The Defeat*, 426, 442–43
Way to Keep Him, The (Murphy), 245, 403, 419, 436–37, 468
West Indian, The (Cumberland), 65, 387, 395–96, 400, 413, 417, 421, 434, 436–37, 447, 457, 467–68, 476
What We Must All Come To (Murphy), 385
Whitehead, William: *The Roman Father*, 26, 40, 47, 186, 276, 280, 296, 393–94, 416, 467; *The School for Lovers*, 246, 253, 276, 284, 296, 424, 445
Wife Well Managed, A (Centlivre), 177
Win Her, and Wear Her; or, Harlequin Skeleton (anon.), 414, 416–17
Witches, The; or, Harlequin Restored (Love), 269–70, 281, 291–92, 298, 327, 352, 358, 361, 468
Witches, The; or, Harlequin Mercury (anon. or same as above?), 420–21, 423
Wit's Last Stake (King), 364
Woman's A Riddle (Bullock), 173

Wonder, The: A Woman Keeps a Secret! (Centlivre), 236, 252, 277, 282, 291, 300, 313, 329, 369, 435, 464
Woodward, Henry: *Genii, The*, 333
Word to the Wise, A (Kelly), 39, 400–402, 410, 414, 432, 458
Wrangling Lovers, The (Lyon), 334, 347

Yarrow, Joseph: *Trick Upon Trick*, 335
Young American in London, The (anon.), 468
Young, Edward: *Revenge, The*, 203, 206, 275, 314, 316, 329, 338, 361, 373, 383, 389

Zara (Hill), 319, 325